270391-5   8/64

REVIEW OF

Child Development

Research

VOLUME ONE

MARTIN L. HOFFMAN
and
LOIS WLADIS HOFFMAN
Editors

Prepared under the auspices of the
Society for Research in Child Development

RUSSELL SAGE FOUNDATION
New York   1964

© 1964
RUSSELL SAGE FOUNDATION
Printed in the United States
of America

*Library of Congress
Catalog Card Number: 64-20472*

WM. F. FELL CO., PRINTERS
PHILADELPHIA, PA.

Contents

Advisory Committee

NANCY BAYLEY, PH.D.
Chief, Section on Early Development
Laboratory of Psychology
National Institute of Mental Health

ORVILLE G. BRIM, JR., PH.D.
President
Russell Sage Foundation

LEON EISENBERG, M.D.
Professor of Child Psychiatry
The Johns Hopkins University

ROBERT J. HAGGERTY, M.D.
Assistant Professor of Pediatrics
and Markle Scholar in Academic Medicine
Harvard Medical School

RONALD LIPPITT, PH.D.
Program Director
Research Center for Group Dynamics
The University of Michigan

WILLIAM E. MARTIN, PH.D.
Head, Department of Child Development
and Family Life, Purdue University

JULIUS B. RICHMOND, M.D.
Chairman, Department of Pediatrics
Upstate Medical Center
State University of New York

SEYMOUR B. SARASON, PH.D.
Professor, Department of Psychology
Yale University

PAULINE SEARS, PH.D.
Associate Professor, School of Education
Stanford University

IRVING E. SIGEL, PH.D.
Chairman of Research
The Merrill-Palmer Institute

LEON J. YARROW, PH.D.
Director, Infant Research Project
Family and Child Services of Washington, D. C.

Preface

To FACILITATE the effective use of child development theory and research by the practicing professions, Russell Sage Foundation has provided funds to the Society for Research in Child Development for periodic publications that will collate and interpret current research in child development. The present volume is the first in this series. Its major purpose is to disseminate the advances in scientific knowledge about children among practitioners in such areas as pediatrics, social work, clinical psychology, nursery and elementary school education, and child psychiatry. Another purpose is to help the practitioner increase his understanding of the scientific study of child development, so that he can evaluate more readily the implications of the research literature for his own work. It is anticipated that these reviews will be useful to administrators and to faculty members in professional schools, as well as to service personnel engaged in work with children and families. The present and ensuing volumes also should be of value to researchers, students, and faculty members in nonapplied areas.

Personnel and procedures. To help assure that these reviews would report useful material for practitioners and provide the coverage deemed necessary, an Advisory Committee, consisting of persons who are experienced researchers and who also have a definite commitment and involvement in the applied professional areas, was appointed. The members of the Advisory Committee are: Nancy Bayley, Orville G. Brim, Jr., Leon Eisenberg, Robert J. Haggerty, Ronald Lippitt, William E. Martin, Julius B. Richmond, Seymour B. Sarason, Pauline Sears, Irving E. Sigel, and Leon J. Yarrow. This Committee aided the editors through all stages in the preparation of the volume: working out the overall approach; suggesting topics, authors, and editorial consultants; and reading some of the chapter drafts.

To prepare the reviews, authors were selected who are engaged in research on the topic and are thoroughly familiar with the theoretical and research literature—published and unpublished—as well as the more subtle methodological issues, problems, and nuances involved. In most cases the authors also have some familiarity with the problems and interests of the relevant professions but being primarily researchers, their knowledge of such matters is inevitably limited. To compensate for this and help assure the relevance of the reviews to the widest possible range of professions, twelve editorial consultants were appointed who are actively involved in applied professional work in child areas and who also have some familiarity with the problems of doing research and interpreting it for the practitioner. These consultants were: Aline B. Auerbach, Joseph E. Brewer, Gerald Caplan, Leonard J. Duhl, David Fanshel, Robert J. Havighurst, Alfred J. Kahn, J. Clayton Lafferty, Richard W. Olmsted, Sally Provence, Julius B. Richmond, and Ruth Updegraff. Each of these consultants read two chapters for their intelligibility and potential usefulness. They prepared reports which included suggestions for topic coverage, alternative organization of the paper, implications for practitioners of the research reported, language changes, and any other points that would help maximize the value of the paper for practitioners.

To be certain that each chapter adequately represented the research in the field, the help of twelve additional editorial consultants was enlisted. These consultants, each of whom had done significant research in one of the topic areas, were: Mary D. Ainsworth, Albert Bandura, Arthur J. Brodbeck, Roger V. Burton, Walter Emmerich, John H. Flavell, Daniel G. Freedman, J. W. Getzels, Jerry Hirsch, William Kessen, L. Joseph Stone, and Stephen B. Withey. Each reported on one chapter in his area of competence, making suggestions dealing mainly with the scientific adequacy of the paper, its coverage of the literature, and the appropriateness of conclusions drawn from the research.

Topic coverage and sequence in this volume. The choice of topics was not based on any overall framework but on practitioner-oriented criteria such as significance for a wide range of the professions, and the existence of an adequate body of research to report. The volume, then, is a sampler of significant topics in child development rather than an attempt to cover the entire field. Comprehensive coverage will come from the series of volumes rather than from any single one.

The first ten chapters in the volume deal with social and psychological aspects of child development. These are arranged in a developmental sequence insofar as possible, ranging from the early periods of socialization by adults, peers, and the mass media, to the development of higher mental processes as reflected in productive thought and moral character. Chapters on the genetic and neurophysiological underpinnings of behavior then follow. A minimum of background knowledge is required of the reader except for the chapter on neurophysiological substrates, which will interest mainly the medical practitioner and others having a prior knowledge of the nervous system.

Plans for the second volume. Plans are under way for a second volume which is scheduled to appear within two years. The second volume will include some of the general child development topics not covered here, as well as more specific topics that have only recently come into their own as subjects for empirical investigation. The chapter topics and authors are tentatively as follows: Effects of Family Structure (John A. Clausen); Psychological Effects of Minority Group Membership (Stuart W. Cook); Trends in Adolescent Behavior (Elizabeth Douvan and Martin Gold); Language Development and Its Social Context (Susan M. Ervin); Advances in Physical Growth (Stanley M. Garn); Social Structure and Social Change in the Classroom (John C. Glidewell); Factors in Preparing and Placing Children in Occupations (John I. Kitsuse); Delinquency: Causes and Efforts at Prevention (Lloyd E. Ohlin); Development of Intergroup Attitudes (Harold M. Proshansky); Psychosomatic Medicine (Julius B. Richmond and Earle L. Lipton); Learning Processes in Mentally Retarded Children (Edward F. Zigler); Testing of Children (Murray Levine and Seymour Sarason).

Acknowledgments. We wish to express our appreciation to the authors, members of the Advisory Committee, and the editorial consultants. The authors were assigned a very difficult task: that of integrating and interpreting the research, organizing it along lines of interest to the practitioner, and communicating it in nontechnical language. An extraordinary amount of effort and thought went into the preparation of their original manuscripts. Yet they were fully cooperative when revisions were requested—and these were usually substantial because of the special purposes of the volume.

The members of the Advisory Committee provided invaluable support and assistance. Meetings with the Committee were stimulating and arduous sessions, and between meetings there was a steady flow of communications between us and the individual members.

The editorial consultants examined the manuscripts with considerable care and their criticisms and suggestions were specific and detailed. As a result, their reports were very helpful to us in formulating guidelines to the authors for revision.

We also wish to thank Margaret R. Dunne, editor for Russell Sage Foundation, Earl K. Brigham, and Joan W. Barth for the editorial aid they provided. Jeanne Taylor, Elsie Kramer, Margaret Julian, Karen Baker, and Athalia Gentry assisted with typing, proofreading, and other clerical work.

Lois Wladis Hoffman
Society for Research in Child Development

Martin L. Hoffman
The Merrill-Palmer Institute

January, 1964

Introduction

PRACTITIONERS in the several professions that provide services to children have a constant need for knowledge in a wide variety of areas. Yet those whose time is fully taken up in such services find it almost impossible to keep up with the large volume of theory and research in child development coming from the various disciplines. The major purpose of this volume is to bring together the relevant research data from the many sources in a form that will be useful to the professional persons who work with children.

In preparing the volume, an attempt has been made to overcome some of the more flagrant hindrances to effective communication and utilization of research findings. The research literature too often gives the appearance of a confusing array of discrete studies which do not add up to anything useful. Individual research reports tend to be delimited by the few variables that can be accommodated within the design, by special characteristics of the sample, and by other factors that prevent a fully adequate portrayal of the complexities of the phenomenon under investigation. Often the problem is further compounded by the use of concepts which, though similar, are enough different to make each study appear to stand alone.

A more basic problem for the practitioner is that most research topics are determined largely by the concerns of a particular scientific discipline. Rather than being addressed to a solution of practical problems, they follow the logic of the guiding theories and the dictates of the research designs. From the standpoint of long-range progress this is as it should be. The researcher should be free to pursue the data wherever they may lead, unhampered by premature pressures toward practical application. But the theoretical and conceptual focus of such research can obscure the relevance for practice even when it exists, because of the difference between the concepts and terminology of the researcher and the practitioner. The practitioner may at times have difficulty even finding the studies that pertain to his work, because they are titled and indexed in ways that give little or no hint of their relevance.

To be useful, the research must be pulled together and interpreted. This volume therefore tries to provide integrative reports of the pertinent studies and advances in a particular area. Most of the chapters include a brief historical overview, to provide the reader with both a sense of continuity and the background for a fuller understanding of current and future research. For similar reasons, methodological issues that may impose limitations on the interpretation of the research findings are discussed. The chapters are not complete reviews or abstracts, however; rather, they are selective and interpretive in nature. The attempt is made to evaluate the significant research, and to point up the convergent and divergent findings which emerge from different research designs and populations.

Applied implications are pointed out for those studies which have obvious utility, but such studies are in the minority. The primary task of the editors and chapter authors has been to organize the relevant research around topics that articulate more with practitioner interests than with the more abstract theoretical or methodological issues which most concerned the investigators who originally reported the studies. In some cases this has called for emphasis upon questions and issues directly relevant to practice. But in most cases the data have been organized around more genotypic concepts that might suggest new ways of thinking about the problem. It is felt that this approach—in contrast to a more direct attempt to answer the practitioner's questions—preserves the integrity of the research, while using to best effect the competence of the authors, which is primarily in research. At the same time it should give perspective to the practitioner's own clinical insights, facilitating his translation of the research to the specific purposes of a particular case.

The aim of the volume will be fulfilled if the reports are found to be maximally useful to the practitioner without straying too far from the actual research findings. Herein lies a dilemma which plagues researcher and practitioner alike. Scientists are often very reluctant to stretch interpretations of their data to make practical applications. Professionals working in applied areas, on the other hand, are in great need of facts that can reduce the guesswork in their decisions. The research workers hesitate to draw action conclusions because the data from any single study, and even groups of studies, are probabilistic and limited by the particulars of the research design. These limitations in method are compounded by the lack of knowledge about the details of the particular case and the fact that any real-life behavior or event exists only in a complex context. Consequently, in every chapter of this volume—whether the variable is a gene, an aspect of parent behavior, or a social event—the point is made that the effects take place only in interaction with any number of other variables.

For example, in the chapter on parental discipline, Wesley Becker tells of several studies showing that punitive discipline by parents produces aggressive children. But he must then modify his conclusions by pointing out that boys and girls may respond differently; that the punitiveness of both parents has to be considered; that the child's aggressiveness is not expressed in all situations; and that there is some evidence that punitiveness in the early years may lead to the *inhibition* of aggression when the child is older. In addition, he points out that the association between parental punitiveness and child aggression may not be directly causal. That is, punitive parents are often hostile or less warm, and perhaps these are the crucial variables. Furthermore, the child's aggression could result from the frustration experience, from modeling an aggressive parent, or possibly because punitive parents actively encourage aggression in their children.

The present volume, then, is not a cookbook for the practitioner. It is an attempt to communicate the results of research in child development with a minimum of technical language, while paying due regard to the limitations of existing research procedures and without stripping the findings of their necessary qualifications. This does not mean that the authors avoid generalizing from the research. On the contrary, generalizations from data, principles, suggestive theoretical notions about underlying processes, and expositions of major theoretical positions make up a very important part of this volume. But these are not prematurely forced into prescriptions for administrative or clinical decisions in child care.

There are some studies, of course, that readily lend themselves to specific suggestions for practice. Examples are the following: (a) studies which show the effectiveness of diagnostic, therapeutic, educational, or child care procedures, and how the effectiveness varies with different kinds of children; (b) studies which add to the practitioner's repertoire of techniques and methods; (c) studies which provide leads to new kinds of data that should be obtained by the practitioner before selecting a course of action; and (d) studies which point up those aspects of the child that are relatively given and unchangeable, and those that are most subject to modification.

Studies having such obvious utility are included in the reviews wherever possible. Much of the research on early separation of children from parents, for example, has grown out of the interest of social workers, pediatricians, and child psychiatrists who were directly concerned with action implications. The chapter by Leon Yarrow on the effects of separation can therefore deal with such very practical issues as defining the dangers of early separation, specifying the ages of the children for whom separation is most perilous, and delineating more precisely the conditions relevant to these adverse effects. Furthermore, Yarrow reports studies which have actually evaluated the effectiveness of various procedures designed to ameliorate these effects. Similarly, part of the research on productive thinking has been stimulated by the concerns of educators. James Gallagher in his chapter on this topic is thus able to report research on techniques for stimulating productive thinking in children. Gallagher also suggests clues for the recognition of productive thinking abilities, and points out aspects of the child's social and educational setting that could inhibit the development of these abilities.

In the main, however, the reviews are seen as being useful in less direct ways. For example, they may make more explicit some of the assumptions that guide professional practice and report the data bearing on their validity, thus enabling the practitioner to examine them more objectively. In some cases the findings reported may buttress the assumptions. Examples are those findings which indicate that the child who spends an excessive amount of time watching television may have emotional problems; that the absence of the parent of the same sex may have harmful effects on the child's ability to adopt his expected adult role; that learning is promoted by teaching techniques which build upon the child's existing needs and interests.

Findings that run counter to prevailing views are perhaps more valuable to the practitioner, even though they tend to diminish certainty rather than increase it. An example is the often accepted belief that maternal employment has negative effects on the child—a belief not supported by current research. The research suggests that other factors must be taken into account before one can determine the effects of maternal employment, such as the mother's attitude toward employment and the age of the child. Two other examples might be mentioned. Jerome Kagan presents evidence that, despite the changing norms for male and female behavior in our society, young children still have traditional views about what is appropriate sex-role behavior. Bettye Caldwell presents evidence that contradicts the presumed advantages of late weaning; that is, prolonged sucking makes weaning more difficult rather than less, and increases the likelihood of non-nutritive sucking. Practitioners may also find it useful to know that certain assumptions and beliefs have not yet been subject to empirical test or that the data are inconclusive—as is the case of breast-feeding versus bottle-feeding.

Identifying group differences is another important contribution of research. The idea of being "culture-bound" or "class-bound" is not new. Educated persons have for some time been aware that attitudes, behavior standards, and behavior are different for different cultures and for different subgroups within a complex culture like our own. Yet the practitioner's perspective may be limited and some of his decisions influenced by subtle biases, because the children with whom he deals represent a narrow range of the population. Studies using diverse populations can help to broaden this perspective. As an illustration, consider a group worker accustomed to planning activity programs for middle-class girls whose new assignment

includes work with lower-income groups. A knowledge of the more traditional feminine interests of lower-class girls, as reported by Jerome Kagan,
might prove to be very useful in working with the new groups.

A more recent variation on this same theme is the discovery that *relationships* that hold for one group may be quite different for another. For
example, researchers who have analyzed their data for boys and girls
separately have discovered that the same experience may have a very
different effect on the two sexes. Wesley Becker reports a study which
shows that leadership in boys is facilitated by having parents who are
indulgent and warm and who also use principled discipline; yet these same
factors were found to discourage leadership and foster dependency in girls.
Eleanor Maccoby reports a study on the effects of television in Japan, in
which boys showed intellectual decrements and girls showed intellectual
increments.

The chapters in this volume indicate other kinds of qualifications which
determine whether certain events or situations will be significant. For
example, the chapter on mass media indicates that the effects of television
depend on the individual child's temperament, his intelligence, needs,
beliefs and values, and the opportunities that occur in real life to put into
practice what he has learned from the programs he watches.

In recent years, investigators have tended to reexamine broad concepts
in order to provide increased specification of the aspects of the general
event that produce a particular effect. An outstanding example of this will
be found in the chapter by Leon Yarrow, in which the broad concept of
"separation from parents" is analyzed into subtypes and then examined
further to determine with increased precision just which are the "dangerous" aspects of separation experiences. Through such specification and
identification of the process by which a given effect takes place, effective
clinical and social action can be facilitated.

Conceptualization in general may be one of the major values of these
reviews to the practitioner. In many of the chapters, the author's organization of the materials, or the category systems and theoretical concepts
reported, should facilitate the development of schemes and points of reference for organizing and conceptualizing the practitioner's experience. In
turn, such schemes should help to make the research findings more meaningful to the practitioner, heightening his awareness to certain important
variables in his work that might otherwise be missed. For example, in
discussing the influence processes in the child's peer group, John Campbell
points out that some of the effects stem from situational factors and he
organizes the relevant data around five of these factors: the physical
setting, the activity, the clarity of the task, the reward structure, and the

social structure. Apart from the actual research reported, organizing the findings so as to highlight the role of these variables can aid a group worker in the systematic analysis of some of the problems he may face. As another example, Joan Swift discusses several category systems for describing the behavior of nursery school teachers. These should help a teacher in assessing and improving her techniques, as well as making her more fully conscious of certain important aspects of her behavior.

In some instances these reviews can contribute by helping reduce the complexities of a class of events or stimuli to a smaller number of concepts. An example is the chapter on discipline which points out how the many aspects of parent practices might be reduced empirically to three bi-polar dimensions. These dimensions could then serve as orienting guidelines to many significant aspects of parent behavior, with due precautions against prematurely ignoring other pertinent factors.

Child development research has traditionally contributed normative standards and frames of reference that can help sensitize the practitioner to the range and variety of child behaviors at different age levels and in different settings. These standards also provide objective baselines for evaluating the child's performance as well as anticipating his potentialities. For example, understanding the child's cognitive potential should be useful in judging school readiness and in planning school curricula. As pointed out by Irving Sigel in the chapter on concept attainment, it might also help in judging the level on which to communicate to the child. Thus an adult might take a more appropriate approach to discipline if informed about the ages at which the child has the time perspective that permits him to defer gratification, the ability to generalize parental teachings beyond the immediate situation, and the ability to distinguish between being punished for his actions and being personally rejected by the parent.

It is true that individual studies often may not be safely used as a basis for drawing conclusions for practice. Yet they may, rather dramatically at times, suggest some new direction for the practitioner's consideration. When such is the case, they are frequently experimental studies. This volume presents several illustrations. Some of them are the findings that children tend to be more aggressive in the presence of permissive adults than when alone; that children tend to imitate the behavior of adults with whom they have a warm relationship, but will imitate aggressive behavior regardless of the relationship; that children can solve problems based on advanced mathematical concepts long before they can organize and articulate them as principles; that when the preschooler who leads his group joins another group, the "traditions" of that group are imposed on him and he may no longer function as leader.

Perhaps the most significant contribution this volume can make is to give the practitioner an opportunity to get a broad view of up-to-date material in many different areas. Though no one can hope to keep up with all of the relevant research, some familiarity with even the less germane areas has its value for good professional practice. Anyone concerned with improving the child's performance by some form of environmental manipulation, for example, should benefit from the chapter by Gerald McClearn, in which he pulls together the basic principles of behavior genetics and some of the recent advances in that field. Pediatricians, who are so often expected to be social workers and psychotherapists as well as physicians, should find much that is useful in the reviews on such topics as early separation, infant practices, and parental discipline.

In sum, this volume presents interpretive and selective reviews of child development research, oriented toward the interests of professionals working in the applied areas. In some places practical implications are discussed or studies are taken up which have obvious utility. More often the chapters will serve less direct functions, such as the assessment of the validity of certain operating assumptions, identification of group differences, and indication of the conditions mediating certain observed effects. The specification of global concepts like parental separation, maternal employment, television watching, and intelligence, and the pinpointing of the process by means of which a given effect is brought about, are extremely important contributions being made by some of the studies reported in these chapters. Often a social condition known to have negative effects cannot and should not be totally abolished; but knowing which particular aspects of the condition are most culpable, and how they operate to produce the effects, can facilitate taking more realistic and effective clinical and social action. In addition, these reviews provide the reader with conceptual schemes for organizing his own professional experiences—perhaps catching new views of familiar situations.

There are very likely other ways in which the interested practitioner who wishes to integrate research data within the framework provided by a fund of day-to-day practical experience, can benefit from a reading of this volume. Where precise answers are not available, reviews such as these can still reduce some of the guesswork in making professional judgments by providing frameworks within which to seek facts and examine problems.

The Effects of Infant Care[1]

BETTYE M. CALDWELL

State University of New York

In the research literature of the past decade, infant care practices have had a difficult time. Buffeted by contradictory or inconclusive empirical findings and assailed by accusations of inadequate theoretical heritage, they have frequently been denounced as inadequate experiential foundations for socialization theory. But in spite of their travail in the research literature, they have retained their popularity in the clinical and lay literature and in the preoccupations of conscientious parents.

Throughout antiquity there has been considerable interest in the effects of patterns of infant care, but the topic received its greatest modern impetus from early psychoanalytic theory. Additional contemporary support has come from cultural anthropology and social learning theory. In the absence of these formal scientific antecedents, however, interest in infant practices would probably have remained at a high level, since many of the hypotheses about the effects of parent behavior on the infant have an appealing face validity. That is, viewed adultomorphically, the infant snuggled up against his mother for repeated breast-feeding *ought* to feel more secure and content than the one abandoned to his own sucking struggle with an indifferent bottle; the baby fed or picked up whenever he cries *ought* to develop feelings of power and confidence that he has some influence over his environment. Thus the prevailing interpretations of the meaning of such experiences to the infant, coming as they do from adult frames of reference, produce little cognitive dissonance and gain ready acceptance.

Within the child care professions there seems to be more ambivalence toward, than either acceptance or rejection of assumptions about, the consequences of infant training patterns. For example, in formulating conclusions from a study concerned with the effects of different patterns of infant care, Sewell (1952, p. 159) stated: "Such practices as breast feeding, gradual weaning, demand schedule, and easy and late induction to bowel and bladder training, which have been so much emphasized in the psycho-

[1] The author wishes to acknowledge the contributions of colleagues and students whose comments and reactions helped structure the final form of this chapter. Particular appreciation is expressed to Dr. Julius B. Richmond and to Dr. Lois W. Hoffman.

9

analytic literature, were almost barren in terms of relation to personality adjustment as measured in this study." That forceful declaration, however, was quickly followed by a scientific apology for inadequacies of methodology (minimal controls, questionably accurate data on training practices, imperfect personality measures) and a formal expression of doubt: "However, it should not be concluded that these results unequivocally refute the claim that infancy is an important period in the development of the individual's personality, or even that the particular training practices studied have a bearing on personality formation and adjustments."

A similar expression of ambivalence is found in the comprehensive review by Orlansky (1949). After a thorough survey and cogent analysis of the empirical studies and the clinical and anthropological literature, he concluded that one would have to reject the hypothesis that specific infant disciplines have an invariant psychological effect upon the child. But in his final paragraph he drops the role of critic and proposes, "There is a good deal of evidence that subtle behavioral cues to maternal emotion are detected by the child in later months of life, and that these cues may be more important in governing its character development than are the gross patterns of discipline which an observer may quickly note" (p. 42). That "good deal of evidence" is buttressed with not a single one of the 149 references listed in his review but stands supported by a lone footnote referring to a clinical paper. Thus occasionally those whose own research or whose surveys of research done by others might seem to warrant closing the door on this topic have carefully left it slightly ajar.

HISTORICAL TRENDS

Almost throughout recorded history much attention has been given to patterns of infant care, especially those concerned with feeding. Current practices lead one to think of some type of cow's milk offered in a nippled bottle as the only alternative to maternal breast milk for the young infant. Yet over the centuries many ingenious nutritional and mechanical improvisations appeared before scientific developments in food chemistry, sterilization, and rubber and plastics provided us with the modern "formula" and the bottle and nipple. Until fairly recently the most common type of substitute feeding was provided by a lactating female who contracted to nurse one or more infants other than her own.

Selection of the wet nurse was apparently attended with all the solemnity currently attending the choice of the baby's pediatrician. Leading medical figures had many prescriptions associated with the choice. Consider, for instance, this priceless formula offered in 1545 by Thomas Phaer in *The Boke of Children:*

Wherfore as it is agreing to nature, so is it also necessary & comly for the own mother to nourse the own child. Wiche if it maye be done, it shal be most commendable and holsome, yf not ye must be well advised in taking of a nourse, not of yll complexion and of worse manners: but such as shal be sobre, honeste and chaste, well fourmed, amyable and chearefull, so that she may accustome the infant unto myrth, no dronkard, vycyous nor sluttysshe, for suche corruptethe the nature of the chylde (Ruhrah, 1925, p. 158).

As recently as the latter part of the nineteenth century, Routh (1879) devoted much attention to the choice of the wet nurse, making an attempt to appear more scientific by presenting gross data on chemical analyses of milk in support of his prescriptions. He insisted that the nurse be of good hereditary predisposition, lest she pass along to the suckling infant diseases known to be hereditary (implicating in this category syphilis, cancer, insanity, and a "deficiency in intellectual power"). Blondes and redheads were to be avoided, as their reputedly sanguine and passionate temperaments were said to cause deterioration in the quality of milk whenever there was any stress. Brunettes, while generally preferable, offered the additional advantage of restraining precocious children and protecting them from undue psychical excitement.

It is of particular interest that, in all the attention to the physical, moral, and mental attributes of the desirable wet nurse, no one seems to have been interested in the nature of the emotional attachment developed by an infant for the substitute-mother. Likewise, the psychological consequences to the mother of failing to nurture her own infant seem not to have been of much historical concern.

It is difficult to arrive at an estimate of the prevalence of wet nursing during any historical period in a particular locality. However, the practice was in general limited to the upper classes and to orphans and other wards of the state. The willingness of unscrupulous women to contract to nurse more children than they could feed satisfactorily, thus indirectly hastening the death of their own or of the contracted infants, perhaps helped to put the practice in disfavor. According to Wickes (1953d), the custom declined sharply toward the end of the nineteenth century and has now virtually disappeared in the western world.

Several formal historical surveys of the available literature pertaining to feeding techniques and other infant care practices have appeared, each commenting on slightly different aspects of the problem. Vincent (1951) analyzed trends in the scientific and lay literature published between 1890 and 1948. In 644 articles dealing with infant feeding, the discussion was entirely one-sided, with the vast majority of articles strongly advocating breast-feeding. The reasons for this recommendation shifted over the years from predominantly physical to predominantly psychological or emotional reasons. Vincent raised the interesting question of why such articles continued to pour forth without the stimulus of controversy, concluding that a fresh wave of exhortations appeared each time some new force in the culture threatened the practice. Also striking was the fact that changes occurred in chorus, with most writers advocating similar policies during any given time period. Thus there would seem to be a fairly rapid diffusion of new ideas which find their way almost in unison into the hands of those who will interpret to the general public.

In a similar survey, Stendler (1950) covered only articles in women's magazines from the 1890's to the middle of the twentieth century. In these materials she detected three distinct phases: (a) the sentimental phase, which exalted the role of the mother; (b) the rigid and disciplinary phase, emphasizing self-control and acquisition of habits by the child; and (c) the phase of self-regulation and understanding of the child. During the same period there was a shift from concern with moral and character development to personality development. In noting that each period studied had offered its share of child-training fads, Stendler concluded incisively that the fad of the present era may well be its overemphasis upon the relationship between specific infant disciplines and subsequent personality.

Wolfenstein (1953) made an impressive analysis of trends discernible in a single source—successive editions of the pamphlet *Infant Care* published between 1914 and 1951—and traced the zigzagging of recommendations offered during this short period of time. Early editions stressed the importance of impulse control, as exemplified by avoidance of autoerotic practices. During the thirties the emphasis shifted abruptly; the chief struggle was no longer between the child and his impulses but between the child and his parents. Feeding and elimination must be regulated and scheduled in order that the child learn the realities of the world to which he must adjust and to subordinate his own desires to the judgments of his parents. During the forties the recommendations took a different tack. Control was inconsequential, for the child was depicted as blameless and harmless in every way. Gratification of his impulses would help to make him less demanding in the future. His chief aim was exploration of his world, including his body and the interpersonal situation in which he lived. Autoerotic activities were merely one instance of this exploratory urge; if he were otherwise occupied such activities would disappear. In the 1951 edition mildness was still advocated, but the concept of limits appeared. Although gratification was still seen as important to security, too much could produce a tyrant. From the first through the penultimate edition, breast-feeding was emphatically recommended, and only in the 1951 edition were mothers given any reassurance that failure to breast-feed would not necessarily jeopardize the healthy development of their infant. Recommendations about bowel training showed sharp fluctuations, ranging from the 1921 advice to begin as soon as the confinement period was over to the 1951 suggestion that one and one-half to two years would be better. Wolfenstein expresses concern about these drastic shifts that show concern only for surface behavior and ignore the fact that deep parental feelings, which cannot be so easily disposed of, remain unaltered.

The zeal with which research was translated into concrete recommendations, and the ease and speed with which abrupt reversals of policy were made, have indeed been impressive. Since the life span of each major trend of the twentieth century has been at most two decades, not even one generation has been given a chance to provide adult validation of the hypothesized child training consequences. A new trend is always appearing to push the old one out of the nest. The 1963 publication of a new revision of *Infant Care*[2] suggests that neither the scientific nor the lay community is too dismayed by these somewhat embarrassing reversals and that the quest for an ever-new temporary answer to the perennially poignant question, "How shall we rear our children?" continues unabated.

DETERMINATION OF EFFECTS

How does one demonstrate that a particular parent practice has a given effect? In order to do so one must deal with factors that relate to the definition of concepts, to choice of criteria in terms of which to determine effects, to techniques of assessment, to methods of obtaining the infant care data, to the subjects who will be used to demonstrate the effects, and to the anticipated duration of effects. Rather than ingenuously attempting to prove that "breast-feeding is important," one must specify carefully what is meant by breast-feeding and then seek to determine its effects within a particular developmental area as measured by a specific technique in a carefully described group of subjects observed for a prescribed period of time. Each of these major design factors which can influence the outcome of research concerned with the effects of early socialization practices warrants brief discussion.

[2] A new edition of *Infant Care* has just been published. Most noticeable in the latest edition is an almost complete absence of dogmatism about the influence of any specific practice and a recognition of the possibility of alternative modes of infant response to similar forms of parent behavior. The potential influence of specific practices is minimized, while the importance of the interpersonal context in which the behavior will occur is stressed. The pamphlet's attention to the importance of a stable mother-child relationship for healthy development reflects the professional concern of the past decade with the topic of maternal deprivation.

Conceptual Factors

In an area which does not seem at all recondite, conceptual problems should not cause much trouble. Yet they do, since the definition of terms in this area is a highly individualized affair. There seems to be imperfect agreement as to what is meant by such terms as breast-feeding, demand feeding, or toilet training, and significantly less consensus about *early* breast-feeding or *coercive* toilet training. Weaning, for example, may be used to indicate the withdrawal of all forms of nutritive sucking, withdrawal of only the breast but continuation of bottle feeding, or the introduction of solid foods into the diet. Likewise, the addition of descriptive adjectives serves to add further confusion, in that one man's "late" (Sears and Wise, 1950) may be another man's "early" (Hoefer and Hardy, 1929). Likewise, "toilet trained" may mean that the child will produce a stool or urine upon request, that he usually announces his desire to relieve himself, that he does this during the day but not at night, or that he has been dry and has not soiled day or night for six months. Yet generalizations from the studies generally ignore the careful definitions and refer only to the generic terms. Brody (1956) has emphasized this point in a discussion of what the term "self-demand" connoted to a group of mothers. It meant not offering food until the infant gave some sort of hunger signal but little else. Missing from the maternal concept were concern with time and method of terminating feeding and an awareness of the importance of need gratification and emotional support.

Benedict (1949) has implied that completely objective definitions are impossible, since parent practice must be defined not only in terms of the behavior involved but also in terms of what is communicated to the child by the particular behavior. She illustrates this with a discussion of swaddling in different eastern European cultures. Swaddling may be practiced in order to ensure that the violent and antisocial impulses of the child will not find bodily expression; it might be used to keep the child's hands away from the genital region; or it might be advocated in order to provide maximal nurturance and protection for the infant. She asserts that one must attend to the subtle communications of a particular act if one is to anticipate correctly its consequences for the infant. This is in effect one approach to controlling for both overt and covert aspects of behavior, very similar to the distinction made later in this chapter between practice and attitude.

Criterion Factors

As criteria against which to evaluate the effects of infant care practices, many studies have used personality variables. These may range from relatively narrow and specific traits (such as tendency to engage in thumb or finger sucking) through more pervasive variables (such as amount of security, dependency, aggression) to essentially global attributes (such as presence or absence of psychopathology). Physical development has not been ignored as a criterion, particularly in the area of effectiveness of patterns of infant feeding, and physiological variables that seem logically related to patterns of infant care have been frequently used as criteria of the effects. Not until very recently has there been much eclecticism about choice of criteria or a strong inclination to examine for the effects of a practice in a different area of behavior (for example, the effects of breast-feeding upon response to toilet training). The availability of computers which can handle large matrices of relationships is now making it possible to do this, and heuristic studies which examine for unpredicted antecedent-consequent relationships are appearing with increasing frequency. It is of interest to note that cognitive criteria, such as intellectual and language development, have been minimally employed.

Assessment Factors

Assessment techniques used in studies concerned with child care practices have been extremely varied, ranging from superficial questionnaires to prolonged depth analyses. The structured interview has been by far the most popular technique for providing data about both the antecedent parent variables and the consequent infant variables. The difficulties associated with this pattern of assessment have been discussed elsewhere (Caldwell, 1962). When all available techniques are to some extent fallible, each investigator is entitled to make his own choice. However, the fact that research employing different techniques to assess the same variable will not necessarily lead to identical results must not be overlooked. Consider the likelihood of obtaining similar results from two studies concerned with the influence of method of toilet training on the degree of disturbance shown by the child, one using a single maternal interview and the other using extended free play sessions with the child to estimate degree of disturbance. Failure of two such studies to corroborate each other demonstrates only that different methods can lead to different results, and any contradiction should not necessarily be interpreted as weakening the hypothesis that method of training may have demonstrable effects.

Methodological Factors

Data about infant care are often obtained through retrospective reports. The types of false inference likely to be drawn from retrospective studies of any criterion group in which a particular pattern of behavior or symptomatology is observed (for example, thumb-sucking, constipation, high aggression) have been more fully grasped in recent years. However, only recently have actual data been offered to substantiate the long-suspected distortion and loss of information involved in retrospective data collection.

Goddard, Broder, and Wenar (1961) interviewed 25 mothers of four- and five-year-old children on whom extensive hospital and clinic records from birth onward were available. Detailed information about pregnancy, delivery, and early development of the child was obtained from the mothers and compared to data available in the medical records. The authors concluded that there was sufficient unreliability of recall to question the use of history given by the parents as a source of information about perinatal events, feeding experiences, and early illnesses.

Similarly, Wenar and Coulter (1962) presented data on the accuracy of retrospective material dealing with early child care. They re-interviewed 25 mothers who, some three to six years previously, had provided information about the early developmental histories of their children for whom admission to a therapeutic nursery school was sought. Results obtained from this second interview were compared with the data obtained at the time of the original application. Only 57 per cent of the directly comparable pairs of statements from the two interviews were exactly the same. Furthermore, almost half of the differing statements involved a considerable deviation from the original report. There is no indication that the mothers tended to describe their children in a more desirable manner with the passage of time, nor that the original diagnostic category of the child affected accuracy of recall. Wenar and Coulter concluded that there was somewhat more reliability in essentially factual areas than in areas dealing with more emotional aspects of the earlier developmental period.

In a study by Bernstein (1955) discrepancies were found between cumulative clinic records based on maternal report at each visit and retrospective information about such events as time of weaning, but data in the records could not be considered infallible. A correlation of only .50 was found for age of weaning as reported by 36 mothers of five-year-old children and the age as recorded in the clinic chart. In two cases where there was an extreme discrepancy, the mothers claimed to have falsified information earlier in order to escape anticipated criticism from the clinic staff for their chosen methods. Thus even currently recorded information based upon maternal report rather than actual observation offers no guarantee of complete accuracy, but it is more likely to be accurate than data based on similar reports given some years later.

Subject Factors

In spite of the general acceptance of the principle of individual differences, most research has tended to disregard factors conducive to reactive differences among subjects and to assume that a given type of parental behavior should be responded to uniformly by all children. Yet there are a number of child characteristics which may monitor the effects of parental behavior. Some of the more obvious variables are age, sex, and ordinal position of the child within the family. Most of the available studies have dealt in some way with age of the child being socialized and some have been concerned with the differential effects of parent behavior on boys and girls. However, there are other subject variables equally deserving of attention which have generally been neglected. For example, intellectual level seems to have been of little interest as a subject variable which might influence a child's reaction to a given form of parental behavior. Recognition that such subject characteristics will already show the influence of extrinsic factors by the time they can be measured does not warrant avoidance of effort to determine their interaction with other relevant variables.

Time Factors

The effects of child-rearing practices may be sought in either the immediate present or at some time in the future. For instance, one might be interested in the immediate tranquilizing effects of extra mothering on colicky babies or in the ease with which individuals who have received such mothering may form social relationships in adolescence. The question of determining a reasonable period of time for assessing effects is a tricky one which has not received adequate consideration. In retrospective studies carried out with adults, demonstration of persistence of effects for twenty or more years is sometimes required. As many of the relationships suggested by psychoanalytic theory refer to adult consequences of infancy experiences, such long-interval testing makes sense. But whether it makes sense to seek to establish straight-line relationships from infancy to adulthood, with no concern for intervening experiences, is another matter. Attenuation of relationships with time is to be expected (see Rheingold, 1956; and Rheingold and Bayley, 1959) since subsequent experiences have the opportunity to reinforce or inhibit earlier patterns of response. Discontinuity from early childhood into adulthood appears to be the pattern for many behavioral variables. (See Kagan and Moss, 1960.) An obvious implication of this lack of behavioral constancy is that parent behavior which would show a relationship to child behavior at one age would fail to show a similar relationship at a later age. Thus in order to understand the total cumulative influence of parental behavior, it is imperative to isolate those variables which will have a delayed action effect as well as those which will have an immediate effect. Only long-term studies can provide the answers to such questions. In view of the hazards associated with retrospective research, it is hoped that the several prospective longitudinal studies now coming to fruition in this country will be able to supply some of the much-needed information in this area.

Omitted from this discussion are such universally important design factors as size of the sample and the application of appropriate statistical tests. The factors highlighted here, while important in all types of scientific investigations, are of particular relevance to research oriented toward identifying variables associated with change in behavior over time.

SCOPE OF THIS REVIEW

If one is willing to ignore the exhortations and examine the evidence, what conclusions can be reached about the effects of infant care? This review will be devoted to a presentation of as much of the empirical literature as could be found which appears relevant to answering this question. Although the author's assignment was to deal only with *specific practices* rather than broad variables of infant care, such as the influence of the maternal personality or the warmth of the mother-child relationship, this distinction was not always easy to maintain. The review cannot claim to be exhaustive, for anthropological and clinical case reports are not included. Clinical studies which meet reasonable standards of methodological adequacy will be discussed when appropriate. Closing off these two major channels of information was necessary in order to keep the chapter to a reasonable length. However, such materials have often served as the major stimulants to the design and execution of an empirical study and are thus indirectly represented.

Specific empirical studies concerned with the effects of various infant care practices have in general assumed one of the following forms:

1. Both the independent and the dependent variables are singular—for example, the effects of duration of sucking upon frequency or intensity of thumb-sucking.

2. The effects of a single independent variable are sought on multiple dependent variables—for example, the effects of duration of nutritive sucking upon personal adjustment, school adjustment, and adaptability.

3. The dependent variable is restricted, and the influence of multiple independent variables is traced. Thus aggression in preschool children might be related to degree of self-regulation permitted in feeding and toileting during infancy.

4. Both the dependent and independent variables cover broad swaths of behavior. These might be designated as omnibus studies. The effects of type of feeding, time of weaning, time and method of toilet training are sought in a variety of areas, such as presence of oral habits, degree of personal and social adjustment, and presence or absence of psychopathology. During recent years this type of design has become increasingly popular, perhaps reflecting the conviction of research workers that meaningful relationships between parent behavior and child behavior will not be established in terms of isolated single variables.

Discussion of empirical studies will be oriented in terms of the major independent variables given research attention over the years. To be considered are the effects of patterns of infant feeding, time and method of elimination training, and other miscellaneous infant care practices. Within each section, however, studies will be discussed in terms of the dependent variables selected by the investigators in terms of which to seek to demonstrate the effects. Following the presentation of research evidence pertaining to specific practices of the infancy period, the influence of the personal-social context in which training occurs, the role of social class, and the influence of the child being trained will be considered.

INFANT FEEDING

Components of Oral Gratification

Food needs are powerful throughout life, but, because of the infant's limited intake and peak growth requirements, they are particularly urgent during early infancy. Since these needs cannot be gratified without the intervention of some other person, the feeding of the infant is a social as well as a nutritional experience. Since the satiated young infant usually goes quickly to sleep, the important social transactions of the early months are likely to occur either just before, during, or just after feeding. Thus the attention of personality theorists of diverse orientations to infant feeding practices is readily understood.

The most insistent theoretical impetus to concern with infant feeding has come from psychoanalytic theory, as formulated by Freud (1905) and Abraham (1921), which stressed that the need for food involves also a need to suck (and later to bite) and that gratification or frustration of this "oral" drive will affect the personality of the developing infant in a variety of ways. For example, a gratifying infancy is said to be conducive to oral optimism—that is, to generosity, sociability, receptivity to new ideas, and an extremely positive outlook on life. Lack of oral gratification is said to lead to oral pessimism—that is, to anxiety and insecurity, to the need for constant reassurance, selfishness, aggressiveness, impatience, and so on. Similarly, Erikson (1950) has postulated that oral gratification for the infant is essential for the development of a basic sense of trust in the people and objects in his environment.

Oral gratification is presumably facilitated by at least three major aspects of the infant feeding situation: (a) source of nourishment, (b) schedule of feedings, and (c) technique of inducing the child to abandon sucking as a means of obtaining nourishment. Maximum gratification is assumed to occur with breast-feeding regulated by the child's hunger rather than the clock, with weaning delayed until the infant is "ready" and carried out gradually rather than abruptly.

Of these three aspects of presumed oral gratification, the one for which it is paradoxically most difficult to make a case is breast-feeding. The proposition that sucking at the breast is somehow more gratifying than sucking from a bottle involves a number of assumptions which probably stem from the realization that breast-feeding is the natural method of infant feeding and should therefore serve some adaptive function. Choice of breast-feeding is often regarded as an index of maternal acceptance of the child, and the position in which the infant is held for breast-feeding may offer more collateral pleasurable stimulation than is likely to be available with other feeding techniques. However, it is a well-known clinical fact that interruption of breast-feeding due to illness of the mother or temporary separation will frequently result in subsequent rejection of the breast by the infant after even brief exposure to some other sucking procedure.

The gratifying nature of relaxed feeding schedules is not an idea of the twentieth century, as a reading of Wickes's (1953a,b,c,d,e) scholarly history of customs of infant feeding will reveal. However, it has been during fairly recent times that the custom received a new label—self-demand—and new status. One of the first formal statements of the importance of this variable appeared in the book by Gesell and Ilg (1937), in which the authors stressed the ability of the infant to regulate his own food intake with respect to both quantity and frequency. They presented data from individual cases in which maternal feeding had followed the cues given by the infant, both as to time of feeding and amount to be ingested, to support their contention that total food intake would not vary greatly from the amount ordinarily offered by the mother, though there might be considerable fluctuation from one feeding period to the next or even from one day to the next.

As the third support of the oral gratification triad, nature of weaning derives its theoretical status from the importance of the urge to suck. The sucking reflex is in most infants well developed at birth and can be elicited by any type of stimulation of the perioral region. If there is, as Freud postulated, a basic oral drive which involves sucking as its primary manifestation, then early and abrupt weaning ought to be frustrating and leave the oral drive unsatiated, whereas prolonged sucking opportunity and a gradual introduction to other eating techniques should help to provide maximal oral gratification. These, then—breast-feeding, flexible schedules, and late and gradual weaning—have been assumed to represent the essentials of oral gratification for the infant.

In reviewing the literature on infant feeding, it is not always possible to separate the influence of these different components of oral gratification. Studies using nutritional or general developmental criteria have been primarily concerned with source of nourishment, with duration of milk feeding as a correlated secondary concern. Investigations using some form of oral behavior as a dependent variable have been most concerned with duration of nutritive sucking and have paid less attention to source of nourishment and spacing of feedings. Research employing personality measures as criteria has frequently dealt with all three components, sometimes in combination and sometimes in what might be described as contaminated isolation. That is, if one were to test for the effects of any one aspect of this triad, the possible effects of the other two should be carefully controlled. In attempting to demonstrate certain correlates of type of feeding, one should have breast-fed and formula-fed groups carefully matched in terms of schedule of feedings and duration of total breast or bottle sucking experience. In actual practice when any one aspect is selected for study, the assumption is made that the other two will vary randomly. Such an assumption is tenuous, as breast-fed infants are probably more likely to be fed on demand, and bottle-fed infants are likely to be permitted a longer duration of nutritive sucking (discounting the possibility that in such an ideal study the breast-fed infants would be permitted a transitional period of nutritive sucking from a bottle). Such controls still leave untouched other important aspects of the feeding situation which might influence results, such as the tactile contact assured in breast-feeding but optional in bottle feeding and the interpersonal context in which any one practice is employed.

Since research of this type can employ only the differential or comparative method, such precision of control can seldom be achieved; as a result, there is frequently some residual ambiguity about the precise aspect of the infant feeding situation likely to have been influential even when an association with a pattern of child behavior has been demonstrated. Because of this complexity, the following discussion is organized around consequences rather than antecedents, and all components of the main independent variable will not always receive individual attention. However, in summarizing the general effects of infant feeding practices an attempt will be made to highlight the contributions of each component.

Normative Data on Infant Feeding

Prior to an examination of some of the findings regarding early feeding gratification and development, it would be well to consider normative data about each of the components. In spite of the previously mentioned flow of persuasive literature extolling the physical and psychological virtues of breast-feeding, its incidence has declined sharply during the current century. It is difficult to arrive at an exact incidence figure that is up-to-date, and extrapolation based on surveys made as recently as five years ago may be inaccurate. Table 1 presents summary data from a number of studies published during the past decade. The studies by Meyer (1958) and Robertson (1961) deal with the broadest United States sample, and both indicate that approximately one-fifth of American mothers breast-feed their infants initially, with the fraction rising to about one-third if one includes supplemented breast-feeding. Both studies also reported wide regional variation in incidence, with the New England states having the lowest incidence and mountain and western states the highest. Data from the Sears, Maccoby, and Levin (1957) and from the Robertson studies suggest that incidence at three months of age is from 10 to 15 per cent. This percentage is somewhat lower than reported estimates for most other countries, but the incidence has declined in all industrialized nations, with the decline being sharper in urban than in rural areas. Geber (1958), commenting on trends in partially westernized African nations, suggests that cultural sophistication and ability to breast-feed are becoming incompatible. For an excellent summary of world trends the reader is referred to that by McGeorge (1960).

Normative data on the use of feeding schedules and age of weaning will be taken from Sears, Maccoby, and Levin (1957). They found that relatively few mothers adopted either extreme of the scheduling continuum, with 12 per cent feeding entirely on demand and only 8 per cent feeding according to a rigid schedule. The modal pattern could be described as one based on a rough schedule modifiable by as much as a half-hour. With respect to weaning, which meant for them initiation of the process of inducing the infant to relinquish nutritive sucking, they reported that 60 per cent of the mothers in their sample began the process when their infants were between five and eleven months of age, with 5 per cent of the mothers beginning before their infants were five months of age and only 1 per cent postponing this step until after the infant was two years of age.

TABLE 1. RECENT TRENDS IN THE FREQUENCY OF BREAST-FEEDING

Author and Date	Source of Data	Major Findings
1. Jelliffe (1955)	Summarized data from British studies.	Decline in complete breast-feeding at three months from 77% to 36%, 1929–1949.
2. Boek, Lawson, Yankauer, & Sussman (1957)	Home visits to 1,433 mothers with infants between 3 and 6 months of age in upstate New York.	Only 3.7% of the infants breast-fed at 3 to 6 months. Slightly higher incidence in middle- and upper-class families.
3. Sears, Maccoby, & Levin (1957)	Interviews with 379 mothers of kindergarten children residing in Boston area.	Some breast-feeding by 39%; only 15% breast-fed for three months or more.
4. Meyer (1958)	Questionnaires sent to 2,000 hospitals throughout the United States.	Decline in breast-feeding from 38% to 21% between 1946–1956. Wide regional differences.
5. McGeorge (1960)	Summaries provided by hospital matrons in New Zealand of type of feeding at time of discharge; data from visiting nurses re breast-feeding at 3 weeks, 3 months, and 6 months; incidence of breast-feeding at 6 weeks postnatal clinic visit. Also summarizes published reports of world-wide trends.	In 1957–1958 incidence range of 62% to 92% in different hospitals. From 1948 to 1958, breast-feeding at discharge declined from 89% to 75%. Breast-feeding at 6 months declined from approximately 70% to 20% from 1938 to 1952. Large differences in world trends but slight decline in all industrialized areas.
6. Robertson (1961)	Questionnaires sent to 1,223 mothers with young infants throughout the United States.	At one week, 30% of infants totally or partially breast-fed; 15% on any breast-feeding at 8 weeks, 7% at 18 weeks. Primiparae more likely than multiparae to breast-feed; middle class had lowest incidence. Marked regional variations in incidence.

In slightly more than half of the infants, weaning was completed within four months, but for 12 per cent of the sample a year or more was required for completion of the process.

Oral Gratification and General Development

The first and perhaps most obvious area in which to look for effects of oral gratification is general health and development. However, since this review is oriented more to psychological consequences of infant care practices, the topic will not receive extensive coverage. With respect to no other aspect of infant feeding does research become so quickly dated, and each study cited here typifies the era in which it was conducted. As mentioned earlier, type of nourishment (breast or substitute milk) has been the most frequently examined antecedent condition. Hoefer and Hardy (1929) evaluated the performance of 383 school children ranging in age from seven to thirteen on a number of physical and psychological measurements. Length of period of exclusive breast-feeding was the major independent variable. The children were placed into subgroups, depending upon whether they had been breast-fed for three months or less, from four to nine months, and from ten to twenty months. On a host of measures (weight, muscle tone, general physical condition, age of walking and talking, age of dentition, intelligence quotient) the four-to-nine month feeding period tended to be associated with more advanced development. The children who were entirely artificially fed were, on the whole, inferior to the other two groups, the only exception being that the extended breast-feeding group had the lowest intelligence test performance. As length of breast-feeding extended beyond nine months, there was a slight but progressive decline in intelligence test performance. Although this was interpreted as being due to the nutritional disadvantage associated with prolonged breast-feeding, it may have reflected a concentration of culturally deprived families in the prolonged breast-feeding group.

Major advances in the development of artificial feeding formulas did not appear until around 1925 (McGeorge, 1960), which would be after the infancy of the children in the preceding study. At that time attention shifted from attempts to humanize cow's milk to the task of discovering the basic nutritional needs of the human infant. With today's wide array of milk formulas available for ready consumption, rare is the infant for whom an apparently wholesome type of substitute milk cannot be found. Thus more recent investigations might be expected to yield different results. A study by Hytten, Yorston, and Thomson (1958), while designed primarily as an investigation of maternal attributes associated with continuation or abandonment of breast-feeding, provides data pertinent to this question. Frequent postnatal visits were made to 106 primiparae who had been breast-feeding their infants at the time of discharge from the hospital. Observations and inquiries were directed toward identifying difficulties encountered in breast-feeding and toward an assessment of the general health and development of the infants. It was found that, at three months of age, the infants of those mothers who had abandoned breast-feeding within the first month gained weight more rapidly, cried less, and were at least as healthy as the breast-fed infants. Furthermore, the physical condition of the mothers who were using bottle feeding seemed better, since chronic fatigue and breast discomfort plagued the mothers who had continued to breast-feed. Heinstein (1963), in a study concerned primarily with psychological correlates of breast versus formula feeding, reported as an incidental finding that children who had been breast-fed were no healthier or better developed physically than the formula-fed children.

In summarizing research dealing with the effects of breast or artificial feeding on physical and nutritional status, Stone and Bakwin (1948) state that one must conclude that, though there may be difficulties, the human infant can thrive on artificial milk. Data accumulated by the World Health Organization on the incidence of Kwashiorkor in underdeveloped countries (Brock and Autret, 1952) point to certain nutritional hazards associated with prolonged breast-feeding. However, the fact that infants gain weight less rapidly and are perhaps a bit fussier under a breast-feeding regimen is not likely to dissuade advocates of the custom. In fact, McGeorge (1960), in commenting on such findings, cautions that maximal rates of growth have not been proven to be optimal rates, and there may be certain advantages at maturity to a less than maximal growth rate during early years. Such a reminder may well constitute the next line of evidence to support the practice of breast-feeding which Vincent (1951) conjectured would always come forth whenever the custom appeared to be in jeopardy. At any rate, at this point in the twentieth century, it is impossible to demonstrate any nutritional or health advantage for the infant or growing child associated with breast-feeding.

Oral Gratification and Personality

In Table 2 is presented a summary of research published within the past two or three decades which deals with the relationship between some aspect of infant feeding gratification and personality. Since many of the studies have dealt with more than one component of the oral gratification triad, it was decided to avoid repetition by presenting one master table which summarizes the nature of all the research relevant to this topic. For every study, information is given about the number and type of subjects used, measures of the major independent variables, measures of the major dependent variables, and obtained results, plus certain comments from the reviewer about design factors which should be kept in mind in evaluating the research. Not every study summarized in the table will be discussed in the text. Although the tabular material appears overwhelming, it actually provides a more concise summary than would be possible in a detailed exposition. Also, by lining up comparable information about each piece of research, it should help to bring into focus the methodological factors which must be considered in arriving at conclusions on the basis of the evidence. An attempt is made to supply enough information to permit the reader to form his own judgment about the merits of each study.

TABLE 2. INFANT FEEDING PRACTICES, PERSONALITY, AND DEVELOPMENT

Author and Date	Subjects	Measures of Major Independent Variables	Measures of Major Dependent Variables	Summary of Findings and Conclusions	Comments
1. Hoefer & Hardy (1929)	383 school children 7–13 years of age.	Duration of breast-feeding as exclusive source of nourishment. Comparisons made of children breast-fed <4 months, 4-9 months, and >9 months.	Measures of physical and mental development—weight, muscle tone, physical condition, age of walking, talking, and dentition, and intelligence quotient.	Advanced development associated with 4-9 month breast-feeding. Prolonged breast-feeding associated with lowest performance on mental tests.	Insufficient data to justify conclusion that association between prolonged breast-feeding and low I.Q. due to nutritional deficit; during that era prolonged breast-feeding more likely to occur in culturally deprived group.
2. Childers & Hamil (1932)	469 children referred to clinic for psychological problems.	Length of breast-feeding, (<1, 1-5, 6-10, >11 mos.) as reported in social history.	Number of symptoms of emotional problems reported.	Undesirable behavior manifestations were common in 1-5 month group.	No statistical analysis or information about type of feeding (cup or bottle) offered to nonbreast group. Retrospective data on feeding.
3. Rogerson & Rogerson (1939)	109 7-year-old children (62 breast-fed and 47 artificially fed).	Clinic records of type of feeding and age of weaning.	Physical and emotional development, based on observations in home visits, and school records.	No difference in age of weaning (introduction of solid foods) for 2 groups; artificially fed group had poorer appetites, enuresis, sibling jealousy, nervousness, (was) below average in school work.	Idiosyncratic definition of weaning (introduction of solid foods rather than cessation of sucking).
4. Peterson & Spano (1941)	126 "normal" children from Fels longitudinal study.	(a) Two indices of duration of breast-feeding: (1) complete breast-feeding—no other milk given child; (2) supplemented breast-feeding—length of time mother provides any milk for child. (b) Fels ratings of maternal rejection.	(a) Measures of several aspects of personality; (1) 13 Fels scales rated in Nursery School; (2) Joël Behavior Maturity Scale; (3) Vineland Social Maturity Scale; (4) Brown Personality Inventory. (b) Length of breast-feeding.	No significant correlations. No evidence that longer breast-feeding is associated with security and good psychological adjustment. Length of breast-feeding unrelated to maternal rejection.	Data on breast-feeding recorded at time it occurred.
5. Maslow & Szilagyi-Kessler (1946)	418 college students.	Length of breast-feeding (information secured by the students from their mothers).	Scores on security inventory.	Curvilinear relationship—highest security scores earned by those breast-fed <3 mos. and >12 mos.	No data on type of feeding offered after termination of breast-feeding; feeding history retrospective.
6. Holway (1949)	17 preschool children, 8 boys and 9 girls.	Degree of self-regulation permitted infant as assessed by maternal interview covering length of breast-feeding, and maternal feelings about feeding.*	Two doll play sessions scored for reality, fantasy, hostile, and tangential behavior.	Positive correlation between degree of self-regulation permitted the child and amount of reality play; inverse relation between self-regulation and fantasy.	Small N, retrospective data re self-regulation. Questionable assumption that reality in doll play is best index of child's ability to deal with stress.

* Other independent variables were also considered in this study.

TABLE 2. INFANT FEEDING PRACTICES, PERSONALITY, AND DEVELOPMENT (Continued)

Author and Date	Subjects	Measures of Major Independent Variables	Measures of Major Dependent Variables	Summary of Findings and Conclusions	Comments
7. Newton (1951)	24 normal kindergarten children.	Maternal interview about early feeding history. Some checks on accuracy by comparing reports with school records.	Teachers' ratings, investigators' observations of behavior and adjustment in kindergarten.	Partially or totally breastfed, and flexibly fed children showed most desirable group behavior. Late-weaned group contained best and worst adjusted children.	Small sample, no statistical treatment. Feeding data retrospective, though checked against possible where medical records.
8. Thurston & Mussen (1951)	91 male psychology students.	Infant feeding gratification data obtained from questionnaires mailed to Ss' mothers.	Oral traits as measured by group Thematic Apperception Test.	No relation found between adult oral traits and infant feeding gratification.	Retrospective data on feeding history obtained by mail.
9. Sewell & Mussen (1952)	162 rural 5-6-year-olds.	Maternal interview about type of feeding, schedule of feeding, and method of weaning.	Maternal report about oral symptoms and adjustment; teachers' ratings of response to frustration and emotional adjustment. Children's scores on California Test of Personality.	No evidence that breast-feeding, demand schedules, and gradual weaning promote personal adjustment.	Retrospective. Forced dichotomization of variables (e.g., each case forced into predominantly breast or bottle though may have received both types of feeding).
10. Goldman-Eisler (1953)	115 normal and neurotic adults; 100 college students.	Duration of breast-feeding.	Relative strength of traits indicative of oral optimism and oral pessimism. Relationship between strength of these traits and breast-feeding history.	Emergence of bi-polar factor or corresponding to oral optimism and oral pessimism. Correlation between later weaning and oral optimism.	Retrospective data on breast-feeding. No information about feeding experience after breast-weaning.
11. Sears et al. (1953)	40 preschool children, 20 boys and 20 girls, and their mothers.	Maternal interview about feeding, weaning, and general permissiveness.*	Teachers' ratings and time sampled observations of dependency and aggression in preschool.	Dependency positively correlated with severity of weaning in both boys and girls; also with rigid feeding schedule. No relation between infantile frustration and aggression.	Data on infant feeding obtained retrospectively but soon after events had occurred. Excellent measures of aggression and dependence.
12. Bernstein (1955)	23 boys and 27 girls.	Three indices of oral gratification, based on maternal interview and clinic records.*	Play interview with child eliciting oral behavior.	Positive relation between sucking in infancy and tendency to constipation; inverse relation between oral gratification and tendency to collect objects (hoard) in childhood.	
13. Klatskin, Jackson, & Wilkin (1956)	50 primiparae and their infants selected from Yale Rooming-In Project through first 3 years.	Degree of flexibility in maternal behavior as noted from Project records in feeding, toilet training, socialization and adjustment to maternal role.	Ratings of presence or absence of problems in child in same 4 areas, and evidence of maladjustment.	Child influenced by deviant maternal behavior in all 4 areas after first year. Direction of deviation (rigid or overpermissive) relatively unimportant.	Preconceived notion about what is "optimal."

* Other independent variables were also considered in this study.

TABLE 2. INFANT FEEDING PRACTICES, PERSONALITY, AND DEVELOPMENT (Continued)

Author and Date	Subjects	Measures of Major Independent Variables	Measures of Major Dependent Variables	Summary of Findings and Conclusions	Comments
14. Sears, Maccoby, & Levin (1957)	379 mothers of 5-year-old Boston area children.	Carefully structured maternal interview securing information about early feeding history, and some data about reaction of child to parent behavior.*	Maternal report (in same interview) of degree of dependency, aggression, conscience, development, feeding problems, etc.	No effects associated with breast- or bottle-feeding. Later and more severely weaned children showed more upset during weaning; no relation to dependency or aggression. Rigid feeding schedule associated with lack of warmth toward infant and high child-rearing anxiety.	Large and representative sample. Data re infancy retrospective. Maternal interview provided data about both dependent and independent variables.
15. Hytten, Yorston, & Thomson (1958)	106 3-month-old infants breast-fed at time of hospital discharge.	Continuation or abandonment of breast-feeding during first three months.	Maternal reactions to breast-feeding experience; amount of crying and irritability, and physical development of the infants.	Infants placed on bottle feeding within first month gained weight more rapidly, cried less, and were as healthy as breast-fed infants; physical condition of mothers in bottle feeding group better than those continuing to breast-feed.	Infants very young at time of evaluation.
16. Durrett (1959)	60 preschool children, 30 boys and 30 girls, from upper- and middle-class homes.	Home interview about feeding schedule and other patterns of parent behavior that give an index of degree of self-regulation permitted the infant.*	Two 20-minute doll play sessions scored for aggression.	No significant relationship between early regulation and doll play aggression. Correlations among measures of early regulation usually low but positive.	Data about early regulation obtained retrospectively. Mothers asked to rate themselves on degree of early regulation.
17. Acheson & Truelove (1961)	152 adult ulcerative colitis patients; 152 controls with other medical disorders.	Establishment of "successful" breast-feeding —i.e., breast-feeding for at least the first 14 days of life.	Presence or absence of ulcerative colitis.	In 18.2% of colitis and 7% of controls breast-feeding was not established; no difference in proportion of cases in 2 groups breast-fed at one month.	Data on weaning secured from the patients themselves; weaning means breast-weaning only.
18. Murphy (1962)	32 preschool children.	Oral gratification in infancy and autonomy permitted infant in feeding situation.*	"Coping behavior."	Oral gratification and feeding techniques correlated positively with many preschool measures of good adjustment.	Prospective; assessment techniques not fully described.
19. Heinstein (1963)	47 males and 47 females who were subjects in Berkeley Guidance Study until 18 years of age.	Duration of breast-feeding without supplementary nursing; duration of total nutritive sucking. Warmth of the mother; nervous stability of the mother; marital adjustment of parents as assessed by interviews when children were between 21 and 36 months of age.	Mild personality problems observed during preschool period and preadolescence; performance on TAT given when children were between 9 and 12, and performance on Rorschach administered at age 18.	Single variable analysis yielded few significant associations. Breast-feeding and length of nursing have different effects, depending on interpersonal situation, with patterns of interaction different for boys and girls.	Excellent study which deals with interaction as well as effects of single variables. Personal-social environment as assessed at 2-3 years not necessarily identical to that which prevailed during first year.

* Other independent variables were also considered in this study.

28

Psychological adjustment. Several studies summarized in Table 2 have used as dependent variables some measure of psychological adjustment or maladjustment. In a number of these (Childers and Hamil, 1932; Rogerson and Rogerson, 1939; Peterson and Spano, 1941; Maslow and Szilagyi-Kessler, 1946; Acheson and Truelove, 1961), duration of breast-feeding was the only aspect of the dependent variable considered. With the exception of the study by Peterson and Spano, all of these pointed to some effect associated with breast-feeding. Taken at face value they suggest that, from the standpoint of later psychological adjustment, even a little breast-feeding is better than none at all but that, if the mother does not plan to continue breast-feeding for at least a half year or so, it might be better if she stops before her infant is much older than one month.

With the exception of the study by Peterson and Spano, the one study in which no effect could be demonstrated, all of these studies were retrospective; furthermore, in two of them information about infant feeding was secured directly from the subjects rather than from the mothers. To this reviewer it comes as no surprise that 44 of the subjects in the Acheson and Truelove (1961) study were unable to answer the question, "Were you breast-fed or bottle-fed from birth?" Likewise, in all of these studies almost no attention was paid to the type of substitute feeding available to the nonbreast-fed infants. That is, it is not made clear whether those who were taken off the breast were subsequently bottle or cup fed or put on solid foods. In the Rogerson and Rogerson (1939) study it is stated that the breast and artificially fed groups were "weaned" at roughly the same times, but weaning meant the introduction of solid foods into the diet and not the total duration of sucking permitted the infants. Thus methodological factors warrant caution in generalizing from the pooled results of this cluster of researches dealing only with duration of breast-feeding.

Several other studies summarized in Table 2 have used psychological adjustment as a major dependent variable but have added other facets of the infant feeding situation as refinements of the independent variable (Newton, 1951; Sewell and Mussen, 1952; Klatskin, Jackson, and Wilkin, 1956; Heinstein, 1963). From her survey of 24 kindergarten children Newton concluded that partial or total breast-feeding and flexible feeding seemed associated with good psychological adjustment; the correlates of weaning age were unclear, as the late-weaned group contained all the best and all the most poorly adjusted children. However, as her sample was very small and as no statistical treatment was used, her findings can only be interpreted as suggestive. The Sewell and Mussen (1952) project was an omnibus study which included as independent variables all aspects of the gratification triad, although with respect to weaning their attention was limited to the gradual-abrupt continuum. These variables were related to maternal interview data about oral symptoms and signs of adjustment, to teachers' ratings, and to scores obtained by the children (162 five-year-olds) on a personality questionnaire. From their results they concluded that there was no evidence that breast-feeding, flexible schedules, or gradual weaning was conducive to good adjustment. Klatskin, Jackson, and Wilkin (1956), whose report was based on children during the first three years of life, disregarded type of feeding and paid most attention to flexibility of feeding program. They found that deviation in either direction (too rigid or too flexible) was associated with problem behavior in the children.

The most comprehensive and best-designed study dealing with early feeding experience and adjustment which has been published is reported in the recent monograph by Heinstein (1963). In his study both type of feeding and duration of nutritive sucking were among the independent variables considered, with incidence of mild behavior problems during the preschool period and early adolescence and a number of personality ratings based on projective techniques administered during adolescence as the major dependent variables. Subjects were 47 boys and 47 girls who remained in the Berkeley Guidance Study (Macfarlane, 1938) from infancy through eighteen years, and all data analyses were made separately for boys and girls. Results of single variable analyses of infant feeding factors revealed no clear adjustment advantage for either boys or girls at any age period as a function of whether breast or bottle had been the major source of nourishment. A longer duration of total nutritive sucking was associated with more problem behavior in boys, especially during the middle childhood period, but not in girls. This important study will be referred to subsequently when the interaction between specific practices and the interpersonal milieu in which they occur is considered.

One would have to conclude from this group of research reports that no clear adjustment patterns had been demonstrated to appear as a consequence of any aspect of infant feeding experience. Although several of the relevant studies have dealt with more than one of the gratification components, possible interaction effects have not been adequately considered.

General personality characteristics. Although there is perhaps no personality characteristic which is not in some way related to psychological adjustment, authors of the studies reviewed in this section appeared to be primarily attempting to delineate some of the personality characteristics observed in children with different feeding histories, making no inferences about whether the observed characteristics indicated good or poor adjustment. They all considered more than one component of feeding gratification. Holway (1949) and later Durrett (1959) both attempted to relate multiple aspects of self-regulation permitted the infant, including feeding gratification, to doll play during the preschool period. Holway concluded that there was a correlation between the degree of self-regulation in feeding permitted the infant and subsequent reality play, equating reality play with the ability to meet the demands of the environment. Durrett, on the other hand, could demonstrate no such relationship.

The studies cited in the table by Sears and associates (Sears *et al.*, 1953; Sears, Maccoby, and Levin, 1957) both reported certain effects associated with the pattern of infant feeding, but the effects were not always in the same direction in the two studies. The first study looked for infant feeding correlates of aggression and dependency, using observational methods for assessing dependency and aggression and a structured maternal interview for eliciting data about infant feeding. There was no correlation between infant feeding frustration and aggression in either boys or girls. With respect to dependency, however, results of the investigation supported the authors' hypothesis that dependency during preschool years would vary positively as a function of rigidity of feeding schedules and severity of weaning in both boys and girls. In the 1957 study, which utilized a maternal interview to supply data about both the maternal behavior and the children's responses, no association between feeding gratification and dependency could be established. No clear effects could be shown for breast-feeding, and few significant relationships pertaining to time and method of weaning could be demonstrated except for the child's response to the weaning process itself. That is, later and more severely weaned children showed more upset during weaning. There were no relationships between weaning variables and either dependency or aggression.

Although the two studies by Sears and associates did not ask the same questions about the effects of feeding schedules, both demonstrated some kind of association between feeding schedules and child behavior or else between feeding schedules and other maternal variables. In the later study they paid more attention to maternal correlates of a particular feeding pattern and reported that adherence to a rigid schedule was associated with lack of warmth shown the infant. The authors hypothesized that choice of this pattern of feeding might be more affected by the pediatric advice the mother had received than by her own inclination and, further, that the least self-confident mothers would be most likely to lean heavily on such advice. This latter hypothesis was confirmed by the finding of a positive correlation between use of rigid scheduling and anxiety about child rearing.

Murphy (1962) has recently reported a number of significant positive correlations between infant oral gratification and preschool measures of coping behavior, including security, sense of self-esteem, strength of interests, ability to regulate the impact of environment, clarity of perception, resistance to fatigue, acceptance of others, flexibility of emotional control, and capacity to maintain internal integration. Similarly, feeding autonomy permitted by the mother correlated positively with such preschool attributes as tolerance for frustration, resistance to discouragement, tolerance of temporary regression, effective energy expenditure, and capacity to maintain internal integration. Significant relationships were also found between the infant's protestation and rejection of unwanted foods and subsequent autonomy, impulse control, general ability, persistence when in difficulty, quickness of orientation in a new environment, drive toward mastery, and self-reliance. On the basis of these correlations Murphy suggested that oral gratification during the first six months tends to leave the baby generally tension-free to facilitate good self-environment differentiation and to foster a wholesome self-concept. She concluded that the basic "coping capacity of the ego" was formed during the first six months of life. It is significant to note that her method of analysis avoided the usual research dichotomies (breast-bottle, schedule-demand) and placed more emphasis upon the reaction of the infant to whatever type of feeding experience he had.

Oral personality. Three studies cited in Table 2 had as one of their major goals testing of certain hypotheses about the oral character as expounded by Freud (1905) and Abraham (1921). In the first of these, Thurston and Mussen (1951) carefully defined 30 Thematic Apperception Test scoring variables which would assess oral traits and then administered the test to 91 male psychology students to whose mothers questionnaires requesting detailed information about feeding histories had been mailed. Data analysis consisted of testing for an association between the 30 oral character traits and three estimates of oral gratification during infancy: duration of breast-feeding as the exclusive source of nourishment; total sucking permitted (breast plus bottle, if relevant); and age at complete withdrawal of the breast. First considering each index of infant feeding gratification separately, they found no more significant associations than would be expected on the basis of chance. In order to determine whether relationships would emerge if only extreme subgroups were considered and if gratification measures were combined, they selected the ten most gratified cases who had also been fed on demand and the scores of the ten least gratified cases who had been fed on a rigid schedule. Again no more significant associations were found than would be expected on the basis of chance alone, which led the authors to conclude that they had found no evidence of a significant association between infant feeding gratification and the presence of adult traits epitomizing the oral personality. Although their study was retrospective, it marked an early attempt to combine indices of gratification by considering simultaneously the effects of type and timing of feeding. Whether their methods provided a very sensitive measure of this interaction is doubtful, however.

Goldman-Eisler (1953) carried out a twofold investigation concerned with oral gratification and the strength of traits indicative of oral character structure. In the first phase of the work she factor-analyzed responses to a questionnaire given to 115 normal and neurotic adults to determine whether some 19 traits co-varied and formed the nucleus of an oral character. The analysis revealed a bi-polar factor, interpreted by the author as corresponding to the psychoanalytic character types of oral optimism and oral pessimism. In an attempt to determine whether scores on this factor were related to age of weaning, 100 college students were given the questionnaire, and an inquiry was made of their mothers about the age at which breast-feeding had been discontinued. (Although the author indicated interest in the amount of sucking allowed the child, she apparently did not consider sucking via the bottle of any consequence.) Results showed a significant difference between scores on oral pessimism for subjects who had been weaned early and weaned late, leading the author to conclude that longer breast-feeding was conducive to the development of oral optimism.

Bernstein (1955), in a well-designed study dealing with several aspects of early child experience, tested certain psychoanalytic hypotheses about oral gratification and personality traits said to reflect orality. He found that prolonged sucking experience was associated with a preference for a confection which could be sucked (lollipop) rather than chewed (chocolate) in a candy choice situation. He also found that prolonged sucking was associated with a tendency toward constipation and that limited sucking experience was associated with a fondness for collecting objects. In psychoanalytic terminology both of these traits are usually interpreted as of anal rather than oral origin.

Oral Gratification and Oral Activities

The specific effects of infant feeding upon the formation of oral symptoms has been a topic of considerable theoretical and practical interest. Although thumb-sucking seems not to be high on many parental lists of desirable child behavior, professional opinions about its significance vary. Bakwin (1948) regards thumb-sucking as no more pathological in a child than smoking in an adult, whereas Kaplan (1950) asserts that the act signals a serious disturbance in interpersonal relationships and a tendency to shut out external stimulation. Explanation of the preference for the thumb as the favorite sucking object must, of course, be highly conjectural. In random arm flexion of the newborn there is probably a greater likelihood that the thumb rather than any other finger will come into contact with the mouth. Palermo (1956) speculates that the choice might be accounted for by stimulus generalization, in that the stimulus properties of the thumb are more similar to those of the nipple on either bottle or breast than any of the other fingers.

Regardless of reasons for preference of the thumb, and regardless of what the behavior might mean to the child or to the parents, it occurs with considerable frequency in infants and children and even in some adults. Table 3 presents a summary of incidence figures as reported in a number of surveys dealing with some aspect of finger sucking. In the two studies concerned with any manifestations of thumb or finger sucking (Kunst, 1948; Brazelton, 1956), the incidence rate is quite high, since almost all the infants were observed to have engaged in some form of nonnutritive sucking at some time. Although the other studies were concerned with the more chronic and habitual form of thumb-sucking, it is doubtful that the behavior was defined uniformly. Some investigators attempted to distinguish between different degrees of intensity, whereas others report in all-or-none fashion. In terms of habitual thumb-sucking, the various incidence figures range roughly from 25 per cent to 50 per cent, with a suggestion of a higher incidence rate in girls than in boys.

Of the studies reporting on spontaneous remission of the habit, only that by Brazelton (1956) would support the common reassurance offered to parents that the behavior will disappear at an early age. He reported that all but four infants stopped the nonnutritive sucking by one year without any sort of parental intervention. In contrast, however, the studies by Klackenberg (1949), Yarrow (1954), and Traisman and Traisman (1958) suggest that the behavior pattern, once established, is durable and persistent. The Traismans found that 81 per cent of those children who had ever sucked their thumbs were still doing so at age two and that the average age for spontaneous abandonment of the habit was just under four years. Thus they felt that, while parents tended to be too concerned about the habit either as an indication of psychological disturbance or a possible cause of dental abnormality, it was inadvisable to tell parents that the behavior would usually disappear around one or two years.

Of more concern than incidence of thumb-sucking have been factors associated with the initiation and perpetuation and/or elimination of this habit. David Levy's original and provocative work on this subject (1928) provided empirical support for the psychoanalytic premise that mouth-

TABLE 3. INCIDENCE OF NONNUTRITIVE SUCKING

Author and Date	Source of Data	Major Findings
1. Levy (1928)	(a) 112 infants and children seen in private practice. (b) 100 infants on welfare.	(a) Thumb-sucking observed in 25%. (b) Thumb-sucking observed in 40%.
2. Kunst (1948)	143 institutional babies, birth to 1 year.	All babies sucked thumb or fingers at some times, boys slightly more than girls. Frequency increases to 3 months, plateaus, declines after 6 months.
3. Klackenberg (1949)	259 Swedish children attending child health center, 4–6 years. Mothers filled out detailed questionnaires.	50% sucked thumbs at some time, onset before 3 months in 54% of those who sucked. By 12 months, 50% stopped; 21% still sucking at 6 years.
4. Yarrow (1954)	68 children followed in longitudinal study.	64% sucked at some time; slightly higher proportion in girls. 50% still sucking at 4 years; 14% at 7 years.
5. Brazelton (1956)	70 cases from private practice. Mothers made 24-hour observations once a week.	Sucking observed in 61 of 70 children. Onset usually 0–3 months, peak usually 7 months. Decreased and stopped by 1 year in all but 4 cases.
6. Traisman & Traisman (1958)	2,650 infants and children, birth to 16 years, seen in private pediatric practice.	45.6% sucked thumbs; no apparent sex differences. Only 4% stopped by 1 year; 81% of those who sucked still sucking at two years.
7. Honzik & McKee (1962)	(a) 184 8-months normal and neurologically suspect infants observed during developmental testing. (b) Maternal reports about habitual thumb-sucking for 743 preschool children, and data from longitudinal study.	(a) Approximately 45% of each sample observed to suck thumbs or fingers; no sex difference. (b) Higher incidence in girls than boys at all ages (50% and 37% in preschool years).

centered activities stem from an oral drive associated with and yet somewhat independent of the hunger drive. Failure to satiate this oral drive with nutritive sucking will lead to compensatory, nonnutritive mouthing or sucking. Reporting on several series of infants, Levy concluded that thumb and finger sucking occurred in response to "incompleteness of the sucking phase of the feeding act" as manifested by spontaneous withdrawal from a rapidly flowing breast or forced withdrawal from the breast or bottle. Onset of the habit frequently occurred almost immediately after a change in feeding schedule which increased the interval between feedings and decreased length of sucking permitted at each feeding session. Outstanding in the feeding histories of children who did not suck their thumbs were unscheduled and untimed feedings, frequent though scheduled feedings, and the use of the pacifier. Age of weaning was not considered in this study.

Levy followed his clinical series with an experimental study (1934) on the effects of restriction of sucking opportunity on nonnutritive sucking and biting activities in puppies. In the tenth day of life he removed from the nest four puppies from a six-pup litter of collies. Two of these were fed from large-hole nipples, and two were fed from small-hole nipples requiring more vigorous and longer sucking to obtain a given quantity of milk. During the 20-day observation period the fast-fed puppies sucked more on the experimenter's proffered finger and on one another than the slow-fed puppies. They were also more active and gained less weight. A similar study by Ross (1951) on puppies fed from either a bottle or an eye dropper from birth substantiated Levy's findings. Puppies nursed by the bitch did not show an appreciable amount of nonnutritive sucking after the sixth day of life, whereas bottle- and dropper-fed puppies engaged in such activities to a great extent until after their return to the mother. Ross concluded that in puppies a sucking need exists which, if not satisfied, will result in excessive nonnutritive sucking.

Levy's hypothesis that thumb-sucking signified insufficient gratification of a sucking drive was subsequently tested in a number of other investigations, a summary of which is presented in Table 4. Scanning of the table will reveal that there has not been consensus in the research dealing with this issue. For a number of years most of the research which was published supported the Levy hypothesis by finding an association between length of individual feedings and thumb-sucking (Roberts, 1944; Klackenberg, 1949). Also the finding by Levine and Bell (1950) and by Klackenberg (1949) that use of pacifier seemed to be a deterrent to the development of thumb-sucking was interpreted as being in support of Levy's hypothesis. However, on the basis of her finding that out of a group of 26 infants, five who had been from birth both breast-fed and demand-fed sucked their thumbs, Simsarian (1947) voiced the conviction that adequacy of sucking provided no guarantee that a child would not suck his thumb and that alternative etiological factors had to be given some consideration.

The discovery of Fredeen's (1948) technique of having nonbreast-fed babies fed directly from a cup led to the initiation of two experiments by Sears and associates (Davis et al., 1948; Sears and Wise, 1950) which polarized the issue of the association between amount of sucking gratification and oral activities. In the Sears and Wise study a comparison was made of the incidence of oral manifestations in children who had been

TABLE 4. FACTORS INFLUENCING NONNUTRITIVE SUCKING

Author and Date	Subjects	Measures of Major Independent Variables	Measures of Major Dependent Variables	Summary of Findings and Conclusions	Comments
1. Levy (1928)	112 infants and children seen in private practice, 100 infants on welfare.	Information secured from the mothers about early feeding, number of feedings per day, length of feedings, change of feeding schedules.	Thumb-sucking	Thumb-suckers had history of shorter feeding times, fewer feedings per day. Onset of habit often coincided with lengthening of interval between feedings.	No data on total duration of nutritive sucking (age of weaning).
2. Roberts (1944)	15 thumb-suckers, 15 nonthumb-suckers, 7–8 months of age.	Type of feeding, number of feedings per day, time per feeding, changes in feeding schedule.	Thumb-sucking	Percentage of thumb- and finger-suckers rose as feeding time decreased.	Subjects very young; some in nonsucking group may later have become suckers.
3. Simsarian (1947)	5 children breast-fed on demand from birth.	Detailed feeding history.	Thumb-sucking	All 5 children sucked thumbs; thus unlimited sucking opportunity no absolute deterrent to sucking.	Small sample.
4. Kunst (1948)	143 institutionalized infants, birth to 1 year.	Time of feeding, amount consumed, contact with other people.	28,000 time samples. Child's sucking score was proportion of observations in which finger sucking occurred.	Sucking increased as a function of time since feeding. Sucking correlated positively with volume of formula, negatively with caloric content. Slightly more in boys than in girls. Less sucking when being stimulated; more when in prone than when in supine position.	Observational study. High reliability of data.
5. Davis, Sears, Miller, & Brodbeck (1948)	60 infants, birth to 10 days.	Method of feeding (20 cup, 20 bottle, 20 breast).	Sucking of proffered finger during first ten days of life.	Duration of sucking increased over the 10-day period in breast-fed babies only. No differences between groups in spontaneous oral activity or crying.	
6. Klackenberg (1949)	259 children, birth to 6 years.	Total duration of breast-feeding, amount of time per feeding, use of pacifier.	Thumb-sucking	Total duration of breast-feeding unrelated to sucking; suggestive association with duration of individual feedings (shorter feeding times—more sucking). No thumb-suckers in group using pacifier at 3 months.	

37

TABLE 4. FACTORS INFLUENCING NONNUTRITIVE SUCKING (Continued)

Author and Date	Subjects	Measures of Major Independent Variables	Measures of Major Dependent Variables	Summary of Findings and Conclusions	Comments
7. Levine & Bell (1950)	28 infants offered pacifiers.	Maternal report on use of pacifiers.	Thumb-sucking.	Only 2 of 28 infants sucked thumbs; both gave up pacifier before 1 year.	No data on time consumed per feeding. Late-weaned group early in terms of current norms.
8. Sears & Wise (1950)	Children 5–8 years from 80 families.	Amount of nutritive sucking in infancy as determined by age at weaning.	Reaction to weaning; frequency and severity of thumb-sucking; feeding and sleeping problems.	Later weaning associated with more severe reaction; tendency for late-weaned to show more thumb-sucking. No association between length of sucking experience and feeding problems.	Efforts made to reduce any retrospective errors. Considered both length of individual feeding periods and total duration of sucking experience.
9. Yarrow (1954)	66 children participating in longitudinal study.	Duration of sucking experience (breast or bottle); length of individual feedings.	Thumb-sucking, reaction to weaning.	No relation between duration of breast-feeding and thumb-sucking; no relation between age of weaning to cup and thumb-sucking. Later weaned group showed more severe reaction to weaning. Children with the shortest feeding time during first 6 months showed significantly more thumb-sucking.	
10. Bernstein (1955)	50 children attending health clinics.	Interview with mothers and medical records about amount of sucking reinforcement permitted child.	Play interview with child, and choice of candy to suck or chew. Maternal interview data on resistance to weaning and thumb-sucking.	Children with more sucking experience show greatest resistance to weaning; no association between amount of sucking and thumb-sucking; children who sucked longer more likely to choose lollipop than chocolate in candy choice.	Though data on feeding are somewhat retrospective, check provided on accuracy of information. Careful use of >1 index of sucking gratification; ingenious behavioral measure of dependent variable.
11. Blau & Blau (1955)	1 male baby, observed for 118 successive feedings between 3 and 7 weeks.	Speed of feeding as controlled by varying size of holes in nipples. Blocks of 26 fast, 34 slow, 51 fast, and 7 slow feedings.	Nonnutritive sucking, general activity, crying.	More sucking activity, crying, restlessness, and more difficulty sleeping associated with slow feeding.	Feeding speeds arranged in blocks rather than randomized, with the fast preceding the slow.
12. Traisman & Traisman (1958)	2,650 infants and children, birth to 16 years, seen in private pediatric practice.	Speed of feeding, type of feeding.	Thumb-sucking	Breast-feeding unimportant; slow feeding, (more sucking) associated with thumb-sucking.	No data on thumb-sucking as related to total duration of nutritive sucking.

38

largely cup fed and others who had been breast or bottle fed for varying lengths of time. They obtained data about early techniques of and response to child training from 80 mothers of children between the ages of two and eight. Weaning occurred quite early in all cases, with only five cases weaned later than seven months. The effects of amount of sucking experience were tested in terms of reaction to weaning, frequency and severity of thumb-sucking, and feeding and sleeping problems. The results showed that there was an association between age of weaning and severity of reaction to weaning, with the later weaned infants showing more severe disturbance. There was a suggestion of greater frequency of thumb-sucking in the late-weaned children, though the difference was not statistically significant. The data from this study suggested that the oral drive is strengthened, not satiated, by continued nutritive sucking and that it is the strength of the oral drive rather than amount of oral frustration (as implied by Levy) which influences reaction to weaning and development of thumb-sucking.

It should be noted here that Levy presented no data about age at weaning in his subjects, basing his interpretation of inadequate sucking opportunity on the length of each individual feeding session. Sears and Wise, on the other hand, presented no data on the length of individual feeding periods but based their estimate of amount of reinforcement of nutritive sucking on the total duration of sucking permitted, that is, age of weaning. Thus the two studies, while frequently interpreted as defining polarized theoretical positions, do not really present contradictory data on the same issue. The later Traisman and Traisman (1958) study considered length of individual feeding periods and found that longer rather than shorter feeding sessions were associated with more thumb-sucking, a finding which was interpreted as supporting the position of Sears and Wise. However, the relationship was not completely linear, as the lowest incidence of thumb-sucking was found in the subgroup of babies taking longer than 60 minutes per feeding session. This reversal of trend could possibly be accounted for by the fact that infants taking so long to feed might be drifting in and out of sleep, thus not receiving constant oral stimulation. In the excellent study by Bernstein (1955), length of individual feeding periods plus number of feedings per day were considered along with total duration of nutritive sucking opportunity in computing a composite index of amount of sucking reinforcement. Although he found no statistically significant difference in the magnitude of this index between the thumb suckers and the nonsuckers in his sample, the direction of difference was similar to that reported by Sears and Wise.

The study by Yarrow (1954) offered a tentative reconciliation of the differences between the two major positions presented thus far. In a group of 66 children (28 males and 38 females) participating in a longitudinal study, he investigated the relationship between thumb-sucking and the following indices of oral gratification: length of breast-feeding, length of individual feeding sessions, and total duration of nutritive sucking. He found no statistically significant differences in duration or severity of thumb-sucking between children who had received no breast-feeding and those who had been breast-fed more than three months (though there was a trend toward an association between longer breast-feeding and a lower incidence of thumb-sucking). Nor was there a statistically significant difference between incidence of thumb-sucking in those who were late-weaned from either breast or bottle and the early-weaned group, although there was a trend toward more thumb-sucking in the later weaned subjects. The late-weaned children reacted to weaning with significantly more upset than the early-weaned group. There was also a statistically significant relationship between thumb-sucking and short individual feeding times during the first six months. Thus his finding that later weaning is associated with a more severe reaction to weaning is in the direction of the Sears and Wise hypothesis; his data on greater incidence of thumb-sucking in children who had short individual feeding sessions during the first six months are in the direction of Levy's findings. In commenting on his results Yarrow offers a cogent refinement of the two major hypotheses which comfortably reconciles these seemingly contradictory positions. If, as the empirical studies suggest, a short feeding time during early infancy and a long overall sucking time are associated with thumb-sucking, an explanation in terms of simple reinforcement theory is not adequate. Therefore, it may be that the strength of the oral drive varies as a function of the developmental level of the child and that it is strongest during the early months of infancy. Thus during early infancy, frustration (fast feeding) may lead to fixation and to non-nutritive sucking. But prolonged satisfaction of this drive after its strength begins to wane (late weaning) may lead to overgratification and to fixation. Yarrow thus formulates a phase-specific hypothesis which implies special sensitivity to frustration at a particular developmental state. Plausible though this explanation may be, more data are needed to resolve the conflict. As yet no one has demonstrated a statistically significant association between late weaning and thumb-sucking, and three trends in that direction cannot be accepted as adequate proof.

Summary

To summarize the material on oral gratification and behavioral development, one can only conclude that the relationship between type and schedule of infant feeding and personality during childhood cannot be fully described at this time. There are hints that gratification for the infant might be more closely related to the degree to which he can program his feeding regime than to whether he is fed from a breast or a bottle. Minimal attention has been given to the infant's individual reaction to various aspects of the feeding situation in appraising the extent of gratification or frustration which he experiences—the avidity with which he sucks, the regularity which he imposes upon himself, his reactions to solid foods, and the amount of biting and chewing he is permitted, and so on. Research which has conducted an eclectic search for possible consequences of feeding patterns suggests that the effects of oral gratification will not be completely understood if one uses as dependent variables only so-called "oral" behaviors and if one is content with single variable analyses.

ELIMINATION TRAINING

Although automatic laundry equipment and diaper services are accessible to most families in America today, elimination training is still a topic of considerable interest to the mothers who have the responsibility of guiding their children through the process. In an early edition of his famous manual (1946), Dr. Spock treated the subject rather casually and implied that, in spite of occasional setbacks and resistance on the part of the infant, training could be accomplished without too much furor and difficulty. In a recent publication, however, Spock (1963) identifies toilet training as the one aspect of child care which has consistently baffled him the most and which seems to provoke more questions from mothers, particularly those with college educations. Thus neither modern technology nor parent education literature at its best has succeeded in removing elimination training from the list of socialization practices deserving of research attention.

Again the major stimulant to professional concern with this topic was Freud's theoretical formulation of stages in pre-genital libidinal development. In a brief paper entitled "Character and Anal Erotism" (1908), he introduced the famous triad of personality characteristics—orderliness, obstinacy, and parsimony—by which an intensification of the anal erotic components of the personality can be identified. To this interpreter, Freud's interest seemed oriented more toward the effects of the drive (erotism) upon toileting behavior rather than the reverse. However, in the course of fifty years or so the influence of toilet training upon manifestations of anal traits seems to have become the focus of interest.

Other theorists have given attention to the sequence of activities involved in elimination training, though obviously for differing reasons. John B. Watson (1928), whose theories formed the basis for the recommendations of early training found in early editions of *Infant Care*, regarded elimination essentially as another arena in which the struggle for control occurred. The child must learn to evacuate at certain times and prescribed places acceptable to the parents; failure to comply suggested refusal of the child to subordinate his desires to those of the adult. Also, Watson considered it imperative that control become automatic in order to liberate the child's energy for more creative forms of endeavor. Dollard and Miller (1950) have also suggested that elimination training is an important socialization activity, describing it as one of the critical learning situations in which anxiety and conflict may develop in the child.

Elimination training is often compared to weaning, in that it involves persuading the infant to abandon a technique of need gratification that has been previously employed and to substitute a technique that meets the specifications of the culture. In some respects, the degree of change involved is greater in elimination training. Complete gratification of the hunger drive, for which sucking serves as the instrumental response, requires that the infant's sucking occur in conjunction with some external object supplied by the mother—either the breast or bottle—and therefore is not entirely at the disposal of the infant. With respect to elimination, however, the degree of gratification is under the infant's control; he can evacuate in complete independence of anyone or anything in his environment. Thus even the most demand-fed infant being weaned is likely to have had some experience of frustration of the instigation to engage in sucking for food (during moments of preparation, and the like), whereas the child undergoing toilet training (at whatever age) encounters such frustration for the first time after a period of complete reinforcement. That such frustration is not beyond the adjustment capacities of the human infant is attested to by the fact that this is a universal training situation—that is, learning not to soil within the immediate living area is expected of infants in every human social group that has been observed.

Most theoretical discussions and articles written for parents distinguish between bowel and bladder training. However, the research investigations themselves have not always made the distinction. In the main, methods of encouraging urinary continence have been neglected, with major attention given to the acquisition of bowel control. In the Sears, Maccoby, and Levin (1957) study, for example, the only mention of urinary control is in connection with parental methods of handling bed-wetting. Inquiries are made about time and methods of initiating *bowel* control, with the information thus secured labeled as methods of "toilet training." This relative neglect of specific urinary training techniques may stem from the fact that only bowel activities are literally "anal" in the psychoanalytic sense, or that bowel training usually occurs first and thus strongly influences subsequent training methods. It may also reflect this author's experience that mothers frequently make no distinction in describing either their training techniques or their children's reactions. Although they might put the baby on the potty in anticipation of a stool, they are not dismayed if instead the child should urinate.

Normative Data on Bowel and Bladder Training

Just as time trends in the incidence of breast-feeding can be discerned, so has age of initiating elimination training changed during the past quarter-century. In an informal survey based on detailed parental interviews in a well-baby clinic, Fries (1935) found that age of initiating bowel training ranged from two to seventeen months, with the modal age being four months and the average age being six months. Length of time required to establish the habit ranged from a few days to eight months, with one or two months sufficing for the majority of the infants. Although similarly detailed information about bladder training was not given, time of initiating training apparently did not differ much from time of initiating bowel training.

Davis and Havighurst (1946) conducted a survey of child-rearing patterns employed by 200 mothers of 567 children. Although their presentation was devoted primarily to social class and ethnic group differences in patterns of child rearing, it is possible to construct the training picture for the total group. With respect to bowel training, in 40 per cent of the children training was begun at six months or earlier; completion by twelve months was achieved in 28 per cent of the total group. Bladder training was begun at six months or earlier in 14 per cent of the children and complete at eighteen months in 49 per cent of the group.

Normative data about the elimination practices of a large group of two-and-a-half-year-old children are contained in two related papers by Roberts and Schoellkopf (1951a,b). Toilet training was still in process in many of the children. Only approximately 88 per cent had achieved bowel control at the time of the maternal interviews which supplied the data. Absence of control was found in 16 per cent of the boys in contrast to 8 per cent of the girls, a difference which was statistically significant. Likewise, with respect to bladder training, about 90 per cent of the girls and 79 per cent of the boys assumed major responsibility for making known their need to urinate. Daytime accidents at this age were fairly common and occurred in 40 per cent of the cases.

Bernstein (1955) obtained information about bowel training history in 47 children attending a well-child clinic in New York City. In 13 cases training was begun by six months; in 18 cases training was started after six months but was accompanied by punishment for failure to comply; in 16 cases training was deferred until the child was older than six months and punishment was not used.

Sears, Maccoby, and Levin (1957) found that eleven months was the average age for beginning bowel training, with average time to complete training being about seven months. Earlier initiation meant, as a rule, that training would take longer, but there were many exceptions. Time for completion of training ranged from a few weeks to a year and a half.

This brief survey would suggest that time of beginning training has been gradually postponed over the past quarter of a century.

Elimination Training and Personality

Research investigations concerned with some aspect of elimination training have generally taken one of the following forms: (a) the relationship between training practices and reaction to training; (b) the relationship between training practices and certain clinical syndromes; (c) a search for an association between training patterns and personality development within the normal range; and (d) the determination of whether personality traits presumably related to anal events actually co-vary and are related to toilet training experience. The available literature dealing with these questions is summarized in Table 5. If the authors distinguished between bowel and bladder training or secured information about both, this has been indicated. However, for those studies where the generic term "toilet training" is used, it is probably accurate to conclude that this refers primarily to bowel training but may also include other aspects of the total elimination training gestalt.

Reaction to training. The reaction of a child to a particular child-rearing practice is a meaningful response measure to use in evaluating the effects of the practice. In the area of elimination training, however, the child's immediate reaction has not received much attention outside of the clinical literature. For example, Huschka (1942, 1943) reports that approximately two-thirds of a group of children who received coercive bowel or bladder training manifested an "undesirable response" to the training procedures. However, she does not specify what is meant by undesirable response; nor does she indicate the percentage of noncoercively trained children who manifested similar responses.

Sears, Maccoby, and Levin (1957) analyzed their data in terms of length of time required to complete training and degree of emotional upset during training as functions of time and method of training. As mentioned previously, on the average training which was started later was completed in a

TABLE 5. ELIMINATION TRAINING AND PERSONALITY

Author and Date	Subjects	Measures of Major Independent Variables	Measures of Major Dependent Variables	Summary of Findings	Comments
1. Huschka (1942, 1943)	(a) 213 emotionally disturbed children, 1–13 years.	(a) Coercive bowel training; begun prior to 8 mos. and completed by 18 mos. Information from case records.	(a) Emotional disturbance, as diagnosed by clinic staff.	(a) More than half trained coercively; $2/3$ of those coercively trained showed undesirable response to training.	(a) Used data in case records, no control group; narrow concept of optimal training period. Figures difficult to interpret.
	(b) 215 emotionally disturbed children, "approximately" the same patients.	(b) Coercive bladder training; begun before 10 months, completed before 2 years.	(b) Same as above.	(b) 68% coercively trained in terms of time, 28% in terms of method. 63% of those coercively trained manifested undesirable response.	(b) Same problem as above.
2. Despert (1944)	60 nursery school children.	Age of beginning and completing bladder training.	Incidence of enuresis and reaction to training.	12.8 months = average age for beginning training; 21.4 months = average age for day control, 27.3 months for night control. 14 enuretic children; training begun relatively late for them.	Does not systematically relate training to enuresis.
3. Holway (1949)	17 preschool children (8 boys, 9 girls),	Maternal interview reporting timing and method of toilet training. Five-point scale describing degree of self-regulation permitted infant.*	Two doll play sessions scored for reality, fantasy, aggression, and tangential play.	Coercively trained had higher aggression, fantasy, and tangentiality scores and lower reality scores.	Small N; retrospective data. Insufficient information given about analysis.
4. Bostock & Shackleton (1951)	73 kindergarten children (43 coercively trained, 30 noncoercively trained).	Early training experiences.	Incidence of enuresis.	26 children coercively trained had enuresis; only 3 of those noncoercively trained had enuresis.	Retrospective; mothers supplied data about both independent and dependent variables.
5. Roberts & Schoellkopf (1951a, b)	779 $2\frac{1}{2}$-year-olds seen in well-child clinic.	Maternal interview data on age of achieving bowel and bladder control.	Sphincter control.	92% of girls, 84% of boys had bowel control; 90% of girls, 79% of boys had urinary control.	
6. Sewell (1952)	162 rural children, 5–6 years old.	Maternal interview on timing of bowel and bladder training; punishment for toilet accidents.*	Scores on several standardized personality tests; maternal reports of symptoms of maladjustment.	Of 460 chi square tests, only 18 significant. Eight of these pertain to toilet training, of which 7 suggest better personal and social adjustment for those trained late and not punished for accidents.	Six (out of 184) chi squares significant at .01 level more than should be expected by chance. Some justification for questioning author's conclusion that there is no evidence of an association between infant training practice and personality.

* Other independent variables were also considered in this study.

45

TABLE 5. ELIMINATION TRAINING AND PERSONALITY (Continued)

Author and Date	Subjects	Measures of Major Independent Variables	Measures of Major Dependent Variables	Summary of Findings	Comments
7. Prugh (1953–54)	(a) 21 boys, 21 girls from Harvard Growth Study on whom data re age of completing training were available. Ages not specified.	Methods of training; time of completion, date of onset culled from records.	Bowel dysfunction (constipation, fecal incontinence).	(a) No statistically significant association between early bowel training and colonic dysfunction, though dysfunction approximately twice as great in group with early as with average training.	Slightly retrospective data re infancy; excellent observational measures of aggression and dependency.
	(b) 30 boys and 15 girls, with established colonic disorder; age range 3–17.			(b) Three-fourths of group with clinical colonic disorder had had coercive bowel training; one-fourth overly permissive training.	
8. Sears et al. (1953)	40 preschool children (20 boys, 20 girls).	Maternal interview on toileting and general permissiveness.*	Teachers' ratings and time sampled observations of dependency and aggression in preschool.	Severity of toilet training unrelated to preschool dependency; suggestive relationship between severe toilet training and aggression.	
9. Alper, Blane, & Abrams (1955)	18 middle- and 18 lower-class nursery school children; 20 middle- and 20 lower-class nursery school children.	Social class level and severity of bowel training.	Performance on two types of art tasks—finger painting and crayon drawing.	MC subjects more often resisted finger painting, tried to avoid getting dirty, and showed more concern for cleaning up afterwards. No differences between groups on crayon tasks.	Evidence that bowel training more coercive for MC children is equivocal; therefore questionable that obtained results related to bowel training rather than some other correlates of class status. Two different groups used for testing hypothesis rather than one group observed twice.
10. Bernstein (1955)	47 kindergarten age children attending health clinic.	Coerciveness of bowel training as estimated from maternal interview.*	Observational measurement of "anal" traits.	Positive relation between coerciveness and reluctance to communicate and between coerciveness and immaturity; no relation between coerciveness and smearing test or collection of objects.	Data re training retrospective, but little time lapse involved. Meaningful observational measures of child variables.
11. Anthony (1957)	76 children with encopresis (63 boys, 13 girls) aged 4–15 years.	Type of toilet training experienced by child as reported in maternal interview.	Type of encopresis (continuous, retentive, or discontinuous); reactions of encopretic children to a variety of perceptual measures of experimental reactions.	Type of encopresis related to type of training; not all who have abnormal training develop pathology and vice versa. Some encopretic children underresponsive, some overresponsive to unpleasant odors.	No nonencopretic control group; ingenious measures of perceptual reactions.

* Other independent variables were also considered in this study.

46

TABLE 5. ELIMINATION TRAINING AND PERSONALITY (Continued)

Author and Date	Subjects	Measures of Major Independent Variables	Measures of Major Dependent Variables	Summary of Findings	Comments
12. Beloff (1957)	120 college undergraduate students and their mothers.	Maternal interview about bowel training procedures. Also questionnaire measuring "anal" traits (the same one given the students).	Students' scores on questionnaires measuring "anal" traits of obstinacy, orderliness, and parsimony.	So-called anal traits describe unitary personality syndrome, but no association between trait score and toilet training. Positive association between scores of mothers and offspring on questionnaire.	Retrospective data about training.
13. Sears, Maccoby, & Levin (1957)	379 5-year olds.	Age and severity of elimination training as reported in maternal interview.*	Emotional reaction to training; length of time required to complete training.	Total time inversely related to age training was begun. Curvilinear relationship between age at beginning and emotional upset, with more reaction shown if training begun under 5 months, and between 15 and 19 months. Child's upset during training related to severity of training.	Retrospective. Both independent and dependent variables based on maternal report.
14. Durrett (1959)	60 4- and 5-year-old children (30 boys, 30 girls) from middle- and upper-class homes.	Self-ratings by mothers on age of beginning training and handling of accidents.*	Two 20-minute doll play sessions scored for aggression.	No correlation between early regulation and fantasy aggression.	Retrospective data on early regulation.
15. Brazelton (1962a)	1170 children seen in private pediatric practice.	Age of instituting training of bowel and bladder. Parents encouraged not to begin before 24 months.	Length of time required to achieve day and night control; incidence of enuresis and other disturbances.	Day training complete by 28.5 months; night by 33.3 months. Author concludes that incidence of enuresis and other disturbances lower than generally seen in pediatric practice.	No direct data on group trained by other methods.
16. Murphy (1962)	32 preschool children.	Type of training, reported by mother.*	Preschool autonomy.	No relationship.	Insufficient information given about techniques of assessment.
17. Hetherington & Brackbill (1963)	20 boys, 15 girls, kindergarten.	Severity of toilet training, reported by mothers. Questionnaire measures of anal personality traits in mothers and fathers.	Observational measures in children of anal triad: orderliness, obstinacy and parsimony.	These traits co-vary to some extent but show no relation to toilet training. Parent-child similarities in "anal" personality traits revealed when family dominance pattern is considered. Different patterns found for boys and girls.	Completely separated measures of dependent and independent variable; ingenious observational measures.

* Other independent variables were also considered in this study.

47

shorter time. The relation between age of initiating bowel training and emotional reaction to the training process was not linear, however, since infants introduced to the training process between five and fourteen months or after nineteen months showed less emotional upset than those infants for whom training was begun prior to five months (which occurred very infrequently) or during the fifteen to nineteen month range. The greater incidence of upset found in children close to a year of age was interpreted as being due to the increased motility drive present at that developmental stage. Anything that made the child sit still for prolonged periods might be unpleasant and likely to stimulate rebellion and resistance. Reaction to training showed a stronger association with severity of training. Over half of the severely trained children showed some upset during the process, while only one-sixth of the mildly trained children showed similar degrees of upset. The training pattern associated with the greatest degree of upset was severe training carried out by a cold and undemonstrative mother.

Training and psychopathology. In a number of investigations summarized in Table 5 an attempt has been made to determine whether timing and method of elimination training are related to psychopathology and to symptomatology involving eliminative functions. There are three clinical studies pertaining to bowel training (Huschka, 1942; Prugh, 1953–54; Anthony, 1957), two to bladder training (Huschka, 1943; Despert, 1944), and one to both bowel and bladder training (Brazelton, 1962a). In addition, there are three empirical studies (Bostock and Shackleton, 1951; Bernstein, 1955; and Sears, Maccoby, and Levin, 1957) which have dealt with some aspect of the relationship between bowel or bladder training and eliminative dysfunction.

Huschka (1942) examined case histories of a group of emotionally disturbed children for details of bowel training methods, with particular attention devoted to whether the training had been coercive. Coercive was defined as "premature institution of a toilet-training regime and overactive, destructive methods." Specifically this meant bowel training begun prior to the age of eight months and completed before eighteen months. Her conclusion was that more than half of the cases for whom information was available had been trained coercively with respect to both time and method. Her implication was that such training may well have influenced the development of psychopathology.

Prugh (1953–54) attempted to investigate the relationship between toilet training experiences and psychogenic colonic disorder (constipation, soiling, and so on) in two groups of children. The first group consisted of 42 cases drawn from the Harvard Growth Study for whom data regarding time of completion of training and, in most instances, time of beginning training were available. Results showed that the incidence of colonic dysfunction (constipation, fecal incontinence) was approximately twice as great in the group of children with early training as in the group with average training, although this difference was of only marginal statistical significance. Boys showed higher incidence of disturbance than girls. In a second sample of 45 children with established colonic disorder of presumably psychogenic origin, three-fourths of the group were found to have received coercive toilet training as defined by Huschka, with most of the remaining subjects having received neglectful or overly lenient training.

Anthony (1957) employed an ingenious experimental approach in studying the relationship between toilet training methods and encopresis (defined for the study as defecation in the clothes, bed, or any receptacle not intended for the purpose). Subjects for the study were 76 encopretic children ranging in age from four through fifteen. Careful study of the children revealed that encopresis was not a unitary symptom but a syndrome of which soiling was but one manifestation. Anthony identified at least three types: (a) continuous—children whose soiling was but one aspect of a general lack of concern with being clean; (b) discontinuous—children for whom the soiling contrasted sharply with overt attitudes toward regularity and cleanliness in other aspects of living; (c) retentive—children with persistent constipation and only occasional encopresis. Statistically significant associations were found between the category of encopresis and type of toilet training, with children in the continuous group having received more neglectful training and children in both the retentive and discontinuous groups having had more coercive training. In a variety of experimental procedures the responses of children in these three groups were compared. For example, the children were exposed to a series of odors generally judged as unpleasant. Children in the retentive and discontinuous groups tended to show strong aversive reactions, whereas children in the continuous group frequently showed no negative reaction. Similarly, when asked to manipulate a shutter that would perceptually equate a plain disc with a circular photograph depicting some phase of toileting, the discontinuous children tended to underestimate the size of toileting scenes. This was interpreted by Anthony as a defense against the anxiety created by stimuli related to elimination procedures.

Although there is a voluminous pediatric and psychiatric literature on enuresis, a far more common dysfunction than encopresis, the possible relationship between bladder training and presence or absence of the symptom has received surprisingly little research attention. Two clinical series (Huschka, 1943; Despert, 1944) were the only studies of the past twenty years that could be found, and neither of these dealt directly with the role of bladder training in the etiology of enuresis. Huschka investigated the incidence of coercive bladder training in "approximately" the same cases considered in her study of coercive bowel training, using coercive to mean training initiated before ten months and completed before two years of age. She found that 68 per cent had been coerced according to her formal criteria and that 28 per cent had been trained by destructive and punitive methods. These were not necessarily the same children who had received coercive bowel training. Although reporting incidence of enuresis for the sample and speculating on the role of coercive bladder training in the etiology of the disorder, she did not compare the bladder training histories of the enuretic group to those of the remaining subsample. In light of the nature of her data, Huschka's conclusion that coercive bladder training is a "seed-bed of psychopathology" can hardly be accepted. Despert examined the histories of bladder training in 60 nursery school children and attempted to relate pattern of training to enuresis, which was found in approximately one-fourth of the group. Although the group of enuretic children tended to be somewhat infantile and to have what Despert referred to as "loose organization of the personality," training history was not remarkable and on the whole had been initiated rather late.

Brazelton (1962a) has presented data on the results of a "child-oriented" approach to toilet training recommended to the parents of 1,170 private pediatric patients over a ten-year period. Crucial to the method is postponement of any training attempts until the child is about two years old, at which time his neurophysiological maturation will have reached the point where true voluntary control is possible and where the child's desire for mastery and autonomy will increase his interest in the development of impulse control. No distinction is made between recommended times for bowel and for bladder control. Although in his sample both bowel and bladder control were developed a little later (28.5 months for day and 33.3 months for night) than reported by Sears, Maccoby, and Levin (1957), it was probably accomplished a little more quickly (approximately four months). The fact that 90 per cent of the parents adopted the recommended procedures was interpreted by Brazelton as indicating that such an educational effort can be effective, provided parental anxieties are anticipated and allayed in advance. As less than 2 per cent of the group showed evidence of enuresis, encopresis, or chronic constipation after the age of five years, in contrast to the range of roughly 10 to 20 per cent usually reported for pediatric practice, Brazelton concluded that the child-oriented method could help to prevent the development of elimination disorders.

Three empirical studies cited in Table 5 also dealt in some way with the relationship between elimination training and psychogenic elimination difficulties. Bernstein (1955), who made inquiries only about bowel training and bowel dysfunction, could find no relationship between coercive training and constipation. Bostock and Shackleton (1951), concerned with urinary dysfunctions, conducted an interview study of 73 kindergarten children and their mothers. They found that 59 per cent of the children had been coercively trained (vaguely defined); 60 per cent of the group who had been coercively trained were enuretic, whereas only 10 per cent of the non-coercively trained children were enuretic. In the study by Sears, Maccoby, and Levin (1957) the relationship between enuresis and elimination training was examined. Age of initiating training was unrelated to enuresis, but severity of training was. Among the maternal variables which showed a correlation with the use of severe training methods were a strong need for order and high sex anxiety.

Attempts to establish a relationship between a specific infant practice and a clinical entity must usually begin with retrospective studies of clinical groups. However, since no explicit control groups were used in the clinical studies (with the exception of the implicit controls available in Prugh's longitudinal group, in Anthony's diagnostic subgroups, and in Despert's nursery group), generalizations based on them must be limited. Findings from the remaining studies suggest a relationship between training and dysfunction, more so for method of training than for time of initiation.

General personality characteristics. The assumption that elimination training is by definition frustrating to the child seems to have led many investigators to examine the relationship between type and timing of training and aggression. Although trends have been suggested in several studies, no clear association has been established. Holway (1949) found a low but positive correlation between coercive training and doll play aggression in a small group of preschool children. In a similar study, Durrett (1959) found no such relation. In their study of antecedents of aggression and dependency in preschool children, Sears and associates (1953) found no relationship between severity of toilet training and dependency but a suggestive relationship between severity of training and aggression.

Bowel and bladder training were two of the socialization variables examined by Sewell (1952) in his omnibus study dealing with child training and personality. Although his conclusion was that there was no evidence to support the existence of a relationship between any aspect of infant training and any of the dependent variables considered in his study, it is of interest to note that the greatest number of statistically significant chi squares dealt with toilet training and that with one exception they pointed to better adjustment associated with delayed initiation of training.

The relationship between type of toilet training experience and autonomy was investigated by Murphy (1962). During the time that toilet training ordinarily occurs, the need for autonomy is theoretically of high potency, and method of training has been assumed to be a factor which could either encourage or inhibit its development. However, Murphy was unable to demonstrate any relationship.

Elimination training and "anal" personality. Four studies were found which pertained in some way to the relationship between elimination training and behavioral manifestations of the personality traits postulated by psychoanalysis to have their origin in anal needs. In the first of these, Bernstein (1955) investigated the relationship between coerciveness (using a slight modification of Huschka's criteria) and a number of behavioral items. He found no relationship between coercive bowel training and either tendency to collect objects or response to a smearing test involving cold cream and finger paints. However, positive associations were found between coercive training and both negativism and separation anxiety. These two findings are not entirely independent, however, since refusal to separate from the mother for the experimental session entered into the rating of negativism. Bernstein concluded that toilet training affected later behavior to some extent, but that the assumptions stemming from psychoanalytic theory about the direction of influence were not entirely verified.

In a somewhat similar study, Alper, Blane, and Abrams (1955) observed the performance on two art tasks of children from different socioeconomic backgrounds, assuming that children from different social class backgrounds would have had different bowel training experiences. They found a greater resistance to finger painting in middle-class children, who had presumably had more severe bowel training experiences, but no class differences in the crayon drawing task. This finding was consistent with their prediction that the task calling for uninhibited smearing (and thus symbolizing manipulation of fecal material) would arouse anxiety in children who had been subjected to early and severe toilet training, whereas the bland crayon task would bring forth no such reaction and thus show no intergroup differences.

Two additional studies (Beloff, 1957; Hetherington and Brackbill, 1963) summarized in Table 5, were concerned not only with whether parental training methods influence the development of putative anal traits but additionally with the important question of whether the classical traits of obstinacy, orderliness, and parsimony are related to one another. Although the two studies used subjects of differing ages and employed dissimilar methodologies, the results were similar. The first of these was conducted by Beloff (1957), who was interested in establishing whether the "anal character" existed as a psychological entity and whether the so-called anal traits could be related to bowel training experiences in infancy. After a survey of the psychoanalytic literature, she developed test items to cover 14 traits which had been suggested by one or another author as representing some aspect of the anal character. Factor analysis of a questionnaire given to 120 undergraduate students revealed only one general factor; however, the factor loading of items measuring parsimony and orderliness was lower than that for items measuring dominance and obstinacy. Then, to permit examination of the relationship between scores on this trait and bowel training experiences, mothers of the subjects were interviewed about their toilet training techniques employed when the students were infants, thus eliciting toilet training data which were retrospective by about twenty years. Results indicated that the range of ages for completing bowel training was from 8 to 24 months, with the median at 13.22 months. The mothers were also given the trait questionnaire previously given to their sons and daughters. The cases were then grouped according to both age of training (early or late) and maternal questionnaire score (above or below the median), with a two-way analysis of variance performed on the scores of the subjects. The only significant source of variation was the maternal questionnaire score. There was a correlation between maternal and off-spring's scores of .51, whereas the correlation between the score of the subject and the age at which toilet training was completed was only .05. On the basis of her data the author concluded that the personality traits ordinarily ascribed to the anal character represent a meaningful dimension for the description of attitudes and behavior but that this dimension is not related to toilet training or anal experiences. It was, however, related to the salience of the same trait in the mothers and could thus reflect the learning experiences of the individual. The finding by Sears, Maccoby, and Levin (1957) of an association between severe toilet training and strong maternal concern with orderliness supports this interpretation. That is, orderliness in an individual may be the result of direct teaching about orderliness; any association with toilet training could be spurious and indicate nothing more than the fact that training for sphincter control is one behavioral area in which this trait can be manifested.

The other study which is concerned both with this trait co-variation and with the relationship to toilet training is a recent study by Hetherington and Brackbill (1963). In a sample of 35 kindergarten children (20 boys and 15 girls), the authors attempted to determine whether there was a relationship between several different behavioral manifestations of *each* component of the anal triad—for example, between task persistence and social stubbornness, both presumably reflecting obstinacy; between reserve in finger painting and keeping a neat locker as indications of orderliness. They also sought to determine whether composite measures of orderliness, obstinacy, and parsimony were related to one another. Strength of these same traits was assessed in the parents by means of an attitude questionnaire covering the same areas. The questionnaire also provided data about the severity of toilet training. Since intercorrelations among measures were patterned differently for girls and boys, all analyses were performed for each sex separately. Neither obstinacy nor orderliness was found to be a unitary trait system in these samples of children. Parsimony was an exception, since there was evidence that if a child was retentive and acquisitive in one situation, he would behave similarly in others. There were fairly substantial intercorrelations among composite measures of obstinacy, orderliness, and parsimony in girls, but none in the boys. Correlations between mothers and daughters for comparable traits (for example, obstinacy with obstinacy) tended to be high and positive, whereas those for fathers and daughters, mothers and sons, and fathers and sons were nonsignificant. However, an analysis which took into consideration the relative degree of dominance of the mother or the father revealed significant parent-child correlations not suggested by correlations based on the total group. That is, for the 12 boys from father-dominant homes, there was some evidence of similarity between the behavior of the sons and the attitudes of the fathers. For the eight boys living in mother-dominated homes, however, there was a negative correlation between paternal and filial personality trait scores. Similar analyses indicated no relationship between mothers and sons from father-dominant homes, but a positive association in the mother-dominant families. Finally, with respect to data about toilet training, results of this study are in agreement with those cited above from the work of Beloff. That is, no association could be found between pattern of toilet training and high degrees of obstinacy, orderliness, and parsimony. The authors in their summary propose a cogent emendation of the semantics of this area as follows:

> From the data on toilet training, one can only conclude that analytic theory is not correct in maintaining that too early, too late, or too severe training leads to high degrees of obstinacy, orderliness, and parsimony. Since previous investigations using the scientific method have come to the same conclusion, one might suggest that it is time for psychoanalysis to reconsider its adamant perpetuation of this aspect of its theory. Most certainly it is time to discard the "anal" from "anal personality traits"—a term that has too long accepted as fact an unproved, perhaps untenable, hypothesis (p. 939).

Summary

To summarize the material on elimination training, it appears possible to suggest a relationship between deviant training and pathology when one examines the training history of children showing some type of disorder associated with bowel or bladder function. However, more information about the incidence of similarly deviant training practices used with children showing no overt pathology is essential before such material can be put into perspective. For unselected groups of children it has been difficult to demonstrate broad personality consequences of elimination training practices, although specific reaction to training appears to vary as a function of both age of initiating training and severity of training procedures. Type of training technique used by the mother is related to her own need for order and to anxiety about sex behavior. Although the so-called anal triad of obstinacy, orderliness, and parsimony constitutes a reasonably unitary trait (at least in adults and in young girls) in which significant parent-child similarities can be demonstrated, there is no consistent evidence that strength of the trait is related to elimination training.

OTHER INFANT CARE PRACTICES

The division of words in this review between feeding-elimination and what are condescendingly labeled "other infant care practices" reflects not only the author's assignment but also the approximate concentration of topics in the research literature. For, while a great variety of infant behavior is available for observation and inquiry, the range sampled has been quite narrow. In a recent publication (Caldwell, 1962) this author made the tongue-in-cheek suggestion that both feeding and elimination training had possibly functioned as *ignes fatui* of socialization research. Pursuit of closure on these problems may have led into a theoretical wasteland in which some of the more important transactions of the infancy period are not to be found. Although it is difficult to pinpoint any one source of interest in infant feeding, there is little doubt that elimination training rose to its position of eminence via psychoanalytic theory. Theory-derived research, while ordinarily conducive to scientific maturity (see McCandless and Rosenblum, 1952), may be stultifying if the theory remains indifferent to the accumulation of empirical data.

Animal researchers with developmental interests have dealt with a wide range of topics and have carried out some of the more exciting developmental research of the past decade. While it is not possible to include animal studies in this review, it is appropriate to mention some of the experiences of the infancy period dealt with in recent animal work merely as a means of spotlighting processes which may play a crucial role in development: the effects of early stress on later behavior, the effects of "gentling," the role of contact comfort in the maturation of the affectional and sexual systems, the influence of the timing of experiences (critical periods), the "following" response and the process of imprinting, the effects of patterns of stimulation on subsequent perceptual and cognitive activities, the effects of modifying certain features of the immediate post-natal period, and a host of others. The theoretical literature of the past decade has contained a number of provocative papers which have offered speculations about the implications of such research for humans, some of which have attempted to modify psychoanalytic theory in the light of data from animal studies (most notably Bowlby, 1958). A safe prediction is that the empirical literature of the next decade will contain studies relating to a far greater breadth of topics than one finds at the present time.

At the present time a potpourri of topics can be presented, each with a few studies to assert its possible importance. Only studies using as inde-pendent variables some specifiable type of overt behavior will be con-sidered; those dealing with affect states and global aspects of the infant's environment will not be included.

Immediate Postnatal Experience

Cross-cultural studies have shown that human neonates in different parts of the world have widely varying experiences in the immediate postnatal period. Within western culture, however, the variation is probably not very great, and with the increasing incidence of hospital births during the past decade, the range of experiences may have narrowed further. However, the encouragement of mother-infant contact throughout the hospital period in the rooming-in programs represents one important type of possible varia-tion. Klatskin and Jackson (1955) have followed the development of a large number of infants who were cared for on a rooming-in arrangement, generally attributing the preference for rooming-in to regular hospital programs as indicative of certain maternal attitudes and thus perhaps as being an effect rather than a cause. Klatskin (1952a) has shown that infants who have this experience encounter more permissive parental behavior and show slightly more accelerated motor and mental development than a control group of infants whose immediate postnatal experience was of the conventional nursery type. Also Jackson, Wilkin, and Auerbach (1956) showed that rooming-in infants were more likely than other infants in the same hospital to be breast-fed throughout their hospital stay and to be given a significantly longer period of breast-feeding (3.5 months as opposed to 2.4).

That even full-term neonates differ in their general maturation and in their sensory sensitivity has been demonstrated by Graham, Matarazzo, and Caldwell (1956), Lipsitt and Levy (1959), and Rosenblith (1963); and a series of detailed studies of differential autonomic sensitivity has been made by Lipton, Steinschneider, and Richmond (1961). Brazelton (1962b) found neonatal differences in time lag prior to commencing to nurse at the breast and in beginning weight gain as a function of maternal premedication during labor and delivery. Although he does not consider this delay to be indicative of nervous system damage, he asserts that it is potentially disruptive of the developing mother-child relationship. How such initial levels of response during the first few days of extrauterine life affect maternal response and interact with parental expectancies and attitudinal reactions is an intriguing subject for future research.

Early Position Arrangements

Throughout antiquity many infants seem to have spent a considerable portion of their sleeping and waking time under conditions that significantly restrained their motor activities. References to swaddling appear in the Bible (see Luke 2) and in historical medical literature (see Ruhrah, 1925). Rousseau (1762) condemned the practice, blaming its use upon the desire of mothers to be partially relieved of the responsibility of caring for their infants.

More recent interest in the practice was aroused by Watson's contention (1928) that restraint of movement invariably evoked a rage reaction in infants. Pratt, Nelson, and Sun (1930) were not only unable to elicit rage reactions to restraint of the arms but found that such limitation of movement would quiet some infants. Their results are usually cited as refuting Watson's theory, but there are indications that the intensity of stimulation applied by those investigators was milder than that employed by Watson. Dennis (1940), examining data from some of his own procedures with a pair of twins reared in partial social isolation and from observed and reported reactions of American Indian children to cradling practices, concluded that restraint produces negative reactions only if the restraint interferes with habits developed by the infant. Similar conclusions were reached by Levy (1944) after a study of head tics observed in hens kept in restraining cages and after reviewing several clinical cases of hypermotility in children following enforced movement restraint. Levy concluded, as had Dennis, that resistance to movement restraint appears only if activity drives have had a prior chance to develop.

In their research on autonomic functioning of the neonate, Lipton, Steinschneider, and Richmond (1960) have shown that newborns tend to be quieter, to sleep more, and to have lower heart rates when tested under swaddled than under free conditions. Individual differences were striking, however, as in one out of the ten infants in their series there was more responsivity under the swaddled than under the free conditions and in four infants there were no detectable differences under the two conditions. The authors suggested that, quite apart from any possible effects of swaddling upon general behavior, this type of motor restraint may be useful in laboratory investigations of neonatal parameters, which require relatively stable conditions for accurate measurement. Benedict's discussion (1949) of the different messages which may be communicated to the infant by the practice of swaddling has already been presented.

As during early infancy all types of positions are imposed on the infant, any position in which the adult places the infant limits the infant somewhat and represents a form of motor restraint. Dennis (1960) presents some very compelling evidence of the importance of regarding habitual placement of the infant as a matter of consequence. He compared the development of infants residing in three institutions in Tehran. In the first of these two institutions the infants were usually admitted below one month of age and never saw their mothers thereafter. They were placed in individual cribs on their backs and received a minimum of interpersonal stimulation. The second institution was the one into which these infants were usually "graduated" after the age of three. Infants in the third institution presumably had comparable genetic and social backgrounds, but the institution differed dramatically from the other two. It had been set up as a demonstration unit to incorporate some of the modern ideas about desirable methods of institutional care; thus there were many more adults available to interact with the babies, and children were held while being fed and were frequently put into the prone position or propped into a sitting position. Motor tests such as sitting, creeping, standing, and walking were given to 174 children in the three institutions. Retardation among children in the first two institutions was severe (for example, only 42 per cent of the children between the ages of one and two could sit alone, and none could walk), whereas in the third institution it was only slight to moderate (90 per cent between the ages of one and two could sit alone and 15 per cent could walk). The author interpreted the extreme retardation of the infants in the first two institutions as being due not only to the lack of handling by adults but also to the failure of such attendants as were available to put the infants into the prone or sitting position. Support for the importance of the postural experiences per se was found in the fact that creeping occurred relatively infrequently among infants in the first two institutions, with the more common form of prewalking locomotion being scooting on the buttocks. On the other hand, scooting did not occur in the third institution, where the more common prone creeping pattern was observed. Dennis concluded that experience affects the patterning of motor development as well as the age at which specific items will appear.

Keitel, Cohn, and Harnish (1960) suggest that position may affect the infant's behavior even during the newborn period. They found that infants kept in the prone position in the hospital were less likely to develop diaper rash, had fewer self-inflicted scratches, and tended to cry less than infants kept in the supine position. Also Kunst (1948) found more nonnutritive sucking behavior when infants were kept in the prone than in the supine position. The work of Blauvelt and McKenna (1961) suggests that the nature of the stimulation received by an infant from its mother will be significantly affected by the position in which the infant is placed with reference to the mother's own body. Likewise Gunther (1961) asserts that success in breast-feeding will be influenced by the position into which the nursing newborn is placed as well as by the shape of the maternal breast. If during nursing the breast or the baby's own upper lip should cover the baby's nostrils, a degree of asphyxia results which causes the baby to fight vigorously when put to breast. She implies further that a very rapid type of learning occurs in the infant, such that after only a few trials the infant cries when turned toward the mother. In turn, the mother finds the baby's fighting unbearable and often quickly decides to change to bottle feeding.

Intensity of Maternal Contact

As the topic of maternal deprivation is considered in another chapter of this volume, discussion in this section will be limited primarily to variations in the quantitative intensity of mother-infant contact within an essentially normal range of mothering activities. Two of the studies to be cited are experimental, as either the experimenter or the mother under the tutelage of the experimenter provided directly for an increase in the quantity of "mothering" made available. The remaining two studies capitalize on variations in intensity of maternal contact found under existing family structures.

Hopper and Pinneau (1957) investigated the effects of additional mothering on the incidence of regurgitations in a group of home-reared infants. Subjects were 21 pairs of infants representing a highly attrited sample of babies whose parents were invited to participate in the study. After the mothers were interviewed regarding their child-rearing and feeding practices and the incidence of regurgitations in their infants during and between feedings, they were given a small pad with attached pencil and asked to record every burp, regurgitation, and new vocalization made by their infants. Although the exact ages of all infants were not given, the authors report that 22 of the infants were between the ages of 99 and 113 days during the study. Infants were randomly assigned to experimental and control groups, and the mothers in the experimental group were asked to increase for a two-week period the stimulation given their infants before each feeding for at least ten minutes, with the diversionary explanation offered that some experts felt that such stimulation would be associated with an advance in speech and language development. No such instructions were given the control mothers. Accuracy of information about both the independent and dependent variables might be questioned, as there was no way of knowing if the mothers actually supplied the extra stimulation or faithfully recorded all burps and regurgitations. Results of the experiment showed that, over the two-week period, incidence of regurgitations diminished slightly but not significantly more in the experimental than in the control group. The authors concluded that extra mothering was ineffective in reducing regurgitations. Data supplied by the mothers on the incidence of vocalizations in the two groups of infants were not reported. Although such information was requested only to disguise the intent of the study, it would have been of considerable interest to know whether additional maternal stimulation affected early vocalization.

A somewhat similar study was conducted by Ourth and Brown (1961) in the hospital nursery during the neonatal period. Subjects were 20 biologically normal newborns and their mothers. Control subjects received routine nursery care stripped of all nonessential contacts, while the experimental subjects were held, wrapped in blankets, and gently rocked for sixty minutes at each daytime feeding period. If the mother herself failed to supply stimulation for the full period, either the experimenter or one of the nurses did so. It is worthy of note here that, in a different decade, the authors might have reported their study as an experimental measure of the effects of breast versus bottle feeding, as all the experimental subjects were breast-fed and all the control subjects were bottle-fed. In view of the general failure of research studies cited in this review to demonstrate any clear effects of breast-feeding, this probably does not vitiate their results or conclusions; however, it seems as though a control group which would have made for a better design was somehow disregarded. Results showed that the "mothered" infants, during the hospital stay of 4.5 days, cried less both during and immediately prior to feeding sessions. Interestingly, the authors interpret their results in a rather negative way—that is, they assume that the control infants were inadequately mothered and that the deficiency in stimulation received by them resulted in disturbed behavior (equating crying with disturbance) rather than that the experimental infants received something extra which resulted in more desirable behavior.

Pease and Gardner (1958) have published a series of reports on the effects of residence during the first few months of life in a home management house situated on a midwestern university campus. This is a center in which home economics students are trained in techniques of infant care and actually provide the total care of the infants until they are placed in adoptive homes, usually within five or six months. Although there is always one house mother available to the infant until adoptive placement, students take turns in performing most of the mothering functions during the infant's residence in the house, thus exposing it to what the authors call noncontinuous mothering. At the age of two years, 37 infants who had resided in the home management house for approximately four months prior to adoption were compared to a control group of 44 adoptive children who had previously resided in foster homes for a similar length of time and to a group of 46 children reared entirely in their natural families (Gardner, Pease, and Hawkes, 1961). On situational tests of response to frustration and to brief maternal separation, no differences among the three groups could be detected.

In another follow-up study of 29 of the home management children and 29 matched controls (age range eight to seventeen), Gardner, Hawkes, and Burchinal (1961) reported that no personality disadvantage associated with earlier residence in the home management house could be demonstrated. However, in spite of their meticulous attempts to match subjects with controls on I.Q., age of child, age of parents, and economic status of the family, they succeeded only on age of the children. Parents of the home management children were slightly older and represented a higher economic status, and group intelligence test scores of the controls were on the average slightly higher than those of the management house children. There was also a difference in personal adjustment scores in favor of the control children which approached statistical significance. Thus while results of this study point to little advantage for the infants who experienced continuous (and thus implicitly more intense) early maternal contact, the data are not entirely unequivocal.

In a final study relevant to this subject, Caldwell and associates (1963) investigated certain types of infant and maternal behavior in what were designated as *monomatric* and *polymatric* families. A monomatric family was defined as one in which the mother was essentially the exclusive female caretaker of her infant; a polymatric family represented one in which such caretaking activities were shared by more than one person either because of maternal employment or extended family arrangements. Subjects for the analysis were 37 women and babies participating in a normative longitudinal study of mother-child interaction, approximately three-fourths of whom represented monomatric family organizations when the infants were six months of age and two-thirds of whom were classified as monomatric when the infants were one year of age. At six months significant differences between the infants in the two groups were almost nonexistent, with the slightly greater irritability observed in the infants from polymatric families probably due to chance. However, a number of significant differences were found between the mothers in the two groups at that time, with mothers from monomatric settings found to be more affectionate, active, sensuous, playful, and vocal with their infants and more concerned about their infants' well-being. They were also more exhibitionistic and less intellectualized in their approach to child rearing. At one year, infants from families that had been monomatric for the preceding six months were found to be more active, more emotionally dependent on their mothers, and more emotional in their interactions with their mothers. At that time maternal differences were less impressive, but they still pointed to a stronger attachment on the part of the mothers from monomatric settings. Analysis of some of the prenatal data available on the women suggested that these differences might have been due more to prenatal personality characteristics than to feedback effects of the mother-infant contact situation. Women who were in the polymatric group when their infants were one year old were found to have been rated as more hostile, dominant, and dependent during the prenatal period. The inverse relationship between prenatal dependency and postnatal attachment to the infant suggested that unresolved dependency needs might interfere with the establishment of a strong and close mother-infant bond.

At this juncture it is not possible to reach definitive conclusions about the effects of intensity of maternal contact during infancy outside of situations that might be regarded as grossly depriving. Of the two experimental studies reported here, one found that more intense maternal stimulation was associated with less irritability during the neonatal period, while the other suggested that additional maternal stimulation was ineffective in reducing burping and spitting during the first few months of life. In the differential studies included by the reviewer under this rubric, the intensity variable, though implicitly similar, was not exactly the same as in the experimental studies. Again one set of investigators reported no effects, although in at least one of their two studies there are grounds for challenging this interpretation, whereas the other reported a closer emotional and dependency bond between mothers and year-old infants with a more intense contact history. There are at present no known studies available which have permitted intensity of maternal contact to vary while controlling for other factors (such as maternal personality and amount and type of paternal contact) which might influence the results.

THE INTERPERSONAL MILIEU OF INFANT CARE

One factor which accounts for an indeterminate amount of variance in any study of the relationship between parent practices and child behavior is the interpersonal milieu in which the behavior occurs. A particular parent practice may occur within a harmonious or disturbed interpersonal environment; it may be performed by a nurturant or a hostile mother; it may be based on fervent intellectual and emotional convictions of the parent or on current social conventions. All such factors undoubtedly interact to some extent with the chosen practice in influencing the child's reaction.

Most frequently examined as aspects of the interpersonal environment which possibly monitor an infant's reaction to the type of care he receives have been maternal attitudes. Extremely divergent attitudes toward child rearing may underlie a given overt act. For example, in one mother the decision to initiate bowel training at six months may have been largely determined by her aversion to fecal matter, in another by her desire to have her child accelerated, in still another by her general annoyance and irritation with the baby. Despite these divergent attitudinal correlates of the selected practice, all these mothers might be placed in the same group for a research project concerned only with overt parental behavior.

Evidence that attitudes were actually more important than overt behavior would probably be welcome to many parents who worry lest an unwise act exert a prolonged negative influence upon the child. There is reassurance in the thought that having one's heart in the right place may nullify the consequences of an assortment of ill-chosen acts. If the child is capable of overlooking the obvious and somehow responding to subtler cues as to the meaning of a particular social event, then he functions in a more stable social environment. Thus the underlying attitudes may integrate and establish continuity among many seemingly diverse aspects of parental behavior. In this section some of the relationships between overt parent behavior and the attitudes which pervade the interpersonal environment will be explored.

The Influence of Attitude on Practice

That the attitude may actually determine the practice appears to be a widely held point of view, particularly with reference to choice of infant feeding technique. The previously discussed decline in the general incidence of breast-feeding has been interpreted by most observers as reflecting the change in attitude on the part of modern women toward this custom. In an attempt to determine whether attitudes held by the expectant mother might influence the choice of whether to breast-feed, Adams (1959) administered a series of projective tests and interviewed 58 women in the last trimester of pregnancy. Those who expressed their intention prenatally to bottle-feed their infants were judged to be more dependent, more rejecting of the unborn child, and more likely to have psychosexual disturbances than those electing prenatally to breast-feed. That attitudinal factors can help to sustain the choice, once it has been made, is supported in the report by Hytten, Yorston, and Thomson (1958) dealing with the breast-feeding experiences of 106 primiparae. Only two women in their series had a completely satisfactory experience of breast-feeding throughout the first three months of their infants' lives. Of the total, 74 women gave up breast-feeding by three months. Although there was usually more than one difficulty that influenced the mother's decision to continue or abandon breast-feeding, the maternal attitude toward the practice seemed to be the most influential. That is, mothers with strong positive feelings toward breast-feeding tended to persist in spite of a multitude of difficulties, whereas those whose attitudes were lukewarm or negative tended to abandon the practice upon encountering any difficulty in lactation or any sign of discomfort in the infant. However, not even an attitude of unqualified acceptance toward breast-feeding guaranteed successful lactation and favorable infant response. Similar findings were reported by Brown *et al.* (1960).

Disparity Between Attitude and Behavior

Although an attitude represents a predisposition to action, there is some evidence that parent practices may occasionally conflict with underlying attitudes. A study by Newton and Newton (1950) is relevant in this context. On the basis of maternity hospital interviews with 91 parturient women, two judges classified the women into three groups in terms of expressed attitudes toward breast-feeding. Of the total, 51 were judged to have positive, 17 doubtful, and 23 negative attitudes. Of the mothers with positive attitudes toward breast-feeding, 74 per cent were able to breast-feed successfully during the hospital period. In the doubtful and negative attitude groups, only 35 per cent and 26 per cent, respectively, breast-fed successfully. Thus while the attitude influenced the behavior to some extent, it did not control it entirely; yet it is likely that the interpersonal situation created for the infants in the positive attitude and the negative attitude groups was not identical. Had follow-up of these women and their offspring been attempted subsequently with the intention of ascertaining the relationship between breast-feeding and child personality, the influence of the attitudinal substrate may have confounded the results.

Also pertinent here are observations made by Brody (1956) in her study of 32 mothers and their infants ranging in age from four to twenty-eight weeks. Her basic hypothesis was that maternal feeding behavior was prototypic of other responses the mother would make to the infant. Rating each behavior unit that related to feeding behavior in terms of maternal sensitivity to the needs of the infant, regardless of the specific type of feeding pattern employed, she found that the practice of breast-feeding offered no guarantee of maternal sensitivity; nor did physical holding of the infant during feeding ensure emotional rapport and intimacy.

The Relative Potency of Attitude and Behavior

If a disparity between attitude and behavior can in fact exist, then it becomes important to know to which aspect of the parental stimulus the infant will respond. Data from the Sears, Maccoby, and Levin study can be directed to this question. Their findings about toilet training suggested that the maternal attitude was crucial in monitoring the effects of severity of training methods. That is, severe toilet training from a cold and unde-monstrative mother with a high degree of sex anxiety seemed most likely to produce the greatest upset in the child. Comparably severe training from a warm and affectionate mother was less likely to produce any adverse effects. Thus such data suggest that a favorable maternal attitude can neutralize an otherwise disruptive type of parent behavior. Of equal relevance is material from the factor analysis carried out on 44 of the 188 scales. Several of the factors which emerged could be described as repre-senting underlying maternal attitudes which spread across many areas of maternal behavior. The factors labeled permissiveness-strictness, warmth of the mother-child relationship, responsible child-training orientation, ag-gressiveness, and orientation toward the child's physical well-being could be described as attitudinal variables which would help to structure parental behavior in many socialization tasks.

The studies of Garner and Wenar (1959) and of Wenar, Handlon, and Garner (1962) offer data relating to maternal attitudes and maternal be-havior. In the first study the authors investigated differences in patterns of mothering available to children who had psychosomatic disorders, chronic illness of a nonpsychosomatic nature, and neurotic disturbance. They hypothesized that the psychosomatic children would be found to have experienced a deficiency of "motherliness" during the first year of life. Q sorts made by clinically trained judges on the basis of maternal interviews yielded significant differences between mothers of children in these three groups in several areas. The mothers of psychosomatic children were described as having fewer "positive" attitudes with respect to quality of total training and care, although negative items did not distinguish the three groups. Likewise, when specific training (feeding and toileting) practices were considered, the mothers of psychosomatic children were found at a marginally significant level, to have used fewer clinically approved training practices, again with no differences among the three groups in incidence of negative practices. As there was only one item in their Q sort universe which could be classified as indicating a positive approach to toilet training, this difference would have to be ascribed to group differences in feeding practices only. Thus both global attitudes and specific practices seemed influential.

In a supplementary study in which a group of severely emotionally disturbed children was added to the original three groups, Wenar, Handlon, and Garner (1962) reported that mothers of severely disturbed children were similar to the mothers of psychosomatically ill children in finding early infant care essentially unrewarding. This was true in respect both to total care and to specific areas of feeding and toileting. The authors state that the mothers of the severely disturbed and of the psychosomatic children were especially similar in their "lack of gratification in feeding the infant." In these studies the authors' basic hypothesis was oriented toward a pervasive and generalized attitude; yet they also found relationships in terms of specific behaviors to which the infants had been exposed.

Compelling data dealing with the question of the relative potency of attitudes and overt behavior appear in the study by Heinstein (1963), discussed previously in the section on infant feeding. Considered to be major independent variables in his study along with type of feeding and total duration of nutritive sucking were maternal warmth, nervous stability of the mother, and the marital adjustment of the parents. When the feeding variables were considered separately, no clear advantage could be demonstrated for breast-feeding with either girls or boys, but there was a suggestion of a higher incidence of problem behavior associated with longer nutritive sucking in boys. Each of the three independent variables which dealt with some aspect of the interpersonal milieu was also analyzed singly. Marital adjustment of the parents showed no relationship to childhood adjustment in either girls or boys; nervous stability was associated with fewer behavior problems in girls but not in boys; warmth of the mother appeared to be a significant variable for both girls and boys, with higher ratings on maternal warmth associated with fewer problems in the children. Following these single variable analyses, Heinstein then examined the interaction effects among practice variables and environmental variables. Thus if testing for the interaction between type of feeding and maternal warmth, the incidence of symptoms would be compared in children breast-fed by a warm mother, breast-fed by a cold mother, formula-fed by a warm mother, and formula-fed by a cold mother. Such analyses revealed many significant interaction effects in contrast to the paucity of significant relationships found when each variable was examined in isolation. Thus girls who had warm mothers had fewer problems if formula-fed. For boys no such interaction effects could be demonstrated on the basis of breast or formula feeding, but equally revealing interactions were found in relation to interpersonal environment and duration of nutritive sucking. Boys in unfavorable interpersonal environments had fewer adjustment problems if nursed for a shorter period of time, whereas boys with good environments showed better adjustment if nursed for a longer period of time. For girls just the reverse was true. It is felt by this reviewer that this type of research represents a major advance in attempts to understand the effects of infant care practices. Analysis in terms of single variables is not likely to lead to a complete understanding of the total pattern of parent influence.

This discussion should not be interpreted as espousing the belief that attitudes are somehow nonbehavioral. The term "attitude" refers to behavior that is more difficult to assess directly, but behavior nonetheless. It is only when the level of observation is macroscopic that one can speak of a disparity between attitude and overt behavior. When the level of observation can deal with smaller units, then the behavior output from a severe method-warm mother and a severe method-cold mother will not be coded as the same behavior. Concern with the relative influence of attitude and behavior is but a way of examining whether those aspects of behavior which can be readily identified and labeled actually comprise the most salient features of the interpersonal stimuli to which the infant responds. The available evidence would suggest that both aspects, considered separately, have some effect, but that their full impact cannot be understood until research is designed to permit their interaction to reveal itself.

THE INFLUENCE OF SOCIAL CLASS

The social class position of the family into which a child is born defines in advance certain aspects of the personal-social environment in which he will be reared. That there are major social class differences in parent attitudes and parent behavior has long been suspected, with the stereotyped image being that of the harsh or punitive lower class parent with abused and neglected children. Thus when Davis and Havighurst in 1946 published the results of a Chicago survey which conflicted with the stereotype, a minor social science revolution was launched. Their results showed that in such activities as feeding and weaning, age of beginning elimination training, and postponement of forced assumption of responsibility, lower-class (or working-class) parents were significantly more permissive than their middle-class counterparts. Data from this study also suggested that any differences in child rearing that might be associated with ethnic group membership were fairly well overshadowed by social class differences.

In the early fifties data began to appear (Klatskin, 1952b; Maccoby and Gibbs, 1954) which did not support the findings of the earlier Davis and Havighurst work and which were in many respects in direct opposition. Within the past decade a series of projects dealing with differences in parent behavior as a function of social class has been published, a summary of which is presented as Table 6.[3] For a more comprehensive summary of data on this question, including several older studies not accessible to this reviewer and information about class differences in post-infancy experiences, the reader is referred to Bronfenbrenner (1958).

The available literature has led to the conclusion that the trend of the fifties is for middle-class mothers to be evaluated as more permissive and supportive, more tolerant of misbehavior, and milder in punishment when such is considered necessary. The greater the social and economic difference between the classes compared, the greater the reported differences tend to be. Differences in specific practices of the infancy period have not been found as frequently as differences in such parental attributes as warmth and pattern of discipline. The currently prevailing interpretation of the time trend is that parent education literature of the past two decades has placed strong emphasis on the values of permissiveness and mildness and that middle-class parents, with a shorter time lag in the assimilation of such cultural influences, have been the first to respond.

While these generalizations about the results of such studies are not out of line with the empirical data on which they are based, they give insufficient recognition to the impressive interclass similarities. Also the semantics of reporting occasionally override the logic of the experimental designs. For example, statistically significant associations frequently consist of differences in proportion of cases employing a particular form of parental behavior—for example, proportion of lower- and of middle-class mothers using a technique designated as lenient or severe. However, from that type of statistical relationship it is easy to fall into the habit of comparing the two groups with respect to degree of severity or leniency. The statement, "More lower-class mothers are severe than middle-class mothers" does not mean the same thing as the statement, "Lower-class mothers are more severe than middle-class mothers." Yet not infrequently when a statistical

[3] Most of the families designated as "middle" class represent professional and business occupations, while these labeled "lower" class include skilled and semi-skilled workers. As many persons have objected to the possible evaluation implicit in the term "lower" class, the label "working" class has been substituted as a synonym in recent years. In Table 6, the terms used by the authors of the original study have been adopted, but it is to be understood that two, not three, social class groups are being described.

TABLE 6. ASSOCIATION BETWEEN SOCIAL CLASS AND TECHNIQUES OF CHILD REARING

Author and Date	Subjects	Dependent Variable	Summary of Major Findings and Conclusions	Comments
1. Davis & Havighurst (1946)	48 middle-class and 52 lower-class mothers (Chicago).	Child-rearing techniques as disclosed in interview.	Lower-class (LC) children reared more permissively; later weaning and toilet training. Middle-class (MC) parents expected earlier assumption of responsibility.	Nonrandom sample; interviewed about "children" rather than specific child.
2. Klatskin (1952b)	223 parents of middle- and lower-classes (New Haven).	Questionnaire data on child-rearing techniques.	LC parents began toilet training earlier. No significant difference in duration of breast- or bottle-feeding or in use of demand schedules. Mothers from LC groups used prohibitive discipline.	Data obtained in longitudinal study though with some lapse of time.
3. Maccoby & Gibbs (1954); Sears, Maccoby, & Levin (1957)	198 middle-class and 174 lower-class mothers (Boston).	Child-rearing techniques as disclosed in interview.	No class differences in feeding; LC mothers more severe in toilet training and sex and modesty training. MC mothers use physical punishment and withdrawal of privilege. MC mothers more affectionate; greater agreement with husband about child-rearing practices.	Retrospective infancy data.
4. Boek et al. (1957)	1,443 mothers of 3–6 month-old infants (upstate New York).	Incidence of breast-feeding at time of home visit by investigator.	Breast-feeding higher in middle-class mothers, and continued somewhat longer.	Untrained interviewers.
5. Littman, Moore, & Pierce-Jones (1957)	206 parents (Eugene, Oregon).	Child-rearing techniques as assessed in separate interviews with mothers and fathers.	Essentially no social class differences.	Provided data on paternal as well as maternal behavior.
6. White (1957)	38 working-class and 36 middle-class mothers with one child between 2 and 5 years (San Francisco).	Child-rearing techniques as disclosed in interview, plus independent personality measures of the children.	Absence of differences in feeding, bowel training, warmth or vigilance. Working class more severe in punishment. MC felt aggression to parents should be expressed. No differences in children.	Study reported independent data on the children.
7. Miller & Swanson (1958)	582 mothers with child under 19 (Detroit).	Child-rearing techniques as disclosed in interview. (Class differences considered separately for different integration settings—bureaucratic and entrepreneurial.)	Entrepreneurial MC bowel train earlier; use symbolic punishment; encourage activity and responsibility more than bureaucratic MC. Entrepreneurial MC encourage activity and responsibility more than either entrepreneurial or bureaucratic lowers. Within bureaucratic settings, essentially no differences between LC and MC patterns.	Retrospective data re infancy. Operational definition of entrepreneurial and bureaucratic settings open to question.

TABLE 6. ASSOCIATION BETWEEN SOCIAL CLASS AND TECHNIQUES OF CHILD REARING (Continued)

Author and Date	Subjects	Dependent Variable	Summary of Major Findings and Conclusions	Comments
8. Kohn (1959a, 1959b)	200 middle-class and 200 working-class parents with children in the fifth grade (Washington, D. C.).	Exercise of parental authority and behavior traits valued by parents.	MC mothers punish behavior signifying child's loss of control, working-class mothers punish inconvenient behavior. MC seems to value internalized standards, working class, compliance with authority.	
9. Kohn & Carroll (1960)	200 middle-class and 200 working-class parents (Washington, D. C.).	Allocation of parental responsibility.	MC mothers want fathers to be emotionally supportive to children; working-class mothers want control from fathers. Working-class fathers view child rearing as woman's work.	
10. Bayley & Schaefer (1960)	56 mothers when children 0–3, 9–14 (Berkeley).	Maternal behavior as observed during testing of infants and assessed by interviewer when same children were 9–14 years.	Few significant correlations, but suggestion of greater warmth and permissiveness for MC parents. Sex differences in relationships.	Dealt with behavior occurring at time of assessment.
11. Wortis et al. (1963)	250 working-class Negro mothers with children born prematurely (Brooklyn).	Child-rearing techniques and attitudes assessed when children were 2½ and again at 5 years.	Class differences more pronounced when extreme groups were used. Relatively little concern about weaning and toilet training. More likely to be intolerant of aggression against parents, more punctual and cold toward child than working class mothers of Boston study. Less restrictive about manners, noise, and cleanliness than Boston working class.	Data obtained concurrently; rater agreement carefully explored. Dealt with segment of working class insufficiently explored previously.

70

finding has been of the first type it is interpreted as though it had been of the second type. Similarly, in those studies in which class differences represent mean rating scores rather than frequencies, the magnitude of the scale differences is extremely small. In the Maccoby and Gibbs study, for instance, differences no greater than .5 of a scale point might achieve statistical significance and yet not represent a just noticeable difference in terms of overt behavior.

The empirical data on social class differences are for the most part limited to differences between middle- and upper-lower-class families. Relatively little is known about child rearing in the upper and lower extremes of the stratification continuum. If educational media are at all influential in modifying parent practices, one would expect the most deviant group to be the one whose lack of educational achievement precludes contact with most of the regular channels of information. Child rearing in such a group has recently been vividly described by Wortis and associates (1963), who interviewed 250 culturally deprived Negro mothers with two-and-a-half-year-old children who had been prematurely born, and subsequently 47 of these mothers when the children were five years of age, using some of the interview items and scales developed by Sears, Maccoby, and Levin (1957). They found that these children lived in extremely disorganized family environments, with almost half of them having no father in the home and many of them having received care from more than one mother figure. Child-rearing practices seemed to be selected in terms of whether they were convenient for the mother rather than because they fit into any maternal philosophy of how to bring up children. Weaning and toilet training were generally handled rather permissively, apparently not because the mother felt that gratification for the child was important but because it was easier to let the child train himself than to engage in a struggle to change his behavior. Corporal punishment was used a great deal, particularly in response to any aggression shown toward the mother herself, but there was minimal concern with instilling habits of neatness and orderliness and control of aggression toward other children. Particularly poignant was the groundwork laid for self-perpetuation of the pattern in virtually every phase of the child-rearing process. Wortis and associates (1963) write:

> Other elements in the environment were preparing the child to take over a lower class role. The inadequate incomes, crowded homes, lack of consistent familial ties, the mother's depression and helplessness in her own situation, were as important as her child-rearing practices in influencing the child's development and preparing him for an adult role. It was for us a sobering experience to watch a large group of newborn infants, plastic human beings of unknown potential, and observe over a 5-year period their social preparation to enter the class of the least-skilled, least-educated, and most-rejected in our society (p. 307).

Social class differences in child-training practices, while producing different learning environments for the children exposed to them, are themselves the products of social forces which thus indirectly influence the way children are reared. In recent years there have been several research programs oriented more toward explaining than delineating class differences. An example of one such approach is the work of Miller and Swanson (1958), whose complex study is summarized briefly in Table 6. They proposed that one explanation of the reported time trend in social class differences is the fact that the middle class is changing from an individuated, risk-taking orientation to one of concern with security and adjustment to the demands of the group—that is, from entrepreneurial to bureaucratic integration settings. Reasoning that integration setting would be perhaps a more powerful influence on parental behavior than social class level per se, they predicted that children reared in entrepreneurial families (of either middle or lower class) would be encouraged to be rational, active, and self-reliant, whereas children reared in bureaucratic homes would be oriented toward being accommodative and alert to cues provided by appropriate organizational structures. Some support of their hypotheses was found in an interview study of 582 Detroit mothers. Entrepreneurial middle-class mothers encouraged activity and assumption of responsibility more than any of the other three groups. Although within the entrepreneurial integration setting there were some differences associated with social class, few such differences could be found within the bureaucratic setting. Thus the bureaucratic orientation seemed to minimize any differences that might otherwise be expected to vary with social class level. Miller and Swanson speculate that one consequence of the increasing bureaucratization of the middle class is that its child-training patterns look increasingly like those of the lower class.[4]

[4] Although this study represents a major theoretical approach to an understanding of the impact of the social organization upon patterns of family care, the authors' conclusion that integration setting is the crucial variable is open to question. The criteria originally established for classifying a family as entrepreneurial—self-employment, employment in a small organization, and a substantial personal income from fees, profits, or commissions—were found to be inapplicable to lower-class families. As a process of individuation is considered basic to the entrepreneurial integration setting, they then looked for other background factors which might contribute to individuation and added two other conditions: farm birth for either of the parents, or foreign birth for either parent. No information was available to support the assumption that the foreign born were probably of rural origin. Only 51 of the 241 families classified as entrepreneurial were done so on the basis of employment conditions only, with the ones remaining representing approximately equal numbers of farm and foreign born and thus comprising the bulk of the entrepreneurial group. Although they attempted to show that entrepreneurial groups established on the basis of these different background factors did not differ significantly from the remainder of the entrepreneurial group in any consistent way, the overweighting of their sample with such families seems unfortunate. Haber (1962), after an examination of some of the data from the original study, noted that the entrepre-

The series of studies by Kohn (Kohn, 1959a,b; Kohn and Carroll, 1960) also represent an attempt to identify certain aspects of social structure which might nourish some of the reported differences in parent behavior associated with social class status. If parents from different class levels do not value the same types of behavior in their children, they will not have the same child training goals and can be expected to employ different child-rearing practices. In an investigation of the values held by middle- and working-class parents, Kohn (1959a) found that, while parents from both class levels held a common core of shared values, there were significant class differences. Working-class mothers tended to place more value on compliance with external authority, whereas middle-class mothers were more concerned about the development of internalized standards of conduct. Conceptions of proper paternal roles also differed in contrasting social class groups, with middle-class mothers viewing the role of the father as involving encouragement and support of the children and working-class mothers regarding the father as one who should supply discipline and control. Paternal views of the proper child-rearing role also showed contrasts, with middle-class fathers wishing to involve themselves in child-rearing and lower-class fathers essentially abrogating such responsibility.

Noteworthy in the literature dealing with social class differences in parent behavior has been lack of concern with possible differences in child behavior associated with the contrasting practices. In neither the Chicago nor Boston studies was any information supplied about social class differences in the behavior of the children. Class differences in children's behavior have been studied extensively, but seldom in the context of these very forms of parent behavior which have been assumed to be important. In White's study (1957) the children were given a number of tests and experimental procedures at the same time that their mothers were being interviewed about their child-rearing practices. Measures included ratings of ability to delay gratification, scores on the Draw-a-Man test, amount of aggression in doll play, and a number of personality ratings. No differences between children from working- and middle-class homes could be found, although in general the middle-class mothers were found to be more permissive, more tolerant of aggressive behavior in the children, and slightly warmer toward the children.

---

neurial parents of both middle- and lower-class status tended to be slightly older than those in the bureaucratic families. This inadequately controlled age difference, he suggested, means that the entrepreneurial families were more likely to have been maximally involved in child rearing during the historical period in which parent education literature advocated early impulse control and greater independence for the child. Thus the obtained findings, while of considerable theoretical significance, may reflect such factors as early rearing in a different cultural milieu or age differences rather than the influence of integration setting per se.

Two studies were found which dealt directly with the question of differences in children as a function of differences in parental behavior. Williams and Scott (1953) investigated the relationship between social class status and performance on the motor items of the Gesell Schedules in a group of Negro infants. Hypothesizing that the frequently reported superiority of Negro infants on this scale (for example, Knobloch and Pasamanick, 1953) might be related to the type of care provided for the infants, they made home visits to the families of 104 Negro babies ranging in age from four to eighteen months, approximately half of whom were middle class and half lower class. Mean motor quotients for infants in the middle- and lower-class groups were, respectively, 107.57 and 114.32, a statistically significant difference. Significant differences in child-rearing practices in the direction of greater permissiveness were also found, with lower-class families having breast-fed longer, used flexible feeding and sleep routines, minimized discipline, and placed fewer restrictions on freedom of movement. To determine whether it was the atmosphere of freedom for the child which fostered the accelerated development of the infant, the total group was dichotomized, regardless of class status, into two subgroups labeled permissive-accepting and rigid-rejecting. Mean motor quotients for the groups resulting from this classification were 114.03 and 100.73, again a statistically significant difference. Thus a significant aspect of infant development was shown to vary as a function of a pattern of child care which in turn varied with social class.

The other study which attempted to relate social class differences in parent behavior to differences in child behavior has already been summarized in Table 5 and will be mentioned only briefly here. Alper, Blane, and Abrams (1955) compared the performance of two groups of middle- and lower-class preschool children on finger painting and crayon drawing, hypothesizing that children who had been frustrated during bowel training would resist the former task and show more concern with getting cleaned up afterward but would show no such reaction in the less messy crayon task. Since only the Davis and Havighurst study had been published at the time these authors collected their first set of data (1948), they expected to find a history of earlier and more frustrating bowel training and observe maximum resistance to smearing of paints in the middle-class children. Results of the experiment supported their hypothesis, leading the authors to conclude that soiling and smearing arouses more anxiety in children who are frustrated during early bowel training. Such frustration, at the time they began their study, was presumably more likely to exist for the middle- than for the lower-class child. However, even though the results supported their hypotheses, one would have to question the inference that the association established between social class and reaction to painting was actually related to bowel training experiences. In the first (finger painting) phase of their study, mean ages for beginning bowel training for the middle- and lower-class samples were 9.0 and 11.2 months, with ages for the completion of the process being 27.0 and 18.0 months, respectively. The significantly later completion age for the middle-class children was interpreted by the authors as indirect evidence of conflict, whereas it may have indicated that middle-class mothers were more relaxed and less stringent in their demands for compliance. In the second (crayon) phase of the experiment, the direction of difference for the beginning of training was reversed, mean ages being 10 and 9 months for middle- and lower-class children, while a later completion age for the middle-class group was again observed (25.9 months for the middle-class and 17.4 for the lower-class children). Thus although this experiment was designed to provide data about the social class—parent behavior—child behavior chain, the nature of the middle link may not have been accurately identified.

In sum, then, it would appear that time trends in social class differences between middle- and what are generally called upper-lower-class families, have been limned by successive researches in the direction of increasing permissiveness in parents of the middle class. At this juncture little is known about the extremes (upper and lower) of the socioeconomic distribution. Data on differences in child behavior associated with differences in parent behavior are in short supply. There is evidence at this time to suggest that social class differences in parent behavior are narrowing, not widening, due in part to the increasing exposure of mothers from all class levels to vanguard research data pertaining to child rearing. A possible exception to this is to be found in the mothers from the lowest echelons of the stratification system for whom mobility for either themselves or their offspring appears too remote to be worth the effort. Lower-class parents are never blind to the values held by the middle class, and if, as research would suggest, these values are changing, then working-class families with mobility aspirations will undoubtedly scan their traditions and the powerful agents of cultural change (child-rearing literature, pediatricians, public health personnel, and so on) for cues as to how the new goals may be implemented.

THE CHILD BEING TRAINED

The lactating breast will rather quickly dry up if presented repeatedly to a nonsucking baby, whereas the same breast might continue to produce a bountiful supply of milk if offered to an avid sucker. Similarly, a mother whose plan for toilet training calls for a late start, much patience, and no punishment might carry out the plan with a docile child and be convinced that her technique was the perfect one; with an intractable and resistant child she might find herself inadvertently changing the plan after the third bowel movement had been deposited in the middle of the living room or the neighborhood supermarket. Thus as surely as infant care practices have an effect upon a child, so does the child being trained have an effect upon infant care practices.

Research attention to individual differences has for some reason not been popular in the area of infant care, although the suspicion that different infants will not react identically to the same experience has long been accepted as a common sense principle to be heeded in dealing with children and as an entirely respectable scientific premise. The design of most of the studies here reviewed has called for the establishment of group trends, a type of design which to some extent precludes attention to individual differences. Yet if one is to understand fully the consequences of child care practices, one must surely pay as much attention to the deviant cases as to those which cluster around the modal response. To look for relationships which ignore the unique monitoring capacity of each individual child is to do an injustice to the magnificence of the complexly evolved human organism which presents itself to be socialized.

Over the years Gesell pleaded eloquently for more serious attention to the intrinsic regulating factors which mediate each child's response to his idiosyncratic psychosocial world. More than thirty years ago (1929) he sounded a tocsin against an overzealous acceptance of the idea that all infant development could be explained by conditioning. Such a pattern could not be biologically adaptive, he argued, as the infant who learned too readily would be at the mercy of a not always favorable environment. He suggested that perhaps maturational factors protected infants from maladaptive conditioning circumstances. Likewise, Shirley (1933), in a longitudinal study of infant personality, voiced her conviction that early personality development reflected innate characteristics and that attempts by the parents to eliminate some traits or to strengthen others by means of specific training practices were usually to no avail.

In their study so frequently mentioned in this review, Sears, Maccoby, and Levin (1957) paid attention to the possible contribution of the child to any given phase of child training. For example, in commenting on the factors associated with the child's reaction to weaning, they stated: "It should be noted that while the age at beginning of weaning, the total duration of weaning, and its severity all seems to have some bearing upon the extent of the child's emotional reaction to weaning, these factors do not by any means fully account for weaning difficulties. It appears quite possible that there are inborn differences among babies, having to do with their activity level or the size (or speed of emptying) of their stomachs, which help to determine how well they can adjust to their infant feeding experiences" (p. 90). In this connection Despert (1944) found that infants who reacted intensely to being wet were trained significantly earlier than infants who did not show this reaction. Similarly, Anthony's finding (1957) of a failure in one subgroup of encopretic children to react aversively to odors ordinarily interpreted as unpleasant implies that such children might be expected to react differently to elimination training procedures.

Over the past few decades several investigators have searched for aspects of infant behavior which would permit predictions to be made as to how a given child would react to his experiential environment, notably Escalona and Leitch (1952), Fries and Woolf (1953), Heider (1960), Bell (1960), Lipton, Steinschneider, and Richmond (1961), and many others. Recently Brazelton (1962b) suggested that even the neonate is capable of regulating his stimulus input to some extent. In a carefully standardized laboratory situation for studying autonomic reactions to strong sensory stimulation (light and sound), he and his colleagues noticed the ability of some newborns to fend off seemingly unwanted stimulation. The response involves a diminution of motor activity, with respiratory and EEG records simulating deep sleep. As soon as the stimulation is terminated, however, the infants may return to an extremely active, perhaps irritable state. Brazelton speculates about the role played by this "stimulus barrier" and wonders if it represents a prototype of subsequent mechanisms of defense.

A tantalizing contemporary approach to the question of individual differences is found in the series of papers by various combinations of Thomas, Chess, and Birch. (See Thomas and Chess, 1957; Chess, Thomas, and Birch, 1959; Thomas, Chess, Birch, and Hertzig, 1960; and Thomas, Birch, Chess, and Robbins, 1961.) These authors are involved in a longitudinal study of 110 middle-class children who have been followed systematically from the age of two or three months, with interviews and observations made five times during the first two years of life and at longer intervals thereafter. In the interview great stress is laid on specific behavior of the infant (rather than any sort of parental interpretation) and details of the child's first response to a new stimulus in relation to subsequent responses to that same category of stimuli. Behavior reported in the interviews is rated on a three-point scale for each of the following categories: activity level, rhythmicity, approach or withdrawal, adaptability, intensity of reaction, threshold of responsiveness, quality of mood, distractability, attention span, and persistence. The authors report an inter-rater agreement of 90 per cent for some 22 independently rated protocols. From patterns of ratings, the investigators arrive at a designation of the child's primary reaction pattern. These have been grouped into clusters qualitatively, with the following five types identified:

> (1) Regularity, adaptability, mild intensity, approach, and positive mood; (2) Irregularity, nonadaptability, high intensity, withdrawal, negative mood, and high activity level; (3) Moderate adaptability, mild intensity, withdrawal, negative mood and low or moderate activity level; (4) Low threshold of response, distractability, short attention span and low persistence; (5) High threshold of response, and nondistractability (Thomas *et al.*, 1960, p. 108).

Details of methodology and of data analysis have not yet been made available by this group, but they have published a number of reports in which general descriptions of their quantitative data have been given. They report that primary reaction characteristics identified in the first two or three months of life persist throughout early childhood at a statistically significant level. Of particular usefulness for identifying a child's primary reaction pattern is exposure to a new situation—whether this be the first bath in infancy, the first solid food, first experience on the toilet, or the first contact with nursery school. If such reaction patterns exist, it is unreasonable to expect specific practices to affect all children in the same manner. While equivocating somewhat about the origins of such patterns, they take a strong position for the importance of inborn attributes, stating:

> Our data thus far do not permit a definite answer to the question of whether these reaction patterns are of an inborn character, or formed under the influence of environmental factors in the first few months of life, or the resultant of the interaction of these two factors. . . . However, our impression from the evidence inclines us to the opinion that these patterns are not experientially determined, but are of an intrinsic character (Chess, Thomas, and Birch, 1959, p. 797).

Publication of their quantitative data and further details of their methods will make it possible to determine the extent to which this new approach at defining important individual characteristics that help to shape the relationship between child training and personality has reached its goals.

THE RESIDUAL

What distillate remains after this empirical assay? What conclusions that are relevant for the everyday world of parents and children can one reach? No matter how scientifically pure or how rigorous one's standards of evidence might be, one must interpret the available data and make judgments. Children must be cared for, socialized, and trained in the customs of their culture. Parents cannot wait until all the answers are in; nor can the professionals who are daily called upon to translate for parents the research upon which they would like to base their recommendations.

On the basis of an examination of the empirical literature available at this time, it seems to this writer that one can reach several conclusions about the effects of varying patterns of infant care and can in addition identify certain guidelines for subsequent research:

1. The breast-bottle dilemma must remain exactly that. One clear fact is that incidence of breast-feeding has declined sharply in recent years, with interesting geographical variations in the reported trends. The two main factors which appear to support the custom at present are (a) lack of industrialization or what is now generally called "westernization," and (b) a positive attitude toward the practice buttressed by the conviction that it is best for the baby. Previous debates about the relative nutritional merits of the two feeding procedures have been made somewhat obsolete by improvements in artificial feeding formulas and wider dissemination of knowledge regarding sterilization techniques. The fragments of evidence that can be mustered in support of possible psychological advantages of breast-feeding are not convincing because of failure to control such factors as duration of total nutritive sucking and degree of physical intimacy offered the nonbreast-fed subjects. However, it is worth noting that while research which has claimed to demonstrate psychological advantages associated with breast-feeding is generally unconvincing, no single piece of research has ever produced evidence of any psychological superiority of formula feeding. Professionals called upon to help a mother make a decision about how to feed her infant might profitably explore such factors as the mother's modesty and whether she would have help in caring for her baby. The counter question, "How do you feel about it?" is more than a nondirective ploy. It is as accurate a compression of the research literature as can be reasonably offered.

2. It is difficult to demonstrate any consistent relationships between oral gratification, defined to include type and scheduling of feeding and time of weaning, and either child or adult personality. Studies designed to elucidate some aspect of this question appear to have resulted in conflicting or inconclusive results more than any other type of investigation concerned with infant care practices. Methodological factors probably account for some of the contradictions, as much of the research has been retrospective in design, and in several investigations adequately separated measures of the dependent and independent variables have not been obtained. Analysis of the available data has usually failed to take advantage of interactions among the variables which could and should be considered. Accordingly

it remains for future research to clarify the nature of the complex relationships between oral gratification and personality.

3. Studies concerned with oral gratification and oral activities provide little support for the hypothesis that sustained gratification leads to drive satiation. Specifically, longer opportunity for nutritive sucking does not guarantee easy transition to other techniques of obtaining nourishment or preclude the development of habits of nonnutritive sucking. Rather, continuing gratification seems to heighten the infant's emotional response to the transition and to increase the likelihood of the development of other types of nonnutritive sucking. There is evidence to suggest that intensity of the sucking drive varies with age, waxing during the first year and waning thereafter. Reactions to prohibition of nutritive sucking may vary both as a function of amount of reinforcement received for this mode of behavior (strength of the secondary drive) and the point in the wax-wane cycle of the primary drive at which a behavior change is demanded.

4. In the research literature it is frequently difficult to determine exactly what is meant by "toilet training," although in general the term seems to have been applied to bowel rather than bladder training. Studies dealing with clinical groups showing some clear disturbance of bowel or bladder functioning have generally been able to implicate coercive or seemingly premature training. However, the absence of information about similarly deviant practices in children showing no overt pathology limits generalizations which can be made from such evidence. For unselected groups of essentially normal children it has usually been possible to demonstrate a relationship between type of training and reaction to the training process but seldom between type of training and broad personality variables. The interpersonal context in which training occurs appears to be more influential than either timing of the training or methods used. Maternal sex anxiety and concern with orderliness appear to influence the choice of harsh methods of inducing bowel and bladder control. While there is evidence of covariation of traits presumed to reflect anal personality characteristics, there is no evidence that strength of the traits is related to type of elimination training. Theoretical interpretations of the impact of elimination training appear to have been largely negative, focusing too much attention on what the child must give up and too little on what he gains in this process.

5. The relationship between parent attitudes and parent behavior is still insufficiently explored and imperfectly understood. In terms of the relative strength of either, the weight of evidence at the present time would appear to be on the side of the attitude. Underlying attitudes may influence not only the choice of a specific parent practice (such as decision to breast-

feed) but may also support the decision when personal needs (comfort, convenience) challenge the wisdom of the choice. Interaction effects may be more important than either attitudes or practices considered separately.

6. Social class differences in patterns of child rearing are generally found, with the controversy regarding identification of which group is more permissive decided for the time being in favor of the middle class. However, the differences found in several studies are of such small magnitude as to be, for all practical purposes, meaningless. Furthermore, associated differences in child behavior have received insufficient attention. In the preoccupation with demonstrating that children from different social classes have different patterns of family life, research designed to demonstrate the effects on young children of these patterns has been neglected.

7. The number of variables in which investigators have shown interest is small indeed. This is undoubtedly related to intense preoccupation with theory-derived research. In addition to the areas of feeding and elimination, there are many other types of behavior of the infancy period that deserve research attention. There has been a tendency to search for the effects of specific practices on certain areas of behavior assumed in advance to absorb the impact of the particular practices. Just as there is need to examine for the effects of a broader range of independent variables, so too is there need for more openmindedness in the pairing of dependent and independent variables. The dawn of the computer era makes a vigorous eclecticism feasible for the first time. It is premature to restrict activities to hypothesis-testing research only; there remains a need for hypothesis-formulating research in this area.

8. Closer attention should be given to important subject variables which may mediate the effects of specific practices. Examining for effects of specific practices on boys and girls separately seems obligatory in future research, as does concern with individual differences in attributes other than those serving as dependent variables in a given study. Cases whose behavior deviates from the modal response must also be accounted for in establishing antecedent-consequent relationships.

9. It is imperative that there be a general improvement of methodology in studies concerned with the effects of infant care. Retrospective methods, with all the inaccuracies and misinterpretations to which they conduce, have been widely employed in research in this area. Except for exploratory studies dealing with new independent-dependent variable relationships, a retrospective design should no longer be acceptable to workers in the field. Only prospective longitudinal studies can provide the answers to many of the perplexing problems in this area, and there is a need for more and better research of this type. Likewise, more attention must be given to

conceptual factors, criterion factors, and appropriate assessment techniques in order to improve comparability of data from different empirical studies. Many of the controversies will be resolved when these methodological problems are solved.

10. Full sequences of attitude-behavior-response must be considered, as for example: parental use by a warm and accepting mother of scheduled feeding (protested by the infant) followed by early elimination training done without punishment (accepted by the infant), and so forth. Thus the ideal study will be concerned with attitude plus practice, with the inherent characteristics of the child as well as his immediate reaction to the process, and with the multiplicity of subsequent experiences through which the specific practice must be filtered before coming to rest as a significant influence in the child's life. Only when such studies are available can the definitive review be written on the effects of infant care.

REFERENCES

ABRAHAM, K. Contributions to the theory of the anal character (1921). *Selected Papers.* 370–392. London: Hogarth Press, 1949.

ACHESON, E. D. & TRUELOVE, S. C. Early weaning in the aetiology of ulcerative colitis. A study of feeding in infancy in cases and controls. *Brit. Med. J.*, 1961, **2**, 929–933.

ADAMS, A. B. Choice of infant feeding technique as a function of maternal personality. *J. consult. Psychol.*, 1959, **23**, 143–146.

ALPER, T. G., BLANE, H. T., & ABRAMS, B. K. Reactions of middle and lower class children to finger paints as a function of class differences in child-training practices. *J. abnorm. soc. Psychol.*, 1955, **51**, 439–448.

ANTHONY, E. J. An experimental approach to the psychopathology of childhood: encopresis. *Brit. J. Med. Psychol.*, 1957, **30**, 146–175.

BAKWIN, H. Thumb and fingersucking in children. *J. Pediat.*, 1948, **32**, 99–101.

BAYLEY, N. & SCHAEFER, E. S. Relationships between socioeconomic variables and the behavior of mothers toward young children. *J. genet. Psychol.*, 1960, **96**, 61–77.

BELL, R. Q. Relations between behavior manifestations in the human neonate. *Child Developm.*, 1960, **31**, 463–477.

BELOFF, H. The structure and origin of the anal character. *Genet. Psychol. Monogr.*, 1957, **55**, 141–172.

BENEDICT, R. Child rearing in certain European countries. *Amer. J. Orthopsychiat.*, 1949, **19**, 342–350.

BERNSTEIN, A. Some relations between techniques of feeding and training during infancy and certain behavior in childhood. *Genet. Psychol. Monogr.*, 1955, **51**, 3–44.

BLAU, T. H. & BLAU, L. R. The sucking reflex: the effects of long feeding vs. short feeding on the behavior of a human infant. *J. abnorm. soc. Psychol.*, 1955, **51**, 123–125.

BLAUVELT, H. & McKENNA, J. Mother-neonate interaction: capacity of the human newborn for orientation. In B. M. Foss (Ed.), *Determinants of infant behaviour.* London: Methuen, 1961. Pp. 3–29.

BOEK, W. E., LAWSON, E. D., YANKAUER, A., & SUSSMAN, M. D. Social class, maternal health, and child care: an interviewing study of mothers with three-to-six months old babies. New York: N. Y. State Dept. Health, 1957.

BOSTOCK, J. & SHACKLETON, M. G. Enuresis and toilet training. *Med. J. Australia*, 1951, **2**, 110–113.

BOWLBY, J. The nature of the child's tie to his mother. *Internat. J. Psychoanal.*, 1958, **39**, 1–23.

BRAZELTON, T. B. Sucking in infancy. *Pediatrics*, 1956, **17**, 400–404.

BRAZELTON, T. B. A child-oriented approach to toilet training. *Pediatrics*, 1962, **29**, 121–128 (a).

BRAZELTON, T. B. Observations of the neonate. *J. Amer. Acad. Child Psychiat.*, 1962, **1**, 38–58 (b).

BROCK, J. F. & AUTRET, M. *Kwashiorkor in Africa*. Geneva: World Health Organization, Monograph Series No. 8, 1952.

BRODY, S. *Patterns of mothering: maternal influence during infancy*. New York: Internat. Univ. Press, 1956.

BRONFENBRENNER, U. Socialization and social class through time and space. In E. E. Maccoby, T. M. Newcomb, & E. L. Hartley (Eds.), *Readings in social psychology*. New York: Holt, Rinehart, & Winston, 1958. Pp. 400–425.

BROWN, F., LIEBERMAN, J., WINSTON, J., & PLESHETTE, N. Studies in infant choices of primiparae. I. Attitudinal factors and extraneous influences. *Psychosom. Med.*, 1960, **21**, 421–429.

CALDWELL, B. M. Assessment of infant personality. *Merrill-Palmer Quart.*, 1962, **8**, 71–81.

CALDWELL, B. M. *et al.* Mother-infant interaction in monomatric and polymatric families. *Amer. J. Orthopsychiat.*, 1963, **33**, 653–664.

CHESS, S., THOMAS, A., & BIRCH, H. Characteristics of the individual child's behavioral responses to the environment. *Amer. J. Orthopsychiat.*, 1959, **29**, 791–802.

CHILDERS, A. T. & HAMIL, B. M. Emotional problems in children as related to the duration of breast feeding in infancy. *Amer. J. Orthopsychiat.*, 1932, **2**, 134–142.

DAVIS, A. & HAVIGHURST, R. J. Social class and color differences in child-rearing. *Amer. Sociol. Rev.*, 1946, **11**, 698–710.

DAVIS, H. V., SEARS, R. R., MILLER, H. C., & BRODBECK, A. J. Effects of cup, bottle, and breast feeding on oral activities of newborn infants. *Pediatrics*, 1948, **2**, 549–558.

DENNIS, W. Infant reaction to restraint: an evaluation of Watson's theory. *Trans. N. Y. Acad. Sci.*, 1940, **2**, 202–218.

DENNIS, W. Causes of retardation among institutional children: Iran. *J. genet. Psychol.*, 1960, **96**, 47–59.

DESPERT, J. L. Urinary control and enuresis. *Psychosom. Med.*, 1944, **6**, 294–307.

DOLLARD, J. & MILLER, N. E. *Personality and psychotherapy: an analysis of learning, thinking, and culture*. New York: McGraw-Hill, 1950.

DURRETT, M. Relationship of early infant regulation and later behavior in play interviews. *Child Developm.*, 1959, **30**, 211–216.

ERIKSON, E. *Childhood and society*. New York: Norton, 1950.

ESCALONA, S. & LEITCH, M. Early phases of personality development. A non-normative study of infant behavior. *Monogr. Soc. Res. Child Developm.*, 1952, **17**, No. 1.

FREDEEN, R. C. Cup feeding of newborn infants. *Pediatrics*, 1948, **2**, 544–548.

FREUD, S. (1905) Three contributions to the theory of sex. In *Basic Writings of Sigmund Freud*. New York: Random House, 1938. Pp. 553–629.

FREUD, S. (1908) Character and anal eroticism. In *Collected Papers*, Vol. II. London: Hogarth Press, 1924. Pp. 45–50.

FRIES, M. E. The formation of character as observed in the well-baby clinic. *Amer. J. Dis. Child.*, 1935, **49**, 28–42.

FRIES, M. E. & WOOLF, P. J. Some hypotheses on the role of the congenital activity type in personality development. *Psychoanal. Study of the Child*, 1953, **8**, 48–62.

GARDNER, D. B., HAWKES, G. R., & BURCHINAL, L. G. Noncontinuous mothering in infancy and development in later childhood. *Child Developm.*, 1961, **32**, 225–234.

GARDNER, D. B., PEASE, D., & HAWKES, G. R. Responses of two-year-old children to controlled stress situations. *J. genet. Psychol.*, 1961, **98**, 29–35.

GARNER, A. M. & WENAR, C. *The mother-child interactions in psychosomatic disorders.* Urbana: Univ. Illinois Press, 1959.

GEBER, M. The psycho-motor development of African children in the first year, and the influence of maternal behavior. *J. soc. Psychol.*, 1958, **47**, 185–195.

GESELL, A. Maturation and infant behavior pattern. *Psychol. Rev.*, 1929, **36**, 307–319.

GESELL, A. & ILG, F. L. *Feeding behavior of infants: a pediatric approach to the mental hygiene of early life.* Philadelphia: Lippincott, 1937.

GODDARD, K. E., BRODER, G., & WENAR, C. Reliability of pediatric histories. A preliminary study. *Pediatrics*, 1961, **28**, 1011–1018.

GOLDMAN-EISLER, F. Breastfeeding and character formation. In C. Kluckhohn & H. A. Murray (Eds.), *Personality in nature, society, and culture.* New York: Knopf, 1953. Pp. 146–184.

GRAHAM, F. K., MATARAZZO, R. G., & CALDWELL, B. M. Behavioral differences between normal and traumatized newborns. II. Standardization, reliability, and validity. *Psychol. Monogr.*, 1956, **70**, No. 21.

GUNTHER, M. Infant behaviour at the breast. In B. M. Foss (Ed.), *Determinants of infant behaviour.* London: Methuen, 1961. Pp. 37–39.

HABER, L. D. Age and integration setting: a re-appraisal of "The Changing American Parent." *Amer. Sociol. Rev.*, 1962, **27**, 482–489.

HEIDER, G. M. Vulnerability in infants. *Bull. Menninger Clinic*, 1960, **24**, 104–114.

HEINSTEIN, M. I. Behavioral correlates of breast-bottle regimes under varying parent-infant relationships. *Monogr. Soc. Res. Child Developm.*, 1963, **28**, No. 4.

HETHERINGTON, E. M. & BRACKBILL, Y. Etiology and covariation of obstinacy, orderliness, and parsimony in young children. *Child Developm.*, 1963, **34**, 919–943.

HOEFER, C. & HARDY, M. Later development of breast fed and artificially fed infants. *J. A. M. A.*, 1929, **92**, 615–619.

HOLWAY, A. R. Early self-regulation of infants and later behavior in play interviews. *Amer. J. Orthopsychiat.*, 1949, **19**, 612–623.

HONZIK, M. P. & McKEE, J. P. The sex difference in thumb-sucking. *J. Pediat.*, 1962, **61**, 726–732.

HOPPER, H. E. & PINNEAU, S. R. Frequency of regurgitation in infancy as related to the amount of stimulation received from the mother. *Child Developm.*, 1957, **28**, 229–235.

HUSCHKA, M. The child's response to coercive bowel training. *Psychosom. Med.*, 1942, **4**, 301–308.

HUSCHKA, M. A study of training in voluntary control of urination in a group of problem children. *Psychosom. Med.*, 1943, **5**, 254–265.

HYTTEN, F. E., YORSTON, J. C., & THOMSON, A. M. Difficulties associated with breast-feeding. *Brit. Med. J.*, 1958, **1**, 310–315.

JACKSON, E. B., WILKIN, L. C., & AUERBACH, H. Statistical report on incidence and duration of breast-feeding in relation to personal-social and hospital maternity factors. *Pediatrics*, 1956, **17**, 700–712.

JELLIFFE, D. B. *Infant nutrition in the subtropics and tropics.* Geneva: World Health Organization, 1955.

KAGAN, J. & MOSS, H. A. The stability of passive and dependent behavior from childhood through adulthood. *Child Developm.*, 1960, **31**, 577–591.

KAPLAN, M. A note on the psychological implications of thumb-sucking. *J. Pediat.*, 1950, **37**, 555–560.

KEITEL, H. G., COHN, R., & HARNISH, D. Diaper rash, self-inflicted excoriations, and crying in full-term newborn infants kept in the prone or supine position. *J. Pediat.*, 1960, **57**, 884–886.

KLACKENBERG, G. Thumbsucking frequency and etiology. *Pediatrics*, 1949, **4**, 418–424.

THE EFFECTS OF INFANT CARE

KLATSKIN, E. H. Intelligence test performance at one year among infants raised with flexible methodology. *J. clin. Psychol.*, 1952, **8**, 230–237 (a).

KLATSKIN, E. H. Shifts in child care practices in three social classes under an infant care program of flexible methodology. *Amer. J. Orthopsychiat.*, 1952, **22**, 52–61 (b).

KLATSKIN, E. H. & JACKSON, E. B. Methodology of the Yale rooming-in project on parent-child relationship. *Amer. J. Orthopsychiat.*, 1955, **25** (1 & 2), 81–108 & 373–397.

KLATSKIN, E. H., JACKSON, E. B., & WILKIN, L. C. The influence of degree of flexibility in maternal child care practices on early child behavior. *Amer. J. Orthopsychiat.*, 1956, **26**, 79–93.

KNOBLOCH, H. & PASAMANICK, B. Further observations on the behavioral development of Negro children. *J. genet. Psychol.*, 1953, **83**, 137–157.

KOHN, M. L. Social class and parental values. *Amer. J. Sociol.*, 1959, **64**, 337–351 (a).

KOHN, M. L. Social class and the exercise of parental authority. *Amer. Sociol. Rev.*, 1959, **24**, 352–366 (b).

KOHN, M. L. & CARROLL, E. E. Social class and the allocation of parental responsibilities. *Sociometry*, 1960, **23**, 372–392.

KUNST, M. S. A study of thumb and finger sucking in infants. *Psychol. Monogr.*, 1948, **62**, No. 3.

LEVINE, M. L. & BELL, A. I. The treatment of colic in infancy by use of the pacifier. *J. Pediat.*, 1950, **37**, 750–755.

LEVY, D. M. Finger-sucking and accessory movements in early infancy (an etiologic study). *Amer. J. Psychiat.*, 1928, **7**, 881–918.

LEVY, D. M. Experiments on the sucking reflex and social behavior in dogs. *Amer. J. Orthopsychiat.*, 1934, **4**, 203–224.

LEVY, D. M. On the problems of movement restraint. *Amer. J. Orthopsychiat.*, 1944, **14**, 644–671.

LIPSITT, L. P. & LEVY, N. Electrotactual threshold in the neonate. *Child Developm.*, 1959, **30**, 547–554.

LIPTON, E. L., STEINSCHNEIDER, A., & RICHMOND, J. B. Autonomic function in the neonate. II. Physiologic effects of motor restraint. *Psychosom. Med.*, 1960, **22**, 57–65.

LIPTON, E. L., STEINSCHNEIDER, A., & RICHMOND, J. B. Autonomic function in the neonate. IV. Individual differences in cardiac reactivity. *Psychosom. Med.*, 1961, **23**, 472–484.

LITTMAN, R. A., MOORE, R. A., & PIERCE-JONES, J. Social class differences in child rearing: a third community for comparison with Chicago and Newton, Massachusetts. *Amer. Sociol. Rev.*, 1957, **22**, 694–704.

MACCOBY, E. & GIBBS, P. K. Methods of child-rearing in two social classes. In W. E. Martin & C. B. Stendler (Eds.), *Readings in child development*. New York: Harcourt Brace, 1954. Pp. 380–396.

MACFARLANE, J. W. Studies in child guidance: I. Methodology of data collection and organization. *Monogr. Soc. Res. Child Developm.*, 1938, **3**, No. 6.

MASLOW, A. H. & SZILAGYI-KESSLER, I. Security and breast-feeding. *J. abnorm. soc. Psychol.*, 1946, **41**, 83–85.

McCANDLESS, B. R. & ROSENBLUM, S. Psychological theory as a determiner of experimental pattern in child study. *Rev. educ. Res.*, 1952, **22**, 496–525.

McGEORGE, M. Current trends in breast feeding. *New Zeal. Med. J.*, 1960, **59**, 31–41.

MEYER, H. F. Breast feeding in the United States: extent and possible trend. *Pediatrics*, 1958, **22**, 116–121.

MILLER, D. R. & SWANSON, G. E. *The changing American parent: a study in the Detroit area*. New York: Wiley, 1958.

MURPHY, L. B. & ASSOCIATES. *The widening world of childhood*. New York: Basic Books, 1962.

NEWTON, N. R. The relationship between infant feeding experience and later behavior. *J. Pediat.*, 1951, **38**, 28–40.

NEWTON, N. R. & NEWTON, M. Relationship of ability to breast feed and maternal attitudes toward breast feeding. *Pediatrics*, 1950, **5**, 869–875.

ORLANSKY, H. Infant care and personality. *Psychol. Bull.*, 1949, **46**, 1–48.

OURTH, L. & BROWN, K. Inadequate mothering and disturbance in the neonatal period. *Child Developm.*, 1961, **32**, 287–294.

PALERMO, D. S. Thumbsucking: a learned response. *Pediatrics*, 1956, **17**, 392–399.

PEASE, D. & GARDNER, D. B. Research on the effects of non-continuous mothering. *Child Developm.*, 1958, **29**, 521–530.

PETERSON, C. H. & SPANO, F. L. Breast feeding, maternal rejection and child personality. *Charac. and Pers.*, 1941, **10**, 62–66.

PRATT, K. C., NELSON, A. K., & SUN, K. H. *The behavior of the newborn infant.* Columbus: Ohio State Univ. Press, 1930.

PRUGH, D. G. Childhood experience and colonic disorder. *Ann. N. Y. Acad. Sci.*, 1953–54, **58**, 355–376.

RHEINGOLD, H. The modification of social responsiveness in institutional babies. *Monogr. Soc. Res. Child Developm.*, 1956, **21**.

RHEINGOLD, H. & BAYLEY, N. The later effects of an experimental modification of mothering. *Child Developm.*, 1959, **30**, 363–372.

ROBERTS, E. Thumb and finger sucking in relation to feeding in early infancy. *Amer. J. Dis. Child.*, 1944, **68**, 7–8.

ROBERTS, K. E. & SCHOELLKOPF, J. A. Eating, sleeping, and elimination practices of a group of two-and-one-half-year old children. IV. Elimination practices: bowel. *Amer. J. Dis. Child.*, 1951, **82**, 137–143 (a).

ROBERTS, K. E. & SCHOELLKOPF, J. A. Eating, sleeping, and elimination practices of a group of two-and-one-half year-old children. V. Elimination practices: bladder. *Amer. J. Dis. Child.*, 1951, **82**, 144–152 (b).

ROBERTSON, W. O. Breast feeding practices: some implication of regional variations. *Amer. J. Public Health*, 1961, **51**, 1035–1042.

ROGERSON, B. C. F. & ROGERSON, C. H. Feeding in infancy and subsequent psychological difficulties. *J. ment. Sci.*, 1939, **85**, 1163–1182.

ROSENBLITH, J. F. Prognostic value of behavioral assessments of neonates. Unpublished manuscript, 1963.

ROSS, S. Sucking behavior in neonate dogs. *J. abnorm. soc. Psychol.*, 1951, **46**, 142–149.

ROUSSEAU, J. J. *Emile* (1762). Great Neck, N. Y.: Barrons's Educational Series, 1950.

ROUTH, C. H. F. *Infant feeding and its influence on life.* New York: William Wood, 1879.

RUHRAH, J. *Pediatrics of the past.* New York: Paul B. Hoeber, 1925.

SEARS, R. R., WHITING, J. W. M., NOWLIS, V., & SEARS, P. S. Some child-rearing antecedents of aggression and dependency in young children. *Genet. Psychol. Monogr.*, 1953, **47**, 135–234.

SEARS, R. R., MACCOBY, E. E., & LEVIN, H. *Patterns of child rearing.* Evanston, Ill.: Row, Peterson, 1957.

SEARS, R. R. & WISE, G. W. Relation of cup-feeding in infancy to thumb-sucking and the oral drive. *Amer. J. Orthopsychiat.*, 1950, **20**, 123–138.

SEWELL, W. H. Infant training and the personality of the child. *Amer. J. Sociol.*, 1952, **58**, 150–159.

SEWELL, W. H. & MUSSEN, P. H. The effect of feeding, weaning, and scheduling procedures on childhood adjustment and the formation of oral symptoms. *Child Developm.*, 1952, **23**, 185–191.

SHIRLEY, M. *The first two years: a study of twenty-five babies.* Vol. III. *Personality manifestations.* Minneapolis: Univ. Minnesota Press, 1933.

SIMSARIAN, F. P. Case histories of five thumb-sucking children breast fed on unscheduled regimes, without limitation of nursing time. *Child Developm.*, 1947, **18**, 180–184.

SPOCK, B. *The pocket book of baby and child care.* New York: Pocket Books, Inc., 1946.

SPOCK, B. Toilet training. *Ladies' Home Journal,* 1963, 80, No. 4, 48–50.

STENDLER, C. B. Sixty years of child training practices. *J. Pediat.,* 1950, **36**, 122–134.

STONE, S. & BAKWIN, H. Breast feeding. *J. Pediat.,* 1948, **33**, 660–668.

THOMAS, A., BIRCH, H. G., CHESS, S., & ROBBINS, L. C. Individuality in responses of children to similar environmental situations. *Amer. J. Psychiat.,* 1961, **117**, 798–803.

THOMAS, A. & CHESS, S. An approach to the study of sources of individual differences in child behavior. *Quart. Rev. Psychiat. & Neur.,* 1957, **18**, 347–357.

THOMAS, A., CHESS, S., BIRCH, H., & HERTZIG, M. E. A longitudinal study of primary reaction patterns in children. *Comp. Psychiat.,* 1960, **1**, 103–112.

THURSTON, J. R. & MUSSEN, P. H. Infant feeding gratification and adult personality. *J. Pers.,* 1951, **19**, 449–458.

TRAISMAN, A. S. & TRAISMAN, H. S. Thumb- and finger-sucking: a study of 2,650 infants and children. *J. Pediat.,* 1958, **52**, 566–572.

VINCENT, C. E. Trends in infant care ideas. *Child Developm.,* 1951, **22**, 199–209.

WATSON, J. B. *Psychological care of infant and child.* London: Allen & Unwin, 1928.

WENAR, C. & COULTER, J. B. A reliability study of developmental histories. *Child Developm.,* 1962, **33**, 453–462.

WENAR, C., HANDLON, M. W., & GARNER, A. M. *Origins of psychosomatic and emotional disturbances.* New York, Paul B. Hoeber, 1962.

WHITE, M. S. Social class, child-rearing practices, and child behavior. *Amer. Sociol. Rev.,* 1957, **22**, 704–712.

WICKES, I. G. A history of infant feeding: Part I. Primitive peoples: ancient works: renaissance writers. *Arch. Dis. Childh.,* 1953, **28**, 151–158 (a).

WICKES, I. G. A history of infant feeding: Part II. Seventeenth and eighteenth centuries. *Arch. Dis. Childh.,* 1953, **28**, 232–240 (b).

WICKES, I. G. A history of infant feeding: Part III. Eighteenth and nineteenth century writers. *Arch. Dis. Childh.,* 1953, **28**, 332–340 (c).

WICKES, I. G. A history of infant feeding: Part IV. Nineteenth century continued. *Arch. Dis. Childh.,* 1953, **28**, 416–422 (d).

WICKES, I. G. A history of infant feeding: Part V. Nineteenth century concluded and twentieth century. *Arch. Dis. Childh.,* 1953, **28**, 495–502 (e).

WILLIAMS, J. R. & SCOTT, R. B. Growth of Negro infants: IV. Motor development and its relationship to child rearing practices in two groups of Negro infants. *Child Developm.,* 1953, **24**, 103–121.

WOLFENSTEIN, M. Trends in infant care. *Amer. J. Orthopsychiat.,* 1953, **23**, 120–130.

WORTIS, H. *et al.* Child-rearing practices in a low socioeconomic group. *Pediatrics,* 1963, **32**, 298–307.

YARROW, L. J. The relationship between nutritive sucking experiences in infancy and non-nutritive sucking in childhood. *J. genet. Psychol.,* 1954, **84**, 149–162.

Separation from Parents
During Early Childhood[1]

LEON J. YARROW

*Family and Child Services
of Washington, D. C.*

THE STRONG AND PERSISTENT EMPHASIS on the importance for healthy
personality development of a close and satisfying relationship with the
mother in infancy and early childhood has been accompanied by a corol-
lary emphasis on the disastrous consequences for the child of an interruption or loss of maternal care. If we accept the basic premise of the importance of good maternal care for personality development, it would seem to
follow logically that separation from the mother will have adverse effects.
This is the essential logic underlying the assumptions about the effects on
the child of maternal separation. The issues, however, are not so simple
and straightforward. Separation from the mother is not a simple delimited
event with simple predictable consequences. There are many varieties of
separation experiences with vastly different implications. The hazards in
trying to formulate simple conclusions about the effects of separation
become evident when one attempts to draw from the research specific implications for practices. The broad generalizations that have grown out of
oversimplified interpretations of the research have tended to obscure a
realistic approach to the practical issues. Global conclusions about the
extremely damaging effects of separation have hindered consideration of
specific factors which might be amenable to manipulation in preventive
and therapeutic programs.

In much of the literature maternal separation and maternal deprivation
have been used synonymously, with the result that the effects attributed to
maternal separation have often been due to other deviating conditions of
maternal care which have been subsumed under this term. The value for

[1] This review was prepared in conjunction with a research project on "The Effects of
a Change in Mother-Figure During Infancy on Personality Development," conducted
under Research Grant 3M-9077 from the National Institute of Mental Health, United
States Public Health Service.

theory development and for research of distinguishing between maternal deprivation, maternal separation, multiple mothering, and distortions in maternal care has been discussed in a previous review (L. J. Yarrow, 1961). These distinctions are useful not only for theoretical clarification but in considering practices in caring for children in various settings outside of their own homes—in institutions, foster homes, day nurseries, and hospitals.

Deprivation of maternal care in the sense of a quantitative lack of tactile, kinesthetic, auditory, and other kinds of stimulation normally provided by a mother-figure, or a lack of sensitive individualized adaptation to the child's needs frequently follows physical separation from the mother. In multiple mothering, which sometimes follows separation, a number of different mother-figures simultaneously provide care for the child, with varying degrees of responsibility and differentiation of functions. Distortions in maternal care, that is, disturbances in the mother-child interaction, involving hostility or ambivalence, which are usually rooted in personality deviations in the mother may be an antecedent of separation and sometimes may follow it. Maternal separation in its purest sense involves a break in the continuity of relationship with a mother-figure after a meaningful focused relationship has been established. Before the point of the formation of an individualized relationship with the mother, physical separation from the mother and from familiar surroundings may result in environmental unpredictability due to changes in the physical environment and changes in the kinds of stimulation and timing of responses given by mother-substitutes in the new environment. After a meaningful focused relationship with the mother has been established, separation from the mother involves the loss of a significant loved person. The reactions of children following this loss have been interpreted by Bowlby as similar to the process of mourning (Bowlby, 1960a,b, 1961).

In analyzing the effects of maternal separation, not only is it important to distinguish separation from other kinds of deviations in maternal care but it is also useful to distinguish among different kinds of separation experiences. It is important, too, to distinguish between the impact of the event itself and experiences subsequent to the event. Separation frequently occurs in the context of other traumatic circumstances which often precipitate the removal of the child from his parents, for example, the death or disability of a parent, sudden economic disaster, external "natural disasters," war. Perhaps most significant are the experiences following the event of separation. Placement in an impersonal institutional environment is a frequent aftermath; often separation is followed by hospitalization with the associated stress of illness, surgery, and painful medical procedures. Separation from natural parents is often the prelude to a series of changes in foster homes.

The meaning to the child of the event of separation and the experiences subsequent to separation will also vary with individual and experiential factors, such as the child's unique vulnerabilities and sensitivities, his developmental stage, and his experiences prior to separation. Separation that occurs after a long period of indifferent parental care or overt rejection and hostility is likely to have a different meaning to the child from that representing a break in an intimate, protective, gratifying relationship. It is also likely that the meaning of separation to the child will vary with such characteristics of the experience as: the degree of concomitant trauma; whether it is permanent or temporary; and if temporary, whether it is of long or short duration; whether any contact is maintained with the parents; and whether it is the first or one in a series of similar experiences.

The psychological ramifications of separation become evident as one differentiates the experience in terms of such dimensions as permanence, duration, and repetition. In terms of these dimensions, we can distinguish six major varieties of separation which on an *a priori* basis one might assume would represent psychologically different experiences to the young child. If these six varieties are further differentiated in terms of degree of external stress at the time of separation, we have at least a dozen different types of separation experiences.

1. Single brief separation followed by reunion with the parents.

   a. Complete separation without concomitant external stress, as occurs when the parent goes on a trip or a vacation and leaves the child with a familiar caretaker, and possibly in a familiar environment.

   b. Complete separation with concomitant external stress, such as the short-term hospitalization of the child or hospitalization of a parent.

   c. Partial separation without concomitant stress, as when the child goes to nursery school.

   d. Partial separation with concomitant external stress, for example, hospitalization in which contact is maintained with the parents.

2. Repeated brief separations with reunion. Four kinds of repeated brief separations can be distinguished:

   a. Repeated complete separations without concomitant external stress.

   b. Repeated complete separations with concomitant external stress.

   c. Repeated partial separations without concomitant external stress.

   d. Repeated partial separations with concomitant external stress.

These involve the same kind of experiences as in "1" above; they differ only on the dimension of frequency of occurrence. One might hypothesize either increasing sensitivity with cumulative experiences, or a desensitization with repeated nontraumatic separation experiences.

3. Single long-term separation with reunion. This type of separation experience differs from the first two in being of relatively long duration. It is usually associated with concomitant stress from other sources, such as hospitalization for chronic illness, severe family crises, or a national emergency, as the wartime separation in England. Contact with the parents may or may not be maintained.

4. Repeated long-time separations with reunion. This type of separation experience occurs to children in families that meet constant crises. It is the type of experience frequently dealt with by social agencies in which the child is placed in a temporary foster home or in an institution, but in which he maintains some contact with his own family. The repeated traumatic separation experiences are likely to be associated with increased separation sensitivity, as distinguished from type 2 separation in which desensitization might be more likely.

5. Single permanent separation. This type of separation usually results from the death or the permanent physical or mental disability of the parents, or because the parents are incapable of providing adequate care for the child. The child is placed in a permanent foster home or an adoptive home. In infant adoption, the child moves from the hospital when one week old into a foster home where he may remain for several months, at which time he is separated from the foster mother and placed in an adoptive home.

6. Repeated permanent separations. This is the most extreme type of separation experience. After permanent separation from the parents, the child may be placed in an institution or a foster home. He usually does not remain in one home sufficiently long to develop a substitute attachment, but experiences a series of changes of foster homes or institutions. Most of the conclusions about the severely destructive effects of maternal separation have been drawn from this type of separation situation involving recurrent separations with frequent change in mothers. The impact of the original loss of the mother is reinforced by repeated separation experiences. The subsequent experiences often involve deprivation and various kinds of trauma.

In looking at separation from the perspective of normal developmental experiences, there are many kinds of partial, physical separations, such as when the child goes to school or the mother is employed, as well as psychological separations which may occur with the arrival of a new sibling. In terms of their meaning to the child, these experiences may be on a conceptual continuum with the permanent or recurrent separation experiences detailed above, but clearly they cannot be equated with them. From a developmental perspective such separation experiences may have constructive as well as destructive aspects. The infant's differentiation of himself from the mother, the child's development of a separate identity and increased autonomy in coping with the environment, are aspects of growth which are dependent on mild doses of separation.

In reviewing the research on separation with reference to its implications for preventive and therapeutic programs, we will attempt to differentiate some of the varieties of separation experiences, and to identify in these different situations some of the significant variables, both the primary variables associated with the experience of separation and the secondary variables, such as the state of the organism, which interact with and modify these primary variables. Much of the research and the theoretical speculation has focused on the significance of separation from the mother, with relatively little consideration given to separation from the father. Although the effects of the loss of the father have not been explicitly considered in the studies of maternal separation, it should be recognized that in most of these situations, paternal separation has also been involved. In this review, only brief consideration will be given to the few studies that have been concerned exclusively with father absence.

HISTORICAL BACKGROUND OF THE RESEARCH

Although much of the research on maternal separation has appeared in the past twenty years, the history of concern for this issue goes back many years. The earliest experiment on the effects of maternal deprivation has been attributed to King Frederick II in the thirteenth century (Stone, 1954). Unfortunately the experimental conditions created such extreme environmental deprivation that all of the subjects died. "For they could not live without the petting and joyful faces and loving words of their foster mothers" (Salimbeme; quoted by Stone and Church, 1957). There is no record of this conclusive experiment having had any significant effect on child care practices. While the psychoanalytic emphasis on the significance of early experiences did much to mobilize concern for the effects of deviations in early maternal care, the first direct observations of such effects were reported by pediatricians—early in the beginning of the twentieth century. Bakwin (1949), reviewing the pediatric literature, describes observations made as far back as 1909 on the physical and psychological deterioration occurring in hospitalized infants. Some research on young children in institutions began to appear in the early 1930's (Durfee and Wolf, 1933), but only in the past twenty years has there been a concerted research attack on the varied aspects of deprivation of maternal care. Many significant studies stimulated concern among professional workers and created a receptive climate for Bowlby's conclusions in his comprehensive review of the literature for the World Health Organization in 1951 (Bender, 1947; Bender and Yarnell, 1941; Goldfarb, 1943a,b,c, 1944a,b, 1945a,b, 1947, 1949; Levy, 1937; Lowrey, 1940; Ribble, 1943; Skeels, 1942; Skeels, Updegraff, Wellman and Williams, 1938; Spitz, 1945, 1946; Spitz and Wolf, 1946, 1949). Bowlby's presentation of the research evidence has served as a rallying point for pediatricians, psychologists, psychiatrists, social workers, and others who had felt the need for reforms in medical and social agency practices.

Although Bowlby's report stimulated loose overgeneralizations about the effects of separation, it also served as a stimulus for more focused and better controlled research. In the ten years following *Maternal Care and Mental Health* (Bowlby, 1951), there appeared several major investigations which have helped to identify more precisely some of the significant variables in institutional environments, and to establish more clearly the relationships between these variations and the intellectual, social, and personality development of children subjected to these influences (David and Appell, 1961; Dennis and Najarian, 1957; DuPan and Roth, 1955; Provence and Lipton, 1962; Rheingold, 1956, 1961). There have also been a few major studies of infants and young children undergoing separation experiences which have helped in arriving at a more differentiated picture of the relationship between the conditions of separation and the reactions of children (Bowlby, 1953a,b; Bowlby, Ainsworth, Boston, and Rosenbluth, 1956; Heinicke, 1956; Robertson and Bowlby, 1952; Schaffer, 1958). Some new retrospective studies, in which the earlier histories of clinic cases were examined for the incidence of separation and institutionalization, began to cast some doubt on the universality and the directness of the relationship between separation and later personality pathology. A few of these studies have begun to consider some of the etiological factors in the context of the life history which differentiate between personality pathology and favorable personality development (Andry, 1960; Barry and Lindemann, 1960; Berg and Cohen, 1959; Brown, 1961; Earle and Earle, 1961; Glueck and Glueck, 1950; Hilgard, Newman, and Fisk, 1960; Howells and Layng, 1955; Maas, 1963a,b; Naess, 1959; Oltman, McGarry, and Friedman, 1952; Pringle and Bossio, 1960; Schofield and Ballan, 1959). Hospital practices designed to mitigate separation anxiety and other traumata associated with hospitalization were evaluated in two major research projects (Faust *et al.*, 1952; Prugh *et al.*, 1953). Plank *et al.* (1959) also described an experimental program to counteract hospitalism. A careful analysis of the differential effects of separation for hospital treatment on children of different ages during the first year was reported by Schaffer (1958; Schaffer and Callender, 1959). After a long period of almost no research, the effects on children of the mother's employment became the subject of a number of investigations in the past few years (Hoffman, 1961; Nye, 1958; Siegel, Stolz, Hitchcock, and Adamson, 1959; Stolz, 1960; M. R. Yarrow, 1961).

Sober reflection on the old data and these new findings resulted in a number of critical re-evaluations of the conclusions regarding maternal deprivation and separation in recent years (Casler, 1961; Glaser and Eisenberg, 1956; Howells and Layng, 1955; O'Connor, 1956; World Health Organization, 1962; L. J. Yarrow, 1961). From the new perspective provided by the recent research and in terms of a more reasoned conceptual orientation, we have arrived at a more balanced point of view regarding the influence of early maternal separation.

In this review which is pointed toward consideration of the applications of the research, the major findings will be summarized with detailed discussion of a few selected studies. These studies were chosen as prototypes of the kinds of investigations from which the conclusions have been drawn. Studies of varying degrees of methodological adequacy have been included. No attempt has been made to consider specifically the adequacy of research designs or the methods used. There has been a selective use of research findings, distinguishing clinical observations from statistically validated results (of which there are few) and attempting to interpret complementary as well as divergent findings in terms of an organizing conceptual framework. Some of the implications of the research for practice will be readily apparent. No attempt has been made in this review to develop in detail specific applications, since we recognize that specific practical measures must be tailored to individual situations.

IMMEDIATE REACTIONS OF INFANTS AND YOUNG CHILDREN TO SEPARATION

Studies of the reactions of young children at the time of separation document the disturbing nature of the experience. Detailed data on the reactions of young children to separation come chiefly from five studies, three of which involved long-term temporary separations with institutional placement (Robertson and Bowlby, 1952; Roudinesco, David, and Nicolas, 1952; Spitz and Wolf, 1946), one, a briefer separation for hospitalization

(Schaffer, 1958; Schaffer and Callender, 1959), and one, a comparison of two types of brief separations—in a day care nursery and in an institution (Heinicke, 1956). The children studied were under three years of age at the time of separation, and in all but one study (Spitz and Wolf, 1946), some contact was maintained with the parents. The subjects in Schaffer's study were infants under one year of age when separated; Spitz and Wolf studied infants six to eight months of age; the cases in the French study (Roudinesco, David, and Nicolas, 1952) were between fifteen and thirty months; and infants in the English study (Robertson and Bowlby, 1952) were between eighteen and twenty-four months.

Three investigations (Spitz and Wolf; Robertson and Bowlby; Roudinesco, David, and Nicolas) report similar reactions of children under two years of age following separation from their mothers and placement in institutional settings. There is a sequence of responses following separation, beginning with crying and strong protest, and followed by progressive withdrawal from the environment and from relationships with people. The immediate reaction of active protest (crying or motor expression of unhappiness) is thought to represent an active effort to regain the lost mother. After this period of active protest, despair and resignation are reflected in increasingly withdrawn and apathetic behavior. This passivity is often interpreted by hospital and institutional personnel as evidence of the child's having settled down and adapted to the situation. If a substitute mother-figure is available, some children may develop a possessive, anxious attachment to the substitute mother. However, if, as is usually the case, there is a series of changing mother-figures, the child does not form an attachment to anyone in the hospital or institution, and shows little feeling toward his parents when they visit. Although on the surface the children seem happy and well adapted to the situation, they act "as if neither mothering nor any contact with humans has much significance for them" (Robertson and Bowlby, 1952, p. 133). This pattern of "detachment" Robertson and Bowlby consider a precursor of the development of the psychopathic personality or affectionless character.

The study made by Spitz and Wolf (1946) was one of the earliest detailed behavioral observations of young infants undergoing a separation experience. From a group of 123 infants being cared for by their own mothers in an institutional setting, some (an unspecified number) were separated from their mothers when they were between six and eight months of age. Of these separated infants, 19 showed severe reactions similar to those described by Robertson and Bowlby, that is, acute anxiety, active rejection of adults, and finally symptoms of severe depression, decreased activity level, loss of appetite, withdrawal from people and from the environment. The depressive syndrome was accompanied by a progessive drop in the developmental quotient, and in physical symptoms, such as loss of weight, recurrent colds, and eczema. In some cases the physical deterioration continued to the point of death. Spitz and Wolf noted a progression in severity of disturbance over time, and concluded that if the infant was not reunited with his mother within five months, irreparable damage occurred.

There are few studies of the behavior of separated children immediately after their return home. Robertson (1953), who observed children in their homes immediately after hospitalization, noted a variety of behavior disturbances, for example, hostility toward the mother intermingled with a pervasive anxiety about losing the mother. Sometimes the children regressed in such areas as toilet training. Robertson found that most children recover in a short time with good handling, but some children continue to show anxiety and disturbance for a long period. He suggests that "it be left an open question how far such disturbances are really resolved, and how often they leave some scar behind which can cause distress to be reactivated much later by some trivial reminder" (Robertson, 1953, p. 385).

The studies by Robertson and Bowlby, by Roudinesco, David, and Nicolas, and by Spitz and Wolf were not designed to provide statistical validation of hypotheses about the effects of separation, but were frankly oriented toward obtaining detailed clinical data on children who had been separated from their mothers at different ages, for different periods of time and under different conditions. They provide interesting and provocative data and describe vividly typical separation reactions of children between one and three years of age. The authors themselves, in most instances, have been aware of the tentative nature of their conclusions.

It seems unlikely that the sequence of increasing disturbance and progressive deterioration in behavior is an inevitable consequence of separation. The studies show that not all children show the severe reactions that have come to be considered typical. Spitz and Wolf comment on several factors which differentiated the infants showing extremely severe reactions from those showing less severe or no symptoms. One important factor was the quality of relationship with the mother prior to separation. Children separated from mothers with whom they had poor relationships showed less overt disturbance than did the children for whom the separation represented the loss of a close relationship. The quality of substitute maternal care also influenced the severity of reactions. Infants who were provided with adequate mother-substitutes did not show the extremely severe reactions. They also found that the duration of separation influenced the possibilities of recovery. They hypothesized that recovery was possible if the infants were reunited with their mothers within three months.

Although studies from a variety of sources indicate that environmental *deprivation* may have serious effects even on very young infants, there are very few data on the important question of how early in infancy *separation* from a mother-figure begins to have an impact. Schaffer's (1958) research (discussed in more detail in the section on hospitalization) is one of the few studies with data directly relevant to this issue. On the basis of findings that overt protest reactions to maternal separation—such as, excessive crying, fear of strangers, clinging to the mother—are not evident before seven months of age, he concluded that separation reactions appear "relatively suddenly and at full force around 7 months of age."

Other research data (Yarrow and Goodwin, 1963) suggest that separation experiences may begin to have effects much earlier. In a study of the impact on infants of a change in mothers in moving from foster to adoptive homes, evidence of reactions was found as early as three months of age. A significant number of infants who were moved at four months of age showed disturbances in the form of withdrawn behavior, increased apathy, and feeding and sleep disturbances. More overt social disturbances—excessive clinging or definite rejection of the new mother—occurred with increasing frequency after six months.

The findings of the latter study emphasize that the immediate reactions of infants following separation from mother-figures need to be interpreted within a broader framework than that of the loss of a significant love object. Separation usually results in significant changes in the total environment for the child—in the kinds and patterns of sensory and social stimulation, in scheduling, in the sequences of gratification, and so on. Both the strangeness and the loss of environmental predictability may be sufficiently strong stress conditions to account for some of the behavioral disturbances noted (L. J. Yarrow, 1961). By definition, true separation reactions cannot appear until after a focused relationship with the mother has developed.

It is clear also that the conclusions based on findings of intense reactions to severe separation experiences cannot be extrapolated to all types of separation conditions as has sometimes been done. Heinicke (1956) studying children, fifteen to thirty months of age, in day care centers and in good residential nurseries found less extreme reactions than were reported in the studies cited earlier. The young children experiencing the partial separation associated with all day care in a day nursery gave no evidence of being seriously disturbed. Although no extremely severe personality disturbances were found in the children in the institutional setting, they did show more overt aggression as well as more regressive behavior than the children in the day nurseries.

On the whole, the findings of the few studies on immediate reactions to separation give little basis for prediction of the long-term impact of separation. Although we might assume that the severity of immediate reactions is an index of the severity of trauma, there are few direct data on this issue (Yarrow and Goodwin, 1963). Inferences about the long-term impact of separation have been based almost completely on the retrospective studies which rarely have adequate information on the experiences around the time of separation.

The studies cited above have focused on the reactions to separation per se. The many studies on institutionalization document the effects of severely depriving experiences which often follow separation.

IMMEDIATE EFFECTS OF INSTITUTIONALIZATION

By far, most of the conclusions about the effects of maternal separation come from studies of children who, after being separated from their families, have been placed in institutions. Although in reality it is difficult to isolate the effects of separation from the effects of institutionalization, it is useful to look for more proximate variables than separation in considering the etiology of the developmental disorders commonly found in institutionalized children. The studies of infants and young children in institutional settings point to a direct relationship between the *characteristics* of the institutional environment—the conditions of stimulation, the learning conditions, and the patterns of maternal care provided by caretakers—and the intellectual, social, and personality development of these children.

Most of the direct studies of institutional settings describe very impoverished environments. The institution is not simply an environment lacking in a mother-figure with whom the child has developed an attachment; institutional environments tend to be deviant in many other respects, such as in the amount, the quality, and the variety of sensory and social stimulation, and in the kinds of learning conditions provided (Goldfarb, 1955; Rheingold, 1960, 1961; Provence and Lipton, 1962; David and Appell, 1962). The low caretaker-infant ratio is associated with significant deprivation in the sheer amount of maternal care. This quantitative deprivation in maternal care, in turn, is associated with inadequate kinesthetic, tactile, social, and affective stimulation. The affective blandness characterizing many institutional environments means that the children are exposed to little strong positive or negative emotional expression. Often the environment is lacking in appropriate equipment, and the conditions for learning or practicing new skills are limited. The changing caretakers and the rigid routinization of care result in deviant learning conditions. The caretakers' actions tend to be based on predetermined schedules and set techniques rather than being responsive to the child's behavior. Thus the child's behavior, for example, smiling or cooing, may frequently be ignored rather than rewarded (Gewirtz, 1961). With multiple caretakers there is often little opportunity for them to become sensitized to individual children, with the result that their handling is rarely adapted to the child's unique sensitivities and characteristics (David and Appell, 1962).

The direct research on the effects of institutionalization has been largely on infants or children under six years of age. The well-known studies of Spitz (1945, 1946) and Goldfarb (1943a,b,c, 1944a,b, 1945a,b), which have served as the basis of many of the conclusions about the effects of maternal separation, and the more recent very detailed study (Provence and Lipton, 1962) of infants in institutions during the first two years document most clearly the impact of extremely depriving environments in infancy and early childhood. Other studies have reported similar, but, on the whole, less serious effects (Freud and Burlingham, 1943; Dennis and Najarian, 1957; Fischer, 1952; Pringle and Bossio, 1958, 1960).

Marked developmental retardation is commonly found in children growing up in institutional environments, with some evidence of progressive retardation with increasing length of institutional residence. Most common among institutionalized children is language retardation. Brodbeck and Irwin's (1946) analysis of speech sounds in young infants suggests that language functions may be affected very early. Freud and Burlingham (1943), Haggerty (1959), Goldfarb (1944a, 1945b), Pringle and Tanner (1958) provide data on language dysfunctions in older children. The direct relationship between verbal stimulation and language development in infancy has been demonstrated in an experimental study by Rheingold, Gewirtz, and Ross (1959). Although motor functions seem to be less vulnerable than other areas of development, deviant motor patterns suggestive of neurological abnormalities have been noted (Spitz, 1946; Fischer, 1952) in infants after an extended period of institutional care. Provence and Lipton (1962) found among institutionalized infants greater impairment in some motor functions than others. Those skills which seem to be primarily dependent on the maturation of the neuromuscular apparatus develop normally, whereas retardation is found in those functions which are dependent on environmental stimulation. They observed two types of motor deviations which they consider derivatives of psychic drives—a diminished impulse to reach out toward people and objects, and an impairment in the capacity to modulate motor impulses to produce smooth motor movements. Emotional responses tend to be limited and stereotyped in institutionalized babies. Both excessive autoerotic activity, for example, rocking, headbanging, masturbation, thumb-sucking, and a complete absence of such activities are reported. Spitz and Wolf (1946) as well as Provence and Lipton (1962) interpret these extremes in autoeroticism as reactions to both deprivation and disturbances in maternal care.

A variety of deviations in social behavior have been reported, ranging from extreme social apathy to an exaggerated demandingness of social response. Infants in institutions often respond indiscriminately to familiar caretakers and to strangers, reflecting a failure in the development of normal social discrimination; and at a later period, they fail to show normal patterns of imitative behavior (Freud and Burlingham, 1943). These deviant patterns of social behavior have been considered precursors of severe disturbances in capacity for relationships at later ages.

It is not clear how early in infancy the institutional environment begins to have impact, since there are very few studies on children under six months of age. Two studies (Freud and Burlingham, 1944; Gesell and Amatruda, 1941) report that deviations in social responsiveness first become evident by six months of age. Deviations in language development (Brodbeck and Irwin, 1946; Provence and Lipton, 1962) and somatic disturbances have been noted as early as two to three months of age. Provence and Lipton's longitudinal data on the development of 75 infants in an institution during their first year provide the clearest data on this issue. They report evidence of retardation and deviation in language, social and motor development as early as the second month. Bakwin (1949) has commented on the failure of institutional infants to make appropriate gains in weight, and on their increased susceptibility to illness during the first few months. Young infants may react to the environmental deprivations associated with inadequate maternal care with undifferentiated physiological disturbances before showing more specific behavioral disturbances. Bakwin has suggested that "a certain amount of conscious cerebral functioning is necessary in order for injury to register itself" (p. 514).

Not all institutionalized children develop severe personality or behavior disorders. There has been a tendency to dramatize the extreme cases and to gloss over those cases which did not show the striking symptoms. In several studies serious intellectual retardation or behavioral disturbances have not been found (Fischer, 1952; Freud and Burlingham, 1943; DuPan and Roth, 1955). These divergent findings clearly suggest that the severity of personality disturbance and the degree of developmental retardation is linked to the degree of environment deviation and deprivation. The findings of the institutional syndrome among children living in very depriving *family* environments (Coleman and Provence, 1957), and also the findings that this syndrome can be reversed by changing the institutional environment (Skeels, 1942), emphasize that the etiological agent in these personal-social and developmental disturbances is not maternal separation per se, or some mysterious attribute of institutional environments, but specific environmental conditions which are commonly associated with institutional care.

During the past ten years a number of studies have begun to delineate more clearly some of the environmental factors which are associated with intellectual and personality disorders among children living in institutions. Other studies have suggested some of the modifying factors in later experiences as well as in the individual child which may increase or decrease the likelihood of later unfavorable outcomes. Freud and Burlingham (1944), who attempted to meet individualized needs of the children within an institutional setting by providing for some consistency in mother-figures and a high level of intellectual and social stimulation, found less extreme deviations than those noted in other institutional studies. There were, however, significant disturbances in interpersonal relationships which they interpreted as reactions to separation.

In institutions in which adequate stimulation is provided, severe developmental retardation is not found (DuPan and Roth, 1955; Fischer, 1952; Freud and Burlingham, 1944; Klackenburg, 1956; Rheingold, 1956). Several studies attest to the possibility of preventing intellectual and personality disturbances in institutionalized children: Skeels and Dye's (1939) striking success in reversing the course of intellectual and social deterioration in young children in an institution by providing specialized care and stimulation; Rheingold's experiment in stimulating social responsiveness by providing individualized social stimulation; and David and Appell's (1962) interesting experiment in which intensive individualized nursing care care was provided in an institutional setting.

Although these findings suggest the possibility of changing institutional environments to modify their pathogenic potential, institutional care seems to have certain limitations which are difficult to overcome. Rheingold (1961) gives impressive evidence that even in "good" institutions there is less contact with mother-figures than in "good" homes. David and Appell (1962) indicate, too, that even under the experimental conditions of intensive, individualized nursing care, the quality of emotional interchange remains limited. The nurses held back from complete involvement with the children, a reaction similar to the kinds of protective defenses observed in foster mothers who avoid becoming too involved with the children from whom they anticipate later separation.

Other factors also need to be considered in attempting to prevent or modify the effects of institutionalization: the timing with regard to the age of the child, and the duration of institutional care. In comparing the early life experiences of children who in adolescence were making satisfactory adjustments with those who were showing maladaptive behavior patterns, Goldfarb (1947) found significant differences between the two groups in the age of admission to the institution and the length of time in the institutional setting. A significantly larger number of the poorly adjusted children entered the institution under six months of age and spent a longer period of time under institutional care. Similarly, Beres and Obers (1950) found differences in intellectual and personality outcomes which seemed to be related to age of institutionalization. All of their cases showing mental retardation in adulthood were admitted to the institution under six months of age; those diagnosed as schizophrenic entered the institution at a later age.

LONG-TERM EFFECTS OF SEPARATION AND INSTITUTIONALIZATION: RETROSPECTIVE AND FOLLOW-UP STUDIES

It is a rather broad jump from the direct data on infants in institutions and infants undergoing separation experiences to data on disturbed patients in psychiatric clinics or hospitals. Yet inferences about the long-term effects of separation and institutionalization have been based mainly on retrospective studies involving analyses of histories of patients in psychiatric clinics, hospitals, prisons, or institutions for juvenile delinquents. There are no longitudinal studies and very few follow-up investigations of cases whose early experiences have been carefully documented. The retrospective studies on the whole do not permit clear-cut differentiation between the effects of institutionalization, separation, and distortions in mothering, and they have only recently included control groups in their designs.

Retrospective Studies

In a clinical study of 44 juvenile thieves, Bowlby (1944) distinguished 14 who were diagnosed as "affectionless characters," a syndrome characterized by serious difficulties in interpersonal relationships. Retrospective analyses of their life histories indicated that 12 of the 14 had been separated from their mothers in infancy or early childhood. The specific pathogenicity of separation experiences for the development of the "affectionless character" was suggested by the fact that separation was more frequent among these thieves than among those who showed neurotic and other kinds of personality pathologies. The life histories of the affectionless characters showed that they had had a variety of pathogenic experiences prior and subsequent to the separation. They had been hospitalized for illness for long periods of time. Some had been placed in institutions; most of them had been subjected to recurrent changes in foster homes or institutions; some had experienced recurrent separations from natural parents—experiences which seem to be typical of the cases in most of the retrospective studies. Bender (1947) in a study of the histories of a large number of psychiatric patients came to conclusions similar to Bowlby's. She found a high incidence of institutional experience in the history of cases diagnosed as psychopathic behavior disorders. The patients' major difficulties were in establishing close interpersonal relationships and in the development of adequate impulse control.

Although Bowlby and Bender concluded that maternal separation is a specific etiological agent in the development of psychopathic personalities, other retrospective studies do not show a direct relationship between separation experiences and this specific personality disorder. Four studies which represent a random selection from the extensive retrospective literature find that separation was a significant etiological factor in four different disorders. In comparing controls and clinical cases with varied diagnoses, they find a significantly higher incidence of separation experiences in the histories of cases in four different diagnostic categories: schizophrenia (Berg and Cohen, 1959); neurosis and psychopathic personalities (Oltman, McGarry, and Friedman, 1952); depression (Brown, 1961); psychosomatic and psychoneurotic disturbances (Gregory, 1958). Several investigations find no significant differences between disturbed patients and normal controls in the incidence of earlier separation experiences (Schofield and Ballan, 1959; Howells and Layng, 1955).

Several studies and analyses of the literature suggest that the variety of disorders found may be related to the diversity of separation experiences and to other modifying variables. Hilgard, Newman, and Fisk (1960), studying the impact of the death of the father during childhood, found that the early relationship with the parents differentiated adults who were functioning well from those who were in mental hospitals. The well-adjusted adults came from homes which had been supportive and provided close affectional relationships prior to the father's death. Following the death of the father, in a significant number of these cases the homes remained intact; the children remained in their homes with their mothers. In analyzing the literature on the frequency of separation experiences in the life histories of delinquents, psychiatric patients, and controls, Gregory (1958) suggests that the differential outcomes may be dependent on the age of the child at the time of separation. He found a higher incidence of loss of the mother through death during the first ten years of life among psychiatric patients than controls. Loss of the mother after ten years of age was not significantly related to psychological disturbance. In another study he found a higher incidence of loss of parent under five years of age among outpatients with psychoneurotic or psychosomatic disturbance than in a control group.

Pringle and Bossio (1958) also found differences in the early histories of institutionalized children who were making an adequate adjustment and those diagnosed as severely maladjusted. Both age of separation and the quality of subsequent relationships with parental figures were important. Nine of the eleven severely maladjusted children had been separated from their parents when they were under one year of age, whereas all but one of the five stable children had been two years or older at the time of separation. Moreover, the stable children had fairly good relationships with parental figures, whereas the maladjusted children had poor relationships with their own parents, and little opportunity to establish adequate relationships with foster parents.

On the whole, the retrospective studies emphasize the pathogenicity of repeated separations and the cumulative effects of depriving environments. They suggest the great vulnerability of the young infant to extreme environmental deprivation. They also point out that there are differing vulnerabilities to separation at different developmental stages. Conversely, they affirm the possibilities of preventing or mitigating extremely adverse effects by manipulating situations to control some of these variables.

Follow-up Studies

The few follow-up studies of cases whose early separation experiences were carefully documented provide firmer evidence than the retrospective studies of the long-term effects of separation. Provence and Lipton (1962) give follow-up observations on 14 preschool children whom they had studied in an institution from the first month of life. These children were placed in adoptive homes at varied ages ranging from nine to twenty-nine months. Their findings suggest that although on the surface these children seemed to be functioning adequately after placement in adoptive homes, they showed on more intensive study residual impairments of varying degrees in the capacity for forming close affectional relationships, in impulse control and modulation, and in conceptual thinking.

Goldfarb's (1943a,b,c, 1944a,b, 1945a,b) series of follow-up studies of older children who had spent the first three years of their lives in an institution indicated serious impairments in complex intellectual and personality functions similar to those noted in the retrospective studies of older children and adults from clinic and mental hospital samples. Intellectual retardation was found in some cases, but more common were the disturbances in conceptual functioning, that is, difficulties in abstracting relationships, difficulties in time concepts, and other learning disturbances. Disturbances in impulse control were also common; both submissive, overly controlled be-havior patterns and uncontrolled expression of aggressive impulses were characteristic. Most striking evidence of failure in normal superego develop-ment was the lack of anxiety or guilt following aggressive or antisocial behavior. The most significant disturbance in these cases was their im-paired ability to form close interpersonal relationships. Low frustration tolerance and a lack of goal-directedness were also common. The develop-ment of delinquent behavior patterns was related dynamically to the in-capacity for close relationships and failure in the development of normal inhibitory controls.

Several follow-up studies indicate that severe personality damage is not an inevitable consequence of early separation experiences (Beres and Obers, 1950; Bowlby *et al.*, 1956; Freud and Burlingham, 1944; Hellman, 1962; Lewis, 1954; Maas, 1963a,b). There were marked differences among these studies in the nature of the separation experience, in the degree of depriva-tion subsequent to separation, and in the depth of personality data obtained.

Only recently has there been follow-up research on persons who, in child-hood, were separated from their families and placed in residential nurseries during World War II. Freud and Burlingham's (1944) report on the imme-diate reactions of these children during the first months after separation suggested that it was a disturbing experience, but also pointed to the possi-bilities of minimizing personality damage by providing substitute individ-ualized relationships. Not all of the evacuated children received as good care as in the Hampstead Nursery, but from the limited data available, the long-term consequences of this experience were not too severe. Maas (1963a,b) made a follow-up study of 20 adults who in early childhood had been evacuated from London and placed in small residential nurseries in the country. He found no severe personality pathology among these cases; most of them were making an adequate adjustment, managing to handle their adult roles and responsibilities capably. There was, however, an inter-esting trend in the data, suggesting that this type of experience may be more damaging to very young infants, under one year of age than to older chil-dren. The individuals who had been separated from their parents under one year of age showed a higher incidence of personal-social disturbance in adulthood than those placed after one year. No serious intellectual impair-ment was found in these adults, all of whom had been placed in nurseries providing adequate stimulation. These findings give further support to the hypothesis that intellectual retardation is not an inevitable consequence of separation.

Hellman (1962) presents a detailed case study of an adult woman who, as a child, had experienced a very traumatic separation from her mother when placed in the Hampstead Nursery during World War II. Although exposed to a number of deviant environmental conditions in the course of her developmental history, as an adult she showed no severe pathology. Hellman noted that "the observers who had seen the child during her traumatic experience in which she reacted with greatest distress had felt that this could not pass without interfering with Jane's further development and personality. Nevertheless, the observations of her development and the assessment of her present personality show that the trauma had neither stopped ongoing development nor left a disturbing mark on her adult life" (p. 174).

The study by Bowlby, Ainsworth, Boston, and Rosenbluth (1956) is one of the few follow-up investigations of the long-term effects of separation based on a substantial number of cases and using a control group design. They studied 60 children between six and fourteen years of age who had been hospitalized at varied ages before their fourth birthday for treatment of tuberculosis; half of them were over two years, fewer than 25 per cent were under one year at the time of hospitalization. The children remained in the sanitarium for varying lengths of time. In the sanitarium they had been subjected to medical procedures for the treatment of tuberculosis which were standard at that time—complete bed rest for the first three months, gastric lavage, and frequent venipunctures for blood analyses. No substitute mothering was provided; there was little continuity in nursing care, but the nursery school teachers provided some continuity in personal relationships. Contact with their own parents was maintained through visiting.

The findings indicate that these children suffered no significant damage to intellectual functions. There were, however, some indications of personality damage. On the basis of teachers' reports and interviews with the parents, the sanitarium children were judged to be showing tendencies toward withdrawal and apathy, as well as aggressiveness. Contrary to expectations, however, disturbance in the capacity to establish relationships with peers was not found in any significant number of these cases. On the basis of judgments of overall adjustment, a fairly high proportion of the children who had been hospitalized during their preschool years were considered maladjusted (63 per cent of the sanitarium children, as compared with 40 per cent of a control group of eight-year-olds).

Interpretations of findings such as these are not simple. The statistically significant differences between the hospitalized children and the controls indicate that there may be some systematic long-term effects of separation. However, it is clear that factors in addition to separation may have influenced these outcomes, for example, concomitant deprivation of maternal care. Moreover, as Bowlby and associates suggest, these children were not only ill and hospitalized, but in many there was also a history of disruption and stress in their families—factors which were undoubtedly important for their subsequent adjustment.

In summing up the findings of this study, the investigators emphasize the great variations in personality patterns among the hospitalized children, and point out that only a small minority developed very serious personality disabilities. On the other hand, they stress that the potentially damaging effects of this kind of experience should not be minimized, and feel that the similarities in personality deviations in some of these children to those in the studies of severely deprived institutionalized children (Goldfarb, 1955) suggest that there may be some degree of "persistence into later childhood of pathological responses having their origin during and immediately following the separation experience" (Bowlby et al., 1956, p. 238). They feel that "the results of the present study, however, give no grounds for complacency . . ." and stress that the potentially damaging effects of separation should not be minimized, but concede that "some of the workers who first drew attention to the dangers of maternal deprivation resulting from separation have tended on occasion to overstate their case" (p. 242).

Lewis (1954) studied a heterogeneous group of children of varied ages, from under five to over fifteen years, who had been admitted to a reception center for temporary care for reasons ranging from juvenile delinquency and emotional disturbance to parental neglect. The largest group, more than 3,000 cases, were admitted because of overt neglect or inability of parents to care for them. Two to three years later, personality evaluations were made by a psychiatrist and a psychiatric social worker on 100 of these children who had been placed in varying kinds of settings. Sixty-one of the children were showing some deviation; only 3 were diagnosed as having marked personality disorders; 22 were having some difficulties in relationships, and 36 were showing mildly neurotic or mildly delinquent behavior. Widely different conclusions regarding the long-term significance of separation and deprivation have been drawn from these findings. The divergent interpretations reflect the lack of normative standards and clear criteria regarding the seriousness of different types of personality and behavior disorders.

Another follow-up study (Beres and Obers, 1950) of adults who had been institutionalized in infancy emphasizes the conceptual and methodological difficulties in assessing mental health in terms of overt functioning or broad social adaptation as contrasted with a psychodynamic assessment of functioning. Beres and Obers found that about half of their cases showed no overt disturbance in work, at school, or in their relationships within their families or among friends. On the other hand, they noted a similar underlying pathology in all the cases—"a distortion in psychic structure . . . an immature ego along with deficient superego development." In discussing the evaluation of the long-term effects of earlier trauma, Hilgard *et al.* (1960) suggest that the ultimate test may be the degree of vulnerability of the individual to similar traumatic events in later life. They conclude that "although personality development may appear to be normal, traumatic losses suffered in childhood may leave scars that can be opened up again at a later time."

The varied findings in the retrospective and the follow-up studies permit one to conclude only that many variables affect the outcome of separation. Although infants and young children may show immediate severe reactions to separation from the mother, it is not an event which will necessarily result in the development of psychopathic or sociopathic personality disorders. Separation in itself cannot be considered a single etiological variable. Its effects undoubtedly are dependent on a variety of factors, probably the most important of which are the age of the child at the time of the experience, the degree of concomitant trauma, and the extent to which subsequent experiences reinforce or mitigate the initial trauma. Separation which is followed by placement in a poor institution or foster home, or which is the prologue to a series of recurrent changes or losses in mother-figures increases the likelihood of personality disturbances. Trasler (1960) has suggested that placement in an institution following separation is likely to lead to temporary repression which is prognostically unfavorable for later development. On the other hand, when children are placed in homes in which they can begin to form trusting relationships, many are able to work through the experience. Although they may show marked disturbances, the assimilation of the trauma is likely to facilitate later adaptation.

The clear implications of these studies are that if the child is given adequate care following separation from his parents, severely adverse effects may be avoided. We have very limited data on attempts to interrupt the sequence of intellectual and personality deterioration following separation, but if one extrapolates from the few studies that have attempted to provide individualized care in hospitals and institutions, it seems likely that serious long-term effects can be diminished. These few studies indicate that the provision of care by substitute mother-figures which is adapted to the individualized characteristics of the child, and the provision of adequate stimulation in the environment may be effective in preventing extreme personality and intellectual deterioration.

In attempting to integrate the findings of these assorted studies, some methodological problems become apparent: the extent to which one's conclusions about personality normality or deviance are dependent on the sensitivity of the measuring instruments used, that is, the kind of test as well as the orientation of the diagnostician, and on the individual investigator's criteria of the seriousness of a given personality or behavior pattern.

MULTIPLE MOTHERING

Following separation, children are sometimes moved to an environment in which there are several mother-figures, with no single person taking over the major mothering responsibilities. There has been some speculation that multiple mothering results in a diffusion of the mother-image, with the consequence that the child is impaired in his capacity to develop significant relationships in later life. It is likely that the effects of multiple mothering will vary with the particular conditions of maternal care provided. Multiple mothering in a depriving environment is likely to have a very different meaning to the child from care by several mother-figures in a culture or a setting where each mother-figure develops a close relationship with the child and responds sensitively and warmly to him, and where the general level of stimulation is high.

The conclusions about the harmful effects of multiple mothering have been derived from situations in which there is extreme inconstancy in mothering, in institutions where the child has no opportunity to relate to one person, and in which multiple mothering has been associated with stimulus-deprivation and inadequate need-gratification. Moreover, in these settings with many mother-figures, there is no opportunity for an individualized relationship to develop between a caretaker and infant, thus hindering the development of sensitivity on the part of the mother-substitute to the unique characteristics and needs of the infant.

Only a few studies have focused on multiple mothering outside of institutional settings. Some research has been done on children in home management houses, a training center for students in home economics. Usually the infants are separated from their foster parents or removed from an institutional environment and placed in a home management house for several weeks to several months. In this setting, the infant is cared for by a variety of young women, each of whom assumes responsibility for the major mothering activities for a period of a week or longer. Some continuity is provided by the instructor in the house, who also assumes some share of the infant's care. In most of these houses the infant receives much stimulation from the several mother-figures. The infant is usually moved from this house to a foster or adoptive home. No evidence of intellectual retardation or gross personality disorder was found in a follow-up study of these children during preschool years (Gardner, Hawkes, and Burchinal, 1961).

The studies of children in the Israeli kibbutzim are also relevant to the issue of multiple mothering. From early infancy the children are placed in a nursery where they are cared for by a substitute mother-figure—the metapelet. Maternal care in the kibbutzim is quite different from that found in the typical institution. The kibbutz infant may experience a lack of continuity in mothering because of the distribution of caretaking functions between the mother and metapelet. Nevertheless, the kibbutz children are in regular contact with their own parents, and close interpersonal relationships tend to be maintained. The parents visit regularly, and some infants are breast-fed by their mothers for several months. Rabin (1958) found some developmental retardation among infants in the kibbutzim which he attributes to a lesser amount of stimulation than is ordinarily provided in family homes. Studies of children in the kibbutzim at later ages, in middle childhood, find no intellectual retardation and no personality distortions. In fact, in one study they were judged as showing "better emotional control and greater overall maturity and greater ego-strength than control children living with their own parents" (Rabin, 1958). There have been some suggestions by observers that the youth and young adults who have spent all of their lives in the kibbutz setting tend to lack emotional depth. They maintain satisfactory relationships with their peers, but there is a tendency for all relationships to be on the same level. It has been pointed out that the pattern of rearing in the kibbutz facilitates a primary identification with the peer group rather than with the family group, thus fostering the kind of personality development most desirable for adaptation in a communal culture.

The data on multiple mothering point up the value of obtaining some cultural perspective in viewing the issues of maternal separation. The meaning of separation undoubtedly will differ for the child in the small, middle-class western family in which his relationships are limited quite narrowly to mother, father, and siblings from that in cultures in which the extended family is customary. Mead (1962) points out that the conviction that the primary child care functions must be taken over by a single mother-figure if the child is to develop adequately is a culture-bound assumption. She gives interesting impressions of personality development in cultures in which multiple mothering is practiced. She suggests that children who grow up in cultures in which there are several good mother-figures learn to trust more people and therefore are better able to tolerate separation. It is her impression that children who are reared in cultures where the child care functions are shared by a number of mother-figures tend to develop more subtle and more complex personality characteristics presumably because of more varied identification figures. Although there are no studies in depth of the personality characteristics of individuals in these cultures, the anthropological reports suggest that they are quite capable of establishing adequate relationships.

Ainsworth (1963) in a recent study of mother-infant interaction among the Ganda presents some evidence to suggest that human infants are basically monotropic. She suggests that even in cultures in which multiple mothering is characteristic, equal division of mothering functions is not likely. She speculates that the infant develops his first attachment to the mother-figure who takes over the major child care functions. Later he may extend his attachment to other figures.

SHORT-TERM HOSPITALIZATION

A common experience in the lives of many children is hospitalization because of an acute illness or surgery. Separation from the parents and from a familiar environment is only one element of this experience (Langford, 1961). Sensitive physicians (Bakwin, 1942, 1949, 1951; Beverly, 1936; Jackson, 1942; Levy, 1945) have pointed to the potentially traumatic implications of the total situation, that is, the feelings of helplessness and the increased dependency associated with illness, the threats to bodily integrity of medical and surgical procedures, as well as the effects of being in a strange environment with unfamiliar people. Although there are many interesting descriptions of the reactions of individual children to hospitalization (Bowlby, Robertson, and Rosenbluth, 1952), research on short-term hospitalization is very limited. Three major studies have been made of this problem (Prugh et al., 1953; Faust et al., 1952; Schaffer and Callender, 1959).

All three studies find that the kinds and severity of reactions to hospitalization vary significantly with the age of the child. Schaffer and Callender, studying the reactions of 25 infants hospitalized less than two weeks, found distinct differences between infants under seven months of age and infants between seven and twelve months of age. In the hospital the younger infants were normally responsive to strange adults; they accepted changes in routines well, and gave little evidence of being disturbed by the separation experience. The older infants—16 cases over seven months of age—showed a variety of disturbances associated with separation: marked anxiety toward strangers, desperate clinging to their mothers, and vigorous crying on their departure.

Prugh and his colleagues (1953), in a study of 200 children between two and twelve years of age, found that the two to three-year-old children showed the most severe reactions. The frequency and type of disturbed behavior decreased with increasing age. The specific anxieties aroused by the hospital experience seemed to differ for children of different ages. The reactions of the younger children seemed to be primarily expressions of anxiety over separation from the parents. At the time of their parents' departure they showed fear and anger, and were acutely anxious with strangers. During the early part of hospitalization, they manifested emotional disturbances and depressive behavior similar to those found in separated children in institutions. Crying and withdrawal from people and from the environment were common. Somatic concomitants of anxiety, such as urinary frequency, diarrhea, and vomiting, also occurred. Regressive behavior manifested in loss of bowel and bladder control, sometimes in demands for a return to bottle feeding, or in refusals to chew solid food was found. Disturbances in activity, such as restlessness or hyperactivity, and rhythmic rocking, were also noted. In the older children, the four to six-year-olds, similar, but less extreme, evidences of disturbance were found, and fewer children showed these patterns. Among the older children, six to ten years of age, there was less anxiety which could be directly attributed to separation. Rather, the anxiety which they showed seemed to be more "free-floating" or was focused on potentially painful or frightening experiences in the hospital.

In interpreting the differences in reactions of children of different ages, the investigators suggest that these reactions may be related to the specific developmental anxieties and conflicts characteristic of the developmental stages. For example, anxieties regarding bodily integrity provoked by the medical measures seemed most intense among the four to six-year-old boys. Among the older children whose major developmental concerns are with the internalization of controls, their anxieties seemed to be derived from feelings of guilt; the illness and hospitalization were seen as retribution for fantasied bad behavior. Children in the latency period handled the hospitalization with the least overt disturbance, a finding which is interpreted in terms of the latency child's capacity for repression, stronger ego defenses, and "more effective superego controls and more varied sublimatory outlets." Anna Freud (1952) has pointed out the significance of variables other than separation in discussing the meaning to young children of such aspects of hospitalization as illness, pain, surgery, and the specific deprivations of hospital routines.

In addition to age differences in the meaning of hospitalization, there are individual differences related to many factors in the child's history. Prugh and associates (1953) found that a most important determinant of the child's capacity to handle this situation was the quality of his relationship with his parents prior to hospitalization. Also very significant were the individual child's capacity to relate to new adult figures and his ability to handle his anxieties fairly directly by talking about them or acting out his feelings in play. The parents' overt behavior in handling the situation, their own anxieties, as well as their feelings of guilt about subjecting the child to these procedures, all influenced the child's reactions. Their feelings of guilt and anxiety were expressed in a variety of ways—ambivalent behavior toward the child, sometimes by overcompensatory indulgence, occasionally by punitive behavior.

More significant than the immediate reactions, of course, are the long-term effects of the hospitalization experience. Schaffer's data on 76 infants under one year of age who had been hospitalized for a two-week period earlier in infancy suggest that this kind of experience may have effects which continue beyond the period of separation. Even the younger infants, those under seven months at the time of hospitalization, who had shown little or no overt disturbance in the hospital, manifested some disturbances immediately after their return home. They vocalized very little; they showed an unusual preoccupation with the environment, that is, they stared with a blank expression and scanned their surroundings with such complete absorption that it was not possible to distract them with toys or to elicit social responses. Some of these young infants also showed sleep and feeding disturbances, but only for a short time. The older infants who had been most anxious about separation in the hospital, upon returning home, showed more severe reactions. They were extremely dependent on their mothers, and were excessively anxious about any separation from them, showing strong anxiety when their mothers went out of their sight; marked fear of strangers was common. Sleep disturbances were also found among the infants over seven months of age. Schaffer concluded from these findings that separation from the mother does not become a crucial factor in hospitalization until the developmental point at which there is differentiation of self from the environment, after seven months of age. He attributes the younger infant's extreme preoccupation with the environment after coming home to a lack of adequate perceptual stimulation in the hospital.

Follow-up studies (Prugh et al., 1953) of older children (two to twelve years of age) three months after discharge from the hospital indicated that about half of them were showing some disturbances in behavior which had not been present prior to hospitalization, although very few were showing severe disturbances. The most common symptoms were expressions of anxiety over separation from the parents, such as recurrent fear that their parents would leave them. These symptoms were particularly intense among the younger children.

Two studies (Prugh et al., 1953; Faust et al., 1952) indicate that the potential traumatic effects of hospitalization can be mitigated by the introduction of special procedures of hospital care designed to reduce separation anxieties and anxieties about bodily injury. Prugh compared the immediate and later reactions of 100 children given special hospital care with a comparable control group cared for under standard hospital conditions. Experimental measures included daily visiting periods for the parents as contrasted with weekly visiting under standard procedures, a special play program comparable to nursery school, careful preparation of the children for potentially traumatic diagnostic or therapeutic procedures. In the course of the study, other special procedures were instituted: the assignment to one nurse of major responsibility for the care of a particularly anxious child; giving special psychological support to particularly anxious parents; and encouraging the parents' participation, particularly the mother's, in the child's care in the hospital. Although disturbances in adaptation to the hospital were noted in both the control and the experimental groups, in general the reactions were less severe, and fewer children in the experimental group were affected. It was concluded that this experimental program was successful in mitigating the traumatic impact of the hospitalization experience for children of all ages.

In the study by Faust and his associates of 140 children who were hospitalized for tonsillectomies, a variety of prophylactic measures were introduced: preparation for the hospital experience through discussion with the parents; helping the parents prepare the children for hospital procedures; careful timing of elective hospitalization in terms of the child's developmental stage and emotional state in relation to other experiences in the home, such as the arrival of a sibling or a move to a new home or school. Significant changes were made in the hospital experience itself, such as arranging for the mother to remain with the child in the hospital, keeping to a minimum potentially traumatic procedures, such as enemas and venipunctures. Study of these children in the immediate postoperative period and three months afterward indicated that the majority of them were "either benefited or scarcely affected by the experience; only a small number—13—evidenced changes of behavior indicative of emotional trauma." On the whole, the younger children showed more adverse behavior changes, but these were considered essentially mild disturbances. The children most seriously affected were those who had been sensitized to separation through previous traumatic experiences and those who had essentially poor relationships with their parents prior to hospitalization.

These findings have significance not only for brief hospitalization but for a variety of conditions of separation. In regard to the effects of hospitalization, these studies suggest that the critical period, that is, the developmental period during which children are likely to be most susceptible to damage by hospitalization, extends roughly from seven months to seven years, with the most vulnerable period being seven months to three years. However, it is also apparent that the experience need not be severely traumatic if the child is given adequate preparation, and if hospital procedures are designed to minimize separation anxiety and trauma regarding bodily injury. The modification in hospital rules which has been made in the United States and in England to permit the mother to "room-in" with a young child prior to and following surgery is one simple practical measure to alleviate the stress of hospitalization (Robertson, 1958).

Clearly separation from the parents is but one among many factors influencing the child's adaptation to a hospital experience. The significance of these other anxiety-evoking experiences and suggestions for modifications in hospital procedures are discussed in detail in several publications (American Academy of Pediatrics, 1960; Bakwin, 1951; Blom, 1958; A. Freud, 1952; Jessner et al., 1952; Langford, 1961; Plank et al., 1959; Robertson, 1958; Spence, 1947).

MATERNAL EMPLOYMENT

Maternal employment is considered in the context of separation because the fact of the mother's working has sometimes been equated with deprivation of maternal care. This assumption, like so many others in the area of maternal separation, has been based chiefly on general impressions of an association between the mother's employment and disturbed and delinquent behavior in children. Many of these impressions are derived from unsystematic case studies of problem families in which maternal employment is observed in the midst of many unfavorable social and psychological conditions, such as, broken homes, poverty, racial discrimination, marital conflict.

Until very recently there has been little systematic research on the effects of maternal employment. The findings which are beginning to emerge indicate that the broad variable of maternal employment cannot in itself be considered an antecedent of intellectual or personality disturbances in children. (For comprehensive reviews of the findings, see Hoffman, 1963; Siegel and Haas, 1963; Stolz, 1960.) The research begins to suggest some of the factors which need to be specified in studies of maternal employment. Hoffman discusses the significance of such variables as social class, full vs. part-time employment of the mother, age of the child, sex of the child, and the mother's attitude toward employment. Siegel (1961) points out the need to consider the personality characteristics of the mother. She suggests that there may be systematic differences between working and nonworking mothers in achievement orientation, in sex role ideology, and in conflict about their sex role. M. R. Yarrow (1961) has emphasized the importance of the mother's feelings about her work role and her maternal role. She found no differences in child-rearing attitudes between working and non-working mothers. Significant differences, however, were found when the mothers were grouped in terms of satisfaction with their role, whether the homemaker or the worker role. Dissatisfied mothers, both working and nonworking, reported undesirable child-rearing practices and attitudes more frequently than mothers who were satisfied with their role.

Data on delinquency in relation to maternal employment are inconclusive. Glueck and Glueck (1957) found no significant relationship between maternal employment and delinquency in children from lower-class backgrounds, whereas both Nye (1958) and Gold (1961) found a significantly higher incidence of delinquency among middle-class children of working mothers than among children of nonworking mothers.

From the child's standpoint, the significance of the mother's working must be considered in terms of how it affects the amount and quality of maternal care provided. If we consider realistically the situation of the mother's leaving the home for work, the physical absence of the mother may be significant quantitatively—in terms of the amount of maternal contact for the infant or young preschool child. For the school-age child the mother's working is likely to be associated with only a very small decrement in amount of contact. Some studies suggest that some mothers may consciously strive to make up for the quantitative deficit (M. R. Yarrow, 1961). Similarly, mother's employment does not uniformly influence quality of maternal care (Hoffman, 1963). Clearly neither the amount nor the quality of contact between mother and child is simply related to mother's employment status.

Even for the youngest child, the fact of separation per se is not likely to be the most relevant psychological variable in maternal employment. Much more research is needed on the interaction between the total family environment and the mother's working. Data are needed, too, on how the impact of maternal employment may be modified by the personality characteristics of the mother and the father and by sociological, economic, and cultural factors. It is likely, as the current studies suggest, that these individual and social factors may outweigh any influences that might be attributed to the mother's employment status per se.

FATHER SEPARATION

In contrast to the vast literature on the significance of the maternal relationship for the infant and young child, there has been relatively little theory and much less research on the father's role in the child's development. It is generally assumed that the absence of the father during early infancy has only an indirect impact on the child, that is, it may be associated with a more intense relationship of the mother to the child or to distortions in this relationship, dependent on the mother's feelings about the absent father. Much of the theoretical writing is concerned with the effects of the father's absence on the development of sex-role identification during the preschool period and middle childhood.

In psychoanalytic theory, the father's influence is first given serious consideration around the Oedipal period of development. Neubauer (1960) in a selective review of the psychoanalytic literature on the effects of the death or absence of the father points out the almost unanimous conviction that lack of an appropriate identification object during early childhood is likely to result in sexual inversion in boys. (See Freud, 1949; Ferenczi, 1950; and Fenichel, 1953.) Fenichel theorizes that later personality disturbances and deviations in the choice of an adult love object may be a result of "the guilt engendered by the fantastic fulfillment of Oedipal wishes when the same sexed parent dies, and the fantasy idealization, based on unsatisfied Oedipal longing, when the opposite sexed parent dies" (Neubauer, 1960, p. 288). Other psychoanalysts have emphasized the disturbances in superego development in boys associated with the lack of a father-figure during the period of superego formation. In Aichhorn's (1935) study of delinquents, he comments on the inadequate ego ideal of the fatherless boy. That the absence of the father may not preclude identification with a male figure, at least in very young boys, is suggested by Freud and Burlingham (1944). In their wartime nursery, they describe very strong attachments to fantasy father-figures among preschool age boys who had no or very meager contact with their fathers. These boys were overtly attempting to pattern their behavior after an idealized image of the father. Freud and Burlingham suggest that if the child has an opportunity for the development of a close substitute maternal relationship, he may be able to develop appropriate superego controls through the blending of substitute and fantasy identification objects. They do not deal with the issue of how the boy acquires sex appropriate behavior patterns in the complete absence of a male figure after whom he can pattern his behavior.

Much of the evidence regarding the impact of father separation comes from two types of studies; studies in which the father is absent because of cultural mores or because of military or occupational obligations, and studies in which the father is permanently absent because of death, desertion, or divorce. All of these studies suggest that the absence of the father during early childhood may lead to difficulties in the development of appropriate sex-role identity in boys. Burton and Whiting (1961), in reviewing cross-cultural data, present evidence that boys reared in societies in which the father is absent during infancy and in which no male figures are available as identification models will have conflicts in sex-role identity. They note that in certain cultures feminine identification in boys is strongly defended against by exaggerated masculine behavior. Similar interpretations of overcompensatory masculine behavior in lower-class delinquent boys have been made.

Lynn and Sawrey (1959) considered the effects upon children of both sexes (eight to nine and one-half years of age) of irregular father absence in a study of the children of Norwegian sailors who are absent from the home for extended periods of time. They found a number of personality differences between these children and children from intact families. Boys were more immature and insecure in their identification with their fathers, and they had difficulties in peer adjustments. In this situation where the fathers were present inconsistently, the boys tended to show compensatory overly masculine behavior. The girls in these families were found to be more dependent on their mothers than girls in intact families. It is likely that these personality differences were not due simply to the father's absence but were also related to changes in the mother's behavior associated with the father's absence. The mothers in the father-absent families were more protective and more authoritarian in their child-rearing patterns than were mothers in the control families.

During World War II a number of studies were made of the impact of the father's absence on the personality development of young children (Bach, 1946; Sears, Pintler, and Sears, 1946; Stolz et al., 1954). Sears and his associates, and Bach, using projective doll play to assess personality and behavior patterns, found less aggressive doll play among boys in families where the father was absent than in boys where the father was present. This pattern of play was interpreted as indicative of a more feminine orientation. Stolz found not only more feminine fantasy behavior but also more overt feminine behavior in boys during their father's absence and after his return. In addition, Stolz noted behavior difficulties among the boys whose fathers had been absent during at least the first year of their lives. They were having difficulties in establishing and maintaining genuine relationships with adults as well as peers. These children showed higher levels of anxiety, and in the doll play experiment conducted after the father had returned, they showed more aggression than did the children in the control group of nonseparated families. Bach suggests that children's attitudes toward the absent father are very much influenced by the mother's basic feelings for the father. In individual case analyses he found that the mother's unfavorable attitudes toward the absent father were reflected in a "curiously ambivalent aggressive-affectionate father fantasy in the children."

Leichty (1960), using a different projective technique from the doll play interview, the Blacky Test, which was designed to study psychosexual development and object relationships, also concluded that the boy's identification with the father was unfavorably influenced by the father's absence.

One aspect of separation that has been given little attention is the effect on the parent's ability after a period of absence to make the necessary adaptations to the child on reunion. The study by Stolz *et al.* highlights the difficulties in adjustment for both father and son which arise following the father's return after a long absence in military service. The father's unfamiliarity with the paternal role and his attempts to establish suddenly a paternal relationship with a son who has been unaccustomed to this kind of relationship frequently led to friction. Other conflicts derived from the father's unfavorable reactions to the feminine interests and characteristics which their sons had developed during their absence.

Several retrospective studies of delinquents, although inconclusive, suggest an association between the development of antisocial behavior patterns in boys and the absence of an adequate male identification model during childhood. In these homes the father may have been absent because of desertion, divorce, or death; or if the father was physically present, he may have been weak or ineffectual, or had little contact with the child. Although Andry (1960) failed to find any relationship between father-absence during early childhood and later delinquent behavior, his findings do suggest an association between delinquency and disturbances in the father-child relationship.

In his discussion of the literature and detailed clinical analysis of a case, Neubauer (1960) emphasizes that the outcomes of father-absence are not simple. It is likely that father-absence increases the probability of disturbances in sex-role identification and in superego development. However, he points out that the effects of this experience will be influenced by such variables as the developmental stage of the child at the time of loss, the child's sex, and most importantly, the child's relationship with the remaining parent.

The limited evidence on father-absence supports dynamic and learning theories in indicating that appropriate sex-role identification is hindered by the lack of a role model of the same sex. Many more data are available on boys than on girls. Curiously the literature on maternal deprivation and maternal separation has not made any attempt to analyze sex differences. There has not even been speculation regarding possible differential effects of maternal absence on girls and boys. The theoretical discussion and research on father-absence has concentrated on the Oedipal period, and it is likely that this period is a particularly vulnerable one for boys with regard to father-absence. Early adolescence might be an equally critical period, although no direct data are available. Some literature on delinquency suggests that the absence of the father may be particularly significant at this time, although delinquent behavior is more often attributed to failure in the internalization of controls at an earlier developmental period. To date, the research has not considered the role of father-substitutes, whether relatives or community group leaders, such as scout leaders and teachers, in providing identification models for boys who have been separated from their fathers.

SUMMARY OF THE EFFECTS OF SEPARATION: ANALYSIS OF ANTECEDENT CONDITIONS AND MODIFYING VARIABLES

Analysis of the literature emphasizes the diversity of experiences associated with separation and their varied meanings for the child. The significance of separation to the child depends on many individual and environmental variables. A temporary interruption in a relationship is likely to have very different significance for personality development from that of a permanent loss of a love object. The significance of separation which is followed by marked deprivation of maternal care in a poor institution or foster home is likely to be very different from separation which is followed by the provision of good substitute maternal care, as in adoptive placement. The effects of separation are modified by individual vulnerabilities and sensitivities, constitutional and acquired, as well as by sensitivities which are characteristic of specific developmental periods. The meaning of separation to the child also depends on the larger experiential context in which it occurs. Its significance is undoubtedly different in the context of a parent's death from that in the context of the parent's going on a vacation. Its meaning may even depend on the larger cultural setting.

The research data can be integrated with regard to their implications in terms of the following major variables: the developmental stage of the child at the time of separation; the character of relationship with the mother prior to separation; the character of maternal care during a temporary separation or following permanent separation; subsequent experiences, that is, experiences which are reinforcing or ameliorating of separation trauma; and individual differences in vulnerability to separation.

1. *Age at time of separation.* Data from varied sources indicate that the age of the child at the time of loss or interruption in relationship with a mother- or father-figure may be highly significant in relation both to the immediate effects and in terms of the implications for later personality development. Reactions to either temporary or permanent separations are apparently less severe very early in infancy, before the establishment of a

stable relationship with a mother-figure, than they are later after a relationship has been formed. If the separation is followed immediately by the provision of an adequate mother-figure, there may be no serious effects, either immediate or long-term. If, however, separation is followed by severe deprivation which continues for a long period of time, even the young infant may be seriously affected.

Chronological age, by itself, may not be a very sensitive index of the depth or level of relationship with a mother. Normative data suggest that focused relationships are established by six months, although as has been indicated elsewhere, the criteria of a focused relationship have not been well-defined (L. J. Yarrow, 1956). Some data from a study of the effects of separation in early infancy (L. J. Yarrow and Goodwin, 1963) indicate that a focused individualized relationship with the mother does not appear suddenly, but develops gradually. There are a number of stages in the development of a focused relationship with a mother corresponding to different degrees of social awareness and of attachment. Moreover, there are great individual differences among infants in the development of relationships, differences which seem to be related to definable characteristics of the mothers, as well as to characteristics of the infants (L. J. Yarrow, 1956; 1963). It is likely that the significance of separation for the child will vary with the stage of development of a focused relationship.

Evidence from a variety of sources indicates that *after* the development of a focused relationship with the mother, infants on being separated show the most severe disturbances (Yarrow and Goodwin, 1963). The significance of these reactions for later personality development has not been established, since we do not know whether immediate severe reactions in young infants are prognostic of serious lasting effects. The intensity of overt disturbance at the time of separation may not be a sensitive indicator of the degree of trauma experienced by an infant. Schaffer's follow-up data (1958) suggest that the lack of strong overt protest in a young infant cannot be taken as evidence that the infant is unaffected by the experience.

The data on age of separation can be interpreted within the framework of the critical period hypothesis. In direct analogy with the data on imprinting in animals, one might hypothesize that there is a specific developmental period during which vulnerability to separation is greatest. The most sensitive time may be the period during which the infant is in the process of establishing stable affectional relationships, approximately between six months and two years. A break in a relationship with a mother-figure during this period would presumably be most traumatic.

To carry the analogy with the imprinting concept further, one might hypothesize that if separation occurs before relationships are established, and the child never has an opportunity to experience intimate personal relationships during this critical period, he would be permanently impaired in the capacity to establish relationships. Some of the retrospective data on the effects of institutionalization might be interpreted within this frame of reference. Definitive studies in which detailed data are obtained on the child's experiences during the period critical for the establishment of relationships have yet to be done. The limited retrospective data on the clinic cases with severe character disorders suggest that many of these adults had been separated from their mothers in early infancy before they had an opportunity to develop a focused relationship. Following the initial separation, they never had an adequate mother-substitute during infancy or childhood. Whether, or at which developmental point, the provision of therapeutic mothering might have halted the progression of this character disorder is not known.

In a broader sense, each developmental stage may be viewed as critical in terms of the child's capacities, in terms of the central developmental tasks or the focal psychological conflicts of specific developmental periods. One might hypothesize that each developmental period has its own sensitivities and vulnerabilities. The psychological situation of the infant during the first six months is very different from that of the infant during the second half of the second year. As a result of the perfection of motor skills and the development of language, the child moves from a situation of complete dependence on the mother to increasing mastery of his environment. At the same time advances are made in conceptual development, particularly in the development of concepts of object constancy and time concepts. On this basis one might assume that separation would be less traumatic to the child past two years of age than to the completely helpless and dependent young infant who has not yet developed the capacity to anticipate his mother's return. There is likely to be a complex interaction between the type of separation and the age of the child. For example, the young infant may be less disturbed by a permanent separation than the child past two years of age who is able to understand more clearly the implications of permanent separation. Thus although vulnerability to loss of a mother-figure may be greatest at one particular period, separation may continue to be a potentially disturbing experience, but to a lesser degree, at other developmental periods. This concept of changing vulnerabilities also suggests that one needs to be aware of the particular developmental sensitivities and focal conflicts at different ages. For example, the data on father-absence suggest that father separation during the height of the Oedipal period may be particularly traumatic. Similarly, hospitalization for surgery may be most traumatic at the developmental period in which there is particular concern about body integrity. The specific procedures developed for minimizing the effects of these experiences might well be based on knowledge of the vulnerabilities of specific developmental periods.

2. *The quality of the relationship with the mother prior to separation.* There is much speculation, but few definitive data, regarding the effects of the quality of relationship with the mother prior to separation on the child's reactions to the separation experience. Spitz and Wolf (1946) noted that the children showing the most severe reactions to separation were those who had the closest relationship with their mothers prior to separation. Mead's observations (1962) on children in cultures where the relationship with the mother is presumably diluted by having the care distributed among several mother-figures indicate that reactions to separation tend to be less acute than in cultures in which more intense individualized mother-child relationships are fostered. The depth of a relationship cannot, however, be completely equated with the singleness of the mothering person.

It has been hypothesized that the child who has had a close relationship with his mother may be better equipped to tolerate separation and to establish a meaningful relationship with a substitute figure than the child who has never experienced an intimate relationship. This variable may, however, have different implications for the immediate and for the long-term consequences. The immediate reactions may be more severe for the child who is deeply attached to his mother, but his later adjustment may be more adequate than the child who has never experienced an intimate relationship. The effects may also depend on the kind of separation experience. A brief, temporary separation with reunion is likely to be less traumatic for the child who has a close relationship with the mother than for the child with a weak or ambivalent relationship. In this close relationship he has presumably developed trust in his mother, and therefore has the confident expectation of being reunited with her. The data on children's reactions to temporary hospitalization support this speculation (Prugh *et al.*, 1953; Faust *et al.*, 1952). On the other hand, it is likely that permanent separation will be more traumatic, the closer the parent-child relationship. The effects of this variable, the quality of relationship with the mother, are undoubtedly interrelated in a complex way with the age of the child at the time of separation and with the specific conditions of separation, especially whether it is temporary or permanent.

3. *The character of maternal care subsequent to the initial separation.* It is clear from the studies on institutionalization that permanent intellectual and personality damage may be avoided if following separation there is a substitute mother-figure who provides adequate stimulation, who develops a personalized relationship with the child, and who responds sensitively to

his individualized needs. Many studies indicate that the provision of adequate substitute mothering following separation may mitigate the shock and prevent the development of serious disturbances. This is true with regard to brief separation as well as long-term and permanent separation. If, after separation, the child moves into an unsatisfactory maternal relationship, the traumatic impact of separation is likely to be strengthened.

4. *The character of the relationship with the parents during temporary separation.* In temporary separations, if the child is able to maintain a relationship with his parents, the impact of the separation is likely to be less severe than if there is abrupt and complete termination of the relationship. This probably holds most clearly for relatively short-term separations, such as in hospitalization where the expectation of reunion is clear. With regard to long-term foster care, the relationships may not be so simple. There are some data suggesting that the overall adjustment of children in foster care tends to be more adequate if the relationship with the parent is maintained by frequent visiting (Maas and Engler, 1959). However, in long-term foster care where the prospects of the child's returning home to his parents are relatively slim, one might speculate about the effects of a continuing ambiguous relationship with the parents on the development of the child's identity feelings.

If the child is reunited with his own parents, after a period of separation, there may be initial difficulties in mutual adaptation of parent and child. These difficulties have been noted on the child's return home after hospitalization (Robertson, 1958); and on the father's return after absence in military service (Stolz *et al.*, 1954). In some experimental studies of separation in animals (Blauvelt, 1955; Rosenblatt, Turkevitz, and Schneirla, 1961), it was found that the animal's adjustment on return to its mother after separation was very much influenced by the mother's capacity to make the necessary adaptations to the needs of the separated animal.

5. *The duration of the separation experience.* With regard to temporary separation, such as hospitalization or temporary foster care, it has been hypothesized that the severity of the impact of the experience is directly related to its duration. Thus the shorter the period of separation, the less serious are the effects. Spitz and Wolf (1946) noted that if infants were reunited with their mothers within three months, recovery was still possible. They have suggested that there may be a crucial time interval after which the effects of maternal separation are irreversible. They place five months as the upper limit for young infants. It is likely that the time interval will vary with such factors as the age of the child, previous separation experiences, and the intensity of stress or degree of deprivation to which the child is being subjected. One might assume that for older children the crucial

time interval might be longer than for young infants. Certainly the significance of the length of the separation experience will also vary with other conditions, such as whether a relationship with the parents is maintained by visiting. It will also be dependent on the child's expectations with regard to reunion with the parents. It would seem likely that duration cannot be considered independent of the nature of the experience; a long separation under good conditions of substitute care will have different effects from a long separation in an extremely stressful or depriving environment.

6. *Subsequent reinforcing experiences.* It is likely that the nature of experiences following separation are of major significance for the long-term effects. Post-separation experiences may in varying degrees reinforce or ameliorate the initial stress. The studies that have stressed permanent impairment of functioning as a result of early traumatic experiences have usually found repetitive or continuous depriving and traumatic experiences during infancy and early childhood—for example, recurrent changes in foster homes, frequent turnover in institutional personnel. Conversely, the meager follow-up data on cases who have made an adequate adjustment in later life suggest that later favorable experiences can modify or undo the impact of earlier stress or deprivation. On the other hand, although there are no statistically reliable data, a number of studies (Goldfarb, 1944b; Trasler, 1960) suggest that children who have experienced separation have been sensitized so that later similar experiences are likely to be especially traumatic for them. This can become a circular process, since separation-sensitive children are more likely to be shifted from one foster home to another because of initial difficulties in adaptation.

7. *The role of constitutional factors.* In recent years there has been renewed consideration of the role of congenital factors in aggravating or modifying the impact of early adverse experiences. Data from a number of sources have begun to document the existence of differences in basic sensitivities and response predispositions among infants at birth or during the first months of life (Chess, Thomas, and Birch, 1959; Bridger and Reiser, 1959; Fries and Woolf, 1953; Richmond and Lustman, 1955; Wolf, 1953). These differential sensitivities and predispositions may influence the intensity of the impact of a given type of deprivation or trauma (Alpert, Neubauer, and Weil, 1956; Bergman and Escalona, 1949). The reactions of infants and young children to separation may be influenced by the degree of change in the kinds and intensity of stimulation in specific sensory modalities. The change in caretakers may also lead to changes in the modalities in which the child is rewarded, for example, one caretaker may respond with caresses and tactile stimulation, whereas another might respond with verbal approval. With regard to the possibilities of reversing

the effects of earlier trauma, there may also be organismic differences in plasticity. These are still unresolved research issues.

Recent reports (Stott, 1956; and Wootton, 1962) have emphasized the necessity for considering the role of congenital factors in the personality and behavior deviations that have often been attributed to separation. They suggest that congenital factors may be operating not simply in the sense of increasing vulnerability to separation or deprivation, but that they may be more direct agents. Wootton emphasizes the fact that children who have been subjected to severe separation experiences are probably not a random sample of the population as a whole but come from a population in which there is a higher incidence of mental deficiency and psychological disturbance. Stott offers the hypothesis that there is a significant association between a range of physical impairments, such as morphological defect and liability to respiratory illnesses, and behavioral abnormalities. Congenital factors cannot be completely ignored in a balanced interpretation of the etiology of some of the behavior disorders which have been attributed to separation. However, the difficulty in locating the beginning of the antecedent-consequent chain complicates clear-cut demonstration of these effects. It is difficult also to distinguish genetic effects from the spiraling effects of parental pathology from one generation to the next.

CONCLUSIONS AND IMPLICATIONS

The controversial issue of the role of maternal separation during childhood in the development of later personality disturbances becomes less controversial when we take a more differentiated view of the concept of separation. It is clear that all separation experiences cannot be equated in their effects. Separation experiences range widely from minor events which are part of the normal experience of most children to the very traumatic disruptions in significant relationships which are often followed by even more traumatic experiences. The retrospective studies indicate that traumatic disruptions in relationships may be directly involved in the etiology of personality pathology. On the whole, the data do not differentiate clearly between the effects of the separation experience per se and the reinforcing conditions following separation. Several kinds of experiences following separation have been repeatedly implicated in the development of personality disorders: placement in a depriving institutional environment and placement in an unstable foster home, with recurrent changes in parental figures.

The accumulated evidence points clearly to the harmful effects of the marked deprivation of sensory, social, and affective stimulation which frequently occurs after placement in an institution. The clear implications are that greater efforts need to be directed toward changing the character of institutional environments or toward providing substitutes for institutional care. If foster homes are to be used as one kind of substitute, then some procedures need to be developed to increase the likelihood of the permannence of foster home placement, in order to avoid the clearly disruptive effects of repeated changes of foster homes.

The research data regarding the long-term effects of brief hospitalizations and brief separations certainly are not definitive. In many respects they are inadequate to permit any firm conclusions. However, they suggest that such experiences have some potentialities for harming young children. In the light of the potentially harmful effects of separation, it is important to examine carefully the reasons for separation and to avoid it whenever possible, and, when there is no alternative, to attempt to manipulate the situation to minimize trauma. Research on the evaluation of different approaches to reducing separation trauma is almost nonexistent.

It is important to consider whether there are justifiable bases for separation, but it is equally important to consider the alternatives to separation. Concern with the ill effects of separation has led to an excessive anxiety about avoiding separation under any circumstances. Decisions often involve a sensitive weighing of risks. This is especially evident with regard to hospitalization; a judgment needs to be made as to whether the potential trauma of hospitalization is likely to be greater than the potential harm of postponing treatment. That there is often a wide gap between general conviction about the indications for medical procedures and the research data has recently been suggested in regard to childhood tonsillectomies (Lipton, 1962). Frequently, however, if we know that surgery is likely to be most traumatic at a given age, it can be postponed until a less sensitive developmental period. With regard to the removal of a child from a very adverse family environment, Lewis (1954) points out that separation under these circumstances may promote mental health rather than damage the child. In the study described earlier, she noted that "some children long exposed to the dislike or indifference of their natural mothers gained rather than lost by separation, provided they passed into kind and sensible hands." Keeping the child with grossly inadequate parents in a depriving and hostile environment or depriving a child of essential medical care does not seem warranted by the research data on the effects of separation. On the other hand, under most circumstances, removing a child from his own family should not be a first course of action. Strong efforts should be made to improve inadequate family conditions or to provide temporary care for children in their own homes when a parent is ill or temporarily hospitalized.

With regard to the separation experience itself, the potentially traumatic effects of the event can be reduced. One aspect of all separation experiences which may contribute significantly to their stressful impact is environmental change (L. J. Yarrow, 1961). For the young infant, the strangeness and the unpredictability of the environment associated with varied changes may be as significant as the loss of the mother-figure. For the older child the traumatic effects of the loss of the mother-figure are likely to be heightened by novelty and unpredictability. There are several practical techniques that might be used in attempting to reduce the degree of change. Attempts might be made to make separation gradual rather than abrupt. For the young infant placed in foster care it is often possible to provide psychological continuity between the old and new caretakers in some simple ways. The degree of change in the physical environment can often be decreased by carrying over familiar objects from the old to the new environment. Although it is not possible to control the change in the physical characteristics of the caretaker, it is quite possible to lessen the degree of change in maternal care by attempting to achieve some continuity in child-rearing techniques, especially in foster home and in adoptive placements. In adoptive home placement frequently the new mother is given extensive information about the routines and schedules of the foster mother, but infrequently is she given specific details about the characteristic modes of stimulation and procedures used in soothing and gratifying the infant or young child.

The value of modifications in hospital practices to lessen the effects of separation and anxieties about bodily injury is quite clear (Schaffer, 1958). Contact between child and parent should be maintained on as close and frequent a basis as possible. Many hospitals in the United States and Great Britain encourage the mother to remain with the child preceding and following operative procedures. The child should be helped in understanding, to the extent of his intellectual capacities, the reasons for various medical procedures, and given preparation for them. It is important that his feelings and anxieties be recognized and his need to express rather than repress feelings be accepted. Although there have been no direct studies on the role of the pediatrician in mitigating separation trauma, it is likely that the degree of support he is able to provide to the parents and the child is of tremendous importance. Such support involves more than reassurance about the likelihood of beneficial outcomes. It requires sensitive awareness of both the parents' and the child's anxieties. There is a thin line between allowing some catharsis and insight to develop through ventilation, and increasing a parent's and child's anxiety level by stimulating expression of feelings which cannot be adequately handled.

The possibility that there may be some adverse effects of a change in mother-figures even in early infancy has clear implications for adoption practices. It suggests that attempts should be made to place infants as early as possible in adoptive homes. Early placement is likely to be advantageous for the parents as well as for the child. There are indications in several studies that some of the difficulties in the separated child's adjustment may be related to the parent's difficulties in making the necessary adaptations to the child.

The harmful effects of recurrent separation associated with repeated changes in foster homes are documented in the retrospective studies. It is clear that new approaches to the management of foster care are needed, approaches which will minimize the likelihood of repeated separations or changes in foster parents.

Currently there is a very optimistic orientation toward the possibilities of prevention and therapy of personality disorders. Creative experimental preventive (Caplan, 1961) and therapeutic (Alpert, 1959) approaches are being tried in a variety of settings. Just as we recognize the complexity of personality development, we must also recognize that many factors in complex interaction determine the extent to which damage from adverse early experiences can be modified by later events or by special therapeutic techniques. If we are able to identify etiological variables with greater precision, we can more effectively manipulate situations to prevent personality damage as well as develop specific therapeutic techniques.

In this area we have few unequivocally established facts, but child care practices and programs cannot wait on definitive findings. We can only proceed on the basis of what seems to be the most adequate knowledge at the present time and avoid extremes in practices that violate "common sense" or good clinical intuition.

REFERENCES

AICHHORN, A. *Wayward youth.* New York: Viking Press, 1935.

AINSWORTH, M. Reversible and irreversible effects of maternal deprivation on intellectual development. In *Maternal deprivation.* New York: Child Welf. League of America, 1962. Pp. 42–62.

AINSWORTH, M. The development of infant-mother interaction among the Ganda. In B. M. Foss (Ed.), *Determinants of infant behaviour II.* New York: Wiley, 1963. Pp. 67–112.

AINSWORTH, M. & BOWLBY, J. Research strategy in the study of mother-child separation. *Courr. Cent. Internat. l'Enfance,* 1954, **4,** 1–47.

ALPERT, A. Reversibility of pathological fixations associated with maternal deprivation in infancy. *Psychoanal. Stud. of the Child,* 1959, **14,** 169–185.

ALPERT, A., NEUBAUER, P., & WEIL, A. Unusual variations in drive endowment. *Psychoanal. Stud. of the Child,* 1956, **11,** 123–163.

AMERICAN ACADEMY OF PEDIATRICS. *Care of children in hospitals.* Evanston, Ill., 1960.

ANDRY, R. G. *Delinquency and parental pathology.* London: Methuen, 1960.

ANDRY, R. G. Paternal and maternal roles in delinquency. In *Deprivation of maternal care*. Public Health Paper No. 14. Geneva: World Health Organization, 1962. Pp. 31–43.

BACH, G. R. Father-fantasies and father-typing in father-separated children. *Child Developm.*, 1946, **17**, 63–80.

BAKWIN, H. Loneliness in infants. *Amer. J. Dis. Child.*, 1942, **63**, 30–40.

BAKWIN, H. Emotional deprivation in infants. *J. Pediat.*, 1949, **35**, 512–521.

BAKWIN, H. The hospital care of infants and children. *J. Pediat.*, 1951, **39**, 383–390.

BARRY, H. J. & LINDEMANN, E. Critical ages for maternal bereavement in psychoneuroses. *Psychosom. Med.*, 1960, **22**, 1661–1681.

BENDER, L. Psychopathic behavior disorders in children. In R. M. Lindner (Ed.), *Handbook of correctional psychology*. New York: Philos. Lib., 1947. Pp. 360–377.

BENDER, L. & YARNELL, H. An observation nursery: a study of 250 children in the psychiatric division of Bellevue Hospital. *Amer. J. Psychiat.*, 1941, **97**, 1158–1174.

BERES, D. & OBERS, S. The effects of extreme deprivation in infancy on psychic structure in adolescence. *Psychoanal. Stud. of the Child*, 1950, **5**, 121–140.

BERG, M. & COHEN, B. B. Early separation from the mother in schizophrenia. *J. nerv. ment. Dis.*, 1959, **128**, 365–369.

BERGMAN, P. & ESCALONA, S. Unusual sensitivities in very young children. *Psychoanal. Stud. of the Child*, 1949, **3-4**, 333–352.

BEVERLY, B. I. The effect of illness upon emotional development. *J. Pediat.*, 1936, **8**, 533–543.

BIRCH, H. G. *et al.* Individuality in the development of children. *Developm. Med. & Child Neurol.*, 1962, **4**, 370–379.

BLAUVELT, H. Dynamics of the mother-newborn relationship in goats. In B. Schaffner (Ed.), *Group processes*. Transactions of First Conference (1954). New York: Josiah Macy, Jr. Found., 1955. Pp. 221–258.

BLAUVELT, H. & MCKENNA, J. Mother-neonate interaction: capacity of the human newborn for orientation. In B. M. Foss (Ed.), *Determinants of infant behaviour*. New York: Wiley, 1961. Pp. 3–35.

BLOM, G. The reactions of hospitalized children to illness. *Pediatrics*, 1958, **22**, 590–600.

BOWLBY, J. Forty-four juvenile thieves. *Internat. J. Psychoanal.*, 1944, **25**, 1–57.

BOWLBY, J. Maternal care and mental health. Monograph Series, No. 2, Geneva: World Health Organization, 1951.

BOWLBY, J. Some pathological processes engendered by early mother-child separation. In M. J. E. Senn (Ed.), *Infancy and childhood*. New York: Josiah Macy, Jr. Found., 1953. Pp. 38–87 (a).

BOWLBY, J. Some pathological processes set in train by early mother-child separation. *J. ment. Sci.*, 1953, **99**, 265–272 (b).

BOWLBY, J. Grief and mourning in infancy and early childhood. *Psychoanal. Stud. of the Child*, 1960, **15**, 9–52 (a).

BOWLBY, J. Separation anxiety: a critical review of the literature. *J. Child Psychol. Psychiat.*, 1960, **1**, 251–269 (b).

BOWLBY, J. Processes of mourning. *Internat. J. Psychoanal.*, 1961, **42**, 317–334.

BOWLBY, J., AINSWORTH, M., BOSTON, M., & ROSENBLUTH, D. The effects of mother-child separation: a follow-up study. *Brit. J. med. Psychol.*, 1956, **29**, 211–247.

BOWLBY, J., ROBERTSON, J., & ROSENBLUTH, D. A two-year-old goes to the hospital. *Psychoanal. Stud. of the Child*, 1952, **7**, 82–114.

BRIDGER, W. H. & REISER, M. Psychophysiological studies of the neonate: an approach toward the methodological and theoretical problems involved. *Psychosom. Med.*, 1959, **21**, 265–276.

BRODBECK, A. J. & IRWIN, O. C. The speech behavior of infants without families. *Child Developm.*, 1946, **17**, 145–156.

BROWN, F. Depression and childhood bereavement. *J. ment. Sci.*, 1961, **107**, 754–777.

BURTON, R. V. & WHITING, J. W. M. The absent father and cross-sex identity. *Merrill-Palmer Quart.*, 1961, **7**, 85–95.

CAPLAN, G. (Ed.). *Prevention of mental disorders in children.* New York: Basic Books, 1961.

CASLER, L. Maternal deprivation: a critical review of the literature. *Monogr. Soc. Res. Child Developm.*, 1961, No. 26.

CHESS, S., THOMAS, A., & BIRCH, H. Characteristics of the individual child's behavioral responses to the environment. *Amer. J. Orthopsychiat.*, 1959, **29**, 791–802.

COLEMAN, R. W. & PROVENCE, S. Environmental retardation (hospitalism) in infants living in families. *Pediatrics*, 1957, **19**, 285–292.

DAVID, M. & APPELL, G. A study of nursing care and nurse-infant interaction. In B. M. Foss (Ed.), *Determinants of infant behaviour.* New York: Wiley, 1961. Pp. 121–141.

DAVID, M. & APPELL, G. Etude des facteurs de carence affective dans une pouponnière. *Psychiat. Enfant*, 1962, **4** (2).

DENNIS, W. & NAJARIAN, P. Infant development under environmental handicap. *Psychol. Monogr.*, 1957, **71**, No. 7 (Whole No. 436).

DIMOCK, H. G. *The child in the hospital: a study of his emotional and social well-being.* Philadelphia: F. A. Davis, 1960.

DOUGLAS, J. W. B. & BLOMFIELD, J. M. *Children under five.* London: Allen & Unwin, 1958.

DUPAN, R. M. & ROTH, S. The psychologic development of a group of children brought up in a hospital type residential nursery. *J. Pediat.*, 1955, **47**, 124–129.

DURFEE, R. & WOLF, K. Anstaltspflege und Entwicklung im erstern Lebensjahr. *Zeit f. Kinderforschung*, 1933, **42**, 28–34.

EARLE, A. M. & EARLE, B. V. Early maternal deprivation and later psychiatric illness. *Amer. J. Orthopsychiat.*, 1961, **31**, 181–186.

FAUST, O. A., JACKSON, K., CERMAK, E. G., BURTT, M. M., & WINKLEY, R. *Reducing emotional trauma in hospitalized children.* Albany, N. Y.: Albany Res. Proj., Albany Med. Coll., 1952.

FENICHEL, O. (1931) Specific forms of the Oedipus complex. In *Collected papers of Otto Fenichel, Vol. I.* New York: Norton, 1953. Pp. 204–220.

FERENCZI, S. (1914) *The nosology of male homosexuality (homoerotism): sex in psychoanalysis.* New York: Basic Books, 1950.

FISCHER, L. Hospitalism in six-month-old infants. *Amer. J. Orthopsychiat.*, 1952, **22**, 522–533.

FREUD, A. The role of bodily illness in the mental life of children. *Psychoanal. Stud. of the Child*, 1952, **7**, 69–81.

FREUD, A. & BURLINGHAM, D. T. *War and children.* New York: Ernst Willard, 1943.

FREUD, A. & BURLINGHAM, D. T. *Infants without families.* New York: Internat. Univ. Press, 1944.

FREUD, S. (1938) *An outline of psychoanalysis.* New York: Norton, 1949.

FRIES, M. & WOOLF, P. J. Some hypotheses on the role of congenital activity type in personality development. *Psychoanal. Stud. of the Child*, 1953, **8**, 48–62.

GARDNER, D. B., HAWKES, G. R., & BURCHINAL, L. G. Noncontinuous mothering in infancy and development in later childhood. *Child Developm.*, 1961, **32**, 225–234.

GARDNER, D. B., PEASE, D., & HAWKES, G. R. Responses of two-year-old adopted children to controlled stress situations. *J. genet. Psychol.*, 1961, **98**, 29–35.

GESELL, A. & AMATRUDA, C. *Developmental diagnosis.* New York: Hoeber, 1941.

GEWIRTZ, J. L. A learning analysis of the effects of normal stimulation, privation and deprivation on the acquisition of social motivation and attachment. In B. M. Foss (Ed.), *Determinants of infant behaviour.* New York: Wiley, 1961. Pp. 213–303.

GLASER, K. & EISENBERG, L. Maternal deprivation. *Pediatrics*, 1956, **18**, 626–642.

GLUECK, S. & GLUECK, E. T. *Unraveling juvenile delinquency.* Boston: Harvard Univ. Press, 1950.

GLUECK, S. & GLUECK, E. T. Working mothers and delinquency. *Ment. Hygiene*, 1957, **41**, 327–332.

GOLD, M. A social-psychology of delinquent boys. Ann Arbor: Inst. for Soc. Res\, Univ. of Michigan, 1961.

GOLDFARB, W. Effects of early institutional care on adolescent personality (graphic Rorschach data). *Child Developm.*, 1943, **14**, 213–223 (a).

GOLDFARB, W. Infant rearing and problem behavior. *Amer. J. Orthopsychiat.*, 1943, **13**, 249–265 (b).

GOLDFARB, W. Effects of early institutional care on adolescent personality. *J. exp. Educ.*, 1943, **12**, 106–129 (c).

GOLDFARB, W. Effects of early institutional care on adolescent personality: Rorschach data. *Amer. J. Orthopsychiat.*, 1944, **14**, 441–447 (a).

GOLDFARB, W. Infant rearing as a factor in foster home replacement. *Amer. J. Orthopsychiat.*, 1944, **14**, 162–173 (b).

GOLDFARB, W. Effects of psychological deprivation in infancy and subsequent stimulation. *Amer. J. Psychiat.*, 1945, **102**, 18–33 (a).

GOLDFARB, W. Psychological privation in infancy and subsequent adjustment. *Amer. J. Orthopsychiat.*, 1945, **15**, 247–255 (b).

GOLDFARB, W. Variations in adolescent adjustment of institutionally reared children. *Amer. J. Orthopsychiat.*, 1947, **17**, 449–457.

GOLDFARB, W. Rorschach test differences between family-reared, institution-reared and schizophrenic children. *Amer. J. Orthopsychiat.*, 1949, **19**, 625–633.

GOLDFARB, W. Emotional and intellectual consequences of psychologic deprivation in infancy: a re-evaluation. In P. Hoch & J. Zubin (Eds.), *Psychopathology of childhood*. New York: Grune & Stratton, 1955. Pp. 105–119.

GREGORY, I. Studies of parental deprivation in psychiatric patients. *Amer. J. Psychiat.*, 1958, **115**, 432–442.

HAGGERTY, A. D. The effects of long-term hospitalization or institutionalization upon the language development of children. *J. genet. Psychol.*, 1959, **94**, 205–209.

HEINICKE, C. Some effects of separating two-year-old children from their parents: a comparative study. *Hum. Relat.*, 1956, **9**, 105–176.

HELLMAN, I. Sudden separation and its effect followed over twenty years: Hampstead Nursery follow-up studies. *Psychoanal. Stud. of the Child*, 1962, **17**, 159–174.

HILGARD, J. R., NEWMAN, M. F., & FISK, F. Strength of adult ego following childhood bereavement. *Amer. J. Orthopsychiat.*, 1960, **30**, 788–798.

HOFFMAN, L. W. Effects of maternal employment on the child. *Child Developm.*, 1961, **32**, 187–197.

HOFFMAN, L. W. Research findings on the effects of maternal employment on the child. In I. Nye & L. W. Hoffman (Eds.), *The employed mother in America*. Chicago: Rand McNally, 1963.

HOWELLS, J. G. & LAYNG, J. Separation experiences and mental health. *Lancet*, 1955, **2**, 285–288.

JACKSON, E. B. Treatment of the young child in the hospital. *Amer. J. Orthopsychiat.*, 1942, **12**, 56–67.

JESSNER, L., BLOM, G. E., & WALDFOGEL, S. Emotional implications of tonsillectomy and adenoidectomy on children. *Psychoanal. Stud. of the Child*, 1952, **7**, 126–170.

KLACKENBURG, G. Studies in maternal deprivation in infant homes. *Acta Paediat.*, Stockholm, 1956, **45**, 1–12.

LANGFORD, W. S. The child in the pediatric hospital: adaptation to illness and hospitalization. *Amer. J. Orthopsychiat.*, 1961, **31**, 667–684.

LEBOVICI, S. The concept of maternal deprivation: a review of research. In *Deprivation of maternal care*. Public Health Paper No. 14. Geneva: World Health Organization, 1962. Pp. 75–95.

LEICHTY, M. M. The effect of father-absence during early childhood upon the Oedipal situation as reflected in young adults. *Merrill-Palmer Quart.*, 1960, **6**, 212–217.

134   REVIEW OF CHILD DEVELOPMENT RESEARCH

LEVY, D. M. Primary affect hunger. *Amer. J. Psychiat.*, 1937, **94**, 643–652.

LEVY, D. M. Psychic trauma of operations in children. *Amer. J. Dis. Child.*, 1945, **69**, 716–729.

LEWIS, H. *Deprived children*. London: Oxford Univ. Press, 1954.

LIPTON, S. On the psychology of childhood tonsillectomy. *Psychoanal. Stud. of the Child*, 1962, **17**, 363–417.

LOWREY, L. G. Personality distortion and early institutional care. *Amer. J. Orthopsychiat.*, 1940, **10**, 576–585.

LUSTMAN, S. L. Rudiments of the ego. *Psychoanal. Stud. of the Child*, 1956, **11**, 89–97.

LYNN, D. & SAWREY, W. L. The effects of father-absence on Norwegian boys and girls. *J. abnorm. soc. Psychol.*, 1959, **59**, 258–262.

MAAS, H. Long-term effects of early childhood separation and group care. *Vita humana*, 1963, **6**, 34–56 (a).

MAAS, H. The young adult adjustment of twenty wartime residential nursery children. *Child Welf.*, 1963, **42**, 57–72 (b).

MAAS, H. & ENGLER, R. E. *Children in need of parents*. New York: Columbia Univ. Press, 1959.

MEAD, M. *Sex and temperament in three primitive societies*. New York: Mentor, 1935.

MEAD, M. Some theoretical considerations on the problem of mother-child separation. *Amer. J. Orthopsychiat.*, 1954, **24**, 471–483.

MEAD, M. A cultural anthropologist's approach to maternal deprivation. In *Deprivation of maternal care*. Public Health Paper No. 14. Geneva: World Health Organization, 1962. Pp. 45–62.

NAESS, S. Mother-child separation and delinquency. *Brit. J. Delinquency*, 1959, **10**, 22–35.

NEUBAUER, P. B. The one-parent child and his Oedipal development. *Psychoanal. Stud. of the Child*, 1960, **15**, 286–309.

NYE, F. I. *Family relationships and delinquent behavior*. New York: Wiley, 1958.

O'CONNOR, N. The evidence for the permanently disturbing effects of mother-child separation. *Acta. Psychol.*, 1956, **12**, 174–191.

OLTMAN, J., McGARRY, J., & FRIEDMAN, S. Parental deprivation and the "broken home" in dementia praecox and other mental disorders. *Amer. J. Psychiat.*, 1952, **108**, 685–694.

O'NEAL, P. & ROBINS, L. N. Childhood patterns predictive of adult schizophrenia: a 30-year follow-up study. *Amer. J. Psychiat.*, 1958, **115**, 385–391.

PLANK, E. N., CAUGHEY, P., & LIPSON, M. J. A general hospital child-care program to counteract hospitalism. *Amer. J. Orthopsychiat.*, 1959, **29**, 94–101.

PRINGLE, M. L. & BOSSIO, V. A study of deprived children. I. Intellectual, emotional, and social development. *Vita humana*, 1958, **1**, 65–92.

PRINGLE, M. L. & BOSSIO, V. Early prolonged separation and emotional maladjustment. *J. Child Psychol. Psychiat.*, 1960, **1**, 37–48.

PRINGLE, M. L. & TANNER, M. The effects of early deprivation on speech development: a comparative study of 4-year-olds in a nursery school and in residential nurseries. *Lang. & Speech*, 1958, **1**, 269–287.

PROVENCE, S. & LIPTON, R. *Infants in institutions*. New York: Internat. Univer. Press, 1962.

PRUGH, D. G. & HARLOW, R. G. "Masked deprivation" in infants and young children. In *Deprivation of maternal care*. Public Health Paper No. 14. Geneva: World Health Organization, 1962. Pp. 9–29.

PRUGH, D. G., STAUB, E., SANDS, H., KIRSCHBAUM, R., & LENIHAN, E. A study of the emotional reactions of children and families to hospitalization and illness. *Amer. J. Orthopsychiat.*, 1953, **23**, 70–106.

RABIN, A. I. Some psychosexual differences between kibbutz and non-kibbutz Israeli boys. *J. proj. Tech.*, 1958, **22**, 328–332.

RHEINGOLD, H. L. The modification of social responsiveness in institutional babies. *Monogr. Soc. Res. Child Developm.*, 1956, **21**, No. 63.

RHEINGOLD, H. L. The measurement of maternal care. *Child Developm.*, 1960, **31**, 565–573.

RHEINGOLD, H. L. The effect of environmental stimulation upon social and exploratory behaviour in the human infant. In B. M. Foss (Ed.), *Determinants of infant behaviour.* New York: Wiley, 1961. Pp. 143–177.

RHEINGOLD, H. L., GEWIRTZ, J., & ROSS, H. Social conditioning of vocalizations in the infant. *J. comp. physiol. Psychol.*, 1959, **52**, 58–73.

RIBBLE, M. *Rights of infants.* New York: Columbia Univ. Press, 1943.

RICHMOND, J. & LUSTMAN, S. Autonomic function in the neonate. *Psychosom. Med.*, 1955, **17**, 269–275.

ROBERTSON, J. Some responses of young children to loss of maternal care. *Nursing Times*, 1953, **49**, 382–386.

ROBERTSON, J. *Young children in hospitals.* New York: Basic Books, 1958.

ROBERTSON, J. & BOWLBY, J. Responses of young children to separation from their mothers. *Courr. Cent. Internat. l'Enfance*, 1952, **2**, 131–142.

ROSENBLATT, J. S., TURKEVITZ, G., & SCHNEIRLA, T. C. Early socialization in the domestic cat as based on feeding and other relationships between female and young. In B. M. Foss (Ed.), *Determinants of infant behaviour.* New York: Wiley, 1961. Pp. 51–74.

ROUDINESCO, J., DAVID, M., & NICOLAS, J. Responses of young children to separation from their mothers: I. Observation of children ages 12 to 17 months recently separated from their families and living in an institution. *Courr. Cent. Internat. l'Enfance*, 1952, **2**, 66–78.

SCHAFFER, H. R. Objective observations of personality development in early infancy. *Brit. J. med. Psychol.*, 1958, **31**, 174–183.

SCHAFFER, H. R. & CALLENDER, W. M. Psychologic effects of hospitalization in infancy. *Pediatrics*, 1959, **24**, 528–539.

SCHOFIELD, W. & BALLAN, L. A comparative study of the personal histories of schizophrenic and nonpsychiatric patients. *J. abnorm. soc. Psychol.*, 1959, **59**, 216–225.

SEARS, R. R., PINTLER, M., & SEARS, P. S. Effect of father separation on preschool children's doll play aggression. *Child Developm.*, 1946, **17**, 219–243.

SIEGEL, A. E. (Ed.) *Research issues related to the effects of maternal employment on children.* University Park, Pa.: Soc. Sci. Res. Center, Pennsylvania State Univ., 1961.

SIEGEL, A. E. & HAAS, M. B. The working mother: a review of research. *Child Developm.*, 1963, **34**, 513–542.

SIEGEL, A. E., STOLZ, L. M., HITCHCOCK, E. A., & ADAMSON, J. Dependence and independence in children of working mothers. *Child Developm.*, 1959, **30**, 533–546.

SKEELS, H. M. A study of the effects of differential stimulation on mentally retarded children: Follow-up report. *Amer. J. ment. Defic.*, 1942, **66**, 340–350.

SKEELS, H. M. & DYE, H. A study of the effects of differential stimulation on mentally retarded children. *Proc. Amer. Assn. Ment. Defic.*, 1939, **44**, 114–136.

SKEELS, H. M., UPDEGRAFF, R., WELLMAN, B., & WILLIAMS, H. M. A study of environmental stimulation: an orphanage preschool project. *Univ. Iowa Stud. Child Welf.*, 1938, **15**, 7–191.

SPENCE, J. C. Care of children in hospitals. *Brit. Med. J.*, 1947, **1**, 125–130.

SPITZ, R. A. Hospitalism: an inquiry into the genesis of psychiatric conditions in early childhood. *Psychoanal. Stud. of the Child*, 1945, **1**, 53–74.

SPITZ, R. A. Hospitalism: an inquiry into the genesis of psychiatric conditions in early childhood: a follow-up report. *Psychoanal. Stud. of the Child*, 1946, **2**, 113–117.

SPITZ, R. A. & WOLF, K. Anaclitic depression. *Psychoanal. Stud. of the Child*, 1946, **2**, 313–342.

SPITZ, R. A. & WOLF, K. Autoerotism. *Psychoanal. Stud. of the Child*, 1949, **3-4**, 85–120.

STOLZ, L. M. Effects of maternal employment on children: evidence from research. *Child Developm.*, 1960, **31**, 749–782.

STOLZ, L. M. *et al. Father relations of war-born children.* Stanford, Calif.: Stanford Univ. Press, 1954.

STONE, L. J. A critique of studies of infant isolation. *Child Developm.*, 1954, **25**, 9–20.

STONE, L. J. & CHURCH, J. *Childhood and adolescence: a psychology of the growing person.* New York: Random House, 1957.

STOTT, D. H. The effects of separation from the mother in early life. *Lancet*, 1956, **1**, 624–628.

TOBY, J. The differential impact of family disorganization. *Amer. Sociol. Rev.*, 1957, **22**, 502–512.

TRASLER, G. *In place of parents.* London: Routledge & Kegan Paul, 1960.

WOLF, K. A. Observation of individual tendencies in the first year of life. In M. J. E. Senn (Ed.), *Problems of infancy and childhood.* New York: Josiah Macy, Jr. Found., 1953.

WOOTTON, B. *Social science and social pathology.* London: Allen & Unwin, 1959.

WOOTTON, B. A social scientist's approach to maternal deprivation. In *Deprivation of maternal care.* Public Health Paper No. 14. Geneva: World Health Organization, 1962. Pp. 63–73.

WORLD HEALTH ORGANIZATION. *Deprivation of maternal care.* Public Health Paper No. 14. Geneva: Author, 1962.

YARROW, L. J. The development of object relationships during infancy and the effects of a disruption of early mother-child relationships. *Amer. Psychologist*, 1956, **11**, 423. (Abstract).

YARROW, L. J. Maternal deprivation: toward an empirical and conceptual re-evaluation. *Psychol. Bull.*, 1961, **58**, 459–490.

YARROW, L. J. Dimensions of early maternal care. *Merrill-Palmer Quart.*, 1963, **9**, 101–114.

YARROW, L. J. & GOODWIN, M. S. *Effects of change in mother figure during infancy on personality development.* Progress Report, 1963. Family and Child Services, Washington, D. C.

YARROW, L. J. & YARROW, M. R. Personality continuity and change in the family context. In P. Worchel and D. Byrne (Eds.), *Personality change.* New York: Wiley, 1964.

YARROW, M. R. Maternal employment and child rearing. *Children*, 1961, **8**, 223–228.

YARROW, M. R., SCOTT, P., DE LEEUW, L., & HEINIG, C. Child rearing in families of working and non-working mothers. *Sociometry*, 1962, **25**, 122–140.

Acquisition and Significance of Sex Typing and Sex Role Identity[1]

JEROME KAGAN

The Fels Research Institute

THE CONCEPT OF SEX ROLE and its close relatives, sex typing and sex role identification, have achieved much prominence during the past decade. It is surprising, however, that this concept has been so tardy in acquiring theoretical popularity among psychologists. For the behavioral differences between the sexes are public and have an ancient and transcultural heritage. Sociology and anthropology have not been as neglectful of this concept, for over a quarter of a century ago Linton (1936) wrote: "The division and ascription of statuses with relation to sex seems to be basic in all social systems. All societies prescribe different attitudes and activities to men and to women." One reason the concept of sex role has played a subordinate theoretical role rests with the history of theory development in psychology. The two major attempts to construct comprehensive schemes for understanding behavior—behavioral and psychoanalytic theory—placed needs at the center of their systems and made strivings for the goals of food, protection from pain, love, security, aggression, sex, and dependency the primary determinants of behavior. These needs are common to both sexes and neither theory directed attention to sex differences in the hierarchy of patterning of these needs. Moreover, an emphasis on needs or motives that require the attainment of external goals to satisfy them camouflaged a more fundamental human motive—the desire to make one's behavior conform to a previously acquired standard.

The motive to match one's behavior to an internal standard—to make one's behavior conform to a standard of masculinity, let us say—differs in two fundamental ways from the traditional description of the motivational process associated with aggression, dependency, or sexuality. The strength of the former set of motives does not wax or wane to the degree that is characteristic of sexual or aggressive motivation. The arousal of sexual or

[1] The preparation of this paper was supported in part by research grant (M-4464) from the National Institute of Mental Health, United States Public Health Service.

aggressive motives is dependent, in large measure, on external provocations. The desire to make one's behavior conform to a standard of masculinity, however, typically does not drift from negligible strength to intense values in different situations or over short periods of time. Further, receipt of whatever reward maintains the tendency to appear masculine does not weaken the motive underlying the response. The performance of masculine acts does not weaken or destroy temporarily the desire to continue such behavior. For sex and aggression, on the other hand, consummation often attenuates the strength of the motive for a period of time.

We shall use the word *standard* to refer to a correlated set of responses (that is, overt acts, attitudes, wishes, or feelings) and external attributes that the individual views as desirable to possess. It is assumed that the cluster of responses and attributes that defines the standard acquires its desirability through three processes: (a) identification with models who possess the cluster, (b) expectation of affection and acceptance for possession of the trait cluster, and (c) expectation that possession of the cluster will prevent social rejection. Once the standard has been acquired, it acts as an internal judge to whom decisions about the initiation of behavior or maintenance of an attitude are referred for evaluation. Thus the probability of a particular action depends, in part, upon the child's standards surrounding the action. It is obvious that children acquire standards for a variety of responses—cleanliness, obedience, honesty, mastery of academic subjects, coherence of speech, and maturity of judgment. Many of these standards are of approximately equal salience for boys and girls. However, a sex role standard dictates the adoption of different responses for boys and girls. The significance of a sex role standard rests with its governing influence on the initiation of a broad band of behaviors.

WHAT IS A SEX ROLE STANDARD?

A sex role standard refers to a learned association between selected attributes, behaviors, and attitudes, on the one hand, and the concepts male and female, on the other. In effect, a sex role standard summarizes the culturally approved characteristics for males and females. During the period three to seven years of age, the child gradually realizes that people fall into one of two related language categories—boys or girls, men or women, fathers or mothers. The early discrimination of social objects into these distinct classes is facilitated by the presence of a variety of clearly discriminable cues, including dress, bodily form and proportion, strength, distribution of hair, depth of voice, posture at the toilet, modal interactive behavior with a child, and characteristic behavior in the kitchen, the garage, or the backyard. Existing empirical evidence clearly indicates that the school-age child has acquired the concepts male and female (Hartup and Zook, 1960; Kagan, Hosken, and Watson, 1961) and this assumption is fundamental for the theoretical discussions that appear later in this essay.

Core Attributes of Masculinity and Femininity

The characteristics that define the concepts male and female can be divided into primary and secondary, depending on the communality of agreement among members of the culture. Both primary and secondary sex role characteristics fall into one of three classes: (a) physical attributes, (b) overt behaviors, (c) feelings, attitudes, motives, and beliefs (that is, covert attributes).

Although the characteristics that are differentially associated with maleness and femaleness among most adults in our culture are not clearly crystallized in the mind of the six-year-old, there is considerable overlap between the standards of the first grader and those of the adult. Let us consider these sex-typed characteristics and note where there appear to be important developmental changes.

Physical Attributes

Analysis of the public media's representation of males and females and the results of studies of preadolescent and adolescent youngsters reveal that American girls regard an attractive face, hairless body, a small frame, and moderate sized breasts as the most desirable characteristics for a girl; boys regard height, large muscle mass, and facial and bodily hair as the most desirable physical characteristics for boys. A girl should be pretty and small; boys, large and strong (Cobb, 1954; Frazier and Lisonbee, 1950; Harris, 1959; Jersild, 1952; Nash, 1958). For the child eight to ten years of age, it appears that an attractive face is a primary sex-typed attribute for girls; a tall, muscular physique primary for boys (Cobb, 1954).

Overt Behaviors

The culture's differential standards regarding the behavioral face to be exposed to the public are not as clearly delineated as the standards for physical attributes, but these rules are strongly felt none the less. One of the primary classes of sex-typed behavior involves aggression. The standard requires inhibition of verbal and physical aggression among girls and women; but gives boys and men license—and even encouragement—to express aggression when attacked, threatened, or dominated by another male. We would expect, therefore, more aggressive behavior from males and the data support this expectation. Indeed, it is difficult to find a sound study of preschool or school-age children in which aggressive behavior was not more frequent among boys than among girls (Bandura, 1962; Bandura, Ross, and Ross, 1961; Dawe, 1934; Hattwick, 1937; Maccoby and Wilson, 1957; Muste and Sharpe, 1947). This difference is also present in the make-believe themes children tell to dolls or to pictures (Bach, 1945; Pintler, Phillips, and Sears, 1946; P. S. Sears, 1951; Whitehouse, 1949), and in the child's differential perception of adult males and females. If children are asked which parent is more dangerous or more punitive (that is, aggressive), both boys and girls agree that the father is more aggressive than the mother (Emmerich, 1959; Kagan, 1956; Kagan and Lemkin, 1960; Kagan, Hosken, and Watson, 1961). The association between maleness and aggression has also been demonstrated in a study in which stimuli symbolic of aggression are used; for example, a tiger versus a rabbit, an alligator versus a bird (Kagan, Hosken, and Watson, 1961). Moreover, adults also regard men as more aggressive than women (Bennett and Cohen, 1959; Jenkins and Russell, 1958), and parents hold differential standards regarding aggression for their children, for they expect more overt aggression from boys than from girls (Kohn, 1959; Sears, Maccoby, and Levin, 1957).

A second class of sex-typed behavior includes the correlated trio of dependency, passivity, and conformity. Girls are allowed greater license to express these behaviors; whereas boys and men are pressured to inhibit them. The data on sex differences in passivity and dependency are less consistent than those for aggression, but there are more studies reporting greater dependency, conformity, and social passivity for females than for males at all ages (Beller and Turner, unpublished; Crutchfield, 1955; Hovland and Janis, 1959; Kagan and Moss, 1962; Lindzey and Goldberg, 1953; McCandless, Bilous, and Bennett, 1961; Sanford et al., 1943; Sears et al., 1953; Siegel et al., 1959). Moreover, affiliative and nurturant behaviors are generally regarded as more appropriate for females than for males, and a majority of investigations of overt behavior or story-telling responses reveal more frequent occurrence of affiliative and nurturant behavior among girls, and greater preoccupation with people and harmonious interpersonal relations among girls than among boys (Goodenough, 1957; Hildreth, 1945; Honzik, 1951; Lansky et al., 1961; Terman and Miles, 1936; Whitehouse, 1949; Winker, 1949).

Correspondingly, children view women as more nurturant than men, and adult women see themselves as more nurturant than their male counterparts (Bennett and Cohen, 1959). The circle is complete with both children and adults expecting and receiving more dependence, passivity, and nurturance from females, more aggression from males.

Additional sets of sex-typed responses include the development of skill and interest in gross motor and mechanical tasks for boys (Kagan and Moss, 1962; Tyler, 1947) and an interest in clothes, dolls, and babies for girls (Honzik, 1951; Tyler, 1947).

During the adolescent and early adult years some refined derivatives of these sex-typed patterns are added to the sex role standard. For females, these include submissiveness with males, inhibition of overt signs of sexual desire, and cultivation of domestic skills (Douvan and Kaye, 1957; Harris, 1959). For males, independence, interpersonal dominance with men and women, initiation of sexual behavior, sexual conquests, and acquisition of money and power become critical sex-typed requirements (Bennett and Cohen, 1959; Child, Potter, and Levine, 1946; Douvan and Kaye, 1957; Harris, 1959; Jenkins and Russell, 1958; Kagan and Moss, 1962; Tuddenham, 1951; Walters, Pearce, and Dahms, 1957).

Game Choices as an Index of Sex-Typed Standards for Behavior

The games, toys, and fantasy heroes chosen by young children corroborate the behavioral standards outlined above. The large body of research on children's game and toy preferences indicates that boys choose objects related to sports, machines, aggression, speed, and power roles; whereas the girls select games and objects associated with the kitchen and home, babies, personal attractiveness, and fantasy roles in which they have a subordinate relation to a male (nurse, secretary). Thus knives, boats, planes, trucks and cement mixers are regarded by school children as masculine; dolls, cribs, dishes, and nurses' equipment are regarded as feminine (Foster, 1930; Honzik, 1951; Rosenberg and Sutton-Smith, 1960; Vance and McCall, 1934).

Many investigators have made up their own tests to assess sex-typed game preferences, and several of these instruments have become popular. The "IT" test (Brown, 1957) presents the child with a figure (the IT), which is supposed to be ambiguous with respect to sex, and a variety of toys and objects. The child is usually asked to select the object or activity the IT figure prefers. It is assumed that the child's choices reflect his personal preferences.

The major results from studies using these kinds of instruments indicate that boys show an increasing preference for sex appropriate games with age. As early as age three, boys are aware of some of the activities and objects that our culture regards as masculine. Among girls, however, preferences are more variable up to nine or ten years of age. Many girls between three and ten years of age show a strong preference for masculine games, activities, and objects; whereas, it is unusual to find many boys who prefer feminine activities during this period. Thus five-year-old boys show a clearer preference for masculine toys than girls show for feminine toys (Brown, 1957; Hartup and Zook, 1960). This difference in game preferences is matched by a relatively greater frequency of girls stating a desire to be a boy or wanting to be a daddy rather than a mommy when they grow up (Brown, 1957).

Since our culture assigns greater freedom, power, and value to the male role, it is understandable that the girl might wish for the more attractive male role. This devaluation of the female role is probably one reason that the typical woman regards herself as less adequate and more fearful than most men (Bennett and Cohen, 1959).

Rosenberg and Sutton-Smith (1960) tested children in Grades 4, 5, and 6 for game preferences. The results suggest that in the year 1960 girls were more masculine in their game choices than they had been thirty years earlier. It may be that the wall separating male and female recreational activities is cracking and some of the traditional differences in sex-typed game choices may be undergoing some change.

Finally, it should be noted that there are social class differences in the game choices of children. Rabban (1950) asked children (age three to eight) in two diverse social groups (middle- and working-class homes) to select the toys they liked the best. The choices of lower-class boys and girls conformed more closely to traditional sex-typed standards than the choices of middle-class children, suggesting that the differentiation of sex roles is sharper in lower-class families. This finding agrees with the fact that lower-class mothers encourage sex typing more consistently than middle-class mothers (Kohn, 1959). Moreover, the difference in sex typing between the classes is greatest for girls (Rabban, 1950). Apparently the middle-class girl, unlike the middle-class boy, is much freer to express an interest in toys and activities of the opposite sex. This finding agrees with the fact that, among girls, there is a positive correlation between the educational level of the family and involvement in masculine activities (Kagan and Moss, 1962).

Feelings, Attitudes, Motives, and Wishes

The cluster of covert attributes that are closely linked to the concept of female in our culture include the ability to gratify a love object and the ability to elicit sexual arousal in a male; the desire to be a wife and mother and the correlated desires to give nurturance to one's child and affection to a love object; and the capacity for emotion. For males, the primary covert attributes include a pragmatic attitude, ability to gratify a love object, suppression of fear, and a capacity to control expression of strong emotion in time of stress (Bennett and Cohen, 1959; Jenkins and Russell, 1958; Parsons, 1955). There are fewer systematic data in support of these covert attributes than there are for the overt behaviors listed earlier. However, clinical studies (Bieber *et al.*, 1962) and self-ratings by adults (Bennett and Cohen, 1959) agree with these statements.

In sum, females are supposed to inhibit aggression and open display of sexual urges, to be passive with men, to be nurturant to others, to cultivate attractiveness, and to maintain an affective, socially poised, and friendly posture with others. Males are urged to be aggressive in face of attack, independent in problem situations, sexually aggressive, in control of regressive urges, and suppressive of strong emotion, especially anxiety. Parsons' (1955) dichotomy of masculine and feminine roles into instrumental versus expressive is consistent with the attributes we have assigned to the categories masculine and feminine.

This list may strike readers as old fashioned or unrealistically traditional, and not representative of contemporary values. Existing data on children indicate that despite a common adult assumption that sex role standards are changing at a rapid rate, children continue to believe that aggression, dominance, and independence are more appropriate for males; passivity, nurturance and affect more appropriate for females (Parsons, 1948; Hartley, 1960a). Hartley writes:

> In response to those who are overly concerned about the effect of apparent recent sex role changes . . . from the child's point of view, there are no changes; he sees only the picture as it appears in his time and this picture . . . shows remarkably little change from traditional values (p. 91).

Moreover, analysis of the areas in which female role changes have occurred reveals that increased license for sexual provocation and work outside the home are the standards that have undergone the most dramatic alteration. The decreased anxiety and inhibition associated with making one's self sexually attractive to males does not contradict—and, in fact, supports—the contention that the ability to attract and arouse a male sexually is a pivotal sex-typed attribute for the female. Parsons writes:

> Emancipation . . . means primarily emancipation from traditional and conventional restrictions on the free expression of sexual attraction and impulses, but in a direction which tends to segregate the element of sexual interest . . . and in so doing tends to emphasize the segregation of the sex roles . . . the feminine glamour pattern has appeared as an offset to masculine occupational status (1948, p. 275).

The increased frequency of working women is predominantly in positions subordinate to males. Moreover, a frequent motivation for this work is to increase the family income. In effect, the work is often viewed as a reflection of a nurturant attitude toward the family, for the increased income is regarded as a way of providing more material goods for the children (Hartley, 1960b).

The fact that the proportion of women in professional and technical occupations has decreased during the last quarter-century (Nye and Hoffman, 1963) suggests that the increasing number of working women does not necessarily reflect a growing tendency for females to assume the masculine role in our society. Moreover, it appears that many working mothers feel guilty about leaving their children to caretakers while they work. They feel they are not "being good mothers." The presence of this anxiety supports the notion that the typical woman believes that a nurturant attitude toward her children is a more essential component of her femininity than a career skill (Hartley, 1960b).

SEX ROLE IDENTITY

We have defined sex role standards as a publicly shared belief regarding the appropriate characteristics for males and females. But the abstracted concept of the ideal male or female, as viewed by the culture, is to be distinguished from a particular individual's conceptualization of his own degree of masculinity or femininity. Such a conceptualization is determined, in part, by the degree to which an individual believes he possesses sex-typed traits. *The degree to which an individual regards himself as masculine or feminine will be called his sex role identity.* This belief is but one component of a complex interlocking set of beliefs the individual holds about himself. The complete set of attitudes is generally regarded as a self-concept or self-identity. Although the individual's assessment of his masculinity or femininity comprises only one aspect of his identity, it is mandatory that the individual assign himself a value on this dimension. Unlike some specialized attributes (for example, knowledge of the habits of birds, ability to prune trees), most individuals cannot declare an indifference to their sex role identity.

The degree of match or mismatch between the sex role standards of the culture and an individual's assessment of his own overt and covert attributes provides him with a partial answer to the question, "How masculine (or feminine) am I?" The belief system we call a sex role identity is not completely conscious, and there is an imperfect correlation between possession of standard sex role attributes and the integrity of one's sex role identity. A man who possesses many masculine behaviors may not necessarily regard himself as highly masculine. But it is probably impossible for a man to possess none of the culturally approved sex-typed attributes and regard himself as highly masculine. Thus possession of some sex-typed traits is necessary but not sufficient for a firm sex role identity.

Unfortunately, there is little empirical information that deals with the mode of establishment of a child's sex role identity. We are forced, therefore, to speculate on this issue and the following suggestions should be regarded as conjecture.

The major determinants of sex role identity for the young child include (a) perceptions of similarity to parents, and (b) degree to which the child adopts the games, and masters the skills that are traditionally encouraged for his sex. The child who perceives major elements of similarity to the parent of the same sex will initially regard himself as masculine (or feminine), for the parents are the original prototypes of masculinity and femininity for the young child. However, when the child enters school, he comes into direct contact with peers and the wider culture's definition of the sex roles. As a consequence of this confrontation, the child gradually is forced to accommodate his definition of maleness and femaleness to the values of this broader community.

A second basic assumption in this essay (the first was that the young child was clearly aware of the sex roles) is that the child wishes to believe that his actions, attitudes, and affects are congruent with the sex role standard. This standard is a condensation of characteristics perceived in the same-sexed parent together with the culture's prescriptive rules for males and females. There will be a core of communality in this concept for all persons in the culture, but there will be slight differences from child to child, depending on the particular family and subcultural milieu in which he is reared.

ACQUISITION OF SEX ROLE IDENTITY AND SEX ROLE STANDARDS

There are two distinct response classes whose acquisition must be explained; namely, a covert label applied to the self (sex role identity), and a set of attributes that the culture has labeled as masculine or feminine (sex role standards). There is no need to dwell on the concept of sex role preference (Lynn, 1959) at this point in the discussion. It is acknowledged that some children either resent or experience anxiety over the behaviors that are assigned to their biological sex. But it is assumed that all children have a need to acquire a self-label that matches their biological sex. This assumption is not inconsistent with the fact some adolescents and adults strive to avoid adoption of sex-typed responses because of anxiety over the behaviors that are prescribed for their sex role. These individuals are typically in conflict and are likely to manifest a variety of psychopathological symptoms. This topic will be treated in more detail in a later section of the paper.

In the discussion that follows we shall not deal with the possible effect of constitutional variables on the adoption of sex-typed characteristics. There is, however, some evidence suggesting that constitutional variables may predispose the male toward activity and dominance; the female toward passivity (DeVore and Jay, in press; Harlow and Zimmerman, 1959; Hebb, 1946).

Acquisition of a Sex Role Identity

There are at least three kinds of experiences that determine the degree to which an individual regards himself as masculine or feminine: (a) differential identification with mother, father, parental surrogates, older siblings, and special peers; (b) acquisition of the attributes or skills that define masculine or feminine behavior; and (c) a perception that other people regard the individual as possessing appropriate sex-typed characteristics. Let us discuss each of these processes in some detail.

Identification as a base for sex role identity. The concept of identification is, to some degree, controversial. There is disagreement as to its usefulness in explaining aspects of human development, and even among those who regard the concept as fruitful there is no unanimity as to definition. Since Freud's original discussion of identification (Freud, 1925) contemporary writers have presented searching analyses of this concept and suggested significant modifications (Bronfenbrenner, 1960; Kagan, 1958; Lynn, 1959; Maccoby, 1959; Mowrer, 1950; Parsons, 1955; Sanford, 1955; R. R. Sears, 1957; Whiting, 1960). A major point of disagreement revolves around the question "To what events or processes does this term refer?" For the term *identification* has been applied to overt behavior, to a motive system (the need to identify with a model), to the process by which behaviors are acquired, and to a belief about the self. In an earlier paper (Kagan, 1958), the author presented a definition and analysis of identification. We shall summarize this position here with special reference to sex role identification.

A definition of identification. An identification is a belief that some of the attributes of a model (parents, siblings, relatives, peers, and so on) belong to the self (Kagan, 1958). If a six-year-old boy is identified with his father, he necessarily regards himself as possessing some of his father's characteristics, one of which is maleness or masculinity. Moreover, if a child is identified with a model, he will behave, to some extent, as if events that occur to the model are occurring to him. If a child is identified with his father, he shares vicariously in the latter's victories and defeats; in his happiness and in his sorrow; in his strengths and in his weaknesses. It has been argued elsewhere that the establishment of an optimally strong identification requires that three conditions be met: (a) the model must be perceived as nurturant to the child; (b) the model must be perceived as being in command of desired goals, especially power, love from others, and task competence in areas the child regards as important; and (c) the child must perceive—before the identification belief begins its growth—some objective bases of similarity in external attributes or psychological properties between himself and the model (Kagan, 1958).

The child's motivation to develop an identification with a model is based on his desire to command the attractive goals possessed by the model. At this point a critical assumption is introduced into the argument. The child assumes that if he possessed some of the external—and more objective—characteristics of the model, he might also possess his desirable psychological properties (for example, power, love from others). In effect, the child behaves as if he believed that objects that appear alike on the outside have similar properties on the inside, and that the greater the external similarity between himself and a model, the greater the possibility that he will possess the model's power, competence, and affection. One of the important consequences of the boy's desire for a strong identification with the father is his attempt to take on the father's characteristics. For each time he successfully imitates a behavior or adopts an attitude of the father he perceives an increased similarity to the latter. This perception of increased similarity strengthens his belief that he possesses some of the father's covert characteristics. One of these covert attributes is the self-label of masculinity. Thus a strong identification with the same-sexed parent at seven years of age facilitates the future establishment of an appropriate sex role identity.

Let us now consider some of the differential consequences attending those parent-child dyads in which one boy identifies with a father who practices traditional masculine behavior; whereas the second boy identifies with a father who does not display sex-typed behavior. We must assume that both fathers are equally nurturant and that each son perceives the same degree of similarity to his father.

The boy with the minimally masculine father will confront the societal standard for masculinity when he enters school. Since his overt behavior will be less sex typed than that of his peers, he will perceive a discrepancy between his actions and those of the "other boys." He will be tempted to conclude that he is not masculine because his behavior does not match that of the male peer group, and because he may be the target of accusatory communications implying that he is not masculine. As a result of these experiences, his sex role identity is likely to be weakened.

The child who has identified with a masculine father does not experience this dissonant discrepancy upon school entrance. This boy's sex role identity becomes based not only on the identification with the masculine father, but also on the perception of similarity between his own attributes and the societal standard for masculinity as displayed by his peers. The boy with a masculine father gains two products from an identification with him—the vicarious power and strength that facilitate future attempts to master sex-typed skills, and the continued exposure to sex-typed behavior. This exposure facilitates the acquisition of sex-typed responses.

The process may be similar for the girl. The girl who identifies with a mother who displays traditionally feminine behavior should display submissiveness with boys, inhibition of aggression, the cultivation of personal attractiveness, and an interest in domestic and nurturant activities. The girl who identifies with a mother who does not manifest traditional feminine attributes is not likely to have adopted sex role characteristics. She will begin to question her femininity when she confronts the values of the peer group, and her sex role identity will be weakened to some degree.

But what of those children who have minimal identifications with their same-sexed parent? If these children adopt the sex role behavior displayed by peers, siblings, or relatives of their own sex, they will possess some basis for an appropriate sex role identity. But it is possible that a weak identification with the same-sexed parent may prevent the child from developing the confidence to master many sex appropriate skills. The boy with a fragile identification with his father and a moderately strong one with his mother would be predisposed to adopt her traits. If she displays feminine attributes, the boy is likely to be passive, to feel inadequate in comparison to his peers, to be reluctant to defend himself against attack, and to have difficulty suppressing anxiety. Since a feeling of strength and a retaliatory posture to stress are masculine traits, this boy will have some difficulty establishing an appropriate sex role identity. The clinical literature, despite its methodological deficiencies, is in general accord in indicating that boys who have a stronger identification with mother than with father (owing to maternal dominance of the family, a perception of greater maternal than paternal competence, and paternal rejection with maternal acceptance) tend to be dependent and more prone to anxiety in threatening situations (Bieber et al., 1962). Moreover, the occurrence of maternal dominance over a passive father, together with maternal rejection of the child, is frequent in the histories of schizophrenic males (Kohn and Clausen, 1956).

Similarly, the girl with a minimal identification with her mother will probably begin to question her potential attractiveness to males and her ability to master feminine attributes. This girl will experience some strain in attaining a firm sex role identity. In sum, both the strength of the child's identification with the same-sexed parent as well as the parents' sex-typed behaviors must be assessed if we are to predict the strength of the child's sex role identity.

One of the implications of this discussion—albeit conjectural—involves the placement of young children in foster homes. If we assume that strong identification with the same-sexed parent is a desirable outcome, then one could argue that a boy should be placed in a home where the father is clearly dominant over the mother; whereas a girl should be placed in a home where the mother has some degree of power and competence. For the child is predisposed to identify with the parental model he perceives to possess power and competence. Unfortunately, there are no definitive empirical tests of these hypothetical ideas. The studies most pertinent to the relation between identification and sex role behavior are subject to multiple interpretations, but we shall consider some of them briefly.

Comparison of the doll play themes of boys whose fathers were absent from the home in contrast to those from intact families revealed less aggressive fantasy from the former than from the latter group (Bach, 1946; Sears, Pintler, and Sears, 1946). Though these results are predictable from several points of view, they are also consonant with the interpretation that absence of the father—who typically displays dominant and aggressive behavior—left the boy without a male model from whom he might imitate aggressive actions. This rehearsal of the model's behavior is one of the concomitants of the identification process. The results of other studies also suggest the relevance of father's presence for an adequate sex role identification.

In a study of Norwegian children with father absent or present (Lynn and Sawrey, 1958), boys with father absent had greater difficulty establishing peer relations than boys from intact families. Failure to develop the masculine skills valued by the peer culture often leads to peer rejection. Thus the relation between father-absence and poor peer relations could result from retardation in the acquisition of masculine interests as a consequent of a weak identification with the father.

A related pair of studies (Mussen and Distler, 1959; Payne and Mussen, 1956) suggests the importance of a nurturant relation between father and son in the formation of an identification. In the Payne and Mussen study, junior and senior high school boys and their parents filled out the California Psychological Inventory. The 20 boys with the highest father identification scores, defined in terms of similarity of father-son answers on the Inventory, were compared with 20 low father-identified boys. The 40 boys were then given an incomplete-stories test to assess perception of the father-son relation. The boys with a strong identification with father produced more frequent evidence of warm father-son relations and a perception of the father as nurturant, than did the low-identified subjects. Moreover, the boys who were identified with the father possessed more sex-typed masculine behavior and attitudes than the boys with minimal identification with their fathers.

In the Mussen and Distler study, kindergarten boys were given a test to assess degree of adoption of sex-typed masculine interests. The ten most masculine and ten least masculine boys were tested in a doll play situation. The doll play themes of the masculine boys contained more evidence of a perception of the father as nurturant and powerful than the themes of the nonmasculine boys. These results support the notion that identification is facilitated when the model is seen as nurturant to the child and powerful vis-a-vis the mother. Finally, a recent experimental investigation (Bandura, 1962) suggests that a child is more likely to imitate the behavior of a nurturant adult model than one who is not nurturant.

Changes in sex role identity as a function of acquisition of sex-typed attributes. In addition to identification with an appropriate model, sex role labels may be altered as a result of the acquisition of desirable sex-typed attributes. The boy who learns to be dominant with peers, sexually aggressive with girls, or competent on the athletic field often begins to regard himself as more masculine. The girl who becomes popular with boys, socially poised with adults, or capable of giving nurturance labels herself as more feminine. It has been suggested that the strength of a sex role identity is a function of the discrepancy between the inventory of actual sex-typed attributes and the ideal attributes prescribed by the culture. We are assuming that acquisition of appropriate attributes can reduce this discrepancy and lead to corresponding modifications in the self-label. The opposite effect is also possible. Loss of attributes or goal states that are essential parts of the self-label "I am (masculine) (feminine)" can widen the gap between actual attributes and the ideal, and make a sex role identity more vulnerable.

A third set of events that influences a sex role identity is closely related to the acquisition of sex-typed skills discussed above. In this process, experiences with other people in ways that are congruent with sex-typed standards may alter self-labels. If men and women react toward Bill as though the latter were dominant and strong, the discrepancy between Bill's idealized model and existing self-concept will be attenuated. Correlatively, if a girl continually hears praises of her attractiveness, she may gradually alter her conception of herself and the self-ideal discrepancy will be reduced. Of course, these experiences comprise only one aspect of the process of sex role identity. The identification with each parent is presumed to form the basic foundation for a sex role identification. There is no guarantee, therefore, that the social experiences mentioned above will always lead to marked changes in the content of the self-labels that characterize sex role identity.

In sum, differential identification with parents and parent surrogate models, acquisition of sex-typed skills, and sex role congruent experiences are each influential in determining the degree to which an individual labels himself as masculine or feminine.

Overt Sex-Typed Behaviors: Establishment and Maintenance

The learning of sex role behaviors—like a sex role identity—is facilitated by the desire to identify with a model of the same sex. But there are other motives that influence this learning, especially desire for receipt of affection and acceptance from parents and peers, and anxiety over rejection by significant others. Most parents punish aggression and open sexuality more consistently in daughters than in sons; they punish passivity, dependency, and open display of fear more consistently in sons than in daughters (Aberle and Naegele, 1952; Kohn, 1959; Sears, Maccoby, and Levin, 1957). Moreover, children feel that their parents want them to adopt sex role attributes (Fauls and Smith, 1956). Thus parental reward of sex appropriate behavior and punishment of inappropriate responses facilitate the adoption of sex-typed traits. The typical child desires the acceptance of parents and peers and wants to avoid their rejection. These motives predispose him to shun sex inappropriate activities and preferentially choose responses that are congruent with sex role standards. It is conceivable, of course, that a child might have a same-sexed parent who displays sex appropriate behavior but an opposite sexed parent who does not reward—and perhaps punishes—sex role attributes. This child should be ambivalent with respect to the display of sex role behavior. Thus in order to predict with maximal accuracy the occurrence of sex role behavior one must assess (a) the degree of identification with the same-sexed parent, (b) degree of sex-typed behavior displayed by each parent, and (c) the pattern of rewards issued by each parent.

It is of interest to note that most of the *overt sex-typed responses the girl must acquire require reactions from other people*. It is almost impossible for a girl to assess whether she is attractive, socially poised, or passive with others without continued interaction and feedback from the social environment. The girl is forced to be dependent upon people and to court their acceptance in order to obtain those experiences that help to establish sex-typed behaviors. The critical significance of adult and peer acceptance for girls probably contributes to the greater degree of conformity and concern with socially desirable behaviors typically found among females (Crutchfield, 1955; Hovland and Janis, 1959).

The boy, on the other hand, develops many important sex-typed behaviors while alone. Many sex-typed skills involve solitary practice for which the boy does not require the reactions of others in order to assess when he has reached an adequate level of mastery. Perfection of gross motor or mechanical skills are examples of such activities. Witness the ten-year-old boy shooting baskets in his backyard or fixing his bicycle. The boy receives from these solitary endeavors information that strengthens his conviction that he is acquiring masculine attributes. Moreover, independence of the attitudes and opinions of others—and this implies relative independence of the wishes of others—is in itself a sex-typed trait. The typical boy, therefore, tries to suppress anxiety over social rejection because these reactions are not regarded as masculine in this culture.

Constraints on the Pattern of Sex Role Behavior

This discussion has placed primary emphasis on the quality of the child's contact with his family and peers as determinants of sex typing and sex role identification. There are two additional classes of variables that play more than a trivial role in this process. These include the child's rate of physical maturation and the social class in which he is reared.

Physical maturation and sex typing. Since physical attributes (attractive face and figure for girls; bodily hair, height, and size for boys) are essential sex-typed qualities, one might expect that children who have early pubertal growth spurts and develop secondary sex characteristics early will be more popular, more confident, and initiate heterosexual behavior earlier and with more frequency than children who mature late. Investigations by Jones and Mussen using the longitudinal data from the University of California Institute of Human Development verify this expectation (Jones, 1957; Jones and Mussen, 1958; Mussen and Jones, 1957; Mussen and Jones, 1958). The late maturing boy who has little facial and bodily hair, small genitals and small physique realizes his deviation from community norms and begins to doubt his ability to interact successfully with females. He is likely to withdraw from social interactions, to engage in more infantile attention getting and dependent behaviors, and is less likely to become a leader among his peers (Mussen and Jones, 1957).

Early and late maturing boys and girls also differ in their interests. As one might expect, early maturing boys obtain more masculine interest scores than late maturing boys, while early maturing girls obtain more feminine interest scores than their late maturing counterparts. A study of premenarcheal and postmenarcheal girls (Stone and Barker, 1939) found that the postmenarcheal girls were more interested in heterosexual activities and personal adornment, and less interested in games requiring vigorous gross motor activity.

Social class differences in sex role behavior. As indicated earlier, lower-class children typically adopt sex-typed traits earlier in development and with greater consistency (Rabban, 1950). This class difference is consonant with the fact that lower-class parents are more concerned with traditional sex typing than middle-class parents. Pope (1953) has found that both lower- and middle-class boys reject the effeminate boy with nonmasculine interests but differ in their attitude toward the academically studious boy. Middle-class boys accept him, while lower-class boys reject him. Among girls, both classes accept the studious girl. However, the middle-class girl rejects the female who displays an excessive interest in heterosexual relations; whereas, the lower-class female is more likely to accept her. Since concern with attractiveness, dating, and establishing love relations with boys are primary in the feminine sex role standard, one would expect the lower-class peer culture—which adopts traditional sex typing with greater enthusiasm—to promote this characteristic with vigor.

SIGNIFICANCE OF THE CHILD'S SEX ROLE IDENTITY

The child's continuing desire for a stable and firm sex role identity plays a central role in directing his development, for it sets strong constraints upon future behavioral choices. In this final section we would like to discuss the relationship of sex role identification to three psychological problems: (a) stability of behavior over time, (b) differential mastery of academic skills, and (c) sexuality and behavior with love objects.

Relationship of Sex Role Identification to Continuities in Behavior

The degree of continuity of selected behaviors is a topic of both practical and theoretical significance. Knowledge of that developmental era during which we can obtain a preview of the future is important for practitioners who wish to initiate prophylactic or immediate treatment procedures, whether the area be delinquency, obsessive-compulsive rituals, or academic difficulties. It is generally acknowledged that asocial behavior, sexual

anomalies, and academic retardation in a fourteen-year-old are often refractory to conventional psychiatric treatment. If we knew when early
manifestation of these behaviors could be regarded as a reliable clue to the
future, we could justifiably begin preventive measures in the hope of blocking nascent psychopathology before it became firmly established. Moreover, knowledge of the critical period during which a particular set of
responses is being established would be theoretically useful. For such information would point to the developmental era during which investigations into the learning of that response would be most profitable.

A recent study of the long-term stability of behavior from birth to adulthood in a group of middle-class subjects from the Fels Research Institute's
longitudinal population has suggested some important conclusions regarding the relationship of sex role identification to behavioral continuities
(Kagan and Moss, 1962). Briefly, the procedure involved study of the relation
between two independent sets of data on the same individuals—ratings of
adult behavior based on interviews when the subjects were between twenty
and thirty years of age, and independent ratings of their behavior during the
four developmental periods of birth to age three, three to six, six to ten, and
ten to fourteen years of age. The childhood ratings were based on behavioral observations in the home, nursery school, day camp, public school,
and interviews at the Institute. The major behavioral variables studied
included aggression, dependency, passivity, intellectual achievement,
social interaction anxiety, heterosexual behavior, and sex-typed activities.

The probability of occurrence of a specific response during the period six
to ten years of age was a moderately sensitive predictor of the occurrence
of a similar response during adulthood *when the response was congruent
with sex role standards.* That is, when sex role standards dictated inhibition
of a particular behavior for one sex, behavioral continuity from childhood
to adulthood was minimal. To illustrate, childhood passivity and dependence in problem and stress situations predicted passivity and dependence
for adult women, but not for men. As indicated earlier, these traits are
acceptable characteristics for females, but violate masculine sex role
standards. Thus a passive or dependent boy would experience considerable
pressure to inhibit overt passive behavior in order to conform to sex role
standards. Aggression and sexuality, on the other hand, are acceptable responses for males, but violate feminine sex role standards. The data revealed that childhood aggression toward adults and heterosexual behavior
predicted anger arousal and sexual behavior for adult men, but not for
women. Involvement in mastery of academic skills is appropriate and encouraged for both sexes, and sex role standards do not dictate strong inhibition of intellectual mastery for either sex. Thus involvement in intellec-

tual tasks should be stable for both sexes. The results affirm this expectation, with the degree of continuity slightly higher for males than for females.

Our interpretation of the finding that behavioral stability depended on congruence with sex role standards is neither complicated nor strained. A preadolescent girl is exposed to models who inhibit aggression and blatant sexuality, and the social environment punishes open display of these behaviors. These social pressures, together with the girl's identification with appropriate models, cause her to inhibit excessive aggression and sexuality. Although these motives may be strong within her, they are not given direct expression. Similarly, boys are pressured to inhibit passivity and dependence upon others. Boys should fight their own battles and solve their problems autonomously. The excessively dependent boy is likely to inhibit undisguised expression of dependency because it is inappropriate for his sex role. Behavior that deviates markedly from sex role standards will be inhibited as a result of the child's desire to avoid social rejection and his desire to model himself after culturally approved role models. This interpretation agrees with Sears's suggestion that aggression-anxiety in girls is closely related to anxiety over maintaining an appropriate sex role identity; whereas, the development of aggression-anxiety in boys is more typically derived from different forces, especially parental handling of aggressive actions in the boy (R. R. Sears, 1961).

The less direct derivatives of child behavior in adult personality were also made comprehensible through a reliance upon the construct of sex role identity. Passivity and dependency in childhood predicted similar behaviors for adult women, but were unrelated to adult behavior in other dimensions such as sexuality, quality of social interaction, competitiveness, dominance, or aggression. For men, there was no relation between child and adult passivity or dependency. But childhood passivity and dependency predicted lack of competitiveness, lack of aggression, and avoidance of sexuality in adulthood—behaviors that have a passive flavor to them.

Childhood aggression predicted undisguised aggression in adult men but was unrelated to other personality dimensions. For women, childhood aggression predicted competitiveness, intellectual mastery, and rejection of feminine sex typing, but not undisguised aggression.

It appears that although the girl inhibits the direct expression of aggression, she may select (unconsciously, in many cases) a substitute behavior that gratifies this motive but is socially more acceptable. Similarly, a passive boy is likely to inhibit direct display of undisguised passivity as an adult, but will manifest behaviors that contain a passive element and are less subject to social rejection.

The data from this project suggest that when a childhood behavior is congruent with sex role standards it is likely to be predictive of similar behavior in adolescence and adulthood. When it conflicts with sex role standards, it is likely to be unrelated to behavior manifestly similar to the childhood response, but predictive of theoretically related behaviors that are socially more acceptable. It appears, therefore, that the sex role appropriateness of a response is a major determinant of its developmental stability, and the degree to which substitute behaviors will appear in the behavioral repertoire of the individual.

It is of importance to note that the tendency to practice sex-typed behaviors was highly stable from early childhood to adulthood. The correlation between practice of sex appropriate activities during age six to ten and adulthood was .63 for men and .44 for women. This finding is supported by data from the Oakland Growth Study (Mussen, 1961, 1962), which revealed a moderately high relationship between degree of masculine interests in males from adolescence through adulthood.

Sex Role Identification and Intellectual Mastery

Although competence in intellectual and academic tasks is not as clearly a sex-typed trait as aggression or dependency, it appears that degree of involvement in most academic problems is greater for adolescent and adult males than for females. Particularly well documented is the fact that skills at problems requiring analysis and reasoning (primarily those involving spatial and mechanical reasoning, science, and mathematics) are viewed as more appropriate for boys than for girls, and girls perform less well on such tasks (Bennett and Cruikshank, 1942; Havighurst and Janke, 1944; Heilman, 1933; Herzberg and Lepkin, 1954; Kostick, 1954; Lord, 1941; Mellone, 1944; Swineford, 1948; Tyler, 1947). To illustrate, Milton (1958) reported that when adolescent or adult subjects were presented with problems involving primarily mathematical or geometric reasoning, the males consistently obtained higher scores than females. Moreover, there was a low positive relation between masculinity scores on the Terman-Miles Masculinity-Femininity Test and problem-solving scores for both sexes. The female who rejected traditional feminine interests performed better on mathematical and geometric problems than the girl who had adopted traditional feminine behaviors. However, if the verbal problem dealt with feminine content (cooking and gardening materials), the females scored better than if the problem dealt with guns, money, or geometric designs, even though the logical steps and computations were identical. It seems that the typical female believes that the ability to solve problems involving geometry, physics, logic, or arithmetic is a uniquely masculine skill, and her motivation to attack such problems is low. This decreased involvement may reflect the fact that the girl's self-esteem is not at stake in such problems, or the fact that she is potentially threatened by the possibility that she might perform with competence on such tasks. For unusual excellence on such tasks may be equated with a loss of femininity.

The sex difference in problem-solving appears early in development and under different guises. Boys are more likely to adopt an analytic attitude toward natural events in the environment and toward formal problems. Smith (1933), for example, reported that preschool boys asked many more "how" and "why" questions spontaneously; whereas girls preferentially asked questions about social rules and the conventional labels to be applied to objects. Milton (1958) gave problems to men and women and asked them to state whether their preference would be to *analyze the situation, go for help*, or *adopt a trial-and-error* approach in the solution of this problem. Males were much more likely to select the analytic alternative. The masculine preference for analysis is also present in the child's tendency to fractionate visual stimuli. The author has unpublished data clearly indicating that eight- and nine-year-old boys are more likely than girls to analyze a complex design into its component parts.

Other sex differences in the approach to problem-solving relate to autonomy and persistence. McDavid (1959) had children three to nine years of age observe an adult perform a task. When the children were later asked to perform the task, the girls were more likely to imitate the adult than the boys. Crandall and Rabson (1960) gave children two puzzles, one of which they solved, the other they failed to solve. When the children were asked subsequently to which one they wished to return, more boys than girls chose the puzzle they had not been able to solve. In sum, boys appear to be more analytic, more independent, and more persistent in problem situations presented in a laboratory setting. This difference increases with time, and by late adolescence and adulthood the typical female feels inadequate when faced with most problems requiring analysis and reasoning.

The sex-typed character of domains of knowledge is most evident in the vocational choices of young adolescents. A recent national survey of thousands of high school students conducted by *Project Talent* asked students about their planned major in college and future occupational choice. The sex-typed character of their choices was already evident in the ninth grade. For example, 25 per cent of the boys and only 3 per cent of the girls selected the physical or natural sciences or engineering; whereas 3 per cent of the boys and 13 per cent of the girls chose elementary or secondary school education as future vocations (Flanagan, unpublished).

A third reason for the girl's lower motivation and performance in science and mathematics—in addition to her belief that females are not supposed to be competent in these areas and her reluctance to analyze problems—is the fact that a girl's sex role identity is more dependent on her ability to attract and maintain a love relationship than on her academic skills. For many males, however, academic excellence is viewed as a necessary antecedent to vocational success. Since vocational success is an essential component of the male's sex role identity, we would expect the adolescent male to be more highly motivated to master those tasks that are linked to his vocational aspirations. It is also possible that the girl more often works to obtain the acceptance and approval of her teacher and parents, while the boy is more likely to view mastery as a test of his personal adequacy. Thus the male's performance may be more frequently oriented to "figure the task," rather than "figure the teacher."

There is one obvious implication of these ideas. Because of the associational link of mathematics, science, and masculinity, it is suggested that the content of the problems given to young children be less biased toward the masculine. To illustrate, one can teach a child that the area of a circle is πr^2 using pie pans as well as missiles or planets as the context in which formulas are taught.

Although an intense involvement in academic mastery is more characteristic of the adolescent and adult male than female, this is not the case in the primary grades. In kindergarten through the fourth grade the girl typically outperforms the boy in all areas, and the ratio of boys to girls with reading problems ranges from three to one to six to one (Bentzen, 1963; Tyler, 1947). Why is there a developmental shift between age six and seventeen? How can we explain the fact that girls' academic performances are superior to boys during the early school years but gradually become inferior during late adolescence and adulthood? One reason is that among late adolescent boys academic proficiency is linked to vocational success, and the boy's motivation is stronger than it was during the early years of school. Moreover, the girl's motivation toward mastery is decreasing with age as a result of anxiety over feeling intellectually more competent than the boy and conflict over excessive competitiveness. Let us explain this last statement on competitiveness. It is not uncommon for an adolescent to view intense intellectual strivings as a competitively aggressive behavior. In order to obtain the best grade in a class one must often defeat a peer in open debate and in examination score. But competition has obvious aggressive overtones. Since the typical female has greater anxiety over aggressive and competitive behavior than the male (Buss, 1961; Kagan and Moss, 1962), she experiences greater conflict over intellectual competition. This conflict can lead to inhibition of intense strivings for academic excellence.

Another reason for the gradually increasing academic superiority of boys is the change in perception of the sex-typed character of school and academic work. It is suggested that first- and second-grade boys have more difficulty than girls in mastering reading, writing, or arithmetic because the average boy perceives the school atmosphere as excessively feminine. Since the six-year-old boy is striving to develop a masculine sex role identification, he resists involvement in feminine situations. The case for a feminine atmosphere in the primary grades rests on the following facts. The child's introduction into school is mediated by female teachers who usually initiate the activities of painting, coloring, and singing. Moreover, most teachers place a premium on obedience, decorum, and inhibition of aggressive and restless motoricity. These activities and values are clearly more appropriate for girls than for boys, and it might be expected that most children would view the school situation as more feminine than masculine. Recent studies (unpublished) at the Fels Institute indicate that children in the second grade do view the school situation as more feminine than masculine. Since one cannot ask a child directly whether a blackboard or a book is masculine or feminine, the experiments used a minor disguise. Second- and third-grade children were taught different nonsense syllables to stand for maleness and femaleness. They were then shown pictures of school-related objects (blackboard, page of arithmetic, book, school desk, library) as well as nonacademic stimuli. The results indicated that second-grade boys and girls were more likely to label the school objects feminine than masculine. This tendency diminished with age, especially for boys. The labeling of the nonacademic objects was in accord with expectation; for example, the children called a bird feminine, and a lion masculine. Moreover, the presence of a male principal or librarian in the school was associated with a stronger tendency to view school as masculine among the boys.

A more sophisticated differentiation of academic work occurs during the adolescent years. This differentiation turns on the schism between the sciences and the humanities. The adolescent begins to classify knowledge as practical or impractical; as having an instrumental effect upon the world or as unrelated to instrumental changes in the environment; as involving machines or words. Since a pragmatic, instrumental, and mechanical orientation to nature is central in the sex role standard for males (Parsons, 1955), some adolescent boys are highly motivated to master the sciences, but poorly motivated to acquire impractical subject matters (for example, language, history) that involve only words and ideas. This difference in involvement and performance results from the implicit association between subject matter and sex role standards. Similarly, the girl who has chosen a masculine career, such as law, medicine, or science, may experience anxiety over exerting effort in an activity that is not traditionally feminine.

It appears that there are strong semantic associations between the words *masculinity* and *femininity*, and specific areas of knowledge for most adult members of western culture. This is an unfortunate marriage, for one would hope that knowledge would retain neutrality amidst the warring factions of the mind. There is, however, cause for some optimism. Unlike many undesirable psychological states, it may be possible to alter the associational link between domain of knowledge and the sex roles through modifications in the procedures and atmosphere of the elementary and secondary schools. If teachers begin to believe that girls can do as well as boys in mathematics and science, and female teachers become more confident about their own abilities in these areas, they will become more desirable role models for young girls. For a country interested in the maximization of intellectual potential, this change would be salutary.

Further, the introduction of men into the primary grades, and an appreciation of the importance of creating a more masculine atmosphere in the primary grades, may reduce the frequency of reading problems in young boys. A significant educational experiment on this issue would involve a comparison of reading progress in Grades 1 and 2 between children taught by male versus female teachers.[2]

Sex Role Identification and Sexuality

Since success in heterosexual relations is a critical component of a satisfactory sex role identity in adults, it is not surprising that disturbances in sex role identification are associated with disturbances in sexual behavior. Sex role standards for males call for sexual initiative with girls, attractiveness to girls, and easy dominance in the boy-girl dyad. Sex role standards for girls call for inhibition of undisguised sexual excitement, passivity in the boy-girl relationship, and attractiveness.

Deviations from these standards lead to different degrees of anxiety and apprehension in relationships with the opposite sex. Thus the sixteen-year-old boy who is small, not shaving, and shy will be afraid to initiate heterosexual relationships for fear that the girl will reject him or find him undesirable. He may fear initiation of erotic activity because he doubts his ability to maintain an erection, or fears that his genitals are too small for him to be an adequate sex partner. Similarly, the girl who feels physically unattractive anticipates that she will not attract boys, and she avoids situations in which such rejection might be realized. There is, of course, no perfect

---

[2] The author is associated with such a study being conducted in an elementary school system in Chillicothe, Ohio.

relationship between an adolescent's perception of his degree of attractiveness and his physical attributes as judged by others. But neither is this relationship negligible. In general, most adolescents have a fairly realistic appraisal of their attractiveness to others, gained, of course, through social experience and exposure to the values of the public media.

We have already discussed the fact that late-maturing boys whose physiques differ from the cultural ideal are late in establishing heterosexual behavior (Mussen and Jones, 1957, 1958). The Fels longitudinal data suggest that adolescent boys with nonmasculine interests during early childhood, in contrast to those with more conventional masculine interests, were anxious about sexuality and less likely to have erotic experiences with girls (Kagan and Moss, 1962).

In sum, the adolescent's expectancy of success in heterosexual contacts is related to the degree to which he or she practices sex-typed activities and possesses sex-typed attributes. There is a circular dynamic involved in the relation between sex role identification and sexual behavior, especially for boys. Since sexual experience with girls is a vital ingredient in attaining a satisfactory sex role identity, most boys strive hard to obtain these goals, in the same way that the boy practices foul shots in his driveway. For every successful sexual conquest helps to close the gap between the existing assessment of the self and the idealized sex role model. Thus much sexual activity among males is motivated by the desire to strengthen a masculine identification rather than by overwhelming biological urges.

The occurrence of homosexual behavior or fear of being a homosexual is often related to anxiety over not attaining the masculine ideal. To most adolescents and adults in our society, the term *homosexual* implies the following trio of characteristics—not interested in girls, slight of build, nonmasculine interests. The adolescent or adult male who feels he possesses these attributes is in the precarious position of beginning to believe that he may be a homosexual. The inaccuracy of this belief is no safeguard against its appearance. The boy who has failed to develop masculine interests (for any one of a variety of reasons) will be anxious about initiating heterosexual behavior because of the anticipation of being rejected. This chronic anxiety soon leads to an avoidance of girls and a growing apathy until the individual comes to believe that he is incapable of becoming interested in girls. He does not interpret his apathy and avoidance as the sequelae of long-standing fear. Instead, he interprets them as an indication that he is a homosexual. The panic that results from this realization leads to a more intense fear of initiating contact with women. For the self-label homosexual often carries with it the expectation of failure in a heterosexual relation.

A recent book on homosexuality by a group of psychoanalysts (Bieber *et al.*, 1962) reports that a high percentage of homosexual men in contrast to a control group were, as children, less likely to play baseball, to participate in competitive group games, or to become involved in fights with other boys. Chang and Block (1960) compared 20 male homosexuals and 20 controls. Each subject described his ideal self, his father, his mother, and himself. The controls and homosexuals did not differ in the characteristics of their ideal self. For example, both homosexual and control men rejected dependency as a trait for the ideal self. But the homosexual male described himself as dependent and not ambitious—traits that are alien to the traditional masculine ideal.

This is not to deny that pathognomonic parent-child relations may be relevant for the development of this complex class of behavior. But it is suggested that a perception of marked deviance from the masculine ideal is one antecedent of the feeling that one has homosexual wishes and facilitates the probability of engaging in homosexual behavior. Fear of interaction with females as a result of a fragile masculine sex role identity is often present in the attitude structure of the homosexual.

CONCLUSIONS

The construct of sex role identification is not without its ambiguity and one could argue for its fragmentation into several better articulated terms. Its retention as a descriptive and explanatory concept rests on the assumption that the concepts *male* and *female* and the dimensions *maleness* and *femaleness* are basic to our language. The evidence supports this assumption. The child as young as four has dichotomized the world into male and female people and is concerned with boy-girl differences. By the time he is seven he is intensely committed to molding his behavior in concordance with cultural standards appropriate to his biological sex and he shows uneasiness, anxiety, and even anger when he is in danger of behaving in ways regarded as characteristic of the opposite sex. The appellation of "sissy" to a boy or "tomboy" to a girl usually has a strong negative affective charge. We have argued that the desire to behave in accordance with sex role standards extends far beyond an interest in sports for boys and cooking for girls. For the desire to establish a sex role identification touches many important domains of behavior, including school work, sexual behavior, and vocational choice, and has a strong effect on behavioral continuities over the course of development.

The emphasis on the motive to match one's behavior to a standard has been central in this paper. It is suggested that one of the most compelling of human motives is the desire to reduce the discrepancy between an internal standard and the ever-changing behavior of the individual. Thus, expression of sexual behavior, verbal aggression, or academic mastery is sometimes an intermediate act that serves a more powerful motive than sex, aggression, or achievement; namely, the desire for congruence between an ideal representation of the self and one's everyday behavior. This appears to be a uniquely human motive and psychology is witness to a refreshing confluence of theoretical writings that emphasize this point of view. Festinger (1957) suggests that cognitive dissonance is an annoying state of affairs that elicits behavior aimed at reducing the dissonance. Heider (1958) argues for the human need for cognitive harmony and balance. One of the central axes around which such harmonies are played is the standard for sex role behavior. It appears that unnecessary conflicts are generated because of anxiety over deviation from sex role standards. Once learned, these standards are not easily altered. But they are modifiable during the early school years and society should perhaps consider the desirability of initiating changes in selected aspects of our current sex role standards.

REFERENCES

ABERLE, D. F. & NAEGELE, K. D. Middle class fathers' occupational role and attitudes toward children. *Amer. J. Orthopsychiat.*, 1952, **22**, 366–378.

BACH, G. R. Young children's play fantasies. *Psychol. Monogr.*, 1945, **59**, No. 2.

BACH, G. R. Father fantasies and father typing and father separated children. *Child Developm.*, 1946, **17**, 63–79.

BANDURA, A. Social learning through imitation. In M. R. Jones (Ed.), *Nebraska symposium on motivation, 1962.* Lincoln: Univ. Nebraska Press, 1962.

BANDURA, A., ROSS, D., & ROSS, S. A. Transmission of aggression through imitation of aggressive models. *J. abnorm. soc. Psychol.*, 1961, **63**, 575–582.

BELLER, E. K. & TURNER, J. LeB. A study of dependency and aggression in early childhood. Unpublished report from progress report on NIMH Project M-849.

BENNETT, E. M. & COHEN, L. R. Men and women: personality patterns and contrasts. *Genet. Psychol. Monogr.*, 1959, **60**, 101–153.

BENNETT, G. K. & CRUIKSHANK, R. M. Sex differences in the understanding of mechanical problems. *J. appl. Psychol.*, 1942, **26**, 121–127.

BENTZEN, F. Sex ratios in learning and behavior disorders. *Amer. J. Orthopsychiat.*, 1963, **33**, 92–98.

BIEBER, I., DAIN, H. J., DINCE, P. R., DRELLICH, M. G., GRAND, H. G., GUNDLACH, R. H., KREMER, M. W., RIFKIN, A. H., WILBUR, C. B., & BIEBER, T. B. *Homosexuality.* New York: Basic Books, 1962.

BRONFENBRENNER, U. Freudian theories of identification and their derivatives. *Child Developm.*, 1960, **31**, 15–40.

BROWN, D. G. Masculinity-femininity development in children. *J. consult. Psychol.*, 1957, **21**, 197–202.

BUSS, A. H. *The psychology of aggression.* New York: Wiley, 1961.

CHANG, J. & BLOCK, J. A study of identification in male homosexuals. *J. consult. Psychol.*, 1960, **24**, 307–310.

CHILD, I. L., POTTER, E. H., & LEVINE, E. M. Children's textbooks and personality development: an exploration in the social psychology of education. *Psychol. Monogr.*, 1946, **60**, No. 3.

COBB, H. V. Role wishes and general wishes of children and adolescents. *Child Developm.*, 1954, **25**, 161–171.

CRANDALL, V. J. & RABSON, A. Children's repetition choices in an intellectual achievement situation following success and failure. *J. genet. Psychol.*, 1960, **97**, 161–168.

CRUTCHFIELD, R. S. Conformity and character. *Amer. Psychologist*, 1955, **10**, 191–198.

DAWE, H. C. An analysis of 200 quarrels of preschool children. *Child Developm.*, 1934, **5**, 139–157.

DEVORE, I. & JAY, P. Mother-infant relations in baboons and langurs. In H. L. Rheingold (Ed.), *Maternal behavior in mammals*. New York: Wiley, in press.

DOUVAN, E. & KAYE, C. *Adolescent girls*. Ann Arbor: Surv. Res. Center, Univ. of Michigan, 1957.

EMMERICH, W. Young children's discriminations of parent and child roles. *Child Developm.*, 1959, **30**, 403–419.

FAULS, L. B. & SMITH, W. D. Sex role learning of five-year-olds. *J. genet. Psychol.*, 1956, **89**, 105–117.

FESTINGER, L. *A theory of cognitive dissonance*. Evanston, Ill.: Row, Peterson, 1957.

FLANAGAN, J. C. Project talent. Unpublished manuscript.

FOSTER, J. C. Play activities of children in the first six grades. *Child Developm.*, 1930, **1**, 248–254.

FRAZIER, A. & LISONBEE, L. K. Adolescent concerns with physique. *School Rev.*, 1950, **58**, 397–405.

FREUD, S. Mourning and melancholia. In *Collected papers of* . . . . Vol. IV. London: Hogarth Press, 1925. Pp. 30–59.

GOODENOUGH, F. W. Interest in persons and aspects of sex differences in the early years. *Psychol. Monogr.*, 1957, **55**, 287–323.

HARLOW, H. F. & ZIMMERMAN, R. R. Affectional responses in the infant monkey. *Science*, 1959, **130**, (3373), 421–432.

HARRIS, D. B. Sex differences in the life problems and interests of adolescents, 1935 and 1957. *Child Developm.*, 1959, **30**, 453–459.

HARTLEY, R. E. Children's concepts of male and female roles. *Merrill-Palmer Quart.*, 1960, **6**, 83–91 (a).

HARTLEY, R. E. Some implications of current changes in sex role patterns. *Merrill-Palmer Quart.*, 1960, **6**, 153–164 (b).

HARTUP, W. W. & ZOOK, E. A. Sex role preferences in three- and four-year-old children. *J. consult. Psychol.*, 1960, **24**, 420–426.

HATTWICK, B. A. Sex differences in behavior of nursery school children. *Child Developm.*, 1937, **8**, 343–355.

HAVIGHURST, R. J. & JANKE, L. L. Relations between ability and social status in a midwestern community: I. Ten-year-old children. *J. educ. Psychol.*, 1944, **35**, 357–368.

HEBB, D. O. Behavioral differences between male and female chimpanzees. *Bull. Canad. Psychol. Assn.*, 1946, **6**, 56–58.

HEIDER, F. *The psychology of interpersonal relations*. New York: Wiley, 1958.

HEILMAN, J. D. Sex differences in intellectual abilities. *J. educ. Psychol.*, 1933, **24**, 47–62.

HERZBERG, F. & LEPKIN, M. A study of sex differences on the Primary Mental Abilities Test. *Educ. psychol. Measmt.*, 1954, **17**, 687–689.

HILDRETH, G. The social interests of young adolescents. *Child Developm.*, 1945, **16**, 119–121.

HONZIK, M. P. Sex differences in the occurrence of materials in the play constructions of preadolescents. *Child Developm.*, 1951, **22**, 15–35.

HOVLAND, C. I. & JANIS, I. J., *et al.*, *Personality and persuasibility*. New Haven: Yale Univ. Press, 1959.

JENKINS, J. J. & RUSSELL, W. A. An atlas of semantic profiles for 360 words. *Amer. J. Psychol.*, 1958, **71**, 688–699.

JERSILD, A. T. *In search of self.* New York: Teach. Coll., Columbia Univ., 1952.

JONES, M. C. The later careers of boys who were early or late maturing. *Child Developm.*, 1957, **28**, 113–128.

JONES, M. C. & MUSSEN, P. H. Self conceptions, motivations, and interpersonal attitudes of early and late maturing girls. *Child Developm.*, 1958, **29**, 491–501.

KAGAN, J. The child's perception of the parent. *J. abnorm. soc. Psychol.*, 1956, **53**, 257–258.

KAGAN, J. The concept of identification. *Psychol. Rev.*, 1958, **65**, 296–305.

KAGAN, J., HOSKEN, B., & WATSON, S. The child's symbolic conceptualization of the parents. *Child Developm.*, 1961, **32**, 625–636.

KAGAN, J. & LEMKIN, J. The child's differential perception of parental attributes. *J. abnorm. soc. Psychol.*, 1960, **61**, 446–447.

KAGAN, J. & MOSS, H. A. *Birth to maturity.* New York: Wiley, 1962.

KOHN, M. L. Social class and parental values. *Amer. J. Sociol.*, 1959, **64**, 337–351.

KOHN, M. L. & CLAUSEN, J. A. Parental authority behavior and schizophrenia. *Amer. J. Orthopsychiat.*, 1956, **26**, 297–313.

KOSTICK, M. M. A study of transfer: sex differences in the reasoning process. *J. educ. Psychol.*, 1954, **45**, 449–458.

LANSKY, L. M., CRANDALL, V. J., KAGAN, J., & BAKER, C. T. Sex differences in aggression and its correlates in middle class adolescents. *Child Developm.*, 1961, **32**, 45–58.

LINDZEY, G. & GOLDBERG, M. Motivational differences between male and females as measured by the TAT. *J. Pers.*, 1953, **22**, 101–117.

LINTON, R. Status and role. In *The study of man.* New York: Appleton-Century-Crofts, 1936. Pp. 113–131.

LORD, F. E. A study of spatial orientation of children. *J. educ. Res.*, 1941, **34**, 481–505.

LYNN, D. B. A note on sex differences in the development of masculine and feminine identification. *Psychol. Rev.*, 1959, **66**, 126–135.

LYNN, D. B. & SAWREY, W. L. The effects of father-absence on Norwegian boys and girls. *J. abnorm. soc. Psychol.*, 1958, **59**, 258–262.

MACCOBY, E. E. Role taking in childhood and its consequences for social learning. *Child Developm.*, 1959, **30**, 239–252.

MACCOBY, E. E. & WILSON, W. C. Identification and observational learning from films. *J. abnorm. soc. Psychol.*, 1957, **55**, 76–87.

McCANDLESS, B. R., BILOUS, C. B., & BENNETT, H. L. Peer popularity and dependence on adults in preschool age socialization. *Child Developm.*, 1961, **32**, 511–518.

McDAVID, J. W. Imitative behavior in preschool children. *Psychol. Monogr.*, 1959, **73**, No. 486.

MELLONE, M. A. A factorial study of picture tests for young children. *Brit. J. Psychol.*, 1944, **35**, 9–16.

MILTON, G. A. Five studies of the relation between sex role identification and achievement in problem solving. Technical Report No. 3, Dept. of Indust. Admin., Dept. of Psychol., Yale Univ., December, 1958.

MOWRER, O. H. Identification: a link between learning theory and psychotherapy. In *Learning theory and personality dynamics.* New York: Ronald Press, 1950. Pp. 573–616.

MUSSEN, P. H. Some antecedents and consequents of masculine sex-typing in adolescent boys. *Psychol. Monogr.*, 1961, **75**, No. 2 (Whole No. 506).

MUSSEN, P. H. Long-term consequents of masculinity of interests in adolescence. *J. consult. Psychol.*, 1962, **26**, 435–440.

MUSSEN, P. H. & DISTLER, L. Masculinity, identification, and father-son relationships. *J. abnorm. soc. Psychol.*, 1959, **59**, 350–356.

MUSSEN, P. H. & JONES, M. C. Self-conceptions, motivations, and interpersonal attitudes of late and early maturing boys. *Child Developm.*, 1957, **28**, 243–256.

MUSSEN, P. H. & JONES, M. C. The behavior inferred motivations of late and early maturing boys. *Child Developm.*, 1958, **29**, 61–67.

MUSTE, M. J. & SHARPE, D. F. Some influential factors in the determination of aggressive behavior in preschool children. *Child Developm.*, 1947, **18**, 11–28.

NASH, H. Assignment of gender to body regions. *J. genet. Psychol.*, 1958, **92**, 113–115.

NYE, F. I. & HOFFMAN, L. W. *The employed mother in America.* Chicago: Rand McNally, 1963.

PARSONS, T. Age and sex in the social structure of the United States. In C. Kluckhohn & H. A. Murray (Eds.), *Personality in nature, society and culture.* New York: Knopf, 1948. Pp. 269–281.

PARSONS, T. Family structures and the socialization of the child. In T. Parsons & R. F. Bales (Eds.), *Family, socialization and interaction process.* Glencoe, Ill.: Free Press, 1955.

PAYNE, D. E. & MUSSEN, P. H. Parent-child relations and father identification among adolescent boys. *J. abnorm. soc. Psychol.*, 1956, **52**, 358–362.

PINTLER, M. H., PHILLIPS, R., & SEARS, R. R. Sex differences in the projective doll play of preschool children. *J. Psychol.*, 1946, **21**, 73–80.

POPE, B. Socioeconomic contrasts in children's peer culture prestige values. *Genet. Psychol. Monogr.*, 1953, **48**, 157–220.

RABBAN, M. Sex-role identification in young children in two diverse social groups. *Genet. Psychol. Monogr.*, 1950, **42**, 81–158.

ROSENBERG, B. G. & SUTTON-SMITH, B. A revised conception of masculine-feminine differences in play activities. *J. genet. Psychol.*, 1960, **96**, 165–170.

SANFORD, R. N. The dynamics of identification. *Psychol. Rev.*, 1955, **62**, 106–117.

SANFORD, R. N., ADKINS, M. M., MILLER, R. B., & COBB, E. A., *et al.*, Physique, personality and scholarship: a cooperative study of school children. *Monogr. Soc. Res. Child Developm.*, 1943, **8**, No. 1, Serial No. 34.

SEARS, P. S. Doll play aggression in normal young children: influence of sex, age, sibling status, father's absence. *Psychol. Monogr.*, 1951, **65**, No. 6.

SEARS, R. R. Identification as a form of behavior development. In D. B. Harris (Ed.), *The concept of development.* Minneapolis: Univ. Minnesota Press, 1957. Pp. 149–161.

SEARS, R. R. Relation of early socialization experiences to aggression in middle childhood. *J. abnorm. soc. Psychol.*, 1961, **63**, 466–492.

SEARS, R. R., MACCOBY, E. E., & LEVIN, H. *Patterns of child rearing.* Evanston, Ill.: Row, Peterson, 1957.

SEARS, R. R., PINTLER, M. H., & SEARS, P. S. Effect of father separation on preschool children's doll play aggression. *Child Developm.*, 1946, **17**, 219–243.

SEARS, R. R., WHITING, J., NOWLIS, V., & SEARS, P. S. Some child-rearing antecedents of aggression and dependency in young children. *Genet. Psychol. Monogr.*, 1953, **47**, 135–234.

SIEGEL, A. E., STOLZ, L. M., HITCHCOCK, A. E., & ADAMSON, J. Dependence and independence in the children of working mothers. *Child Developm.*, 1959, **30**, 533–546.

SMITH, M. E. The influence of age, sex, and situation on the frequency of form and function of questions asked by preschool children. *Child Developm.*, 1933, **3**, 201–213.

STONE, C. P. & BARKER, R. G. The attitudes and interests of premenarcheal and postmenarcheal girls. *J. genet. Psychol.*, 1939, **54**, 27–71.

SWINEFORD, F. A study of factor analysis: the nature of the general, verbal, and spatial bi-factors. *Supp. Educ. Monogr.*, 1948, No. 67.

TERMAN, L. M. & MILES, C. C. *Sex and personality studies in masculinity and femininity.* New York: McGraw-Hill, 1936.

TUDDENHAM, R. D. Studies in reputation: III. Correlates of popularity among elementary school children. *J. educ. Psychol.*, 1951, **42**, 257–276.

TYLER, L. E. *The psychology of human differences*. New York: Appleton-Century-Crofts, 1947.

VANCE, T. F. & McCALL, L. T. Children's preference among play materials as determined by the method of paired comparisons of pictures. *Child Developm.*, 1934, **5**, 267–277.

WALTERS, J., PEARCE, D., & DAHMS, L. Affectional and aggressive behavior of preschool children. *Child Developm.*, 1957, **28**, 15–26.

WHITEHOUSE, E. Norms for certain aspects of the Thematic Apperception Test on a group of nine- and ten-year-old children. *Personality*, 1949, **1**, 12–15.

WHITING, J. W. M. Resource mediation and learning by identification. In I. Iscoe & H. W. Stevenson (Eds.), *Personality development in children*. Austin: Univ. Texas Press, 1960. Pp. 112–126.

WINKER, J. B. Age trends and sex differences in the wishes, identifications, activities and fears of children. *Child Developm.*, 1949, **20**, 191–200.

Consequences of Different Kinds of Parental Discipline[1]

WESLEY C. BECKER

University of Illinois

ACTIVE INTEREST by social scientists in the consequences of disciplinary techniques can be traced to three main influences in the early part of this century: the focus on learning processes by the early functional and behavioristic psychologists, the developmental focus of psychoanalytic theory, and the repeated findings in clinical practice of a high incidence of atypical disciplinary practices in the backgrounds of problem children and adults. The delinquency studies during the 1910's and 1920's were the first to provide some semblance of systematic information on the effects of discipline. The 1930's saw a sharp increase of research in this area from many points of view. David Levy and Helen Witmer fostered research on many aspects of parent behavior relevant to discipline. Longitudinal studies were initiated at the University of California and the Fels Research Institute. Persons in many centers began to explore the correlates of strictness, permissiveness, consistency, and type of reinforcement. Research designs were generally weak and conclusions not especially exciting, but progress was slowly being made. Kurt Lewin's work, particularly the group atmosphere studies, had considerable influence in supporting a general shift (already in process) toward more permissive approaches to child training. By the 1940's, the behavior theorists (particularly at Iowa and Yale) had focused their attention on the consequences of child-rearing practices. Experimental manipulations were mixed with naturalistic observations under the guidance of theory. New insights were gained and a better realization of the complexities was engendered. The growth of computers in the 1950's led to the use of larger samples and more complex statistical procedures in attempting to pull apart the multiple influences. During this period, the

[1] The author wishes to express his gratitude to Barbara Anderson for her diligent assistance in obtaining references and preparing the manuscript, to Gordon Paul, Leigh Triandis, and especially Martin Hoffman for their helpful comments on the manuscript, and to the National Institute of Mental Health whose support of our research on parents and children (Grant M-4881) made this undertaking possible.

research community belatedly acknowledged that father was a parent, too, by including him in research. In the present decade, the fruits of the longitudinal studies initiated in the early 1930's are beginning to appear. Early reports suggest an array of additional complications in the interactions of age and sex variables which cross-sectional research has missed. Understanding these interactions should keep us busy for some time. The tempo of active research on the consequences of child-rearing practices continues to accelerate at a phenomenal rate. The next ten years should produce an output volume far in excess of that achieved in the past sixty years.

Because of the nature of this review, an attempt has been made to avoid encumbering the discussion with technical issues, particularly those associated with measurement problems. In trying to formulate generalizations from the empirical research, we have relied heavily (but not exclusively) on a convergence of implications from several studies. Perhaps it is unnecessary to say that no study in this complex area can be considered definitive. However, some tentative generalizations are possible when several studies using different methods and populations produce congruent findings. It should also be noted that no attention has been given in this review to the possible interaction of genetically based temperamental characteristics with the disciplinary practices. From animal research, there is every reason to believe that such interactions are important, but it may be another twenty years before implications for the human situation are clarified even in a preliminary way.

SOCIAL CLASS, SEX, AND CHILD'S AGE

Children grow up in different social and economic circumstances, and in families of varying role structure. How these various aspects of the social context of discipline affect the interpretation and generality of findings is as yet very poorly understood. At this point, a number of studies have demonstrated mean differences in the frequency and/or intensity with which different kinds of discipline are used in middle and working classes, by mothers or by fathers, with boys or with girls. A brief overview of some of the more important differences may help to temper the broader generalizations to be presented later.

Social Class

Social class is most typically defined in terms of the prestige level of the father's occupation. Systematic research has focused primarily on the middle class (professionals, proprietors, managers, and white-collar workers), and the working class (skilled manual workers with steady jobs). Little attention has been paid to the upper classes or to the "down and outers." Needless to say, these are gross categories with wide individual differences in social and economic conditions within each. Generally, the research has shown that middle-class parents provide more warmth and are more likely to use reasoning, isolation, show of disappointment, or guilt-arousing appeals in disciplining the child. They are also likely to be more permissive about demands for attention from the child, sex behavior, aggression to parent, table manners, neatness and orderliness, noise, bedtime rules, and general obedience. Working-class parents are more likely to use ridicule, shouting, or physical punishment in disciplining the child, and to be generally more restrictive (Bronfenbrenner, 1958; Kohn, 1963; Kohn and Carroll, 1960; Miller and Swanson, 1960; Sears, Maccoby, and Levin, 1957).

Attempts to account for these social class differences have called attention to the higher intelligence and education of middle-class parents, and the fact that they are more exposed to the current expert opinion through their readings on child rearing (Bronfenbrenner, 1958). Kohn (1963) has suggested that the life conditions of the "classes" and the resulting parental values may provide a more basic explanation. Working-class parental values center more on conformity to external proscriptions (as do their occupational roles), while middle-class parental values center more on self-direction. Kohn believes that it is this value orientation which leads middle-class parents to seek out and accept expert opinion congruent with their goals.

A little study by Roy (1950) serves to illustrate that there may be a number of environmental factors in the structure of daily living which in part condition disciplinary practices. She found a direct increase in the permissiveness of child-rearing attitudes as the number of rooms in the house increased. The number of children, their closeness to each other, physical space, safeness of the neighborhood, adequacy of sanitation, and a series of other factors, in addition to values conditioned by occupational circumstances or educational experiences, are possibly relevant to understanding social class differences in disciplinary practices.

Sex of Parent—Sex of Child

It will be noted throughout this review that results will sometimes be significant for one sex and not the other, or for one parent and not the other. It is becoming more and more apparent that separate evaluations of developmental issues for the sex groups (parent and child) may be needed to encompass fully the individual differences. A number of studies, largely based on children's reports, have revealed differences in the parent-child interaction patterns for sex groups (Droppleman and Schaefer, 1961; Emmerich, 1959a,b; Finch, 1955; Gardner, 1947; Hawkes, Burchinal, and Gardner, 1957; Kagan, 1956; Kagan and Lemkin, 1960; Kagan, Hosken, and Watson, 1961; Sears et al., 1957; Tasch, 1952). Some of the more salient findings are that: (a) mother is usually seen as more loving and nurturant than father; (b) father is perceived as being stricter; (c) mothers are viewed as using more psychological control, especially with girls; (d) fathers are viewed as using more physical punishment, especially with boys; (e) the opposite-sexed parent is rated as more likely to grant autonomy than the same-sexed parent; (f) boys feel they get punished more than other members of the family; (g) the same-sexed parent is seen as being less benevolent and more frustrating, particularly by older children; and (h) father is viewed as more fear-arousing.

It is reasonable to expect that differences in the agent, level, and mode of treatment for boys and girls would lead to different consequences. The greater nurturance and psychological discipline given to girls may partly account for the typical findings of better socialization of girls than boys. To date, only a small beginning in research on these issues has been undertaken. A few illustrations of some of the possibilities will be given later.

Finally, we should note that age differences markedly affect disciplinary practices, and possibly their consequences. Again, a few illustrations of age effects will be provided in this review, although by and large systematic study of this variable has not been undertaken. For the most part, the generalizations discussed in subsequent sections of this review are those which have been supported in studies of children at several age levels.

THE "GROSS ANATOMY" OF PARENT BEHAVIOR

To develop a reasoned understanding of the research on discipline, it is also important to realize that discipline is but a part of the interaction that occurs between parent and child. The line between discipline and other aspects of parent behavior which influence the child (particularly affectional relations) is difficult to determine from the naturalistic research literature. However, by studying the ways in which various aspects of parent behavior relate to each other, we stand a better chance of gaining some perspective on the problem and are in a better position to know when certain findings may be confounded by the effects of other variables. In recent years, a number of investigators have used a method of analyzing correlations, called factor analysis, in an attempt to simplify the conceptualization of relations between various parent behaviors. Factor analysis is a tool which can help to determine a minimum number of orthogonal dimensions necessary to account for the empirical correlations among variables. (Orthogonal dimensions are dimensions which are uncorrelated with each other, or, in the language of plane geometry, perpendicular to each other.) For example, in Figure 1, rather than thinking in terms of 14 different aspects of maternal behavior, factor analysis would suggest that it might be more reasonable to think of two dimensions of maternal behavior—Love versus Hostility and Control versus Autonomy. *Within this framework*, a democratic mother would be one who is both loving and autonomy granting, while a protective mother is loving and controlling. A considerable economy in conceptualization can thus be achieved.

The model presented in Figure 1 was developed by Schaefer (1959, 1961) to summarize a number of studies which suggest that most of the concepts developed over the past two decades to describe types of parents can be reduced to a combination of two main dimensional concepts. It is important to realize that these factor concepts, while derived from empirical analysis,

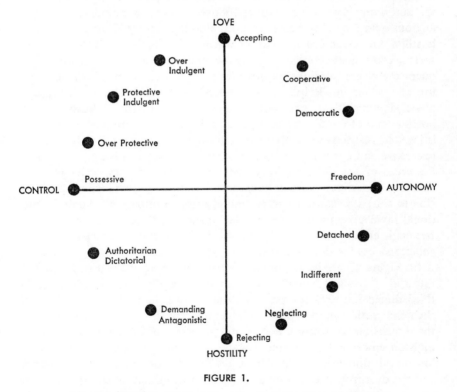

FIGURE 1.

Schaefer's (1959) Hypothetical Circumplex Model for Maternal Behavior

Reproduced with permission from *J. abnorm. soc. Psychol.*, 1959, **59,** 226–235.

are *not necessarily* of any greater scientific value than the typological concepts which preceded them. They certainly are not any more *real*. Like any other construct created in the mind of man, they are created to help achieve a better understanding of the phenomena under study, and if they achieve this goal, can be considered useful.

In recent years, several studies have correlated a wide range of variables pertaining to discipline as well as other aspects of parent behavior (Baldwin, Kalhorn, and Breese, 1945; Becker *et al.*, 1959; Becker *et al.*, 1962; Roff, 1949; Sears *et al.*, 1957; Takala, Nummenmaa, and Kauranne, 1960). During the past year, this author has attempted to tie these studies together through a series of factor analyses. The results of this work suggest that it may be important to consider at least three general dimensions in looking at parent behavior. Figure 2 provides a graphic representation of the three-dimensional model generated from the series of factor analyses. This alternative model differs from Schaefer's in that we have subdivided his control vs. autonomy dimension into restrictiveness versus permissiveness and anxious-emotional involvement versus calm-detachment. The warmth versus hostility dimension is defined at the warm end by variables of the following sort: accepting, affectionate, approving, understanding, child-centered, frequent use of explanations, positive response to dependency behavior, high use of reasons in discipline, high use of praise in discipline, low use of physical punishment, and (for mothers) low criticism of husband. The hostility end of the dimension would be defined by the opposite characteristics. The restrictiveness versus permissiveness dimension is defined at the restrictive end by: many restrictions and strict enforcement of demands in the areas of sex play, modesty behavior, table manners, toilet training, neatness, orderliness, care of household furniture, noise, obedience, aggression to sibs, aggression to peers, and aggression to parents. Anxious emotional involvement versus calm-detachment is defined at the anxious end by: high emotionality in relation to child, babying, protectiveness, and solicitousness for the child's welfare.

In Figure 2 we have attempted to show how the various concepts referring to types of parents fit into the model and point to the need for the third dimension to encompass important distinctions. For example, both the democratic parent and the indulgent parent (by definition) are high on the dimensions of warmth and permissiveness, but the indulgent parent is high on emotional involvement while the democratic parent tends to be low on this dimension (calm-detached). Both the organized-effective parent and the overprotective parent are high on warmth and restrictiveness, but the overprotective parent again shows more emotional involvement than the organized-effective parent. The argument can be thus carried around

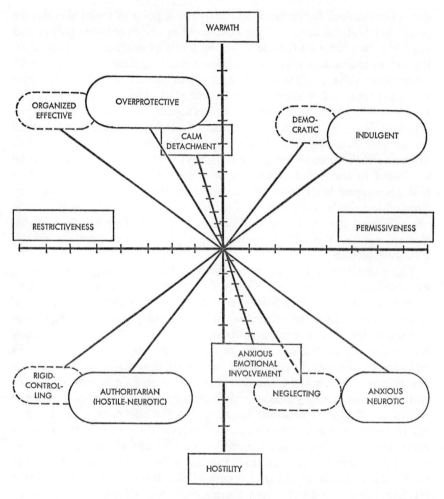

FIGURE 2.

Becker's Hypothetical Model for Parental Behavior

the model, showing how the typical concepts for types of parents can be thought of as being defined by various combinations of three dimensions of parent behavior.

Relevance for Discipline Research

In addition to providing a conceptual framework which may be useful in integrating research, the results of these factor analytic studies carry more direct implications for research on discipline. A point of major significance is the fact that the nature of the affectional relations between parent and child is correlated with the use of certain kinds of discipline. In particular, the use of praise and reasons has been repeatedly found associated with warmth variables, and the use of physical punishment with hostility variables (Bandura and Walters, 1959; Becker *et al.*, 1962; Sears *et al.*, 1957; Unger, 1960, 1962). This point is of significance, since (a) there is a considerable body of research where use of praise, reasons, and physical punishment has played an important role in the definition of types of discipline without considering the possibility that the results could also be attributed to correlated differences in affectional relations, and (b) other findings suggest both kinds of variables—discipline and affectional relations—have similar consequences for child behavior. Thus it is necessary to exercise great care in trying to disentangle special effects of type of discipline, per se. We will document these points more carefully in the following section.

The examination of the more global relations among child rearing variables also leads to a conclusion that there is a general dimension of restrictiveness versus permissiveness in dealing with children which is relatively independent of affectional relations. By independent, we mean that *on the average* restrictive (or permissive) parents are neither predominantly hostile nor warm, but can show all degrees of warmth and hostility. In addition to pointing to a possibly important dimension to examine for consequences in the child, the fact that this dimension is independent of warmth versus hostility makes it theoretically possible to average out the effects of affectional relations in examining the effects of restrictiveness versus permissiveness. Actually, as we interpret the research, some of the more interesting implications occur when the effects of restrictiveness versus permissiveness are examined in a hostile or warm context, rather than independently of either. Because of the absence of direct research relating emotional-involvement versus calm-detachment to disciplinary practices, this dimension is not elaborated later in this paper.

LOVE-ORIENTED AND POWER-ASSERTIVE TECHNIQUES

Since 1938 there have been a large number of investigations of the consequences of discipline, which, for convenience, will be considered under the general classification of love-oriented versus power-assertive techniques. Definitions of types of discipline have varied considerably, as have the populations studied and consequent child behaviors. Love-oriented techniques have generally included positive methods, such as use of praise and reasoning; and negative methods which threaten the love relation to the parent, such as isolating the child from the parent, showing disappointment, and withdrawing love. As will be seen, some results suggest that it may be important in considering the effects on children to separate love-oriented discipline into positive and negative methods. Power-assertive techniques most typically have included physical punishment, but in some cases have been extended to include yelling, shouting, forceful commands, and verbal threats. The consequent variables in the child have focused primarily on the inhibition and expression of aggression by the child, the child's reaction to transgressions, and the child's resistance to temptation. In an overly simplified way, the research in this area may be summarized as suggesting that approaches to discipline which focus on using the love relationship with the child to shape his behavior are more likely to be correlated with internalized reactions to transgression (feelings of guilt, self-responsibility, confession) and with nonaggressive or cooperative social relations. On the other hand, power-asserting techniques in controlling the child are more likely to correlate with externalized reactions to transgression (fear of punishment, projected hostility), and with noncooperative, aggressive behaviors. The effect of type of discipline on resistance to temptation has produced highly conflicting findings.

In trying to understand the implications for child rearing of this complex body of literature, we will first look in some detail at the findings concerning aggression in the child. In these studies of aggression, the antecedent parent variables have centered largely on power-assertive techniques, although the positive love-oriented methods (praise, reasons) are also frequently involved in defining low power-assertion. It is important throughout this section for the reader to keep in mind possible variations in definitions for the parent variables from study to study.

Aggression

As part of a rather extensive study of nursery school children, Sears, Whiting, Nowlis, and Sears (1953) examined the consequences of punitiveness of mother for aggressive behavior. Punitiveness was defined largely by the degree of physical pain or discomfort generated by the mother when the child acted in an aggressive or asocial manner. Physical punishment is the key variable defining the punitive end of the scale, and use of reasons is central to the definition of the nonpunitive end of the scale. Contrary to the investigators' expectations that punishment for aggression would act to inhibit its expression, the findings were as follows. For boys, there was a positive relation between punitiveness and overt aggression in school. For girls, the relationship was curvilinear. Girls of both high and low punitive mothers showed less aggression in school than girls of moderately punitive mothers. Using 30 of these same subjects a year later and the same ratings of maternal punitiveness, Hollenberg and Sperry (1951) found a direct *positive relation* between maternal punitiveness and aggression in doll play for both boys and girls. This suggests that high maternal punitiveness had actually produced as strong an aggressive reaction in girls as in boys, but that for some reason, its expression was inhibited in the schoolroom situation.

Becker and his colleagues (1962) reproduced almost exactly the findings relating punitiveness of mother to teacher's ratings of aggression in children. Boys' school aggression was directly related to mothers' use of physical punishment (and low use of reasoning), while girls' aggression showed the curvilinear relation. However, *home* ratings of aggression (averaged parent ratings) showed direct positive relations to mothers' punitiveness for both boys and girls. Similar relations to home ratings are reported by Eron, Banta, Walder, and Laulicht (1961) and by Sears and associates (1957). If high punitiveness is producing the inhibition of aggression for girls at school, one would have expected even more evidence of inhibition of aggression in the presence of the punitive agent. This apparently was not the case. Further perplexing effects were found when Becker *et al.* (1962) examined the relationship of fathers' punitiveness to child aggression. For girls, positive linear relations are found at school and home; while for boys, more aggression is found when father is either high or low in punitiveness. Closer examination of the data suggested that the perplexing results might be a product of the failure to consider the frustrating effects of *both parents.* When hostility and punitiveness for both parents were summated, approximately linear relations to child aggression were found for both boys and girls at home, and boys at school. For girls at school, as the summated index increased, aggression increased but quickly reached an asymtote; it is as if sex-role appropriateness set a limit on the expression of aggression for girls outside of the home. (See Kagan and Moss, 1962.) In general, these results suggest a positive relation between parental power-assertion and child aggression, although the aggressive effects are not apparent in all situations and the effect of type of discipline has not been untangled from other sources of frustration.

Hoffman (1960) provides further evidence on the relation between a punitive approach to discipline and child aggression. Parents' reports of a full day's interaction with their nursery school child were coded for evidence of *initial unqualified power-assertion* and *reactive unqualified power-assertion.* The first variable reflects the frequency with which the initial attempts to control the child consist of direct commands, threats, material deprivations, and physical force (without explanation), and the second variable reflects the frequency with which the same procedures are used when first attempts to gain compliance fail. Strong relations were found between mothers' (but not fathers') reactive power-assertion and the child's hostility toward other children, power-assertion to other children, resistance to influence by other children, and resistance to influence by teacher. Hoffman speculates that the failure to find consistent relations between initial power-assertion and child aggression may be due to the fact that the parents' power-assertion has more lasting effects when used in situations of heightened conflict and involvement, that is, when the child fails to comply to the initial influence procedure.

Beverly Allinsmith (1960) extended the generality of findings of this sort to a group of junior high school boys. Six story beginnings were used where a loved or feared older person was unfair or was unintentionally a source of frustration. The responses to story beginnings were classified according to the directness of the aggression expressed. When physical punishment was the predominant form of discipline by mother, the boys were more likely to express aggression directly. When psychological discipline (appeals to pride and guilt, expressions of disappointment, shaming) predominated, aggression was likely to be expressed indirectly (or not at all). These relations held for both middle-class and working-class samples, even though psychological discipline was more likely to be used by middle-class mothers and physical punishment by working-class mothers. Using peer judgments, it was also found that boys who received physical punishment were more likely to respond to frustrations from their teachers by getting mad or talking back.

A cross-cultural study by Lambert, Triandis, and Wolf (1959) also supports a relationship between the use of power-assertive techniques and aggression. Where more pain-generating punishment is used in child rearing, the gods were perceived primarily as aggressive rather than benevolent. The perceptions of the gods in this study are assumed to be a projective manifestation of emotional attitudes generated by the child-rearing practices.

The aforementioned studies, while containing some unresolved complexities, suggest that one "consequence" of a punitive approach to discipline is aggression. In trying to understand the meaning of this relationship, we are faced with difficulties. First, a series of studies (too numerous to list) provide rather overwhelming evidence that hostile parents have aggressive children. Earlier we noted that hostile parents also tend to use more physical punishment and less reasoning and praise. We are faced with a situation where certain techniques of discipline and certain emotional attitudes of the parent tend to occur jointly and have similar consequences for the child. Thus we do not know for sure that the obtained relation between physical punishment and aggression is primarily a result of the kind of discipline used, a joint effect of hostility and type of punishment, or primarily an effect of the parents' hostility. If we could find enough warm parents who relied primarily on physical punishment, or enough hostile parents who were not physically punitive, it might be possible to disentangle such effects. The only direct evidence on this question is not very conclusive. Sears and associates (1957) used partial correlations to show that maternal coldness and physical punishment contributed about equally to aggression in the child. There is a need for research to give this question closer consideration.

Given the empirical association between physical punishment (separately or in combination with hostility) and child aggression, how might this relation be accounted for? Three hypotheses stand out in the literature. The first has already been mentioned and assumes that physical punishment is frustrating and thus instigates anger. The second notes that the physically punitive parent is setting a model of aggressive behavior for the child, which in effect sanctions aggression as well as showing the child how to be aggressive. The third postulates a direct reinforcement of aggression behavior by hostile-punitive parents.

Direct evidence for the first hypothesis has not been collected, even though it is the leading hypothesis to account for the relation between power-assertive methods and aggression in the child. The authors of *Frustration and Aggression* (Dollard *et al.*, 1939, p. 40) were the first to formulate explicitly such a relationship on the basis of observational evidence. They would put it this way: the punishment of acts of direct aggression serves as additional frustration which instigates aggression against the punishing agent. It is easy to understand why research with children has not attempted to test this proposition through direct experimental manipulation. At present, the correlational evidence presented in this section provides the strongest support for this hypothesis.

The possible importance of modeling effects has been carefully explored in a series of laboratory experiments by Bandura (1962). The models provided the child have been demonstrated to be very potent in shaping the child's behavior. For example, in one study (Bandura, Ross, and Ross, 1961), a group of nursery school children was exposed to aggressive adult models, while another group was exposed to subdued and nonaggressive models. A control group was not exposed to any model. The children were then mildly frustrated and tested for the amount of imitative (behavior like that of the model) and nonimitative aggressive behavior in a new setting with the model absent. The children who had been exposed to an aggressive model displayed significantly more aggression than the control group, while those exposed to a passive model displayed significantly less aggression than the control group. The children in the aggressive-model condition also showed, with a high frequency, the specific kinds of aggressive responses used by the model. These responses occurred very rarely in the other groups. The tenability of the modeling hypothesis is strengthened by findings such as these, but these studies do not tell just how important modeling is in the real life situation. Some naturalistic studies are a little more helpful on this point. McCord, McCord, and Zola (1959) found that boys with deviant parental models were more likely to participate in criminal activities. This effect of models was over and above that contributed by the hostility or warmth of the parent-child interaction. In a subsequent study of aggression (McCord, McCord, and Howard, 1961), it was found that parental deviance (aggression, escapism, or an eccentric role in the family) correlated with aggression in boys, but an aggressive model by itself did not. They suggest that the absence of a model of inner control was common in the background of aggressive children. The findings by Hoffman (1960) discussed previously also point to a modeling effect. Children with power-assertive mothers were more likely to use power-assertive techniques in attempting to influence other children. In general, the importance of modeling in mediating aggression in children has been quite well supported by the evidence.

The possibility of a direct reward of aggression by power-assertive parents has not been clearly established. In a study of aggressive and withdrawn boys, Bandura (1960) found that mothers of the aggressive boys, while quite punitive when aggression was expressed toward them, were more permissive than mothers of inhibited boys when the aggression was expressed toward peers or siblings. The findings for fathers of aggressive boys, however, indicated that they were more punitive for aggression toward parents, as well as *less* permissive of aggression to peers. In our own work (Becker *et al.*, 1962), we have found that when mother is high in use of physical punishment, she is also likely to insist that her children fight for their rights with other children. As will be seen in the section on permissiveness, it is clear that implicit or direct reward for aggression increases its expression. However, the evidence is not clear in demonstrating that this hypothesis can account for the positive relation between power-assertive methods and child aggression.

Power-assertive discipline and the inhibition of aggression. Laboratory studies of the effects of punishment on animals have rather consistently shown that punishment will inhibit a strongly motivated behavior by arousing anxiety (Skinner, 1938; Estes, 1944). There is some evidence to suggest that inhibition also takes place in the naturalistic setting as a consequence of the consistent use of punitive techniques over a period of time. In a follow-up of his kindergarten study, R. R. Sears (1961) found that early punishment by mother, which at the age of five was positively associated with aggression in the home, lost this association with open aggression by age twelve and tended to relate to inhibited or deflected forms of aggression (prosocial aggression, for example, "When a person has broken a rule, he should be punished for it," and self-aggression). In a similar vein, McCord and associates (1959) found the lowest crime rates to occur where both parents were consistently punitive during the early years. Assuming low crime rates among these boys to imply that they tended to be less aggressive and more inhibited, these results support Sears in suggesting that given enough time or consistency of application, power-assertive approaches to discipline do appear capable of promoting inhibition of aggressive behavior.

Reactions to Transgressions

Several studies have produced suggestive relations between love-oriented disciplines and signs of guilt, or acceptance of self-responsibility in reaction to transgressions. In a cross-cultural study, Whiting and Child (1953) rated the prevalence of use of love-oriented techniques of discipline (use of praise, isolation, withdrawal of love) in a variety of different cultures. They then evaluated the degree to which responsibility for cause of illness was attributed to the individual's own behavior, in order to obtain a projective index of level of guilt for each culture. Higher guilt scores were found for cultures where love-oriented techniques predominated. W. Allinsmith (1960) provides evidence that middle-class mothers of junior high boys who used predominantly psychological punishment (appeals to pride and guilt, expressions of disappointment, shaming), in contrast to physical punishment, had boys who manifested greater guilt on a story completion test. The relationship was not found to hold for lower-class families. In a later study with middle-class college students (Allinsmith and Greening, 1955), it was found that male students who reported greater use of psychological discipline by their parents were found to have higher guilt-over-aggression scores on a story completion test than subjects whose parents used physical punishment. The female subjects in their sample showed only a slight relationship in the same direction. The authors point out that this difference may be due to the fact that the story situation was more appropriate for boys. Similar results were obtained in Heinicke's (1953) study of five-year-old boys. His measure of guilt was based on the boys' responses to interview questions dealing with problems of right and wrong, and how they would react when they had done something wrong. Frequent use of praise and infrequent use of physical punishment and isolation related to high guilt. Expression of affection toward the child also was positively related to guilt reactions in the child.

Aronfreed (1961) examined post-transgression behavior in terms of whether it was motivated by internal or external forces. Using incomplete stories in which the central figure commits an aggressive act, the responses of a group of sixth-grade children were coded in terms of whether the central figure sought to correct the situation, accepted responsibility for his action, and did not focus on external punishment; or whether the focus was on externally motivated actions and punitive consequences. Techniques of discipline were classified into *induction* and *sensitization* categories on the basis of parent interviews. Induction techniques are those which are capable of arousing unpleasant-feeling reactions in the child about his misbehavior, independently of external threat, and which encourage the child to accept responsibility for his actions. Some examples are insisting on restitution or apology, asking why he did that, explaining to the child why it was wrong, or not punishing if the child shows recognition that he has done wrong. Sensitization techniques are those aimed only at inhibiting the child's unacceptable behavior by focusing on the painful consequences. Physical punishment, yelling, shouting, and so on, would be included here. The high similarity to the love-oriented versus power-assertive groupings is apparent. As expected, use of induction techniques was positively related to internally motivated, self-corrective actions, while use of sensitization techniques was related to externally motivated actions and punitive consequences.

A highly similar result was obtained by Hoffman and Saltzstein (1960). Children's moral judgments about violations were classified as expressing an internalized standard or merely the fear of detection and punishment. The boys who tended to have internalized standards reported that their mothers were less likely to use force, threat of force, deprivation, or direct commands (power-assertive techniques) in disciplining them, and that mothers were more likely to stress how the child's misbehavior hurt the parent. Mothers of internalizers were also reported to be more affectionate. Internalization in girls was related only to use of rational appeals by father, and the absence of threats by the mother to have father discipline them. Internalized subjects of both sexes gave more guilt responses in a story completion test.

Two studies suggest that the negative love-oriented disciplines (withdrawal of love, expressions of disappointment, and the like) relate to signs of conscience only when mother has a warm relation with the child. Using their full sample, Sears and associates (1957) found no correlation between withdrawal of love and conscience. However, when only warm mothers were considered, use of withdrawal of love related positively to signs of conscience. Similar results were reported by LeVine (1961). Withdrawal of love was positively associated with remorse after transgression only when warm mothers were considered. It might also be noted that in the study by Allinsmith reported earlier, his definition of psychological discipline involved primarily negative love-oriented methods (appeals to pride and guilt, expressions of disappointment, shaming). His finding that psychological discipline related to guilt only for middle-class mothers might possibly be attributed to a frequently obtained difference in warmth between the middle-class and working-class families. The fact that negative love-oriented techniques seem to be effective primarily where there is love to lose makes good sense.

It is of interest that LeVine also found use of reasoning to be the best predictor of confession and remorse after transgression. Sears and associates (1957) also found use of reasons and praise (the positive love-oriented techniques as we have classified them) to be the best predictors of signs of conscience (along with low physical punishment). In addition, Burton, Maccoby, and Allinsmith (1961) fully replicated these findings, as well as the relationship between warmth and signs of conscience. There is a strong suspicion from the patterning of the evidence, that the positive love-oriented techniques (praise, reasons) which are highly correlated with warmth variables, need to be considered separately from the negative love-oriented methods (withdrawal of love, isolation, expressions of disappointment). The latter relate to guilt indices primarily when there is love to lose.

Unger (1960, 1962) made an attempt to disentangle the effects of warmth versus hostility and type of discipline with respect to guilt-after-transgression. He related a projective measure of guilt-after-transgression to psychological (praise, reasons) versus physical punishment and to the warmth versus hostility of each parent. Evaluations of parent behavior were obtained from the questionnaire responses of sixth-grade children. The effects of type of discipline were examined separately for parents high and low in warmth. The warmth of each parent was found to have the *major* influence on guilt scores, but type of discipline showed significant effects (in the expected direction) for mothers low in warmth and fathers high in warmth. Also, the trend for mothers high in warmth was in the expected direction. Type of discipline had no effect for fathers low in warmth. LeVine (1961) provides additional evidence for an effect of reasoning, independent of warmth. When the mothers in her study were divided into warm and cold groups, the relationship of reasoning to confession and remorse remained for each group.

In summary, these various studies suggest that internalized reactions to transgression in the form of guilt or acceptance of self-responsibility for misdeed are more likely to occur when the parent is warm and uses techniques of discipline which utilize the love relations to the parent for their effects. The use of praise and reasoning appears to have the most predictable effects across studies, while love-withdrawing methods seem effective primarily when the parent is high in warmth.

A number of hypotheses have been proposed to help account for the empirical relations. The importance of anxiety over displeasing the parent has been stressed by many investigators since Freud originally emphasized it (1933). The fact that love-withdrawing methods seem to be more effective when there is more love to lose adds some support to this notion. However, research to date has not pinned down this variable in a way to demonstrate its explicit role. A modeling effect has also been hypothesized as being important. The parent using love-oriented discipline provides a model of self-restraint in dealing with the child. But whether the parent also provides a model of self-criticism after misdeed has not been demonstrated, though it is not unlikely. The frequent concurrence of use of reasons by the parent and internalized reactions to transgressions by the child suggests two further possibilities. First, the parent who talks and reasons with the child about his misbehavior is more likely to provide the child with a clear understanding of what he did wrong, so that the anxiety about misbehavior is connected to the right cues. Secondly, as Aronfreed has suggested, explanations and reasons provide the child with internal resources for evaluation of his own behavior; that is, the child gains explicit training in making moral judgments.

Both Aronfreed and Hill have taken a closer look at the differences in learning conditions likely to be present when love-oriented or power-assertive techniques are used. Hill (1960) proposed that the love relation itself may not be the critical factor, but rather the reinforcement by the parent of explicit reactions from the child. Love-oriented discipline is likely to continue until the child makes some symbolic renunciation of his wrong-doing. Thus self-admission and verbal recognition of wrong-doing may be reinforced by regaining parental approval and ending the punishment. Physical punishment is more likely to occur all at once and be over, and what the child does toward the end of preventing future occurrences is not related to the ending of punishment. LeVine (1961) has taken a preliminary step toward testing Hill's hypothesis. Mothers completed a questionnaire concerning the degree to which their children tended to confess and show remorse after transgression (and the degree to which the children resisted temptation). They also described their techniques of

discipline, with care being taken to have them describe the conditions leading to the ending of punishment. The mothers who continued discipline
(regardless of its nature) until the child verbalized that he was sorry were
more likely to have children who confessed wrong-doing and expressed
remorse.

Aronfreed (1963; in press; Aronfreed, Cutick, and Fagan, 1963) has developed another theoretical model to account for the learning of self-
criticism in response to transgression. Hill assumed that confession of
wrong-doing and expressions of remorse were learned because they were
reinforced by escape from punishment. Aronfreed postulates that the
criticizing responses from the parent are adopted by the child if the *parents'*
responses (rather than the child's) are associated with the termination of
anxiety induced by transgression and punishment. Thus the parents' responses become cues that punishment is over, and the child, after a transgression, can reduce his own anxiety about punishment by reproducing
these cues. Self-criticism is, then, reproducing the parent criticism which
signals the end of the anxiety. The paradigm is a general one to account for
the learning of responses generally classified as identification with the
aggressor. "After a child has had some experience with a transgression,
punishment itself may come to serve as a cue signifying the termination of
anxiety that accompanies its anticipation" (Aronfreed, 1963). Aronfreed
suggests that the occasionally obtained associations of love-oriented
discipline with signs of conscience may be due to the intertwining of withdrawal of love with a high degree of cognitive structuring (reasons) and
certain properties of the timing, rather than being a special effect of withdrawing love.

Resistance to Temptation

The consequences of love-oriented and power-assertive classifications of
discipline have also been explored in a series of studies of resistance to
temptation. In contrast to the previous group of studies, the question
focuses on what the subject does under pressure to violate his standards
rather than on his reactions after transgression. Also, in contrast to the
previous section, the results of various studies show greater inconsistencies.

MacKinnon (1938) initiated research on this question with an experimental study of cheating by college males. The subjects were asked to solve
20 problems, each on a separate page. For some of the problems they could
look at the solutions in a book on the table, but were prohibited from
looking at others. Without their knowing it, the subjects were observed
through a one-way screen. MacKinnon found that those who cheated

reported that their fathers used predominantly physically aggressive forms of punishment rather than love-oriented techniques (parental indications that they were not worthy of love, fall short of parents' ideals). Consistent with the results discussed earlier, MacKinnon also noted that violators tended to vent their anger outwardly during the frustrations of the test, while nonviolators tended to blame themselves. Also, nonviolators indicated that they would feel badly if they had violated a prohibition, while violators indicated that they would not.

Findings partially consistent with these were obtained by Allinsmith in the study cited earlier. Two story-beginnings were used where the central figures had not yet transgressed, but were tempted to do so. Resistance to temptation was assessed by whether or not the hero transgressed in the completed story. While his measure of psychological and physical discipline did not relate to resistance to temptation, the use of explained requests (reasons) rather than arbitrary demands did.

Several more recent studies have adapted the experimental paradigm used by MacKinnon for use with younger children (Burton *et al.*, 1961; Grinder, 1962; Sears, Rau, and Alpert, 1960). The test for resistance to temptation involved placing the child in a game situation where he was tempted to violate the rules to win a prize. A one-way screen was used to observe the child's behavior during the game. The trend of the findings in the Sears and Grinder studies was for resistance to temptation to relate to love-oriented (praise, reasoning, withdrawal of love) rather than physical forms of control. Burton and associates found just the opposite direction of effects; that is, higher resistance to temptation tended to be associated with use of physical punishment and scolding. In the study discussed previously, LeVine (1961) obtained findings consistent with Burton's. Higher resistance to temptation was positively associated with use of physical punishment and deprivation of reward, and negatively associated with use of reasoning.

In his recent review of research on moral development, Hoffman (1963) considered in detail some of the possible reasons for the inconsistent results in this area. Experimental temptation situations attempt to set a desire for a certain reward against a competing sanction against cheating. To measure accurately the strength of resistance to temptation one must be sure that subjects are equated in their desire for the prize. No attempts were made in these studies to control for this desire. Also, since the tasks used usually involved competition with a standard of excellence, it would be important to control for the children's achievement strivings.

Another source of difficulty may be with the theory itself. Studies of resistance to temptation have started with the expectation that the child-rearing antecedents would be similar to those obtained for guilt, since one is assumed to resist temptation in order to avoid strong guilt. As Hoffman points out, this assumption can be questioned not only by the lack of consistent empirical evidence for common parental antecedents, but also because indices of guilt and resistance to temptation have not been consistently found to be correlated with each other. MacKinnon (1938), Grinder (1962), Sears and associates (1960), and Grinder and McMichael (1963) reported a low positive relation between resistance to temptation and guilt; W. Allinsmith (1960) and Maccoby (1959) reported no relation; while Burton and associates (1961) and LeVine (1961) reported a negative relation. It seems quite possible, particularly for the young child, that the presence of guilt reactions to transgression do not necessarily imply that the child will resist temptations in order to avoid guilt. The possible reasons for this are largely speculative. Hoffman (1963) suggests that the child may lack the cognitive apparatus to discriminate relevant cues and anticipate consequences, or the child may be aware of consequences and lack the necessary controls. Those who approach the problem from a learning theory point of view have suggested that the learning of guilt in response to transgression and the learning of controls in the face of temptation involve separate problems. A guilt response to transgression is more likely to occur when the punishment follows the transgression, whereas punishment at the onset of the deviant act is more likely to tie anxiety to the preparatory responses themselves and thus serve to inhibit the deviant act. Burton, Maccoby, and Allinsmith attempted to test this hypothesis by asking the mothers in their study the following question: "Suppose you wanted him to learn not to play with something—like the TV set or matches. If you saw that he was tempted to touch it, would you stop him before he touched it or wait to see if he really played with it and *then* correct him?" (1961, p. 703). The results were contrary to the hypothesis. Allowing the child to "touch" the object and then stopping him was significantly related to resistance to temptation. The authors suspect that their results may be deceptive. They suggest that the notion of "wait till he actually plays with it" reflected the mother's waiting to be sure what the child was up to before punishing, and that in fact, their mothers did not let the child go very far with the act. Thus "wait till he actually plays with it" may have actually been punishment at the onset of the deviant act. This example serves to illustrate further some of the methodological difficulties in reaching firm conclusions in this area.

Probably the most coherent generalization we can draw from the studies of resistance to temptation is that how one reacts to misdeed is not necessarily related to whether one will resist temptation in the first place.

Summary: Love-Oriented and Power-Assertive Techniques

Power-assertive techniques of discipline tend to be used by hostile parents, and in this context, tend to promote aggression in young children, resistance to authority, power assertion to other children, and externalized reactions to transgression (fear of punishment, projected hostility). There is suggestive evidence that, in time, consistent use of power-assertive techniques leads to an inhibition of overt aggression, but the hostility generated is still detectable in the form of prosocial-aggression and self-aggression. The aggression-inducing effects of power-assertive techniques are assumed to be mediated by the following mechanisms: (a) occurring in a hostile context, power-assertion is more likely to serve as a further frustration of the child and lead to a counter-aggressive anger reaction; (b) the model of aggressive behavior set by the parent shows the child how to be aggressive as well as implicitly sanctioning it; and (c) there is also some evidence to suggest that hostile-punitive parents actually directly reinforce or encourage aggressive behaviors to others.

Love-oriented techniques of discipline tend to be used by warm parents and in this context tend to promote acceptance of self-responsibility, guilt, and related internalized reactions to transgression. Their effectiveness in promoting these behaviors are probably due to four characteristics of the parents' behavior: (a) warmth, which makes the parent important to the child and obviates the need for more severe forms of discipline to gain compliance; (b) the providing of a model of controlled behavior; (c) the providing of verbal cues (reasons) which facilitate understanding of what is expected and aid the child's development of an anticipation of consequences; and (d) certain aspects of the timing of punishment termination.

While a number of studies have attempted to relate love-oriented and power-assertive techniques to the child's ability to resist temptation, the results at present do not suggest any consistent generalizations.

RESTRICTIVE AND PERMISSIVE APPROACHES TO DISCIPLINE

The degree to which parents place demands and restrictions on the child in a broad grouping of task areas, and insist on compliance to these demands and restrictions, has been found in recent statistical analyses to form a global dimension useful in describing parent-role behavior. In the study by Sears and associates (1957), a permissiveness versus restrictiveness factor was found which included both level of restrictions and the degree of strictness in enforcing them in the areas of sex play, modesty, table manners, toilet training, neatness, orderliness, care of household furniture, noise, obedience, aggression to sibs, aggression to peers, and aggression to parents. Becker and associates (1962) replicated this factor almost exactly for mothers and for fathers of five-year-olds. The statistical evidence implies that there is a strong tendency for parents who are strict or restrictive in one area to be so in other areas of child rearing. Thus it is reasonable to conceptualize a global dimension of restrictiveness versus permissiveness and consider its possible consequences for the child. This global dimension might be thought of as reflecting the degree of control exerted over the child without specifying the way in which such control is achieved. Yet the statistical evidence also implies that there is considerable room for individual parents to be more restrictive or permissive in some areas than in others. That is, the correlations among the various child-rearing areas are not so high as to preclude some differentiation in the degree of restrictiveness or permissiveness of individual parents in their treatment of, for example, sexual behavior versus aggressive behavior, or aggression to parents versus aggression to peers. It is quite likely that a more careful examination of such differential effects will be undertaken in the near future.

A major difficulty in integrating the present research literature in this area is the wide variety of definitions which have been used. Only a few studies have used definitions which even approach the one discussed above. Generally, studies which have classified parents as dominant or submissive have used definitions which are good approximations to restrictiveness and permissiveness. A number of other terms also have some relevance for the question at hand. For example, indulgence can be thought of as a combination of permissiveness, warmth, and emotional involvement (see Figure 2); overprotectiveness as a combination of restrictiveness, warmth, and emotional involvement. Differences between indulgent and overprotective parents would presumably reflect the effects of restrictiveness versus permissiveness in a warm, emotional context. Similarly, the laxity of the neglecting parent who fails to supervise the child can be thought of as a variety of permissiveness combined with a detached hostility (rejection), and the behavior of the authoritarian parent can be considered a combination of restrictiveness, hostility, and emotional involvement. Surprisingly, when simple semantic assumptions of this sort are made, a fairly consistent picture of the consequences of restrictiveness versus permissiveness emerges.

The organization of this section is as follows. First, a few studies will be examined where the warmth or hostility of the parent is probably not seriously contributing to the results. These studies will serve to give an overview of some of the general trends. After this, the research will be grouped to bring out certain interactions of restrictiveness and permissiveness with warmth and hostility.

General Implications

Generally, the results support the common-sense supposition that restrictive discipline fosters inhibited behaviors, and permissive discipline more uninhibited behaviors. For example, in an early study in the area, Symonds (1939) compared children with dominating parents with those whose parents were submissive. Dominance was defined as the use of much control, restrictiveness, strictness, severe punishment, criticism, or excessive planning for the child's needs (overprotectiveness). Submission was defined as giving the child a great deal of freedom, acceding to the child's demands, indulging the child, being permissive, deserting and neglecting the child, and/or showing lax and inconsistent discipline. Children of dominating parents were better socialized and more courteous, obedient, neat, generous, and polite. They were also more sensitive, self-conscious, shy, and retiring. Children of submissive (permissive) parents were more disobedient, irresponsible, disorderly in the classroom, lacking in sustained attention, lacking in regular work habits, and more forward and expressive.

In her study of nursery school children, Radke (1946) provides support for the findings that children with restrictive parents (defined in terms of the amount of freedom available to the child) show inhibited (passive, non-rivalrous) and socially withdrawing (unpopular) behaviors. R. R. Sears (1961), on the other hand, provides data to support the relation between permissiveness and overtly aggressive behavior. His permissiveness factor (defined earlier), based on ratings of mother when the child was five, was positively correlated with antisocial aggression in boys at both age five and at age twelve, but not in girls. As Kagan and Moss (1962) have suggested, the sex-role sanctions against the expression of aggression in girls makes the prediction of consistent effects in the aggression area for girls a much more difficult task.

Probably one of the most significant contributions to our understanding in this area in recent years comes from the Fels longitudinal study (Kagan and Moss, 1962). It is the only available study that considers the effects of age of the child in relation to the mother's restrictiveness, and systematically explores the consequences for the child over a thirty-year period. Restrictiveness of mother was defined as the degree to which mother attempted to force the child, through punishment and threat, to adhere to her standards, and the degree to which deviations from standards were punished. Mother's restrictiveness was evaluated from all the available home observation and interview material, and averaged ratings were determined for three age periods (birth to three, three to six, and six to ten). The children were rated on a wide variety of behaviors for the same time periods, and for age ten to fourteen and as adults (by interview).

For mothers of girls, there was a high degree of consistency in restrictiveness between age periods. This consistency, as well as sex-typing goals, may account for the broader range of significant effects in girls. For boys, mothers' early restrictiveness was not related to later restrictiveness, but consistency was present after the early period (birth to three). For both boys and girls, later restrictiveness was more highly associated with maternal hostility. Restrictiveness during the first three years appeared to have lasting inhibiting effects on both boys and girls. Restricted children were more conforming, less aggressive, less dominant and competitive with peers, more dependent on adults, and showed less mastery behavior. It is of interest that in adulthood, girls who were restricted in the early years remained dependent on parents as permitted by sex-typing mores, but restricted boys did not.

Examination of the effects of maternal restrictiveness assessed when the child is between three and six years of age revealed some interesting variations in effects. For boys, fearful and dependent behaviors were present from age three to ten, but a shift occurred at adolescence to more competitive and aggressive behaviors. In adulthood, the tendency not to criticize parents remained, but was accompanied by an anger indicator (retaliation to frustration or attack). It would appear that restrictiveness at ages three to six is more likely to generate aggression, but the aggression is manifested in socially approved forms (competitiveness, indirect aggression to peers, and justifiable retaliation). These trends became clearer for boys when mothers' restrictiveness was considered for the six-to-ten-year period. At this time, both dependency behavior and aggression toward mother and peers related to restrictiveness. During adolescence, recognition seeking, fear of peer rejection, and dominance of peers all suggest an attempt to gain peer acceptance and rebellion from mothers' control. The adult indicators confirmed the presence of suppressed hostility in measures of the readiness to retaliate and ease of anger arousal.

For girls, a change appeared in the correlates of restrictiveness at the three-to-six period. The girls under the most restrictions were aggressive and not withdrawn, but low in achievement mastery and independence. Beyond this period, the aggressive elements appeared to drop out and restrictiveness led to a passive, dependent girl. But in adulthood, though one does not criticize one's mother, anger is easily aroused and justified retaliation strong. A consistent consequence in adulthood for girls of restrictive mothers was low criticism of *mother*, and for boys, low criticism of *father*.

These most interesting findings imply some complex interactions of age and sex variables. Early restrictiveness appears to have far greater inhibiting power than later restrictiveness. Restrictiveness at later ages, whether it succeeds in producing a conforming-dependent child or not, is likely to generate more hostility in the child, albeit, controlled hostility. At these later ages, the child is more likely to be aware of the "unfairness" of a restrictive parent and resent excessive control. Also at the later age, the child is more capable of retaliating with aggression, even though it is eventually inhibited. The data further imply that boys are more likely to fight against a restrictive mother successfully. It would be nice to know to what degree father enters into this successful battle.

Restrictiveness vs. Permissiveness in a Hostile Context

A proportionately large number of studies have explored the consequences of restrictiveness versus permissiveness in groups of parents who are primarily warm or hostile. Others have measured both restrictiveness versus permissiveness and some aspect of warmth versus hostility and examined the interactions of the two. In general, the studies show that permissiveness combined with hostility maximizes aggressive, poorly controlled behavior, while restrictiveness combined with hostility maximizes self-aggression, social withdrawal, and signs of internal conflict.

Parents of delinquents repeatedly have been shown to have poor affectional relations with their children and to use poor disciplinary techniques. While delinquency is not a homogeneous psychological category, one might expect differences between delinquents and nondelinquents to have some relevance for understanding the antecedents of aggressive and poorly controlled behavior. One of the earliest studies to stress the importance of parental discipline was that by Healy and Bronner (1926). Although they lacked control data, they noted a high incidence (40 per cent) of parental neglect and lack of exercise of control (lax about discipline) among 4,000 court referred delinquents. Later studies by Burt (1929), the Gluecks (1950), McCord and associates (1959), and Bandura and Walters (1959) have essentially shown that mothers of delinquents are very likely not to attempt to exert much control over their children, place few restrictions on them, and do not enforce obedience. These studies have consistently shown, however, that a relatively higher incidence of overly strict discipline occurs among fathers of delinquent boys. While fathers of delinquents on the average tend to be lax in discipline, there are some who use a brutal kind of strict control. In these families, mother is usually lax in discipline. Coupled with other findings on defective affectional relations, this evidence suggests that maximum generation of noncompliant, aggressive, and poorly controlled behavior occurs largely under lax-hostile conditions, that is, where hostility is generated and no controls are demanded from the child when he rebels.

A number of widely divergent studies of "normal" children lead to implications which are very similar to those from the delinquency studies. McCord and associates (1961) classified largely working-class mothers of boys into three levels of control (over, normal, subnormal). Overcontrol was defined as mother's insistence that the boy should be close at all times and submit completely to her direction. Normal control reflected concern with shaping the child's activities in some areas but granting freedom in others. Subnormal control reflected a neglecting or unconcerned attitude. Because lower-class parents tend to show less warmth, and the "permissive" category used was primarily neglect, we have considered these findings as fitting into the permissive-hostile group. The findings indicated that nonaggressive boys came most frequently from homes where mother was overcontrolling; assertive boys came most frequently from homes where mother used normal control; while aggressive boys came from homes with both subnormal control and overcontrol. In both this study and the delinquency studies, the occurrence of high rates of aggression or nonconformity has been associated with overly strict *and* overly permissive discipline. As we shall note later, the evidence suggests that overt aggression is likely to occur in the child with an overly strict parent only if the other parent is permissive or lax about discipline, that is, where there is one type of inconsistency (McCord *et al.* 1959, 1961). In brief, this study adds support to the notion that lax discipline can contribute to aggressiveness.

Meyers (1944) examined the effects of certain aspects of discipline under experimental conditions where the child was faced with a variety of conflicting commands from two adults. Nursery school teachers rated the parents on attitudes of rejection, dominance, submission, and overprotection. Dominance and submission were very similar in meaning to restrictiveness and permissiveness as we have used them here. Consistent with the delinquency studies, parents of the children who exhibited noncompliance in the experiment were higher on rejection and submission (hostile-lax) than other parents. Of further interest for understanding the effects of restrictiveness versus permissiveness, was the fact that parents who were both rejecting and submissive had children who were noncompliant; while parents who were rejecting and dominant had compliant children. Results of a similar nature, but focusing on aggression rather than noncompliance, were found by Sears and associates (1957). Both permissiveness for aggression to mother and punitiveness for aggression to mother were found to increase aggression, even though these two variables were negatively correlated with each other. Maximal aggression was associated with high permissiveness-high punishment (analogous to the lax-hostile condition of the delinquency studies or Meyers' submissive-rejecting condition).

Several studies suggest that more neurotic-like conflicts are generated under a restrictive-hostile condition. Although these studies are in no sense replications, their implications are consistent with each other. First, in the follow-up study mentioned earlier, R. R. Sears (1961) showed that low permissiveness-high punishment (restrictive-hostile) leads to maximum self-aggression (self-punishment, suicidal tendencies, accident proneness) for twelve-year-old boys. In an early study of self-reports of 230 graduate students, Watson (1934) related self-descriptions to the students' reports of parental discipline on a strictness vs. permissiveness dimension. Watson (1957) noted later that his definition of strictness was probably confounded with severe punishment and rejection. The way in which his students' reports fit other findings for restrictive-hostile parents supports this hunch. Students with parents in the strictest quartile reported more hatred and constraint in relations to parents, more rejection of teachers, poorer relations with classmates (more quarrels and more shyness), more unsatisfactory love affairs, more worry, anxiety, and guilt, more unhappiness and crying, and more dependence on parents. It is difficult to understand why they also reported better grades and stronger ambition, unless this represented some sort of compensatory striving for acceptance. Lewis (1954), Rosenthal, Finkelstein, Ni, and Robertson (1959), and Rosenthal, Ni, Finkelstein, and Berkwits (1962) all present evidence from clinical studies that inhibited, neurotic children tend to have more constraint or excessive control in their family backgrounds than aggressive or delinquent children. By and large, these studies suggest that the combination of restrictiveness and hostility fosters considerable resentment, with some of it being turned against the self, or, more generally, experienced as internalized turmoil and conflict.

Restrictiveness vs. Permissiveness in a Warm Context

Watson (1957) has carried out one of the few studies to investigate directly the consequences of strictness and permissiveness in intact families offering an adequate level of warmth to the child. Consistently strict and consistently permissive families were selected through nominations from parents, teachers, and social workers, and were finally screened after home interviews by social workers. Parent self-ratings and the children's ratings of their parents' discipline confirmed the classifications with a high degree of accuracy. The children were evaluated through direct observation under experimental conditions, and through projective techniques (doll play, thematic stories, and Rorschach). The results showed that children reared in a warm-permissive home were more independent (ease of assuming responsibility for own behavior), more friendly in interaction with adults (cooperation), moderately persistent in the face of an impossible task (rather than either extreme), more creative, and less hostile on projective measures. Children reared in a warm-restrictive home were more likely to be dependent, unfriendly, to be either very high or very low in persistence, less creative, and to show more fantasy hostility. The similarity of these results to the general patterning of the findings in the study by Kagan and Moss is more than striking.

Maccoby (1961) pursued another aspect of the effects of warmth and permissiveness. Using the same children followed-up by Sears at age twelve, she studied the antecedents of the tendency to enforce rules with peers. Maccoby found that parents who had been restrictive in the early years (evaluated when the child was five) had boys who were strict rule-enforcers at age twelve. Rule-enforcing boys also showed less overt aggression (teacher ratings), less misbehavior when the teacher was out of the room, and were highly motivated to do school work. On examining the interactions with warmth, she found maximum rule enforcement when mother was warm and restrictive, and the least rule enforcement when mother was warm and permissive. The results for girls were again perplexing, and suggest that we are going to have to do some different thinking about development in girls. The rule-enforcement measures for girls were associated with more misbehavior when the teacher was out of the room, and in other ways contained more aggressive rather than conforming implications. Consistent with this was the fact that mothers' punitiveness rather than restrictiveness predicted rule enforcement for girls. Maccoby's results for boys are consistent with the findings by R. R. Sears (1961) of least aggression in boys when mother was low in permissiveness and low in punitiveness (restrictive-warm), and with Meyers' (1944) findings of maximal conformity when mother was dominant and accepting (restrictive-warm).

There are a few studies to suggest that permissiveness in a warm context can also facilitate aggressive behavior, but perhaps of a different character, which might better be called social assertiveness. Baldwin (1949) related the nursery school behavior of children to home-observation ratings of mothers. Children from homes high in democracy (warmth, permissiveness, and rationality) were higher on socially outgoing behaviors of the hostile and domineering kinds as well as the friendly kind (as noted by Watson). In contrast to the aggression of children with hostile parents, however, the aggressing and bossing of children from democratic homes was quite successful and led to acceptance by the group. A somewhat related finding comes from a study by Levy (1943). When he divided his overprotective mothers into an indulgent type (warm, permissive, emotionally involved), and a dominant type (warm, restrictive, emotionally involved), he found that where mother was mainly indulgent, the child was rebellious, aggressive, disrespectful, and disobedient at home, but a model of deportment in school. Where mother was dominating, the child was more submissive, dependent, timid in school, neat, obedient, and polite. While both of these studies leave much to be desired in determining just which parental antecedents relate to the child behaviors, they both suggest the possibility that the kind of aggression which emerges from a warm-permissive environment is more easily turned on and off in response to reinforcing conditions, rather than being an uncontrolled, reflexive, emotional reaction.

Levin (1958) has suggested the possible importance of another dependent variable in thinking about the consequences of warmth and permissiveness. Levin measured the frequency with which children used adult dolls as agents of action in doll play (adult-role taking). The maximum adult-role taking occurred under the combination of warmth and permissiveness. If adult-role taking is assumed to reflect a positive modeling of the parent and the learning of adult ways of doing things, these findings are theoretically consistent with the greater independence (Watson) and achievement mastery (Kagan and Moss) noted earlier to be associated with permissiveness.

Summary: Restrictiveness vs. Permissiveness

The research literature indicates a number of consistent consequences of restrictive and permissive approaches to child training. This dimension reflects the degree to which control is exerted (or not exerted) over the child, but the manner in which control is achieved can vary considerably. The consensus of the research suggests that both restrictiveness and permissiveness entail certain risks. Restrictiveness, while fostering well-controlled, socialized behavior, tends also to lead to fearful, dependent, and submissive behaviors, a dulling of intellectual striving and inhibited hostility. Permissiveness on the other hand, while fostering outgoing, sociable, assertive behaviors and intellectual striving, tends also to lead to less persistence and increased aggressiveness.

Longitudinal analysis suggests that early restrictiveness by mother (prior to age three) leads more consistently to conforming, dependent behavior than later restrictiveness. Both boys and girls show some aggressive reactions (although of an inhibited form) to mothers' later restrictiveness.

The interactions of restrictiveness vs. permissiveness with warmth vs. hostility are particularly informative. Some of the salient findings are summarized in the accompanying table. The counter-aggression generating properties of hostility are apparent in the child of both permissive-hostile and restrictive-hostile parents. In the former, the aggression is expressed directly with little control. In the latter, the aggression is expressed in certain safe areas (with peers), but is more likely to be inhibited and turned against the self, or be revealed in manifestation of internal conflict. On theoretical grounds, the restrictive-hostile condition would be expected to produce the most defensive identification or identification with the aggressor. The many parallels between the effects of this condition with the results of the authoritarian personality studies should be apparent.

INTERACTIONS IN THE CONSEQUENCE OF WARMTH vs. HOSTILITY
AND RESTRICTIVENESS vs. PERMISSIVENESS

	Restrictiveness	*Permissiveness*
Warmth	Submissive, dependent, polite, neat, obedient (Levy) Minimal aggression (Sears) Maximum rule enforcement, boys (Maccoby) Dependent, not friendly, not creative (Watson) Maximal compliance (Meyers)	Active, socially outgoing, creative, successfully aggressive (Baldwin) Minimal rule enforcement, boys (Maccoby) Facilitates adult role taking (Levin) Minimal self-aggression, boys (Sears) Independent, friendly, creative, low projective hostility (Watson)
Hostility	"Neurotic" problems (clinical studies) More quarreling and shyness with peers (Watson) Socially withdrawn (Baldwin) Low in adult role taking (Levin) Maximal self-aggression, boys (Sears)	Delinquency (Gluecks, Bandura and Walters) Noncompliance (Meyers) Maximal aggression (Sears)

The findings for the warm-permissive condition are consistent with the recommendations of child-rearing specialists concerned with maximizing socially outgoing characteristics and individuality. The child with warm-permissive parents is socialized mainly through love, good models, reasons, and a trial-and-error learning of how his actions (which are a bit uncontrolled at times) have an impact on others.

A detailed examination of the processes by which permissiveness and restrictiveness have their effects has yet to be undertaken. A step in this direction is the experimental research on the effects of permissiveness which comes from a series of studies of doll play techniques (Hollenberg and Sperry, 1951; P. S. Sears, 1951; Yarrow, 1948). When the child's behavior is measured over a series of experimental sessions under warm-permissive interaction conditions, a general increase in a variety of response patterns is found. Such results are consistent with the common-sense notion that permissiveness serves as a generalized reinforcer for a wide range of responses, just as restrictive attitudes appear to have a generalized inhibitory effect. Future research might well address itself to a more careful examination of how breadth of control (variety of areas in which control is demanded), intensity of control, mode of control, and age of the child influence the generality of inhibited behavior in the child. The present research implies that all of these factors are important, but does not permit one to specify their relative importance. Research might also give closer consideration to the relative effectiveness of father and mother as inhibitory agents.

CONSEQUENCES OF INCONSISTENT DISCIPLINE

The concept of consistency in discipline is multifaceted and quite poorly understood, although everyone is quite ready to agree that inconsistency is *bad* for children. It is reasonable to assume that consistent behavior by the parent will increase the degree of predictability of the child's environment and lead to more stable behavior patterns. A problem arises, however, in understanding the effects of inconsistency, since inconsistency can take many forms, and research has by and large neglected to examine the effects of different types of inconsistency. Certain behaviors may be permitted at one time and not at others on a capricious basis, or because mother is present at one time and not another, or because mother's moods change from one time to another, or because one parent is present and not the other. Inconsistency might also be expected to have different effects as a function of the patterns of rewards and punishments utilized. For example, threatening punishment and not following through could have different effects from rewarding a behavior at one time and punishing it at another, or punishing at one time and doing nothing the next time. A kind of inconsistency can also arise when there is a discrepancy between what the child is rewarded for doing, what he is told to do, and what he sees others doing.

Confusion may also arise about the term *consistency*, depending upon the standards for judgment of what constitutes consistency. One parent might be literally and rigidly consistent, and another might be consistent with her rational goals for the child, though showing behavioral variability. Subtleties of this sort have not been closely examined.

Research on inconsistency has taken several approaches. Some have derived a conglomerate rating of the general stability of the parent-child interactions; some have evaluated the consistency over time for a single parent; and others have contrasted the severity of demands placed on the child by one parent with those of the other.

Probably the clearest and most consistent evidence on inconsistency comes from the delinquency studies (Andry, 1960; Bandura and Walters, 1959; Burt, 1929; Carr-Saunders, Mannheim, and Rhodes, 1944; Glueck and Glueck, 1950; McCord et al., 1959). These studies have repeatedly shown a higher incidence of erratic or inconsistent discipline, both within and between parents, to contribute to antisocial behavior. The evidence from McCord and associates (1959) is particularly clear in demonstrating that intra-parental inconsistency makes a contribution to crime rates in addition to that produced by a lack of warmth. A subsequent study of nondelinquent boys (McCord et al., 1961) also revealed greater consistency in discipline for mothers of nonaggressive boys than for mothers of aggressive boys.

Three additional studies have investigated the effects of inconsistency produced by differences in the parents' approach to discipline. Read (1945) provides suggestive evidence that when one parent of nursery school children is strict and the other permissive, more "unfavorable behavior" (aggression?) is displayed by the child than when both parents are strict or permissive. Considering only the cases where low demands are placed on the child, McCord and associates (1961) found that when one parent was punitive and the other was nonpunitive, boys were more likely to be aggressive than when both parents were punitive or nonpunitive. A similar positive association between interparental inconsistency and crime rates was demonstrated in an earlier study (McCord et al., 1959).

A few other consequences of inconsistency (not clearly defined) are suggested in studies by Terman and associates (1938) and by Sanford and associates (1943). Terman found that a category of irregular discipline (in contrast to strict or permissive) tended to be selected as descriptive of their upbringing by persons who later scored low on a marital happiness scale. Sanford defined a syndrome which he called "unstable home" in his study of a group of five- to fourteen-year-olds. Unstable home was defined in terms of the use of capricious discipline and overstimulation of the child. Families high on "unstable home" would repeatedly arouse the child to a high pitch through fatigue effects and overstimulation, and then punish the child for the resulting behavior. Unstable home was positively associated with anxious emotionality, low social feelings, and low conscientiousness.

Inconsistent discipline apparently contributes to "maladjustment," conflict, and aggression in the child. There is obviously a need for more carefully controlled research on different kinds of inconsistency, and a need to articulate the processes by which types of inconsistency affect the child.

A LOOK TO THE FUTURE

It is painfully apparent that the social scientists who have set for themselves the task of unraveling the consequences of child-rearing practices are faced with a problem with infinite complexities. The literature reviewed implies that the research strategy has been one of first establishing the more salient themes and then moving cautiously toward the variations on the themes produced by a more complex interaction of variables. To illustrate more concretely the potential rewards of pursuing these more complex interactions, we would like to close this review by summarizing a rather stimulating analysis by Bronfenbrenner (1961a). His data are based on teachers' ratings of responsibility and leadership for 192 tenth-grade boys and girls. Evaluations of parental child-rearing practices were obtained from the adolescents themselves, who by and large have been shown to be rather accurate observers of the parents.

Starting on familiar ground, Bronfenbrenner first found that rejection, neglect, and lack of discipline from father were associated with irresponsible behavior in boys. High levels of responsibility were related to warmth and nurturant attitudes, especially from mother, and with *moderately* strong discipline, especially from father. Bronfenbrenner also found that *too much* discipline impeded the development of responsibility. For girls, a dramatically different picture emerges. While rejection and neglect lead to low responsibility as for boys, the presence of strong *paternal* discipline is particularly debilitating, much more so than for boys. Again, the effect is curvilinear, but highest responsibility in girls is associated with a low-moderate level of discipline rather than the high-moderate level found for boys. There appear to be optimal levels of authority, with the optimum level higher for boys than for girls.

The results for leadership gave a similar picture with a slight change in focus. Rejection, neglect, parental absence, and protectiveness all related to low leadership for both sexes. For boys, leadership was facilitated by high nurturance, warm relations with parents, and principled discipline; however, these same factors served to discourage leadership in girls and foster dependency.

As noted earlier, girls receive considerably more affection and less physical punishment than boys. With greater earlier affection and less punitive or more love-oriented discipline, there is a risk of oversocialization in girls (parental power is high). The familiar findings that girls are more obedient, cooperative, anxious, and dependent are consistent with this analysis. Boys, on the other hand, are more likely to receive less affection, have greater demands for independence placed on them, and be disciplined with techniques which have less inhibitory power. With less affection, greater discipline is required to achieve a given effect. The net result, according to Bronfenbrenner, is a greater risk of undersocialization in boys. The upshot of this thinking is the hypothesis that the optimal balance of affection and control is different for the two sexes. The danger for girls is an overdose of both and for boys an underdose of both. These dangers are probably conditioned by sex differences in sensitivity, sex-typed parent-child relations, and sex-typing training goals.

Bronfenbrenner also examined the relative amount of authority wielded by each parent, apart from type of discipline used, and found this to relate to the child's behavior. Thus, paternal authority was found to facilitate responsibility in boys and impede it in girls. Taking this one step farther, both responsibility and leadership are facilitated by relatively greater salience of the same-sexed parent. The evidence indicates, however, that too much dominance of either parent leads to lower levels of responsibility and leadership (Bronfenbrenner, 1961b).

IMPLICATIONS

It is apparent that the consequences of disciplinary practices cannot be fully understood except in the context of the warmth of the parent-child relation, the prior history of disciplinary practices and emotional relations, the role-structure of the family, and the social and economic conditions under which a particular family unit is living. In view of these complexities, it also becomes apparent that many of the generalizations drawn from the research literature must be restricted to the kinds of populations studied. In essence, this means that our knowledge is most firm where mothers of working- and middle-class families are involved. Because of the difficulties in obtaining the cooperation of families at the lowest class levels, and fathers of all class levels, our knowledge is less complete for these sub-groups. Obviously, these gaps need to be pursued. It should also be noted that research has tended to focus initially on extreme practices. The majority of parents do not fall at these extremes and typically use a large variety of mixed procedures in discipline. There are probably many routes to being a "good parent" which vary with the personality of both the parents and children and with the pressures in the environment with which one must learn to cope. Analysis of the purer examples provided by extreme groups aids in understanding basic principles, but still leaves one somewhat at a loss when more complex interactions are involved.

Many potential readers of this chapter are faced daily with the problems of evaluating the adequacy of parents as parents. Such evaluations are particularly crucial when there is a question of removing a child from a home or placing him in a foster home. The development of the Parent Attitude Research Instrument (PARI) by Schaefer and Bell (1958) has seemed to some to offer a hopeful procedure for aiding in their decisions. The failure even to mention research on the PARI in this review should not be interpreted as an oversight. With very few exceptions, the research with this instrument has not supported its usefulness (in its present form) for making valid predictions about parents. There is some research on questionnaire methods in progress which may eventually aid in such practical decisions, but the stage of practical utility is probably ten years off. On the other hand, research covered in this review does offer some practical suggestions for conceptualizing parental behavior in terms of a few elemental dimensions (and related consequences) which can be of aid in sensitizing one to things to look for in forming judgments about parents.

Some rather basic convictions about the consequences of various modes of child rearing have received support in this review. The importance of warmth and permissiveness in facilitating the growth of sociable, independent children has found repeated support. The debilitating effects of parental hostility in its many forms is certainly apparent. Even here, however, it should be noted that it is primarily extreme forms of hostility which have been demonstrated to have undesirable consequences. It is not yet clear to what degree a certain amount of openly hostile interaction between parent and child may actually facilitate the child's ability to cope with the realities of independent living in our society. The preliminary work by Bronfenbrenner is particularly provocative in suggesting that we should perhaps be thinking more in terms of optimal levels rather than "this is good and that is bad." In this same vein, caution should be exercised in supposing that use of love-oriented techniques of discipline is "good" and use of power-asserting techniques is "bad." This review has focused on specifying consequences, not evaluating their desirability. Illustrations of different values which might be placed on these various approaches to discipline are not difficult to find. Acceptance of boys by their peers in our culture requires an ability to react to provoked attack with an adequate counter-attack. Disciplinary procedures which strongly inhibit or fail to provide models for such behavior, could foster adjustment problems for boys with their peers. Needless to say, one could go too far in generating feelings of anger and aggressive responses, as suggested by the delinquency studies. In evaluating the potential "goodness" and "badness" of love-oriented methods, there appears to be no evidence that the positive love-oriented methods (use of praise and reasons) have undesirable consequences. However, there is a possibility that the use of threats to the love relationship (negative love-oriented methods) may be so powerful a control method that the development of independence is jeopardized. The research also has suggested both "desirable" and "undesirable" consequences of more extreme forms of both restrictiveness and permissiveness. It is apparent that the task of the professional serving in a consultant role to parents requires considerable wisdom in judging the potential implications of a series of complexly interacting processes.

Possible further implications for those concerned with attempts to modify the behavior of parents and children can be drawn from the research findings and the speculation about the processes by which certain consequences in the child occur. First, where both mothers and fathers have been studied, most of the research has shown the father's influence on the child's behavior to be at least equal to that of the mother. Such findings should help to reinforce the growing trend toward inclusion of the father in treatment efforts. Next, where the disciplinary approach to the child does not seem to be producing the desired effects, this review suggests that it might be profitable to give attention to a detailed analysis of what the parent is rewarding and punishing, the timing of punishment in relation to what the child does, the degree of frustration involved, the clarity with which expectations are communicated to the child, the consistency of reinforcement within and between parents, and the types of models for the child implied by the parents' behavior. In many instances it is possible that making the parent more aware of how his or her behavior is having an impact on the child can motivate a change in the parent's handling of the child. As an aside, it should be pointed out that the effectiveness of various educational procedures in modifying parent behavior has not been adequately researched. A summary of the studies that have been made is presented by Brim (1959, pp. 290–317).

Scientific knowledge on discipline is progressing rapidly or slowly, depending on one's perspective. From the viewpoint of history, the gains in systematic knowledge over the past thirty years have been close to the spectacular. From the viewpoint of persons who must daily face the complex and seemingly impossible problems of troubled families, the gains must appear to border on the trivial.

REFERENCES

ALLINSMITH, B. B. Expressive styles: II. Directness with which anger is expressed. In D. R. Miller & G. E. Swanson (Eds.), *Inner conflict and defense*. New York: Holt, 1960. Pp. 315–336.

ALLINSMITH, W. Moral standards: II. The learning of moral standards. In D. R. Miller & G. E. Swanson (Eds.), *Inner conflict and defense*. New York: Holt, 1960. Pp. 141–176.

ALLINSMITH, W. & GREENING, T. C. Guilt over anger as predicted from parental discipline: a study of superego development. *Amer. Psychologist*, 1955, **10**, 320 (Abstract).

ANDRY, R. G. *Delinquency and parental pathology*. London: Metheun, 1960.

ARONFREED, J. The nature, variety, and social patterning of moral responses to transgression. *J. abnorm. soc. Psychol.*, 1961, **63**, 223–240.

ARONFREED, J. The effects of experimental socialization paradigms upon two moral responses to transgression. *J. abnorm. soc. Psychol.*, 1963, **66**, 437–448.

ARONFREED, J. The origin of self-criticism. *Psychol. Rev.*, in press.

ARONFREED, J., Cutick, R. A., & Fagan, S. A. Cognitive structure, punishment, and nurturance in the experimental induction of self-criticism. *Child Developm.*, 1963, **34**, 281–294.

BALDWIN, A. L. The effect of home environment on nursery school behavior. *Child Developm.*, 1949, **20**, 49–61.

BALDWIN, A. L., KALHORN, J., & BREESE, F. Patterns of parent behavior. *Psychol. Monogr.*, 1945, **58**, No. 3 (Whole No. 268).

BANDURA, A. Relationship of family patterns to child behavior disorders. Progress Report, USPHS, Project No. M-1734, Stanford Univ., 1960.

BANDURA, A. Social learning through imitation. In M. R. Jones (Ed.), *Nebraska symposium on motivation, 1962*. Lincoln: Univ. Nebraska Press, 1962.

BANDURA, A., ROSS, D., & ROSS, S. A. Transmission of aggression through imitation of aggressive models. *J. abnorm. soc. Psychol.*, 1961, **63**, 575–582.

BANDURA, A. & WALTERS, R. H. *Adolescent aggression*. New York: Ronald Press, 1959.

BECKER, W. C., PETERSON, D. R., HELLMER, L. A., SHOEMAKER, D. J., & QUAY, H. C. Factors in parental behavior and personality as related to problem behavior in children. *J. consult. Psychol.*, 1959, **23**, 107–118.

BECKER, W. C., PETERSON, D. R., LURIA, Z., SHOEMAKER, D. J., & HELLMER, L. A. Relations of factors derived from parent-interview ratings to behavior problems of five-year-olds. *Child Developm.*, 1962, **33**, 509–535.

BRIM, O. G. *Education for child rearing*. New York: Russell Sage Found., 1959.

BRONFENBRENNER, U. Socialization and social class through time and space. In E. E. Maccoby, T. M. Newcomb, & E. L. Hartley (Eds.), *Readings in social psychology*. New York: Holt, 1958. Pp. 400–425.

BRONFENBRENNER, U. Some familial antecedents of responsibility and leadership in adolescents. In L. Petrullo & B. M. Bass (Eds.), *Leadership and interpersonal behavior*. New York: Holt, 1961 (a).

BRONFENBRENNER, U. Toward a theoretical model for the analysis of parent-child relationships in a social context. In J. C. Glidewell (Ed.), *Parental attitudes and child behavior*. Springfield, Ill.: Charles C Thomas, 1961 (b).

BURT, C. *The young delinquent*. New York: Appleton, 1929.

BURTON, R. V., MACCOBY, E. E., & ALLINSMITH, W. Antecedents of resistance to temptation in four-year-old children. *Child Developm.*, 1961, **32**, 689–710.

CARR-SAUNDERS, A. M., MANNHEIM, H., & RHODES, E. C. *Young offenders*. New York: Macmillan, 1944.

DOLLARD, J., MILLER, N. E., DOOB, L. W., MOWRER, O. H., & SEARS, R. *Frustration and aggression*. New Haven: Yale Univ. Press, 1939.

DROPPLEMAN, L. F. & SCHAEFER, E. S. Boys' and girls' reports of maternal and paternal behavior. Paper read at Amer. Psychol. Assn., New York, August, 1961.

EMMERICH, W. Parental identification in young children. *Genet. Psychol. Monogr.*, 1959, **60**, 257–308 (a).

EMMERICH, W. Young children's discriminations of parent and child roles. *Child Developm.*, 1959, **30**, 404–420 (b).

ERON, L. D., BANTA, T. J., WALDER, L. O., & LAULICHT, J. H. Comparison of data obtained from mothers and fathers on childrearing practices and their relation to child aggression. *Child Developm.*, 1961, **32**, 457–572.

ESTES, K. W. An experimental study of punishment. *Psychol. Monogr.*, 1944, **57**, No. 263.

FINCH, H. M. Young children's concept of parent roles. *J. Home Econ.*, 1955, **47**, 99–103.

FREUD, S. *New introductory lectures on psychoanalysis.* New York: Norton, 1933.

GARDNER, L. P. An analysis of children's attitudes toward fathers. *J. genet. Psychol.*, 1947, **70**, 3–28.

GLUECK, S. & GLUECK, E. T. *Unraveling juvenile delinquency.* Cambridge, Mass.: Harvard Univ. Press, 1950.

GRINDER, R. E. Parental childrearing practices, conscience, and resistance to temptation of sixth grade children. *Child Developm.*, 1962, **33**, 803–820.

GRINDER, R. E. & McMICHAEL, R. E. Cultural influence on conscience development: resistance to temptation and guilt among Samoans and American Caucasians. *J. abnorm. soc. Psychol.*, 1963, **66**, 503–506.

HAWKES, G. R., BURCHINAL, L. G., & GARDNER, B. Pre-adolescents' views of some of their relations with their parents. *Child Developm.*, 1957, **28**, 393–399.

HEALY, W. & BRONNER, A. F. *Delinquents and criminals: their making and unmaking.* New York: Macmillan, 1926.

HEINICKE, C. M. Some antecedents and correlates of guilt and fear in young boys. Unpublished doctoral dissertation, Harvard Univ., 1953.

HILL, W. F. Learning theory and the acquisition of values. *Psychol. Rev.*, 1960, **67**, 317–331.

HOFFMAN, M. L. Power assertion by the parent and its impact on the child. *Child Developm.*, 1960, **31**, 129–143.

HOFFMAN, M. L. Child-rearing practices and moral development: generalizations from empirical research. *Child Developm.*, 1963, **34**, 295–318.

HOFFMAN, M. L. & SALTZSTEIN, H. D. Parent practices and the child's moral orientation. Paper read at the Amer. Psychol. Assn., Chicago, September, 1960.

HOLLENBERG, E. & SPERRY, M. Some antecedents of aggression and effects of frustration in doll play. *Personality*, 1951, **1**, 32–43.

KAGAN, J. The child's perception of the parent. *J. abnorm. soc. Psychol.*, 1956, **53**, 257–258.

KAGAN, J., HOSKEN, B., & WATSON, S. Child's symbolic conceptualization of parents. *Child Developm.*, 1961, **32**, 625–636.

KAGAN, J. & LEMKIN, J. The child's differential perception of parental attributes. *J. abnorm. soc. Psychol.*, 1960, **61**, 440–447.

KAGAN, J. & MOSS, H. A. *Birth to maturity: the Fels study of psychological development.* New York: Wiley, 1962.

KOHN, M. L. Social class and parent-child relationship: an interpretation. *Amer. J. Sociol.*, 1963, **68**, 471–480.

KOHN, M. L. & CARROLL, E. E. Social class and the allocation of parental responsibilities. *Sociometry*, 1960, **23**, 372–392.

LAMBERT, W. W., TRIANDIS, L. M., & WOLF, M. Some correlates of beliefs in the malevolence and benevolence of supernatural beings: a cross-societal study. *J. abnorm. soc. Psychol.*, 1959, **58**, 162–169.

LEVIN, H. Permissive childrearing and adult role behavior. In D. E. Dulany, R. L. DeValois, D. C. Beardsley, & M. R. Winterbottom (Eds.), *Contributions to modern psychology.* New York: Oxford Univ. Press, 1958. Pp. 307–312.

LEVINE, B. B. Punishment techniques and the development of conscience. Unpublished doctoral dissertation, Northwestern Univ., 1961.

LEVY, D. M. *Maternal overprotection.* New York: Columbia Univ. Press, 1943.

LEWIS, H. *Deprived children.* London: Oxford Univ. Press, 1954.

MACCOBY, E. E. The generality of moral behavior. *Amer. Psychologist,* 1959, **14,** 358. (Abstract)

MACCOBY, E. E. The taking of adult roles in middle childhood. *J. abnorm. soc. Psychol.,* 1961, **63,** 493–503.

MACKINNON, D. W. Violations of prohibitions. In H. A. Murray (Ed.), *Explorations in personality.* New York: Oxford Univ. Press, 1938. Pp. 491–501.

McCORD, W., McCORD, J., & HOWARD, A. Familial correlates of aggression in non-delinquent male children. *J. abnorm. soc. Psychol.,* 1961, **62,** 79–93.

McCORD, W., McCORD, J., & ZOLA, I. K. *Origins of crime.* New York: Columbia Univ. Press, 1959.

MEYERS, C. E. The effect of conflicting authority on the child. *Univ. Iowa Stud. Child Welf.,* 1944, **20,** No. 409, 31–98.

MILLER, D. R. & SWANSON, G. E. *Inner conflict and defense.* New York: Holt, 1960.

RADKE, M. Relation of parental authority to children's behavior and attitudes. *Univ. Minnesota Inst. of Child Welf. Monogr.,* 1946, No. 22.

READ, K. H. Parents' expressed attitudes and children's behavior. *J. consult. Psychol.,* 1945, **9,** 95–100.

ROFF, M. A factorial study of the Fels Parent Behavior Scales. *Child Developm.,* 1949, **20,** 29–45.

ROSENTHAL, M. J., FINKELSTEIN, M., NI, E., & ROBERTSON, R. E. A study of mother-child relationships in the emotional disorders of children. *Genet. Psychol. Monogr.,* 1959, **60,** 65–116.

ROSENTHAL, M. J., NI, E., FINKELSTEIN, M., & BERKWITS, G. K. Father-child relation-ships and children's problems. *AMA Arch. Gen. Psychiat.,* 1962, **7,** 360–373.

ROY, K. Parents' attitudes toward their children. *J. Home Econ.,* 1950, **42,** 652–653.

SANFORD, R. N., ADKINS, M. M., MILLER, R. B., & COBB, E. Physique, personality and scholarship: a cooperative study of school children. *Monogr. Soc. Res. Child Developm.,* 1943, **8,** No. 1.

SCHAEFER, E. S. A circumplex model for maternal behavior. *J. abnorm. soc. Psychol.,* 1959, **59,** 226–235.

SCHAEFER, E. S. Converging conceptual models for maternal behavior and for child behavior. In J. C. Glidewell (Ed.), *Parental attitudes and child behavior.* Springfield, Ill.: Charles C Thomas, 1961.

SCHAEFER, E. S. & BELL, R. Q. Development of a parental attitude research instrument. *Child Developm.,* 1958, **29,** 339–361.

SEARS, P. S. Doll play aggression in normal young children: influence of sex, age, sibling status, father's absence. *Psychol. Monogr.,* 1951, **65,** No. 6.

SEARS, R. R. The relation of early socialization experiences to aggression in middle childhood. *J. abnorm. soc. Psychol.,* 1961, **63,** 466–492.

SEARS, R. R., MACCOBY, E. E., & LEVIN, H. *Patterns of child rearing.* Evanston, Ill.: Row, Peterson, 1957.

SEARS, R. R., RAU, L., & ALPERT, R. Identification and child training: the development of conscience. Paper read at the Amer. Psychol. Assn., Chicago, September, 1960.

SEARS, R. R., WHITING, J. W. M., NOWLIS, V., & SEARS, P. S. Some child-rearing ante-cedents of aggression and dependency in young children. *Genet. Psychol. Monogr.,* 1953, **47,** 135–234.

SKINNER, B. F. *The behavior of organisms.* New York: Appleton-Century, 1938.

SYMONDS, P. M. *The psychology of parent-child relationships.* New York: Appleton-Century, 1939.

TAKALA, M., NUMMENMAA, T., & KAURANNE, U. I. Parental attitudes and child-rearing practices: a methodological study. *Acta Academiae Paedogogicae Jyvaskylaensis,* 1960, **19,** 1–75.

TASCH, R. J. The role of the father in the family. *J. exp. Educ.,* 1952, **20,** 319–361.

TERMAN, L. M., *et al. Psychological factors in marital happiness.* New York: McGraw-Hill, 1938.

UNGER, S. M. On the development of guilt-response systems. Unpublished doctoral dissertation, Cornell Univ., 1960.

UNGER, S. M. Antecedents of personality differences in guilt responsivity. *Psychol. Rep.,* 1962, **10,** 357–358.

WATSON, G. A comparison of the effects of lax versus strict home training. *J. soc. Psychol.,* 1934, **5,** 102–105.

WATSON, G. Some personality differences in children related to strict or permissive parental discipline. *J. Psychol.,* 1957, **44,** 227–249.

WHITING, J. W. M. & CHILD, I. L., *Child training and personality.* New Haven: Yale Univ. Press, 1953.

YARROW, L. J. Effect of antecedent frustration on projective play. *Psychol. Monogr.,* 1948, **62,** No. 6.

The Attainment of Concepts[1]

IRVING E. SIGEL

The Merrill-Palmer Institute

OUR PHYSICAL AND SOCIAL WORLD is made up of a host of diverse stimuli. Sounds, lights, textures, shapes are among the innumerable sources of stimulation consistently impinging on our senses. For us, as adults, diversity is neither distressing nor chaotic, for we have created order out of the seeming disorder. Having acquired this order, we are able to move about our environment with considerable accuracy and security. By learning to behave appropriately toward the many objects, events, and people with whom we come in contact, we adapt and function in our environment with the necessary precision and confidence.

One major reason we function so efficiently is that we have developed a system of concepts that ". . . serves as an experiential filter through which impinging events are screened, gauged, and evaluated, a process that determines in large part what responses can and will occur" (Harvey, Hunt, and Schroder, 1961, pp. 2–3). In short, concepts function as an adaptive mechanism through which we cope with reality.

Concepts are learned and are attained through a variety of complex processes. In the discussion here we will describe how concepts are acquired, the psychological processes necessary for that acquisition, and the concepts and conceptual abilities available to children as they develop.

FUNCTION OF CONCEPTS

As implied above, concepts serve as crucial links between the environment and the individual. They are intellectual tools that man uses in organizing his environment and attacking his problems. When man employs concepts, he thinks in terms of symbols and classes. When he orders diversity into classes or categories, he begins to reduce ambiguity and imprecision.

Associated with most concepts or categories, moreover, is a set of appropriate behaviors, be they thoughts, motoric acts, or fantasies. Man

[1] Financial assistance for the preparation of this manuscript came from a Social Research Foundation grant to The Merrill-Palmer Institute.

209

thereby has a repertoire of behaviors with which to deal effectively with the environment. In fact, his response may become virtually instantaneous, since he quickly identifies and classifies environmental cues within the context of a particular concept. Thus concepts perform a vital function in enabling us to cope with the complexities of the physical and social world (Harvey, Hunt, and Schroder, 1961).

CONCEPTS ARE ACQUIRED

Concepts are acquired through a complex set of processes. The child has to learn to recognize and identify objects. That is to say, he has to learn that objects exist, have permanence, and differ one from the other. Identification and subsequent naming follow. Further, he must learn not only to identify the whole object but also to define its manifold characteristics. He learns that various objects have multiple characteristics and attributes; a chair is more than something to sit in. In addition to such discrimination, he learns to perceive commonalities among diverse stimuli. Diverse items are organized into classes or categories that are labeled in conventional terms. Language both facilitates and directs the categorization process, since it provides the tools by which to identify the commonalities. Not every language, however, has the same sets of labels for categories of physical or social reality (Brown, 1958; French, 1963).

This complex set of learnings is based on such processes as discrimination, perception, transposition, and generalization—all facilitated by language. These have been studied intensively (Kendler, 1961). *Discrimination learning*, for example, has been demonstrated to be a primary step in the long road toward concept acquisition (White, 1963). *Perceptual learning* studies have been undertaken to determine how children perceive; what information they get from the environment; and the kinds of stimuli that are attended to and how these change with age (Gibson, 1963). *Transposition*, the ability of children to respond to new stimuli with responses learned under a different set of conditions, has been receiving increased attention— especially in relation to the acquisition of concepts (White, 1963). Other studies have focused on the age changes of children's ability to make *generalizations* (Kendler and Kendler, 1956, 1962; Welch, 1940; White, 1963). Here we will only touch upon some directly germane studies. There are comprehensive reviews available, however, that will provide the reader with the details of the developmental trends for each of these psychological processes (Stevenson, 1963; G. G. Thompson, 1962).

On the basis of such complex learning, the individual evolves a schema that encompasses a class of items judged as belonging together even in their diversity. The ability to recognize a cat, a dog, a lion, and a sheep as animals would demonstrate a particular schema—vertebrate. The individual learns at least three characteristics of a schema or a class of items. First, he learns what is its central tendency; that is, what is the most common aspect of it. Second, he learns how items within the class differ from one another; for example, vertebrates may be carnivorous or herbivorous, yet still judged within the vertebrate class. Third, he learns how members within the class differ from one another, as well as how items may have multiple class membership (Attneave, 1957). For example, a group of geometric figures, such as blue triangles, blue squares, blue rectangles, could be classified on the basis of blueness while ignoring their difference in shape—thus employing a color category. The items could also be categorized on the basis of shape, ignoring similarity in color and attending to diversity of form. Reclassifying objects in this way provides the flexibility needed in organizing the environment. Because of this capacity, humans are able to make a variety of adaptations to the environment.

To recapitulate, the individual through complex learning processes acquires data from the environment. Stimulation is reciprocal: environmental sensations stimulate the person and the various sensations eventually become identified, named, and organized. Through his increased ability to discriminate and to generalize, he develops schemata. In so doing, the individual becomes increasingly emancipated from the perceptual and sensory aspect of the environment, and is able to approach it in a conceptual way.

THEORIES OF DEVELOPMENT

Development refers to change that occurs through time. One basic question is whether development always follows the same general pattern; or, stated more formally, whether it proceeds in a sequential, invariant order. There are those who hold that it does (Goldstein and Scheerer, 1941; Tanner and Inhelder, 1960; Werner, 1948; Piaget, 1952, 1954, 1960, 1961; Inhelder and Piaget, 1958; Laurendeau and Pinard, 1962; Kohlberg, 1963). These stage-dependent theories maintain that for the child to arrive at stage B in his development, he must first have reached and passed through stage A. The order is fixed; stage B cannot be arrived at until stage A has been mastered.

For some investigators, this invariant order is accepted as being hereditarily based (Gesell and Amatruda, 1941). But for others "the order is assumed to be a fixed feature of the organism-environment interaction, to be both organismic and experiential" (Hunt, 1961, p. 256; Tanner and Inhelder, 1960).

Those assuming a fixed order also accept the position that the age at which stages appear and their length will vary as a function of hereditary potential and experience (Tanner and Inhelder, 1960). Studies with mental defectives indicate that the order of the stages is present but appears at different chronological periods, and that the rate of change varies from that of normal children (Inhelder, 1944; Woodward, 1961). Thus ages and stages are not necessarily linked, although in normal situations some correspondence is generally found.

There are others who believe that stages as invariant sequences do not hold but, rather, that the child is a product of learning experiences, showing different levels of ability, knowledge, and skills as a function of such experience. Order of development is not an invariant order; instead, the rate and quality of change depends on the particular kinds of experiences (Ausubel, 1957; Estes, 1956; Hunt, 1961; Sears, 1958).

Laurendeau and Pinard (1962) provide a concise summary of the issues involved in this controversy. They give three reasons for the criticisms of the stage-dependent theory. The first is that there is considerable over-lapping among chronological age groups in all kinds of responses and concepts children employ. Not all children at chronological age four, for example, are in the same stage but show a variety of stages. Second, there is apparent continuity in the development of the child so that gaps are not directly observable. Finally, the tremendous instability found among many young children results in their giving inconsistent answers, so that it is difficult at times to determine whether a child is or is not at a particular stage. Some studies tend to refute the stage concept because they find no evidence supporting it (Deutsche, 1937; Ezer, 1962; Estes, 1956; Mogar, 1960; Sears, 1958).

Another critique raises the question that if stages have this invariant sequence, then "of what do the individual differences in the intelligence of children from seven to nine (for example) consist . . . ?" (Hunt, 1961, p. 257). Individual differences in performance still have to be accounted for in stage-dependent theories.

Those upholding a stage-dependent theory assert that stages are not found frequently because of the methods employed in working with children. The experimental studies must be set up so as to ensure the child an opportunity to express himself completely and clearly. In refuting the argument of instability or inconsistency, Laurendeau and Pinard (1962) maintain that it is illogical to insist that children always reason the same way when attacking different kinds of problems. The stages are not to be described as universal but, rather, as particular to particular classes of situations. For example, one of the concepts widely described in stage terms is *animism:* attributing life to inanimate objects. Laurendeau and Pinard report that the child goes through a variety of steps before he shifts from an animistic point of view to an objective one. When and how he does so depends upon the kinds of objects with which he is dealing. Where rocks and tools are concerned, he loses his sense of animism earlier than would be the case if he were dealing with such objects as automobiles and airplanes. Children tend to lose the concept of animism in relation to the amount of knowledge they gain about particular kinds of things. Several investigators have provided empirical support for the stage theory through such techniques as scaleogram analysis, making use of various scales on which the points represent developmental stages (Dodwell, 1961; Kohlberg, 1963; Wohlwill, 1960b; Wohlwill and Lowe, 1962).

Another critical question facing proponents of the stage theory is how to explain the transition from one stage to another. A pertinent discussion is presented by Laurendeau and Pinard. It may be said that what is presumed to happen is that the child goes through a set of steps, which are then transformed into a new level. During this period, as he proceeds from one stage to the next, continuous integrations and reintegrations are made (Laurendeau and Pinard, 1962; Piaget, 1952; Werner, 1948).

Development from one stage to another can also occur through the substitution of one kind of activity for another. In this case, an inferior performance disappears and a superior kind emerges. Development explained this way does not imply integration of one stage with another but, rather, that some kinds of approaches, habits, and ideas drop out and others occur. The implication is that continuity does not necessarily exist in development, but that a new process may appear with no apparent previous manifestation. For example, the child's walking is not continuous with his crawling; rather, crawling drops out and walking emerges.

The best test of the validity of the invariant order of concept development would require longitudinal studies, with the same children being consistently studied over long periods of time. Only in this way could investigators trace the invariant order of stages for each child. To date, no published studies of this type are available.

A second test is to ask whether external influences, such as teaching, affect the stage development. Laurendeau and Pinard, again, maintain that home or school experiences are not of sufficient moment to alter the natural processes of adaptation which take place in the child's adjustment to his objective world. Even though the child's verbalizations suggest he is at a more advanced stage, the child will "quickly abandon the explanations received and revert to his primitive schemata or else he distorts the adult interpretation to adjust it to his own current beliefs" (Laurendeau and

Pinard, 1962, p. 260). This fixed evolution is presumed to be natural and cannot be altered by external forces. Other writers do not take such a firm position, considering the question to be still open (Flavell, 1963). The evidence on the reaching of concepts, like that on the invariant order of their emergence, is as yet inconclusive.

Although the invariant order of stages awaits clarification, its acceptance by some writers is based on inferences from cross-sectional studies (Elkind, 1961a,b; Kooistra, 1963; Laurendeau and Pinard, 1962; Piaget, 1950; Wohlwill, 1960a,b). In such studies children of different ages are compared as to their ability to perform various tasks. The younger children usually perform at a stage inferior to that of the older. It is assumed that if the same child were followed from one chronological age to another, he would show the same developmental pattern as do the cross-sectional groups. Some of the empirical studies employing such cross-sectional procedures will be discussed later.

Let us now turn to a schematic description of the major stages of intellectual development before proceeding to a detailed discussion of each of a number of specific concepts.[2]

STAGES OF INTELLECTUAL DEVELOPMENT

Sensory-Motor Period (Birth to Two Years)

The first two years of life have been described by Piaget (1954) and Werner (1948) as the sensory-motor period. In this period the infant moves from a primarily reflexive organism responding in an undifferentiated way to his environment to "a relatively coherent organization of sensory-motor actions vis-a-vis his immediate environment" (Flavell, 1963, p. 86). The evolution of cognitive operations begins at birth with the initial use of inherent reflexes, part of the child's biological endowment. Through stimulation and responses of such apparatus, the infant increasingly strives to interact with his environment.

The infant's movements, physical and intellectual, lack precision and his activities like his attention are dominated by external stimulation. The infant has been described as approaching his environment in an undifferentiated, unreflective, and unspecified manner (Koffka, 1928; Lewin, 1946; Werner, 1948).

Piaget studied the infant's development and this sensory-motor period in detail (1954). In general, he reports that the child accomplishes the following kinds of tasks: he attains rudimentary knowledge that is the

[2] We will adapt Piaget's overall schema to our present purposes as the basis of organizing this discussion.

prototype of concepts—the stuff out of which concepts are made; he establishes a differentiation of himself from objects; he localizes himself in space; he establishes a beginning awareness of cause and effect, of time and space—in part because he has acquired the ability to identify the permanence and substantiality of objects early in this period.

In the course of such development the child goes through six stages which have been reviewed very clearly by Flavell (1963). These stages can be summarized as follows: the first stage, which lasts about a month, is one where the child shows little besides reflexive behavior. In the second stage, from about one to four months, various reflex activities become modified with experience and coordinate with one another. In stage three, between four and eight months, the infant begins to act toward objects and events outside his own body as though they have some permanence and stability. In effect, he is beginning to demonstrate intention or goal-directed activity; he is purposeful in his search. Intentionality of purpose is observed in children between eight and twelve months, stage four, where the beginnings of what are called "means-end relationships" are defined. He tends to use what he has already learned in searching for objects, as well as repeating patterns of behavior. When the child reaches stage five he is between twelve and eighteen months. He now begins to experiment, to search for new ways to solve problems; and he begins to get excited about novelty for its own sake. Finally, at stage six, at eighteen months to approximately two years, the child shows the capacity for primitive symbolic representation. He may invent solutions mentally; that is, symbolically, rather than by trial and error. As the child begins to be symbolic, he approaches the next phase of development.

Much of the accomplishment of intellectual development during this period occurs because the child is developing and learning to coordinate motorically, for example, reaching precisely for an object and bringing it to his mouth. This coordination provides him with some basis for responding to the environment.

Piaget has called these major learnings schemata—that is, each of them is an organization of particular behaviors all relevant to one another. Even as the child moves to the end processes of this period, he is still dominated by the physical attributes of the environment. He is still a perceptually dominated organism. For the child under two years of age, the world is not experienced as an integrated unit but, rather, as a series of stills moving one from the other.

The schemata are acquired by means of two central processes, *assimilation* and *accommodation*. Assimilation is a concept that Piaget has borrowed from biology, which in effect holds that the individual takes within himself certain aspects of the environment and these become organized within classes or groups. It is analogous to the idea of our assimilating food, where food is taken in and becomes part of the blood stream. In the course of the process, the child is also making adjustments to these new assimilations. This is referred to as accommodation. The child's intellectual development proceeds by the assimilation of new information; this, in turn, results in modification of some existent schema (accommodation). His possessing this modified schema results in an altered behavior toward the environment. For example, the child has learned to attribute the word *animal* to four-legged creatures. He then learns that two-legged creatures can also be defined as animals. As this new information is assimilated, he alters his concept of animal to include a wider variety of instances. These two inter-related processes, assimilation and accommodation, are operative through the entire developmental period (Flavell, 1963).

Such judgments of infant behavior by Piaget and others have also been inferred by observers who have watched infants in naturalistic situations and in a naturalistic environment. Piaget, however, made some experimental studies with his own children (Piaget, 1954).

The observations of Piaget and others do not tell us what the capacity of the infant is to respond in a differentiated way. Current evidence suggests that the infant differentiates at earlier than six months of age and shows preference for particular visual patterns. As an example, infants fixated longer on horizontal stripes than concentric circles (Fantz, 1958). It also appears that the infant responds selectively to sound and movement, with movement being attended to earlier (Koffka, 1928; Werner, 1948).

The long-term significance of the intellectual development from birth to two years still needs examination. The early significance of these periods relative to the eventual attainment of concepts and intellectual functioning needs to be studied longitudinally. To illustrate, it may well be that one reason children from so-called culturally disadvantaged homes have difficulty in kindergarten and first grade is that they did not have appropriate stimulation during these early years. The assumption, of course, is that adequate or inadequate experience in the first two years of life influences the rate of development, and therefore intellectual stimulation must begin earlier if we are to help children acquire necessary knowledge.

To summarize the accomplishments of the child's first two years, we can say in more general terms that he begins with undifferentiated views of himself and the environment, then gradually begins to differentiate himself from the environment. In the process he also learns that the environment functions on a basis of certain physical properties, such as space, object permanence, and causality. The child at this period has also been called preabstract. He is not able to grasp what is called in biology a "genus-specie" relationship. That is, he is not yet able to grasp a higher class concept. For example, he cannot yet understand that a dog is in the broad general class, Animal—although he can handle the fact that a particular dog, Rover, is a member of a smaller class, Dog (Welch, 1940). At the end of the second year, the child has acquired a number of intellectual skills that enable him to function on a more symbolical level. He now enters a time of preparation for and organization of concrete operations. This is divided into crucial periods, the *preoperational* and the one of *concrete operations*. We shall deal with each of these separately.

Preoperational Thought Period (*Two to Seven Years*)[3]

Preoperational phase (two to four). This period of life can be broken down into two phases, a preoperational one from age two to four, and an intuitive one from age four to seven. Now instead of thinking and reasoning motorically (that is, he has to try things out and have things operate in their external concrete way), the child is approaching the point at which he can function symbolically. He is able to distinguish between the signifier —that which stands for something—and the actual object. We have here the beginnings of symbolic thought with language playing an increasing role. The distinction is presented very clearly by Flavell, as follows:

> First, the sensory motor intelligence is capable of only linking, one by one, the successive actions of perceptual stages with which it gets involved. Piaget likens it to a slow motion film which represents one static frame after another, but can give no simultaneous and all encompassing purview of all the frames. Representational thought, on the other hand, through symbolic capacity has the potential for simultaneously grasping, in a single, internal epitome, a whole sweep of separate events. It is a much faster and more mobile device which can recall the past, represent the present, and anticipate the future in one temporally brief, organized act (1963, pp. 151–152).

Let it not be thought, however, that this preoperational thought is mature. During the preoperational period (two to four) the child is egocentric, using himself as the standard of judgment, and unable to take the viewpoint of other people. He is egocentric with respect to representations and his symbolic activities. He still judges things on face value and is not reflective in his thought. He categorizes on the basis of single characteristics of objects, and is unable to classify the multi-faceted aspects of stimuli simultaneously. For example, he cannot take into account an object having width and height simultaneously. The child is conceptualizing on single salient features of the environment.

[3] These ages are approximate and should be viewed as estimates.

This inability to handle multiple characteristics of objects is one reason that Piaget refers to this time of the child's life as one in which he is operating on preconcepts. Although the child has already acquired the concept of the object and has some idea of classes of objects, he is not able to incorporate the variety of characteristics of an object into a single classification. He can grasp such ideas as men and women being classified as people, or that potatoes and apples are food. These are called first-level concepts (Welch, 1940). But he cannot employ two attributes of the same object, that is, break up a group of apples along the multiple dimensions of big red apples and small green apples.

The child's conceptualization is perceptual-dominant, since his organization, classification, and primitive conceptions are determined to a large measure by the potency of the physical attributes. However, what makes this different from the sensory-motor stage is that he can approach these materials in a symbolic way rather than through direct motoric action. Werner cites an example of the child using the word *papa* not only for his father, but for all objects belonging to his father. These ways of relating different kinds of objects, by applying to them either the same name or the same behavior, reflect the child's selecting a particular characteristic deemed relevant as the basis of organizing diverse materials. Or as Werner (1948, p. 227) states: "The grouping operation (that is, the seeing things as belonging together) is derivative from a realistic concrete unity." In effect, the child sees things as belonging together because from his experience and his view of things they are, in fact, together.

At this point the child's thinking is what Piaget calls *transductive*, that is, the child tends to relate the particular to the particular. If A is like B in one respect, then A must be like B in other respects.

For some writers children's conceptualizations have been described as syncretic, since diverse items are grouped together in an egocentric fashion, often in disregard of their intrinsic relationships. For children at this period, all kinds of events may be related one to the other—even assumed to be causally related—not on the basis of objectivity nor on an accurate cause-effect basis, but rather because of juxtapositions in time and space. In the most literal sense, then, the children are realistic; whatever they see is taken on its face value and accepted (Piaget, 1954; Werner, 1948).

Intuitive phase (four to seven). The next period, that of intuitive thought (age four to seven), is still somewhat part of the same epoch but with a transition to increased symbolic functioning (Flavell, 1963; Hunt, 1961; Piaget, 1950). The child is still egocentric, dominated by his perceptions with his judgments subjective. Three fundamental operations now make an appearance: the ability to think in terms of classes, to see relationships, and to handle number concepts. The child can classify material on the basis of objective similarity. When presented with a group of squares and triangles, he can classify objects on the basis of triangularity or color. But he is still categorizing on the basis of one of these characteristics. At the same time he is increasingly able to comprehend the meaning of similarity and classification. It is now possible for him to see relationships such as "Mrs. Smith is the mother of John," as a result of the ability to perceive relations as well as to compare and order items. The child is now said to be intuitive because he does not necessarily verbalize or indicate awareness of his classification. He is also beginning to utilize numbers and to order things in terms of quantity. Because he is becoming able to disregard certain properties of items and see that a relationship can exist on a numerical basis, even though the objects differ structurally, he can now count different kinds of things. In so doing he is able to produce a sum, which is an abstraction.

Concrete Operations (Seven to Eleven Years)

During the period from approximately seven to eleven years of age our reasoning processes begin to appear logical. At this stage even logicians would be satisfied that a child is thinking in logical terms. The term *operation* refers to the child's internalized responses, that is, mental acts which are "in imagination the thing or concept thought about in order to reach some conclusion. According to Piaget, a concept or classification is not a mere task of labeling of a set of stimuli, it is an actual imaginative 'piling together' of objects included in the class" (Kohlberg, 1963, p. 16).

Piaget describes a number of such operations, such as the logical operations involved in simple arithmetic (reversibility), or in organizing objects into hierarchies of classes (classification), or arranging items along continua of increasing values (seriation). One important consequence of the child's acquisition of these concrete operations is his increasing ability to handle number concepts.[4] For Piaget, the acquisition of the number concept requires the child to perform (a) reversible operations, that is, for every action or operation there is one that cancels it, such as eight times six is 48 and 48 divided by six equals eight; (b) the development of the logic of class, that is, grouping of diverse items into a single classification; and (c) the comprehension of and the development of an understanding of asymmetrical relations, that is, the ability to arrange items in order. In effect, the child has to be able to treat objects as alike even though diverse, and also be able to count this one first and that one second.

[4] Detailed studies of number acquisition and the stages involved are to be found in Dodwell, 1960; Ilg and Ames, 1951; Martin, 1951; D. Russell, 1956; Wohlwill, 1960a, b.

Dodwell, working with children five to eight years of age, specifically examined the interdependence of class concepts with the acquisition of numbers. He did not find the correspondence reported by Piaget, but rather that the "ability to answer correctly questions which involve simultaneous consideration of the whole class and its (two) component subclasses appears to develop to a large extent independently of understanding of the concept of cardinal numbers" (1962, p. 158).

To impose hierarchical ordering of classes on objects, the child has to be able to ascertain that certain properties of objects are invariant in the face of certain changes. This awareness is called *conservation*. Two eight-inch pies are still equal, even though one is cut into six slices and the other into five. The quantity of pie remains the same in the face of changes irrelevant to the quantity. The ability to conserve in Piaget's system is a critical test to determine whether the child has acquired such concepts as number, mass, weight, volume, and area (Flavell, 1963; Hunt, 1961; Kessen and Kuhlman, 1962; Piaget, 1952, 1961; Piaget, Inhelder, and Szemenska, 1960). We shall discuss later some of the studies dealing with conservation.

A concrete operation which enables seriation to appear is *transitivity*. For example, if A is heavier than B, and B is heavier than C, then A is heavier than C. The child is able to arrange items in a series along particular continua. Conservation and transitivity appear between ages five and seven, depending on the particular content involved (Braine, 1959; Kessen and Kuhlman, 1962; Kooistra, 1963; Smedslund, 1960).

The child's ability to perform these various operations is critical to the establishment of a conceptual approach (Hunt, 1961). He must be able to see how some items can be in more than one class and that some classes can be subordinated to others. Because he can now combine these various operations to form new ones and is able to handle opposites and other characteristics, he is increasingly able to deal symbolically with various kinds of materials, for example, words, numbers, and so on. As we shall see later, considerable research by Piaget and others has demonstrated the intense intellectual and conceptual growth that occurs during this period from age seven to eleven.

Piaget's theory is of an interweaving as well as interdependent set of concrete operations—in effect, the mental operations are integrated into a cognitive system (Piaget, 1950). The entire system evolves during this period to provide a mental structure increasingly capable of developing concepts for representational thought.

Other studies tend to confirm the general trends described by Piaget. They have, moreover, described the kinds of classificatory behavior children show as well as pertinent bases for ordering stimuli. Children at seven and eight tend to categorize on the basis of the perceptual or concrete aspects of a stimuli. Many of these studies employ sorting tasks containing familiar everyday objects, for example, cars, furniture, geometric figures, and the like. The child is asked to sort these on any basis he wishes and usually he is asked to give the reason for his grouping. The results tend to agree that children perceive similarity on the basis of perceptual factors such as *structural similarities* (items all have legs, or a speck of brown), or on the basis of similarity of *use* (these tools are used to build). With increasing age, the basis of categorization shifts to conceptual or categorical labels such as animals, tools, and the like, at least with lower and middle-class boys between eight and nine (Bolles, 1937; Sigel, 1953). For the younger children, seven to nine, the concepts are still limited in inclusiveness, that is, not all instances of a category are included. The employment of categorical labels still has elements of concrete aspects—as evidenced in the child's applying the name *animal* only to animals that are structurally similar, for example, four-legged ones. Gradually this increases to extensive categorization (J. Thompson, 1941), especially between nine and eleven years of age.

These results provide a further rationale as to why one should heed Werner's (1957) admonition, that the child's employment of conceptual labels does not necessarily mean the underlying intellectual process is conceptual. The popular usage of the concept *animals* accounts for the label, rather than the level of conceptualization (Sigel, 1961).

The nature of the items influences how children categorize. When meaningful materials are used (for example, animals) children at ages seven, nine, and eleven tend to ignore such structural properties as color, texture, or material the objects are made from, and focus on the meaning of the item (Sigel, 1954). Items depicting human figures are categorized on different bases from those depicting objects or animals (Sigel, 1961, 1963). Children aged seven and eight were presented with pictures depicting such human figures as a fireman, cowboy, nurse, and so on. They were asked to classify these stimuli on the basis of similarity. They tended to use labels which were descriptive of parts of the stimuli; for instance, selecting the fireman and the soldier "because both have uniforms," or the boy and the girl "because they both have shoes." Given pictures of familiar objects and animals—furniture, tools, livestock—they tended to sort them by applying functional or class labels. Typical were the responses for a hammer and saw, "these are used to build with," or for the cow, sheep, and chicken, "these live on a farm" (Sigel, 1961).

Younger children of four and five using similar type materials respond differently from the older children. Boys aged four tended to pay more attention to the background and structural aspects of the stimuli; for example, these have grey lines, or these have dark backgrounds. Girls, however, tended to organize materials on the basis of the more meaningful parts of the pictures; for example, these have legs, or these have arms (Sigel, 1963). The kind of content, then, with which the child is working influences the basis of organization.

The child during this period, age seven to eleven, has evolved a conceptual organization that begins to be coherent and stable, possessing characteristics of logic, the ability to think in categorical terms. He is increasingly objective and manifests increasing emancipation from the perceptual dominance of the environment. He is now becoming able to use his conceptual framework as a way of organizing the diverse world about him. It is during these particular four or five years that the child makes the great strides toward formal and adult conceptual functioning. What has preceded and what follows, however, should be considered as interdependent.

Period of Formal Operations (*Eleven to Fifteen Years*)

The final period, that of formal operations which are truly logical, occurs from eleven to fifteen years of age. It is at this point (according to Piaget) that the child is able to take the final steps to true abstract thinking and conceptualization. He now may be guided by the forms of various argument situations. For the first time, he can ignore the content. Both as preadolescent and adolescent he is able to make inferences and evaluate hypotheses. He can now operate in what is called the hypothetical deductive procedure of logical thought, since he can create hypotheses and deduce logical conclusions (Inhelder and Piaget, 1958).

A variety of intellectual skills become available at this time of life. In mathematics considerable development occurs, for the child is now able to handle calculus of proportions and logical reasoning of the inductive and deductive type in which he employs propositions. During this period Piaget holds that the child can truly plan scientific investigations because he is now ready to handle all kinds of combinations in a systematic order whereas previously he could only handle one variable at a time.

Some Interpretations and Conclusions

We have presented schematically a review of the stages of development, using Piaget's system as an organizing framework. Unfortunately, condensation of this monolithic and complicated theory into a few short pages may provide the reader with mere tastes and glimpses of the actual complexity. Other reviewers might have chosen other conceptual frameworks. Piaget was selected here because he provides the most meaningful system dealing with cognitive development. The reader is referred to the excellent and recent work by Flavell (1963), which provides a comprehensive review in great detail of Piaget's entire system. Hunt (1961), Wallach (1963), and Kessen and Kuhlman (1962) provide more schematic reviews. The theory is a stage-dependent one in which the child is said to move in an invariant order through major stages and substages, each denoting the necessary operations required. That is, he moves from sensory-motor intelligence, age 0 to 2, to preoperational thought, age 2 to 7; then into the concrete operations, age 7 to 11; and finally, at age 11 to 15, into the period of formal operations. Passage through these stages results in transformations, substitutions, and integrations.

The reader may be concerned about the fact that these stages are tied to rather specific ages. These ages have been established by Piaget, but he has indicated that they are only guidelines and not to be treated as fixed (Piaget, 1960; Tanner and Inhelder, 1960). In fact, as mentioned in our introductory statements, children at any given chronological age are found to function within different stages. Thus the chronological ages can be used only as estimates of when certain kinds of functions may be expected.

The child's utilization of concepts is influenced by the kinds of materials with which he is dealing. His mode of thought does not "reach the operational level in all areas simultaneously, but is rather subject to horizontal time lags whereby the same intellectual structures are successively applied to different contents" (Laurendeau and Pinard, 1962, p. 251). To illustrate, consider integrating items into a class. The success a child has in building such classes depends on the extent to which the elements to be integrated are endowed with properties readily accessible to perception or intuition. For example, the integration of the subclasses "boys and girls" into a general class of children is easier to make than that of the subclass "blue beads and red beads" into the class of wooden beads. For the same reason, the development of the concept of conservation of mass is grasped earlier than conservation of weight, even though both problems call for operational thinking.

Language is another factor which influences the acquisition of concepts. In fact, according to some theories language is the key determinant of the developmental sequence of concept attainment and thought in general. The structure of language influences the system one employs to organize and understand the environment (Johnson, 1962). From this point of view, the acquisition of language determines how the environment is discriminated, what objects can be integrated, and what kinds of abstract concepts can be invoked. Lacking a name in English for a category encompassing the relationship between two mothers-in-law, English-speaking children do not have this category. But it is not so in Yiddish, for example. It follows that organizational concepts of kinship would differ among English-speaking groups, in contrast to Yiddish-speaking groups. Thus availability of categories can even be said to be determined by the language structure (Brown, 1958; Whorf, 1956).

The acquisition of language and the particular linguistic system employed must be viewed as an important explanatory factor determining the kinds of concepts a child will develop. The exact role of language is still being investigated (Brown, 1958; Bruner, Goodenow, and Austin, 1956; Church, 1961; French, 1963; Vygotsky, 1962; Whorf, 1956).

ACQUISITION OF SOME COMMON CONCEPTS

Let us now turn to some of the major concepts. We cannot discuss them all but shall focus on the acquisition of concepts organizing apparent relationships of the physical world—object permanence, space, form, color, and size. Then we will proceed to those depicting relationships of physical and natural phenomena—causality, mass, weight, and volume.

Concept of Object Permanence

One of the most fundamental and taken-for-granted concepts a child has to acquire is that of object permanence. The acquisition of the concept of an object as different from oneself, as possessing its own intrinsic and independent permanence, is a necessary prerequisite for conceptual thinking. Piaget (1954) is one of the few investigators who have examined this problem in some detail.

By the time the child is eighteen to twenty-four months old, he realizes that objects have substance, take up space, and are permanent (that is, exist when out of sight). Initially an object or sensation or perception is viewed by the child as an extension of himself (Piaget, 1954; Wallach, 1963; Werner, 1948). When he is able to differentiate the object from himself, he tries to recapture or maintain the relationship with it. If the object is out of sight, however, he does not seek to locate it because he presumably believes it no longer exists. During this stage he is beginning to identify an object by its parts. Thus identification of a particular attribute—for instance, the handle of a rattle—is adequate for him to recognize that the whole object is there. He is now beginning to anticipate and to accommodate. He can anticipate the future position of objects as they move through space. For example, if he drops an object to the floor while sitting in his high-chair, he follows this with his eyes by looking over the edge. Yet earlier he would have gazed at the hand which had released the object. According to Piaget, if the child cannot recapture the object immediately, he still gives up interest.

Following this stage, the child begins to show active searching for an object no longer in his sight, by continuing to search randomly when someone suddenly hides it from him. Still later, he will search specifically at the place where he last saw the object. The last stage of object permanence is evidenced by his indicating an awareness that the object could be in any number of places. He now sees it as a thing apart from other objects and himself, subject to its own laws, and taking up space.

The significance of acquiring this concept becomes clear when we consider it as a prerequisite to two major aspects of the child's development. One is the identification that objects have their own integrity and exist independently of the person; the other, that the individual is differentiated from the environment and can himself be treated as an object (Piaget, 1954; Witkin, Dyk, Faterson, Goodenough, and Karp, 1962).

The attainment of the concept of object permanence occurs during the preverbal stage. The child does not know the specific labels for particular items and does not have a linguistic structure which enables him to identify what he has just seen. In spite of this, the child can think of the object independently of what he can do with it.

Space and Spatial Relations

Concomitant with the acquisition of concepts of object permanence is the acquisition of spatial concepts. Piaget theorizes that the infant's earliest ideas are that there are many kinds of spaces, each dependent upon where the child is at that point. A series of developmental stages follow in which he learns to comprehend a single objective space, encompassing objects, persons, and events. Here, Piaget identifies six stages. First, the child's concept of space is that of unrelated separate spaces. Next, space perception occurs. Perhaps Piaget's own words best describe the complex and yet critical developmental task that then follows.

> How, then, can we form an image of this space of the third stage? . . . Before the prehension of visual objects the child is in the center of a sort of moving and colored sphere, whose images imprison him without his having any hold on them other than by making them reappear by movements of head and eyes. Then when he begins to grasp what he sees the sphere expands little by little and the objects grasped are regulated in depth in relation to the body itself; distant space merely appears then as a kind of neutral zone in which prehension is not yet ventured while near space is the realm of objects to be grasped (1954, pp. 145–146).

As the child moves into the fourth phase, he is beginning to increase the differentiation between subjective and objective space. For example, as he searches for objects he is able to perceive the spatial relationships between himself and the place of the objects. If an object is behind the screen, he distinguishes between it and the screen, or if it is under the pillow he makes a similar distinction. He is beginning to show very primitive concepts of distance perspective, and thus to maintain a certain notion of constancy of size of the object. The child during the two subsequent stages shows an increase in his understanding of the relationship among objects in space, for example, stacking objects one on top of the other, putting them into containers, and so on. In the final stage the child is able to understand relationships of objects in their spatial concepts.

Both the concepts of space and object permanence and the stages of their acquisition are highly related, because the child is continuing to differentiate not only spaces but objects in it. Further, he separates himself from objects and realizes that he, too, is an object in space. He is moving toward objectivity.

Piaget was interested in determining the degree to which knowledge of spatial concepts has an ontogenetic order of appearance. What he wanted to demonstrate was that the perception of space and the representation of space are intellectual concepts, the end products of a long and arduous development sequence. The development of these spatial concepts depends upon actions in space rather than just the perception of it. As Flavell says, "Adult representation of space . . . results from active manipulations of the spatial environment rather than from any immediate 'reading off' of this environment by the perceptual apparatus. For example, we eventually come to 'see' objects as together or separated in space, much less as a function of past visual enregistrations of their proximity or separation than from past actions of placing objects together and separating them" (1963, p. 328).

Piaget has categorized space in three ways, similar to fields of mathematics. He speaks of topological, projective, and Euclidean space. Topological space refers to such things as order, enclosure, and continuity. Projective space refers to the perceptually invariant features of objects even when the point from which the object is viewed changes (object constancy). Euclidean space deals with such concepts as angularity, rectangularity, and parallelism. What Piaget finds is that discrimination of topological properties is made fairly early in life. In fact, during the preoperational period topological properties are apparent and become integrated into stable operations around age seven. It is only when the child is about nine or ten that he is able to handle projective and Euclidean space concepts. Flavell

(1963) points out that, in the history of science, man's study of space did not proceed in the developmental order cited by Piaget but rather in the order of Euclidean, projective, and topological concepts. Our educational system also teaches Euclidean space concepts earlier than topological and projective, but the work of Piaget implies that the reverse might be more effective.

In view of the educational implications of these concepts, it might be of interest to describe how Piaget studied them. In one experiment, the child was seated in front of a screen behind which were objects. He could handle the objects through an opening in the screen but could not see them. He was asked to match the objects behind the screen with duplicates which were visible. In a second experiment, the child was asked to draw pictures of the unseen objects after handling them. It was found that between the ages of three and four the child was able to discriminate objects in his drawings mainly on the basis of the topological characteristics. He was able to identify objects that were open compared to those that were closed. The ability to discriminate between curvilinear and rectilinear forms occurred later. Piaget concluded that the child of three or four years can readily distinguish an open from a closed circle, but is unable to discriminate between the closed circle and closed rectilinear figures such as squares. The implication of these cross-sectional studies is that the child passes through a sequential order in his acquisition of these space concepts.

A study reported by Meyer (1940) also indicates a developmental sequence from practical space to subjective space, beginning about age two-and-a-half. And at four years on, the child responds to objective space. He sees himself as one object among others. This report by Meyer corresponds generally to Piaget's description.

Related to spatial concepts is the ability of children to respond to relationships between items in space. It has been found that the position objects are in provides a very early clue which children can employ in ordering objects in the environment (Miller, 1934). The specific concept *middleness* has been studied by Graham, Jackson, Long, and Welch (1944) in children seven, eight, and nine years of age. The ability to form a generalized concept of middleness was found to increase between the ages of seven and nine, the period when children are able to handle the relationship of one set of objects to another.

We have suggested in this section that identification of space is related to the development of identification of the characteristics of objects. Further, there is interdependence between space concepts and spatial relations. The evidence suggests the detailed step-by-step developmental process. Related to the concepts of space and object permanence are other

major characteristics of objects—form, color, and size. Let us now turn
to those.

Development of Form Concepts

Since form is a salient feature which must be discriminated to identify
objects in space and to differentiate between objects, specific attention has
been paid to the development of form discrimination. Ling (1941) has
reported that children as young as six months were able to discriminate
forms and manifest "primitive abstraction." The infant in this experiment
was sitting in a crib, with a tray containing a semicircle of five holes in
front of him. Blocks of different shapes could be fastened into the holes or
left free. Various shapes such as circles and triangles were used. One form
would be fastened down, and the other left free. Since the infant would
naturally attempt to put the blocks in his mouth, that fact was taken
advantage of in the experiment. The unfastened form was sweetened with
saccharin, giving him a "reward" for picking it up and an inducement to
experiment with other forms that were not fastened down. Ling found that
the infant could learn to choose the correct block (the sweetened one) when
the two differed in shape. To ascertain preferences among form, it was also
possible for the experimenter to leave all the blocks free so as to observe
which ones the child selected. Infants were able to differentiate triangularity
and circularity from other forms, even when the form varied in size and
color. This type of discrimination is, in fact, a primitive abstraction.

Fantz (1958) found that infants could discriminate form even earlier than
reported by Ling. Fantz presented infants simultaneously with two visual
patterns, one containing horizontal stripes and the other, concentric circles.
He observed which type of pattern the infant fixated on longer. He found
that pattern preferences change toward a preference for complexity. Discrimination of pattern was found to occur as young as three weeks. Other
studies than that of Ling have reported that the child can learn form concepts as young as six months (Munn and Steinung, 1931).

During the sensory-motor period there is consistent and rapid development in which the infant is learning to make refined and precise judgments,
such as reaching for and identifying objects visually and physically (Fantz,
Ordy, and Udelf, 1962; Rheingold, 1961). The child not only has to
learn to distinguish one object from another by comparing their intrinsic
features; he also has to learn to identify forms, even when the background
or context within which he sees the forms changes. This is a necessary
abstraction that enables him to acquire object constancy (for example, to
find a familiar face in a strange crowd). Children as young as fifteen months
were able to learn to differentiate a cross from a square, even when the

object's position and color of background varied (Munn and Steinung, 1931). Crudden (1941) found that intelligent children between the ages of sixty-five months and seventy-eight months were able to make form abstractions when the position of objects changed. A diamond lying on its side was difficult for children below five years to identify, but between age five and six children were able to identify the sameness of the object even when it was oriented differently (Rice, 1930). Ling reports some semblance of such behavior even earlier.

Children in these early years, then, are acquiring concepts of object constancy as well as of object permanency. Objects, therefore, can be abstracted from their context and identified. At the preverbal period as well as in the subsequent early years, children show the beginnings of generalization ability and skill in differentiation. However, it must be kept in mind that the addition of language enchances a child's ability to categorize as well as influencing the kinds of dimensions he elects to categorize (Whorf, 1956).

The degree to which a child can generalize the identification of a form concept has been studied by Long (1940). He investigated generalization of the concept of roundness by training children between the ages of three and six years to make discriminations between a ball and a block. He varied the degree of roundness of the stimuli from spheres to ovals, and so on. The more the child continued to respond to an orange, for example, or to the more circular of the ovals, the more he had grasped the concept of roundness. While all of Long's subjects showed some ability in this respect, it was easier for the older children. The younger children had difficulty in extending the concept of roundness to cylinders and other figures.

These results indicate that a child of about five or six can show abstraction ability, since he can ignore irrelevancies—an intellectual feat similar to what Piaget has called "conservation." Perhaps we have here conservation of form. The findings indicate that children may be less dominated by the perceptual aspects of the environment somewhat earlier than our previous discussion implied.

Development of Color Concepts

Color as a basis of organization plays a significant role in psychological theory. On projective tests such as the Rorschach Ink Blot Test, color responses are interpreted as indicating expressions of emotionality (Klopfer, Ainsworth, Klopfer, and Holt, 1954). The individual who produces color-based percepts is considered less mature emotionally than one who emphasizes form. This is based on the assumption that color is a more primitive response, developing earlier and consequently reflective of immaturity.

It is true that children are able to discriminate colors early. In fact, they are able to do so before they can name those colors (Hurlock and Thomson, 1934; Reichard, Schneider, and Rapaport, 1944). Cook (1931) reports that more children at two years of age can match colors than can name them. By approximately four years of age, about 90 per cent of the children could match colors and about 80 per cent could name them. Children apparently discriminate and identify color before being able to apply the label.

That such discrimination appears early, even prior to verbalizations about color, does not mean it is the earliest feature of the object environment attended to. We have already observed the primitiveness of form discrimination. The question is, then, whether color has a greater attraction than form. A number of studies have been undertaken investigating this question.

One of the earliest experiments of this nature was performed by Katz prior to World War I. Working with children aged three to six he found that, for the youngest children, color was a much more important attribute than form (reported in Werner, 1948). Descoudres (1914) studied the problem more rigorously to determine the preference of color, form, or number concepts. She found that some children as young as three used color or form consistently, while others vacillated and tried to use both. She noted that even those who preferred form could change to color preferences when necessary. The preference for form was found to increase regularly from preschool to adulthood, while color choices diminish steadily. On the whole she concluded that color is favored over form between the ages of two and six, while with adults form is dominant. Descoudres added another important dimension to her experiment, the employment of realistic figures. Here she found that children tended to respond more readily on the basis of form than of color.

Other studies using younger subjects—such as that of Brian and Goodenough (1929)—found that children as young as twenty-one months of age tended to match various shaped and colored blocks on the basis of form rather than color. Their study indicates that after an initial preference for form, color becomes preferred about the age of three; color preference then gradually decreases until age six, when form again becomes dominant. For children seven to eleven, color is not a meaningful basis of organization when the items are familiar and realistic (Sigel, 1953). The findings of Brian and Goodenough can be integrated with Piaget's (1952) report on children within the sensory-motor period where the children are motoric and manipulatory. It may be more adaptive for children to deal with objects on the basis of form. The comprehension of permanence may come about just because of form saliency. Further, if the children during the preschool period are oriented toward objects on a topological basis, it would appear that form is a salient criterion in differentiating the environment. This may explain the dominance of form.

The previous studies, however, did not attempt to discover the degree to which children are consistent in their preference for form or color. Colby and Robertson (1942) studied the distribution and stability of types of responses within a limited age group between the ages of three and one-half and nine and one-half. The children were allowed to organize the material freely either on a color or a form basis, but not on both. The authors reported a small group of very stable types at all age levels, although the main developmental trend was toward form. At no age level did they find an overwhelming color dominance, as reported in other studies.

The Colby and Robertson study agrees with the Brian and Goodenough study that form is a salient basis for organization of objects at various times in the developmental cycle. It may well be that for most children it develops early, since it usually involves meaningful stimuli and may be essential for communicating the meaning of objects. Color may be less salient in the world of objects because it is less relevant to identification and interaction with objects. The form "chair" may have more significance for the child than the chair's particular color. Assimilation and accommodation to the form may enable the child to attend to color.

The findings of the Colby and Robertson study provide some evidence to show that a few children before five years of age can handle color, form, and size simultaneously as bases for classification. This is surprising in view of the contrast to Piaget's findings (1950), which indicate that multiple abstractions do not occur until the period of concrete operations (seven to eleven years). This is a further illustration of the need to be sensitive to the individual differences in the stages in which various phenomena appear, rather than being overly dependent on age levels.

The variability in color-form preferences found by Colby and Robertson might be due to personality differences. Honkavaara (1958a,b,c) set out to examine the degree to which color and form preferences can be interpreted as signs of primitiveness in personality or function. This problem pertains to the interpretation of projective tests, pointed out previously, that color dominance is an index of primitiveness in emotional expression. Honkavaara (1958b) was able to identify two types of respondents: *color reactors*, who prefer to organize material on the basis of color; and *form reactors*, who prefer form. She found that children of lower I.Q. were more often form reactors. Children and adults who tended to react predominantly with color orientation were more perceptive and sensitive to other people, whereas form reactors tended to be more practical, realistic, and socially conforming. Form reactors were also more common among women than men. These sex differences are consistent with those of Kagan and Lemkin (1961), who reported girls to be more form-dominant than boys.

Honkavaara maintains that particular preference for color or form reflects basic personality orientation. She even goes so far as to propose psychotherapeutic programs which take into account the color or form reactivity of the individual. The results of her voluminous research indicate some of the potential significance of the color-form issue in regard to the larger questions of personality functioning.

Development of Size Concepts

Size is less salient an organizational cue than color or form for the very young child (Kagan and Lemkin, 1961; Sigel, 1953, 1954, 1961). Abstraction of size-attributes requires the child to ignore the other potent and observable attributes of color, form, and meaningfulness. The size of an object is relative to an external measure or to other objects, whereas color and form are judged by intrinsic attributes.

The degree to which children classify objects as biggest, middle-sized, and "littlest" was studied by Thrum (1935). Working with subjects aged two to five years, she found the most difficult concept for children to select correctly was "middle-sized"; the next most difficult was "biggest"; and the easiest was "littlest." The youngest child who chose all three of the relative sizes correctly was three years and three months of age.

Long (1941) attempted to train children between the ages of four and seven years to discriminate a large stimulus from a small one. Candy was given as a reward for the correct choice. He found that children required from five to 437 trials to succeed. Once the children learned to discriminate differences of a wide range, they could generalize to narrower ones. They had difficulty, however, when the gross size differences were maintained but the forms were of different shapes.

Judging from the evidence, the concept of relative size seems a difficult one to learn even though form discriminations are possible early. It may well be that relative size concepts have similar prerequisites to relative position, for example, "middleness." The child must be able to abstract the size and see its relativity—which requires the ability to conserve and to relate.

Causality

Integral to our intellectual functioning is the ability to understand cause-and-effect relationships. The attainment of such concepts comes about through a sequence of developmental steps. Although children as early as the sensory-motor period show awareness of cause-effect relationships, an objective understanding of the causal nature of events does not blossom until late childhood. The explanations given by children prior to achievement of objective causality have been called *precausal* because they are infused with subjective thinking and based on limited knowledge.

Piaget has investigated the child's concepts of physical reality and causality to determine what kinds of ideas the child has about the physical world, and his work has influenced many others (Dennis, 1953; Dennis and Russell, 1940; Deutsche, 1937; Huang, 1943; Klingensmith, 1953; Laurendeau and Pinard, 1962; Mogar, 1960; Nass, 1956; Oakes, 1947; R. W. Russell, 1940, 1942). Piaget designed a series of experiments to uncover developmental changes in the child's concepts of psychic and physical phenomena. By questioning the child regarding the origin of such physical phenomena as movements of clouds or origin of night, Piaget uncovered the developmental stages for each kind of phenomenon (Piaget, 1928, 1930).

Piaget described three basic orientations children have to reality, each of which is said to derive from the initial lack of differentiation between self and the world. Children are initially egocentric and unable to discriminate "between psychological and physical events; human experiences (thoughts, feelings, wishes) constantly interpenetrate and get confused with the objective reality on which these experiences bear" (Flavell, 1963, p. 281). As an example, one type of such an inability to discriminate is to interpret dreams or thoughts as possessing thing-like qualities. This form of conceptualization is called *realism*. A complementary form coexisting at this time of life is *animism*, which, as indicated earlier, is the attributing of life to inanimate objects. In addition to *realism* and *animism*, there is the tendency to regard physical phenomena as products of human and divine creation. This is called *artificialism*.

Each of these orientations proceeds toward objective reality and causality through a succession of stages. Although the stages for each are interrelated, they are not perfectly synchronized. To illustrate, the second stage of animism, where consciousness is attributed to moving objects (for example, bicycles), occurs about ages six to eight; whereas the second stage of artificialism, in which mythological bases are offered in explanation of natural events, occurs about ages five to seven.

Piaget's (1930) findings on reality and causality can be summarized as follows: the first stage lasts until two to three years of age; the child confuses objective and subjective reality. There is magical thought with the belief that any desire can influence external objects and that external things can obey. The second stage, which lasts from two or three to seven or eight, is characterized by the child's egocentricity. There is no desire to find logical justification for one's statements of belief. The child is precausal. Causal concepts are based on a confusion between psychological activity and physical mechanism, and between motive and cause. In the third stage, logical and real categories develop: the child gives objective and logical causal explanations; for example, consciousness is limited to the animal world (Piaget, 1929).

Piaget's findings raised two basic questions: (a) Do these types of causal concepts in fact exist? (b) If they do, do they follow developmental stages? A number of investigations have been undertaken to test these. Deutsche (1937) conducted one of the major investigations in which Piaget's findings were not replicated. She did find four types of explanations but *no* animistic thinking. Working with children from age eight (Piaget had children below seven) and using group procedures (Piaget worked with individuals), Deutsche set out to determine if stages were necessary to describe the development of causality. She reported four types of causal thinking: *phenomenistic explanations,* in which two facts appearing together in perception are perceived as related simply because they exist continuously in time and space; *dynamic causality,* where objects are seen as having inherent forces capable of explaining their activity and movement; *mechanical causality,* where explanation is by contact and transference of movement rather than by internal forces (pedals make bicycles go, wind pushes clouds); and *logical deductions,* where explanations are based on principles.

Phenomenistic explanations are prevalent at age eight and decline steadily by age fifteen. Dynamic explanations are not frequent at any age but are found occasionally among children of ages eight to sixteen. Mechanical explanations increase slowly with age. Logical deduction increases with age, reaches its peak at fourteen years, then levels off. Since Deutsche did not find a sequence in the use of these causal explanations—but rather found that all appeared during the ages studied—she concluded stages do not exist. Other investigations tend to support her thesis that some of the types of causal explanations found are congruent with those of Piaget, but not the stage sequence (Ezer, 1962; Mogar, 1960).

Considerable disagreement exists about the degree to which animism is found in young children (Honkavaara, 1958a; Huang and Lee, 1945; Jahoda, 1958a,b; R. W. Russell, 1940, 1942). Some researchers have found it (R. W. Russell, 1940, 1942); others have not (Huang, 1943). The inconsistencies appear to be partly due to the methodologies employed. Apparently when children attribute "life" or consciousness to objects, it is not done indiscriminately; rather, selected aspects of "aliveness" are being attributed. "Aliveness" for children means activity (Klingensmith, 1953). Life is also attributed to things a child likes or thinks are pretty (Honkavaara, 1958a). However, research has not yet verified whether the use of terms like "life" and "alive" in reality expresses a belief that the object is, in fact, alive. Frequently, we employ personal pronouns and animistic concepts for automobiles, ships, and the like. Information must be obtained to clarify the underlying conceptualization before we can be certain whether or not the child is truly animistic.

Laurendeau and Pinard (1962) analyzed the various relevant studies in conjunction with their intensive investigation of causal thinking. They concluded that differences and contradictions reported by other investigators are due to the varieties of testing procedure, types of subjects used, and the techniques of analysis.

In their own studies they worked with 250 boys and 250 girls from various socioeconomic and intellectual levels, between the ages of four and twelve. They interviewed each child about concepts of dreams, concepts of life, origin of night, movement of clouds, the floating and sinking of objects. Stages were found for each of these particular concepts. Although each had its own stage sequence, they summarize the overall results as follows: "Realism disappears at approximately six and a half years of age, artificialism around nine, animism and dynamism around ten. Before these ages, precausal thinking is preponderant" (p. 248).

Thus precausal explanations decline with age but disappear at different rates, depending on the particular types of causal problems. Laurendeau and Pinard's findings (1962, p. 252) show time lags, since "some areas of reality are more easily or rapidly objectified than others, according to the complexity of the phenomena, the child's experience, and the formal teaching he has received."

This study suggests caution in the acceptance of ages at which certain stages occur. An implication from Laurendeau and Pinard is that experience and knowledge may influence the onset of causal thinking stages and the lags in certain areas, but the order is fixed.

Many of the studies which tested Piaget's findings unfortunately varied too much in many of the conditions to provide crucial tests of the theory. For example, Ezer's study (1962) on the effect of religious belief and physical causality concludes that the stages do not exist. But his findings are based on causal situations very different in content from Piaget's and categorized so differently that comparability is not possible.

We can conclude that children do provide different kinds of explanations for physical and psychical phenomena, that there is a crude correspondence with age but not a one-to-one relationship, and that the existence of stages of causal explanations is still a tenable hypothesis. The invariance of these stages needs more precise and rigorous testing, assessing the role of experience and knowledge in the onset of particular stages.

Development of Conservation of
Mass, Weight, and Volume

The major works in the understanding of the child's attainment of concepts of mass or quantity, weight, and volume also stem from the investigations of Piaget and the research he has stimulated. D. Russell (1956), in his survey of the literature, reports studies which summarize the pertinent research here. The findings point to a steady improvement with age, but provide little insight regarding the developmental levels or the specific trends for each of these concepts.

Piaget studied these concepts in connection with his interest in the development of conservation. Two questions posed by him and his co-workers are: (a) "Do children understand concepts of the invariance of continuous quantity when the size of the container for liquids or the shape of an item varies?" (b) "Are they able to understand that volume remains the same even though the shape of the container may vary?"

One experiment Piaget and Inhelder (1941) carried out in order to understand children's comprehension of continuous quantity of weight, for example, employed two identical balls of clay. One ball was used as the standard and the other was manipulated by the experimenter who cut it, rolled it out, or similarly altered its shape. After the shape of one ball was changed, the child was asked whether the two pieces of clay weighed the same, more, or less. Experiments using such procedures discovered that there is a natural ordinal scale of conceptualization of quantity, weight, and volume. Quantity is understood in conservational terms by the age of seven or eight; weight by the ages of nine and ten; and volume around the age of eleven or twelve.

Studies in the United States (Elkind, 1961a,b,c) and in Great Britain (Lovell and Ogilvie, 1960, 1961a,b) systematically repeated Piaget's experiment. They confirmed the developmental sequence for quantity and weight even to the extent of age ranges. An exception was that conservation of volume was difficult for twelve-year-old American children. Like most of the others, however, these studies employed cross-sectional samples. A better test of whether the stages are invariant would be to determine whether for child A, for example, the sequence described will hold.

Kooistra's research (1963) with children of four through seven years of age emphasized the importance of the child's intellectual level in performance of a conservation task. Working with a sample of children of superior intelligence (average Stanford-Binet I.Q. of 135), his results using mental age as a criterion were comparable to previous findings in which chronological age was the criterion. When the children's explanations of the various conservation procedures were classified according to chronological age, the ages at which 50 per cent or more of the responses displayed that conservation had been achieved were: age five for mass, age six for weight, and age seven for volume. Only seven of the 96 children in Kooistra's experiment showed any deviation from the mass-weight-volume sequence reported by Piaget.

Conservation, like other intellectual operations, develops in a sequence. This has been consistently supported by a number of studies. To date, the evidence points to what appears to be an invariant order—at least so far as concepts of mass, weight, and volume are concerned. Of particular interest is the study of Kooistra in which such an order of development was found, but at relatively younger chronological ages because the children were intellectually superior. This suggests that the mental age of a child is an important factor, determining the onset of a stage. Notwithstanding, the sequence is consistent with reports in the literature.

FACTORS AFFECTING THE ATTAINMENT OF CONCEPTS

We have described to this point the sequence of concept attainment as well as the cognitive context in which it occurs. We have not, to any extent, specified those factors which might influence the course of such development, positively or negatively. The stages described have been based, for the most part, on normally developing children of unspecified social or intellectual level. Some exceptions have been reported in the studies of Lovell and Ogilvie (1960, 1961a,b); Kooistra (1963); Dodwell (1962); Laurendeau and Pinard (1962). The degree to which variations result from social status or intellectual level still needs further specification.

While it seems reasonable to assume that intelligence and concept attainment should be highly correlated, much of the research reported in the literature does not present a consistent picture (Hoffman, 1955; Stuart, 1935). That high-level abstract concepts (for example, "living things") have been found among seven-year-old children of average mental ability would suggest that mental ability, as usually measured, is not the crucial factor in the child's attainment of concepts (Sigel, 1953). Recently, two studies were carried out which shed considerable light on this question. Osler and Fivel (1961) working with children ages six to fourteen, one group with an average I.Q. of 101 and a second with an average I.Q. of 121, found that the higher I.Q. group acquired more quickly and showed sudden acquisition of such concepts as bird, animal, and living—in contrast to the average I.Q. group who showed a gradual acquisition. Both groups do acquire the concepts, however. Efficiency of concept attainment, then, is associated with the higher I.Q. In attempting to explain the sudden acquisition of concepts among the brighter children, a second study was undertaken by Osler and Trautman (1961). This one sought to test the idea that the brighter children employ hypotheses in their concept attainment. This expectation was confirmed. The high I.Q. child does try out hypotheses in learning concepts. Once he hits upon the correct hypotheses, he immediately learns the concept and thereafter makes no errors. The experiment, however, sheds no light on the processes used by the average I.Q. group.

The evidence to date thus indicates that the higher I.Q. children attain concepts more readily than less-bright children. However, children of average I.Q. do eventually have available abstract as well as concrete concepts.

If all normal children pass through the entire sequence of stages described, and acquire the ability to conserve or to handle class relations, then how can we explain individual differences in cognitive functioning? The theory of the invariant order of concept attainment allows for the effect of I.Q. and experience on the *onset* of a given stage, although all individuals are expected to progress through all stages. That is, individual differences in conceptual level reflect differential growth *rates*. Pursuing this point further, the following question may also be asked. As the individuals begin to level off, will the less-bright individual catch up with the brighter one, so that at a later mature age all persons will operate at the same cognitive level? We know that this is not true—that, in fact, there is considerable variation in the ability of adults to solve reasoning and logical problems. The lack of concern with such individual differences is reflected in the experimental designs and the system of categorizing responses used by Piaget and his followers. The experimental problems they pose do not employ items sufficiently graded in level of difficulty within particular areas. For example, take the task used to determine a child's ability to conserve mass. After all, to comprehend the continuous quantity of weight of a clay ball is easy. The clay balls should be followed by more difficult items, testing the same principle. In this way, individual differences in ability will be brought out. All the children at a particular age level will pass some, but not all, of the items testing the same concept.

From the work with mentally retarded children, it is clear that the degree of retardation influences the level of conceptualization. There are some groups at I.Q. less than 30 who are incapable of any abstract thinking and of only minimal concrete thinking. The groups between 30 and 70 I.Q.

show considerable variation in the kinds of concepts they have available. The mildly retarded show even greater variability; some do attain concepts of conservation of weight and quantity, though at a later chronological time (Inhelder, 1944; Woodward, 1961).

Research in concept learning is beginning to experience a revival of interest, particularly in the study of mental retardation. With increased precision of measures and more research, we may be able to identify more specifically the deficits in concept learning and the processes involved.

Emotional attitudes, motivational states, states of adjustment, and acquired predispositions as to approaches to the environment can also influence the attainment of concepts (Anthony, 1956). Children who are prejudiced, for example, have greater difficulty in handling abstract concepts than those low on prejudice (Kutner, 1958). Children who are autistic—a psychotic condition in which the child is nonresponsive to the environment—show considerable defects in concept attainment (Finch, 1960). The level of anxiety that children show also influences their attainment and use of concepts (Sarason, Davidson, Lighthall, Waite, and Ruebush, 1960). Children who are highly anxious tend to employ concepts dealing with the emotional aspects of the situation more than do those who are not (Sigel, 1961).

Children with brain damage also have difficulty in attaining abstract concepts. Brain-injured children tend to be more concrete in their vocabulary level, appear less capable of shifting from one approach to another, and have difficulty in integrating various kinds of information. In fact, one of the important diagnostic tools for brain injury is the degree to which a child has difficulty in coping with abstractions (Goldstein and Scheerer, 1941; Harvey, Hunt, and Schroder, 1961; Hebb, 1949; Strauss and Werner, 1942; Werner, 1946, 1948). Differences in color-form perception and the learning of such concepts have been found in comparisons of deaf children with children who can hear (Gaines, 1963).

The concepts a child acquires are influenced by the predisposition he shows to attend to particular features of the environment (Harlow, 1959). Children attain and employ different concepts, depending on the kinds of information they possess. For some children the manifest features of stimuli—parts or apparent common elements—are the basis of organization. Others may organize materials by drawing inferences rather than dealing with the obvious. Such differences in patterns are called cognitive style, and are presumed to influence the kind of content a child will employ in evolving his concepts (Kagan, Moss, and Sigel, 1963; Sigel, 1961). Gallagher, in another chapter in this volume, discusses the relationship between cognitive style and productive thinking.

The strategy the child employs in seeking out relevant information from stimuli has also been studied, since it has been found to relate to the efficiency and quality of concept attainment. Bruner and his associates (1956) have identified a number of such strategies. The particular one employed may depend on the individual child's cognitive style as well as on the content of the material. These investigators have not discovered what accounts for those strategies, up to the present time, but have presented convincing evidence that they do, in fact, exist.

EFFECTS OF TRAINING

A number of studies have been reported in which attempts were made to teach new concepts to young children. Attempts have been made to determine the child's ability to learn conservation of quantity, weight, and volume (Smedslund, 1961a,b,c,d,e,f); conservation of area (Beilin and Franklin, 1962); logical thinking (Ervin, 1960a,b); hierarchically ordered concepts (Welch, 1940); and the conservation of number (Wohlwill and Lowe, 1962). The accumulating evidence strongly suggests that a child cannot be taught the concept in question unless he has already attained a particular cognitive level of maturity. In each of these studies the authors tried to teach the child some concept just before he was "ready" and failure was attributed to his immaturity and lack of experience. Possibly they did not employ sufficiently long training periods, *nor ascertain with any precision the necessary sequences as preludes to the learning*. This lack of success has been interpreted as reflecting "deep developmental reality about these structures, and in this sense the learning studies confer a degree of backhanded validity to Piaget's previous assertions that they are, in fact, real existents which exert weight in the young child's intellectual life" (Flavell, 1963, p. 377).

Nevertheless, one investigator has reported some change in the development of conservation of substance (Smedslund, 1961 e,f). The research is of significance since a theoretical basis for the change is provided. Smedslund holds that the essential condition for the shift from nonconservation to conservation is introduction of cognitive conflict. This conflict induces a cognitive reorganization which results in the concept of conservation. To test this hypothesis (Smedslund, 1961e) 13 five and one-half to six and one-half-year-old children who indicated no prior evidence of conservation of substance were subjected to a training procedure as follows. The child was presented with two objects (pieces of plasticine). One was intact and the other was transformed in two ways: changed in shape; and either a piece of it removed or another piece added. The child was asked "Do you think there is *more* or the *same amount* or *less* in this one than in that one?" To create conflict, the change in shape was always in opposition to the addition or subtraction. For example, the object might have been both elongated (to make it appear larger) and a piece taken from it (to make it appear smaller). Of the five subjects who consistently answered only in terms of addition or subtraction—correctly ignoring the change in shape— four gave a number of conservation responses in the posttraining test, complete with the logical rationale. Although the number of subjects in this experiment is small, Smedslund points out that such shifts from no con- servation to conservation with a logical explanation are extremely rare in the research literature. In a later experiment (1961f), Smedslund used a similar training procedure, but added a control group that received no training. Whereas in previous studies training had been ineffective, with the introduction of cognitive conflict and with no rewards for correct responses, the training groups performed better than the controls. This has interesting implications for education, suggesting that to teach a concept, juxtaposition of two competing ones will force a child to reflect and think rather than to respond with what he already knows. Further, when such conflict is inherent in the task, rewarding the child is not necessary.

Of further interest is an earlier study by Smedslund in which he reports that children who had acquired conservation in the course of their normal experience did not give up that concept in the face of challenging experi- mental conditions. This was in contrast to those who had acquired the concept during an experiment (Smedslund, 1961c). Subjects were presented with two plasticine objects. One was changed in shape but the experimenter surreptitiously stole a piece from it. When the child said the quantity was the same despite the change in shape, the experimenter proved this answer wrong by weighing the object on a scale. The children who had acquired the concept of conservation naturally were resistant—insisting for example, that a piece of plasticine must have fallen to the floor. The children who had acquired conservation experimentally, on the other hand, quickly reverted to nonconservation.

Acquisition and retention of the concept of conservation reflects an inner logical necessity. If these results continue to be confirmed, it indicates that training for concept acquisition in other areas—number, space, geometry, quantity—will have to take into account the child's general intellectual structure. Induction of concepts into an inadequately mature cognitive organization can result in a hollow core of concept acquisition.

These findings and interpretations are, again, consistent with Werner's admonition (1957): that the child's observed facility in reproducing or producing concepts does not necessarily mean that the underlying intellec- tual process is accurately reflected. That the child can use the *term* animal does not necessarily mean he has the *class concept* animal. It may be parroting, or involve meanings applied in a limited way. The underlying process can be ascertained only by appropriate questioning. Isolated instances of emerging concepts have to be assessed with caution.

IMPLICATIONS FOR EDUCATION

The most direct application of the insights and knowledge available from this review is for curriculum development and diagnosis of the child's intellectual status. In view of the findings on stages of concept attainment, curricula could be organized to take these into account. Take the teaching of physical concepts as an example. If the child's comprehension of quantity, weight, and volume does appear in sequential order, it may make sense to arrange elementary school science curriculum accordingly. Science experiments dealing with quantity could be introduced possibly as early as ages six to seven, especially with above-average children, followed by experiments dealing with weight. But the change should not be viewed as a mere translation or mechanical application to younger levels of present teaching content. It would require a comprehensive reexamination of a quantity of materials in the areas of mathematics, science, causality, and so on. This ambitious undertaking may be well worthwhile.

If the stage-dependent conceptualization continues to hold up, it can provide a valuable ordinal scale for diagnosing the child's intellectual ability. Determining which stage a child is in enables the diagnostician to know those already achieved and what the child's next steps are to be.

Since experience and language so influence our ability to conceptualize, exposure to a wide variety of relevant experiences and encouragement in the acquisition of verbal skills may increase both the quality and quantity of a child's concepts; and may facilitate his application of concepts by providing a more coherent and stable cognitive organization. Here we invoke once more the concern of several investigators about building concepts on a foundation of insufficient intellectual maturity.

A direct teaching implication emerges also from Smedslund's cognitive-conflict theory: both the utilization and the acquisition of concepts may be furthered when the child must solve a problem involving concepts that are juxtaposed. Intolerance of cognitive conflict may well be one of the motivating variables that influence concept acquisition (Festinger, 1957).

From Piaget's work, in particular, we find that children are able to handle many kinds of problems intuitively. That is, they are able to solve the problems without being able to verbalize them. What is suggested is a need for teaching techniques in which children can work on certain problems without necessarily having to provide verbal explanations. True, this may seem contradictory to the proposition that the child's verbalization facilitates the acquisition of concepts; but it would appear that there is sometimes reason to limit such emphasis. It is the present writer's contention that a willingness of the teacher to accept relatively poorly articulated expressions without negative evaluation may sometimes have a positive effect, potentially providing a basis for the child to enhance his intellectual development. This may be particularly important in the education of children from culturally underprivileged groups, where verbal facility often lags considerably behind intellectual potential. Excessive demand for verbalization may bring about a withdrawal or rebellion from other aspects of learning.

There is no question that much more research must be done in this area. A host of fascinating research problems emerge. For example, to what degree can teaching modify the order or development rate of the sequential stages, and what are the psychological, cognitive, and affective consequences? What kinds of teaching procedures are required? Whether or not appropriate teaching increases the rate of development, there is still the question of the long-term consequences of such enrichment.

IMPLICATIONS FOR CHILD REARING

Finally, in the research we have reviewed, several implications seem present with respect to the parent's communication with the child. The verbal statements parents use, for example, to discipline their children should be viewed in relation to the child's intellectual status. Although we do not have much empirical evidence here, we can make some inferences.

Thus, it has been frequently stated by child-rearing experts that in disciplining, the parent should distinguish between the child and his behavior. From our knowledge of the child's conceptual development, to the young child, his action and self are one. He does not make this objectification; attempting to separate behavior from self may therefore be meaningless. The parent might better be concerned with dealing with the child as an integrated unit, until the child is ready to handle the separation of self from behavior. Another inference is that the child is concrete during his early years; consequently, he will comprehend specific statements better than generalized principles. Further, since the child's concept of time is limited in preschool periods and in the early elementary grades, promises or expectations of long-term behaviors would also seem to be unrealistic. The parent, reflecting on the child's intellectual status, should employ techniques which are consistent with it. How parent-child practices influence conceptual development, however, needs further study.

REFERENCES

ANTHONY, E. J. The significance of Jean Piaget for child psychiatry. *Brit. J. med. Psychol.*, 1956, **29**, 20–34.

ATTNEAVE, F. Transfer of experiences with a class-schema to identification-learning of patterns and shapes. *J. exp. Psychol.*, 1957, **54**, 81–88.

AUSUBEL, D. P. *Theory and problems of child development.* New York: Grune & Stratton, 1957.

BEILIN, H. & FRANKLIN, I. C. Logical operations in area and length measurement, age and training effects. *Child Developm.*, 1962, **33**, 607–618.

BOLLES, M. M. The basis of pertinence. *Arch. Psychol., N. Y.*, 1937, **212**, 51.

BRAINE, M. D. S. The ontogeny of certain logical operations: Piaget's formulation examined by nonverbal methods. *Psychol. Monogr.*, 1959, **73**, No. 5 (Whole No. 475).

BRIAN, C. R. & GOODENOUGH, F. L. Relative potency of color and form perception at various ages. *J. exp. Psychol.*, 1929, **12**, 197–213.

BROWN, R. W. *Words and things.* Glencoe, Ill.: Free Press, 1958.

BRUNER, J. S., GOODENOW, J. J., & AUSTIN, G. A. *A study of thinking.* New York: Wiley, 1956.

CHURCH, J. *Language and discovery of reality.* New York: Random House, 1961.

COLBY, M. G. & ROBERTSON, J. B. Genetic studies in abstraction. *J. comp. Psychol.*, 1942, **33**, 385–401.

COOK, W. M. Ability of children in color discrimination. *Child Developm.*, 1931, **2**, 303–320.

CRUDDEN, C. H. Form abstraction by children. *J. genet. Psychol.*, 1941, **58**, 113–129.

DENNIS, W. Animistic thinking among college and university students. *Sci. Mon., N. Y.*, 1953, **76**, 247–249.

DENNIS, W. & RUSSELL, R. W. Piaget's questions applied to Zuni children. *Child Developm.*, 1940, **11**, 181–187.

DESCOUDRES, A. Couleur, forme ou nombre. *Arch. de Psychol.*, 1914, **14**, 305–344.

DEUTSCHE, J. M. The development of children's concepts of causal relations. *Univ. Minn. Inst. Child Welf. Monogr.*, 1937, **13**.

DODWELL, P. C. Children's understanding of number and related concepts. *Canad. J. Psychol.*, 1960, **14**, 191–205.

DODWELL, P. C. Children's understanding of number concepts: characteristics of an individual and of a group test. *Canad. J. Psychol.*, 1961, **15**, 29–36.

DODWELL, P. C. Relations between the understanding of the logic of classes and of cardinal numbers in children. *Canad. J. Psychol.*, 1962, **16**, 152–160.

ELKIND, D. The development of quantitative thinking: a systematic replication of Piaget's studies. *J. genet. Psychol.*, 1961, **98**, 37–46 (a).

ELKIND, D. Children's discovery of the conservation of mass, weight, and volume: Piaget replication study II. *J. genet. Psychol.*, 1961, **98**, 219–227 (b).

ELKIND, D. Quantity conceptions in junior and senior high school students. *Child Developm.*, 1961, **32**, 551–560 (c).

ERVIN, S. M. Training and a logical operation by children. *Child Developm.*, 1960, **31**, 537–554; 555–563 (a).

ERVIN, S. M. Experimental procedures of children. *Child Developm.*, 1960, **31**, 703–719 (b).

ESTES, B. W. Some mathematical and logical concepts in children. *J. genet. Psychol.*, 1956, **88**, 219–222.

EZER, M. Effect of religion upon children's responses to questions involving physical causality. In J. Rosenblith & W. Allinsmith (Eds.), *The causes of behavior: readings in child development and educational psychology.* Boston: Allyn & Bacon, 1962. Pp. 481–487.

FANTZ, R. L. Pattern vision in young infants. *Psychol. Rec.*, 1958, **8**, 43–47.

FANTZ, R. L., ORDY, J. M., & UDELF, M. S. Maturation of pattern visions in infants during the first six months. *J. comp. physiol. Psychol.*, 1962, **55**, 907–917.

FESTINGER, L. A. *Theory of cognitive dissonance*. Evanston, Ill.: Row, Peterson, 1957.

FINCH, S. M. *Fundamentals of child psychiatry*. New York: Norton, 1960.

FLAVELL, J. H. *Developmental psychology of Jean Piaget*. Princeton, N. J.: Van Nostrand, 1963.

FRENCH, D. The relationship of anthropology to studies in perception and cognition. In S. Koch (Ed.), *Psychology: a study of a science*. Vol. VI. New York: McGraw-Hill, 1963.

GAINES, R. Color-form response patterns in perception, discrimination ability, and learning in deaf and hearing children. Unpublished doctoral dissertation, Univ. of Chicago, 1963.

GESELL, A. & AMATRUDA, C. S. *Developmental diagnosis: normal and abnormal child development*. New York: Hoeber, 1941.

GIBSON, E. Perceptual development. In H. Stevenson (Ed.), *Child psychology. 62nd Yearb. nat. Soc. Stud. Educ.* Chicago: Univ. Chicago Press, 1963.

GOLDSTEIN, K. & SCHEERER, M. Abstract and concrete behavior: an experimental study with special tests. *Psychol. Monogr.*, 1941, **53**, No. 2 (Whole No. 239).

GRAHAM, V., JACKSON, T. A., LONG, L., & WELCH, L. Generalizing concepts of middleness. *J. genet. Psychol.*, 1944, **65**, 227–237.

HARLOW, H. F. Learning set and error factor theory. In S. Koch (Ed.), *Psychology: a study of a science*. Vol. II. *General systematic formulation, learning and special processes*. New York: McGraw-Hill, 1959.

HARVEY, O. J., HUNT, D. E., & SCHRODER, H. M. *Conceptual systems and personality organization*. New York: Wiley, 1961.

HEBB, D. O. *The organization of behavior*. New York: Wiley, 1949.

HOFFMAN, H. N. A study in an aspect of concept formation, with subnormal, average, and superior adolescents. *Genet. Psychol. Monogr.*, 1955, **52**, 191–239.

HONKAVAARA, S. The "dynamic affective" phase in the development of concepts. *J. Psychol.*, 1958, **45**, 11–23 (a).

HONKAVAARA, S. A critical reevaluation of the color and form reaction, and disproving of the hypothesis connected with it. *J. Psychol.*, 1958, **45**, 25–36 (b).

HONKAVAARA, S. The color form reaction as a basis for differential psychotherapeutic approach. *J. Psychol.*, 1958, **46**, 39–51 (c).

HUANG, I. Children's conception of physical causality: a critical summary. *J. genet. Psychol.*, 1943, **63**, 71–121.

HUANG, I. & LEE, H. W. Experimental analysis of child animism. *J. genet. Psychol.*, 1945, **66**, 69–74.

HUNT, J. McV. *Intelligence and experience*. New York: Ronald Press, 1961.

HURLOCK, E. B. & THOMSON, J. L. Children's drawings: an experimental study of perception. *Child Developm.*, 1934, **5**, 127–138.

ILG, F. & AMES, L. B. Developmental trends in arithmetic. *J. genet. Psychol.*, 1951, **79**, 3–28.

INHELDER, B. *Le diagnostic du raisonnement chez les debiles mentaux*. Neuchatel: Delachaux et Niestle, 1944.

INHELDER, B. & PIAGET, J. *The growth of logical thinking from childhood to adolescence*. New York: Basic Books, 1958.

JAHODA, G. Child animism: I. A critical survey of cross-cultural research. *J. soc. Psychol.*, 1958, **47**, 107–212 (a).

JAHODA, G. Child animism: II. A study in West Africa. *J. soc. Psychol.*, 1958, **47**, 213–222 (b).

JOHNSON, R. C. Linguistic structure as related to concept formation and to concept content. *Psychol. Bull.*, 1962, **59**, 468–476.

KAGAN, J. & LEMKIN, J. Form, color, and size in children's conceptual behavior. *Child Developm.*, 1961, **32**, 25–28.

KAGAN, J., MOSS, H. A., & SIGEL, I. E. Psychological significance of styles of conceptualization. In J. E. Wright & J. Kagan (Eds.), Basic cognitive process in children. *Monogr. Soc. Res. Child Developm.*, 1963, **28**, No. 2.

KENDLER, H. H. & KENDLER, T. S. Inferential behavior in preschool children. *J. exp. Psychol.*, 1956, **51**, 311–314.

KENDLER, H. H. & KENDLER, T. S. Vertical and horizontal processes in problem solving. *Psychol. Rev.*, 1962, **69**, 1–16.

KENDLER, T. S. Concept formation. *Ann. rev. Psychol.*, 1961, **12**, 447–472.

KESSEN, W. & KUHLMAN, C. (Eds.) Thought in the young child. *Monogr. Soc. Res. Child Developm.*, 1962, **27**, No. 2.

KLINGENSMITH, S. W. Child animism: what the child means by "alive." *Child Developm.*, 1953, **24**, 51–61.

KLOPFER, B., AINSWORTH, M. D., KLOPFER, W. G., & HOLT, R. R. *Developments in the Rorschach technique*. Vol. I., *Techniques and theory*. New York: World Book, 1954.

KOFFKA, K. *The growth of the mind: an introduction to child psychology*. Transl. by R. M. Ogden. (2nd rev. ed.) New York: Harcourt Brace, 1928.

KOHLBERG, L. Stages in children's conceptions of physical and social objects, in the years four to eight. A study of developmental theory. Unpublished manuscript, 1963.

KOOISTRA, W. H. Developmental trends in the attainment of conservation, transitivity, and relativism in the thinking of children: a replication and extension of Piaget's ontogenetic formulations. Unpublished doctoral dissertation. Wayne State Univ., 1963.

KUTNER, B. Patterns of mental functioning associated with prejudice in children. *Psychol. Monogr.*, 1958, **72**, 1–48.

LAURENDEAU, M. & PINARD, A. *Causal thinking in the child*. New York: Internat. Univ. Press, 1962.

LEWIN, K. Behavior and development as a function of the total situation. In L. Carmichael (Ed.), *Manual of child psychology*. New York: Wiley, 1946. Pp. 791–844.

LING, B. Form discrimination as a learning cue in infants. *Comp. Psychol. Monogr.*, 1941, **17**, No. 2, 66.

LONG, L. Conceptual relationships in children: the concept of roundness. *J. genet. Psychol.*, 1940, **57**, 289–315.

LONG, L. Size discrimination in children. *Child Developm.*, 1941, **12**, 247–254.

LOVELL, K. & OGILVIE, E. A study of the conservation of substance in the junior school child. *Brit. J. educ. Psychol.*, 1960, **30**, 109–118.

LOVELL, K. & OGILVIE, E. The growth of the concept of volume in junior school children. *J. Child Psychol. Psychiat.*, 1961, **2**, 118–126 (a).

LOVELL, K. & OGILVIE, E. A study of the conservation of weight in the junior school child. *Brit. J. educ. Psychol.*, 1961, **31**, 138–144 (b).

MARTIN, W. E. Quantitative expression in young children. *Genet. Psychol. Monogr.*, 1951, **44**, 147–219.

MEYER, E. Comprehension of spatial relations in preschool children. *J. genet. Psychol.*, 1940, **57**, 119–151.

MILLER, N. E. The perception of children: a genetic study employing the critical choice delayed reaction. *J. genet. Psychol.*, 1934, **44**, 321–339.

MOGAR, M. Children's causal reasoning about natural phenomena. *Child Developm.*, 1960, **31**, 59–65.

MUNN, N. I. & STEINUNG, B. B. The relative efficacy of form and background in a child's discrimination of visual pattern. *J. genet. Psychol.*, 1931, **39**, 73–90.

NASS, M. L. The effects of three variables on children's concept of physical causality. *J. abnorm. soc. Psychol.*, 1956, **53**, 191–196.

OAKES, M. E. Children's explanations of natural phenomena. *Teach. Coll. Contr. Educ.*, 1947, No. 926.

OSLER, S. F. & FIVEL, M. W. Concept attainment: I. The role of age and intelligence in concept attainment by induction. *J. exp. Psychol.*, 1961, **62**, 1–8.

OSLER, S. F. & TRAUTMAN, G. E. Concept attainment: II. Effect of stimulus complexity upon concept attainment at two levels of intelligence. *J. exp. Psychol.*, 1961, **62**, 9–13.

PIAGET, J. *Judgment and reasoning in the child.* New York: Harcourt Brace, 1928.

PIAGET, J. *The child's conception of the world.* New York: Harcourt Brace, 1929.

PIAGET, J. *The child's conception of physical causality.* New York: Harcourt Brace, 1930.

PIAGET, J. *The psychology of intelligence.* London: Routledge & Paul, 1950.

PIAGET, J. *The origins of intelligence in children.* New York: Internat. Univ. Press, 1952.

PIAGET, J. *The construction of reality in the child.* New York: Basic Books, 1954.

PIAGET, J. The general problems of the psychobiological development of the child. In J. M. Tanner & B. Inhelder (Eds.), *Discussions on child development.* Vol. IV. New York: Internat. Univ. Press, 1960. Pp. 3–27.

PIAGET, J. The genetic approach to the psychology of thought. *J. educ. Psychol.*, 1961, **52**, 275–281.

PIAGET, J. & INHELDER, B. *Le developpement des quantités chez l'enfant.* Neuchatel: Delachaux et Niestle, 1941.

PIAGET, J., INHELDER, B., & SZEMENSKA, A. *The child's conception of geometry.* New York: Basic Books, 1960.

REICHARD, S., SCHNEIDER, M., & RAPAPORT, D. The development of concept formation in children. *Amer. J. Orthopsychiat.*, 1944, **14**, 156–161.

RHEINGOLD, H. L. The effect of environmental stimulation upon social and exploratory behavior in the human infant. In B. M. Foss (Ed.), *Determinants of infant behaviour.* New York: Wiley, 1961.

RICE, C. The orientation of plane figures as a factor in their perception by children. *Child Developm.*, 1930, **1**, 111–143.

RUSSELL, D. *Children's thinking.* Boston: Ginn, 1956.

RUSSELL, R. W. Studies in animism: II. The development of animism. *J. genet. Psychol.*, 1940, **56**, 353–366.

RUSSELL, R. W. Studies in animism: V. Animism in older children. *J. genet. Psychol.*, 1942, **60**, 329–335.

SARASON, S. B., DAVIDSON, K. S., LIGHTHALL, F. F., WAITE, R. R., & RUEBUSH, B. K. *Anxiety in elementary school children.* New York: Wiley, 1960.

SEARS, P. S. Developmental psychology. In P. R. Farnsworth & Q. McNemar (Eds.), *Annual review of psychology.* Vol. IX. Palo Alto, Calif.: Annual Reviews, Inc., 1958. Pp. 119–156.

SIGEL, I. E. Developmental trends in the abstraction ability of children. *Child Developm.*, 1953, **24**, 131–144.

SIGEL, I. E. Dominance of meaning. *J. genet. Psychol.*, 1954, **85**, 201–207.

SIGEL, I. E. *Cognitive style and personality dynamics.* Interim progress report for National Institute of Mental Health, M2983, 1961.

SIGEL, I. E. Sex and personality correlates of styles of categorization among young children. *Amer. Psychologist*, 1963, **18**, 350. (Abstract)

SMEDSLUND, J. Transitivity of preference patterns as seen by pre-school children. *Scand. J. Psychol.*, 1960, **1**, 49–54.

SMEDSLUND, J. The acquisition of conservation of substance and weight in children: I. Introduction. *Scand. J. Psychol.*, 1961, **2**, 11–20 (a).

SMEDSLUND, J. The acquisition of conservation of substance and weight in children: II. External reinforcement of conservation of weight and of the operations of addition and subtraction. *Scand. J. Psychol.*, 1961, **2**, 71–84 (b).

SMEDSLUND, J. The acquisition of conservation of substance and weight in children: III. Extinction of conservation of weight acquired "normally" and by means of empirical controls on a balance. *Scand. J. Psychol.*, 1961, **2**, 85–87 (c).

SMEDSLUND, J. The acquisition of conservation of substance and weight in children: IV. Attempt at extinction of the visual components of the weight concept. *Scand. J. Psychol.*, 1961, **2**, 153–155 (d).

SMEDSLUND, J. The acquisition of conservation of substance and weight in children: V. Practice in conflict situations without external reinforcement. *Scand. J. Psychol.*, 1961, **2**, 156–160 (e).

SMEDSLUND, J. The acquisition of conservation of substance and weight in children: VI. Practice on continuous versus discontinuous material in conflict situations without external reinforcement. *Scand. J. Psychol.*, 1961, **2**, 203–210 (f).

STEVENSON, H. (Ed.) *Child psychology: the sixty-second yearbook of the National Society for the Study of Education.* Chicago: Univ. Chicago Press, 1963.

STRAUSS, A. A. & WERNER, H. Disorders of conceptual thinking in the brain injured child. *J. nerv. ment. Dis.*, 1942, **96**, 153–172.

STUART, H. N. A study of sensori-motor and conceptual thinking in children between the ages of nine and eighteen. *J. exp. Educ.*, 1935, **4**, 147–153.

TANNER, J. M. & INHELDER, B. (Eds.) *Discussions on child development.* New York: Internat. Univ. Press, 1960.

THOMPSON, G. G. *Child psychology.* Boston: Houghton Mifflin, 1962.

THOMPSON, J. Ability of children of different grade levels to generalize on sorting tests. *J. Psychol.*, 1941, **11**, 119–126.

THRUM, M. E. The development of concepts of magnitude. *Child Developm.*, 1935, **6**, 120–140.

VYGOTSKY, L. S. *Thought and language.* Transl. by E. Hanfman & G. Vakan. New York: Wiley, 1962.

WALLACH, M. A. Research on children's thinking. In H. Stevenson (Ed.), *Child psychology. 62nd Yearb. nat. Soc. Stud. Educ.* Chicago: Univ. Chicago Press, 1963.

WELCH, L. A preliminary investigation of some aspects of the hierarchical development of concepts. *J. genet. Psychol.*, 1940, **22**, 359–378.

WERNER, H. The concept of rigidity: a critical evaluation. *Psychol. Rev.*, 1946, **53**, 43–52.

WERNER, H. *Comparative psychology of mental development.* (Rev. ed.) Chicago: Follett, 1948.

WERNER, H. The concept of development from a comparative and organismic point of view. In D. B. Harris (Ed.), *The concept of development.* Minneapolis: Univ. Minnesota Press, 1957.

WHITE, S. Learning. In H. Stevenson (Ed.), *Child psychology. 62nd Yearb. nat. Soc. Stud. Educ.* Chicago: Univ. Chicago Press, 1963.

WHORF, B. L. *Language, thought and reality.* Cambridge, Mass.: Technology Press, 1956.

WITKIN, H. A., DYK, R. B., FATERSON, H. F., GOODENOUGH, D. R., & KARP, S. A. *Psychological differentiation: studies of development.* New York: Wiley, 1962.

WOHLWILL, J. F. Absolute versus relational discrimination of the dimension of number. *J. genet. Psychol.*, 1960, **96**, 353–363 (a).

WOHLWILL, J. F. A study of the development of the number concept by scalogram analysis. *J. genet. Psychol.*, 1960, **97**, 345–377 (b).

WOHLWILL, J. F. & LOWE, R. C. Experimental analysis of the development of the conservation of numbers. *Child Developm.*, 1962, **33**, 153–167.

WOODWARD, M. Concepts of number of the mentally subnormal studied by Piaget's method. *J. Child Psychol. Psychiat.*, 1961, **2**, 249–259.

Effects of Early Group Experience:
The Nursery School and Day Nursery

JOAN W. SWIFT

The Thresholds

AN UNDERSTANDING of the nature of group experience and its effect on the young child is of both theoretical and practical importance in the field of child development today. The theoretical importance stems from the relevance which this problem has to the processes of socialization and those through which group identification is achieved. The practical importance lies primarily in its relevance for practice in the fields of education and child welfare; yet also, in the implications for all practitioners concerned with the health and development of the young child.

A number of trends in our society point up the importance of the problem. The increasingly large proportion of mothers in the labor force—and the resulting need of better provision for care of their children during the working day—has led to an expansion of those programs offering day care for preschool children. The importance we accord to good social adjustment, and to the ability to function effectively in the group, has led to a concern for providing the child with opportunities for group experiences at an early age. The value that educators and others place upon utilizing the child's full potential for learning during the preschool years, for the stimulation of creative interests and intellectual skills, has helped to create a pressure for the extension of schooling downward into those years. The rising rate of juvenile delinquency and school dropouts (related by many to the high incidence of school failures and learning disabilities among children from disadvantaged homes) has aroused an interest in providing the culturally deprived child with the sort of preschool experiences that will increase his chances of successful school adjustment.

Counteracting these trends is the concern expressed by those who feel that greater group participation in the preschool years may interfere with the fulfillment of the child's need for a close relationship with his mother during this period, a need much emphasized in psychiatric literature today. Concern is also expressed over the effects upon the young child of the greater routinization of care in the group situation and the necessity of conforming to group demands before the child has fully defined himself and his role as an individual.

The group experience we shall consider in the present review—namely, that which occurs in the nursery school or day nursery—is only one of several types to which the young child may be exposed. The number and variety of situations in which he may participate as a member of a group are many, ranging from the informal, often short-lived, backyard play group to formal communal living situations in which he may live permanently. Limitations of space preclude discussion here of the research relating to the full gamut of such experience. Our selection is based upon the relevance of nursery school and day nursery experience to the trends mentioned above. The equally important topic of the effects of communal living upon the young child merits separate attention at another time.

As we shall use them here, the terms *nursery school* and *day nursery* refer to two types of group program that have developed from quite different backgrounds. The former developed from the fields of child development and education; the latter, from the welfare field. Originally far apart in practice and theoretical approach, as well as in purpose or function, both share a common concern today for providing the preschool child with an environment geared to his emotional and developmental needs. In the structuring of this environment, both must draw on the same body of knowledge concerning basic child development principles.

Differences in socioeconomic background of the children served are no longer key factors in distinguishing the two programs. In the past, the children served by the day nursery (particularly those nurseries sponsored by public or private social agencies) came from homes of lower-than-average socioeconomic status; those attending nursery schools tended to come from above-average homes. But as more professional women combine motherhood with a career, more children from upper middle-class homes are attending full day nursery programs. In addition, the interest in providing enrichment programs for the culturally deprived has meant that more lower-class children are participating in nursery school programs.

The essential differences in the two types of program today lie in (a) the functions served for the community; (b) the relative proportions of the child's time spent in the program; and (c) the central emphasis of the program. The day nursery serves the function of substituting for maternal care of the child during a major part of the day. It puts its emphasis upon meeting the basic developmental needs of the child—physical, emotional, social, and intellectual—during that period. The nursery school serves as a supplement to the home experience of the child, covers a relatively shorter period of time, and places its primary emphasis upon selective educational experiences.

Significance for the Practitioner

The practitioner is interested in two kinds of knowledge about the effects of group experience on the young child: the general overall advantages or disadvantages of group programs for preschool children, on the one hand, and the specific effects to be expected in terms of a particular child, on the other. These questions are of concern to practitioners in several fields. For the social worker engaged in civic planning to meet the needs of the community's children, it is important to understand the values and dangers inherent in the use of group care for large numbers of young children. Before day care centers are provided on a large scale as a solution to the problem of the working mother, as a method for lightening relief rolls, or as a means of increasing the supply of women in the labor market by enabling more mothers to work, the effects of the group experience on the child's development need to be considered. For the caseworker engaged in planning with parents the best solution to a family problem, a thorough understanding of what is involved in the use of a group care program for a given child is necessary—or the plan made may be worse than the problem it proposes to solve.

The pediatrician called upon to advise parents as to the desirability of nursery school for a young child needs to have a basic understanding of what the nursery experience may mean. He needs to know the possible assets and liabilities, and what factors in the personality or developmental status of the child must be considered in assessing a readiness for the experience.

In addition, other practitioners have special questions of their own. The nursery school teacher and others concerned with administration of the group program need to know more about the specific effects of different teaching techniques, the range of learning experiences that can take place in the group setting, and those developmental needs of the child which must be considered in planning a sound nursery program.

In the present chapter, therefore, we shall first briefly review research that is designed to give answers to questions regarding the global effects of nursery school or day nursery experience on various aspects of development. We shall next turn to an analysis of the factors which make up the nursery experience, those which must be considered in assessing the possible effects of the experience for the individual child. We shall then review research relevant to these components of the group situation. An attempt will be made throughout to draw implications for the practitioner from the findings reported.

EFFECTS OF NURSERY ATTENDANCE
ON DEVELOPMENT

Group care of the young child is not a recent development in the child welfare field. The first day nurseries were established for the children of working mothers over a hundred years ago. The utilization of group settings for research in child development, however, did not get under way until the 1920's when a number of nursery school programs were established specifically for research and training purposes. In general, it is from the latter type of setting—the nursery school connected with a university or training center—that the major part of the research in this field has come.

Historically, the first approach to a determination of the effects of nursery experience on the child involved was the measurement of changes following nursery school attendance. Studies attempting to measure such changes have been numerous, and the literature covers nearly forty years. The period of greatest research concentration fell between 1925 and 1940. It can be said to have begun with the study by Woolley (1925) reporting changes in intelligence scores following attendance at the Merrill-Palmer School, and to have culminated with the publication of the 1940 edition of the Yearbook of the National Society for the Study of Education, in which a large number of pertinent studies were brought together. The research of this period concerned itself most intensively with the question of whether nursery school attendance could bring about acceleration of mental growth, as reflected in changes in intelligence test performance. The issue became a highly controversial one, part of the larger question of the relative effects of nature and nurture in child development to which no single answer has been found. A large body of more recent research has concerned itself with the effects of such attendance upon the child's social and emotional adjustment, upon later work-orientation and relations with authority in the school situation. A smaller number of studies have been concerned with physical status and motor development.

In general, two approaches to the problem of assessment of change have been utilized. In the first, the child's status on a given trait is assessed before exposure to nursery school and again after a period of nursery school attendance. The changes, if any, are taken as evidence of the effect of the nursery experience. The more carefully carried out studies taking this approach have included use of a control group, made up of children of the same age and general characteristics who have not attended nursery school during a similar period. Evaluation is then made in terms of the degree of change in a given variable obtained from the nursery group as compared with changes observed in the nonnursery group.

In the second approach, a particular trait is assessed in a given group of children (often at the first or second-grade level), of whom some have and some have not attended nursery school during their preschool years. The assumption is made that the nursery school experience affected those traits on which the nursery children differ significantly from the nonnursery children.

Effects of Nursery Attendance on Intellectual Development

It has been hypothesized that the nursery school setting, designed to provide those experiences necessary to increase intellectual curiosity and add to the child's knowledge, would produce accelerated mental growth in the children attending. The most extensive work pertinent here was carried out at the Iowa Child Welfare Research Station, as part of a larger series of studies on the effect of a variety of environmental conditions upon intellectual development. The overall findings have been reported by Wellman (1932, 1934, 1940); Skeels, Updegraff, Wellman, and Williams (1938); Skeels (1940); and others (Skodak, 1939; Stoddard and Wellman, 1940). Wellman (1943) has summarized the studies on nursery attendance, whose findings generally reflected gains in I.Q. by children attending nursery school. This was interpreted by the respective investigators to demonstrate that such attendance can bring about positive changes in intellectual functioning—changes which do not occur during similar periods of non-attendance and which are maintained over a period of later school attendance. These findings, however, while similar in direction to those originally reported by Woolley (1925) and others (Starkweather and Roberts, 1940; Frandsen and Barlow, 1940), have not been duplicated by the majority of investigators at other institutions (Kawin and Hoefer, 1931; L. D. Anderson, 1940; Bird, 1940; Olson and Hughes, 1940; Jones and Jorgensen, 1940; Lamson, 1940; Goodenough and Maurer, 1940). Their studies report no significant changes in I.Q. associated with nursery attendance.

Attempts to account for such differences have included the following factors as possibly influencing the results: practice effects, bias of testers, coaching by parents or nursery school teachers, inadequate standardization of the tests used, inadequacies in statistical handling of the data, selective factors in the populations studied, and differences in parental characteristics. On the basis of the data available, it is probable that none of these is sufficient to have caused all the differences in results obtained—though in a specific study, one or more may have been operative. Important factors that should be more carefully considered are the specific nature and content of the program provided for the children, its relation to the changes expected, and its relation to the children's experiences outside the nursery.

As generalizations about nursery school attendance, the results from these studies are inconclusive and contradictory. The possibility that certain nursery programs can contribute to increases in mental functioning, however, is not ruled out.

Effects of Nursery Attendance on Social Development

Since the social element is the one which distinguishes the nursery setting most markedly from the other situations to which the young child is exposed, it is natural to expect that here, most of all, differences in behavior will follow attendance. This expectation leads many parents to send a child to nursery school. Lack of playmates of the same age, the child's inability to share, his insistence on being the center of attention, or similar patterns of problem behavior which are seen by the parents as stemming from the child's lack of opportunity for social experience, are often offered as reasons for enrolling the child in the nursery. It has been hypothesized that the opportunity to interact with other children in a controlled setting will result in better social adjustment and the acquisition of social skills.

A number of early studies in this area were based on repeated observations of the same child over a period of attendance in the nursery school. The findings, while interesting and suggestive, cannot be taken as evidence that nursery attendance caused the changes noted, since the effects of maturation cannot be ruled out in the absence of either a control group or standardized norms for evaluating social development. Among such studies are those of Ezekiel (1931), Mallay (1935), Andrus and Horowitz (1938), Horowitz and Smith (1939), Joel (1939), and Vitz (1961). In general, their investigations point to a greater degree of socially outgoing behavior, more successful use of social techniques, and greater maturity and independence over the period of observation. Andrus and Horowitz found that certain traits considered symptomatic of "insecurity" persisted in several nursery groups despite attendance in the school.

Studies using the methodologically sounder approach of comparing nursery attenders with a matched group of nonattenders have been carried out by Walsh (1931), Cushing (1934), Hattwick (1936), Jersild and Fite (1939), Van Alstyne and Hattwick (1939), and Brown and Hunt (1961). The majority of these used teachers' ratings of various aspects of social behavior as the method for assessing social adjustment. Jersild and Fite utilized data collected through direct observations of nursery school behavior. Others have recently employed sociometric techniques of assessing popularity, along with teachers' ratings, to evaluate the extent to which nursery school and/or kindergarten experience can be shown to make a difference in social adjustment in the elementary school years (Allen and Masling, 1957; Bonney and Nicholson, 1958). While a number of these studies have reported positive findings consistent with the hypothesis of better social adjustment following nursery attendance (Walsh, Cushing, Hattwick, and Allen and Masling), others have not (Bonney and Nicholson, and Brown and Hunt). In general, there are no clear-cut findings which reflect superior social adjustment on the part of children who have attended nursery school over those who have not.

Possible factors in producing differences in the results are the following: the wide variety of behaviors used by different investigators as measures of "social adjustment"; differences in sophistication, training, and experience of the teachers doing the ratings; differences in the later school environment in which the children were observed; and selective factors operating in the initial decision to send the child to nursery school. This latter point seems an especially important one. In many cases such a decision is based on the child's inadequate social adjustment; in others, the good adjustment of the child in the nursery is a factor operating to keep him in, once enrolled. It cannot be assumed that these factors are operating in a random fashion in the nursery school populations studied. Most important of all, it would seem, is that here (as was the case with studies of intellectual development) material is not available concerning the kind of social experiences and guidance the children were receiving in the various programs.

Effects of Nursery Attendance on Physical Development and Motor Skills

Another of the expectations around which the nursery school curriculum was developed was that the provision of adequate space, properly designed equipment, and sound health routines—combined with the stimulation afforded by a group of agemates—would lead the child to greater and more purposeful physical activity, the establishment of better health habits, and hence better physical health (H. M. Johnson, 1928). The few research studies which have concerned themselves with a global approach to assessment of nursery experience in terms of physical status have found little support for this hypothesis (Kawin and Hoefer, 1931; Lamson, 1940). Skeels and associates (1938), using as subjects preschool children in an orphanage setting, found little difference in motor skills between a group of children who took part in a nursery school program within the orphanage and those who did not. The only exceptions were with regard to a small number of specific skills for which no opportunity for practice was available to the children outside of the nursery program.

Effects of Special Programs

The studies reported so far have come almost entirely from nursery school settings with children of average or above-average intelligence, from primarily middle and upper middle-class backgrounds. It is likely that the families selecting these nursery school experiences for their children in general valued, and also provided at home, many of the same kinds of experiences: reading of stories, encouragement of verbal communication, and opportunity for creative activity. Where similar studies have been carried out on groups of children from less advantaged backgrounds, more consistently positive findings regarding change in functioning after nursery attendance have been obtained.

In general, studies which have measured intelligence of children from severely limited backgrounds (whether the limitation was due to parental inadequacy, the nature of the institutional setting, or cultural deprivation) have found these children to be functioning at a lower level than those from advantaged homes—and in many cases to show a generally decreasing trend in I.Q. over a period of time (Skeels and Fillmore, 1937; Crissey, 1937; Skeels *et al.*, 1938; Kirk, 1958). Programs designed to offset these trends have been carried out in a number of settings. Most frequently used has been the institutional setting where special programs were being introduced for the first time (Woolfolk, 1929; Barrett and Koch, 1930; Skeels *et al.*, 1938; Dawe, 1942). The setting made it possible to select and treat two groups of children whose life experiences were extremely similar, with the exception of the time spent in the nursery school itself. Matching on the basis of age, sex, length of residence, I.Q., and physical status was usually possible. In general, the findings have shown gains on the part of the children who participated in the programs, particularly in language skills, in contrast to those who did not.

Positive findings are also reported in a study by Kirk and his colleagues (1958) of a preschool program for educable mentally retarded children. While the overall effects of the nursery school program were generally positive for the children attending, the group for whom it provided such accelerating effects on development as could not otherwise be expected to appear were from inadequate, psychosocially deprived homes.

It would seem, therefore, that where the experiences offered provide an opportunity which the child has not had at home for acquiring developmental skills, the nursery school experience can be valuable for him. It must be offered in a setting, however, in which there is understanding of the special problems of the deprived child; for as Skeels and associates (1938) and Riessman (1962) have pointed out, many of the methods perfected in the laboratory nursery schools with children of high educational status were found to be ineffective with those from deprived backgrounds. Limitations in experience, information, attention span, verbal ability, and a general lack of orientation for learning prevent these children from making constructive use of the conventional nursery school program.

Effects of Nursery Attendance on Emotional Adjustment

The studies reported to this point have been concerned with attempts to determine the positive benefits to be derived from nursery school experience. Fewer studies have approached the question from the opposite direction: that of determining possible negative effects. One study attempting to assess possible deleterious effects of the full day nursery experience is that by Glass (1949). She studied a group of children two to five years of age whose mothers worked and who attended a day nursery for from six and a half to ten and a half hours daily. A control group of children cared for at home by their mothers was also studied. The two groups were compared with respect to eating, sleeping, and elimination habits, and with respect to the incidence of problem children (children showing either one marked habit disturbance, or a habit disturbance allied to a personality or behavior difficulty). The findings indicated only slight differences between the two groups. The author concluded there was no evidence, therefore, to suggest that children cared for in a day nursery are more likely to present developmental problems than those cared for by their mothers. A slight preponderance of problem behavior in children in the day nursery group seemed related to the presence of specific problem situations in the home, problems often the cause of the child's need for day nursery care in the first place. Since these findings held despite the fact that over half of the nursery group had entered before two years of age, they were interpreted as discounting the belief that nursery care for the child around two is especially harmful.

The greater part of the research concerned with the deleterious effects of early group experience has come from studies of institutionalized children who have been separated from their parents. The work of Spitz, Goldfarb, Freud and Burlingham, and others have been summarized by Bowlby (1951) and more recently by Yarrow (1961). Many practitioners have feared that the negative effects of this kind of experience might also result when the young child experiences parental separation in attending the day nursery. A study by Heinicke (1956) shed some light on the validity of this concern through a comparison of the relative effects of full residential care and day nursery care. The behavior of two groups of two-year-old children during the period of their first separation from their parents was compared. One group was made up of children placed in a residential nursery situation; the second, of children in a day nursery setting. Using direct observations of behavior in the everyday living situation in the nursery and in individual doll play sessions, Heinicke studied the children's reactions to the separation from their parents. Both groups showed initial disturbance over the separation, particularly during the first two days; but following this, the day nursery children showed a lessening of concern, while the residential group continued to show significantly greater disturbance in a number of areas. Initial attempts to regain their parents were made by both groups —but children in the day nursery tended to be free of overwhelming concern with this problem and were able, seemingly, to work through whatever concern they felt in fantasy and mild hostility. Their need was satisfied by the physical proximity of adults and they spent a greater percentage of time in activities with other children and doll play than they did in seeking out adults for attention. Reactions to their parents when the latter returned were appropriate and showed no disruption of relationship. Children in the residential nursery, on the other hand, showed massive reactions: loss of sphincter control, severe hostile reactions, greed for sweets, active seeking for adult affection, resistance to adult demands even while seeking greater attention, an increase in autoerotic behavior, and a high incidence of illness (colds). There were some refusals to recognize the parents when the latter visited, despite the relatively short duration of the separation (a total of three weeks). These observations on the residential nursery children are consistent with those reported by other investigators on institution children.

While no broad generalizations can be made on the basis of a single study, it would seem that there is evidence that the separation effects of day care cannot be equated with those of residential care. The day care child maintains his essential relationship and identification with his parents, despite the long day away from home, and is free to participate in the social and play opportunities afforded by the nursery.

Summary and Implications for the Practitioner

In summary, the findings reported so far have been inconclusive and conflicting with respect to the extent to which attendance in a nursery school, in and of itself, brings about positive changes in intellectual, social, and physical development of young children. There is, on the other hand, no evidence that children receiving nonresidential group care have been negatively affected in their development or adjustment as a result of the experience. Where special programs have been developed and adapted to the needs of special groups of children, there is evidence that these experiences can have positive effects on development, particularly in the intellectual and language area.

The findings reported thus far, therefore, do not support the conclusion that nursery school experience is an essential one for every child. It has not been demonstrated that nursery experience itself is of such value that the child for whom it is not available is under a handicap in entering kindergarten or first grade. Differences in I.Q. scores, which may have been brought about as the result of nursery school attendance, can generally be expected to level off over time in the grade school. The social skills which the child develops in his relationships with peers in the nursery are also picked up by the average child during his early elementary school years; some he will have developed in his informal play experiences at home.

The findings do support the conclusion that when dealing with children from culturally deprived backgrounds, or children who present special learning problems, active intervention in the form of special programs may bring about important gains for the child and indirectly for the community.

These general conclusions must remain provisional, however, subject to further definition of relevant aspects of the nursery situation and the variables which make it up. It is evident from the studies reviewed so far that there is no simple answer to the question, "What are the effects of nursery experience upon the young child?" "Nursery experience" does not represent a constant or given set of social and/or environmental stimuli that can be expected to have a specified effect on every individual or group exposed to it. Yet in the majority of these studies there has been a tendency to treat the nursery situation in just this way. While some investigators have described briefly the general physical setup and educational philosophy operative in the school being studied, few have attempted to define the nursery situation psychologically, with reference to the particular situational variables that are presumed to bring about the expected changes in behavior.

COMPONENTS OF THE NURSERY EXPERIENCE

It is thus necessary to break down the global concept of nursery experience into its component parts, and attempt to define it more accurately and more meaningfully in terms of the variables operative within it. It will then be possible to differentiate those variables likely to have positive effects from those of little relevance to development, and from those that may actually have deleterious effects upon the child.

To one who is familiar with a number of nurseries, this conclusion may seem an unnecessarily complicated way of saying what he has known all along: that nurseries differ in many ways; that some are "good," and others "poor"; that one would expect a child to benefit from one and not from another. It is less easy, however, to define with any degree of certainty what factors are of greatest relevance to the evaluation of "good" and "poor." Even in the field of nursery education, concepts have changed over the years. Research findings have challenged some of the theories held earlier as to what constitutes the most salutary environment for the healthy growth and development of the young child. It is our purpose here to identify some of the variables that make up the nursery experience and to review research dealing with their effects on the preschool child.

The nursery experience may be considered to be influenced by five major factors: the physical setting; the program of activities and routines; the teacher or teachers; the peer group; and the child's own personality, abilities, and interests.

Physical Setting

Though nursery educators have described the "ideal" nursery setting—including the arrangement of space and provision of materials and equipment—relatively little research has been concerned specifically and systematically with the physical setting. Some of the early observational studies of children's play, however, provide findings relevant to this aspect of the group situation. Certain conditions have been found to be more conducive to certain types of behavior and learning than have others.

In an extensive study of children's motor abilities and use of equipment in the nursery, Gutteridge (1939) found that the curve of motor achievement rose rapidly during the early preschool years but dropped off sharply after the age of three. This was attributed to the lack of environmental stimulation and challenge to further effort offered by the standard nursery equipment, rather than to the attainment of a physiologically determined level of skill. It was felt that the usual equipment provided in the nursery, while adequate for the two- and three-year-old, was too stereotyped, inflexible, and limited in function to provide the necessary opportunity and stimulation for maximum development of motor skills in the four- and five-year-old child.

A number of studies have noted the effect of amount of space upon the incidence of aggressive behavior in the nursery (Green, 1933b; Jersild and Markey, 1935; and Murphy, 1937). In general, these studies have shown that conflicts between children are more numerous where play space is more restricted. Certain types of equipment and play facilities have also proved conducive to a greater number of conflicts. Green, for example, found that sand play was accompanied by the highest incidence of quarreling of any play activities observed; while M. W. Johnson (1935a), comparing the incidence of quarrels on the playground with and without toys and other movable equipment, found that the absence of such equipment was accompanied by more quarreling. Johnson found social interaction in general to have been stimulated to a greater extent by the absence of the equipment. Other investigators have also found the type of equipment and facilities offered to affect the kind of social interaction that takes place (Updegraff and Herbst, 1933; Markey, 1935; Murphy, 1937; Body, 1955). Murphy, for example, found cooperation stimulated by such equipment as swings, tricycles with place for a rider, and wagons. Markey found blocks to be a good medium for cooperative play, while Updegraff and Herbst found that, with two- and three-year-olds, clay tended to provide more cooperative interaction than did blocks. Green found the most cooperation in conjunction with opportunities for dramatic play (doll corner activities). Markey also reports greater imaginative play to occur under conditions of greater play space.

Such findings indicate the large number of variations that can be utilized by the imaginative teacher to stimulate certain types of activity. No single setting or arrangement of equipment can be considered "ideal"; the setting must always be considered in relation to the needs of the child and the purpose of the program. For the child with little opportunity to play with other children, or for the withdrawn child whose need is for stimulation toward social play, a setting designed to stimulate cooperation and social interaction may be most appropriate. For the child from a crowded home with many siblings, a setting in which he can remove himself from the group and play quietly alone may be equally important. In considering the day nursery setting as contrasted with the nursery school, it may be appropriate for the former to provide more opportunity for solitary play, through the provision of greater space and appropriate equipment, in order to offset the fatiguing effects of prolonged social interaction. The nursery school which emphasizes social learning might more appropriately utilize limited space and more, rather than fewer, stimulants to social interaction in order to provide opportunity for directed social learning.

Research on provision and use of the physical setting and equipment is also relevant to the development of program; in practice it is difficult to separate the two factors. The provision of physical space with certain characteristics and equipment is in itself a form of program.

Program

The typical nursery school program attempts to stimulate creative expression, provide for the acquisition of information, and offer learning opportunities in such areas as language, communication, motor and social skills. Various studies have been concerned with the development and assessment of specific programs for such learning (Jersild and Bienstock, 1931; Hilgard, 1932; Jersild, 1932; Hissem, 1933; Colby, 1935; Jersild and Bienstock, 1935; Updegraff, Heiliger, and Learned, 1938; Dawe, 1942; Williams and Mattson, 1942; Dubin, 1946). Early studies in this area also included several emphasizing the handling of routines and habit training as a major aspect of the nursery program (Hill and Van Alstyne, 1930; Dunshee, 1931; Campbell, 1933; Dales, 1941).

Much of the material regarding specific aspects of the nursery program has been consolidated into an accepted body of practice. This is available to the nursery school or day nursery practitioner in a number of texts and pamphlets (Read, 1960; Child Welfare League, 1960), as well as in a more detailed review by Sears and Dowley (1963). Several specific points deserve consideration here, however.

Certain programs have been successful in stimulating achievement and interest in given areas, while others seem to have little immediate or lasting effects. Reference has already been made to Dawe's (1942) study of the positive effects of an enriched language program upon a group of orphanage preschool children. Wann, Dorn, and Liddle (1962), in an extensive study of the way in which children learn about their social and physical environment, have described a program which stimulated such learning in children from several nursery schools and day nurseries, representing a wide range of socioeconomic backgrounds. Studies by Jersild and Bienstock (1931), Hissem (1933), and Updegraff et al., (1938) have presented evidence that children of three and four can increase their singing ability in a number of ways when exposed to a specially designed program, and that this increase in skill is accompanied by an increased interest in and enjoyment of music. However, Jersild and Bienstock (1935), in another study, reported that a similar program designed to increase skill in rhythmical activities was unsuccessful in producing significant gains in the ability to keep time to music. Equally unsuccessful was a program designed to teach preschool children to play a musical instrument (Colby, 1935). Hilgard (1932) studied the effects of practice on three motor skills: cutting with scissors, climbing, and buttoning. The children studied were two and three years old. At the end of a twelve-week practice period, children in the experimental group exceeded those in the control group in tests of these three skills; but practice over a one-week period subsequent to the tests increased the skill of the control group to the level obtained by the experimental group. The rapidity with which the children in the control group caught up with the experimental group seemed to reflect differences in developmental readiness for such learning.

Certain principles of learning in the preschool years—particularly as these relate to developmental stages, the acquisition of skills, and the conditions conducive to learning—are important for understanding why some programs have failed while others have been successful. Much of our understanding of these principles comes from research on animals (for example, King, 1958); from studies on twins (Gesell and Thompson, 1929; McGraw, 1935); and from the work on developmental stages by Gesell and his associates (1940). A fuller discussion of such studies will be found in Thompson (1962).

The acquisition of a skill is dependent upon both maturation and experience, the relative importance of each varying with the skill involved. Certain skills seemingly develop regardless of the opportunity for practice (Dennis and Dennis, 1940); others may develop only when specific training and opportunity for practice are provided at the appropriate time in the developmental sequence (McGraw, 1935). Practice alone, offered without regard to maturational readiness, will not produce learning (Hicks, 1930). Most skills lie between the two extremes and require a certain degree of maturational readiness before practice or even specific training can be effective, but improve where opportunity for practice is provided (Hilgard, 1932; Williams and Scott, 1953). Motivation and interest in learning a skill is greatest when the child is developmentally ready for such learning (Gutteridge, 1939). Planning a program for children in the preschool years when growth is so rapid, depends upon identifying the child's readiness for certain types of learning and providing appropriate opportunities for practice. While there are certain relatively consistent sequences of developmental stages through which children in our culture pass, the chronological age at which a given child reaches a given stage varies from child to child (Gesell, 1940). This means that there will be children at many different stages of development even within a relatively homogeneous nursery group. The determination of readiness must be made on an individual as well as chronological basis.

Other research indicates that much important learning takes place in a nonspecific way as the child explores his environment, is exposed to different types of experience, and has the opportunity to experiment at first hand with many kinds of materials. Behavior that often seems purposeless to the observer supplies the child with basic experiences from which he draws the data to solve problem situations which may arise later (Hicks and Ralph, 1931).

A good nursery program will be based on an understanding of these factors. Carefully planned opportunities for a wide range of experiences with materials appropriate to the age and developmental level of the child provide for the most fruitful learning. Routine practice of skills or exposure to overly complicated materials at an age when maturation and interest are not appropriate not only may not result in learning, but may even interfere with the child's interest and motivation to learn in this area at a later time.

Teacher Behavior and Teacher-Child Relationships

The provision of equipment and materials is not enough in itself to make the program. In choosing appropriate equipment and materials, in planning their presentation, and in adapting the program to the needs of the individual child and the larger group, the role of the teacher is a central one. She must have a knowledge and an understanding of developmental principles, the ability to recognize developmental readiness in the children she teaches, and the know-how to present ideas and materials in stimulating and constructive ways.

Considering this central importance of the teacher's role, there has been comparatively little research on teacher behavior and its effects on the child. This relative disregard can be understood historically as a reflection of two factors: (a) many of these studies were carried out in nursery schools set up as research laboratories for studying children's "natural" behavior; (b) the prevailing educational philosophy held that the young child should be provided with an environment as free from restraint and direction as possible. To allow free exercise of the child's developing physical and social skills, adult supervision was minimal. It was concerned primarily with routines of physical care, habit training, and leadership of specific program activities (singing, story-telling). But as more has been learned about the young child's social and emotional needs, the emphasis has changed and the teacher's role has become a more active and significant one.

There are three kinds of studies dealing with this component of the nursery experience: descriptive studies of teacher behavior, studies relating teacher behavior to child behavior, and experimental studies of single variables relevant to the teacher-child relationship.

Classification of teacher behavior. A number of investigators have attempted to develop reliable methods of observing and classifying teacher behavior in the nursery setting. Among these have been Bain (1928), Foster (1930), H. H. Anderson (1939a,b), Appel (1942), Landreth et al., (1943), Thompson (1944), and Reichenberg-Hackett (1962). Tucker (1940) and Bishop (1951) have developed categories for classifying the behavior of mothers in an experimental and a group situation which are equally relevant to a classification of teacher behavior.

Early classifications tended to emphasize the specific activity in which the teacher engaged (Bain, 1928; Foster, 1930); others have been concerned with the methods used by the teachers (Tucker, 1940; Appel, 1942; and Landreth et al., 1943). Such descriptive classifications become most meaningful when the behaviors described have been organized around concepts of broader educational significance, or when the behavior items have been broadened to take into account the situation in which the action has taken place, the purpose of the action, and its relationship to the child's own goals and activities.

An early attempt to develop a more meaningful categorization of teaching behavior was that of H. H. Anderson (1939a,b), who adapted to teacher-child relationships the concepts of *domination* and *integrative behavior*, developed originally in connection with child-child relationships (H. H. Anderson, 1937a,b). Domination occurs, according to Anderson, when one individual attempts to impose upon another his own wishes, methods, and goals without considering those of the other. Integrative behavior includes the wishes and goals of the other person as important considerations in the working out of a common goal or solution. Thompson (1944) has classified teacher-child contacts as *extensive* or *restrictive*: the former refers to behavior generally supportive of the child's activities (through giving information or help, offering structuring suggestions, and so on); the latter involves restriction or inhibition of the child's actions. Bishop (1951) classified adult behavior observed in an experimental situation along three continua: *degree of contact with the child, degree of specificity of adult control*, and *degree of interference or facilitation of child's activity*.

A recent study by Reichenberg-Hackett (1962) has combined a number of the dimensions of teacher behavior included in other studies into a meaningful and comprehensive approach to studying factors in teacher behavior that determine the nature of the nursery experience for the child. Among the behaviors included are teacher motivating techniques of *encouragement* and *discouragement*, similar to the domination-integration, restrictive-extensive, interference-facilitation dimensions (respectively) of Anderson, Thompson, and Bishop. In addition, the *values* supported by the teacher's behavior, the specific kinds of *activities* provided for the children, and the *availability* of the teacher to the children are variables this classification makes available for study.

The classification of teacher behavior and classroom techniques is of greatest significance when the variables so defined and classified can be related differentially to variables in child growth and development. Many of the studies reported have taken a first step in this direction by demonstrating that there are observable and consistent differences between teachers, with respect to the methods they use and the climate or atmosphere they create in the classroom. Landreth and associates (1943), for example, contrasted teacher-child contacts in a WPA nursery with those in a university nursery school and found differences in methods used and in method goals. The two situations differed with respect to amount of physical handling of the children, number of commands, physical compulsion and disapproval, information given, and number of questions asked. The WPA nursery was characterized by an insistence on having orders carried out and rigid routines followed, in contrast to the educational atmosphere of the other nursery. Both Tucker (1940) and Bishop (1951) found consistent individual patterns of behavior in the mothers observed.

In the study by Reichenberg-Hackett (1962), teachers in ten nursery groups were observed and their behavior classified according to the categories described above. Striking differences among teachers were found with respect to certain of the categories—such as the ratio of encouragement to discouragement, the values stressed, and the amount of child-centered behavior exhibited. Such differences reflect the wide range of experiences to which children attending different nursery groups may be exposed. Not all of these types of experience are conducive to healthy development. On the basis of the findings, the author concluded that it is the personality of the teacher, her outlook and convictions, that constitute the most important single factor in the shaping of the child's nursery experience. No relationships between the behavior of the teachers and the children's behavior in the classroom have been included in the findings of this study, though specific observations of differences in child behavior are reported that provide leads for future research.

Studies attempting to define the antecedent conditions for certain types of teacher behavior in the classroom have been of three kinds: those having to do with the characteristics of the particular children in the group, those related to the teacher's professional experience and training, and those dealing with the teacher's personality and background.

Relatively consistent differences in teacher behavior related to the age of children in the group have been observed by several investigators (Foster, 1930; Appel, 1942; Landreth, 1943; and Reichenberg-Hackett, 1962). In her study of mothers in a cooperative nursery, Tucker (1940) found that despite the generally consistent individual patterns of behavior exhibited by the mothers, certain children were found to elicit certain reactions in all the mothers.

Differences in teacher behavior reflecting professional experience and/or training have been postulated by studies of Landreth and associates (1943) and Nesbitt (1943). Reichenberg-Hackett (1962), while concluding that the most important factor is the personality of the particular teacher, found differences in the teachers' professional and the socioeconomic backgrounds to be important. The bulk of the literature pertaining to attempts to relate teacher personality and characteristics with classroom behavior has been concerned with teaching at the elementary school level. An extensive review of this literature has been presented by Getzels and Jackson (1963). In general, while there is widespread agreement that personality and attitudes are crucial factors in determining the individual's ability to function effectively as a teacher of young children, there is no clear-cut agreement as to what specific attributes are most relevant. More research on these factors in regard to nursery teaching is needed.

Effects of teacher behavior upon child behavior. A major study relating teacher techniques to child behavior is that of Thompson (1944). Two groups of children matched for age, sex, I.Q., socioeconomic status of parents, and performance on a number of measures of social and emotional development, were exposed to contrasting types of teacher behavior over a period of eight months' attendance in nursery school. In one group the teachers were instructed to adopt an impersonal and uninvolved attitude; they gave information and help only upon the specific request of the child. In the other group, teachers were instructed to help the child in his relations with other children and in his use of play materials to the extent appropriate to his social and emotional needs. The two groups were compared at the end of the period on a number of experimental and observational measures in the following areas: *ascendance, social participation, leadership, constructiveness in the face of failure, number of nervous habits,* and *intellectual growth.* Significant differences favoring the group receiving greater teacher involvement were found with respect to ascendance, social participation, leadership, and constructiveness. Increases were noted in each of these areas. No significant differences were found with respect to intellectual growth or reduction in nervous habits. Since the same head teacher served in each group, the differences found between the children seemed to reflect directly the differences in techniques adopted, rather than teacher personality.

H. H. Anderson (1939a,b) studied the relation between dominative and integrative behavior on the part of the teacher and child behavior in the classroom. His results indicate that, while the relation is not a simple one, in general the hypothesis that domination in the teacher calls forth dominative behavior in the child is borne out.

Studies relating specific teacher techniques to child behavior have been made by M. W. Johnson (1935b), McClure (1936), Moore (1938), and Appel (1942). In general, their findings have indicated that children tend to respond most positively and to achieve most success when they are given positive, unhurried, specific, and encouraging types of directions. Appel, in a study of the handling of aggression, found these techniques effective in ending quarrels: diverting and separating, interpreting the wishes and feelings of one child to another, explaining property rights, and suggesting solutions. Disapproval and moralizing were ineffective, as were overly general techniques, such as suggesting that the children "talk it over."

In general, the research findings indicate that techniques which take into account the child's own interests and goals, which build on these to further educational goals, and which are specific and clearly understandable to the child, will be most effective in promoting learning. In order to carry out these techniques the teacher must be child-centered in her approach, aware of the child's needs, and willing to adapt to his goals while pursuing her own (educational goals) for him. While research has not yet determined the relative degrees to which personality, background, experience, and professional training influence the classroom behavior of the teacher, all can be presumed to play a part. There is a real need for more studies to define the relationship between teacher behavior, classroom atmosphere, and child behavior and development.

Studies of adult-child relationships. Research findings regarding specific types of adult-child interaction provide valuable leads to other variables involved in teacher-child relationships. A number of these have been concerned with the effects on the child's behavior of adult availability, ranging from absence through differing degrees of adult attention and responsiveness.

Findings generally have demonstrated that the child shows greater dependence, and tends to seek attention and approval from adults more actively when such attention has been limited or denied, than when it has been continuously available (Gewirtz, 1954; Gewirtz and Baer, 1958a,b; Gewirtz, Baer, and Roth, 1958).

Studies in which children have been exposed to differing amounts of adult attention immediately prior to participation in learning experiments have demonstrated that the children who experienced deprivation (either social isolation or inconsistent nurturance) were the ones who learned more quickly. The increase in learning performance under these conditions has been considered to reflect the child's increased motivation to secure adult approval (Gewirtz and Baer, 1958a,b; Hartup, 1958).

The tendency of the child to model his behavior on that of a nurturant adult has been demonstrated by Bandura and Huston (1961). In an experimental problem-solving situation, children tended to imitate certain aspects of the experimenter's behavior that were irrelevant to the performance of the task. This imitation was shown more strongly in the case of an adult model with whom the child had had a rewarding and warm period of interaction prior to the experimental situation than in the case of an adult who had remained aloof and cold. This relationship broke down with respect to aggressive behavior; the adult's aggressive behavior was imitated by the children regardless of the nurturance received in the preexperimental session. Rosenblith (1959) has also noted the preschool child's tendency to imitate adult behavior not directly relevant to the task at hand.

The withdrawal of adult attention or responsiveness has been shown to represent a frustration for the child to which he may react with anger as well as with increased attention-seeking behavior (Hartup and Himeno, 1960). In an experiment with young children eleven to thirty months of age, Arsenian (1943) has demonstrated the importance of the presence of a familiar adult to the child's ability to adjust in an insecurity-provoking situation. The withdrawal of the adult in such a situation commonly resulted in a high degree of insecurity reflected in nonadaptive behavior—such as crying, regression, or withdrawal—while the adult's continued presence freed the child to explore and to manipulate the environment constructively. Withdrawal of the adult after the child had become familiar with the new situation did not precipitate such anxiety. The return of the adult following an initial period of isolation (and consequent disturbance) resulted in recovery from anxiety only in children whose initial anxiety had not been extreme. Nonadaptive behavior continued even in the presence of the adult in children whose initial reaction was one of great anxiety.

The role of the adult as the interpreter of standards of conduct for the child is demonstrated in an interesting way in a study of children's aggression (Siegel, 1957; Siegel and Kohn, 1959). It was found that children in an experimental play situation exhibited more aggression in the presence of a permissive adult than when no adult was present. It was suggested by the authors that the permissiveness of the adult was not seen by the child as neutral or nonjudgmental, as adults tend to think of it, but as actively condoning the behavior observed. The adult's lack of response to initial aggressive acts was interpreted by the child to mean that such behavior was acceptable and that he was free to continue to act in this way. The decrease in aggressive behavior in the absence of an adult was accounted for in terms of the child's reliance on his own learned standards of conduct (that is, aggression in social play is not acceptable), which were called into play when no adult was present to define the social situation and to express expectations regarding the child's behavior in it.

These studies have further emphasized the importance of the teacher's role. The preschool child is still dependent upon the adult for approval, direction, and attention. He will seek clues to the adult's judgments of his behavior where these are not clear to him. Some of his interpretations may be incorrect—based on distortions brought from home, or on insufficient knowledge—but he will react to the situation as it appears to him. Guidance from the teacher in defining the situation more realistically and communicating the values which she seeks to reinforce, will make the situation a more effective learning experience for the child.

The Arsenian study points up the importance of another aspect of the adult's role: that of providing the child with the sense of security he needs in order to approach and master new and frightening experiences. The adult's presence nearby encourages rather than discourages independence. As the child becomes more secure, this need decreases.

Peer Relationships

The most distinctive feature of the nursery experience for the child is the opportunity it provides for play with a group of agemates. The use he makes of this opportunity and the nature of the relationships he forms within his peer group represent significant aspects of social adjustment. The importance of this area of development is attested to by the large number of studies dealing with social relationships in the preschool years.

Social behavior has been studied by means of variables relating to *social interaction:* social participation, initiation of social contacts, resistance, aggression, sympathy, and cooperation; and also by means of variables relating more directly to the *status of the individual in the group:* leadership roles, ascendance, submission, and social acceptance or popularity. A summary of methodological approaches to the study of social behavior can be found in Thomas (1929), Arrington (1932, 1943), and in chapters by Kesson, Thompson, and Wright in Mussen (1960).

One of the earliest and most frequently cited studies of social interaction is that of Parten (1932, 1933b) on the social participation of preschool children. In it she differentiated six categories of social participation: unoccupied behavior, solitary play, onlooker behavior, parallel play, associative play, and organized or cooperative group play. Studies by Beaver (1932) on initiation of social contacts, and by Caille (1933) on resistant behavior, have provided further pertinent data.

Studies of aggressive behavior in children have been made by a number of investigators. Among these have been Jersild and Markey (1935), Fite (1940), Appel (1942), Muste and Sharpe (1947), and Body (1955). Studies by Dawe (1934) and Green (1933a,b) have been concerned more specifically with children's quarrels. Murphy (1937) included observations of aggressive behavior in her larger study of social behavior and personality.

Studies of friendship and positive social relations have also been carried out (Green, 1933a; Challman, 1932). Murphy's (1937) study on sympathy and cooperation in young children is among the most extensive works in this field.

In general, these studies have reported markedly similar findings with respect to patterns of social development. There is an increase in all forms of social interaction with increasing chronological age in the preschool years—three-year-olds showing a greater degree of initiation, interaction, and participation than two-year-olds, and four-year-olds showing a greater degree than three-year-olds. These findings hold whether one is referring to such socially acceptable methods of interaction as cooperation and sympathy, or to less acceptable methods such as aggression. In addition, the relative proportion of acceptable to unacceptable methods tends to increase with age. The older child relies more heavily on verbal than on physical or material contacts, and shows less dependent behavior toward adults.

A second consistent finding is that the child who ranks high with respect to one area of social activity is likely to rank high with respect to other types of social behavior. For example, the child who is the most actively sympathetic in the group is likely also to rank among the children showing the greatest number of aggressive contacts. This fact has led a number of investigators to postulate a dimension of personality along a continuum from passivity to activity (Murphy, 1937; Andrus and Horowitz, 1938).

The wide range of individual differences observed in all areas of social interaction is another consistent finding. Generalizations made with respect to any of the variables discussed may be found invalid when applied to a given child. Just as in other areas of development, the child proceeds through the developmental stages at his own pace and is ready for certain experiences in relation to his own level of development. The added factor of differences in basic temperament makes generalizations even more difficult to apply to the individual.

These studies have implications with regard to the age at which the average child is ready for the nursery experience, the factors to be considered in determining a specific child's readiness, and program planning for the preschool ages.

With regard to the age at which the child is ready for group experience, the following facts are relevant. The two-year-old is generally not ready to participate actively in social activities with other children. His main social behavior will take the form of onlooker behavior, with some parallel play and solitary play making up the major part of his play activity. Since chronological age seems to be the critical factor here, it is unlikely that early entrance into the nursery group will speed social adjustment to any particular extent, nor will the child necessarily be stimulated to greater social participation. The three-year-old, on the other hand, is beginning to spend a greater proportion of his time in more active social interaction and, if outgoing and secure, may derive real enjoyment from the opportunity for social play. The four-year-old, unless unusually shy or withdrawn, will enjoy and benefit from the opportunity for cooperative group play.

In considering the readiness of a particular child, age is not the only consideration involved. The research indicates that individual differences in rates of development and in temperament must also be considered. The active outgoing child may find the nursery a challenge and an opportunity, or he may find the degree of social stimulation so great as to be overtiring. A more passive, less outgoing child, in a similar situation, might make an easier adjustment because he is less responsive to the social stimulation. There is no single rule that can be used to assess with certainty a given child's ability to utilize the nursery experience in a positive way. It will be necessary to look at the individual child, the level of his play with his age-mates, and his general activity level, as well as the purpose for which a group program is being considered. If it is primarily for social learning, readiness to participate in social play must be present before the experience can be meaningful. If the need is for care, the group experience may be acceptable even without this readiness, if provision is made for solitary play and onlooker behavior.

The findings with regard to friendship groupings among preschool children are relevant to the question of whether the nursery experience is a necessary one for all children. Social play within the nursery group takes place generally within small groups, of two or three children, during the early preschool years. Even during the later preschool years, groups are usually limited to three, four, or five children. Groups of this size are often available to the child in his own neighborhood. The more formal group activities will be available to the child in kindergarten and first grade, when he is ready for participation in a larger group.

Program planning for children in the preschool years must take into account the wide range of individual differences found within any age group. Provision must be made for a balance of individual and group activities so that individual children can find activities suited to their own levels, inclinations, and abilities. No nursery program should be designed for a single level of social participation. The teacher must realize that social learning takes place in relation to conflicts as well as in cooperative play, and that many of the situations which stimulate cooperative interaction may also stimulate aggressive behavior.

Studies of certain patterns of behavior that distinguish one child from another have grown out of the observations described above. Individual differences reflecting stable behavior traits have been subjected to analysis and classification. Among these, the traits of *leadership* and *social acceptance* (popularity) have been given the most careful attention, and are most relevant to the nursery group experience.

Leadership. Parten (1933a) used behavioral observations in the nursery school to obtain valid and reliable measures of leadership in preschool children. Two distinct types of leaders were identified: the "diplomat" and the "bully"; the former "by artful and indirect suggestions" controls a large number of children, while the latter employs brute force in bossing the small group he has chosen for his "gang." Individual differences in directing, following, and independent pursuit were found to be greater than the differences which were attributable to age. While sex differences in leadership were found to be negligible, leaders somewhat exceeded non-leaders in intelligence, and tended to come from higher occupational classes.

In a study of social structure of a group of kindergarten children, Hanfmann (1935) found some interesting patterns of dominance emerging, even within the small group of ten children whom she studied. Her findings are similar in many ways to those of Parten. The method used differed from Parten's, in that it involved ranking each child for dominance in relation to each other child in the group on the basis of a play session alone with that child. She distinguished: the "objective leader," the child who dominates by strong interest in constructive play; the "social leader," whose dominant interest is play with the other child and who bases his demands on the requirements of play but takes into account the needs of others; the "gangster," who uses social play as a means of expanding and displaying his own power; and the "destroyer," who deliberately disrupts orderly play and achieves domination by immobilizing the other person. She points out that there is not a simple linear relationship between these types of domination. For example, dominance by destruction was found to be the most effective but also the least stable, because it tended to disappear as soon as an interest in play was aroused. Neither the "destroyer" nor the "gangster" patterns of dominance were truly accepted by the dominated children. Only those who led through an interest in play as such or in social play were followed willingly.

A more extensive study of patterns of ascendance and submission was made by Jack (1934). Later work extending Jack's study has been done by Page (1936) and Mummery (1947). Jack was interested not only in identifying characteristics of ascendant behavior but also in devising methods for its modification. Ascendant behavior was defined to include both pursuit of one's own purposes against interference and directing the behavior of others. On the basis of ascendance scores, obtained for each child through observations of his play with one other child in an experimental situation, the children were divided into an ascendant, a moderately ascendant, and a nonascendant group. Since the aspect of social behavior in the free play situation most closely associated with nonascendance was "lack of confidence," training in a variety of skills designed to increase the child's self-confidence was provided for children in the nonascendant group. Increases in ascendant behavior were found following this training. Comparable increases were not found in a control group of nonascendant children who did not receive this training. A similar relationship between lack of confidence and nonascendance had been noted in a study by Emmons (1933).

H. H. Anderson (1937a,b), whose studies of dominative and integrative behavior in teachers have already been mentioned, has made an important contribution to an understanding of the variables relevant to ascendant behavior. In a series of studies of children of different ages and in different settings, he has attempted to differentiate two aspects of ascendant behavior, domination and integration, and to establish certain relationships between them and other behavior. While both dominative and integrative behavior represent attempts by one person to achieve a personal goal through interaction with another, the dominating person seeks to achieve his goal without regard to the desires or interests of the other person involved, and without consideration of alternative courses of action. Integrative behavior is directed flexibly toward the achievement of goals which take into consideration the variety of alternatives possible and includes consideration of the feelings, interests, and opinions of others. Anderson's studies with preschool children found the following hypotheses supported by the data obtained: that domination incites dominative behavior in others; that integrative behavior induces integrative behavior in a companion; and that domination and integration as defined are not only different techniques of responding to differences in others, but are not necessarily related.

The development of a group identity with values and mores of its own is a subject which has received considerable attention with respect to children in the elementary and high school years. Less attention has been accorded the subject in regard to the preschool years. The existence of some group identification in the preschool child, however, cannot be doubted by anyone who is familiar with groups of children of this age.

An extensive and interestingly conceived study of this phenomenon and its relationship to individual leadership has been carried out by Merei (1949). In this study a number of small groups were set up, consisting of children characterized as nonascendant in their nursery classroom behavior. These groups tended to develop a group tradition and set of standards which gave structure and content to the group activities. An older, more ascendant child, accepted as a leader in the nursery, was introduced into the group after such traditions had become established. Despite the fact that in the regular nursery setting these leaders could direct the behavior of any individual in the experimental group, in the small group situation the group absorbed the leader—forcing its traditions upon him, and ignoring his suggestions or accepting them only in modified form within the traditions of the group. Individual differences in handling the problem of imposing one's leadership upon the already formed group mores were found that paralleled in many ways those observed by Hanfmann, Parten, and others.

Other results of this study included the finding that the degree of group activity was strengthened by providing only one object for the group, while group activity was weakened by the provision of a toy for each child. Setting a concrete task for the group also strengthened the group.

Studies of preschool children living in the Kibbutzim of Israel (Irvine, 1952; Faigin, 1958; Spiro, 1958)—as well as the findings reported by Freud and Burlingham (1944), and Freud and Dann (1954)—attest to the reality and strength of group identification for children of this age. Further research on social development in the preschool years is needed to provide a fuller understanding of the meaning of this identification in the development of the young child. Still unanswered is the question of whether it represents a positive extending of the individual's capacity for forming relationships through identification with others, or whether it tends to interfere with the development of personal goals and standards and strengthens conformity at the expense of individuality. (See also Rabin, 1957, 1958a,b.)

The attribute of flexibility in adapting to the needs and interests of other individuals in the pursuit of realistic goals of one's own, has been discussed in connection with teacher behavior (H. H. Anderson, 1939a,b; Thompson, 1944; Reichenberg-Hackett, 1962), and with leadership (Hanfmann, 1935; Merei, 1949). It is an important factor in assuring the success of leadership, and in successful interpersonal relationships in general.

Such flexibility requires, among other things, the ability to perceive and to interpret correctly the relevant factors in a social situation. Chittenden (1942) developed a method for increasing the young child's ability to perceive and to interpret social situations involving peers, and of teaching appropriate ways of responding in such situations. Two types of "assertiveness," domination and cooperation, were differentiated—paralleling to a considerable extent the concepts of ascendance, domination, and integration described earlier. Following a procedure similar to Jack's (1934),

Chittenden provided children who were highly dominative with a series of training sessions, using dolls to play out situations involving potential social conflict. Through discussions which included interpretation of the situation portrayed and a consideration of the types of behavior that would be most appropriate to solving them, the child was helped to a better understanding of social relationships. The group of children who participated in the experimental sessions showed a significant decrease in dominative behavior and an increase in cooperative behavior.

Social acceptance. A more recent development in the study of peer relationships has been the application of sociometric techniques for determining the child's status in the group. These techniques have provided valuable data concerning social acceptance and the structure of groups. While they were developed originally for use with elementary school children whose peer group relations are more firmly structured, a number of investigators have adapted them to use with preschool children. Early studies relied on verbal questioning of the child only; more recently a picture sociometric technique has been devised by McCandless and Marshall (1957a). Other variations in technique include one reported by Dunnington (1957a,b), in which choices were not limited to "best-liked" but each child indicated the extent to which he liked or did not like to play with each of the others. A given child's sociometric score was based on the ratings he was assigned by all the others.

A number of studies have been concerned with the validity of the sociometric method as a measure of children's actual feelings toward each other, and as predictors of social behavior in the nursery. Among these are the following: Koch (1933), Hagman (1933), Lippitt (1941), Moreno (1942), Frankel (1946), Marshall (1957), Marshall and McCandless (1957a), McCandless and Marshall (1957a), Horowitz (1961). Later studies have involved the relating of other variables with social acceptance. Specific variables studied in this way have been: dependence on adults (Marshall and McCandless, 1957b; McCandless, Bilous, and Bennett, 1961); sex differences (Marshall and McCandless, 1957b; McCandless and Hoyt, 1961); social participation and play preferences (McCandless and Marshall, 1957b; McCandless and Hoyt, 1961); social behaviors in a classroom situation (Bonney and Powell, 1953); aggressive, imaginative, and verbal behavior (Dunnington, 1957b; Marshall, 1961).

In general, dependence on adults has been found to be negatively correlated with social acceptance by peers, as this has been measured through sociometric scores, teacher judgments of popularity, observed social acceptance in play, and number of observed friendly interactions in play (Marshall and McCandless, 1957b). The strength of this relationship is increased when "dependence on adults" is further qualified as to whether it is "instrumental dependency" or "emotional dependency" (following Heathers, 1955). The former consists of requests for help from the adult to further an objective goal of the child; the latter, of requests for nurturance from the adult (McCandless, Bilous, and Bennett, 1961). As would be expected, emotional dependence was related to low social status; the degree to which a child requested help from the adult to further an activity of his own was unrelated to social acceptance by others.

Dunnington (1957b) found generally similar relationships with respect to attention-seeking behavior on the part of children with high and low social status in their group. Low-status children showed greater attention-seeking behavior toward the adult in an experimental play situation than did high-status children, and with this, a greater resistance to adult suggestion or direction.

The relationship between hostility (and/or aggressive behavior) and social acceptance is somewhat less clear-cut. Dunnington found that children with high social status showed a greater proportion of positive affect than did the low-status children, and their aggression tended to be expressed within the context of dramatic play. The aggression shown by high-status children in dramatic play was more frequently ascribed to single, more definite characters, and directed toward specific recipients; the aggression shown by the low-status child in this setting was more likely to be diffuse, and less frequently structured. Marshall (1961) found hostility exhibited within the context of dramatic play to be positively related to social acceptance. Marshall and McCandless (1957b) found that hostile interactions within the peer group were not related to social acceptance.

The child's development of a positive self-image is touched on by these studies. While we know that the child's concept of himself and his evaluation of himself and his abilities during the preschool years are fashioned in large part by parental attitudes toward him, there can be no doubt that he also develops an image of himself in relation to his peers, based upon their reactions to him. How he is perceived by the children and adults around him will influence his own perception of himself as a social person. Hence, behavior which leads to unpopularity in the group, despite its relative harmlessness otherwise, may need to be considered seriously by those working with the child, and modified where possible.

Studies reviewed here suggest ways in which this modification can be carried out. The teacher can use her good relationship with the group to help them model their behavior toward the child on hers. She can increase the child's self-confidence by helping him develop skills and to experience successes that will add to his feeling of personal worth. She can help him increase his social perceptiveness through discussion of incidents that occur in the classroom. The possibility of creating leadership experience for the nonleader, through the careful selection and formation of subgroups of nonascendant children, is suggested by the Merei study. Through utilization of program, equipment, and an understanding of the factors involved in social interaction, the teacher can provide important social learning experiences for the child in the nursery setting.

The studies on ascendance, leadership, dominance, and social acceptance point in a similar direction: the child who is free of dependence on adults, who has confidence in himself and reacts appropriately and flexibly (perhaps because of freedom from the inner conflicts which would distort his ability to perceive the social environment accurately), is the child most accepted in the group. He leads out of an interest in the activity shared with other children, rather than out of a need to dominate or have his own way. As he is free to consider the desires of others, he can be expected to become increasingly more perceptive and adept at integrating the needs of others toward common goals.

Personality Factors in Nursery Adjustment

The effect of the nursery experience on the individual child will, in the last analysis, depend upon the child's own personality, abilities, and interests. These in turn will have been shaped by earlier experiences in the home. Some of the variables important in determining the nature of the experience for a particular child have been mentioned previously. The child's familiarity with the kinds of activities which make up the nursery program, the degree to which he has resolved his own problems of dependence, his level of self-confidence, his ability to perceive and adapt himself to the essential social and reality aspects of a play situation, and the nature and degree of the hostility he shows have been demonstrated to influence the child's functioning in the group situation and the role he is assigned in the group.

There have been a number of studies attempting to establish specific relationships between factors in the home situation and the child's adjustment in the nursery. Among these are studies by Baldwin (1948, 1949, 1954), Highberger (1955), Hartup (1959), and Marshall (1961).

Baldwin attempted to relate school adjustment to parental attitudes. On the basis of ratings of parental behavior in the home, using the Fels Behavior Rating Scale, a measure of "democracy" was obtained which was found to be associated with free and active participation in nursery school activities, successful aggression and self-assertion, and creative and constructive behavior. Other syndromes of parental behavior, subsumed under the heading "indulgence," were found to be associated with physical apprehension and inhibition in development of large muscle skills.

The Early-Adjustment-to-School Scale was developed by Highberger (1955) as a measure of the child's adjustment in the nursery, based on ratings of behavior in the initial period of attendance. While the scale proved to be a reliable predictor of the child's adjustment in the nursery at the end of a six-month period, it did not reflect differences in the maternal attitudes Highberger studied. In an attempt to define the usefulness of the EAS Scale further, Hartup (1959) found essentially similar results. Reasons suggested for the failure of this scale to correlate with maternal attitudes were the global nature of the scale and the possible inappropriateness of the particular maternal variables selected.

Marshall (1961) measured child behavior in the nursery and the home as well as parental attitudes and behavior in order to investigate the relationships between certain home experiences and children's social behavior in school. One of the important nursery school behaviors studied was the dramatic play activity so often observed in children—play in which the child pretends to be an animal, object, or another person. It was found that the child's ability to get along with his peers and his status in the nursery group were related to the frequency with which he indulged in such dramatic play. His ability to indulge in these types of activities was in turn dependent upon wide informational experiences with adults in the home; and was negatively related to parental attitudes of suppression, punitive control, and overpermissiveness. The greater the opportunity the child had to learn about topics capable of translation into dramatic play, through talk with parents and other meaningful adults at home, the greater the social acceptance achieved in the group.

The results of these studies indicate that many of the traits which the child brings to the nursery, and which ensure his success or failure in the nursery group, are related directly to parental attitudes and the experiences the parents have provided for the child in the home. The conclusion implicit in this would seem to be that the child for whom the nursery will be most successful is the child whose home experience has already developed the emotional independence, the ability to get along with peers, and the good communication skills which the nursery itself is designed to provide. Yet it is the dependent child, the child whose own needs interfere with his ability to perceive social situations realistically, or whose background of language and information is inadequate to provide him with tools of effective communication, whose need for the nursery experience is the greatest. One answer to this dilemma has been discussed in the previous section.

Techniques are available for the teacher to provide corrective experiences for the child within the nursery setting itself.

A second answer is to be found in the opportunity which the nursery can provide for parent education. The cooperative nursery school in which the mother participates in a teaching role, parent education programs (including lectures and discussion groups in conjunction with the regular nursery school or day nursery), and the use of social workers as counselors in conjunction with the day nursery represent methods of handling this problem in current practice. The subject of influencing child-rearing practices and parental attitudes, while directly relevant to the present discussion, is too large for inclusion in the present review. However, the observation that behavior in the preschool years tends to persist throughout childhood (Van Alstyne and Hattwick, 1939; Macfarlane, Allen, and Honzik, 1954) serves to underline the importance of intervention during the preschool years.

SUMMARY AND CONCLUSIONS

This review has concerned itself with research on the effects of early group experience on young children, with specific reference to the nursery school and day nursery. The importance of the topic for practice lies in its relevance to (1) the issue of providing group care for young children as a community resource for working mothers, for socialization experience for the child, and for the intellectual and cultural enrichment of the preschool child; (2) the determination of the advisability of nursery experience for a specific child; and (3) the need of the nursery educator for sound knowledge concerning child development principles as these are related to practice in the classroom.

Studies which have attempted to evaluate the nursery experience globally, in terms of the effects of attendance upon intellectual, social, and physical development, were reviewed. Results from such studies have generally proved inconclusive because they have failed to relate the changes expected to the specific variables expected to bring about the changes. A more fruitful approach to the assessment of the nursery experience has been in terms of the components which make it up: the physical setting, the program, teacher-child relations, peer group interaction, and the personality characteristics of the individual child.

Findings from the specific studies reviewed have emphasized the fact that the effectiveness of a given program (in terms of effecting changes in the individual) will depend on its appropriateness to the child's developmental level and its provision of experiences which supplement, rather than merely duplicate, experiences he is receiving elsewhere. The most important single factor in determining the nature of the experience for the child is the teacher. The range of actual teacher behavior in the classroom is wide, and varies in terms not only of specific methods used but also in degree of support given the child in the pursuit of his interests and in the goals and values that are stressed. The teacher's use of program and equipment makes these factors effective learning experiences. Her ability to help the individual child improve in skill, in perceptiveness of social situations, and in his interpersonal relationships will determine the progress he will make in social skills.

The child's responsiveness and ability to utilize the peer group aspect of the nursery increases with chronological age, but is also profoundly affected by the child's own temperament and individual makeup, and by the experiences he has had at home.

Questions specifically relevant to the use of day nurseries (day care centers) have not been studied as fully as those pertaining to nursery schools. More research is needed on the effects of the long hours and the necessarily greater degree of routine and regimentation in the full day program. There is as yet no evidence that these are likely to prove deleterious to the child, if carried out within a professionally adequate program. Therefore, the provision of day care centers cannot be said to be contraindicated by the research available. The use of such a center for a specific child, however, should be evaluated in terms of his personal readiness for the group experience, the purpose of the program, and the characteristics of the nursery under consideration.

If the child primarily needs care during the day, his readiness to enter the nursery should be gauged primarily in terms of his ability to separate from his mother without trauma or serious deprivation. The ability to utilize the group aspects of the experience itself is less important. Onlooker behavior and solitary or parallel play are acceptable forms of group participation at appropriate ages. However, if the aim is to provide an enriching experience, readiness to utilize the group situation constructively is the crucial factor, and sometimes nursery school attendance might better be delayed until the child has indicated a readiness for a higher degree of social participation with peers. If the purpose is to provide a corrective experience for the child, a different criterion of readiness would need to apply. The decision that the child should enter the nursery would be based on the belief that the child's separation from his mother and placement in a group of peers would be of therapeutic value in spite of, or because of, the child's inadequacies in social and emotional development.

All statements regarding readiness must be qualified with respect to the specific group experience available. The child of three may be ready to leave his mother for a period of several hours to enter a small group of other three-year-olds under the guidance of an attentive and experienced teacher;

he may not be ready to spend an eight-hour day in a large group of children of mixed ages, with little adult attention and support. The child with special problems may be able to profit from the group experience because of his close personal relationship with an especially well-trained teacher, but he might be unable to function at all within a larger, less well-staffed program.

If the community is to rely on group programs for the preschool child to solve the problem of day care needs, to offset cultural deprivation, or to enrich development, it must be prepared to provide these programs with adequately prepared staff, sufficient in number to meet the needs of young children. Consultation services should be available to help differentiate the children who are able to use the group experience in a positive way from those to whom the group setting might actually prove damaging. The provision of these professional safeguards makes group care of preschool children an expensive service, but one which can meet a real need—both for the community and the individual family. Without adequate safeguards, however, it can be a factor detrimental to the healthy social and emotional development of the child.

REFERENCES

ALLEN, G. B. & MASLING, J. M. An evaluation of the effects of nursery school training on children in the kindergarten, first and second grades. *J. educ. Res.*, 1957, **51**, 285–296.

ANDERSON, H. H. An experimental study of dominative and integrative behavior in children of preschool age. *J. soc. Psychol.*, 1937, **8**, 335–345 (a).

ANDERSON, H. H. Domination and integration in the social behavior of young children in an experimental play situation. *Genet. Psychol. Monogr.*, 1937, **19**, 341–408 (b).

ANDERSON, H. H. Domination and social integration in the behavior of kindergarten children and teachers. *Genet. Psychol. Monogr.*, 1939, **21**, 287–385 (a).

ANDERSON, H. H. The measurement of domination and of socially integrative behavior in teachers' contacts with children. *Child Developm.*, 1939, **10**, 73–89 (b).

ANDERSON, L. D. A longitudinal study of the effects of nursery school training on successive intelligence test ratings. *Yearb. nat. Soc. Stud. Educ.*, 1940, **39**, Part II, 3–10.

ANDRUS, R. & HOROWITZ, E. L. The effect of nursery school training: insecurity feelings. *Child Developm.*, 1938, **9**, 169–174.

APPEL, M. H. Aggressive behavior of nursery school children and adult procedures in dealing with such behavior. *J. exp. Educ.*, 1942, **11**, 185–199.

ARRINGTON, R. E. Interrelations in the behavior of young children. *Monogr. Soc. Res. Child Developm.*, 1932, No. 8. Teach. Coll., Columbia Univ.

ARRINGTON, R. E. Time sampling in studies of social behavior. *Psychol. Rev.*, 1943, **40**, 81–124.

ARSENIAN, J. M. Young children in an insecure situation. *J. abnorm. soc. Psychol.*, 1943, **38**, 225–249.

BAIN, W. E. *An analytical study of teaching in nursery school, kindergarten, and first grade.* New York: Teach. Coll., Columbia Univ., 1928.

BALDWIN, A. L. Socialization and the parent-child relationship. *Child Developm.*, 1948, **19**, 127–136.

BALDWIN, A. L. The effect of home environment on nursery school behavior. *Child Developm.*, 1949, **20**, 49–61.

BALDWIN, A. L. Effect of home environment on nursery school behavior. In W. E. Martin & C. B. Stendler (Eds.), *Readings in child development*. New York: Harcourt Brace, 1954.

BANDURA, A. & HUSTON, A. C. Identification as a process of incidental learning. *J. abnorm. soc. Psychol.*, 1961, **63**, 311–318.

BARRETT, H. E. & KOCH, H. L. The effect of nursery school training upon the mental test performance of a group of orphanage children. *Pedagogical Seminary & J. genet. Psychol.*, 1930, **37**, 102–121.

BEAVER, A. P. The initiation of social contacts by pre-school children. *Monogr. Soc. Res. Child Developm.*, 1932, No. 7. Teach. Coll., Columbia Univ.

BIRD, G. E. Effect of nursery school attendance upon mental growth of children. *Yearb. nat. Soc. Stud. Educ.*, 1940, **39**, Part II, 81–84.

BISHOP, B. M. Mother-child interaction and the social behavior of children. *Psychol. Monogr.*, 1951, **65**, No. 11.

BODY, M. K. Patterns of aggression in nursery school. *Child Developm.*, 1955, **26**, 3–11.

BONNEY, M. E. & NICHOLSON, E. L. Comparative social adjustments of elementary school pupils with and without preschool training. *Child Developm.*, 1958, **29**, 125–133.

BONNEY, M. E. & POWELL, J. Differences in social behavior between sociometrically high and sociometrically low children. *J. educ. Res.*, 1953, **46**, 481–495.

BOWLBY, J. *Maternal care and mental health*. World Health Organization Monographs, Geneva, 1951, No. 2.

BROWN, A. W. & HUNT, R. Relations between nursery attendance and teachers' ratings of some aspects of children's adjustment in kindergarten. *Child Developm.*, 1961, **32**, 585–596.

CAILLE, R. K. Resistant behavior in young children. *Monogr. Soc. Res. Child Developm.*, 1933, No. 11.

CAMPBELL, E. H. The effect of nursery school training upon the later food habits of the child. *Child Developm.*, 1933, **4**, 329–345.

CHALLMAN, R. C. Factors influencing friendship among preschool children. *Child Developm.*, 1932, **3**, 146–158.

CHILD WELFARE LEAGUE OF AMERICA. *Standards for day care service*. New York: Author, 1960.

CHITTENDEN, G. E. An experimental study in measuring and modifying assertive behavior in young children. *Monogr. Soc. Res. Child Developm.*, 1942, **7**, No. 1.

COLBY, M. G. Instrumental reproduction of melody by preschool children. *J. genet. Psychol.*, 1935, **47**, 413–430.

CRISSEY, O. L. The mental development of children of the same IQ in differing institutional environments. *Child Developm.*, 1937, **8**, 217–220.

CUSHING, H. M. A tentative report of the influence of nursery school training upon kindergarten adjustment as reported by kindergarten teachers. *Child Developm.*, 1934, **5**, 304–314.

DALES, R. J. Afternoon sleep in a group of nursery school children. *J. genet. Psychol.*, 1941, **58**, 161–180.

DAWE, H. C. An analysis of two hundred quarrels of preschool children. *Child Developm.*, 1934, **5**, 139–157.

DAWE, H. C. A study of the effect of an educational program upon language development and related mental functions in young children. *J. exp. Educ.*, 1942, **11**, 200–209.

DENNIS, W. & DENNIS, M. G. The effect of cradling practices upon the onset of walking in Hopi children. *J. genet. Psychol.*, 1940, **56**, 77–86.

DUBIN, E. R. The effect of training on the tempo of development of graphic representation in preschool children. *J. exp. Educ.*, 1946, **15**, 166–173.

DUNNINGTON, M. J. Investigations of areas of disagreement in sociometric measurement of preschool children. *Child Developm.*, 1957, **28**, 93–102 (a).

DUNNINGTON, M. J. Behavioral differences of sociometric status groups in a nursery school. *Child Developm.*, 1957, **28**, 103–111 (b).

DUNSHEE, M. E. A study of factors affecting the amount and kind of food eaten by nursery school children. *Child Developm.*, 1931, **2**, 163–183.

EMMONS, A. L. A study of the relations between self-assurance and skill in young children. *Child Developm.*, 1933, **4**, 323–328.

EZEKIEL, L. F. Changes in ego-centricity of nursery school children. *Child Developm.*, 1931, **2**, 74–75.

FAIGIN, H. Social behavior of young children in the Kibbutz. *J. abnorm. soc. Psychol.*, 1958, **56**, 117–129.

FITE, M. D. Aggressive behavior in young children and children's attitudes toward aggression. *Genet. Psychol. Monogr.*, 1940, **22**, 153–319.

FOSTER, J. Distribution of teachers' time in nursery school and kindergarten. *J. educ. Res.*, 1930, **22**, 172–183.

FRANDSEN, A. & BARLOW, F. P. Influence of the nursery school on mental growth. *Yearb. nat. Soc. Stud. Educ.*, 1940, **39**, Part II, 143–148.

FRANKEL, E. B. The social relationships of nursery school children. *Sociometry*, 1946, **9**, 210–225.

FREUD, A. & BURLINGHAM, D. *Infants without families.* New York: Internat. Univ. Press, 1944.

FREUD, A. & DANN, S. An experiment in group upbringing. In W. E. Martin & C. B. Stendler (Eds.), *Readings in child development*. New York: Harcourt Brace, 1954.

GESELL, A. L., et al. *The first five years of life.* New York: Harper, 1940.

GESELL, A. L. & THOMPSON, H. Learning and growth in identical twins. *Genet. Psychol. Monogr.*, 1929, **6**, 1–124.

GETZELS, J. W. & JACKSON, P. W. The teacher's personality and characteristics. In N. L. Gage (Ed.), *Handbook of research on teaching*. Chicago: Rand McNally, 1963.

GEWIRTZ, J. L. Three determinants of attention-seeking in young children. *Monogr. Soc. Res. Child Developm.*, 1954, **19** (2), 1–48.

GEWIRTZ, J. L. & BAER, D. M. The effect of brief social deprivation on behaviors for a social reinforcer. *J. abnorm. soc. Psychol.*, 1958, **56**, 49–56 (a).

GEWIRTZ, J. L. & BAER, D. M. Deprivation and satiation of social reinforcers as drive conditions. *J. abnorm. soc. Psychol.*, 1958, **57**, 165–172 (b).

GEWIRTZ, J. L., BAER, D. M., & ROTH, C. H. A note on the similar effects of low social availability of an adult and brief social deprivation on young children's behavior. *Child Developm.*, 1958, **29**, 149–152.

GLASS, N. Eating, sleeping, and elimination habits in children attending day nurseries and children cared for at home by mothers. *Amer. J. Orthopsychiat.*, 1949, **19**, 697–711.

GOODENOUGH, F. L. & MAUER, K. M. The mental development of nursery school children compared with that of non-nursery school children. *Yearb. nat. Soc. Stud. Educ.*, 1940, **39**, Part II, 161–178.

GREEN, E. H. Friendship and quarrels among preschool children. *Child Developm.*, 1933, **4**, 237–252 (a).

GREEN, E. H. Group play and quarreling among preschool children. *Child Developm.*, 1933, **4**, 302–307 (b).

GUTTERIDGE, M. V. A study of motor achievements of young children. *Arch. Psychol.*, *N. Y.*, 1939, **34**, No. 244.

HAGMAN, E. P. The companionships of preschool children. *Univ. Iowa Stud. Child Welf.*, 1933, **7**, No. 4.

HANFMANN, E. P. Social structure of a group of kindergarten children. *Amer. J. Orthopsychiat.*, 1935, **5**, 407–410.

HARTUP, W. W. Nurturance and nurturance withdrawal in relation to the dependency behavior of preschool children. *Child Developm.*, 1958, **29**, 191–201.

HARTUP, W. W. An evaluation of the Highberger Early Adjustment to School Scale. *Child Developm.*, 1959, **30**, 421–432.

HARTUP, W. W. & HIMENO, Y. Social isolation vs. interaction with adults in relation to aggression in preschool children. *J. abnorm. soc. Psychol.*, 1960, **59**, 17–22.

HATTWICK, B. W. The influence of nursery school attendance upon the behavior and personality of the preschool child. *J. exp. Educ.*, 1936, **5**, 180–190.

HEATHERS, G. Emotional dependence and independence needs in nursery school play. *J. genet. Psychol.*, 1955, **87**, 37–57.

HEINICKE, C. M. Some effects of separating two-year-old children from their parents: a comparative study. *Hum. Relat.*, 1956, **9**, 105–176.

HICKS, J. A. The acquisition of motor skill in young children: a study of the effects of practice in throwing at a moving target. *Child Developm.*, 1930, **1**, 90–105.

HICKS, J. A. & RALPH, D. W. The effects of practice in tracing the Porteus Diamond Maze. *Child Developm.*, 1931, **2**, 156–158.

HIGHBERGER, R. The relationship between maternal behavior and the child's early adjustment to nursery school. *Child Developm.*, 1955, **26**, 49–61.

HILGARD, J. R. Learning and maturation in preschool children. *J. genet. Psychol.*, 1932, **41**, 36–56.

HILL, A. B. & VAN ALSTYNE, D. *Learning levels of the children in the nursery school with reference to the eating situation.* New York: Teach. Coll., Columbia Univ., 1930.

HISSEM, I. A new approach to music for young children. *Child Developm.*, 1933, **4**, 308–317.

HOROWITZ, E. L. & SMITH, R. B. Social relations and personality patterning in preschool children. *J. genet. Psychol.*, 1939, **54**, 337–352.

HOROWITZ, F. D. Latency of sociometric choice among preschool children. *Child Developm.*, 1961, **32**, 235–242.

IRVINE, E. Observations on the aims and methods of child rearing in communal settlements in Israel. *Hum. Relat.*, 1952, **5**, 247–275.

JACK, L. M. An experimental study of ascendant behavior in preschool children. *Univ. Iowa Stud. Child Welf.*, 1934, **9**, 7–65.

JERSILD, A. T. Training and growth in the development of children. *Monogr. Soc. Res. Child Developm.*, 1932, No. 10.

JERSILD, A. T. & BIENSTOCK, S. F. The influence of training on the vocal ability of three year old children. *Child Developm.*, 1931, **2**, 272–291.

JERSILD, A. T. & BIENSTOCK, S. F. Development of rhythm in young children. *Monogr. Soc. Res. Child Developm.*, 1935, No. 22.

JERSILD, A. T. & FITE, M. D. The influence of nursery school experience on children's social adjustments. *Monogr. Soc. Res. Child Developm.*, 1939, No. 2.

JERSILD, A. T. & MARKEY, F. V. Conflicts between preschool children. *Monogr. Soc. Res. Child Developm.*, 1935, No. 21.

JOEL, W. The influence of nursery school education upon behavior maturity. *J. exp. Educ.*, 1939, **8**, 164–165.

JOHNSON, H. M. *Children in the nursery school.* New York: John Day, 1928.

JOHNSON, M. W. The effect on behavior of variation in amount of play equipment. *Child Developm.*, 1935, **6**, 56–68 (a).

JOHNSON, M. W. The influence of verbal directions on behavior. *Child Developm.*, 1935, **6**, 196–204 (b).

JONES, H. E. & JORGENSEN, A. P. Mental growth as related to nursery school attendance. *Yearb. nat. Soc. Stud. Educ.*, 1940, **39**, Part II, 207–222.

KAWIN, E. & HOEFER, C. A. *Comparative study of a nursery school vs. a non-nursery school group.* Chicago: Univ. Chicago Press, 1931.

KING, J. A. Parameters relevant to determining the effects of early experience upon the adult behavior of animals. *Psychol. Bull.*, 1958, **55**, 46–58.

KIRK, S. A. *Early education of the mentally retarded: an experimental study.* Urbana: Univ. Illinois Press, 1958.

KOCH, H. L. Popularity in preschool children: some related factors and a technique for measurement. *Child Developm.*, 1933, **4**, 164–175.

LAMSON, E. E. A follow-up study of a group of nursery school children. *Yearb. nat. Soc. Stud. Educ.*, 1940, **39**, Part II, 231–236.

LANDRETH, C., GARDNER, G. H., ECKHARDT, B. C., & PRUGLE, A. D. Teacher-child contacts in nursery schools. *J. exp. Educ.*, 1943, **12**, 65–91.

LIPPITT, R. Popularity among preschool children. *Child Developm.*, 1941, **12**, 305–332.

MACFARLANE, J. W., ALLEN, L., & HONZIK, M. P. *A developmental study of the behavior problems of normal children between twenty-one months and fourteen years.* Berkeley: Univ. California Press, 1954.

MALLAY, H. Growth in social behavior and mental activity after six months in nursery school. *Child Developm.*, 1935, **6**, 303–309.

MARKEY, F. V. Imaginative behavior of preschool children. *Monogr. Soc. Res. Child Developm.*, 1935, No. 18.

MARSHALL, H. R. An evaluation of sociometric-social behavior research with preschool children. *Child Developm.*, 1957, **28**, 131–137.

MARSHALL, H. R. Relations between home experiences and children's use of language in play interactions with peers. *Psychol. Monogr.*, 1961, **75**, 1–76.

MARSHALL, H. R. & McCANDLESS, B. R. A study in prediction of social behavior of preschool children. *Child Developm.*, 1957, **28**, 149–159 (a).

MARSHALL, H. R. & McCANDLESS, B. R. Relationship between dependence on adults and social acceptance by peers. *Child Developm.*, 1957, **28**, 413–419 (b).

McCANDLESS, B. R., BILOUS, C. B., & BENNETT, H. L. Peer popularity and dependence on adults in preschool-age socialization. *Child Developm.*, 1961, **32**, 511–518.

McCANDLESS, B. R. & HOYT, J. M. Sex, ethnicity, and play preferences of preschool children. *J. abnorm. soc. Psychol.*, 1961, **62**, 683–685.

McCANDLESS, B. R. & MARSHALL, H. R. A picture sociometric technique for preschool children and its relation to teacher judgments of friendship. *Child Developm.*, 1957, **28**, 139–147 (a).

McCANDLESS, B. R. & MARSHALL, H. R. Sex differences in social acceptance and participation of preschool children. *Child Developm.*, 1957, **28**, 421–425 (b).

McCLURE, S. C. The effect of varying verbal instructions on the motor responses of preschool children. *Child Developm.*, 1936, **7**, 276–290.

McGRAW, M. B. *Growth: a study of Johnny and Jimmy.* New York: Appleton-Century-Crofts, 1935.

MEREI, F. Group leadership and institutionalization. *Hum. Relat.*, 1949, **2**, 23–39.

MOORE, S. B. The use of commands, suggestions, and requests by nursery school and kindergarten teachers. *Child Developm.*, 1938, **9**, 185–201.

MORENO, F. Sociometric status of children in a nursery school group. *Sociometry*, 1942, **5**, 395–411.

MUMMERY, D. An analytical study of ascendant behavior of preschool children. *Child Developm.*, 1947, **18**, 40–81.

MURPHY, L. B. *Social behavior and child personality.* New York: Columbia Univ. Press, 1937.

MUSSEN, P. H. (Ed.) *Handbook of research methods in child development.* New York: Wiley, 1960.

MUSTE, M. J. & SHARPE, D. F. Some influential factors in the determination of aggressive behavior in preschool children. *Child Developm.*, 1947, **18**, 11–28.

NESBITT, M. Student and child relationships in the nursery school. *Child Developm.*, 1943, **14**, 143–166.

OLSON, W. C. & HUGHES, B. O. Subsequent growth of children with and without nursery school experience. *Yearb. nat. Soc. Stud. Educ.*, 1940, **39**, Part II, 237–244.

PAGE, M. L. The modification of ascendant behavior in preschool children. *Univ. Iowa Stud. Child Welf.*, 1936, **12**, No. 3.

PARTEN, M. B. Social participation among preschool children. *J. abnorm. soc. Psychol.*, 1932, **27**, 243–269.

PARTEN, M. B. Leadership among preschool children. *J. abnorm. soc. Psychol.*, 1933, **27**, 430–440 (a).

PARTEN, M. B. Social play among preschool children. *J. abnorm. soc. Psychol.*, 1933, **28**, 136–147 (b).

RABIN, A. I. Personality maturity of kibbutz and non-kibbutz children, as reflected in Rorschach findings. *J. proj. Tech.*, 1957, **21**, 148–153.

RABIN, A. I. Behavior research in collective settlements in Israel: infants and children under conditions of "intermittent" mothering in the kibbutz. *Amer. J. Orthopsychiat.*, 1958, **28**, 577–586 (a).

RABIN, A. I. Some psychosexual differences between kibbutz and non-kibbutz Israeli boys. *J. proj. Tech.*, 1958, **22**, 328–332 (b).

READ, K. H. *The nursery school: a human relations laboratory.* Philadelphia: W. B. Saunders, 1960.

REICHENBERG-HACKETT, W. Practices, attitudes and values in nursery group education. *Psychol. Rep.*, 1962, **10**, 151–172.

RIESSMAN, F. *The culturally deprived child.* New York: Harper, 1962.

ROSENBLITH, J. F. Learning by imitation in kindergarten children. *Child Developm.*, 1959, **30**, 69–80.

SEARS, P. S. & DOWLEY, E. M. Research on teaching in the nursery school. In N. L. Gage (Ed.), *Handbook of research on teaching.* Chicago: Rand McNally, 1963.

SIEGEL, A. E. Aggressive behavior of young children in the absence of an adult. *Child Developm.*, 1957, **28**, 371–378.

SIEGEL, A. E. & KOHN, L. G. Permissiveness, permission, and aggression: the effect of adult presence or absence on aggression in children's play. *Child Developm.*, 1959, **30**, 131–141.

SKEELS, H. M. Some Iowa studies of the mental growth of children in relation to differentials of the environment: a summary. *Yearb. nat. Soc. Stud. Educ.*, 1940, **39**, Part II, 281–308.

SKEELS, H. M. & FILLMORE, E. A. The mental development of children from underprivileged homes. *J. genet. Psychol.*, 1937, **50**, 427–439.

SKEELS, H. M., UPDEGRAFF, R., WELLMAN, B. L., & WILLIAMS, H. M. A study of environmental stimulation: an orphanage preschool project. *Univ. Iowa Stud. Child Welf.*, 1938, **15**, No. 4.

SKODAK, M. Children in foster homes: a study of mental development. *Univ. Iowa Stud. Child Welf.*, 1939, **16**, No. 1.

SPIRO, M. E. *Children of the kibbutz.* Cambridge, Mass.: Harvard Univ. Press, 1958.

STARKWEATHER, E. K. & ROBERTS, K. E. IQ changes occurring during nursery school attendance at the Merrill-Palmer School. *Yearb. nat. Soc. Stud. Educ.*, 1940, **39**, Part II, 315–335.

STODDARD, G. D. & WELLMAN, B. L. Environment and the IQ. *Yearb. nat. Soc. Stud. Educ.*, 1940, **39**, Part I, 405–442.

THOMAS, D. S. (Ed.) *Some new techniques for studying social behavior.* New York: Teach. Coll., Columbia Univ., 1929.

THOMPSON, G. G. The social and emotional development of preschool children under two types of educational program. *Psychol. Monogr.*, 1944, **56**, No. 5 (Whole No. 258).

THOMPSON, G. G. *Child psychology.* Boston: Houghton Mifflin, 1962.

TUCKER, C. *A study of mothers' practices and children's activities in a cooperative nursery school.* New York: Teach. Coll., Columbia Univ., 1940.

288   REVIEW OF CHILD DEVELOPMENT RESEARCH

UPDEGRAFF, R., HEILIGER, L., & LEARNED, J. The effect of training upon singing ability and musical interest of three-, four-, and five-year-old children. *Univ. Iowa Stud. Child Welf.*, 1938, **14,** 85–131.

UPDEGRAFF, R. & HERBST, E. K. An experimental study of the social behavior stimulated in young children by certain play materials. *J. genet. Psychol.*, 1933, **42,** 372–391.

VAN ALSTYNE, D. & HATTWICK, L. A. A follow-up study of nursery school children. *Child Developm.*, 1939, **10,** 43–72.

VITZ, P. C. Some changes in behavior of nursery school children over a period of seven weeks. *J. Nursery Educ.*, 1961, **16,** 62–65.

WALSH, M. E. The relation of nursery school training to the development of certain personality traits. *Child Developm.*, 1931, **2,** 72–73.

WANN, K. D., DORN, M. S., & LIDDLE, E. A. *Fostering intellectual development in young children.* New York: Teach. Coll., Columbia Univ., 1962.

WELLMAN, B. L. The effect of preschool attendance upon the IQ. *J. exp. Educ.*, 1932, **1,** 48–69.

WELLMAN, B. L. Growth in intelligence under differing school environments. *J. exp. Educ.*, 1934, **3,** 59–83.

WELLMAN, B. L. Iowa studies on the effects of schooling. *Yearb. nat. Soc. Stud. Educ.*, 1940, **39,** Part II, 377–399.

WELLMAN, B. L. The effects of preschool attendance. In R. G. Barker, J. S. Kounin, & H. F. Wright (Eds.), *Child behavior and development.* New York: McGraw-Hill, 1943. Pp. 229–243.

WILLIAMS, R. & MATTSON, M. L. The effect of social groupings upon the language of preschool children. *Child Developm.*, 1942, **13,** 233–245.

WILLIAMS, J. R. & SCOTT, R. B. Growth and development of Negro infants: IV. Motor development and its relationship to child rearing practices in two groups of Negro infants. *Child Developm.*, 1953, **24,** 103–121.

WOOLFOLK, A. S. Social adjustment through kindergarten training. *Child. Educ.*, 1929, **5,** 264–268.

WOOLLEY, H. T. The validity of standards of mental measurement in young children. *Sch. & Soc.*, 1925, **21,** 476–482.

YARROW, L. J. Maternal deprivation: toward an empirical and conceptual reevaluation. *Psychol. Bull.*, 1961, **58,** 459–490.

Peer Relations in Childhood[1]

JOHN D. CAMPBELL

National Institute of Mental Health

THE CHILD is a member of two worlds: the world of adults and that of his peers. His experiences in each of these worlds are crucial aspects of his daily living and are significant agents in molding his subsequent development. This chapter focuses on research primarily concerned with one of these worlds, that of the peer culture of childhood. Discussion will center to a considerable extent, but not exclusively, on the middle years of childhood, on the elementary school-age child's relations with other children of approximately the same age and general development.[2] Of the complex of factors involved in the total picture of peer relations, three principal facets have been singled out for consideration: (a) the role of the broader environmental context in which peer processes occur, (b) the peer group as a socializing agent, and (c) aspects of interpersonal influence within the peer group situation.

Although the broad environmental context need not be viewed as an integral part of peer relations, it is an important determinant of the impact of children's groups and affects the nature of relationships within them. Thus general cultural and subcultural factors and family influences serve to establish the framework within which peer relations operate, to set the stage on which the drama of peer relations unfolds. While this drama may have several themes, that concerned with the peer group's role as a socializ-

[1] Grateful acknowledgment is given to Katherine C. Rigler and Margaret D. Vogel for their valuable bibliographic assistance, to Nancy F. Gist for manuscript typing and proofreading, and to Harriet S. Murphy, Roger V. Burton, Marian Radke Yarrow, Melvin L. Kohn, and the editors of this volume for their comments and suggestions in the preparation of this chapter.

[2] Group experiences of the preschool child are largely ignored, since these are dealt with more fully in another chapter of this volume. Although adolescent groups do enter the picture at various points throughout the course of this chapter, a detailed appraisal of the adolescent subculture poses a sufficient number of unique issues to warrant separate consideration. These will be the focus of a chapter in the second volume of this series.

Peer groups considered will include school and neighborhood groups, clubs, cliques, and gangs; delinquent groups will, however, be bypassed in this chapter. Delinquency, which has generally been treated by research worker and practitioner alike as a separate area of inquiry, will also be considered in the second volume.

ing agent has been chosen for primary consideration here, for the task of growing up in a social world is a central one for childhood's middle years. Hence we may view the peer group as a determinant of acceptance and stability in social relations, as a contributor to the child's developing self-concept, and as one of the factors operating to form the child's attitudes and values concerning the world about him. The processes at work determining the group's influence in shaping the child in such respects are several. Those highlighted in a later portion of this chapter include characteristics of the situation, variations in children's susceptibility to influence, other children as influence agents, and the impact of the adult on children's peer groups.

Before embarking on the general survey, two preliminary tasks need to be accomplished. Since conclusions from research can be no better than the methodology on which they are based, some brief considerations in this area are required. Further, since the bulk of the research reviewed is of recent vintage, it is pertinent to place it within a larger frame, to orient it in relation to some of the earlier work in the area.

A METHODOLOGICAL NOTE

Research conclusions are at least partial captives of research methods. Thus, although an appraisal of the methodology of each study included in this review cannot be attempted, a brief reminder concerning some major recurring issues is warranted. Because of problems in research design, problems not always easy to overcome, there are limitations in the extent to which results may be accepted and generalized. Two major methodological provinces restricting the nature of conclusions to be drawn from research on peer relations are (a) the research subjects and the situations in which they are studied, and (b) the measurement techniques employed.

Research findings applicable to children of one type may not necessarily hold true for those of a different type. For example, information relevant to middle-class children may not be tailored in quite the same fashion for children in working-class homes; data from preadolescents may not apply to a sample of adolescents; and, of course, though sometimes research reports may not hint of it, the difference between the sexes may remain an important one. Situational factors, too, limit research generalizations. Thus the circumstances in which data are obtained are highly relevant to the interpretation of findings. Results in studies of play groups cannot be freely generalized to the classroom; the response in a brief laboratory encounter may have a different meaning from that occurring in certain more enduring relations of daily life.

In the appraisal of peer relations no measurement technique is problem-free. Whether to rely on verbal reports or to attempt direct measurement of behavior is an issue that remains as difficult to solve as it is familiar. Acceptance of evidence from interviews and questionnaires must necessarily be qualified; such meaningful verbal data are not identical with the behavior they attempt to describe. Although direct observation of behavior does avoid some of the pitfalls of interview and questionnaire procedures, observational methods are themselves far from foolproof. If an observer is known to be present, children's behavior may be altered, and not always in a uniform fashion. Some highly relevant acts may be less likely to be displayed in the presence of the observer than would be the case in his absence. Other significant types of behavior may occur with very low frequency; hence obtaining observational information on their incidence might be a very costly operation.

No matter what the techniques of data collection, cause-and-effect relationships are most frequently the research aim. Yet measurement difficulties, at times, lead necessarily to a Scotch verdict of "not proven." Correlational analyses of data obtained from a single source or at a single point in time may lead to the appearance of strong relationships, but they preclude truly effective separation of concomitance from causation. On the other hand, some low relationships may be more attributable to a lack of good measurement instruments than to inadequacy of theory. Further, a given variable or set of variables, while yielding statistically significant findings, may yet fail to account for much of the variation in behavior of particular children.

Thus research on peer relations (as is true of most research in the behavioral sciences today) has its methodological imperfections. While these place limits on the nature of the inferences that may be made, they do not negate the value of such research inquiries. The skilled practitioner may use findings and interpretations of research data to buttress his own insights, to test out the adequacy of his hunches, and to serve as partial contributors to his action decisions.

LANDMARKS AND MILESTONES

A comprehensive historical view of the study of children's peer relations is, of course, beyond the scope of this chapter. But a brief scrutiny highlighting a few of the landmarks and milestones in the area may serve to place the subsequent survey in its proper perspective. Social scientific interest in and recognition of the importance of children's peer relations dates back at least to the turn of the century. One of the earlier and still significant theorists is Charles H. Cooley, who gave explicit recognition to the relevance of peer group processes in socialization and general societal functioning. In 1909 he stated it thus: "The general fact is that children, especially boys after about their twelfth year, live in fellowships in which their sympathy, ambition and honor are engaged even more often, than they are in the family" (1955, pp. 24–25). And he went on to cite with approval a remark made by Jane Addams, in discussing children's gang activities, "in these social folk-motes, so to speak, the young citizen learns to act upon his own determination."

Terman's (1904) research on leadership and suggestibility in elementary school children is a noteworthy pioneer effort by an American psychologist. This investigation, conducted with considerable methodological sophistication, examined qualities of leadership and stability of status within experimentally constituted groups. Much of subsequent research is of the same lineage. More sociologically oriented early work on children's peer groups focused on the gang and stemmed, in large part, from a concern for social amelioration.[3] These studies clearly recognized the importance of the peer group as a socializing influence. Thus Puffer, who collected case histories of gangs and gang members, stated, "three boys in every four are members of a gang; and the character of this gang determines in no small degree what sort of men these boys shall become" (1912, p. 8).

During the latter part of the 1920's, research interest in peer groups began to mount. Theory was often sketchy or absent entirely, but empirical work was beginning to add significant bits of information. The year 1927 stands as a banner one in this respect. Several studies are illustrative of the contributions of that year. Hurlock presented experimental work showing the way in which group rivalry served as an incentive. Furfey reported on factors influencing boys' friendship choices, an area of inquiry that continues to remain of interest today. Thrasher collected case histories and statistics on boys' gangs and, in so doing, formulated significant insights on the role of the primary group. He noted the occurrence of specialized roles in the gang and commented on group cohesiveness and the emergence of common codes. He characterized the gang as developing "an elaborate tradition, almost a culture of its own, and in this sense it is . . . like a society in miniature . . ." (1927, p. 296). Studies such as these have a significance that extends beyond their specific contributions to the understanding of group processes. They ushered in a considerable volume of research during the decade that followed—work that in many respects has

---

[3] Such early studies usually included conflict with other groups as an important general characteristic of gangs. But the pejorative implications in some current definitional distinctions between the concepts of *clique* and *gang* (with the latter being characterized as behaving in a less socially acceptable fashion than the former) were not always an integral part of the early definitions.

served to define the issues and methods that remain of principal concern to students of peer group functioning at the present time.

During the 1930's, research interest in children's group processes clearly burgeoned. Hare, Borgatta, and Bales's annotated bibliography (1955) of small group research lists more than five times as many references to children's groups in the period 1930 to 1939 than for the preceding decade. (A similar emphasis on children's groups did not hold true for the 1940's. Though the number of references to research on groups cited by Hare and associates rose considerably for that period, references to *children's* groups declined, suggesting that group research had gone to war.)

Along with the increase in volume of research during the 1930's came an increase in sophistication of approach along both methodological and conceptual lines. The first years of this decade marked the conscious systematizing and perfecting of techniques for blueprinting the nature of relationships in children's groups. Dorothy Thomas and her collaborators were among several whose efforts were channeled into devising suitable procedures for direct observation. They formulated statistically reliable methods for recording data on children's behavior by using rating categories to evaluate behavior in systematically specified time periods (Thomas, Loomis, and Arrington, 1933). About the same time, sociometric procedures became soundly established as a means for measuring acceptance within a group. In this technique, devised by Moreno (1934), individuals indicate group members with whom they prefer to associate in specified activities or situations; examination of patterns of choice yields a picture of interpersonal relations within the group. Though ways of collecting and handling observational and sociometric data have become increasingly sophisticated, both of these approaches remain clearly recognizable friends to current students of group process.

In the late 1930's, Lippitt and White (1947), under the guidance of Kurt Lewin, used experimental procedures to study the way variations in adult leadership affected individual and group behavior in clubs of eleven-year-old boys. This examination of reactions to "authoritarian," "democratic," and "laissez faire" leadership is a major landmark in small group research. In its application of experimental method to meaningful social situations, in its detailed observation and recording of data, and in its concern with theoretical issues in the study of group process, this inquiry climaxed the early phases of research on children's peer relations and served as a transition point to the current era.

The bulk of the discussion in the pages that follow is based on an appraisal of research initiated after 1940. Yet the debt of such research to earlier work is frequently quite evident: it is apparent in definition of research problems, in methods employed, and in conceptualization and theory undergirding research. Research and theory since 1940 have been not so much new as they have represented a refinement and an extension of the work of this earlier period.

PEER RELATIONS AND THE BROADER SOCIAL CONTEXT

Children in groups act within the framework of social forces at work in the society at large. In addition to serving to establish limits within which peer processes operate, such forces affect specific aspects of children's relationships with one another. The influences of the social context cover a considerable range. At the broadest levels are general cultural factors and subcultural influences (such as social classes and ethnic groups within the larger society). At a considerably more specific level, the family also helps to channel the nature of the child's functioning with his age mates. A consideration of peer relations would be incomplete if the perspective provided by such contextual factors were not introduced.

Cultural Variations in the Relevance of the Peer Group

Peer groupings are found among all societies; however, societies differ from one another both in the degree to which peer relationships are salient in the course of child development and in the extent to which adults recognize and explicitly use such groups as agents of socialization. In most cultures the role of the peer group is defined by an emergent process, rather than by any clearly articulated societal definition of what peer group functioning should be. Although sound supporting research is lacking, a number of plausible theories have been offered to account for the extent to which such groups assume major roles. Ausubel states, "it is mostly in heterogeneous urban cultures that values during preadolescence (and especially adolescence) tend to acquire a wider base and peers tend to replace parents as interpreters and enforcers of the moral code" (1958, p. 393). Davis points to the significance of rapid social change as a factor "creating a hiatus between one generation and the next," thus contributing to the role of age mates in the socialization process (1940, p. 523). A recent and apt expression of this same point of view is the statement that "the relations between the generations are weakened as the rate of social innovation increases" (Keniston, 1962, p. 153). From ethnographic comparisons Eisenstadt (1956, 1962) has concluded that youth groups are most likely to develop "in those societies in which the family or kinship unit cannot ensure . . . the attainment of full social status on the part of its members" (1962, p. 34).

As a rule societies do not consciously use the peer group in the socialization process. Yet the Israeli kibbutz and the Soviet method of character training alike attest to the fact that such intentional utilization is possible. Spiro's (1958) detailed anthropological portrait of a single kibbutz and Diamond's (1957) historically oriented probing for the sources of kibbutz institutions and values present a picture of a social system explicitly based on certain ideological convictions of its founders. To achieve their formulated goals, the kibbutz founders greatly altered traditional patterns of family relationships and devised a pattern of living that maximized peer contacts. For children so reared, the frequency and intensity of contact within the primary peer group makes it in many ways the most important influence on the child. Bronfenbrenner (1962), reporting his impressions on certain aspects of child rearing in Russia, has indicated that the Soviet educational system relies to a marked extent on the children's group (with initial guidance from adult leadership) as the principal agent of socialization. The group, rather than the individual, is the focal point for the organization of the educational system. Between-group competition, evaluation of individual behavior in terms of its relevance to the collective, and administration of punishment and reward on a group basis are among the key principles in the Soviet approach to child rearing.

Although such pervasive conscious use of the network of peer relations may not be the case in America, this need not greatly lessen the impact of its influences. In a large sample of a cross-section of eleven- to thirteen-year-old boys, nearly three out of four of those interviewed reported that they had "a bunch of fellows" with whom they spent "a lot" of their time (Withey, Foster, and Billingsley, 1960). Such a report gives an indication of the extent to which the peer group enters in as a meaningful aspect of the American child's daily life. Several writers have suggested that the peer influences play a stronger part in this country than they do in some other cultures. Such a view appears plausible, though evidence on which it is based is sometimes too sketchy for comfort. Hsu, Watrous, and Lord (1960/61) attributed differences in behavior of Chinese youths in Hawaii and American youths in Chicago in part to the likelihood that American youths were far more under the tyranny of their peers than were their Chinese counterparts. Differences between Mexican and American children have been interpreted in a similar fashion by Maslow and Diaz-Guerrero (1960), who see the Mexican child learning to live more by adult values, because in comparison with the American child, he lives far more in the family and less in a peer society.

Within the American scene, some subcultural variations lead to differential impact and relevance of the peer group. Parents in lower socioeconomic levels apparently show less concern about children's activities outside the home than do parents higher in the status scale. Thus working-class parents exercise less control and supervision over their children in the latter years of childhood (Psathas, 1957). Further, middle-class parental values are more likely to emphasize self-direction and internal standards of conduct; among working-class parents, an important value cluster is that of conformity to external proscriptions (Kohn, 1959, 1963). Given such class differences, it is reasonable to hypothesize that this in effect provides greater opportunity for the peer group to assume an important role in shaping the course of social development of working-class children.

Specific Cultural and Subcultural Influences

Not only do cultural and subcultural variations make a difference in the extent to which children's peer groups assume positions of salience; such variations also help to determine the specific course of peer relations by inculcating values, shaping behavior, and influencing friendship and association.

Values and behavior. Different cultures probably inculcate different prestigious aspirations and self-images. Among 859 American graduate students who reported they were members of the "leading crowd" when they were in high school, only 43 per cent considered themselves intellectuals. In contrast, of 126 foreign graduate students now studying in American universities, 63 per cent of those in the leading crowd in high school saw themselves as intellectuals (Coleman, 1961a,b). At the subcultural level, variations in socioeconomic status have been found to be associated with differences in children's values and aspirations (Sherif, 1962). Such differences create for children images of different styles of life, images which when translated into behavior have immediate consequences on peer relations. Illustrative of this is information on children's activities both in and out of school. Ten- to twelve-year-old children from different social classes have been found to use leisure time in quantitatively and qualitatively different fashions, even though they lived in the same heterogeneous urban neighborhood (Macdonald, McGuire, and Havighurst, 1949). Also, among high school students, the higher the family income level, the greater the likelihood that students participate in a variety of organized school and community activities (Coster, 1959).

The extent to which children use particular modes of behavior relevant to interpersonal processes is also linked to the culture and the subculture. For example, cross-cultural study shows that predominant belief systems may affect the behavior of individual children. Independent and self-reliant acts of children are more likely in societies with aggressive gods, and children's nurturant behavior is related to cultural beliefs in benevolent gods and spirits (Lambert, Triandis, and Wolf, 1959). In America some class-linked differences in children's behavior have been described. Lower-class children are physically more aggressive (Pope, 1953; McKee and Leader, 1955), and among boys (but not girls) there is a strong negative relationship between socioeconomic status and conformity (Tuma and Livson, 1960). Such behavior influences the nature of children's relationships in group situations.

Friendship and association. To what extent is parental class or ethnic or racial status a significant determinant of children's friendships and social contacts? Even at the preschool age young children are *aware* of ethnic and racial differences (Clark and Clark, 1952; Goodman, 1952; Radke and Trager, 1950; Stevenson and Stewart, 1958). It is probable that such perceived differences are also early reflected in children's actions, but there is conflicting research evidence on this point. Using standard sociometric techniques, Criswell (1939) did not find racial cleavages until children were eight to ten years old. But other studies (Lambert and Taguchi, 1956; McCandless and Hoyt, 1961) have detected evidence of such cleavage in the preschool years.

Information on the extent to which friendship ties are classbound is also slightly contradictory, but there is reasonable support for a generalization that socioeconomic status does make a difference. In his community study of a midwestern town, Hollingshead (1949) concluded that clique membership tended to be homogeneous with respect to prestige class. In the same community, Neugarten (1946), using a modified sociometric procedure, found that both elementary school children and high school children discriminated along class lines in their selection of friends. (Only among the younger children, however, was social status also clearly linked to rejection of peers.) In a partial replication of the Hollingshead work, Udry (1960) concluded that, among students in a new suburban community in a southern California high school, the tendency to choose friends from one's own social class was negligible. Bonney (1946) reported that socioeconomic status played a small but consistent part in determining friendships. And among eighth-graders, Elkins (1958) found significant correlations between sociometric preference and socioeconomic status, a finding noteworthy in view of the relatively homogeneous population from which the research subjects were initially drawn.

What factors account for the extent to which parental class and ethnic status are related to children's peer relations? No single item can be isolated, but it seems obvious that frequency of contact, ecological separation, and differences in value orientations all play a part, and these may reinforce one another. Two groups of Israeli youth, one children of European Jews and the other, Yemenite, lived in separate areas of the same town. This spatial separation worked hand in hand with existing cultural differences to reduce contacts and keep friendships between the two groups at a minimum (Katz and Zloczower, 1961).

On the American scene residential segregation similarly reinforces value differences between children of different status groups. Warner and Lunt in 1941 reported that ecological distribution of children among elementary schools operated to keep children of different socioeconomic status levels separated. That such residential segregation of social classes influences aspirations of high school boys is a major conclusion emerging from A. B. Wilson's (1959) extensive survey of student interests. The American class system has been criticized for the way in which it "limits the associations of children to their own class group and so limits and patterns the learning environment" (Martin and Stendler, 1953, p. 182). The probable impact of this has been described as "increasingly irreversible. The longer a lower-class child is deprived of *intimate* contact with middle-class children the less opportunity he has of acquiring their values and sanctioned patterns of behavior" (Ausubel, 1958, p. 433).

The impact of status differences on peer relations is not, of course, via ecological segregation alone. In some instances in which such segregation is not marked, differential association, differential behavior, and differential values appear to be associated with such status variations (Macdonald, McGuire, and Havighurst, 1949). Other general social forces operating in the community frequently contribute to the impact of adult status differences on children's peer groups. Further, although status differences are clearly operative, they are not all pervasive. Among older children, socioeconomic status is not markedly related either to prestige and recognition (Jones, 1958) or to criteria for accepting and rejecting peers (Feinberg, Smith, and Schmidt, 1958). Coster (1959) has reported that though children from different socioeconomic levels differed with respect to their participation in various school activities, they shared essentially the same attitudes about the school and its program. And (lest we forget the obvious) sex and grade in school are both more important determinants of children's clique membership than is prestige class (Hollingshead, 1949).

Age and Sex

The grouping of persons in terms of age and sex (along lines partially determined by cultural factors) limits the nature of peer relations. Membership in a given age-sex category appears to be a prerequisite for the occupation of almost any status in a society (Linton, 1942). Although such typings are universal throughout different societies, there is no universal agreement on the number and definition of such groupings. For example, not all societies have a separate term for or give recognition to the period of adolescence, nor do all give equal emphasis to the transition from one age grouping to another.

The most visible indicator of the impact of age and sex categories on children's peer relations is the widespread evidence of segregated groupings in terms of these two factors and of concomitant pressures for behavioral differentiation. From preschool up to adolescence, sex homogeneity is a prime element in friendships and clique memberships, and, next to sex, age carries the most weight in peer group formation (Challman, 1932; Hollingshead, 1949; Tuddenham, 1951b). Segregation by sex is associated with differences in group activity interests; for example, adolescent girls are more interested in social activities and less interested in competitive sports and games than boys (Douvan and Kaye, 1957). As they mature, of course, children of both sexes become more involved in heterosexual friendships and coed group activity (Withey, Foster, and Billingsley, 1960). That girls become interested in such activity at an earlier age than boys constitutes a special problem for the practitioner engaged in group work.

It is clear that age and sex groupings do have functional utility in a child's learning a succession of differentiated roles. And cross-cultural evidence supports the view that, from the early years of childhood, cultural pressures train the child in sex-differentiated behavior (Barry, Bacon, and Child, 1957). It is thus not surprising that children reflect such training in their peer relations. One indication of this appears in the tendency for children to hold more favorable attitudes toward members of their own sex than those of the other sex (Harris and Tseng, 1957; Meyer, 1959).[4] Further, the children who have learned the behavior prescribed for their sex are rewarded with peer acceptance. Thus, among preschool boys, the use of dramatic play hostility was associated with peer acceptance, though this was not the case for girls (Marshall, 1961). Early sex-differentiated behavior persists, tends to conform to the cultural stereotype, and is reinforced both by the adult world and the child's own age mates.

Changes in social relationships associated with age have been well documented. An insightful review of the literature made in 1939 remains quite pertinent today. In this statement Anderson traced the evidence showing that as children grow older their social attachments become more pro-

[4] While the general trend is clear, relevant qualifiers should be introduced: among grade school children, heterosexual friendship choices appear to be influenced to some extent by socioeconomic level (Kanous, Daugherty, and Cohn, 1962). Further, in a sample of fifth graders, the extent to which boys were accepted by girls was associated with the boys' acceptance by other boys (Reese, 1962).

nounced, functioning within the group becomes increasingly differentiated, social activities become more organized, and the effectiveness of the group in motivating behavior increases. As the child matures, he is given greater opportunity for group membership beyond the family circle, and the likelihood of peer influence increases concomitantly. That the peer group then becomes a more salient factor is implied both from observational and experimental data. Among children in a midwestern community, it was observed that the average amount of time spent in family settings decreased and that spent in community settings increased with age throughout childhood and adolescence (Wright, 1956). Research on developmental trends in group problem-solving revealed that interdependence of group members clearly increased with age in four-person groups (homogeneous in age and sex) ranging from the nursery school to the university level (A. J. Smith, 1960). Thus the age of group members becomes a relevant factor in the strategic considerations of any adult who wishes to use peer influences to achieve particular goals.

Family Influences

In his early years, the principal agent for transmitting culturally determined values, attitudes, and behavior to the child is his family. Yet its influence extends, of course, well beyond the role of culture mediator. Both the objective structural characteristics of the family and its interpersonal processes help to shape the unique nature of the child's relations to his peers and his attitudes to the larger social world of which he becomes increasingly a part.

Family structure. Research evidence is accumulating to show the effect of prolonged absence of either parent (as a result of death, divorce, or other factors) and to clarify the role of the structure of sibling relationships.

Boys' general peer adjustment and also their specific behavior with others are altered in households in which the father is not present. Among eight- and nine-year-old boys in Norwegian sailor families, the absence of the father for at least nine months of the year was linked with lessened adequacy of peer adjustment (as determined from the mother's report on the number of friends her child had, the extent to which he had problems with peers, and so forth) (Lynn and Sawrey, 1959). That boys with no father in the home also deviate from others in the expression of aggressive impulses is suggested by evidence from studies of children of servicemen in wartime (Bach, 1946; Sears, Pintler, and Sears, 1946).[5]

[5] A pertinent summary of research evidence and a theoretical statement concerning the impact of father absence on the child's developing identity may be found in Burton and Whiting (1961).

Although it is possible to find studies dealing with the impact of father-absence when other aspects of the family and household remain relatively unchanged, in most instances the effects of maternal absence are not readily separated from such other influences as institutionalization, multiple mothering, and the like. As Clausen and Williams (1963) have stated, "the expression 'mother-absent family' seems a contradiction in terms." The impact of maternal deprivation has been documented elsewhere in this volume and hence will not be treated here. Additional systematic appraisals are presented in Casler (1961) and L. J. Yarrow (1961).

In addition to the structural characteristics deriving from presence or absence of parents, the structure of sibling relationships (that may be linked to particular child-rearing concomitants) also enters the picture of the child's orientation to his peer group, affecting both his interest in his peers and the way he relates to others. Schachter (1959), in a study that has the fascination of a good detective story, blended data from experiments and natural situations to demonstrate that first-born children, compared with those later in the birth order, want more to be with others, rather than to remain alone, when they are placed in a stressful setting.[6] In a rigorously formulated and thorough study, Koch (1957) traced the way age and sex of siblings influenced children's preferences for playmates. She found that first-born children were more likely than second-born to play with children younger than themselves. Also, though children generally preferred others of the same sex as playmates, preference for those of the opposite sex was more frequently expressed by those with a sibling of the opposite sex than by those with a same-sex sibling. Thus the child tends to build peer relationships along the lines of the model provided in the sibling structure of his own family.

Family processes and peer relations. Family structure is by no means the only familial influence on children's functioning in groups. Values and attitudes in the home and the quality of interaction within the family also contribute significantly. Parents both intentionally and unintentionally help to provide the child with knowledge of social relationships and to crystallize his views of the world about him, views that may be translated into behavior in his associations with other children. Information concerning ethnic and race relations serves as a case in point. Parents influence such intergroup relations by directly controlling contacts (Yarrow, Trager, and

---

[6] Though other research has tended to confirm this (for example, Schooler and Scarr, 1962), a recent replication by Weller (1962) failed to obtain similar results. Thus the role of birth order in affiliative inclination remains in need of some clarification. Perhaps future work in which additional dimensions such as sibling spacing and sex of siblings are introduced and in which more concern is given to child-rearing practices associated with particular family constellations will resolve ambiguities in this area.

Miller, 1952), by explicitly or implicitly indoctrinating their children (Goodman, 1952; E. L. Horowitz, 1936), and probably also by inculcating value patterns and styles of life that lead the child to feel more comfortable when he is associating with other children ethnically similar to himself (McCandless and Hoyt, 1961).

The child's general adjustment in his peer group also shows the influence of interpersonal relationships in the home. In a careful study comparing, with a control group, the families of twenty preadolescents who had been referred either by parents or by school authorities for psychological guidance, Clark and van Sommers (1961) concluded that unsatisfactory relationships between the adults in the home (as indicated by evidence of argument, physical violence, avoidance of interaction) accompanied unsatisfactory relationships between the adults and the child. The contradictory demands on the child's allegiance in the home contributed to his maladjustment with his classmates and in other aspects of the school situation. In a longitudinal study using independent sets of data on characteristics of children's families and characteristics of the children themselves, Peck (1958) found that ego strength (defined by a cluster of highly intercorrelated items measuring an individual's capacities to react to events) was associated with measures, made several years earlier, of stable consistency and warmth in family life, and that children's friendliness and spontaneity were linked with a lenient democratic family atmosphere. From this same source of data Peck and Havighurst conclude that "an adolescent's social and moral adjustment to his agemates is a reflection of the attitudes and behavior he earlier learned in his home" (1960, p. 127).

The fact of parental impact on peer relations remains clear when particular types of children's behaviors are considered. For example, children's overt dependent behavior is heightened in cases where there is parental rejection of the child and lack of cohesion in the family; those children who are dependent on their peers but avoid close adult relationships "appear to have been encouraged by their parents to leave their homes and to disregard the wishes of adults" (McCord, McCord, and Verden, 1962, p. 323). Well covered are parental antecedents of children's aggressive behavior. Parents' punitiveness, hostility, and restrictiveness toward the child serve to evoke with devastating effectiveness aggression in the child and hostility toward his peers (Bandura and Walters, 1960; Marshall, 1961). The pattern is not, however, without complexities. Among the relevant bits of clarifying and sometimes complicating information are these: Bandura and Walters suggest that parents who strongly disapprove of aggression in the home nevertheless encourage and reward aggression outside the home; thus aggressive impulses may be displaced toward peers as a result of discrimination learning. Boys who characterize their fathers as more likely to discipline them than are their mothers, are not only rated by their teachers as high on aggressiveness and use of physical force but also on friendship initiation (Hoffman, 1961). Further, evidence supports Hoffman, Rosen, and Lippitt's (1960) hypothesis that boys' hostility needs that are aroused by parental coerciveness are softened and more effectively expressed in the peer group by those children who are high in autonomy. Such items as these should thus serve as a cautionary reminder that in this area, as in many others, the pattern has its complications.

This brief inspection of the role of a number of aspects of the broader social context has indicated that, while the exact functioning of cultural, subcultural, and familial processes cannot yet be delineated with complete clarity, variations in such factors do make a difference. They affect the attitudes, values, and behavior of children and also the general relevance of their peer groups.

THE PEER GROUP AS A SOCIALIZING AGENT

Although the family is rightfully viewed as a prime influence in the child's individuality, his activities in the company of other children contribute to his developing picture of the social world, help to establish his identity, and provide him an opportunity for group experience relevant not only to present functioning but to future social relationships as well. The peer group has generally been recognized as a socializing agent, but it has not yet been given the same sort of systematic research attention that has been focused on the family. Bronfenbrenner has suggested that limited consideration of the socialization function of group processes in collective settings outside the family is attributable to

> . . . the traditional emphasis in Western culture, reflected in scientific work, on the centrality of the parent-child relationship in the process of upbringing. It is this circumscribed conception which probably accounts for the fact that Western personality theory and research, highly developed as they are in comparison with their Russian counterparts . . . offer little basis for ready-made hypotheses bearing on processes and effects of socialization in collective settings (1962, p. 556).

Although much still needs study, several aspects of this area yield promising research results.

The child in the group is part of a complex network of relations with other children in the environment. Each child observes and evaluates the events around him, responds with feelings of liking or disliking, acts in the situation, and is the recipient of actions of others. Through such processes as these the role of the individual child becomes established and the particular nature of the peer group as a social product emerges. The Robbers Cave experiment, a stimulating and productive study directed by Sherif, illustrates some general aspects of this process (Sherif, Harvey, White, Hood, and Sherif, 1961). Twenty-two fifth-grade boys, homogeneous with respect to such criteria as age, family background, and intelligence, were brought together as members of two separately functioning camp groups, generally isolated from the outside world. At the end of one week, these boys, initially strangers to one another, had formed cohesive groups. Ratings by adult observers showed that a stable status structure had been established within the seven-day period; differentiation of function had taken place along hierarchical lines. Joint participation of group members in pursuit of the common goals of camp led to the formation of stable attitudes about one another and about places and objects in the camp environment. Since such attitudes were shared by members of the group, norms governing behavior in various aspects of the situation were established concomitantly with the formation of the group structure itself. When the boys discovered the presence of another group of campers, this added a heightened awareness of group membership and an emphasis on group solidarity. The "natural history" of Sherif's experimental groups reasonably closely approximates the pattern followed in many children's group situations. Such experiences contribute to the crystallization of the child's role and status among his peers, aid in establishing his own self-concept, and serve as an important resource for the formation of the child's attitudes and values concerning his social world.

Peer Acceptance and Stability of Peer Relations

As the description of Sherif's experiment suggests, early in a child's group experience his peers form an impression of him. On the basis of such impressions, the child is assigned status and is accepted or rejected accordingly.

What are the criteria for acceptance or rejection? These can conveniently be classed broadly as pertaining either to personality and social characteristics or to skills and abilities. Ample research information exists to indicate some of these factors that enter into children's assessments of one another. Among the personality and social characteristics contributing to differential status, friendliness and sociability are, as one would certainly expect, associated with acceptance (Feinberg, Smith, and Schmidt, 1958; Tuddenham, 1951), and social indifference, withdrawal, rebelliousness, and hostility are attributes of low-status or rejected children (Northway, 1944;

G. H. Smith, 1950). In the area of skills and abilities, the picture continues to build up that the more intelligent and creative are generally more accepted by their age mates; the slow learners and the retarded, less well accepted (Baldwin, 1958; Barbe, 1954; Gallagher, 1958; Northway and Rooks, 1956; Peck and Galliani, 1962; Porterfield, and Schlicting, 1961). Body size, muscular strength, and athletic ability also appear as criteria for acceptance among boys (Clarke and Clarke, 1961; Tuddenham, 1951a). And developmental maturity is associated with prestige of adolescent girls (Faust, 1960). In general, the qualities evaluated positively by peers are similar at different ages, but some variation does occur during the course of development. For American children such changes are apparently more marked among girls. In comparing shifts in values placed on personality traits by twelve- and fifteen-year-old children, Tryon (1939) reported that values for girls underwent some revolutionary changes. For boys, the same three-year age difference revealed only minor shifts, slight changes in emphasis on particular values.

The evidence is clear that, once children have been constituted into a group, patterns of relationships are quickly established and remain stable over time. Young boys were asked to state friendship preferences on the first day of attendance in a summer camp and at weekly intervals thereafter. A week-to-week comparison of such choices showed considerable consistency of choice. Complete stability was not, of course, achieved at the very outset of group formation, but the progress was rapid; although patterns of personal preference altered frequently during the very earliest phases of camp, consistency of preference and stabilization of status of group members rapidly increased (Hunt and Solomon, 1942). In groups that have been established for some time, stability in preferences is the rule. Singer (1951) reported a high degree of constancy in friendship choices among a group of seventh- and eighth-grade children throughout a year and a half of study. And among children in the second, third, and fourth grades, general social acceptance was found to be about as constant over a three-year period as were measures of intelligence (Bonney, 1943).

As one might expect, stability of relationships is positively related to age (Horrocks and Thompson, 1946; Thompson and Horrocks, 1947). But even among preschool children, sociometric preferences remain reasonably consistent over ten- to twenty-day intervals (McCandless and Marshall, 1957). Emotional disturbance or its absence also enters as a factor. Hospitalized emotionally disturbed boys, ranging in age from seven to thirteen years, were significantly less stable in friendship patterns than were a group of campers and a group of schoolboys of approximately the same age (Davids and Parenti, 1958).

Relationships among children are, of course, also expressed along lines other than those of choice and rejection. Do children also show stability in the behavior they display in the group situation? The answer is yes, with reservations. Thus in an experimental study of sixteen pairs of preschool children, Gellert (1961) found that, despite a fair amount of inter-session variability, children maintained reasonably consistent positions of dominance and submission, although such was not the case for the expression of resistance (that is, noncompliance, self-defense, and counterdomination). Somewhat different results were obtained with newly formed preadolescent groups (Campbell and M. R. Yarrow, 1961). In these groups there was stability over a two-week period in the extent to which children initiated friendly and aggressive behavior, but on two much less frequently occurring dimensions of interaction, assertive and submissive behavior, there was much less consistency. Other evidence in this study suggested that children's reputations were more stable than their behavior. Further, information on changes in reputation and behavior led to the inference that reputations, which were quickly established, shaped expectations and, in part, drew out behavior from the children that accorded with such expectations. Polansky, Lippitt, and Redl reached a similar conclusion in their "contagion" studies: "So far as we can tell . . . the relative 'prestige' assigned to an individual in his group will be a fairly powerful determinant of his own behavior" (1950, p. 347). Such interpretations as these point to the potentially powerful role that the group may play in shaping a child's social development.

Peer Acceptance and the Self-Concept

One of the most important and enduring functions of peer relationships is to help the growing child in his attempt to paint the picture of his own identity. Early in his group experiences, he becomes aware that his peers place him along particular lines, and, as he grows older, he develops proficiency in interpreting his own status in the eyes of other children (Ausubel, Schiff, and Gasser, 1952). That his assessment by others is related to his own self-picture is suggested by a number of studies. F. D. Horowitz (1962) found that, in the middle grades of elementary school, the less popular children tended to think less well of themselves. Rosen, Levinger, and Lippitt (1960), studying boys in their early teens, obtained evidence supporting the view that a boy's desire for change in himself is partly contingent on the extent to which he is well liked and viewed by his peers as a desired role model. In his extensive study of high school students, Coleman (1961a) saw much the same phenomenon. Students having elite status in their schools (named as being in the leading crowd, as a desired friend, or as someone to be liked) were much less likely than others to want to "be someone different from myself." High status in the group may, then, be a source of a positive self-concept; lack of status and security, a source of dissatisfaction with one's self.

In which direction does the causal relation go? Does popularity lead to self-esteem, or does self-esteem lead to popularity? It is perfectly possible that both alternatives are true. That some of the freight of influence, however, *does* travel from the group's appraisal to the individual's self-assessment is suggested by a conclusion by Polansky and his colleagues that "by and large those children to whom prestige position is attributed are aware of the fact; their awareness is facilitated by the behavior of others toward them . . ." (1950, p. 334). Rosenberg's (1962) extensive questionnaire study of high school students lends further research support to this view. His data reveal that those students who were reared in a neighborhood in which the predominant religious affiliation was different from that of their own families were more likely to have low self-esteem, to report psychosomatic symptoms, and to have feelings of depression. Such children growing up in dissonant religious contexts more often reported having experienced discrimination, and such experiences of rejection presumably contributed to psychic disturbance.

It is clearly an oversimplification to suggest that acceptance by peers directly determines the extent of a child's self-esteem. More rigorous evidence on the nature of this relationship needs to be obtained. Further, it is probable that additional factors (including the extent to which adults reinforce the child's self-picture, and the importance of peer-group membership to the child) play an influential role. Yet the likelihood that a child's age mates may contribute to his developing identity is a possibility for the practitioner to consider in determining strategy for action with children's peer groups.

Attitudes, Values, and the Peer Group

Just as peer relations play a part in the formation of concepts of the self, so, too, do they influence the formation of attitudes and values. To some extent, of course, such influences cannot readily be separated from those of the broader social environment. Indeed, it is probable that such peer influences often do not counter, but rather tend to reinforce predominant values in the adult culture. Yet peer influences do indeed aid in forming and changing attitudes and values; this can be quite clearly inferred from a number of studies differing in general orientation and in methodological approach. In a charming description, supplemented by quotations from interviews with Swiss children, Piaget has described the way that the child, in simple social games such as marbles, learns the rules of the game. The peer group is the one social agency primarily responsible for this process; as Piaget states, ". . . we are in the presence of rules which have been elaborated by the children alone" (1948, p. 2). A. B. Wilson (1959) studied the influence of the predominant values in membership groups on the educational, occupational, and political values of high school students. He classified 13 schools into three categories in terms of the general socioeconomic level from which the student body came. He then examined the data obtained from the students to ascertain the extent to which their values reflected the socioeconomic level of their parents and the extent to which they reflected the predominant socioeconomic level of the student body of their high school. It was apparent that status characteristics of a student's parents did influence his values. Yet when such parental characteristics as occupation and education were controlled, the hypothesis was clearly sustained that the bulk of the students in a school affected the values of individual students whose parents came from social strata differing from that of a major portion of the students' families.

Coleman's (1960, 1961a,b) inquiries present a similar picture. He found that social climates influenced values concerning academic achievement. In schools where such achievement was valued by the peer group, academic excellence was more closely related to measures of intelligence than was the case in schools where academic performance was less valued. Moreover, the impact of the peer value system tends to show some increment with time. Thus freshman students in a private school in a seriously oriented university setting valued "good looks" as an attribute for membership in the leading crowd to about the same extent as did freshmen in other high schools. But, in this one school, the importance of this factor went down sharply over the course of the four years, whereas the pattern in the average of the other schools showed no such decline.

From "natural experiments" with children's groups comes further confirmation of the proposition that the group serves to shape attitudes and values. Two weeks of equalitarian contact in a racially integrated summer camp led to significant reduction in, but not elimination of, feelings of social distance (as expressed by friendship preferences) between Negro and white preadolescents (Campbell and M. R. Yarrow, 1958). Among eleven-year-olds in international summer camps, a summer of such international living reduced ethnocentrism (Bjerstedt, 1961). Attitudes toward children differing in language and nationality were clearly more favorable. The work of Sherif and Sherif (1953) indicates the way in which group membership may influence interpersonal attitudes. After three days together in a summer camp, twelve-year-olds were separated into two experimental groups in which friendship preferences for members of the experimental in-group were substantially less than for those of the experimental out-group. When sociometric choices were again made after a five-day period in which the two groups lived in separate bunkhouses, the pattern of choice was reversed; preferences for the experimentally created in-group predominated. Such experiments as these show that favorable contact situations can modify interpersonal attitudes. How deeply seated or how permanent are such changed orientations remains, of course, another question.

Such studies clearly support the proposition that the peer group is a potent factor in the child's coming to terms with his environment.[7] Some facets of the *process* by which aspects of the group experience operate to shape the child will be presented in the subsequent portion of this chapter.

INFLUENCE PROCESSES IN THE PEER GROUP

Patterns of peer relations show considerable variability. The individual child and the group as a whole are subject to a number of factors that tend to channel actions in particular directions. The forces at work are of various sorts. Some are inherent in the character of the situation; others derive from characteristics of children—as recipients of influence as well as influence agents; and when adults are participants, they too shape the course of children's functioning in groups. These various factors do not, of course, function in isolation from one another, but, for ease of dealing with available research information, each can reasonably be brought into central focus, while the others remain temporarily in the background.[8]

Situational Influences

At least five different types of situational factors exert some degree of control over individual and group functioning. First, the physical setting itself, the actual structure of the environment plays a meaningful part in determining the course of group relations. Among preadolescent campers who were initially strangers to one another, friendship preferences within the cabin were significantly influenced by the physical structure of the cabin (Campbell and M. R. Yarrow, 1958). Blood and Livant (1957) noted

---

[7] For relevant consideration of the role of the peer group in shaping attitudes and values of delinquent youth, see Cloward and Ohlin (1960); Cohen (1955); and Sykes and Matza (1957).

[8] Influence processes at work in groups of children do not, of course, differ in kind from those operating among adults. Thus, while it is not included in the present discussion, much of the work on influence in adult groups would be of some relevance to the reader.

that not only was interaction concentrated heavily within cabin groups, but children actively used cabin space (by relocating bunks, and the like) to express relations, to implement friendships, and to secure protection.

One step removed from the physical characteristics of the situation is the process whereby different activity settings lead to differences in behavior. In studies of normal and disturbed children, Raush, Farbman, and Llewellyn (1960) found that specific settings tended to induce particular patterns of behavior. For both groups of subjects, food settings were associated with friendly actions and competitive games were associated with unfriendly behaviors. In a similar vein Gump, Schoggen, and Redl (1957) noted that milieu factors affected behavior and experience; the amount and quality of interaction of eleven-year-old campers were quite different in different activity settings. Consistent with this theme are Spiro's observations in an Israeli kibbutz. Noting that children's classroom behavior was highly informal, he attributed this in part to the fact that, for these children, "the dormitory and the classroom building are one" (1958, p. 263). The situation became so defined that the lack of a physical transition from the setting for sleep and play to that for school was accompanied by a similar lack of psychological transition.

The clarity of definition of the task for the group member is a third factor affecting the nature of his response. Thus Berenda (1950), studying effects of group pressures on children's judgments of perceptual stimuli, and Patel and Gordon (1960), examining the extent to which children yielded to influence in a vocabulary test, found that the more ambiguous the stimulus, the greater the likelihood that children would accept the views of others. Further, Kitano (1962) reported that "problem children," as well as "normal children," showed a high degree of adjustment in situations where role expectations were clear and where prescriptions for performance were readily enforceable.

Still a fourth situational factor, the reward structure, has been shown to relate to group cohesiveness in experimental studies of children in the elementary grades (Lott and Lott, 1960). Three-member groups played a game in which some were rewarded, others were not. Those who were rewarded subsequently indicated more positive attitudes toward their fellow group members than did the unrewarded.

The fifth situational factor that plays a part in the influence process is the social structure. Group size was linked to consensus among Boy Scouts: smaller groups achieved more consensus after a discussion, and their members were more likely to change their views as a result of the discussion (Hare, 1952). Interpersonal communication is also affected by the social structure of the group. In a study of boys in a summer camp,

Larsen and Hill (1958) concluded that the more stable the social structure, the greater was its influence on interpersonal communication.

Although no group leader could be reasonably expected to take into account all of the diverse elements that might influence the course of individual and group development, the continually mounting evidence for the role of situational factors suggests that this aspect of the interaction equation warrants much thoughtful consideration. An assessment of the setting, the activity, the clarity of the task, the rewards, and the social structure of the group may lead to specific program modifications that can be used to obtain desired consequences in individual and group performance.

Variations in Susceptibility to Influence

What children are most responsive to the various forces shaping behavior in the peer group? No blanket generalizations can be made, but research evidence throws light on the extent to which such characteristics as age and sex, status in the group, and personality factors are associated with susceptibility to influence.

Information on the role of age and sex presents a slightly inconsistent picture. But the one that does emerge suggests that, as one might expect, younger children are more susceptible to the views of others than are older children, and, in line with cultural stereotypes about differences between the sexes, girls are more likely to yield to peer pressures than boys. Perceptual judgments of children under ten were more influenced by the reports of others than those of children over ten years old (Berenda, 1950). Patel and Gordon (1960) found girls more likely to accept suggestions than boys, and twelfth graders less likely to yield to influence than tenth or eleventh graders, but the trend was not strictly linear over the three grades. In a clinical evaluation of available data on the extent to which 48 adolescents conformed to the authority of their peers, Tuma and Livson (1960) concluded that, over the limited age range studied, girls apparently increased in conformity, while boys became slightly less conforming. Such a conclusion fits reasonably well with Coleman's (1961b) survey results, which showed, in general, that cliques and crowds had far greater importance for the high school girls studied than for the high school boys.

The extent to which the child is influenced by others appears to be linked with his status in the group. Among boys and girls in the third, sixth, ninth, and eleventh grades, those whom peers accorded low status in terms of leadership criteria were more likely to change their opinions when faced with a contrary judgment supposedly given by a peer (Harvey and Rutherford, 1960). When members of 27 cliques in a training school for delinquent boys judged perceptual stimuli, the group members ranking just below the leaders conformed more to views held by others than did either the leaders or the bottom ranking boys (Harvey and Consalvi, 1960). In yet another experimental situation, high school boys with indefinite status conformed more than did either popular or unpopular boys (R. S. Wilson, 1960). While one might like to see such experimental evidence supported with additional data coming from observations of more natural situations, the findings do suggest that status and status strivings help to account for conformity to the norms of the peer group.

The role of personality factors in children's susceptibility to influence when faced with an ambiguous judgmental situation has been indicated in two experiments using the autokinetic phenomenon as the judgmental stimulus. (This phenomenon, effectively "socialized" by Sherif in 1935, is the illusory movement of an actually fixed pinpoint of light in an otherwise dark room.) In one of these experiments (Jakubczak and Walters, 1959), nine-year-old boys who were high on dependency (who were willing to accept help in tasks even when none was required) proved to be more susceptible to suggestions of others than boys who were low on dependency. In the second experiment (Walters, Marshall, and Shooter, 1960), adolescent boys who reported anxiety about being experimental subjects were more suggestible; that is, they conformed more in response to contrary judgments than nonanxious boys. We may contrast these findings with information from a comparison of hyperaggressive boys aged eight to ten and a matched group of normals studied in a residential therapeutic center (Raush, Farbman, and Llewellyn, 1960). Observation of behavior revealed that the normal children varied their behavior according to the social setting to a greater degree than did the hyperaggressive boys. Another way of phrasing this finding is that normal boys conformed more to situational demands than did the other group. The reasonable implication is that "conformity" is not solely the province of the anxious, the dependent, the maladjusted; unwitting conformity in the face of ambiguity may be so, but conformity to the socially accepted demands of clearly defined situations seems a perfectly healthy response for a child (or for an adult, for that matter).

Children as Influence Agents

Various personal characteristics have been singled out as associated with children's ability to affect the functioning of their peers. Intelligence relates significantly to children's social power, though the degree of the relationship is not nearly as profound as many an intellectual might wish (Zander and Van Egmond, 1958). Suggestions attributed to children in a higher age-grade status are more likely to be accepted than are those from children with lower age-grade status (Patel and Gordon, 1960). The child who is chosen with a high degree of frequency on sociometric measures is also the one who is observed to take definite stands on issues, insist on impersonal fairness, and enlist others to aid in controlling deviant group members (Jennings, 1947). Children who have power and influence are more likely than others to be perceived as possessing those characteristics valued by their peers (Gold, 1958). Summer campers who received high peer ratings on such qualities as athletic skill, independence of adults, and independence of social pressures were the more influential members of the camp group. They attempted to influence their peers more often than did low-power members, and they were also more successful in such influence attempts; other group members were more likely to imitate the behavior of these high-power members, were more likely to accept their direct attempts at influence, and were more likely to initiate deferential behavior toward them (Lippitt, Polansky, and Rosen, 1952; Polansky, Lippitt, and Redl, 1950).

While some of the information on characteristics of children who are able to influence others may at first glance seem obvious, careful scrutiny at times qualifies the obvious in an illuminating fashion. Lippitt and associates (1952) provide a case in point. Although perceived fighting ability was strongly associated with attributed power among boys in two different camps, neither height nor weight was significantly related to attributed power. In one of these camps, composed primarily of normal boys from middle-class homes, height and weight were significantly related to perceived fighting ability. But in the other, with more disturbed boys and boys coming from low-income families, no such relationship was found. In the former instance, actual fighting was a rarity, so that potential was assessed in terms of the most obvious cues. In the latter case, perception was based on actual performance, and this did not necessarily correlate very highly with physical size.

Interest understandably tends to focus primarily on the influence and power of the high status child; yet influence is not the exclusive property of the esteemed individual. For example, the single impulsive child, given the right circumstances, may be an important determiner of group action. Thus a "contagious" response in the group may result when the impulsive child triggers off an action the group is ready for but has not yet done (Polansky et al., 1950). Such children are peculiarly effective in stressful situations when their expressional freedom is in accord with the group needs of the moment. Furthermore the group itself has an impact. Berenda's (1950) experimental work indicated that children's judgments were subject to the pressure of the views of a majority of fellow group members.

Children's Peer Groups and the Adult

The impact of the adult may range from an effect on quite specific functioning of individual children to a broad, pervasive influence on the group as a whole. One of the landmark studies of the late 1930's clearly indicated that the adult leader's role was a strong determiner of social interaction and emotional development in several experimentally organized boys' clubs studied over an extended period of time (Lippitt and White, 1947). When adult experimenters adopted either "authoritarian" or "laissez-faire" leadership styles, boys expressed more irritability and aggression toward fellow group members than in groups with "democratic" leadership. There was greater group unity and less use of scapegoating as a channel of aggressive release in the democratic than in the authoritarian groups. Further, experimentally contrived absences of leaders revealed that work motivation was more leader-induced in authoritarian situations while the presence or absence of the leader in democratic groups had practically no effect on work motivation.

In a natural experiment examining racial desegregation among groups of preadolescent campers, adult leaders were viewed as pivotal figures in determining the success of this process (Yarrow and Yarrow, 1958). The adults influenced children's reactions to the initial ambiguity of the interracial setting by structuring activities, defining behavioral possibilities, and setting the tone of affective relations.

The extent to which an adult can influence sociometric status of specific children was experimentally verified by Flanders and Havumaki (1960). When 17 groups of tenth-grade students met for a single discussion session with a teacher-trainer not known to any of the students, the teacher gave praise for participation only to those seated in odd-numbered seats. Subsequently obtained sociometric information indicated that the praised students received more choices. The relevance of this finding becomes increased in the light of evidence that teachers' responses to high status children differ from their responses to those with low peer-ascribed status (Lippitt and Gold, 1959). This leads to the possibility of a vicious circle, in which (a) the child may be negatively evaluated by teacher and peers alike; (b) such negative evaluations may mutually reinforce one another; (c) the child may become aware of his own rejected status in the eyes of others; and (d) he may respond in such a fashion that his behavior serves further to confirm his disvalued position in the group. While heightened awareness of group processes and personal evaluations would not alone be sufficient to permit the adult leader to circumvent the sort of situation just described, such an awareness might constitute a reasonable positive step toward the creation of an effective environment for the social and emotional development of the group members.

The Adult vs. the Peer Group?

Given evidence that adults and children alike are significant in plotting the course of peer relations, the query as to the relative impact of these two sources of influence readily arises. The issue is sometimes posed as a conflict between the world of the adult and that of the child, a conflict that presumably reaches its peak during adolescence. And many suggest that when the smoke has cleared from the battlefield, youth emerges victorious. Certainly support can be mustered for such a contention. Berenda's (1950) systematic experimentation has shown that children's judgments yield much more to the pressure of a majority of their classmates than to that of their teacher. At the broad descriptive level, Davis, Gardner, and Gardner (1941) have suggested that the clique has more influence over the behavior of its members than do parents. The cross-pressures and the way they are frequently resolved by the bright girl are described by Coleman (1961b) in his careful survey of school climates. Urged by parents and teachers to do well in school but faced with norms of the peer culture that dissuade them from a role of "brilliant student," many of the girls who could be top scholars are constrained not to work so hard. Rosen's (1955) research indicates that among a group of Jewish high school students, when attitudes of family and peer group conflicted concerning the use of kosher meat, the peer group tended to exert more influence.

Such evidence fits a picture suggesting that the child's peer group wields greater influence than do significant adults. But at the same time this should not be equated with a conclusion that a major intergenerational conflict, a conflict that is resolved by youth's compulsive conformity to the peer culture, is occurring. A number of studies clearly restrict such an interpretation. To a considerable extent children select friends on the basis of values acquired from their parents (Westley and Elkin, 1956). A convincing majority of the teenagers in Coleman's (1961b) extensive study reported that, despite a personal preference, they would not join a particular club in school if parents disapproved of the group. The adolescent's own values, in some respects, seem to be a compromise between the values of his parents and those of his peers as he sees them; further, his expectations about his subsequent adult values clearly approach those of his parents as perceived by him (Riley, Riley, and Moore, 1961). Thus whatever the gap between the generations, youth has every intention of bridging it. Such items as these are entirely consonant with Bandura and Walters' (1963) conclusion that there is no serious conflict of generations.

The seemingly contradictory bits of evidence cited in the two preceding paragraphs suggest that the query concerning the relative impact of the adult and the peer group and the amount of conflict between these influence agents has not yet been satisfactorily answered. However, at least a limited clarification is possible. To ask whether the adult or the peer group has more influence on the child may actually be an inappropriate way to frame the question. It is quite likely that the functioning of these two sources of influence is contingent on several factors, including the characteristics of the situation, those of the participants, and the particular attitudes, values, or behaviors that are the outcome issues in question. And while it would be inappropriate to ignore evidence of dissonance between the world of the adult and that of the child, it is probable that the differences between adult values and those of the peer group are ones of degree, rather than kind. A fuller recognition of *particular* differences may result when they are placed within a context indicative of *general* similarity of values.

CONCLUDING REMARKS

For anyone wishing to put to use knowledge deriving from the currently available data on children's peer relations, three useful ingredients are a modicum of skepticism, justifiable optimism, and a willingness to experiment. Knowledgeable skepticism is in order, for despite the apparent abundance of findings, some "facts" on the role of peer relations are subject to a number of qualifications deriving to a large extent from problems in research design and methodology considered in a prior portion of this chapter.

Yet such skepticism should not be equated with pessimism. That research on peer relations will be able to make an increasing contribution to the practitioner is a very real prospect, as a casual inspection of some of the trends over recent years suggests. Three lines of progress are in evidence: first, methodological and conceptual sophistication in research approaches has increased. No single theoretical orientation appears to hold a commanding lead in the area, but efforts at broader, integrative conceptual schemes do seem to be assuming more prominence. Second, the increasing attempts to examine the way several factors in the behavioral equation are simultaneously related to one another are a significant development. Noteworthy explorations of the interaction of the environment with personal and social characteristics of the individual child have been made (for example, Raush, Dittmann, and Taylor, 1959; Rosen, 1955; Rosenberg, 1962). While such orientations do introduce additional complexities in analysis, they clarify the underlying nature of certain peer group processes, and they serve as a reminder of the multidimensional world that is the focal point for research worker and practitioner alike. Still a third indication of strides toward integration of research and practice appears in efforts to bridge the gap between the laboratory and the natural setting in studies of children's peer relations. Illustrative is the work by Sherif and his associates (1961); thoughtfully contrived experimental procedures incorporated in a meaningful real-life situation enduring over time have led to additional insights concerning processes for the reduction of intergroup conflict.

There is increasing evidence of a willingness to experiment, to explore the potential of the peer group in a more systematic fashion, and to attempt to capitalize on its possibilities as a significant agent for personality development. Bronfenbrenner (1962) has recently suggested that more consideration be given to the study of extrafamilial groups as socializing forces. Coleman (1961a,b) has pointed to ways that the peer group, its attitudes and values, might effectively be used to alter the motivational structure in secondary education. Ideas deriving from research and theory have led to the use of the peer group as a major force in an experiment in delinquency rehabilitation (Empey and Rabow, 1961). It is likely that the practitioner, using some of the concepts and methods of the research worker, and the research worker, sensitizing himself to the informational requirements of the practitioner, will be able to strengthen their lines of communication in a fashion that will benefit all concerned.

REFERENCES

ANDERSON, J. E. The development of social behavior. *Amer. J. Sociol.*, 1939, **44**, 839–857.

AUSUBEL, D. P. *Theory and problems of child development.* New York: Grune & Stratton, 1958.

AUSUBEL, D. P., SCHIFF, H. M., & GASSER, E. B. A preliminary study of developmental trends in socioempathy: accuracy of perception of own and others' status. *Child Developm.*, 1952, **23**, 111–128.

BACH, G. R. Father-fantasies and father-typing in father-separated children. *Child Developm.*, 1946, **17**, 63–80.

BALDWIN, W. K. The social position of the educable mentally retarded child in the regular grades in the public schools. *Except. Child.*, 1958, **25**, 106–108.

BANDURA, A. & WALTERS, R. H. *Adolescent aggression.* New York: Ronald Press, 1960.

BANDURA, A. & WALTERS, R. H. *The social learning of deviant behavior.* New York: Holt, Rinehart & Winston, 1963.

BARBE, W. B. Peer relationships of children of different intelligence levels. *Sch. & Soc.*, 1954, **80**, 60–62.

BARRY, H., III, BACON, M. K., & CHILD, I. L. A cross-cultural survey of some sex differences in socialization. *J. abnorm. soc. Psychol.*, 1957, **55**, 327–332.

BERENDA, R. W. *The influence of the group on the judgments of children.* New York: King's Crown Press, 1950.

BJERSTEDT, A. Informational and non-informational determinants of nationality stereotypes. *Acta Psychol.*, 1961, **18**, 11–16.

BLOOD, R. O. & LIVANT, W. P. The use of space within the cabin group. *J. soc. Issues*, 1957, **13** (1), 47–53.

BONNEY, M. E. The relative stability of social, intellectual, and academic status in grades II to IV and the inter-relationships between these various forms of growth. *J. educ. Psychol.*, 1943, **34**, 88–102.

318   REVIEW OF CHILD DEVELOPMENT RESEARCH

BONNEY, M. E. A sociometric study of the relationship of some factors to mutual friendships on the elementary, secondary, and college levels. *Sociometry*, 1946, **9**, 21–47.

BRONFENBRENNER, U. Soviet methods of character education: some implications for research. *Amer. Psychologist*, 1962, **17**, 550–564.

BURTON, R. V. & WHITING, J. W. M. The absent father and cross-sex identity. *Merrill-Palmer Quart.*, 1961, **7**, 85–95.

CAMPBELL, J. D. & YARROW, M. R. Personal and situational variables in adaptation to change. *J. soc. Issues*, 1958, **14** (1), 29–46.

CAMPBELL, J. D. & YARROW, M. R. Perceptual and behavioral correlates of social effectiveness. *Sociometry*, 1961, **24**, 1–20.

CASLER, L. Maternal deprivation: a critical review of the literature. *Monogr. Soc. Res. Child Developm.*, 1961, **26**, No. 1.

CHALLMAN, R. C. Factors influencing friendships among preschool children. *Child Developm.*, 1932, **3**, 146–158.

CLARK, A. W. & VAN SOMMERS, P. Contradictory demands in family relations and adjustment to school and home. *Hum. Relat.*, 1961, **14**, 97–111.

CLARK, K. B. & CLARK, M. K. Racial identification and preference in Negro children. In G. E. Swanson, T. M. Newcomb, & E. L. Hartley (Eds.), *Readings in social psychology*. (2nd ed.) New York: Holt, 1952. Pp. 551–560.

CLARKE, H. H. & CLARKE, D. H. Social status and mental health of boys as related to their maturity, structural, and strength characteristics. *Res. Quart. Amer. Assn. Hlth. Phys. Educ. & Recrn.*, 1961, **32**, 326–334.

CLAUSEN, J. & WILLIAMS, J. Sociological correlates of child behavior. In H. W. Stevenson (Ed.), *Yearb. nat. Soc. Stud. Educ.*, 1963, **62**, Part I.

CLOWARD, R. A. & OHLIN, L. E. *Delinquency and opportunity*. Glencoe, Ill.: Free Press, 1960.

COHEN, A. K. *Delinquent boys*. Glencoe, Ill.: Free Press, 1955.

COLEMAN, J. S. The adolescent subculture and academic achievement. *Amer. J. Sociol.*, 1960, **65**, 337–347.

COLEMAN, J. S. Social climates in high schools. *U. S. Office of Education Cooperative Res. Monogr. No. 4*, 1961, OE-33016 (a).

COLEMAN, J. S. *The adolescent society*. Glencoe, Ill.: Free Press, 1961 (b).

COOLEY, C. H. *Social organization, and Human nature and the social order*. 2 vols. in 1. Glencoe, Ill.: Free Press, 1955.

COSTER, J. K. Some characteristics of high school pupils from three income groups. *J. educ. Psychol.*, 1959, **50**, 55–62.

CRISWELL, J. H. A sociometric study of race cleavage in the classroom. *Arch. Psychol., N. Y.*, No. 235, January, 1939.

DAVIDS, A. & PARENTI, A. N. Time orientation and interpersonal relations of emotionally disturbed and normal children. *J. abnorm. soc. Psychol.*, 1958, **57**, 299–305.

DAVIS, A., GARDNER, B. B., & GARDNER, M. R. *Deep south*. Chicago: Univ. Chicago Press, 1941.

DAVIS, K. The sociology of parent-youth conflict. *Amer. Sociol. Rev.*, 1940, **5**, 523–535.

DIAMOND, S. Kibbutz and Shtetl: the history of an idea. *Social Problems*, 1957, **5**, 68–100.

DOUVAN, E. & KAYE, C. *Adolescent girls*. Ann Arbor: Inst. Soc. Res., Univ. of Michigan, 1957.

EISENSTADT, S. N. *From generation to generation*. Glencoe, Ill.: Free Press, 1956.

EISENSTADT, S. N. Archetypal patterns of youth. *Daedalus*, Winter, 1962, 28–46.

ELKINS, D. Some factors related to the choice-status of ninety eighth-grade children in a school society. *Genet. Psychol. Monogr.*, 1958, **58**, 207–272.

EMPEY, T. L. & RABOW, J. The Provo experiment in delinquency rehabilitation. *Amer. Social. Rev.*, 1961, **26**, 679–696.

FAUST, M. S. Developmental maturity as a determinant in prestige of adolescent girls. *Child Developm.*, 1960, **31**, 173–184.

FEINBERG, M. R., SMITH, M., & SCHMIDT, R. An analysis of expressions used by adolescents at varying economic levels to describe accepted and rejected peers. *J. genet. Psychol.*, 1958, **93**, 133–148.

FLANDERS, N. A. & HAVUMAKI, S. The effect of teacher-pupil contacts involving praise on the sociometric choices of students. *J. educ. Psychol.*, 1960, **51**, 65–68.

FURFEY, P. H. Some factors influencing the selection of boys' chums. *J. appl. Psychol.*, 1927, **11**, 47–51.

GALLAGHER, J. J. Social status of children related to intelligence, propinquity, and social perception. *Element. Sch. J.*, 1958, **58**, 225–231.

GELLERT, E. Stability and fluctuation in the power relationships of young children. *J. abnorm. soc. Psychol.*, 1961, **62**, 8–15.

GOLD, M. Power in the classroom. *Sociometry*, 1958, **21**, 50–60.

GOODMAN, M. E. *Race awareness in young children.* Cambridge, Mass.: Addison Wesley, 1952.

GUMP, P., SCHOGGEN, P., & REDL, F. The camp milieu and its immediate effects. *J. soc. Issues*, 1957, **13** (1), 40–46.

HARE, A. P. A study of interaction and consensus in different sized groups. *Amer. Sociol. Rev.*, 1952, **17**, 261–267.

HARE, A. P., BORGATTA, E. F., & BALES, R. F. (Eds.) *Small groups.* New York: Knopf, 1955.

HARRIS, D. B. & TSENG, S. C. Children's attitudes toward peers and parents as revealed by sentence completions. *Child Developm.*, 1957, **28**, 401–411.

HARVEY, O. J. & CONSALVI, C. Status and conformity to pressures in informal groups. *J. abnorm. soc. Psychol.*, 1960, **60**, 182–187.

HARVEY, O. J. & RUTHERFORD, J. Status in the informal group: influence and influencibility at differing age levels. *Child Developm.*, 1960, **31**, 377–385.

HOFFMAN, L. W. The father's role in the family and the child's peer-group adjustment. *Merrill-Palmer Quart.*, 1961, **7**, 97–105.

HOFFMAN, L. W., ROSEN, S., & LIPPITT, R. Parental coerciveness, child autonomy, and child's role at school. *Sociometry*, 1960, **23**, 15–22.

HOLLINGSHEAD, A. B. *Elmtown's youth.* New York: Wiley, 1949.

HOROWITZ, E. L. The development of attitudes toward the Negro. *Arch. Psychol., N. Y.*, 1936, **28**, No. 194.

HOROWITZ, F. D. The relationship of anxiety, self-concept, and sociometric status among fourth, fifth, and sixth grade children. *J. abnorm. soc. Psychol.*, 1962, **65**, 212–214.

HORROCKS, J. E. & THOMPSON, G. G. A study of the friendship fluctuations of rural boys and girls. *J. genet. Psychol.*, 1946, **69**, 189–198.

HSU, F. L. K., WATROUS, B. G., & LORD, E. M. Culture pattern and adolescent behavior. *Internat. J. soc. Psychiat.*, 1960/61, **7**, 33–35.

HUNT, J. McV. & SOLOMON, R. L. The stability and some correlates of group-status in a summer-camp group of young boys. *Amer. J. Psychol.*, 1942, **55**, 33–45.

HURLOCK, E. B. The use of group rivalry as an incentive. *J. abnorm. soc. Psychol.*, 1927, **22**, 278–290.

JAKUBCZAK, L. F. & WALTERS, R. H. Suggestibility as dependency behavior. *J. abnorm. soc. Psychol.*, 1959, **59**, 102–107.

JENNINGS, H. H. Leadership and sociometric choice. *Sociometry*, 1947, **10**, 32–49.

JONES, M. C. A study of socialization patterns at the high school levels. *J. genet. Psychol.*, 1958, **93**, 87–111.

KANOUS, L. E., DAUGHERTY, R. A., & COHN, T. S. Relation between heterosexual friendship choices and socioeconomic level. *Child Developm.*, 1962, **33**, 251–255.

KATZ, E. & ZLOCZOWER, A. Ethnic continuity in an Israeli town: I. Relations with parents. *Hum. Relat.*, 1961, **14**, 293–308.

KENISTON, K. Social change and youth in America. *Daedalus*, Winter, 1962, 145–171.

KITANO, H. H. L. Adjustment of problem and nonproblem children to specific situations: a study in role theory. *Child Developm.*, 1962, **33**, 229–233.

KOCH, H. L. The relation in young children between characteristics of their playmates and certain attributes of their siblings. *Child Developm.*, 1957, **28**, 175–202.

KOHN, M. L. Social class and parental values. *Amer. J. Sociol.*, 1959, **64**, 337–351.

KOHN, M. L. Social class and parent-child relationships: an interpretation. *Amer. J. Sociol.*, 1963, **68**, 471–480.

LAMBERT, W. E. & TAGUCHI, Y. Ethnic cleavage among young children. *J. abnorm. soc. Psychol.*, 1956, **53**, 380–382.

LAMBERT, W. W., TRIANDIS, L. M., & WOLF, M. Some correlates of beliefs in the malevolence and benevolence of supernatural beings: a cross-societal study. *J. abnorm. soc. Psychol.*, 1959, **58**, 162–169.

LARSEN, O. N. & HILL, R. J. Social structure and interpersonal communication. *Amer. J. Sociol.*, 1958, **63**, 497–505.

LINTON, R. Age and sex categories. *Amer. Sociol. Rev.*, 1942, **7**, 589–603.

LIPPITT, R. & GOLD, M. Classroom social structure as a mental health problem. *J. soc. Issues*, 1959, **15** (1), 40–49.

LIPPITT, R., POLANSKY, N., & ROSEN, S. The dynamics of power: a field study of social influence in groups of children. *Hum. Relat.*, 1952, **5**, 37–64.

LIPPITT, R. & WHITE, R. K. An experimental study of leadership and group life. In T. M. Newcomb & E. L. Hartley (Eds.), *Readings in social psychology*. New York: Holt, 1947. Pp. 315–330.

LOTT, B. E. & LOTT, A. J. The formation of positive attitudes toward group members. *J. abnorm. soc. Psychol.*, 1960, **61**, 297–300.

LYNN, D. B. & SAWREY, W. L. The effects of father-absence on Norwegian boys and girls. *J. abnorm. soc. Psychol.*, 1959, **59**, 258–262.

MACDONALD, M., McGUIRE, C., & HAVIGHURST, R. J. Leisure activities and the socioeconomic status of children. *Amer. J. Sociol.*, 1949, **54**, 505–519.

MARSHALL, H. R. Relations between home experiences and children's use of language in play interactions with peers. *Psychol. Monogr.*, 1961, **75**, No. 5.

MARTIN, W. E. & STENDLER, C. B. *Child development: the process of growing up in society*. New York: Harcourt Brace, 1953.

MASLOW, A. H. & DIAZ-GUERRERO, R. Delinquency as a value disturbance. In J. G. Peatman & E. L. Hartley (Eds.), *Festschrift for Gardner Murphy*. New York: Harper, 1960. Pp. 228–240.

McCANDLESS, B. R. & HOYT, J. M. Sex, ethnicity, and play preferences of preschool children. *J. abnorm. soc. Psychol.*, 1961, **62**, 683–685.

McCANDLESS, B. R. & MARSHALL, H. R. A picture sociometric technique for preschool children and its relation to teacher judgments of friendship. *Child Developm.*, 1957, **28**, 139–148.

McCORD, W., McCORD, J., & VERDEN, P. Familial and behavioral correlates of dependency in male children. *Child Developm.*, 1962, **33**, 313–326.

McKEE, J. P. & LEADER, F. B. The relationships of socio-economic status and aggression to the competitive behavior of preschool children. *Child Developm.*, 1955, **26**, 135–142.

MEYER, W. J. Relationships between social need strivings for the development of heterosexual affiliations. *J. abnorm. soc. Psychol.*, 1959, **59**, 51–57.

MORENO, J. L. *Who shall survive?* Washington, D. C.: Nervous & Mental Disease Pub. Co., 1934.

NEUGARTEN, B. L. Social class and friendship among school children. *Amer. J. Sociol.*, 1946, **51**, 305–313.

NORTHWAY, M. L. Outsiders: a study of the personality patterns of children least acceptable to their age mates. *Sociometry*. 1944, **7**, 10–25.

Northway, M. L. & Rooks, M. McC. Creativity and sociometric status in children. *Sociometry*, 1956, **18**, 450–457.

Patel, A. S. & Gordon, J. E. Some personal and situational determinants of yielding to influence. *J. abnorm. soc. Psychol.*, 1960, **61**, 411–418.

Peck, R. F. Family patterns correlated with adolescent personality structure. *J. abnorm. soc. Psychol.*, 1958, **57**, 347–350.

Peck, R. F. & Galliani, C. Intelligence, ethnicity and social roles in adolescent society. *Sociometry*, 1962, **25**, 64–72.

Peck, R. F. & Havighurst, R. J. *The psychology of character development*. New York: Wiley, 1960.

Piaget, J. *The moral judgment of the child*. Glencoe, Ill.: Free Press, 1948.

Polansky, N., Lippitt, R., & Redl, F. An investigation of behavioral contagion in groups. *Hum. Relat.*, 1950, **3**, 319–348.

Pope, B. Socio-economic contrasts in children's peer culture prestige values. *Genet. Psychol. Monogr.*, 1953, **48**, 157–220.

Porterfield, O. V. & Schlichting, H. F. Peer status and reading achievement. *J. educ. Res.*, 1961, **54**, 291–297.

Psathas, G. Ethnicity, social class and adolescent independence from parental control. *Amer. Sociol. Rev.*, 1957, **22**, 415–423.

Puffer, J. A. *The boy and his gang*. Boston: Houghton Mifflin, 1912.

Radke, M. J. & Trager, H. G. Children's perception of the social roles of Negroes and whites. *J. Psychol.*, 1950, **29**, 3–33.

Raush, H. L., Dittmann, A. T., & Taylor, T. J. Person, setting, and change in social interaction. *Hum. Relat.*, 1959, **12**, 361–378.

Raush, H. L., Farbman, I., & Llewellyn, L. G. Person, setting, and change in social interaction. II. *Hum. Relat.*, 1960, **13**, 305–322.

Reese, H. W. Sociometric choices of the same and opposite sex in late childhood. *Merrill-Palmer Quart.*, 1962, **8**, 173–174.

Riley, M. W., Riley, J. W., & Moore, M. E. Adolescent values and the Riesman typology: an empirical analysis. In S. M. Lipset & L. Lowenthal (Eds.), *Culture and social character, the work of David Riesman reviewed*. Glencoe, Ill.: Free Press, 1961. Pp. 370–385.

Rosen, B. C. Conflicting group membership: a study of parent-peer-group cross pressures. *Amer. Sociol. Rev.*, 1955, **20**, 155–161.

Rosen, S., Levinger, G., & Lippitt, R. Desired change in self and others as a function of resource ownership. *Hum. Relat.*, 1960, **13**, 187–193.

Rosenberg, M. The dissonant religious context and emotional disturbance. *Amer. J. Sociol.*, 1962, **68**, 1–10.

Schachter, S. *The psychology of affiliation*. Stanford, Calif.: Stanford Univ. Press, 1959.

Schooler, C. & Scarr, S. Affiliation among chronic schizophrenics: relation to intrapersonal and birth order factors. *J. Pers.*, 1962, **30**, 178–192.

Sears, R. R., Pintler, M. H., & Sears, P. S. Effect of father separation on pre-school children's doll play aggression. *Child Developm.*, 1946, **17**, 219–243.

Sherif, M. A study of some social factors in perception. *Arch. Psychol., N. Y.*, 1935, No. 187.

Sherif, M. The self and reference groups: meeting ground of individual and group approaches. *Ann. N. Y. Acad. Sci.*, 1962, **96**, 797–813.

Sherif, M., Harvey, O. J., White, B. J., Hood, W. R., & Sherif, C. W. *Intergroup conflict and cooperation: the robbers cave experiment*. Norman: Univ. Oklahoma Press, 1961.

Sherif, M. & Sherif, C. W. *Groups in harmony and tension*. New York: Harper, 1953.

Singer, A., Jr. Certain aspects of personality and their relation to certain group modes, and constancy of friendship choices. *J. educ. Res.*, 1951, **45**, 33–42.

SMITH, A. J. A developmental study of group processes. *J. genet. Psychol.*, 1960, **97,** 29–30.

SMITH, G. H. Sociometric study of best-liked and least-liked children. *Element. Sch. J.*, 1950, **51,** 77–85.

SPIRO, M. E. *Children of the kibbutz.* Cambridge: Harvard Univ. Press, 1958.

STEVENSON, H. W. & STEWART, E. C. A developmental study of racial awareness in young children. *Child Developm.*, 1958, **29,** 399–409.

SYKES, G. M. & MATZA, D. Techniques of neutralization: a theory of delinquency. *Amer. Sociol. Rev.*, 1957, **22,** 664–670.

TERMAN, L. M. A preliminary study of the psychology and pedagogy of leadership. *Pedagogical Seminary*, 1904, **11,** 413–451.

THOMAS, D. S., LOOMIS, A. M., & ARRINGTON, R. E. *Observational studies of social behavior:* vol. 1. *Social behavior patterns.* New Haven: Inst. Human Relat., Yale Univ., 1933.

THOMPSON, G. G. & HORROCKS, J. E. A study of the friendship fluctuations of urban boys and girls. *J. genet. Psychol.*, 1947, **70,** 53–63.

THRASHER, F. *The gang.* Chicago: Univ. Chicago Press, 1927.

TRYON, C. M. Evaluation of adolescent personality by adolescents. *Monogr. Soc. Res. Child Developm.*, 1939, No. 23.

TUDDENHAM, R. D. Studies in reputation: III. Correlates of popularity among elementary school children. *J. educ. Psychol.*, 1951, **42,** 257–276 (a).

TUDDENHAM, R. D. Studies in reputation: I. Sex and grade differences in school children's evaluation of their peers. *Psychol. Monogr.*, 1951, **66,** No. 1 (b).

TUMA, E. & LIVSON, N. Family socio-economic status and adolescent attitudes to authority. *Child Developm.*, 1960, **31,** 387–399.

UDRY, R. J. The importance of social class in a suburban school. *J. educ. Sociol.*, 1960, **33,** 307–310.

WALTERS, R. H., MARSHALL, W. E., & SHOOTER, J. R. Anxiety, isolation, and susceptibility to social influence. *J. Pers.*, 1960, **28,** 518–529.

WARNER, W. L. & LUNT, P. *The social life of a modern community.* New Haven: Yale Univ. Press, 1941.

WELLER, L. The relationship of birth order to anxiety: a replication of the Schachter findings. *Sociometry*, 1962, **25,** 415–417.

WESTLEY, W. A. & ELKIN, F. The protective environment and adolescent socialization. *Social Forces*, 1956, **35,** 243–249.

WILSON, A. B. Residential segregation of social classes and aspirations of high school boys. *Amer. Sociol. Rev.*, 1959, **24,** 836–845.

WILSON, R. S. Personality patterns, source attractiveness, and conformity. *J. Pers.*, 1960, **28,** 186–199.

WITHEY, S. B., FOSTER, B., & BILLINGSLEY, P. *A study of boys becoming adolescents.* Ann Arbor: Inst. Soc. Res., Univ. of Michigan, 1960.

WRIGHT, H. F. Psychological development in Midwest. *Child Developm.*, 1956, **27,** 265–286.

YARROW, L. J. Maternal deprivation: toward an empirical and conceptual reevaluation. *Psychol. Bull.*, 1961, **58,** 459–490.

YARROW, L. J. & YARROW, M. R. Leadership and interpersonal change. *J. soc. Issues*, 1958, **14** (1), 47–50.

YARROW, M. R., TRAGER, H., & MILLER, J. The role of parents in the development of children's ethnic attitudes. *Child Developm.*, 1952, **23,** 13–53.

ZANDER, A. & VAN EGMOND, E. Relationship of intelligence and social power to the interpersonal behavior of children. *J. educ. Psychol.*, 1958, **49,** 257–268.

Effects of the Mass Media

ELEANOR E. MACCOBY

Stanford University

IT IS EVIDENT that television, comic books, radio, and movies are absorbing a substantial segment of the time and concentrated attention of today's children. Exposure to these media begins very early. In some households the one-year-old's playpen is located in the same room with a television set that other family members are watching, and there are instances in which a child's first word is the name of a television star or a product being advertised. What is happening to a child as he absorbs TV and radio programs, or reads the comic strips? Is he merely being entertained, or is he carrying something away from these experiences that will affect his later beliefs or actions? Certainly some of the great polemic dramatists of history (such as Aeschylus, Shaw, and Ibsen) have hoped that their work would have some impact after the audience had left the theater. But whether a television viewer or playgoer can be changed or guided by the passive vicarious experience he has had is a matter that is little understood.

Parents, educators, and others dealing professionally with children have long been concerned about the possible effects of the media. Beginning fairly early in this century, children's literature became a target for reformers who claimed that many children's classics, from *Little Red Riding Hood* to Grimm's and Anderson's fairy tales, with their violence, themes of children being abandoned and mistreated, were unduly frightening for children. Countering these views, some writers held that if one tried to take all the frightening or aggressive material out of children's stories there would be nothing interesting left; that the dramatic value of literature depended upon generating emotions in the reader or viewer; and that children enjoyed such experiences in the same way they enjoy being moderately scared on carnival rides. During the rapid growth of the motion picture industry in the 1920's, when children began to attend movies once or twice a week, public concern was aroused over the possible effects of the movies on children's moral values and behavior. In this instance, for the first time, systematic research was undertaken to assess the effects. A group of emi-

323

nent psychologists and sociologists carried out a series of studies known as the Payne Fund Studies, published in 1933, which deal with the effects of movies on social attitudes, on delinquent behavior, and on emotional responsiveness (Blumer and Hauser; Charters; Dysinger and Ruckmik; Peterson and Thurstone). Following the Payne Fund Studies, which did indeed detect some significant effects of exposure to movies (some of these findings will be reported below), little further research was done.

During the early 1950's, there was a resurgence of interest in the mass media and their effects. Part of this interest stemmed from the concern that rising rates of juvenile delinquency might be traced, at least in part, to the widespread reading of crime and horror comic books and viewing of crime programs on television. A Senate committee, investigating juvenile delinquency, conducted hearings on the media in relation to delinquency (U. S. Senate Hearings, 1955). There was impressive evidence that criminal activity is a central theme in the mass media offerings for the juvenile audience; that the criminal is sometimes presented sympathetically, the law-enforcement officer unsympathetically; that methods of executing crimes are sometimes presented in great detail. It was also made clear that young delinquents are, on the average, avid consumers of this kind of fare from the mass media. It is a large step, however, from pointing out these facts to demonstrating any causal relationship between them. Obviously, the young criminal's interest in crime comic books and crime TV shows might be a result, rather than a cause, of his antisocial tendencies.

The public concern over the contents of the mass media had some direct effects. The comic book industry organized a system of self-censorship, establishing a code which was applied to comic publications, and most comic books now distributed bear the seal of approval indicating that they have complied with this code. The kind of sadistic and depraved offerings (see U.S. Senate, Committee on the Judiciary, 1955) which outraged the public in the early 1950's is not now to be found on open newsstands. Television was never guilty of the excesses in content which characterized part of the comic book industry, and there has been less change in program content as a result of public pressure. But public interest in the possible effects of mass media on children has continued, and has been directed not only toward a possible connection with juvenile delinquency but toward other possible effects, potentially beneficial as well as potentially harmful. Since the early 1950's, a substantial amount of research has been done and a considerable body of knowledge has accumulated concerning children's viewing and reading habits, and preferences, as well as concerning the effects of their mass media experiences. It is the purpose of this review to summarize and evaluate the findings relevant to the impact of movies, television, and comics. But first it may be useful to discuss the nature of the problem and the nature of the material which should be relevant to an understanding of it.

THE NATURE OF POSSIBLE EFFECTS

There are several ways in which exposure to the mass media could influence children. The first is indirect. The media can exert an influence by taking children away from other activities. If the other activities would be harmful to the child (including, for example, activities of a delinquent gang), then the effect of the media would be wholesome. If, however, extensive TV-watching or comic book reading were taking the child away from needed physical exercise, or from cultural activities such as practicing on a musical instrument, then we would be more likely to judge the effects to be harmful. In any case, if we wish to appraise the effects of the media, it is clear that we must be concerned with the child's total pattern of activity, so as to discover if possible what is being given up in favor of the hours spent with the media.

The more direct effects of repeated exposures to the media may be either immediate or long-range. Under immediate effects we would include the emotional reactions of the child while he is viewing, listening, or reading, and the immediately ensuing repercussions of these in defensive reactions, fatigue, excitement, dreams, and so on. The long-range effects concern the *learning* that is produced: both the learning of content (vocabulary, items of information, beliefs) and the strengthening or weakening of certain personality traits of the child, such as aggressiveness, passivity, and the like.

The connotation of the word *learn* is such as to make one think of the classroom, or at least of the documentary film, whose intent is to impart information. As we will see later, by far the largest portion of children's exposure to the mass media is not of this instructional sort, yet it is clear that he learns from the mass media nonetheless. The child's interest lies primarily in being entertained, and he achieves entertainment primarily, we believe, through putting himself in the place of one or more of the characters depicted in the film or book and experiencing vicariously the events that involve this character. Although the viewer may be sitting quite still while the hero shoots it out with the villian, the fact that he is sharing the hero's experiences to some extent is suggested by the nature of his emotional reactions while viewing. Many years ago, Dysinger and Ruckmik (1933) took physiological measures of children's emotional responses (galvanic skin response, breathing, heart rate) and noted that the viewers showed changes in emotion that reflected the action on the screen. Furthermore, which screen characters and which action most fully engaged the viewer were found to be a function of certain characteristics of the viewer. For example, boys became most aroused during fight scenes and other adventurous episodes; girls were most emotionally responsive during romantic scenes.

We must assume from this that the kind and degree of vicarious experiencing depends upon the individual viewer's preexisting interests and motives to some degree, and upon the match between these characteristics of the viewer and the events on the screen. It is possible, by watching the eyes of movie viewers as they watch a movie, to determine which screen character they are looking at most of the time. In one study (Maccoby, Wilson, and Burton, 1958) it was found that male viewers spent more time watching the hero, and female viewers more time watching the heroine, during romantic scenes involving just the male and female leading characters. We assume that in stories which present more than one leading character, a viewer makes a choice of a character who will be his primary "identificand," and experiences the actions vicariously through this character. It follows that he learns more about this character's actions (and those elements of the stimulus situation that are most relevant for triggering this character's actions) than about other elements in a story. We also assume that the depth of the viewer's involvement with the character will vary, depending on the nature of the action and the extent to which the action meshes with the viewer's own motivational system. A demonstration of these phenomena may be found in a study of seventh-graders and their learning (memory) of the content of a class-B entertainment movie (Maccoby and Wilson, 1957). Boys remembered aggressive content better, girls remembered romantic content; *but* this preferential memory was found only for the aggressive or romantic content for which the same-sexed leading character was the actor. Thus boys remembered best the aggressive actions performed by the boy hero, but were not especially good at recalling aggressive actions of the heroine. We see then that similarity between the viewer and the actor, both in role (for example, sex) and in preferred action systems, influences which elements of movie content will be absorbed.

It should be noted here that the differences among viewers in what is seen and remembered from films is small, though reliable. Many films offer little choice of an identificand, having essentially a single hero, and the efforts of the writer and the director are to draw the viewer into empathic engagement with that character. The question of just what characteristics of a screen character will produce fullest identification among viewers is a fascinating and still largely unexplored issue. The ability to lead viewers into identification with the characters is a major part of the screen writer's skill, and so far belongs more to the sphere of art than science. We merely wish to indicate here that we believe that the nature and degree of this identification is important in determining what the viewer will take away from the viewing experience.

For this and other reasons, then, it would be a mistake to assume that the impact of the mass media would be constant, or even similar, from one child to the next. The child is not a passive entity, simply absorbing like a sponge whatever is offered to him. He is an active selector of what mass media materials he will expose himself to in the first place; and even during exposure, as noted above, he deploys attention selectively, and what he remembers varies accordingly. Furthermore, what a child does take in has a different effect, depending on his preexisting level of information, the nature of his needs, and the quality of his adjustment to his life situation. So when we ask about the effects of the mass media, we must not phrase the question in terms of *whether* the media have an effect, but rather *how much* effect on *what kind* of children, and under *what circumstances* will the effects be exhibited. The mass media may teach children skills they will never perform (for example, how to take the oath as President of the United States), or attitudes that will never be elicited (for example, toward men from Mars). So the effects depend in some degree on the probability that situations relevant for the application of the content acquired from the mass media will occur in the real life of the child.

METHODS OF STUDYING MASS MEDIA EFFECTS

Before we attempt to evaluate existing knowledge concerning mass media effects, it may be well to consider how we can discover what these effects are. If present-day children are different in some ways from the children of previous generations, it is tempting to attribute the changes to television and the other mass media. But it is obvious that modern children are growing up in surroundings which differ in many ways from earlier patterns of life. In recent years, society has been recovering from the effects of a major war and living in the shadow of another one; population has grown rapidly, with crowding of houses and schools, and population has shifted from rural to urban to suburban areas, with accompanying changes in the demands that are placed upon children; more mothers are working; and income and living standards have been rapidly rising. To sort out the effects of the mass media in the complex of changes that are occasioned by all these other shifts in our pattern of life is difficult indeed.

The advent of television has created a few "experiments of nature"— situations in which certain areas share in most of the social changes of modern times but for some reason are late in acquiring television. Such areas may be contrasted with other similar areas which do have television, and the characteristics of children in these pairs of areas may be compared. There are certain risks in these comparisons. For example, if a particular town is late in getting television, the reason is likely to be that it is geographically isolated to some degree, and the residents may be exposed to fewer cultural influences of many sorts in addition to being unexposed to television. Still the findings of several such studies have proved instructive.

Another related technique for studying the effects of television has been to contrast the behavior and attitudes of children who live in homes with television with those of children whose homes are without television. Here the problem is that in most American communities the saturation of television sets is extremely high, with more than 90 per cent of all homes having a set. In such a situation, the homes which do not have TV are an unusual population in many respects. The group without TV includes intellectuals who believe that the quality of programs offered is too poor to justify their buying a television set, and it also includes a small group of very poor or very disorganized families who cannot obtain credit for the purchase of a set. Obviously, children growing up in these homes are subject to many other special influences from their environment—they are likely to be different from the children in the TV-owning households in many ways other than those produced by the influence of television. Valid comparisons between set-owners and nonowners may be made only during the early days of the introduction of TV into a community, when it is possible to find groups of owners and nonowners who are reasonably well matched with respect to characteristics other than set ownership; and even here, as will be noted later, it is necessary to be cautious about inferring effects of television. For when one compares a family who bought television as soon as it was introduced with another family having the same income, same number of children, same age parents who did not buy it, the two families must have different philosophies concerning the allocation of their economic resources—differences which undoubtedly have implications for the values taught to children.

Perhaps the most powerful technique for the study of the effects of television has been the before-after study. In a few notable instances, it has been possible to study a community *in advance* of the introduction of television, and then to restudy the same population (including the same children) after television has been established and individuals have had a year or two of exposure to it. The most notable example of a study of this kind is the one made by Himmelweit, Oppenheim, and Vince (1958) in Great Britain. A later, highly valuable before-after study, patterned upon the British one, was made by Furu (1962) in Japan. We shall draw upon these studies extensively in the report below.

Even with a carefully executed before-after study, however, there are limitations in how much can be learned with this method. Our knowledge of the effects of exposure to the mass media has been much advanced through the use of smaller experimental studies in which one group of children are shown a movie, comic book, or television program, and another pre-matched group are *not* exposed to this material. The two groups of children can then be tested to see whether there are any differences in beliefs or behavior that might be related to the content of the material. Experimental procedures of this sort cannot tell us much concerning the long-term, cumulative effects of continued exposure to the media. But they can serve to pinpoint specific effects of individual exposures with a high degree of precision. And they can provide better tests of theoretical issues concerning effects, since they permit control of irrelevant variables to a degree not possible in studies which are conducted in preexisting natural settings.

In the summary that follows we shall draw upon all these varieties of research, keeping in mind the advantages and limitations of each approach.

MEDIA USAGE AND THE DEPLOYMENT OF TIME

Schramm, Lyle, and Parker (1961) have provided us with an excellent, detailed account of American children's usage of media at different age levels. With respect to television specifically, they point out that the measurement of viewing habits is not a simple process. Asking people to estimate how much time they spent viewing, for example, usually results in an underestimate of the time they actually spent. They employed a variety of techniques to obtain as accurate estimates as possible. Here is a summary of some of their findings:

1. From ages three through sixteen the average American child spends about one-sixth of his waking hours watching television—somewhat more than he devotes to school during these years, when one considers weekends and vacations.
2. In terms of hours spent, television-watching reaches its peak at the age when the child is in the sixth through the eighth grades in school. Older children, during adolescence, spend more time with one another and TV-viewing drops off somewhat (from a high of twenty-three or twenty-four hours a week to eighteen or nineteen), with radio assuming more importance as a form of entertainment that can be more easily assimilated into group social activities.
3. TV-viewing is related to I.Q.; especially at high school age, the brighter children spend considerably less time viewing.

4. Much of children's viewing time is devoted to "adult" programs. In the first grade, 40 per cent of viewing time is spent on programs not intended primarily for children, and by the sixth grade, this figure is nearly 80 per cent. Favorite programs are "Westerns" and situation comedies, with crime programs emerging as favorites by the eighth-grade level.

Himmelweit and her colleagues (1958) report a lower total volume of television-viewing in their study of British children. These children were spending about eleven to thirteen hours a week with TV, but it is well to remember that the study was made during a period in the early 1950's when most of the children studied had access to only a single BBC channel, and when broadcasting was restricted in various ways (for example, no programs were broadcast during the dinner hour). The British study, like the American one reported above, showed that the amount of TV watching was inversely related to intelligence, and that a substantial proportion of children's TV time is devoted to watching adult programs.

Clearly, the advent of television, with its very substantial inroads upon children's time, must have produced a change in the pattern of their other activities. What activities are given up or reduced in favor of TV? The studies which have obtained data on this question (Maccoby, 1951; Himmelweit et al., 1958; Furu, 1962) are in agreement on certain major points: First, some TV time is taken from sleep time; after the acquisition of TV children go to bed a little later. Second, a substantial segment of TV time is taken from other mass media. Radio listening among children declines when the family acquires television; so does the reading of comic books and attendance at movies. Himmelweit and her associates have generalized this finding into a principle of "functional similarity"; that is, activities that will be given up most readily in favor of television are those that satisfy the same needs but less effectively. They cite as an example of this principle the fact that movie attendance is greatly depressed by the advent of TV among younger children, but that among older children the effect is much smaller, because movie-going has social functions for these children that TV will not satisfy. Similarly they note that comic book reading is permanently displaced by television, while the reading of more serious books (fiction and nonfiction) is not.[1]

The principle of functional similarity appears to be one that makes a good deal of sense *a priori*. Yet it is not always easy to tell when to invoke

[1] While the authors conclude that book reading is not affected by television, their appendix tables do show a displacement of about .2 of a book per month. E. B. Parker reports that this table shows a near-significant effect of television — p <.06 by one-tailed test.

it. Furu, in his recent study in Japan, found that not only comic book reading but the reading of serious books (both fiction and nonfiction) claimed less time from children after they acquired television. Can it be that television and book reading are more "functionally similar" in Japan than they are in England? The question makes it clear that we require an independent definition of the functions which different media experiences serve before we can make a rigorous test of the principle of functional similarity. Yet the principle has led to some useful predictions. It led Parker (1963) to predict that when TV broadcasting began in a set of communities, the public library circulation of fiction would decline and the circulation of nonfiction would not. This prediction was borne out.

Himmelweit and her associates make a second generalization: that it is the marginal, unorganized activities which tend to be displaced by television. Consistent with this would be their finding that the amount of time devoted to homework is unaffected by television. Maccoby (1951) also found no effect on homework in her American study, but Furu did find a loss of about a quarter-hour a day in home study among the television-owning children in Japan, and a greater loss than this among a subgroup of older boys. Television also appears to have less impact on structured play activities (for example, organized team sports) than on casual play.

EFFECTS ON PERFORMANCE IN SCHOOL

In general, the American and English studies agree that television has had little effect on school performance. Schramm and associates (1961) did note, in their comparison of the two communities "Radiotown" and "Teletown," that children who have been growing up with television appear to come to school with about a one-year advantage in vocabulary. Thus, to quote these authors, "so far as vocabulary represents general knowledge, then, we can say with some confidence that television appears to help children get off to a fast start."[2] Yet this advantage was not maintained. In the sixth and tenth grades, the children in the two towns did not differ in their total information level. The kind of information possessed, however, did appear to be related to media usage: TV viewers could name singers and band leaders with greater accuracy; children in the town without television were more able to name writers and statesmen.

There have been many studies in which academic achievement has been studied in relation to (a) the amount of time a child spends viewing television, or (b) whether there is television in the child's home. It is not uncommon to find a negative correlation between the amount of viewing and

[2] The improvement in vocabulary appears to have occurred primarily among the brightest and dullest children, the "middle" I.Q. group showing little effect.

school grades. But this finding can be an artificial product of intelligence. That is, the children with higher I.Q.'s view less on the average, and, of course, they also obtain higher grades in school. When intelligence is controlled, the relationship between grades and television ownership, or hours of viewing, tends to be small if indeed it does not disappear altogether. Himmelweit *et al.* (1958), in comparing carefully matched groups of viewers and nonviewers, found that the two groups did not differ in general information level; that the nonviewers obtained slightly better grades, although the difference was not large enough to be statistically significant; and that the slight loss in grades that might be attributed to television occurred primarily among the more intelligent children. It is notable in this British study that two-thirds of the children were required to finish their homework before being allowed to watch television.

The situation in Japan is different. Furu (1962) does find some effects of television on school performance. In his study it was possible to study a large group of children (nearly 4,000) before television was available to the community in which they lived. Then these children were restudied two years later, after television had been introduced. The sample of TV children was made up of those who had had TV in their homes for at least three months at the time of the second survey, and the comparison group were classmates matched with respect to grades, sex, and intelligence, who did not have television at home. Furu found a loss of reading ability among the children who had acquired television (by comparison with their controls), especially among boys in school grades 5 to 7. These same boys spent less time on general outside reading, and (as noted above) less time on their homework, which may account for their failure to keep up with their classmates in school reading tests. By contrast, TV girls showed *gains* in their scores on science achievement.[3]

These cross-cultural differences in the effects of television on school achievement raise some fascinating questions—questions which become important if we wish to predict the effects of the introduction of television into new areas of the world. In these days of rapid social change in Japan, are the after-school activities of Japanese adolescent boys subject to less parental control than would be true for British children? Are Japanese girls unlikely to be exposed to scientific concepts except through television? To interpret Furu's results, knowledge of Japanese culture is required. And this fact underlines the danger of attempting to extrapolate from British and American studies to cultures where initial information level, educational practices, and family organization may be different.

[3] Himmelweit *et al.* did not examine their data separately for each sex; thus it is possible that the findings of the two studies are not so different as it at first appears.

EFFECTS ON AGGRESSIVE BEHAVIOR

As we noted earlier, many parents and educators have been especially concerned over the possibility that the existing content of the mass media might make children more aggressive. Both casual viewing and more formal content analysis reveal enormous amounts of violence and aggression in mass media programs. (See Schramm *et al.*, 1961, pp. 139–140.) Do children learn techniques for aggression by watching fights in movies and on TV? Do they come to believe that aggressive behavior is more legitimate than they would believe it to be if it were not so frequently presented? Are there any hostile feelings aroused by watching fight scenes, which last after the exposure is terminated, or do emotional effects dissipate as soon as the story plot has been resolved? Does the effect of fight scenes depend in any way upon *who* commits aggressive acts on the screen, or on the depicted consequences of the actor's aggression?

These questions relate to some theoretical issues which are of current importance in the thinking of psychologists studying personality. While the issues are not specific to any particular class of actions, let us discuss them as they relate to aggression. It has long been held, by psychodynamic theorists and learning theorists alike, that expression of aggression reduces aggressive motivation or aggressive "drive." This position is known as the "catharsis" hypothesis, and it has had wide acceptance and application not only among theoretical psychologists but among practitioners dealing with children; note, for example, the nursery school teachers who encourage children to hit a Bobo doll in order to "release their pent-up feelings" and "get the anger out of their systems." Following a clear statement of the hypothesis in 1939 (Dollard *et al.*), there has been much experimentation and theoretical writing on the subject. A good summary of the work that has been done appears in Berkowitz's book, *Aggression* (1962). The issues have become complex, and it is not possible to present the entire range of arguments with supporting data here. I will attempt to select the materials most relevant to aggression in the mass media and its effects on children.

The first question is this: While it may be true that there will be a cathartic release through directly expressing aggression against the instigator of the aggressive motivation, is it also true that *vicarious* experience (through fantasy or through watching aggressive acts performed by others) will also provide cathartic reduction in aggressive motivation? There is some evidence that this is so with adults. Feshbach (1955) performed an experiment in which a group of adults had been made angry. Some of them had an opportunity to express aggression in stories they wrote during a waiting period, others did not. Subsequently those who had "discharged" aggression in their stories expressed less aggression directly toward the instigator when they had an opportunity than did the subjects who had spent their waiting period in some other way than writing aggressive stories. Similarly, a group of adults who had been made angry and then saw an aggressive movie were less aggressive subsequently than other adults, also angered, who saw a neutral movie during their waiting period (Feshbach, 1961).

The work so far done with children points to quite different effects of fantasy aggression. Bandura, Ross, and Ross (1961) allowed children of nursery school age to see movies of adult aggressive models who interacted in a novel and aggressive way with a set of play materials. They sat on a Bobo doll and hit it on the nose; then they raised the doll and hit it on the head with a mallet; they called out certain aggressive phrases, such as "kick him," "hit him down." By contrast, some children did not see this movie. Subsequently, all the children were subjected to a mild frustration experience (not being allowed to play with some attractive toys), and then they were led, one child at a time, into a room which contained the same play materials that had been depicted on the screen, as well as other materials. The children who had seen the aggressive film imitated the actions they had seen there: they sat on the Bobo doll and punched it on the nose, then they raised the doll and hit it on the head with a mallet; they called out the identical aggressive phrases they had heard the models say. In addition, they were more aggressive in nonimitative ways: they made more aggressive use of toy guns which were available, even though these had not been part of the scene they had witnessed in the film. In all, the movie-exposed children exhibited approximately twice as much aggressive behavior in the test situation as the children who had not seen the film. The authors, in discussing their results, emphasized that it is often claimed that filmed aggression has an effect only upon children who already have strongly deviant tendencies. The results are directly contrary to this assumption, for the experimental group was a randomly selected group of children from a normal nursery school population and the children quite uniformly showed the effect.

Another study by Ivar Lövaas (1961) produced results which are entirely consistent with those of Bandura and associates. Lövaas wished to discover whether cartoons that emphasized fighting would make child viewers feel more aggressive or less so after viewing the cartoon. He showed an aggressive program to one group of children, and some nonaggressive material to another group. Immediately after viewing, each child was given a choice between two toys to play with, one of which was an aggressive toy. If the child turned a lever activating the aggressive toy, he could make two dolls hit each other on the head. The other toy which the child could choose had moving doll figures which did not hit one another. The children who had seen the aggressive cartoon tended to play with the aggressive toy immediately afterward, while the children seeing the nonaggressive cartoon preferred the nonaggressive toy.

Similarly, a study by Mussen and Rutherford (1961) compared three groups of children: one group had seen an aggressive cartoon, one a nonaggressive cartoon, and a third group no cartoon. Subsequently the children were offered an opportunity to engage in aggressive play (popping balloons), and the children who had seen the aggressive cartoon were more willing to do so.

A final study should be mentioned, although it had inconclusive results. Siegel (1956) showed children an aggressive cartoon, and on another occasion, a nonaggressive cartoon. She compared the amount of aggression the children showed toward nursery school playmates after the viewing of each of these films. Following the aggressive cartoon, there was slightly more aggression displayed by the children, but the difference was not significant. The primary finding, then, was that seeing an aggressive film did not reduce subsequent aggression.

Why are these results of studies with children so different from the Feshbach (1961) studies with adults? Feshbach emphasizes that one should expect a cathartic effect only if the subject has been made angry *before* being being exposed to the film, and in the adult studies cited above this was the case. In the Bandura *et al.* (1961) work, the children were frustrated *after* seeing the film but before being tested for imitative aggression. And in the Lövaas (1961) study, there was no experimental arousal of the children's emotions at any point. In the Mussen and Rutherford (1961) study, however, one group of children was frustrated before seeing the cartoons, another was not; and this condition made no difference in the amount of subsequent aggressive impulse produced by the film.

In the instances in which some reduction in aggressive impulses have been observed following exposure to aggressive film material (as in Feshbach's research), it is possible to interpret the findings differently from Feshbach. Berkowitz (1962) points out that the reduction in aggressiveness may be due, not to any cathartic effect of having experienced aggression vicariously in fantasy but to the arousal of guilt or anxiety over the aggression seen in the film, with a resulting inhibition of normal aggressive responses. This point of view, if valid, would help to explain why we sometimes get reduction of aggression following viewing of aggressive film sequences in adults but not in children. Possibly, anxiety and guilt over aggression are more fully learned in adults, through their longer period of socialization, and children have fewer inhibitions over the enjoyment of aggressive fantasy. Or possibly, for children, seeing aggressive behavior enacted on the screen in a context where it is "justified" by the plot may serve to make such behavior appear more legitimate and may release some of the not very strongly established inhibitions against displaying it. In any case, the existing evidence appears to us to indicate that over a normal population of children, with a normal range of preexisting aggressive motivation, the effect of aggression in films is to *arouse*, rather than discharge or inhibit, aggressive impulses.

The reader may have noted that in three out of four of the studies with children cited above, the increased aggressiveness of the children was measured in play situations, where the aroused aggression could be expressed with little danger of retribution. Is it likely that aggressive impulses aroused through watching aggressive movie scenes, and the aggressive actions learned imitatively through exposure to such scenes, would be manifest in real life? Bandura *et al.* (1961) make the point (and we concur with it) that the likelihood of such transfer depends on whether similar situations arise in real life. The children in their study learned, through watching adult models, how to perform certain specific aggressive actions toward a Bobo doll. But this learning may never have been elicited later unless the child found himself in the presence of a Bobo doll. Similarly, from watching Westerns, children may learn many things concerning guns, and many impulses to use them, but they are not permitted to have real guns in their everyday life. They may learn something about how to rob a safe from seeing it done, but if they are never subsequently in a situation where they are alone with a safe and a set of burglar's tools the learning would remain "underground" indefinitely.

It follows that the more realistic the setting in which filmed aggression is portrayed, the more likely that the child viewer will make use in his real life of what he has learned from observing the movie. Evidence for this may be seen in the fact that imitative aggression is more frequent following portrayal by a live model than a cartoon model (Bandura, Ross, and Ross, 1963). But there is the further matter of sanctions imposed on the child's real-life actions. A child might, for example, acquire a tendency to say "you big stupid" to his mother from hearing a child say this to his mother on a television program; but whether he would ever actually say it would depend on the range of behavior his own mother permitted, her consistency in reacting to undesired behavior, and the nature and severity of the disciplinary measures she commonly employed. All we may safely assume from the experiments cited is that tendencies toward performing certain actions may be acquired (or augmented) from watching others perform them in the mass media. These tendencies will then enter as one element in the set of behavior tendencies aroused later in some relevant situation, and whether the particular item of behavior will actually occur will be a function of the strength of competing responses and the restraints acting upon the media-acquired behavior. One should seldom expect to find a one-to-one matching of the child's behavior to that of the movie model (although in the special circumstances Bandura and associates established, they did find something close to this). But a child's behavior may show the effects of exposure all the same, even without direct matching, in the sense that his real-life actions may represent a compromise between the newly acquired element and previously established patterns of behavior. Furthermore, if the behavior is of a kind that is usually subject to sanctions, it may require stronger sanctions to suppress it after the film exposure.

We might note that while the discussion above has been confined to the learning of aggression through the imitation of film characters, it ought to be possible to transmit other specific kinds of behavior in this way too. That is, we might expect that children ought to be able to learn to tell the truth, to help others in distress, and so on, through imitation of screen characters showing these kinds of behavior. Unfortunately, it is not entirely clear which kinds of behavior are most easily transmitted through observation of screen characters. One experiment by Bandura and Huston (1961) bears upon this point. They used two experimenters, one of whom interacted in a nurturant and friendly way with a group of nursery school children, the other of whom did not. The two experimenters then performed some distinctively different sets of actions (including some aggressive actions), and the children were observed to see which of the two models they imitated. The findings were that the children more often imitated the model who had interacted nurturantly with them for all categories of behavior *except aggression*. Aggressive behavior was imitated regardless of the previously established relationship between the model and the child. This experiment would appear to suggest that while aggressive behavior on the part of screen characters might be fairly readily imitated by viewers, other categories of behavior would not be so easily copied from screen characters as they would be from real-life models to whom the child was emotionally attached. But this is speculation, and so far we have little direct information on the imitative learning of nonaggressive behavior from screen models. It would be reasonable to assume, however, that under proper conditions of motivation it does occur.

In the preceding discussion of the effects of the mass media upon aggressive behavior, we have focused upon the possible aggression-arousing effects of seeing fights and crimes on television. We have not mentioned the fact that screen stories frequently depict evildoers being punished, and sometimes show the serious consequences to others of antisocial behavior. Such scenes may well contribute to the moral education of the child; he is learning not only about aggression itself, but about the consequences of such behavior when it is directed toward antisocial ends. So it is probably not only the real-life restraints imposed upon aggression that limit the imitation of such behavior seen on television, but also the inhibitions acquired from the outcomes of the stories themselves; such inhibition would serve to limit the imitation of antisocial aggression, but not of prosocial aggression of the sort displayed by the "Western" hero, who is shown as being aggressive only in the service of "right" and "justice."

EFFECTS UPON MOOD AND DEFENSES

Being exposed to aggressive behavior enacted by heroes in the mass media may, of course, have other effects than arousing or shaping the viewer's specifically aggressive behavior. This point has been emphasized by Emery and Martin (1957), Australian investigators who have made an analysis of the nature of the identification that usually exists between a child viewer and the hero of a "Western" film. They hold that the boy viewer "is unconsciously living out his problems of controlling his asocial tendencies in a social environment that threatens to punish lack of control and rewards successful control." The classic Western depicts a struggle between good and evil. Emery showed boy subjects a "Western" in which the hero, during part of the film, allies himself with the forces of evil (which are depicted as of great strength). While the moral outcome of the film is successful, it is depicted as the result of a chance occurrence rather than the hero's possessing greater power than the power of the evil forces. The boys were given projective tests before and after seeing this film, in which they were asked to tell a story about a still picture showing a little boy sitting on a doorstep. After seeing the Western, the subjects depicted the little boy in the picture to be in worse circumstances; they showed him more often being the victim of circumstances beyond his own control; in short, the film appears to have increased the viewers' feelings of being surrounded by a "powerful and actively hostile environment."

R. J. Thomson (1959) also stresses that programs may have effects other than the direct transmission of certain action tendencies via imitation. Thomson was especially interested in the effects of viewing crime dramas, and he showed two such dramas to a group of teenage children in Melbourne, Australia, giving them projective tests subsequently to discover the effects of the viewing experience. He did not find any increases in manifestations of aggression or fear in the projective stories the children told following exposure to the crime programs. He did find evidence, however, of certain defensive reactions. While photographs taken of the audience during the showing of the programs did indicate that a considerable degree of tension was being built up in the viewers, the stories told afterward indicated a drop in the "general buoyancy level" (increase in depressive affect) —which the author takes to be an indicator of a "natural safeguard, operating to protect the typical adolescent crime drama audience from stress effects." It appears that there is a reaction to the intense emotions generated by crime shows, and the author suggests that one consequence of frequent viewing of such shows might be a fairly general repression or discounting of normal emotional reactions. He reports that frequent viewers of such shows "did not exhibit as high a degree of emotional responsiveness, either on their pre-film or post-film protocols," as infrequent viewers matched with them for relevant aspects of personality. He points to the danger that the crime-viewer might become relatively insensitive to the sufferings of others, and sterotyped in his reactions to real-life situations. However, Thomson does not provide us with any direct evidence on this point.

There is another indication in the literature of changes in "feeling tone" occurring as a consequence of TV-viewing: Himmelweit and associates (1958) report that adolescent girls whose families have television (and who tend to see many daytime serials) are more anxious about the future than a matched group of girls whose families do not have television. To quote these authors:

> The difficulties of adult life which form the principal theme of so many television plays seem to have influenced the adolescent viewers, making them more anxious than the controls about their competence in dealing with adult life, more reluctant to leave home and school, and more worried about going out to work and about marriage (p. 258).

The authors note that the adolescent children in homes with television do not differ from their matched controls in other indicators of emotional instability. Thus it appears unlikely that having anxious and tense children in the home was related to a family's decision to buy television when others of like income were not doing so. It becomes more plausible, then, to conclude that the greater anxieties of the TV-viewing adolescents can be traced directly to the effects of television, rather than to preexisting differences between the viewers and their controls, especially since the nature of these anxieties reflects the specific content of the programs these children so often see. Nevertheless, the causal connection cannot be completely pinned down in this research.

EFFECTS UPON ATTITUDES, VALUES, AND BELIEFS

In the early 1930's, as part of the series of studies entitled "Motion Pictures and Youth" (Payne Fund Studies), Peterson and Thurstone (1933) undertook to discover whether children's social attitudes could be influenced by movies. Some preliminary studies made in Chicago showed slight but not significant effects; subsequent studies were made in small towns where the children were more "naive," and it proved possible to change children's attitudes significantly toward war, toward minority racial and national groups, toward gambling, and toward capital punishment. Such changes could be brought about by single showings of certain pictures. For example, the film "Birth of a Nation" shifted a large group of children from the most favorable end to the most unfavorable end of a scale of attitudes toward the Negro. Effects were tested both immediately and after the passage of time, and the lasting nature of some of the effects was striking. For example, the effect of having seen "Son of the Gods" (a picture that depicted Chinese characters in an admirable light) could still be detected among high school students nineteen months after they had seen it: they still had a more favorable attitude toward Chinese people than students who had not seen the film.

More recently, Siegel (1958) demonstrated that second-grade children who heard three fifteen-minute "radio programs" about an aggressive taxicab driver expected taxi drivers in real-life situations similar to those depicted in the "program" to behave more aggressively than did children who heard programs about nonaggressive taxi drivers, but the effects did not spread to an expectation of aggressiveness from taxi drivers in all situations. This appears to show that mass media experiences can create a *limited* stereotype concerning an occupational group. But it should be noted that the occupational group chosen for study was one with which children had had little first-hand experience, and it does not follow that their attitudes could be so easily influenced with respect to more familiar occupations such as doctor or teacher.

There are documented instances, then, in which the formation of a particular attitude among children may be traced to a movie or radio program. If one considers the impact of the total exposure children have to the mass media, the effects on their attitudes ought to depend, among other things, on how consistent the values and stereotypes are which are being presented to them. If the media presented a wide range of values and attitudes, then the effects of different media experiences might cancel each other. Himmelweit and her colleagues (1958) approach this question through content analysis of a sample of television shows. They found the values to be remarkably consistent from show to show. They summarize their findings as follows:

> The world of television drama tends to be that of upper middle-class urban society. The occupations of people of this social level are depicted as worthwhile, while manual labor is presented as uninteresting. Television plays teach that self-confidence and toughness are needed to achieve success—goodness of character is not enough; that life is difficult, especially for women; that marriages are frequently unhappy, and parent-child relationships often strained. Events rarely turn out satisfactorily and virtue seldom brings happiness in its train. Violence is an inevitable part of life, and good people often resort to it (p. 17).

How much of this system of values "rubs off" on the young viewer? These investigators found some instances in which it did. It affected their wishful fantasies about occupations, for example, and their beliefs concerning the factors that make for personal success (self-confidence being more emphasized by the viewers). It increased their attention to the cues of status. Viewers were more likely than their controls to believe, for example, that "you can tell how important a man is from the way he is dressed."

Bailyn (1959) contributed to our knowledge on value-acquisition through her study of the relationship between the media-usage habits of fifth and sixth-grade children and certain of their cognitive characteristics. She thought it possible that one effect of high exposure to television, movies, and comic books would be to increase the stereotyping in children's thinking. By stereotyping, she meant the tendency to see things as all black or all white, and to ignore motivations as a basis for judging other people's actions. She did find that children who spent more time with the mass media were more stereotyped in their thinking. For example, high-exposure children were more likely to agree to these statements: "People are either all good or all bad," and "There are only two types of people in the world, the weak and the strong." Furthermore, when asked why some people tell lies, or why some people commit crimes, the high-exposure children were more likely to answer "because they are just naturally bad," while the low-exposure children would refer to specific motivational or environmental causes.

One faces the chicken-and-egg problem in interpreting these findings. Were high-exposure children more stereotyped because they had been influenced by the stereotyped nature of the stories they had so frequently encountered, or did they seek out unduly high levels of exposure to the media because their thinking was stereotyped in the first place? Bailyn attempted to answer this question by selecting a subsample of children and having them read a comic book under experimental conditions and testing them before and after. She found some increase in stereotyping (especially among children who normally did not see much of this sort of material) as a result of the reading. Hence, there are some grounds for believing that exposure to the pictorial media does bear some direct responsibility for building up stereotyped thinking in children. In the same way, Bailyn found some evidence that the pictorial media produce a belief that the world is a threatening place in which to live (although this correlate of high viewing frequency was found only among girls). This result is consonant with the findings by Emery and Martin (1957), Thomson (1959), and Himmelweit *et al.* (1958) reported above on feelings of depression and anxiety associated with heavy exposure to the media.

The effect of the media in producing stereotyped thinking is not unequivocal. Himmelweit and her colleagues found that their sample of "viewers" (by contrast with their controls) were *less* likely to make value judgments about minority groups, they shifted from describing such groups as "unhappy," or "swindlers," to delineating their objective characteristics ("They have dark skins," or "They don't believe in Christ"). At the same time there was an increase among the viewers in labeling the French as witty and gay, the Germans as vicious and arrogant—nationality stereotypes which were consonant with the way individuals with these national labels had been depicted on television.

Himmelweit and associates list the values which do *not* appear to be influenced by television, and it is instructive to keep this point in mind, for there is some danger that in listing the effects which have been found we should come to assume that the effects are more general than they are. In the British study there was, for example, little influence on the children's occupation plans, or on their expectations of getting married. From this and other findings, Himmelweit and associates offer the generalization that children are more likely to be influenced by the media the less complete their knowledge is from other sources. This view would be consistent with the Peterson and Thurstone (1933) experience: that social attitudes could be more easily influenced by movies in small towns, where the children had little personal experience with members of minority groups or with gambling, than would be true for urban children. While the point has not been fully demonstrated, it is reasonable to suppose that in value areas where the parents have strong, explicitly stated views, and where the parents serve as models for their children's actions, the media would have little effect. The values and attitudes which should be most vulnerable to media influence should be those concerning which the significant people in the child's life have not taken a stand. Furthermore, children in homes where the parents do not interact frequently with their children should be more susceptible to media influences than children whose relationship with their parents is more intense.

INDIVIDUAL DIFFERENCES IN SUSCEPTIBILITY TO INFLUENCE

It has been pointed out earlier that we should not expect all children to be influenced in the same degree by the mass media. In the first place, given equal opportunities, some children choose to spend much more time with the media than others do. In a few cases, a child's absorption in comic books and television is so great that it can best be described as an addiction; in other cases, children almost completely ignore these sources of entertainment. There has been a good deal of research on the correlates of the number of hours devoted to the media, and there is a good deal of uniformity in the findings. It has been repeatedly shown that the state of a child's emotional and social adjustment has a bearing upon his media usage. Maccoby (1954) found that children who were subject to many restrictions, who were treated punitively rather than warmly by their parents, spent more hours watching television; but this relationship held only for middle-class children: working-class children had a high level of viewing without regard to their relationship with their parents. Schramm and his colleagues (1961) replicated this finding. They had a measure of the degree of conflict between the child and his parents, and found that among families in the higher social strata the more the conflict the more the children watched television. Bailyn (1959) reports a similar finding for total usage of the pictorial media. Himmelweit and associates (1958) directed their attention to the children's relationships with age-mates, and found that it was the shy, withdrawn child who had few friends and felt insecure, who spent the most time watching television. We surmise, then, that for many children the pictorial media serve to provide an escape—escape from tension or escape from boredom—and the extent of their need for such escape will govern their viewing frequency. But there are other reasons for becoming a frequent viewer. For example, children are guided in this matter by their parents' example, and parents who view frequently tend to have children who do so also; hence, we see that in some instances it is closeness to a parent which leads to heavy viewing, in other instances it is distance and conflict.

The temperamental characteristics of the child seem to have a bearing on how much he views. Schramm and his colleagues (1961) report that children who are characterized by a high level of antisocial aggressive tendencies (as revealed by paper-and-pencil personality tests) are high users of television, movies, and comic books. (This finding was replicated for girls by Bailyn, 1959.) They also find that high users of these media prefer immediate gratification. According to their answers to questions on the subject, they tend to have a philosophy of "eat, drink and be merry." They more often agree, for example, with the statement "The best way to live is to enjoy today and not think about tomorrow." Schramm and his colleagues assume that children who are aggressive, or oriented toward immediate gratification, will choose to spend much time with the "fantasy" media (instead of more reality-oriented newspapers and books) because these media offer them immediately gratifying content. It seems possible, however, that at least to some extent, the cause and effect sequence may be running the other way. We grant that highly aggressive or immediate-pleasure-seeking children might be more motivated to seek out television, movies, and comics because of the high concentration of aggressive and sensational content; but once having done so, we suspect that the mass media may serve to reinforce, or augment, these preexisting temperamental tendencies.

It is likely that the child's choice of how many hours to devote to the media will be a determiner of their effect upon him. But the effects may be different upon different children who watch for the same number of hours, or indeed, who watch the same programs. The Rileys (1954) noted that children who do not have many friends among their age-mates will daydream about a program after it is over; the socially well-integrated child, on the other hand, will not use the program so much for escape (either during or after viewing), but will be more interested in its social utility, and will be more likely to get ideas from it for subsequent discussion or application with his friends. So the same material from the media may be put to different uses, depending on the needs of the viewer.

IMPLICATIONS FOR THOSE DEALING PROFESSIONALLY WITH CHILDREN

It appears clear from the foregoing summary of research findings that children's values, beliefs, and actions can be shaped to some degree through exposure to mass media. While we have long been aware that mass media in the form of visual aids are valuable instructional tools in the classroom (and recent work on school uses of instructional television strongly supports their effectiveness), it has not been clear whether the very large amounts of time children spent being *entertained* by the mass media had any consequences other than the pleasure they gave. We now know that they do. The nature of the effects depends upon many limiting conditions: on the nature of the individual child's temperament, intelligence and needs, and the quality of his personal adjustment; on the amount of information a child has, and the strength of his existing beliefs and values, before exposure to relevant mass media contents; and on the opportunities which occur in real life for the child to put into practice what he has learned from the mass media. But the impact of the media is real. What the child absorbs while he is being "entertained" he uses in the interpretation of his real-life experiences, and in preparing himself for roles that he will play in the future, as well as for immediate action. And the media may influence moods (for example, produce a mood of pessimism) or transmit pervasive beliefs (for example, that the world is a threatening place), as well as present bits of information or bits of action for imitation.

The findings summarized above have been predominantly negative in their implications concerning mass media effects. This has been partly due to the nature of the problems researchers have chosen to study. For example, the research on imitation of behavior depicted on the mass media has been confined almost entirely to the imitation of aggression; and in studying emotional effects, Thomson investigated the impact of *crime* dramas; so that any effects noted were, of course, much more likely to be in the direction of anxiety or depression than in the direction of increased optimism and gaiety. Quite possibly, studies of the after-effects of viewing some of television's popular family comedies would show increases in feelings of happiness and well-being, but no one has carried out such studies. Yet "bias" in the choice of research problems is not the entire explanation of the results. The work of Schramm and Himmelweit, to mention only two, was set up in such a way that the results could have shown television to be a strong positive stimulant in the intellectual growth of the child; and on the whole, their findings show that it has not proved to be so. It has not appreciably broadened children's knowledge or interests, at least not so far.

But this is not to say that it could not do so. Our review of the literature has shown that the kind of mass media fare children are exposed to does have an impact upon them. It follows from this that it ought to be possible to provide fare which would have a *different* impact, and perhaps a more constructive one. Would it not be possible, for example, to show children programs which would hold their interest and which would at the same time convey the feeling that the individual can take effective action in achieving his own destiny, rather than being a helpless pawn at the mercy of external (often malevolent) forces? Could not children's programs offer a wider range of issues and their solutions than the rather stereotyped fare now presented?

For people engaged in professional dealings with children, there would appear to be three implications of what has been said so far.

First: If a child becomes an addict of the pictorial mass media (movies, television, comic books), this is a dependable danger signal. There is a strong relationship between such addiction and problems of interpersonal adjustment, and for children who spend inordinate amounts of time with the pictorial media exploration of the possibility of therapeutic action would appear to be justified.

Second: The effects of the mass media in shaping values are subject to being counteracted, and perhaps nullified altogether, by teachings (explicit or otherwise) from the significant people in the child's life. If the beliefs and values being transmitted by the media are contrary in any instances to what the people responsible for a child's welfare would like to see him adopt, they can minimize the effects of the media through counter-training. Discussing with the child the implications of the values he is being exposed to, and making explicit the range of other possible value positions, should be useful means, in many instances, but the practitioner would have to make use of his knowledge of the individual child to decide how best to reach him.

Third: The nature of the contents offered to children on television and the other media are important elements in the influential environment which surrounds the child. People working professionally with children make it their business to do what they can to see that the conditions which affect the health, safety, and intellectual development of children are as wholesome as possible. They exert pressure when they can to have an overpass built over a dangerous road-crossing, or to see that children get inoculations, milk with school lunches, and so on. This public spirited pressure applied in the interests of children might well be extended to the mass media. The dangers of censorship are very real, and probably more would be lost than gained by the creation of a board of citizens who would insist on the deletion of this fight scene or that crime from the television screen (although a code governing what may be shown is necessary and desirable for the industry). But the nature of the material offered through the mass media is a product of the decisions of many people; some of these people are more concerned about the welfare of the child audience than others; public pressure serves to strengthen the hands of those who are so concerned. There are creative people in the mass media who could provide young audiences with a greater variety of programs, a less stereotyped kind of fare, than they are now getting; and people dealing professionally with children might well address themselves to the question of how they could help to support the efforts of these people.

REFERENCES

BAILYN, L. Mass media and children: a study of exposure habits and cognitive effects. *Psychol. Monogr.*, 1959, **73**, No. 1 (Whole No. 471).

BANDURA, A. & HUSTON, A. Identification as a process of incidental learning. *J. abnorm. soc. Psychol.*, 1961, **63**, 311–318.

BANDURA, A., ROSS, D., & ROSS, S. Transmission of aggression through imitation of aggressive models. *J. abnorm. soc. Psychol.*, 1961, **63**, 575–582.

BANDURA, A., ROSS, D., & ROSS, S. Imitation of film-mediated aggressive models. *J. abnorm. soc. Psychol.*, 1963, **66**, 3–11.

BERKOWITZ, L. *Aggression: a social-psychological analysis.* New York: McGraw-Hill, 1962.

BLUMER, H. & HAUSER, P. M. *Movies, delinquency, and crime.* New York: Macmillan, 1933.

CHARTERS, W. W. *Motion pictures and youth: a summary.* New York: Macmillan, 1933.

DOLLARD, J., DOOB, L. W., MILLER, N. E., MOWRER, O. H., & SEARS, R. R. *Frustration and aggression.* New Haven: Yale Univ. Press, 1939.

DYSINGER, W. S. & RUCKMIK, C. A. *The emotional responses of children to the motion picture situation.* New York: Macmillan, 1933.

EMERY, F. E. & MARTIN, D. *Psychological effects of the western film: a study in television viewing.* Melbourne: Dept. Audio-Visual Aids, Univ. of Melbourne, 1957.

FESHBACH, S. The drive reducing function of fantasy behavior. *J. abnorm. soc. Psychol.*, 1955, **50**, 3–11.

FESHBACH, S. The stimulating vs. cathartic effects of a vicarious aggressive activity. *J. abnorm. soc. Psychol.*, 1961, **63**, 381–385.

FURU, T. *Television and children's life.* Radio & Television Cultural Res. Inst., Japan Broadcasting Corp., 1962.

HIMMELWEIT, H. T., OPPENHEIM, A. N., & VINCE, P. *Television and the child.* Published for the Nuffield Foundation. New York, London, Ontario: Oxford Univ. Press, 1958.

LÖVAAS, O. I. Effect of exposure to symbolic aggression on aggressive behavior. *Child Developm.*, 1961, **32**, 37–44.

MACCOBY, E. E. Television: its impact on school children. *Publ. Opin. Quart.*, 1951, **15**, 421–444.

MACCOBY, E. E. Why do children watch television? *Publ. Opin. Quart.*, 1954, **18**, 239–244.

MACCOBY, E. E. & WILSON, W. C. Identification and observational learning from films. *J. abnorm. soc. Psychol.*, 1957, **55**, 76–87.

MACCOBY, E. E., WILSON, W. C., & BURTON, R. V. Differential movie-viewing behavior of male and female viewers. *J. Pers.*, 1958, **26**, 259–267.

MUSSEN, P. & RUTHERFORD, E. Effects of aggressive cartoons on children's aggressive play. *J. abnorm. soc. Psychol.*, 1961, **62**, 461–464.

PARKER, E. B. The effects of television on public library circulation. Paper read at the annual convention of the Pacific Chapter, Amer. Assn. Publ. Opin. Res., Stanford Univ., Stanford, Calif., 1963.

PETERSON, R. C. & THURSTONE, L. L. *Motion pictures and the social attitudes of children.* New York: Macmillan, 1933.

RILEY, M. W. & RILEY, J. W., JR. A sociological approach to communications research. In W. Schramm (Ed.), *The process and effects of mass communication.* Urbana: Univ. Illinois Press, 1954.

SCHRAMM, W., LYLE, J., & PARKER, E. B. *Television in the lives of our children.* Stanford, Calif.: Stanford Univ. Press, 1961.

SIEGEL, A. E. Film-mediated fantasy aggression and strength of aggressive drive. *Child Developm.*, 1956, **27**, 365–378.

SIEGEL, A. E. The influence of violence in the mass media upon children's role expectations. *Child Developm.*, 1958, **29**, 35–36.

THOMSON, R. J. *Television crime drama.* Melbourne: Dept. Audio-Visual Aids, Univ. of Melbourne, 1959.

U. S. SENATE, COMMITTEE ON THE JUDICIARY. *Comic books and juvenile delinquency.* Interim Senate Report No. 62, 84th Congress. Washington: U. S. Government Printing Office, 1955.

U. S. SENATE HEARINGS, SUBCOMMITTEE TO INVESTIGATE JUVENILE DELINQUENCY. *Hearings on television programs, June and October, 1954.* Washington: U. S. Government Printing Office, 1955.

Productive Thinking

JAMES J. GALLAGHER

University of Illinois

THIS CHAPTER is concerned with recent research on productive thinking in children below college age. The study of productive thinking has had an illustrious history extending back to the early philosophers and their attempts to understand thought processes through a study of logic. The names of the great men of psychology can be found who have struggled with these problems. From Dewey to Freud, from Galton to Hull—all of the giants have had something to say on how the human organism generates new ideas or performs analytical or creative operations.

In this section *productive thinking represents the result of the individual's operation upon information from internal or external sources in order to change it into some different product.* In this sense, it would include problem-solving, analytical and logical dimensions, as well as creative thinking.

This problem area of productive thinking has served as a theoretical proving-ground for many conflicts. The struggle between associationism and Gestalt psychology revolved around many issues, raised by antagonists such as Wertheimer (1945) and Thorndike (1932), on whether or not there was something called "insight," and on how problem-solving behavior actually took place.

Kohler (1925), Yerkes and Learned (1925), and others introduced the concept of the thinking animal. The distance between the mental processes of higher and lower organisms was debated. This debate has had recent echoes with investigators concerning themselves with the problem as to whether or not computers can think.

The approach to inner thought production through introspection was stressed by Freud and the psychoanalytic group interested in pathology. The study of how creative persons in various fields pursued their mental tasks occupied the attention of others (Patrick, 1935, 1937, 1938).

The field of child development, however, seemed to be more affected by theories related to personality or learning theory than to cognition. The child, far from being seen as "the father to the man" in cognitive research, was often ignored in favor of adult subjects, or was used in making comparisons with animals to determine continuity or discontinuity in the phylogenetic scale. Cognition was recognized as important mainly in the development of measures of intellectual abilities and their applications to the educational setting.

While there is a general recognition of the important role played by more basic information-processing skills, such as perception, language, memory, and concept formation, these will not be reviewed in this section. Furthermore, no historical treatment of the voluminous material available is attempted, since this has been adequately covered in other reviews such as Russell (1956), Duncan (1959), and Inhelder and Matalon (1960). Instead, more recent studies are reviewed that have some potential application to persons working with children.

CHANGING VIEWPOINTS

For more than a generation, the field of cognitive processes and productive thinking has been dominated by several main concepts regarding the development of intellectual processes.

1. *A valid I.Q. score was generally considered to measure practically all that was of importance in cognitive development.* Creative abilities, productive thinking, and problem-solving were all assumed to be more or less synonymous with I.Q. test performance. Only isolated skills such as musical talent or motor abilities were assumed outside its domain. While this idea was rarely stated in such bald form, the practical applications of the idea are all around us. The I.Q. score was made the predominant and often the only definition of mental retardation.

For many years the I.Q. score was the sole determining factor for the definition of gifted children. Arguments about the definition of giftedness usually revolved around whether a cut-off point should be placed at an I.Q. score of 125 or 130 or 140. Rarely was consideration given for the point of view that I.Q. scores might not be measuring all that was important in "giftedness."

Another major use of the I.Q. score was to define *underachievement.* If the child's achievement level did not reach a point comparable to his I.Q. score or to a formula combining I.Q. score and age, the child was considered to be an "underachiever." No such label could be applied unless one first assumed that the I.Q. score *should* be the major determinant of academic expectation.

2. *Intellectual development was considered to be mainly a process of maturation that would resist change except under extreme conditions.* A functional statement of this idea would be that I.Q. tends to be constant. Undue fluctuations from one I.Q. score to another in the same child were viewed

as evidence of technical problems of the instrument or the fact that the child was poorly motivated or emotionally disturbed at the time of test administration.

3. *Training of mental abilities was not considered to be possible.* The experimental work of Thorndike (1932) and others was used as proof that attempts to "train the mind" in formal disciplines were useless. The presumption of the heavy weighting of genetic factors in intelligence in the work of such men as Goddard (1914) also discouraged attempts at intellectual training.

These concepts are being modified on the basis of further experience. At a recent conference (Gallagher, 1963), 12 research scientists working in the field of gifted children and productive thinking accepted the following tenets as a basis for their philosophy regarding cognitive development:

1. Intellectual talent should be considered multidimensional. It needs to be, in some respects, redefined.

2. There exists a close relationship between motivation and personality variables, and the growth of intellectual abilities.

3. The development of intellectual talent is, to some unknown extent, capable of modification.

What has caused this shift in emphasis from one generation to another? Generally, three trends can be discerned: recognition of the limited validity of the I.Q. constancy notion, the development of specific interest areas, and recognition of the limitations of measuring instruments.

I.Q. Constancy

Concern over the validity of the "I.Q. constancy" concept has been heightened by the evidence of longitudinal studies following children from infancy to adulthood (Bayley, 1955). The reports of the Fels Research Institute project which systematically examined youngsters from a few months of age to ten years indicated that over 60 per cent of the sample fluctuated more than 15 I.Q. points over this period of time (Sontag, Baker, and Nelson, 1958).

Perhaps more important, however, was the discovery of factors influencing consistent increases or decreases in I.Q. over time. Sontag, Baker, and Nelson (1955) studied the 35 students who gained the most I.Q. points on re-tests and the 35 who lost the most in a longitudinal study. They found the "ascenders" to be characterized by independence, mastery, and an attitude that competition was emotionally comforting.

The I.Q. "descenders" were characterized by lack of parental love, dependence, and an attitude that competition was not emotionally comforting. A subgroup of these "descenders"—those who seemed to go down in

I.Q. scores relatively late in the developmental period—were all girls. These girls were characterized by the attitude that the role of femininity was, in itself, anxiety-reducing, so that high school attainment or performance was not necessary for anxiety reduction.

Kagan, Sontag, Baker, and Nelson (1958) found that the children in the Fels research project who consistently improved in I.Q. showed more tendencies in their fantasies and story-telling to indicate need for achievement, curiosity, and lack of passivity than did groups of children who consistently decreased in I.Q. scores. This close relationship between motivation and personality characteristics and the developing cognitive abilities is indicated also in the cognitive style studies which will be discussed later.

Development of Special Interest Areas

Another factor relevant to the change in orientation in the study of productive thinking is the development of special areas of interest and investigation such as *learning, problem-solving, creativity, cognitive style,* and *intelligence tests*. Many of these special areas have become almost separate fields of study in which very little attempt is made at cross-reference from one to the other.

One example of how this fragmentation of the cognitive area can cause confusion has been the studies comparing "intellectual behavior" (as measured by I.Q. test scores) and "creativity." Torrance (1962b), Holland (1961), and Getzels and Jackson (1962), all of whom studied groups of highly intelligent children, found only a small relationship or correlation between "intelligence" and "creativity."

It appears that above a certain level, perhaps the upper 10 per cent of the population, I.Q. scores do not necessarily predict greater creative abilities as measured by commonly used tests. The intelligent lay person may ask, however, "Isn't 'creativity' intelligent behavior? Isn't it, in fact, the highest manifestation of intellectual behavior? How can there be no relationship between the two?"

Sigel (1963) commented on these seemingly small relationships found between scores on creativity tests and intelligence tests:

> It may well be that the reason IQ and creativity are not frequently related is just because we have used the IQ in a narrow restricted way. . . . Such findings are essentially artifacts of our test construction (p. 55).

Measuring Instruments and Their Power to Define

One of the crucial ideas presented here is the important role played by measuring instruments. No matter how complex the formal definition of the thinking processes, in the final analysis they are defined operationally by the measuring instruments used in the research. Thus "intelligence" becomes Stanford Binet I.Q. score; "creativity" becomes the production of clever plot titles to a given story; and "problem-solving" becomes the ability to traverse a maze successfully.

For this reason, the drawing of interpretations or inferences from research studies in such complex areas as problem-solving, productive thinking, or creativity is fraught with peril. One serious problem is determining whether the task chosen by the investigator really is representative of the characteristic he is trying to measure as noted above.

This task-sampling problem is the reason that careful consideration of large numbers of studies using large numbers of different tasks is needed before one draws even tentative inferences. While the experimenter deals with small and sometimes isolated pieces of behavior, the persons interested in the application of research evidence, parents, teachers, and the like, must deal with the whole person in a complex environment. Procedures that seem to work very well in a carefully defined experimental situation might not work well at all in the more amorphous environment of the classroom, the home, or the clinic.

TABLE 1. DIFFERENCES BETWEEN LABORATORY EXERCISES AND
REALITY IN PRODUCTIVE THINKING

Laboratory	*Reality*
Problem selected for subject.	Problem must be chosen from many other stimuli competing for attention of the subject.
Extraneous stimuli reduced or systematically introduced.	Extraneous pressures and distractions randomly presented.
Problem chosen so it can be solved in a short period of time.	Difficult problems often extend for weeks and months before solution.
Emotional involvement limited.	Emotional involvement often severe, affecting self-status, livelihood, family, professional career, etc.

Table 1 summarizes some of the main reasons that caution needs to be invoked in transferring laboratory research results into real life. As the table indicates, there are a number of important factors present in reality situations that are not present, or may even be systematically excluded, in the laboratory environment.

One of the most important differences between life problem-solving and laboratory problem-solving is the choice of the problem itself. In the laboratory, the experimenter has already selected the problem to be presented to the subject. In real life, the problem to be worked on often must be chosen from many other problems competing for the attention of the subject. The individual thus must exercise judgment in the choice of the problem to be attacked. Such judgment is not often required in a laboratory setting.

The championship golfer, by tradition, is allowed complete silence in which to concentrate upon his putt. Few other positions in life allow such luxury. Productive thinking often has to occur in the face of a multiplicity of distractions. The ability to screen out extraneous stimuli can be an important factor governing productivity. The experimenter is usually as solicitous of his subjects as the "galleryite" is of his favorite golfer. Noise is reduced; lighting is controlled; and anything that would interfere with the subject's concentrating on the task at hand is eliminated. Thus a subject may perform well in such a situation but becomes psychologically unglued when he has to solve problems or think creatively with auto horns, crying babies, bill collectors, and other miscellaneous stimuli intruding on his attention.

Whether one is attempting to measure creativity or problem-solving, another serious limitation of the laboratory is that the task must be of relatively short duration. This is in marked contrast to the difficult problems in life situations which can often extend for weeks and months before being solved. Therefore, the ability to persist in the face of chronically unsolved problems becomes a necessity in real life but may not be necessary for high performance in short-term laboratory situations.

Finally, and perhaps most important, is the ability of the effective problem solver or creative individual in real life to operate efficiently often under constant and severe emotional pressure. His work is often done with the very real threat that poor performance will affect his earning power, self-esteem, social status, and professional career. Even in laboratory situations where stress is deliberately provoked, it is not, and cannot be, of the magnitude and scope of the real-life situation.

For all of these reasons, caution is required in transferring the results of "problem-solving" or "creativity" from the limited experimental setting to more complex situations. With all of these problems it is fair to ask, "Wouldn't it be better to do research in a setting closer to reality such as in the neighborhood or in the classroom?" Some of the research reported below makes beginning attempts in this direction. The difficulty here is that the researcher loses control over the multitude of variables that seem to be fluctuating wildly before him and this lack of environment control makes statements on cause and effect very difficult, if not impossible.

Recognition of these two major difficulties, the translation of laboratory results to real life and the establishment of antecedent-consequent relationships in the observation studies, can do much to help the reader understand the problems involved in attempting to translate *science* into *service*.

THE MODEL BUILDERS

A certain disdain for theory that was not based on readily available empirical findings could be noted in American child development and psychology in preceding decades. Only recently has the need been recognized for comprehensive theoretical models that can provide a framework for conceptualizing. Several different approaches have placed an indelible mark upon our present view of cognitive processes. One is presented by the Swiss psychologist, Jean Piaget, another by an American statistician and psychologist, J. P. Guilford, and a third by computer specialists, Newell, Shaw, and Simon.

Piaget

Piaget's (1930, 1947, 1954) contributions extend over three decades but he has had a meaningful impact on American thought mainly in the last half of this period. The delay in Piaget's impact was due partly to the well-known American aversion to reading in a foreign language and partly due to Piaget's casual approach to the statistics and research design that Americans felt were the *sine qua non* of the serious research person. Piaget's theories which carefully delineate various developmental stages in cognition are reviewed effectively in a recent volume by Hunt (1961).

Hunt identifies five main themes that have dominated Piaget's theoretical formulations:

1. Continuous and progressive changes take place in the structures of behavior and thought in the developing child.
2. Successive structures make their appearance in a fixed order.
3. The nature of accommodation (adaptive change to outer circumstances) suggests that the rate of development is, to a considerable degree, a function of the child's encounters with his environment.
4. Thought processes are conceived to originate through a process of internalizing actions. Intelligence increases as thought processes are loosened from their bases in perception and action and thereby become reversible, transitive, associative, and so on.
5. A close relationship exists between thought processes and properties of formal logic.

Among the more striking implications of these major principles abstracted from Piaget's lifetime of investigation are the potential modifiability of intelligence (point 3 above), the ability to locate a child in a given stage of development such as "concrete operations" (point 1), the opportunity to plan methods for stimulating cognitive abilities based on the fixed nature of the appearance of stages (point 2), and the careful analysis of the logic of thought (point 5).

Bruner has made one such application by maintaining that the child in the intuitive phase of concrete operations (approximately ages four to eight) is capable of grasping many of the basic ideas of mathematics, the sciences, the humanities, and the social sciences. Bruner (1960, p. 35) defines an operation as "a means of getting data about the real world into the mind and there transforming them so that they can be organized and used selectively in the solution of problems." The apparent mistake of past generations of teachers was to assume that the child had to be able to present a formal structure of thought (for example, the formulation of a proof for a geometric theorem) in order to demonstrate his grasp of the concept. The child in the stage of concrete operations cannot give a formal organization of complex theoretical ideas, but he *can* solve many problems depending upon such ideas.

Thus the child of seven or eight may well be able to understand the basic principle of *conservation* and correctly answer questions about it or solve problems based on it. No matter how the shape of a plastic ball may be changed, or how many pieces it may be broken into, the child can steadfastly maintain that the weight of the parts remains the same as the weight of the whole. It may be too much for him to realize that he is maintaining the general rule:

$$A + (B + C) = (A + B) + C$$

but he is showing an intuitive understanding of order in the physical world. Cronbach (1963) suggests that it is the function of the school curriculum to teach these basic concepts, or the basic structure of the physical and social world, at different levels as the child's intellectual development progresses. This includes teaching such mathematical concepts as *probability* (Page, 1959) and *set theory* (Suppes, 1960), and such physical constructs as *systems* (Karplus, 1962) and properties such as *space, time,* and *measurement* to elementary school children (Atkin and Wyatt, 1962).

Piaget's theories have been applied more to the field of problem-solving and analytic thinking than to creativity. The systematic development of his ideas may well rescue the field of problem-solving from the scattered appearance seen by Duncan (1959) in a recent review:

The field of problem solving is poorly integrated. The reasons for this seem to be the use of a great variety of tasks to provide problems, the frequent use of unanalyzed and nondimensionalized variables, the lack of agreed upon taxonomy and, to some extent, the failure to relate data to other data or theory (p. 426).

In a similar review Corman (1958) commented that the lack of agreement on definition between investigators was so severe that he could only conclude that "Problem solving meant the behaviors that researchers, who say that they are studying problem solving, study."

Guilford

While Piaget has been interested in the developmental nature and process of cognition, Guilford has placed his emphasis upon individual differentiation of cognitive skills (Guilford, 1956, 1959). His familiar *structure of intellect* is shown in Figure 1. This model was built, to a large extent, on

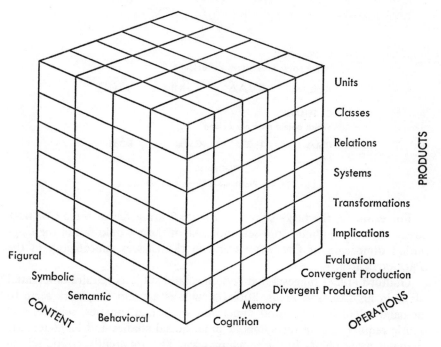

FIGURE 1.

Theoretical Model for the Complete "Structure of Intellect"

Data from Project on Aptitudes of High-level Personnel, Department of Psychology, University of Southern California, June, 1960.

factor analytic studies on adults but recently Guilford has included junior high school students in his groups (Guilford, Merrifield, and Cox, 1961).

No doubt some of the popularity of Guilford's model has been due to the attempt to encompass all of cognitive behavior in one systematic framework, instead of investigating a fragment of cognitive behavior such as "rigidity" or "fluency."

As indicated in Figure 1, Guilford sees three major dimensions of the intellect:

CONTENT—the medium in which thought takes place.

OPERATIONS—the particular mental operation or process performed on the material.

PRODUCTS—the results of the Operation on the particular Content dimensions.

A. FIGURAL
Which figure does not belong?

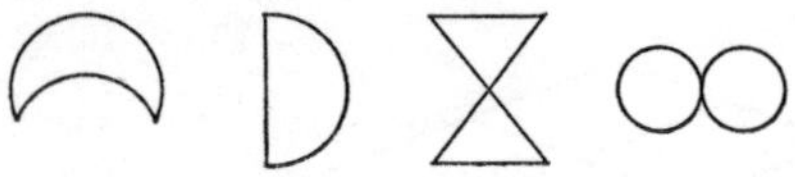

B. SYMBOLIC
Which letter group does not belong?

XECM   PVAA   QXIN   VTRO

C. SEMANTIC
Which object does not belong?

CLAM   TREE   OVEN   ROSE

FIGURE 2.

Classification Problems in Three Content Areas

For example, the tasks shown in Figure 2 are given in three CONTENT areas: figural, symbolic, and semantic. All of these would fall in the Cognition dimension of OPERATIONS and in the Classes subcategory in the PRODUCTS area.

Guilford (1958) suggests that certain school subjects require differential skills in his CONTENT areas. Subjects such as art and shopwork seem to demand talent in the figural dimension while mathematics, science, and music require skill in the symbolic area. Social studies and language arts demand more ability in the semantic area. The apparently erratic school performance of individual children might be profitably reexamined to see if their poor work could be explained by a weakness in one or more of the content areas.

Most of the current applications of Guilford's theories have come from the OPERATIONS dimension, with particular stress placed on the divergent production area. This is due, in part, to an assumed relationship between creativity and divergent production. Guilford refers to *divergent thinking* as the generation of new information out of known information where there is variation of thinking in different directions and where a variety of responses is the rule.

Some of the more common tests used to measure this variation are:

Intellectual fluency—measured by the number of answers given to questions such as "How many different ways can you think of for using a brick?"

Sensitivity to problems—measured by the answers to such questions as "What would happen if everyone in the world would suddenly become deaf?"

Originality—measured by the number of unusual or clever titles given to short stories.

Spontaneous flexibility—measured by the number of category shifts made to questions such as "How many different ways can water be made to work for you?"

A factor of divergent thinking has also been noted in similar studies by Flanagan and associates (1962), McGuire and associates (1961), and Kaya (1960). Little use has yet been made of the PRODUCTS dimension of this model. While Piaget's theory has been applied in the area of problem-solving, most of the Guilford concepts have been used to study creative thinking. Guilford's tests, or adaptations of his tests, are often used to distinguish "creative" from "noncreative" students. Again we can observe the importance of the measuring instrument as a shaping force in research.

Creative process. Those who create, and those who study creative persons, practically all agree that there is a process or sequence of stages through which the creator passes in his production. These conclusions are based on the retrospective analyses of creative persons and on the observations of creative persons at work. While many different terms are used to describe these stages—Russell (1956) presents nine different versions of the stages by nine different researchers—those suggested by Wallas (1926) probably have received the most widespread usage. He observed four main stages in the creative process as follows:

1. *Preparation.* This is the stage in which the problem is investigated from all directions and is primarily a problem-identification and fact-gathering period.

2. *Incubation.* In this stage, the person is not consciously thinking about the problem. There is some kind of internal process of associating new in-

formation with past information. Some type of reorganization of the information seems to be going on without the individual being directly aware of it.

3. *Illumination.* This is the stage during which the "happy idea" occurs. It has been referred to as the "Aha Phenomenon." In this stage, the creator suddenly sees the idea, concept, or solution to the problem.

4. *Verification.* This is the stage in which the idea, which has been obtained through the first three stages, is put to the test to see whether or not it has validity.

There is general agreement that these stages are not discrete and overlap one another, and that conscious effort alone cannot produce creative achievements (Stein and Heinze, 1960).

TABLE 2. DIFFERENT EXPECTATIONS FOR DIFFERENT STAGES
OF THE CREATIVE PROCESS[a]

Stages of Creative Process	Expected Form	Predominant Thinking Operation	Personality Factor or Attitude Required
Preparation	Neat Well Organized Well Stated	Cognitive Memory	Studiousness Sustained Attention
Incubation Illumination	Sloppy Often Confused Incoherent	Divergent Thinking	Intellectual Freedom Risk Taking Tolerance of Failure and Ambiguity
Verification	Neat Well Organized Clearly Stated	Convergent Thinking Evaluative Thinking	Intellectual Discipline Following Logical Sequence

[a] Reprinted from Gallagher, J. J. *Teaching the gifted child.* Boston: Allyn and Bacon, 1964.

One speculative application of the Guilford model has been made by Gallagher (1964) who has presented a concept of the different types of thinking and different personality factors that seem to be needed for the various stages of creative thinking, suggested by Wallas. (See Table 2.) The requirements for the first and last stages of *preparation* and *verification* are easily recognized. They require memory and close attention to logical sequences and evaluation. This is the type of thinking expected in our highly intelligent students. Yet for the stages of *incubation* and *illumination*, there is apparently a quite different kind of thinking required. Here divergent thinking becomes important and with it the accompanying characteristics of risk taking, tolerance of ambiguity, and the willingness to take a flyer on unusual ideas come into play. This would seem to represent, in other terms, Kris's (1952) "regression in the service of the ego." There is such a contrast, and even contradiction, between the characteristics demanded of the different stages, that it is an extraordinary person who can deliberately turn the necessary cognitive styles on and off at will. Yet it would seem that attempts at training persons in creative performance must, at the very least, help persons become aware of the stages and the various demands at each level.

Computer Programming and Model Building

The theoretical models introduced in this field often owe their development to some specific methodology. Much of Piaget's model seems to be based on concepts derived from systematic logic, while Guilford's structure of intellect owes much of its present status to factor analytic methodology. A third model developed to explain productive thinking has been presented by Newell, Shaw, and Simon (1962) and is based upon the technology of the digital computer and the construction of programs for that computer. These authors believe that it is possible to use, as a basis for generating a model of thinking behavior, a kind of computer programming which simulates problem-solving.

As illustrations of the productive thinking potential of computers, the authors have developed the following programs:

1. *The logic theorist.* This is a program capable of discovering proofs for theorems in elementary symbolic logic.

2. *The chess player.* This program solves chess problems by using techniques and processes which resemble, more or less closely, the techniques or processes used by humans.

3. *Musical composition.* Computer programs that can compose music for string quartets have been written and executed on ILLIAC (a digital computer at the University of Illinois).

4. *Design of electric motors.* In this program, the computer not only makes the calculations needed in the designing process but carries out the analysis itself and makes the decisions that were formerly the province of engineers.

As an example of how computer-based programming can simulate productive thinking, the authors (Newell, Shaw, and Simon, 1958) stored the axioms of *Principia Mathematica*, the classic work of Whitehead and Russell, and presented to the machine the first 53 theorems in the order presented by Whitehead and Russell. With this particular program, and the order of presentation of problems, the *logic theorist* was able to *prove* 73 per cent of the theorems presented. Such performance in a child, adolescent, or adult would be regarded as the highest level of productive thinking. The computer programming can also simulate "insight" if it is defined as lack of trial and error and sudden solution of a problem. The lack of a developmental process in the programming similar to that found in children, makes for unknown differences in the analogy between computers and the developing child. While it is not to be expected that there is a one-to-one relationship between the computer operation and human behavior, it seems quite likely that a number of interesting hypotheses can be generated through this particular methodology.

An example of a possible avenue of investigation with many applications is the realization, derived from attempts at programming, of the important role evaluative thinking plays in productive thought. In many instances, such as chess playing or in deriving proofs for theorems, there are an astronomical number of possible solutions that the computer could explore. The important aspect of programming then lies in giving instructions to the computer as to which of the solutions can be discarded as worthless and which need further consideration. Is this also an important aspect of productive thinking in human beings? The sheer generation of unique ideas may not be productive unless accompanied by an evaluative component which enables the individual to select the ones most appropriate for the particular problem or situation.

FACILITATING AND INHIBITING CONDITIONS

In any complex sample of human behavior, as productive thinking certainly is, it makes little sense to ask whether intelligence, personality, social adjustment, or attitude might influence productive performance. It is more realistic to ask to what extent all of these factors relate to it, and to each other. Barron and Roe (1958) presented a committee report at a research conference on scientific talent, suggesting that the important attributes of scientifically creative persons could be found in four general areas: intellectual aptitude, temperament, motivation (including values), and personal history.

Such a hypothetical multivariate situation is given in simplified form in Figure 3. Productive thinking is considered a resultant of the operation of various factors in the motivational, personality, and cognitive areas operating in different environmental situations.

If Figure 3 is a reasonably pertinent model, then there are a large number of different patterns of intellect, motivation, personality, and environment

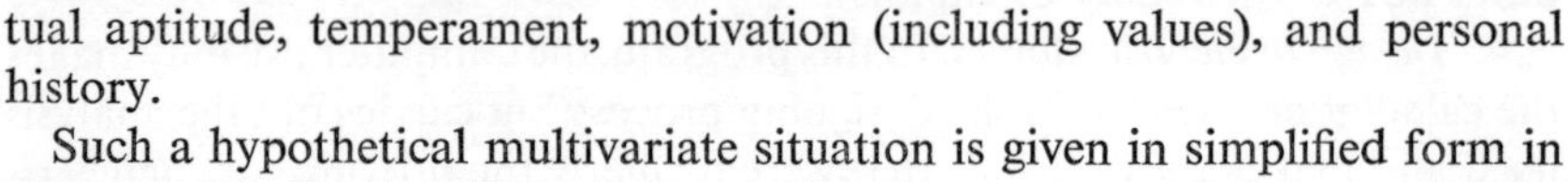

PRODUCTIVE THINKING ⇄ Motivational Factors $f(A)(B)(C)\ldots \left(\begin{matrix}+\\ or\\ -\end{matrix}\right)$ Personality Factors $f(F)(G)(H)\ldots \left(\begin{matrix}+\\ or\\ -\end{matrix}\right)$ Cognitive Abilities $f(J)(K)(L)\ldots \left(\begin{matrix}+\\ or\\ -\end{matrix}\right)$ Environmental Situations $f(P)(Q)(R)\ldots \left(\begin{matrix}+\\ or\\ -\end{matrix}\right)\ldots$

FIGURE 3.

Theoretical Concept of Factors Influencing Productive Thinking that could lead to productive thinking. For one individual a heavy weighting of motivational factors might overcome an indifferent environment or for another, a good environment and intellect could compensate for some negative personality factors. Such a general formulation makes it easier to see the folly of searching for the one road to productive thinking, or worse, trying to force young minds to follow the one pattern that is believed to lead to creative thinking.

Personality

What is the role played by personality in the generation of productive thinking? This question often stems from observation of the conjunction of creativity and emotional disturbance in such noted persons as Poe, Van Gogh, and Wilde.

A glance at any list of creative persons leaves little or no doubt that emotional disturbance can be an accompanying factor and, indeed, sometimes seems to be a causal factor in the creative production of a particular individual. On the other hand, few authorities in the field today would accept the extreme view of Bergler (1947) concerning the inevitable neuroticism of the creative person. "I have never encountered a normal writer, neither in my office nor in private life, nor in studying life history of writers. I doubt that anyone has ever met such a phenomenon as a normal writer."

Rogers (1959), speaking from the psychotherapeutic standpoint, gives a description of constructive creativity which also bears a strong resemblance to the productive cognitive styles discussed below. He identifies three inner conditions: (a) an openness to experience which includes a lack of rigidity and a tolerance of ambiguity, (b) an internal locus of evaluation which is in terms of one's own needs and not dependent on outside valuations, and (c) the ability to experiment with concepts, to shape wild hypotheses, and so forth.

Distinctive attitude and personality constellations have been noted in successful persons in various occupations. Terman (1954) found that there were important differences between the scientists and nonscientists in his group of 800 gifted men. One major dimension discovered was sociability, with the scientists showing significantly less sociability than the nonscientists. The desire for social interaction extends back into childhood and perhaps plays a central role in the choice of the area and occupation to be followed. Roe (1953) found similar distinctions in personality and attitude characteristics in the different occupational groups she studied. McClelland (1962) also has summarized a long list of characteristics distinguishing the creative physical scientist.

The forty-year longitudinal research of Terman and his associates on gifted children (1947, 1959) has added additional information on the personality characteristics which differentiate successful from nonsuccessful persons in a number of different career fields. They compared the 150 most successful with the 150 least successful men (chosen from an original group of children of 140 Binet I.Q. and above) as measured by judges' ratings of performance in adulthood. Self-ratings, together with the ratings of wives and parents, consistently identified four distinguishing characteristics. The successful men were superior on ratings of self-confidence, perseverance, integration to goals, and absence of inferiority feelings. Of particular importance from a developmental standpoint is that these personality and motivational characteristics were observably different in these two groups even as early as preadolescence.

One personality construct which relates the creative process to emotional life is the psychoanalytic notion of "regression in the service of the ego" (Kris, 1952). This term refers to a temporary, partially controlled use of primitive and nonlogical methods of thinking in the earlier stages of the creative process. This reverting back to primitive processes is reported both by the creative producer and by observers of the creative process (Stein and Heinze, 1960). What is accomplished by such regression? One important aspect of the earlier, more childlike, production is the lack of, or suspension of, critical judgment for a period of time. This allows greater freedom for the individual to explore associations or combinations of ideas which seem illogical or unrelated. If he applied a normal yardstick of evaluative thinking, he might reject some combinations. Yet one of these unusual combinations may well provide the basic material for the creative product.

Case histories of creative persons seem to indicate that the lack of repression and their ability to regress or become more childlike or become more naive *temporarily*, in the middle of the creative process, is of great usefulness. The possession of these personality characteristics is not without disadvantages. While repression when used as a defense mechanism is damaging to the creative process, since it cuts off a source of ideational supply, it often serves as a source of great comfort to human beings. The ability to shut out painful experiences, such as a horrifying battle scene, a memory of one's past inadequacies, or of destructive family quarrels, helps to reduce anxiety. These persons who lie open and naked before such past experiences and cannot shut them out, can use them for creative expression but also suffer again the pain they once delivered.

MacKinnon (1962), in summarizing research on creative architects, mathematicians, writers, and research workers, emphasized the role played by personality characteristics.

. . . What seemed to characterize the creative person—and this is especially so for the artistically creative—is a relative absence of repression and suppression as mechanisms for the control of impulse and imagery. Repression operates against creativity . . . because it makes unavailable to the individual large aspects of his own experience, particularly the life of impulse and experience which gets assimilated to the symbols of aggression and sexuality. . . .

It is the creative person's openness to experience and his relative lack of self-defensiveness that makes it possible for him to speak frankly and critically about his childhood and family, and equally openly about himself and his problems as an adult (p. 16).

Cognitive Styles

A different approach to the link between personality factors and productive thinking is found in the recent rebirth of interest in cognitive style. The cognitive style studies are concerned with the characteristic way in which an individual approaches his environment. A number of investigators have observed two distinctly different patterns or strategies which begin in childhood and extend to all aspects of life. One of these patterns is characterized by freedom and striving for expression, the other by caution and concern for the opinions of others.

TABLE 3. DIFFERENT LABELS FOR SIMILAR COGNITIVE STYLES

Investigator	Productive	Nonproductive
Getzels and Jackson (1962)	"High Creative"	"High I.Q."
Witkin and associates (1962)	Field Independent	Field Dependent
Schachtel (1959)	Allocentric	Autocentric
Maslow (1956)	Growth	Defense

Table 3 indicates the different terms that various investigators have used to describe these two approaches. Getzels and Jackson (1962) report some of their distinctions between "high creative" and "high I.Q." adolescents. The term "high creative" refers to students selected because they were in the top 20 per cent on creativity tests *but not* on I.Q. scores and "high I.Q." refers to students selected because they were in the top 20 per cent of the group in I.Q. scores *but not* on creativity scores. They point out that "Whatever terms are used, it is clear that one process represents intellectual acquisitiveness and conformity, the other, intellectual inventiveness and innovation. One focuses on knowing what is already discovered, the other focuses on discovering what is yet to be known" (p. 14).

Witkin and associates (1962) used the terms "field dependent" and "field independent" to describe what seems to be a very similar differentiation. Their discoveries stem from experiments in perception in which they constructed a "rod-and-frame" test. A rod is attached to a frame in such a way that both parts can move independent of one another. The frame can be tilted at various angles and the subject is asked to place the rod in a vertical position. Witkin and his associates found that certain individuals were strongly influenced by the frame position in their attempt to place the rod vertically. They found further that people who characteristically performed poorly on this task also had other consistent cognitive and personality traits and concluded that this "field dependent" behavior was part of an entire pattern and style of life.

Witkin and associates describe the "field dependent" people as follows:

> These people are likely to change their stated views on a particular social issue in the direction of the attitudes of an authority. . . . Their impressions of people are usually based on the physical characteristics these people show and the actions they engage in. . . . When shown a TAT picture that portrays an aggressive act, "field dependent" people are likely to give immediate expression to the ideas and feelings of aggression stimulated by the picture (1962, p. 3).

The "field independent" person reacts with more autonomy but not necessarily with less pathology, since the opposite of the extreme dependence is complete isolation. The characteristic of "field independence" appears developmental in nature, with younger children being much more "field dependent" than older children.

Schachtel's conception of *autocentric* closely approximates many of the elements of Witkin's term of "field dependence." He complains that psychoanalytic personality theory is based primarily on the idea that persons are motivated entirely by efforts to reduce tension. While this is characteristic of the *autocentric* person, many of the activities of the *allocentric* person seem devoted to the sustaining of tension. Schachtel maintains that in the autocentric person "*Hope* is . . . an expectation of, and wish for, magic change to be brought about by some external agency or event, without one's own effort" (Schachtel, 1959, p. 37).

In contrast, the *allocentric* person strives toward experience, and rewards of experience. As such, he can take a large amount of unpleasant experience, such as a child will take in falling while trying to learn to walk, without its diminishing his motivation for the experience itself.

Maslow (1956) sees two opposing characteristics of *defense* and *growth* in the individual. One set of forces clings to safety and defensiveness and is "afraid to take chances, afraid to jeopardize what he already has, afraid of independence, freedom, separation." The other set of forces drives toward "wholeness of self and uniqueness of self, toward confidence in the face of the external world, at the same time he can accept his deepest real unconscious Self." As Maslow conceptualizes it, life is a long series of decision-making situations in which one must choose between these alternate modes of performance. To use his exact words, "Safety has both anxiety and delights; growth has both anxiety and delights." While it can be noted that the conceptions of Getzels and Jackson and Witkin and his colleagues are based mainly on cognitive constructs and Schachtel's and Maslow's are based on personality characteristics, they all appear to be perceiving the same basic patterns from different points of view.

A number of other theoretical formulations touch closely on these modes of behavior. Festinger (1957) suggests that one of the predominant motivations of the individual is for self-consistency and the reduction of "cognitive dissonance." A possible hypothesis can be formulated that the individual who is "field independent," or "high creative," or "allocentric," or motivated toward "growth" is able to sustain a condition of *cognitive dissonance*, which is anxiety-producing, much longer than the person whose predominant mode of action is "defense," "field dependent," "autocentric," of "high I.Q."

Maw and Maw (1962) found that children with high ratings on curiosity indicated a preference for unbalanced and unfamiliar designs when presented with a series of paired figures. They also found (1961) that children high on curiosity retained more information about a story read to them than did a group of children, matched on I.Q., who were rated low on curiosity.

Haggard (1957) has pointed out that certain styles may result in differential performance on various school subjects. The conforming and anxious child seems more likely to be superior in such well-defined areas as spelling and language, but not in areas such as mathematics where the more stable and well-adjusted student seems to excel.

The study of cognitive styles highlights the important interrelationships between cognition and personality. Whenever the emphasis is on production rather than potential, both cognition and personality seem to be important predictors of thinking performance.[1]

Social Environment

To what extent is the productive thinking of the child influenced by his environment? In this case, environment can be viewed as his family, his peers, his school, and the total culture in which he lives.

---

[1] The study of decision-making processes or strategies has been stimulated by developments in games theory (Luce and Raiffa, 1957) but has been used in psychological research mainly in simple perceptual tasks. Some exceptions to this have been the work of Bruner, Goodnow, and Austin (1956) and Atkinson (1957), but generally the potential of this approach has not been fully realized.

Family. The family would seem to be one important influence in the development of cognitive styles or personality factors which remain consistent over time, and affect many levels of the individual's performance. Getzels and Jackson (1961) examined the families of "high creative" and "high I.Q." adolescents and found results confirming their hypothesis.

> The overall impression of the high I.Q. family is one in which individual divergence is limited and risks minimized; the overall impression of the high creative family is one in which individual divergence is permitted and risks are accepted (p. 359).

Witkin and associates (1962) also have found relationships between mother-child interaction consistent with the "field dependence-field independence" continuum. The mothers of field dependent children had the kind of relationship with their children that tended to inhibit the children's progress toward differentiation; mothers of children with a more analytical field approach interacted with their children in a way that tended to foster the development of differentiation in their children.

These authors also report an earlier study by Seder (1957), who found more coerciveness and fewer opportunities for independent behavior in the families of "field dependent" children. Similar results have been obtained on college age populations (Bieri, 1960; Mussen and Kagan, 1958).

Peers. Torrance (1960b) established a laboratory situation for studying the peer pressures on children who score high on creativity tests. In each of 25 groups of five children apiece, grade levels second through sixth, one of the five members was a high scorer on creativity tests. The groups were given the task of discovering a scientific principle through the manipulation of a collection of science toys.

Torrance found evidence of pressure against the most creative member in each of the groups. A majority of the most creative children initiated more ideas than any other member of the group, but only one-fourth of the other group members felt that the creative person was making the most valuable contribution to the group's performance. Torrance also found tendencies for groups to develop a repertoire of techniques for controlling the most creative members. Such techniques of control included: open aggression or hostility, criticism, rejection and/or ignoring, use of organizational machinery to limit scope of operation, and imposing sanctions.

Torrance (1960c), in another experiment, chose the most creative boy and the most creative girl out of 23 classrooms on the basis of his battery of tests of creative thinking. These children were distinctive in three areas. First, they gained a reputation for having wild or silly ideas, a concept held by both peers and teachers. Second, their work was characterized by a high

productivity of off-the-beaten-track ideas. Third, their work was characterized by humor and playfulness. Torrance pointed out that these characteristics can make life unpleasant for the creative student and that one of
the responsibilities of the counselor is to help the creative student avoid
social problems without sacrificing his creativity. Such problems were not
considered a serious issue by Rivlin (1959) and Wallen and Stevenson
(1960), however, who found high social acceptance of the "creative"
students in their studies.

Teacher. Getzels and Jackson (1961) and Torrance (1962b) have reported
that teachers prefer the "high I.Q." to the "high creative" child in both
secondary and elementary classes. Apparently, the unique ideas, the
divergent thinking, and independence of the "creative" child make him
something of an abrasive and less desirable than his more conforming but
less original companions. The "high creative" children still received above
average ratings by the teachers and it should not be imagined that they
were actively rejected.

Cultural Environment. One of the ways of determining whether certain
dimensions of creative abilities are influenced by cultural environment is to
give the same task in a number of different cultures. Torrance (1962a) presented three nonverbal and six verbal tasks used for assessing originality to
approximately 1,000 pupils in grades one through six in Australia, Western
Samoa, Germany, India, segregated Negro schools in Georgia, and in
middle-class, white, American schools. Interestingly, he found a dip in
originality performance in the middle-class American group at the fourth-
grade level, whereas there was no comparable dip in the German, Samoan,
or Australian populations.

Torrance points out that there are a number of changes or cultural discontinuities in the lives of typical youngsters in the fourth grade in our
middle-class culture. Their classroom activities become more organized and
formal; the children sit in orderly rows in the classroom; and they, in effect,
"get down to business." These changing expectations on the part of the important figures in the child's life are given credit for the very unusual dip
in the developmental curve in American culture which is not repeated in
other groups. Rather distinctive curves were found for each culture. In
Samoa, for instance, where the atmosphere was consistently repressive, the
children showed much lower but consistent growth in their test performances.

Sex Differences

There has been growing interest in possible sex differences in cognitive
development. The investigation of such differences was difficult during the
era when I.Q. tests were a predominant measure of cognitive abilities,

since many of the I.Q. test constructors made an *a priori* decision that there were no differences between boys and girls, and therefore eliminated tasks revealing such differences from their tests.

With the reconsideration of a variety of dimensions of cognitive skills, possible differences between the sexes has become an issue again. Table 4 is a summary of studies on sex differences regarding various aspects of cognitive development (Oetzel, 1962). These studies have been divided into four major areas: language development, vocabulary, numerical reasoning, and spatial abilities. Out of the 26 studies cited in the area of language development, 23 of them showed girls significantly higher than boys in language development and verbal fluency, while only one study showed the boys higher. As the table indicates, girls appear consistently higher in language development, fluency, and vocabulary, whereas boys appear consistently higher in the areas of reasoning and spatial ability.

TABLE 4. SUMMARY OF STUDIES ON SEX DIFFERENCES IN COGNITIVE DEVELOPMENT[a]

Characteristic	Studies in Which Boys Appeared Higher	No Difference	Studies in Which Girls Appeared Higher
Language Development and Verbal Fluency	1	2	23
Vocabulary	4	16	8
Reasoning and Numerical Reasoning	13	8	4
Spatial Abilities	14	5	0

[a] Adapted from Oetzel, R. *Selected bibliography on sex differences.* Mimeographed report, Stanford University, 1962.

Some of the research findings on sex differences and cognitive processes are briefly noted below:

1. Preadolescent high I.Q. boys showed more divergent thinking on a battery of Guilford-type tests than high I.Q. girls (Smith, 1962).

2. Elementary school boys were found to be consistently superior to girls in the ability to produce inventive or creative ideas (Torrance, 1960a).

3. There were large differences in I.Q. between teacher-rated creative high school boys and noncreative but able (high I.Q. scores) boys. Little difference in I.Q. scores was found between creative and noncreative girls (Rivlin, 1959).

4. Adolescent girls were found to show more ideational fluency than boys (Riers, Daniels, and Quackenbush, 1960).

5. The factors found for superior girl students were different from those for boys in the area of ideational fluency (Bereiter, 1960).

Little is yet known of the stability of these findings nor is there a solid explanation for these differences. There is some tendency to speculate on a sex-role factor and to discuss differential expectations for girls and boys in this culture. The reader is referred to the chapter on sex roles for further elaboration.

MODIFICATION OF PRODUCTIVE THINKING ABILITIES

Few controlled research studies on the effectiveness of methods to stimulate productive thinking in children can be found in the literature, with the possible exception of attempts at raising the general intellectual level of slow learning children. Kirk (1958) reviewed the literature in this area with a moderately hopeful attitude.

> It would appear that, although the upper limits of development for an individual are genetically or organically determined, the functional level or rate of development may be accelerated or depressed within the limits set by the organism (p. 213).

Training of the Mind

It is only natural that past attempts to modify thinking abilities were centered on the educational program. In past decades, the presence of certain school subjects such as Latin or mathematics in the curriculum was justified by the claim that they were "training the mind" even though they were not of direct value as content subjects themselves. A series of research studies, particularly those of Thorndike (1932), purported to show these claims to be incorrect. These studies, however, appear to have generalized beyond their task sampling. As Bruner commented, while the original case for formal discipline was poorly stated, it is a fact that general transfer of skills can be achieved by appropriate learning.

Vygotsky, an eminent Russian psychologist, pointed out in one of his works, recently translated, that the research studies which criticized the possibility of "training the mind" only measured specialized skills. He commented:

> It stands to reason that in the higher processes emerging during the cultural development of the child, formal discipline must play a role that it does not play in the more elementary processes; all the higher functions have in common, awareness, abstraction and control (1962, p. 97).

This viewpoint that one can "learn how to learn" and transfer ideas from one experience to another has lead to massive efforts to revise school programs in the sciences under curriculum projects supported by the National Science Foundation (1962). While these projects differ in content, their common goal is the attempt to teach the basic structure of the subject matter, often by means of the "discovery" method. The goal is to help the children reproduce, as closely as possible, the kind and sequence of thinking that the scientist actually goes through in discovering new principles and ideas and, through this experience, develop the attitude or set of the scientist.

New curriculum programs such as the Biological Sciences Study Group (Glass, 1962) and the Physical Sciences Study Group (Finlay, 1962) try to get the student to learn not only content but also the strategies and approaches of the scientist. In other words, they are trying to teach a set or approach to problem-solving that will lead the student to adopt a pattern of behavior more conducive to productive thinking. Emphasis has been placed upon the discovery method in many of the new curriculum programs in mathematics (Hendrix, 1961). This approach presents to the students a series of problems carefully arranged and chosen to illustrate a larger principle or generalization. (It really should be labeled the "guided discovery" method to honor the important teacher role in the process.) The children are not told what the principle is, but discover it for themselves through this inductive thinking, problem-solving approach. Interestingly, Ferris (1962) found that when the emphasis is placed on this type of approach, established aptitude tests are no longer effective as predictors of student success.

As Gallagher (1964) has pointed out, the I.Q. test was validated on school performance during an era when successful school performance often depended on sheer memory work. No wonder vocabulary played so important a role in most I.Q. tests! When the cognitive skills of inventiveness and problem-solving are stressed in schools, new or modified aptitude or ability tests may be needed to predict the successful student. The definition of giftedness or retardation itself is likely to undergo some change.

Bruner (1960) emphasizes the importance of teaching for *structure* or the basic concepts in a field of study. Once the structure is learned, individual facts can be forgotten but are easily reconstructed into the system.

The importance of knowing the "structure" of the situation in problem-solving is illustrated in a study by Ervin (1960). A group of third- and fourth-grade children were trained to shoot a ball so that it would ricochet off a backboard and strike a target. Some of the children were able to formulate an explanation for the operation in terms of reflected angles, and some could not even think of an explanation, even though they were intuitively successful in performing the task. When transfer of this knowledge was required by aiming a flashlight at a mirror in order to hit a target, both groups of children were still successful *until* the task was made difficult. Then only those who could formulate the general principle were able to continue their success.

Gagné and Smith (1962) found similar results with high school boys on a different task. Cronbach (1963, p. 384) summarizes the point: "When a problem becomes too complex for intuition and informal use of cues to regulate response, the formal principle is of great value."

In a similar vein, Ausubel and Fitzgerald (1961) report that the presence of "verbal organizers" result in more successful performance in a variety of studies.

Stimulation of Cognitive Abilities

There is some evidence that purposeful intervention is profitable for slow-learning children and for brighter children as well.

Tisdall (1962) compared samples of retarded children in special classes with a control group of retarded children in the regular elementary grades on divergent thinking abilities. These children were randomly placed in experimental and control groups. Tisdall predicted a difference in favor of the special class children based on the greater individual attention given in the smaller special classes and on a curriculum which was more appropriate for the mental age of the child. He hypothesized that continued failure would be a likely experience of the retarded child in the regular class and would result in lower confidence, less risk taking, and consequently lower divergent ability scores. He found that after two years, the children in the experimental classes were generally superior to the control group children on tests of verbal fluency, flexibility, and originality but not on measures of nonverbal creative abilities.

Torrance (1960d) divided all of the pupils in a university experimental school from the first to the sixth grade into four experimental groups at each grade level. Two groups were taught the principles suggested by Osborn (1953) for the development of new ideas, while the other two groups were told that prizes would be awarded for the best performance but were not given the special training. In addition, two of the four groups were motivated by verbal instructions to produce as many ideas as possible, while two other groups were motivated to produce clever, original, and unusual ideas.

Those children who received the special training exercises produced more responses and more clever responses than the untrained children. There was a general tendency for specific instructions (to produce clever and unusual responses) to be more effective in producing such responses than specific requests for quantity. However, this was a short-range experiment in which the evaluation was carried out shortly after the training period. The most important question, of course, is "Would such training have an influence on the pattern or style of the child on a long-range basis?" or, put another way, "Would a series or pattern of exercises or training produce a permanent change in thinking abilities or the cognitive style of a student?"

Suchman (1961) has embarked on a program of "inquiry training" for preadolescent children. He uses films illustrating scientific principles (for example, he shows a bimetallic strip bending in different directions, depending upon which side is heated) and asks children to inquire into the "why" of what they have seen by asking questions that can be answered "yes" or "no." He has found that children generally are not able to inquire systematically or productively in this situation without training.

A special training program was given to the children which involved teaching them to follow certain phases of operation: (a) *episode analysis*, or the establishment of the properties of the object or system involved in the problem; (b) the *determination of relevance*, or the discovery of which of the existing objects or systems are necessary to the solution of the problem; and (c) *induction of relational constructs*, which is the discovery of why these objects or systems are necessary to the solution of the problem.

As Suchman (1962) points out, stage three demands the most productive or creative thinking and depends upon existing conceptual systems in the child. Initial attempts at evaluation have been encouraging but not definitive, for the changes studied dealt only with short time periods.

While experimental evidence is sparse on the permanent effects of any training program to improve productive thinking ability in children, numerous suggestions for the stimulation of productive thinking can be found in the literature. Three major factors seem to appear and reappear in factor analytic studies on creativity: *fluency*, *flexibility*, and *originality*. Certain suggestions and exercises have been made for improvement of each of these factors.

In the area of intellectual fluency, the predominant method that has been suggested is the technique of "brainstorming" pioneered by Osborn (1953). This technique has been most popularly used in industry and with college students, but it can be easily transferred to educational settings with children.

One essential element of the method is to have a group focus on a problem which has some meaning and importance to them. Students are invited to give all the ideas or solutions to the problem they can think of. There are important ground rules to be observed if the technique is to work. Among these are:

1. *No criticism is allowed.* During the period when ideas are pouring forth, no critical comments are allowed. This is based on the belief that premature evaluation smothers creative ideas.

2. *Emphasis is placed on the number of ideas to be produced rather than their quality.* The assumption is that, all things being equal, the more ideas produced the greater will be the quality.

3. *Integration and combination of ideas are welcomed.* The student is alerted to the possibility of combining two prior ideas or building on an idea that has been suggested by someone else.

4. *Evaluation comes after the initial period when the ideas were presented.* Eventually, some judgment or evaluation must take place, if progress is to be made; however, if it is delayed, evaluation is more likely to become fixed on the idea, rather than on the person delivering the idea. Evaluations of this technique have been limited to adult subjects and are not entirely positive.

Other suggestions for improving fluency have encouraged students to become used to thinking in terms of multiple answers to questions. Such directives or questions as "Think of as many different things as you can that are square," and "How many things can you think of that taste sweet?" are suggested to establish a *set* for the student so that he will think in terms of "many answers" rather than only one correct answer. In effect, an attempt would be made to train the student in the area of divergent thinking.

Another presumably important component in creative thinking is flexibility, or the ability to see alternative answers or the alternative uses of objects. One exercise suggested by Myers and Torrance (1961, p. 9), for this specific purpose was as follows:

"What would you sweeten so that it would taste better?"
"What would you make smaller so that it would be nicer?"
"What would you make louder so that it would be more pleasant?"
"What would you give wings to so that it would be prettier?"
"What would you make round so that it would be more comfortable?"

Wilson (1958) also has suggested many exercises to help improve the creative abilities. Some of his suggestions for originality are the following:

In presenting reports, as in connection with a social studies unit, pupils are told that they are to use any method *other* than reading to or telling the class. . . . The possibilities are innumerable, but the important aspect is that the particular method of presentation decided upon originate with the pupils and that the obvious methods of reading or telling be ruled out.

Let the pupils pretend they are going to write a poem about spring (or any season of the year). Suggest to them "Everyone will have an opportunity to go to the window and look outside for a few minutes; when you come back to your seats, you will write down all the things you saw that you would not have seen on a rainy winter day. If you write something that no one else noticed, your score on that word will be *ten*. If only two or three people in the room noticed it, your score on that word will be *five*. . . . You will see that the closer you observe and the more uncommon are your responses, the higher your score will be. . . ."

. . . Read several tall tales . . . have the children discuss the elements which make a good tall tale by comparing different tall tales. What is the role of exaggeration? What is the role of plausibility? . . . Have the children write their own tall tales (pp. 122–123).

For these kinds of exercises to be effective, children must perceive them as continuing efforts in a serious cause and not merely as relaxation from the dull but important school lessons or family routine.

Torrance and Myers (1962) believe it is possible to teach the essence of the scientific method directly to children. They presented some simple research problems to 46 gifted children in a fifth grade, high-achieving class and had them collect their data and write research reports. The instructions for writing the report give a flavor of the instructional goal.

One important aspect of the research process is the communication of your results to others. When we find out something, we want to tell others about it. A good research report should tell the following five things:

1. THE PURPOSE OF THE STUDY: Why did you perform this study? What was it that you didn't know? What were you trying to find out?

2. PROCEDURE: What was done? Who performed the experiment? What materials did they use? Who were the subjects? How many were there? What did the experimenter do and what did the subjects do? These things should be described in such a way that someone else could carry out the study and expect to obtain the same results.

3. RESULTS: What happened? What did you find out? This should include a presentation of your data in tables, charts, or the like.

4. DISCUSSION: What do your results mean? Try to explain your findings and their meaning.

5. CONCLUSIONS: What does it all add up to? What can you be reasonably certain about? How certain can you be? (p. 31).

Although no comparative data were obtained, the children did master the concepts of the scientific method as indicated by a review test and inventory taken at the end of the unit.

The multivariate composition of factors influencing productive thinking as shown in Figure 3 also implies that the total production could be improved by influencing factors other than the cognitive abilities mentioned above.

If ways could be found to increase personal autonomy and reduce dependence, it may be possible to improve productive thinking, perhaps even in the absence of specific cognitive exercises or training. Such a supposition needs to be put to the test. General methods for improving personality or attitudinal components are beyond the scope of this chapter but should receive consideration in planning training programs for productive thinking.

FUTURE DIRECTIONS AND CAUTIONS

Several encouraging steps have been taken recently to revitalize the investigations of productive thinking with children. Among these have been the search for new measuring instruments to describe more adequately the scope of the cognitive processes, the development of theoretical models which allows for the conceptualization of the interrelationship of cognitive processes, and a greater concern for facilitating and inhibiting conditions surrounding productive thinking. Also encouraging is a trend toward using such information to devise training methods in an attempt to aid the developmental growth of these abilities. Much remains to be done.

In the area of measuring instruments, the new tests of divergent abilities still must establish their stability and validity. While test performance on such a characteristic as originality does seem related to teachers' ratings (Riers, Daniels, and Quackenbush, 1960), there are indications that the test results are quite sensitive to such factors as the wording of instructions or working time available (Christensen, Guilford, and Wilson, 1957).

Relationships that hold true with adults do not necessarily hold true with children. Reid, King, and Wickwire (1959) reported different findings in the comparison of creative and noncreative children from those obtained with creative versus noncreative adults. Unfortunately, there has been a tendency to label tasks as "creativity tests" without satisfactory validation against external criteria. Before such a label is placed on a measure, it would seem judicious to make sure that the test can identify satisfactorily those children who are manifestly creative in their life situation and also to ensure that these same characteristics would predict similar creative performance in adulthood. It would be safer to label these tests as ideational fluency, or flexibility, or whatever the manifest character of the test may be.

The development of theoretical models is of immense significance. It means that we have a hypothetical road map for cognition. We must, however, keep in mind that these models should be sketched in light pencil, with a large eraser nearby. They are not constructed to be "right." Rather, they are an aid to further exploration. This further exploration will show defects in the original model, which needs to be repaired and modified. Thus the models of Piaget and Guilford are not stone pillars set in concrete; they are springboards or launching pads for a more sophisticated understanding of productive thinking in the future.

Finally, persons interested in attempting to facilitate productive thinking should not wait for definitive and carefully controlled research evaluation of methods before they initiate training programs. In any substantially new area, it seems unrealistic to call immediately for tightly designed research.

Before careful evaluation studies can be made, there must be some kind of tangible and consistent training program to evaluate. The development of such a program would seem to be the first order of business. Also the development of good measuring instruments should be given top priority. Without these two steps, an evaluation study is wasted effort no matter how carefully designed.

While the teacher, clinician, or parent, who attempts to apply research evidence is to be commended, it would not seem to be taking too great a risk to use information now available, rather than wait for the crucial and controlled research programs which seem some years away. In other words, the risk of applying inappropriate new techniques needs to be balanced against the risk of applying no new techniques at all. The author feels that the latter course entails the greater loss.

The rapid and interesting developments of the past few years and the continued evidence of financial support for research give promise of exciting new vistas in the study of productive thinking during the next decade. In this area, it is reasonable to suggest that the past is only prologue.

REFERENCES

ATKIN, J. M. & WYATT, S. P. *Charting the universe*. Elementary School Science Project. Urbana: Univ. of Illinois, 1962.

ATKINSON, J. W. Motivational determinants of risk taking behavior. *Psychol. Rev.*, 1957, **64**, 359–372.

AUSUBEL, D. P. & FITZGERALD, D. Meaningful learning and retention: intrapersonal cognitive variables. *J. educ. Res.*, 1961, **31**, 500–509.

BARRON, F. & ROE, A. Predictor committee report. In C. W. Taylor (Ed.), *The second University of Utah research conference on the identification of creative scientific talent*. Salt Lake City: Univ. Utah Press, 1958.

BAYLEY, N. On the growth of intelligence. *Amer. Psychologist*, 1955, **10**, 805–818.

BEREITER, C. Verbal and ideational fluency in superior tenth grade students. *J. educ. Psychol.*, 1960, **51**, 337–345.

BERGLER, E. Psychoanalysis of writers and of literary productivity. In G. Roheim (Ed.), *Psychoanalysis and the social sciences*. Vol. I. New York: Internat. Univ. Press, 1947.

BIERI, J. Parental identification, acceptance of authority and within-sex differences in cognitive behavior. *J. abnorm. soc. Psychol.*, 1960, **60**, 76–79.

BRUNER, J. S. *The process of education*. Cambridge, Mass.: Harvard Univ. Press, 1960.

BRUNER, J. S., GOODNOW, J., & AUSTIN, G. A. *A study of thinking.* New York: Wiley, 1956.

CHRISTENSEN, P. R., GUILFORD, J. P., & WILSON, R. C. Relation of creative responses to working time and instructions. *J. exp. Psychol.*, 1957, **53**, 82–88.

CORMAN, B. R. Learning II: problem solving and related topics. *Rev. educ. Res.*, 1958, **28**, 459–467.

CRONBACH, L. J. *Educational psychology.* New York: Harcourt Brace & World, 1963.

DUNCAN, C. P. Recent research and human problem solving. *Psychol. Bull.*, 1959, **56**, 397–429.

ERVIN, S. Transfer effects of learning a verbal generalization. *Child Developm.*, 1960, **31**, 537–554.

FERRIS, F. L., JR. Testing in the new curriculum: numerology, tyranny or common sense. *School Rev.*, 1962, **70**, 112–131.

FESTINGER, L. *A theory of cognitive dissonance.* Evanston, Ill.: Row, Peterson, 1957.

FINLAY, G. C. The physical science study project. *School Rev.*, 1962, **70**, 63–81.

FLANAGAN, J. C., DAILEY, J. T., SHAYCOFT, M., GORHAM, W., ORR, D. B., & GOLDBERG, I. *Design for a study of American youth.* Boston: Houghton Mifflin, 1962.

GAGNÉ, R. M. & SMITH, E. C., JR. A study of the effects of verbalization on problem solving. *J. exp. Psychol.*, 1962, **63**, 12–18.

GALLAGHER, J. J. (Ed.) A report on a conference of research on gifted children. Washington, D. C.: Cooperative Research Branch, U.S. Office of Education, 1963.

GALLAGHER, J. J. *Teaching the gifted child.* Boston: Allyn & Bacon, 1964.

GETZELS, J. W. & JACKSON, P. W. Family environment and cognitive style: a study of the sources of highly intelligent and highly creative adolescents. *Amer. Sociol. Rev.*, 1961, **26**, 351–359.

GETZELS, J. W. & JACKSON, P. W. *Creativity and intelligence.* New York: Wiley, 1962.

GLASS, B. Renascent biology. *School Rev.*, 1962, **70**, 16–43.

GODDARD, H. H. *Feeblemindedness: its causes and consequences.* New York: Macmillan, 1914.

GUILFORD, J. P. The structure of intellect. *Psychol. Bull.*, 1956, **53**, 267–293.

GUILFORD, J. P. Creative intelligence in education. Address delivered at Calif. Educ. Res. & Guid. Assn., November, 1958.

GUILFORD, J. P. Three faces of intellect. *Amer. Psychologist*, 1959, **14**, 469–479.

GUILFORD, J. P., MERRIFIELD, P. R., & COX, A. *Creative thinking in children at the junior high school levels.* Report #26, Psychol. Lab., Univ. Southern California, Los Angeles, 1961.

HAGGARD, E. A. Socialization, personality and academic achievement in gifted children. *School Rev.*, 1957, **65**, 388–414.

HENDRIX, G. Learning by discovery. *Math. Teacher*, 1961, **54**, 290–299.

HOLLAND, J. Creative and academic performance among talented adolescents. *J. educ. Psychol.*, 1961, **52**, 136–147.

HUNT, J. McV. *Intelligence and experience.* New York: Ronald Press, 1961.

INHELDER, B. & MATALON, B. The study of problem solving and thinking. In P. Mussen (Ed.), *Handbook of research in child development.* New York: Wiley, 1960. Pp. 421–455.

KAGAN, J., SONTAG, L. W., BAKER, C. T., & NELSON, V. Personality and IQ change. *J. abnorm. soc. Psychol.*, 1958, **56**, 261–266.

KARPLUS, R. A concept of science education. Mimeographed report, Univ. California, Berkeley, 1962.

KAYA, E. Developing a test of creative thinking in young children. Mimeographed report, New York Univ., New York, 1960.

KIRK, S. A. *Early education of the mentally retarded.* Urbana: Univ. Illinois Press, 1958.

KOHLER, W. *The mentality of apes.* New York: Harcourt Brace & World, 1925.

380   REVIEW OF CHILD DEVELOPMENT RESEARCH

KRIS, E. *Psychoanalytic explorations of art.* New York: Internat. Univ. Press, 1952.

LUCE, R. D. & RAIFFA, H. *Games and decisions.* New York: Wiley, 1957.

MACKINNON, D. W. What makes a person creative? *Saturday Rev.*, 1962, **69**, 15–17, 69.

MASLOW, A. H. Defense and growth. *Merrill-Palmer Quart.*, 1956, **3**, 37–38.

MAW, W. H. & MAW, E. Information recognition by children with high and low curiosity. *Educ. res. Bull.*, 1961, **40**, 197–201, 223.

MAW, W. H. & MAW, E. Selection of unbalanced and unusual designs by children high in curiosity. *Child Developm.*, 1962, **33**, 917–922.

MCCLELLAND, D. C. On the psychodynamics of creative physical scientists. In H. Gruber, G. Terrell, & M. Wertheimer (Eds.), *Contemporary approaches to creative thinking.* New York: Atherton Press, 1962. Pp. 141–174.

MCGUIRE, C., HINDMAN, E., KING, F., & JENNINGS, E. Dimensions of talented behavior. *Educ. psychol. Measmt.*, 1961, **21**, 3–38.

MUSSEN, P. & KAGAN, J. Group conformity and perceptions of parents. *Child Developm.*, 1958, **29**, 57–60.

MYERS, R. E. & TORRANCE, E. P. *Invitation to thinking and doing.* Minneapolis: Perceptive Pub. Co., 1961.

NATIONAL SCIENCE FOUNDATION. The role of the National Science Foundation in course content improvement in secondary schools. *School Rev.*, 1962, **70**, 1–15.

NEWELL, A., SHAW, J. C., & SIMON, H. A. Elements of a theory of human problem solving. *Psychol. Rev.*, 1958, **65**, 151–166.

NEWELL, A., SHAW, J. C., & SIMON, H. A. The process of creative thinking. In H. Gruber, G. Terrell, & M. Wertheimer (Eds.), *Contemporary approaches to creative thinking.* New York: Atherton Press, 1962. Pp. 63–119.

OETZEL, R. Selected bibliography on sex differences. Mimeographed report, Stanford Univ., Stanford, Calif., 1962.

OSBORN, A. F. *Applied imagination.* New York: Scribner's, 1953.

PAGE, D. A. *Probability.* In Twenty-Fourth Year Book. Washington, D. C.: Nat. Council Teachers of Math., 1959. Pp. 229–271.

PATRICK, C. Creative thought in poets. *Arch. Psychol., N. Y.*, 1935, **26**, 1–74.

PATRICK, C. Creative thought in the arts. *J. Psychol.*, 1937, **4**, 35–73.

PATRICK, C. Scientific thought. *J. Psychol.*, 1938, **5**, 55–83.

PIAGET, J. *The child's conception of physical causality.* (Translated by M. Gabain.) New York: Harcourt Brace, 1930.

PIAGET, J. *The psychology of intelligence.* London: Routledge & Kegan Paul, 1947.

PIAGET, J. *The construction of reality in the child.* (Translated by M. Cook.) New York: Basic Books, 1954.

REID, J. B., KING, F. J., & WICKWIRE, P. Cognitive and other personality characteristics of creative children. *Psychol. Rep.*, 1959, **5**, 729–737.

RIERS, E., DANIELS, J., & QUACKENBUSH, J. L. The identification of creativity in adolescents. *J. educ. Psychol.*, 1960, **51**, 346–351.

RIVLIN, J. Creativity and the self-attitudes and sociability of high school students. *J. educ. Psychol.*, 1959, **50**, 147–152.

ROE, A. *The making of a scientist.* New York: Dodd, Mead, 1953.

ROGERS, C. R. In H. H. Anderson (Ed.), *Creativity and its cultivation.* New York: Harper, 1959. Pp. 69–82.

RUSSELL, D. H. *Children's thinking.* Boston: Ginn, 1956.

SCHACHTEL, E. G. *Metamorphosis.* New York: Basic Books, 1959.

SEDER, J. The origin of differences in extent of independence in children: developmental factors in perceptual field dependence. Unpublished bachelor's thesis, Radcliffe College, 1957.

SIGEL, I. How intelligence tests limit understanding of intelligence. *Merrill-Palmer Quart.*, 1963, **9**, 39–56.

SMITH, R. M. Perceptions of self, others, and certain environmental aspects of high and low divergent, intellectually superior children. Unpublished doctoral dissertation, Univ. of Illinois, 1962.

SONTAG, L. M., BAKER, C. T., & NELSON, V. Personality as a determinant of performance. *Amer. J. Orthopsychiat.*, 1955, **25**, 555–563.

SONTAG, L. M., BAKER, C. T., & NELSON, V. Mental growth and personality development: a longitudinal survey. *Monogr. Soc. Res. Child. Developm.*, 1958, **23**, No. 86.

STEIN, M. I. & HEINZE, S. *Creativity and the individual.* Glencoe, Ill.: Free Press, 1960.

SUCHMAN, J. R. Inquiry training: building skills for autonomous discovery. *Merrill-Palmer Quart.*, 1961, **7**, 147–169.

SUCHMAN, J. R. *The elementary school training program in scientific inquiry.* Urbana: Univ. Illinois Press, 1962.

SUPPES, P. *Sets and numbers. Book 1. (Teacher's manual).* Palo Alto, Calif.: Stanford Univ., 1960.

TERMAN, L. M. Scientists and non-scientists in a group of 800 gifted men. *Psychol. Monogr.*, 1954, **68**, 7.

TERMAN, L. M. & ODEN, M. *The gifted child grows up. Genetic studies of a genius. Vol. IV.* Stanford, Calif.: Stanford Univ. Press, 1947.

TERMAN, L. M. & ODEN, M. *The gifted group at mid-life.* Stanford, Calif.: Stanford Univ. Press, 1959.

THORNDIKE, E. L. *The fundamentals of learning.* New York: Teach. Coll., Columbia Univ., 1932.

TISDALL, W. J. Productive thinking in retarded children. *Except. Child.*, 1962, **29**, 36–41.

TORRANCE, E. P. *Explorations in creative thinking in the early school years. VI. Highly intelligent and highly creative children in a laboratory school.* Minneapolis: Bureau Educ. Res., Univ. of Minnesota, 1959.

TORRANCE, E. P. Sex-role identification and creative thinking. *Res. Memo, BER-59-10.* Minneapolis: Univ. Minnesota Press, 1960 (a).

TORRANCE, E. P. Laboratory studies of peer pressures against highly creative group members. In E. P. Torrance, J. E. Bowers, H. J. Radig, N. Palamatu, & P. R. Krishnarah, The Minnesota studies of creative thinking in the early school years. *Res. Memo. BER-60-1.* Minneapolis: Univ. Minnesota Press, 1960. Pp. 22–23 (b).

TORRANCE, E. P. Personality development of the highly creative child. In E. P. Torrance *et al.*, The Minnesota studies of creative thinking in the early school years. *Res. Memo. BER-60-1.* Minneapolis: Univ. Minnesota Press, 1960. Pp 27–29 (c).

TORRANCE, E. P. An experimental attempt to increase quantity and quality of ideas. In E. P. Torrance *et al.*, The Minnesota studies of creative thinking in the early school years. *Res. Memo. BER-60-1.* Minneapolis: Univ. Minnesota Press, 1960. Pp. 30–31 (d).

TORRANCE, E. P. Cultural discontinuities and the development of originality in thinking. *Except. Child.*, 1962, **29**, 2–13 (a).

TORRANCE, E. P. *Guiding creative talent.* Englewood Cliffs, N. J.: Prentice Hall, 1962 (b).

TORRANCE, E. P. & MYERS, R. E. *Teaching gifted elementary pupils how to do research.* Minneapolis: Perceptive Pub. Co., 1962.

VYGOTSKY, L. S. *Thought and language.* (Translated by E. Hanfmann and G. Vakar.) New York: Wiley, 1962.

WALLAS, G. *The art of thought.* New York: Harcourt Brace, 1926.

WALLEN, N. C. & STEVENSON, G. M. Stability and correlates of judged creativity in fifth grade writings. *J. educ. Psychol.*, 1960, **51**, 273–276.

WERTHEIMER, M. *Productive thinking.* New York: Harper, 1945.

WILSON, R. C. Creativity. In R. J. Havighurst (Ed.), *Yearb. nat. Soc. Stud. Educ.*, 1958, **57**, Pt. II. Pp. 108–126.

WITKIN, H. A., DYK, R. B., PATTERSON, H. F., GOODENOUGH, D. R., & KARP, S. A. *Psychological differentiation.* New York: Wiley, 1962.

YERKES, R. & LEARNED, B. W. *Chimpanzee intelligence and its vocal expression.* Baltimore: Williams & Wilkins, 1925.

Development of Moral Character and Moral Ideology

LAWRENCE KOHLBERG

University of Chicago

APPROACHES TO THE STUDY OF CHILDREN'S MORALITY

FOR MANY GENERATIONS, morality was the central category for defining social relationships and development, and the social sciences were termed "the moral sciences." The great theorists of the early twentieth century also considered morality to be the key to understanding social development, as indicated by McDougall's (1908) statement that "the *fundamental problem* of social psychology is the moralization of the individual by the society," or Freud's (1930) statement that "the sense of guilt is the most important problem in the evolution of culture."

In more recent periods, morality has slipped in and out of focus as a central interest in child development (Albert and Kluckhohn, 1959; Jones, 1954). The important work of Hartshorne and May (1928–1930) on children's moral conduct and of Piaget (1932) upon moral judgment was followed by two decades of relative inactivity in the area. In the 1930's and 1940's discussions of children's social adjustment absorbed thought about moral character, and discussions of socialization processes absorbed specific concerns about moral development. In the past decade, however, there has been a great increase both in research investigations and in theoretical statements about conscience and moral values.

This increased interest in moral development seems to be partly the result of recent history, which has sharpened awareness of the distinction between internal moral development and outward socialization and social adjustment. The barbarities of the socially conforming members of the Nazi and Stalinist systems and the hollow lives apparent in our own affluent society have made it painfully evident that adjustment to the group is no substitute for moral maturity.

A concern with internal aspects of socialization, then, has formed the distinctive focus of recent research on children's morality. This research has been addressed to the general question, "How does the amoral infant become capable of morality?" Answers have been sought by isolating factors such as punishment, identification with parents, and role-taking opportunities, and correlating them with the presence or absence of moral development. Morality has generally been defined as conscience, as a set of cultural rules of social action which have been internalized by the individual. Moral development has been conceived of as the increase in such internalization of basic cultural rules. Various theories and researches have stressed three different aspects of internalization: the behavioral, emotional, and judgmental aspects of moral action.

A *behavioral* criterion of internalization is that of intrinsically motivated conformity or *resistance to temptation*. Such a conception is implicit in the common-sense notion of "moral character" which formed the basis of the earlier American research on morality. In this tradition, Hartshorne and May (1928–1930) defined moral character as a set of culturally defined virtues such as honesty, which were measured by observing the child's ability to resist the temptation to break a rule (for example, against cheating) when it seemed unlikely that he could be detected or punished.

A second criterion of the existence of internalized standards is the *emotion* of *guilt*, that is, of self-punitive, self-critical reactions of remorse and anxiety after transgression of cultural standards. Both psychoanalytic and learning theories of conscience have focused upon guilt as the basic motive of morality. It is to avoid guilt that the child behaves morally.

In addition to conduct in conformity with a standard and emotional reactions of remorse after transgression, the internalization of a standard implies a capacity to make judgments in terms of that standard and to justify maintaining the standard to oneself and to others. This *judgmental* side of moral development has formed the focus of recent work and theory inspired by the earlier studies of Piaget (1932).

A common interest in the basic psychological processes of moral internalization has given direction to studies of moral conduct, moral judgment, and moral emotion. In addition, a certain degree of empirical consistency is to be found between these various aspects of children's moral character. Nevertheless, the findings and theories based on these various aspects of morality tend to lead in quite different directions. Accordingly, we shall deal with each area of moral development separately, while pointing out implications of findings in one area for those in another.

In dealing, first, with moral conduct, we consider the extent to which moral behavior is determined by underlying moral character as opposed to nonmoral situational and emotional factors. We then take up the major interpretations of the nature of moral character and of the period in life in which character is formed. Turning next to moral judgment, we consider stages of moral development, their determination by forms of social experience and role-taking, and their relationships to moral conduct. We then review studies of guilt formation as it is related to parental discipline and identification, and to other aspects of conscience development.

We then turn from a consideration of aspects of moral development to a consideration of the role of morality in children's personality functioning. First, we consider studies of the role of guilt and of other moral reactions in delinquency and neurosis. We then consider studies of authoritarian and humanistic moral ideologies as related to personality integration.

Finally, we offer some implications of the findings for moral education. These implications are considered in terms of some basic philosophic and value issues necessarily involved in moral research and moral education.

This last section expresses directly a point of view which has had some selective and organizing influence throughout the chapter. The writer considers the study of moral development as raising a distinctive set of questions basic to researchers, practitioners, and educated men alike. Much of the research in the area has not been specifically addressed to these questions, but has viewed morality as a type of social behavior learned like any other social behavior.

The chapter by Wesley Becker in this volume provides a summary of many of the morality studies from this latter, more representative, point of view. Becker concludes that warmth, use of love-oriented discipline techniques, and consistency of parental control facilitate learning of "guilt" or moral expectations. He also reports studies suggesting that these same child-rearing conditions facilitate learning of "nonmoral" types of parental expectations concerning aggression, dependency, and so on. These findings suggest the very plausible conclusions that the factors effective in the learning of any desired behavior play a role in moral learning.

Rather than directly exploring the detailed implications of such a conclusion, the present chapter attempts to focus on more distinctively "moral" questions. In so doing, research findings are often considered outside of the context or conclusions reported by their authors.

MORAL CHARACTER AND MORAL CONDUCT

As used in psychological studies, "moral character" has generally retained its common-sense meaning as the sum total of a set of virtues. Virtues or character-traits are conceived of as "those traits of personality which are subject to the moral sanctions of society" (Havighurst and Taba, 1949). For Hartshorne and May (1928) these traits included honesty, service (willingness to sacrifice something for a group or charitable goal), and self-control (persistence in assigned tasks). For Havighurst and Taba they included honesty, loyalty, responsibility, moral courage, and friendliness. With the exception of friendliness (which has doubtful status as a moral character trait), all these traits involve some notion of adhering to cultural norms of action, where such adherence involves effort, self-control, or sacrifice.

Psychologists have agreed with common opinion that moral character traits should be assessed from actions, rather than from judgments and feelings. In general, they have followed Hartshorne and May's basic method of measuring honesty by adding together occurrences of obedience to rules in situations allowing cheating or stealing with no apparent risk of detection. These measurements corresponded quite closely to the judgments of honesty made by peers and teachers. For the most part teachers did not agree with one another in judging honesty but when they did agree, they also agreed with the Hartshorne and May experimental measurements.

The first question raised by the concept of moral character is whether the general and stable moral character traits assumed by common opinion actually exist. Recent work with five-year-olds which bears upon this issue (Rau, 1964) is consistent with the earlier extensive findings of Hartshorne and May (1928–1930) concerning preadolescent moral behavior. These findings suggest that the most influential factors determining resistance to temptation to cheat or disobey are situational factors rather than a fixed individual moral character trait of honesty. The first finding leading to this conclusion is that of the low predictability of cheating in one situation for cheating in another. Correlations between cheating in one type of situation and in others ranged from .00 to .45 (Hartshorne and May, 1928; Rau, 1964). Service, self-control, and sympathy have been found to be equally specific to the particular situation (Hartshorne and May, 1930; Murphy, 1937). A second related research finding is that children are not divisible into two groups, "cheaters" and "honest children." Children's cheating scores were distributed in bell-curve fashion around an average score of moderate cheating. A third finding is the importance of the expediency aspect of the decision to cheat; that is, the tendency to cheat depends upon the degree of risk of detection and the effort required to cheat. Children who cheated in more risky situations also cheated in less risky situations (Hartshorne and May, 1930). Thus noncheaters appeared to be primarily more cautious than more honest. Other important aspects of the immediate situation were peer group approval and example. Some classrooms showed a high tendency to cheat, while other seemingly identically composed classrooms in the same school showed little tendency to cheat.

These research findings on situational variation suggest that moral conduct is in large part the result of an individual decision in a specific moral conflict situation. This aspect of moral conduct tends to be ignored by common views of moral character as a set of general "good habits" or as a "strong conscience."

To some extent, however, Hartshorne and May's conclusion that moral conduct is specific to the situation must be qualified by the results of a recent factor analysis by Burton (1963) of the Hartshorne and May data. This analysis indicated a small general factor in the various experimental tests of classroom cheating. While most of the variation in cheating seems due to reactions to the individual situations, part is a product of stable individual differences in attitudes toward classroom cheating.

We need not interpret this personality factor in cheating as a specific trait of honesty, however. It may simply represent differential cautiousness or sensitivity to possible punishment (an interpretation suggested by the fact that Hartshorne and May were able to place children's cheating behavior on a scale of willingness to risk detection). More probably, the personality factor represents a character tendency that is more general than a specific attitude toward honesty or a fear of being caught. The evidence for this is that Hartshorne and May found low positive correlations ($r = .21$ to $.33$) between their experimental measures of honesty and their measures of service and self-control (persistence and nondistractibility). These correlations were about as high as the correlations between various types of honesty and could not have been based on simple cautiousness.

These findings suggest a core of truth to common-sense notions of general good character, and provide some justification for adding up measures of various aspects of moral conduct into a total assessment of moral character. Common sense seems to exaggerate this consistency, however. Thus the consistency found in teacher ratings of moral traits is much higher than the consistency found in experimental measures.

Character as Superego Strength

How is this "moral character" factor in moral conduct to be conceived or interpreted? The prevalent recent interpretation has been that it represents variations in strength of conscience or "superego strength." The "conscience strength" interpretation of "honest" behavior implies that the highly honest person holds a strongly motivated internal rule prohibiting stealing, cheating, or lying. Such a person should have especially strong beliefs that such acts are wrong, and especially painful feelings after their performance. The research findings to date bearing on this interpretation are inconclusive.

Conformity to a moral rule has not been found to bear much relationship to the strength of stated belief in that rule.[1] More importantly, strength of conformity to a rule has not been found consistently to relate to intensity of guilt following transgressions, as will be discussed later in the section on guilt.

Character as Good Habits

A second prevalent interpretation of the moral character factor is that it is a set of general "good habits" produced by training, example, punishment, and reward. In many ways similar to the "conscience" interpretation, this more behavioristic view differs in minimizing the direct role of beliefs and guilt feelings in moral conduct. This interpretation lies behind much philanthropic and parental thinking about moral education. Philanthropic practice has assumed inadequate moral character to be the result of insufficient moral training which it hopes to supplement through character-education classes, Sunday school, or Boy Scouts. The parental faith that early and extensive training and reinforcement in obedience, care of property, and so on will lead directly to later good character also rests on this "good habits" interpretation.

The research results, however, have rather consistently failed to support such notions. Hartshorne and May found no relationship between behavioral tests of honesty or service and exposure to Sunday school, Scouts, or to special character-education classes. More recent research on parental practices has found no positive or consistent relationships between earliness and amount of parental demands or training in good habits—obedience, caring for property, performing chores, neatness, or avoidance of cheating —and measures of children's obedience, responsibility, and honesty (Burton, Maccoby, and Allinsmith, 1961; Grinder, 1963; Harris and Valasek, 1954; Rau, 1964).

With regard to the effects of punishment and reward, the findings are somewhat more complex. Amount of use of praise and amount of deprivation of physical rewards are uncorrelated with either resistance to temptation (Burton, Maccoby, and Allinsmith, 1961; Grinder, 1962), or with absence of delinquent behavior (Bandura and Walters, 1959; Glueck and Glueck, 1950). One study reports a correlation between resistance to temp-

---

[1] The most thorough study of moral beliefs in relation to ratings of conduct was made by Havighurst and Taba (1949). They found only a small average correlation ($r = .24$) between paper and pencil measures of strength of belief in a set of virtues and character ratings on these virtues. No significant correlation has been found between resistance to cheating and stated belief in the badness of cheating or stated unwillingness to cheat (Hendry, 1960; Hartshorne and May, 1930). The relationships between moral judgments and moral conduct are more complex than these negative findings suggest and are discussed in detail later.

tation and amount of physical punishment in preschoolers (Burton, Maccoby, and Allinsmith, 1961); one study does not (Rau, 1964). This possible correlation with physical punishment does not appear to persist as children become older and as their moral behavior becomes less fear-motivated (Grinder, 1962; Glueck and Glueck, 1950; Bandura and Walters, 1959).

There are several possible explanations of these negative findings on the results of direct training in the home and in character-education groups. Regardless of interpretation, they stand in contrast to the recent experimental studies indicating the short-term effectiveness of various conditions of training and direct punishment upon school children's resistance to temptation, as well as observational studies of the effectiveness of punishment in brainwashing and in initiation rites. (This effectiveness is especially apparent under certain conditions of timing, Aronfreed and Reber, 1963; Walters and Demkow, 1963; Solomon and Whiting, reported in Mowrer, 1960.) The contrast between these experimental studies and the child-rearing studies suggests that direct training and physical types of punishment may be effective in producing short-run situational conformity but do not directly produce general internalized habits of moral character carried into later life, carried outside the home, or carried into permissive situations.[2]

Character as Ego Strength

The third major interpretation of the character factor in moral conduct views it in terms of ego abilities rather than moral habits or feelings. In common-sense versions, moral character is believed to indicate strength of will. In a tradition of moral psychology dating back to the British associationists and utilitarians (Sidgwick, 1901), moral character is believed to result from practical judgment or reason. In this view, morality (action based on consideration of how one's action affects others) requires much the same capacities as does prudence (action based on consideration of how it affects the self's long-range interests). Both involve foresight or the ability to predict long-range consequences of action, to weigh probabilities, and to

[2] Indeed, the longer range effects of punishment may essentially rest on cognitive situational decisions by the child. As an example, a recent experiment (Aronson and Carlsmith, 1963) suggests that the impact of punishment upon preschool children is determined by cognitive mechanisms of self-justification or "dissonance-reduction" (Festinger, 1957), which lead individuals to devalue things they give up relatively "voluntarily" but not to devalue things they give up under external coercion. In one experimental condition, Aronson and Carlsmith "strongly threatened" a group of preschool children if they played with certain toys ("I'll be very angry if you do and leave with all the toys") and in another experimental condition, they "mildly threatened" the children ("I'd be annoyed"). Under "severe threat," children increased their liking for the prescribed toys ("forbidden fruit"), while under "mild threat," they decreased their liking of the toys ("sour grapes").

prefer the distant greater gratification to the immediate lesser gratification. Both also involve empathy, the ability to predict the reactions of others to one's action. In psychoanalytic theory these factors of will, foresight, and empathy are included with other aspects of decision-making and emotional control in the concept of "ego strength." Recent psychoanalytic theorizing has given increased prominence to the role of "ego strength" in moral conduct (Redl and Wineman, 1952; Hartmann, 1960).

Support for the view of moral character as will was provided by an early factor-analysis of ratings of adult personality by other adults (Webb, 1915). This study yielded a "will-factor" which included both moral traits and nonmoral will traits. Hartshorne and May (1930) found self-control (or persistence and nondistractibility on achievement tests) correlated with the moral traits of honesty and service. These early studies of "will" have been supported by a more recent factor analytic study of personality traits (Cattell, 1950) and by Peck and Havighurst's (1960) study of moral character development. In the latter study, psychologists' ratings of 35 small-city adolescents on ego strength correlated well ($r = .69$) with total moral character scores (honesty, responsibility, loyalty, courage, friendliness) as rated by community informants (schoolmates, teachers, and other adults). It is quite possible that these correlations were inflated by halo effects, since the raters had some knowledge of the moral character ratings. Nevertheless, the correlations with ego strength were considerably higher than correlations with any other "good" aspects of personality.

These global findings are clarified by findings on particular aspects of ego strength. The first such variable is general intelligence. While studies which use ratings of moral character (Peck and Havighurst, 1960; Sanford et al., 1943) report higher correlations between intelligence and moral character than do studies using experimental measures (Hartshorne and May, 1928), or using delinquency criteria, the correlations are in any case substantial ($r = .20$ to $.50$). While artifacts like social class, the lesser necessity of bright children to cheat, and their greater cleverness in avoiding detection may influence these correlations, some relationship seems to be present when these factors are absent or controlled.

The second ego-strength variable contributing to moral conduct is the tendency to anticipate future events and to choose the greater remote outcome over the lesser immediate outcome. A greater use of future time in projective test stories has been found to discriminate nondelinquents from delinquents (Barndt and Johnson, 1955). Successfully treated delinquents showed much longer time perspective after therapy than nontreated controls (Ricks and Umbarger, 1963). Preference for a larger reward in the future (a large candy bar available next week) over a smaller reward in the present (a small candy bar available at the moment) discriminated non-cheaters from cheaters in an experimental situation, with I.Q. and age controlled (Mischel, 1963).

The third type of ego-strength variable which seems to contribute to moral conduct is the capacity to maintain stable, focused attention. Stability of attention has been measured by the lack of variation in reaction time to presentation of simple repetitive task stimuli, and by the lack of variation in level of galvanic skin responses elicited by such simple stimuli. These measures have been found to correlate well with experimental measures of resistance to cheating ($r = .68$ and .40), as well as with teacher ratings of "conscience strength" (Grim, Kohlberg, and White, 1964). It should be noted that cheating was found related to instability of autonomic reactivity (galvanic skin response) rather than to a high level of autonomic reactivity. Lack of "moral control" in the cheating situation did not appear to be the result of the high potential for emotional arousal, but of the low potential for keeping attention fixed upon the appropriate stimuli and instructions in the situation.

A fourth type of ego-strength variable (possibly related to attentional control) which seems to contribute to moral conduct is the capacity to control unsocialized fantasies. Expression of aggressive fantasy in doll play by preschool children was quite predictive of cheating and disobedience as measured by experimental situations ($r = .63$; Rau, 1964) and by teacher ratings (Bach, 1945). These relationships of moral conduct to absence of aggressive fantasy are not matched by relationships of moral conduct to absence of aggressive behavior. The permissiveness of a doll play situation, like the "permissiveness" of a resistance to temptation situation, appears to bring out unsocialized impulses which are externally or punishment-controlled, but which are not internally controlled (Sears et al., 1953). Control of aggressive fantasy, like resistance to temptation, does not seem to be positively correlated with guilt and other superego-control factors, so much as it is with ego-control factors (Peck and Havighurst, 1960).

A fifth type of ego-strength variable which seems to contribute to moral conduct is self-esteem or satisfaction with the self and the environment. Correlations between a pencil and paper test of satisfaction with self and environment (California Personality Inventory) correlated well ($r = .20$ to .88) with community ratings of adolescent character traits (Havighurst and Taba, 1949).

The above findings, in the aggregate, provide some support for the interpretation of moral character as ego, rather than superego, strength. This interpretation implies that the major consistencies in moral conduct represent decision-making capacities rather than fixed behavior traits. It is thus consistent with the findings on situational variation, which suggested that moral conduct was the product of a situational decision. The "ego-strength" interpretation also seems consistent with the difficulties in distinguishing situational factors stimulating prudential caution from situational factors stimulating moral obligation in the production of honest behavior. Both sets of factors appear to appeal to "ego-strength" dispositions in the personality.

The Age at Which Moral Character Is Formed

An ego-strength interpretation also suggests that moral character is a gradual product of development, since morally relevant "ego-strength" variables increase regularly with age throughout early and middle childhood. In contrast, superego or conscience-strength interpretations have tended to assume that the core of character develops and is stabilized in the first few years of life. As stated by Sears, Maccoby, and Levin (1957, pp. 367–368): "So far as we can tell, there is a learning of internal control that goes on mainly in the years before puberty, perhaps chiefly in the first six to ten years, determining the extent to which conscience will operate throughout all the rest of life." These differing assumptions as to a critical age period in moral development are obviously important for both theory and practice in this area. Unfortunately, research findings on this topic are as yet inconclusive.

The findings on age development in morally conforming conduct are reasonably clear-cut in their actual results, although not in their interpretation. Experimental measures of resistance to cheating or stealing do not increase significantly or regularly with age in the whole period from nursery school to high school (Grinder, 1963; Hartshorne and May, 1930; Rau, 1964). Ratings by adults of honesty, responsibility, or altruism also fail to show age increases during childhood (Harris, 1954; Hartshorne and May, 1930; Turner, 1952). Incidents of stealing and lying reported by parents decrease markedly after the years six to eight (MacFarlane, Allen, and Honzik, 1954), but stealing seems to increase again in adolescence insofar as can be judged by arrest statistics. The finding that the average level of moral conformity is the same in early childhood as in later life suggests that the basic forces of moral character develop very early. The findings may be the result of other factors, however. Experimental measures have tapped very simple types of moral conduct, and rating measures have built-in adjustments to the adult's expectations for given age groups. More basically, the results on age variation can be interpreted in light of the situational findings which suggested that morally conforming conduct poorly represents underlying moral attitudes or "moral control." At younger ages, "moral" conduct may be based primarily on fear or on lack of arousal to transgress (for example, to win by cheating), while at older ages it may be based more on moral beliefs, guilt, and ego factors. Age declines in fear-induced conformity may be counterbalanced by age increases in moral and ego-strength forces for moral conduct. This view is consistent with the data on age differences in the effect of punishment on moral conduct already discussed.

The concept of early conscience or character formation raises a second question: that of whether or not individual differences in moral conduct are set early and remain stable over time; for example, whether the "good" children of age five are the "good" children of age fifteen. Only a few re-sults of longitudinal studies bear upon this issue. Neither psychologists' ratings of aggressiveness nor parents' ratings of selfishness showed a sub-stantial stability between age six and age thirteen (MacFarlane, Allen, and Honzick, 1954; Kagan and Moss, 1962). In contrast, Peck and Havighurst (1960) report considerable stability in moral character ratings by com-munity informants throughout the period of ten to seventeen. In large part, however, this finding may represent the stabilization of the child's reputa-tion and role in a small city rather than "deeper" fixity of moral character. Recent unpublished reports of longitudinal findings in later adolescence suggest the relatively frequent occurrence of marked changes in moral character from high school to college years.

The question of a critical age in character formation may be viewed in terms of the organization of character, as well as in terms of its quantitative growth and stability. Havighurst and his colleagues have attempted to study moral character from both these perspectives. They have defined moral character as an "organization or dynamic patterning of traits" lead-ing to definite character types. Five such types were defined in a population of 35 small-city adolescents using projective tests, interviews, and behavior ratings (Peck and Havighurst, 1960). These types were hypothesized to form a developmental order of personality maturity. The least mature was considered to be the amoral-defiant type, followed by the expedient, the conforming, the irrational-conscientious, and finally, the rational-altruistic type. This order corresponds to neo-psychoanalytic conceptions of ma-turity as self-direction, productive work, and the capacity to love (Fromm, 1947).

Ratings of character maturity in terms of these types were highly corre-lated with community ratings of specific character traits or virtues; that is, rational-altruistic adolescents tended also to be most honest, responsible, and so on. While these high correlations may have been partly the product of rater bias or "halo effects," they do suggest considerable correspondence between character viewed in terms of clinician's conceptions of social maturity and character viewed as community judgments of conformity to moral standards of the culture. As this correspondence suggests, Peck and Havighurst conclude that maturity of moral character is set and stabilized early. They also conclude that parental warmth, trust, and firmness or consistency are necessary and primary factors in the production of mature moral character. This conclusion is based on high correlations between ratings of the family on these variables and ratings of the adolescent's moral maturity. As these correlations have not been replicated by a number of other studies using less personal and global methods of measurement of most of these family variables, Peck and Havighurst's conclusions must be accepted with caution. It is unlikely that the correlations correspond to causal relations between child-rearing practices and fixed internal character structures. What the correlations do seem to suggest is that families have definite moral atmospheres, probably created not only by the parents but also by the children.

THE DEVELOPMENT OF MORAL IDEOLOGY AND JUDGMENT

While moral behavior has not lent itself to age-developmental analysis, the study of moral judgment has readily suggested basic stages of development. Moral judgment has been primarily studied as the child's use and interpretation of rules in conflict situations, and his reasons for moral action, rather than as correct knowledge of rules or conventional belief in them. Studies of "moral knowledge" and belief (Hartshorne and May, 1930) at younger ages indicate that most children know the basic moral rules and conventions of our society by the first grade. Studies and tests of moral knowledge at older ages have not been especially enlightening. While showing relations to conduct, moral knowledge scores seem primarily to indicate intelligence, cultural background, and desire to make a good impression, rather than basic moral development.

An example of data on moral thought and judgment, as opposed to moral knowledge or belief, is provided by answers to a question as to whether a boy should tell his father a confidence about a brother's misdeed. In reply, Danny, age ten, said: "In one way, it would be right to tell on his brother or his father might get mad at him and spank him. In another way, it would be right to keep quiet or his brother might beat him up." Obviously whether Danny decides it is right to maintain authority or right to maintain peer "loyalty" is of little interest compared to the fact that his decision will be based on his anticipation of who can hit harder.

The "stage" approach to understanding such responses characteristic of an age group involves the analysis of their underlying thought structures and the comparison of such structures found in different age groups in order to define the general direction of development. Such "stages" are then used to understand developmental differences among children of a given age and to isolate major social and intellectual influences upon development.

It seems obvious that moral stages must primarily be the products of the child's interaction with others, rather than the direct unfolding of biological or neurological structures. The emphasis on social interaction does not mean, however, that stages of moral judgment directly represent the teaching of values by parents or of their direct "introjection" by the child. In the theories of moral stages of Piaget (1932), Mead (1934), and Baldwin (1906), parental training and discipline are viewed as influential only as a part of a world or social order perceived by the child. The child can internalize the moral values of his parents and culture and make them his own only as he comes to relate these values to a comprehended social order and to his own goals as a social self. In these stage theories, the fundamental factor causing such a structuring of a moral order is social participation and role-taking. In order to *play* a social role in the family, school, or society, the child must implicitly *take* the role of others toward himself and toward others in the group. Moral role-taking involves an emotional empathic or sympathetic component, but it also involves a cognitive capacity to define situations in terms of rights and duties, in terms of reciprocity and the perspectives of other selves. In Danny's reply just quoted, "role-taking" seems to be limited to a prediction about retaliation, which not only represents a limitation of empathic feelings but a primitive structuring of concepts of family rights and duties. In analyzing the bases of such role-taking, the theories mentioned have variously focused upon the family (Baldwin), the peer group (Piaget), and the larger social institutions (Mead).

The theory which has most directly inspired recent research on moral judgment has been that of the Swiss psychologist Piaget (1932). His account of moral development springs largely from his general theory of the development of the child's conception of the world (Piaget, 1928). Piaget believes that the cognitive limitations of the child of three to eight lead him to confuse moral rules with physical laws and to view rules as fixed external things, rather than as the instruments of human purposes and values. Piaget believes that the child sees rules as absolutes and confuses rules with things because of his "realism" (his inability to distinguish between subjective and objective aspects of his experience) and because of his "egocentrism" (his inability to distinguish his own perspective on events from that of others). In addition to seeing rules as external absolutes, the young child feels his parents and other adults are all-knowing, perfect, and sacred. This attitude of "unilateral respect" toward adults, joined with the child's "realism," is believed to lead him to view rules as sacred and unchangeable.

Piaget (1932) attempts to demonstrate the truth of this characterization of the young child's attitudes toward rules by observations of children's behavior and beliefs about the rules of the game of marbles. Swiss children are quoted as saying that the rules of the game can never be changed, that the rules have existed from the beginning of time and have been invented and handed down by God, the head of state, or the father. While the more colorful aspects of these observations have not been found by others, Bobroff (1960) reported attitudes of rigidity toward game rules to steadily decline with age and intelligence in American children of six to twelve.

Piaget believes that intellectual growth and experiences of role-taking in the peer group naturally transform perceptions of rules from external authoritarian commands to internal principles. In essence, he views internal moral norms as logical principles of justice. Of these, he says: "In contrast to a given rule imposed upon the child from outside, the rule of justice is an immanent condition of social relationships or a law governing their equilibrium. The sense of justice is largely independent of adult precept and requires nothing more for its development than mutual respect and solidarity among children" (Piaget, 1932, p. 196).

By the sense of justice, Piaget means a concern for reciprocity and equality between individuals. Norms of justice are not simply matters of abstract logic, however; rather they are sentiments of sympathy, gratitude, and vengeance which have taken on logical form.

Piaget believes that an "autonomous" justice morality develops at about age eight to ten and eventually replaces the earlier "heteronomous" morality based on unquestioning respect for adult authority. He expects the autonomous justice morality to develop in all children, unless development is fixated by unusual coerciveness of parents or cultures or by deprivation of experiences of peer cooperation.

Piaget and his followers have made observations of age changes in eleven different aspects of development of moral judgment which are implied by his stage concepts. Among these are:

1. *Intentionality in judgment.* Young children tend to judge an act as bad mainly in terms of its actual physical consequences, whereas older children judge an act as bad in terms of the intent to do harm. As an example, chil-

dren were asked who was worse—a child who broke five cups while helping his mother set the table or a boy who broke one cup while stealing some jam. Almost all four-year-olds say the child who committed the larger accidental damage was worse (as do about 60 per cent of six-year-olds); whereas the majority of nine-year-olds say the "thief" was worse (Boehm and Nass, 1962; Caruso, 1943; Janis, 1961; Lerner, 1937a; MacRae, 1954; Piaget, 1932).

2. *Relativism in judgment.* The young child views an act as either totally right or totally wrong, and thinks everyone views it in the same way. If the young child does recognize a conflict in views, he believes the adult's view is always the right one. In contrast, the older child is aware of possible diversity in views of right and wrong. As an example, children were told a story in which a lazy pupil is forbidden by his teacher to receive any help in his homework. A friendly classmate does help the pupil. The children were then asked whether the friendly classmate thinks he is right or wrong for helping, whether the lazy pupil would think he was right or wrong, what the teacher would think, and so on. The majority of six-year-olds expected only one judgment, on which everyone would agree; for example, they would say that the helping classmate would think he was wrong to help. By age nine, a majority of children recognized that there would be more than one perspective on moral value in the situation (Lerner, 1937b; MacRae, 1954).

3. *Independence of sanctions.* The young child says an act is bad because it will elicit punishment; the older child says an act is bad because it violates a rule, does harm to others, and so forth (Kohlberg, 1963b). For example, young children were asked to judge a helpful, obedient act (attentively watching a baby brother while the mother is away) followed by punishment (the mother returns and spanks the baby-sitting child). Many four-year-olds simply say the obedient boy was bad because he got punished, ignoring his act. More mature four to five-year-olds say the boy was bad because he must have done something bad to get punished; that is, they invent a misdeed to account for the punishment. By age seven, a majority say the boy was good, not bad, even though he was punished (Kohlberg, 1963b).

4. *Use of reciprocity.* Four-year-old children do not use reciprocity as a reason for consideration of others, whereas children of seven and older frequently do. Even seven-year-olds show mainly selfish and concrete reciprocity concerns, including anticipation of retaliation and anticipation of

return of favors. Most ten-year-olds who were asked "What would the Golden Rule say to do if a boy came up and hit you?" interpreted the Golden Rule in terms of concrete reciprocity and said, "Hit him back. Do unto others as they do unto you." By age eleven to thirteen most children can clearly judge in terms of ideal reciprocity, in terms of putting oneself in the place of someone in a different position, and in terms of sentiments of gratitude for past affection and favors (Kohlberg, 1958; Durkin, 1959).

5. *Use of punishment as restitution and reform.* Young children advocate severe painful punishment after stories of misdeeds; older children increasingly favor milder punishments leading to restitution to the victim and to the reform of the culprit (Harrower, 1934; Piaget, 1932; Johnson, 1962).

6. *Naturalistic views of misfortune.* Six to seven-year-old children have some tendency to view physical accidents and misfortunes occurring after misdeeds as punishments willed by God or by natural objects ("immanent justice"). Older children do not confuse natural misfortunes with punishment (Caruso, 1943; Lerner, 1937a; MacRae, 1954, Medinnus, 1959).

These six aspects of moral judgment have proved to define genuine dimensions of development in the grammar school years. They increase regularly with age, regardless of the child's nationality in western cultures (Swiss, English, Belgian, American, Spanish), his social class, his religion, or the particular stories or situations about which the child is questioned. The absolutism, nonintentionalism, and orientation to punishment of the young child do not appear to depend upon extensive parental use of physical punishment, punishment for committing accidental damage, and the like (MacRae, 1954; Kohlberg, 1964a). Even the permissively reared child appears to have a "natural" tendency to define good and bad in terms of punishment, a tendency which his awareness of punishment by teachers, police, and other parents seems sufficient to stimulate. While specific punishment practices or cultural ideologies do not appear necessary for the formation of the young child's moral ideology of punishment, they may lead to the persistence of this ideology into adolescence or adulthood (Johnson, 1963; Havighurst and Neugarten, 1955). In other words, specific cultural factors appear to stimulate or retard age trends of development on the Piaget dimensions but they do not appear actually to cause the age shifts or trends observed.

The six aspects of moral judgment (especially the first four) seem primarily to reflect cognitive development, as is suggested by the fact that they are related to I.Q. as well as age. All the dimensions suggest a development from judging in terms of immediate external physical consequences to judging in terms of subjective or internal purposes, norms, or values.

In contrast to the six aspects listed, five others suggested by Piaget's stage theory do not hold up as general dimensions of moral development. The five questionable dimensions are those derived from the social-emotional rather than the cognitive components of Piaget's stages, for example, from his concept of a shift from unilateral respect for adults to a mutual respect for peers.[3] The findings do not support the notion of Piaget and others that there is a general trend of moral development in childhood from an authoritarian to a democratic ethic, although they do support the notion that the child's earliest morality is oriented to obedience, punishment, and impersonal forces, and that it progresses toward more internal and subjective values. Piaget's theory of a shift from unilateral to mutual respect also has suggested a number of factors which would be associated with development on all the dimensions he has described. On the whole, research findings have not supported Piaget's theory with regard to these factors. The first factor stressed by Piaget is differential peer group participation. While peer group participation (measured by friendship choice) is an important factor associated with general development of moral judgment, it has not been found to be specifically associated with advance on measures of intentionality or reciprocity (Kohlberg, 1964a). Children reared on an Israeli kibbutz in a communal peer setting are not more intentionally oriented than Israeli children reared in conventional families.[4] A second factor suggested by Piaget's theory is a democratic or permissive home atmosphere. Parental democracy or permissiveness, however, has not been found to relate to development on the Piaget dimensions (Johnson, 1962; MacRae, 1954).

The research results introduce a third qualification into Piaget's interpretation of his dimensions of development. Piaget's dimensions do not represent definite unitary stages which cut across the separate aspects of moral judgment. Within age and I.Q. groups, a child who is at the autonomous stage on one aspect of morality (for example, intentionality) is not especially likely to be autonomous on another aspect of morality,

[3] These five dimensions are: modification of obedience to rules or authority because of situational demands or human needs; maintaining peer loyalty demands as opposed to obedience to authority; favoring direct retaliation by the victim rather than punishment by authority; favoring equality of treatment rather than differential reward for virtue or for conformity to authority; punishment based only on active individual responsibility rather than collective responsibility. On these dimensions, periods of increase with age tend to be followed by periods of decrease; age increases are not found with all cultural or class groups; trends vary widely depending upon the particular stories or situations used, etc. A more detailed summary of the findings of the Piaget studies in relation to these and other points is presented elsewhere (Kohlberg, 1963a).

[4] Personal communication from S. Kugelmass.

for example, naturalistic justice or reciprocity (MacRae, 1954; Johnson, 1962).

While the results of the Piaget studies provide only limited support for his theory, they do suggest the possibility of uncovering basic trends in the development of moral judgment. Further aspects of moral judgment have formed the subject of stage analyses by the writer. In an initial study of 72 boys of ages ten to sixteen, with Piaget procedures, six types of moral judgment were defined after extensive case study. They fell into three major levels of development as follows:

Level I. Premoral

Type 1. Punishment and obedience orientation.

Type 2. Naive instrumental hedonism.

Level II. Morality of Conventional Role-Conformity

Type 3. Good-boy morality of maintaining good relations, approval of others.

Type 4. Authority maintaining morality.

Level III. Morality of Self-Accepted Moral Principles

Type 5. Morality of contract, of individual rights, and of democratically accepted law.

Type 6. Morality of individual principles of conscience.

Each of the six general types of moral orientation could be defined in terms of its specific stance on 32 aspects of morality. In addition to areas suggested by the Piaget dimensions, the aspects ranged from "Motives for Moral Action" to "Universality of Moral Judgment," from "Concepts of Rights" to "Basis of Respect for Social Authority." As an example, the six types were defined as follows with regard to Aspect 10: "Motivation for Rule Obedience or Moral Action":

Stage 1. Obey rules to avoid punishment.

Stage 2. Conform to obtain rewards, have favors returned, and so on.

Stage 3. Conform to avoid disapproval, dislike by others.

Stage 4. Conform to avoid censure by legitimate authorities and resultant guilt.

Stage 5. Conform to maintain the respect of the impartial spectator judging in term of community welfare.

Stage 6. Conform to avoid self-condemnation.

Examples of actual statements of children corresponding to these stages of motivation are presented in Table 1.

TABLE 1. CHILDREN'S STATEMENTS ILLUSTRATING DEVELOPMENTAL
STAGES ON TWO ASPECTS OF MORALITY

Aspect 10: Motivation for Moral Action

Stage 1: Punishment—Danny, Age 10:
(Should Joe tell on his older brother to his father?)
"In one way it would be right to tell on his brother or his father might get mad at him
and spank him. In another way it would be right to keep quiet or his brother might
beat him up."

Stage 2: Exchange and Reward—Jimmy, Age 13:
(Should Joe tell on his older brother to his father?)
"I think he should keep quiet. He might want to go someplace like that, and if he
squeals on Alex, Alex might squeal on him."

Stage 3: Disapproval Concern—Andy, Age 16:
(Should Joe keep quiet about what his brother did?)
"If my father finds out later, he won't trust me. My brother wouldn't either, but I
wouldn't have a *conscience* that he (my brother) didn't."
"I try to do things for my parents; they've always done things for me. I try to do
everything my mother says; I try to please her. Like she wants me to be a doctor, and
I want to, too, and she's helping me to get up there."

Stage 6: Self-condemnation Concern—Bill, Age 16:
(Should the husband steal the expensive black market drug needed to save his wife's
life?)
"Lawfully no, but morally speaking I think I would have done it. It would be awfully
hard to live with myself afterward, knowing that I could have done something which
would have saved her life and yet didn't for fear of punishment to myself."

Aspect 3: Basis of Moral Worth of a Human Life

Stage 1: Life's Value Based on Physical and Status Aspects—Tommy, Age 10:
(Why should the druggist give the drug to the dying woman when her husband couldn't
pay for it?)
"If someone important is in a plane and is allergic to heights and the stewardess won't
give him medicine because she's only got enough for one and she's got a sick one, a
friend, in back, they'd probably put the stewardess in a lady's jail because she didn't
help the important one."
(Is it better to save the life of one important person or a lot of unimportant people?)
"All the people that aren't important because one man just has one house, maybe a
lot of furniture, but a whole bunch of people have an awful lot of furniture and some
of these poor people might have a lot of money and it doesn't look it."

Stage 2: Life's Value as Instrumental to Need-Satisfaction—Tommy at Age 13:
(Should the doctor "mercy-kill" a fatally ill woman requesting death because of her
pain?)
"Maybe it would be good to put her out of her pain, she'd be better off that way. But
the husband wouldn't want it, it's not like an animal. If a pet dies you can get along
without it—it isn't something you really need. Well, you can get a new wife, but it's
not really the same."

Stage 4: Life Sacred Because of a Social and Religious Order—John, Age 16:
(Should the doctor "mercy-kill" the woman?)
"The doctor wouldn't have the right to take a life, no human has the right. He can't
create life, he shouldn't destroy it."

Stage 6: Life's Value as Expressing the Sacredness of the Individual—Steve, Age 16:
(Should the husband steal the expensive drug to save his wife?)
"By the law of society he was wrong but by the law of nature or of God the druggist
was wrong and the husband was justified. Human life is above financial gain. Regardless of who was dying, if it was a total stranger, man has a duty to save him from
dying."

The stages just listed would be generally taken to reflect moral internalization rather than cognitive development. Cognitive development is more immediately apparent in the following stages of thought about Aspect 3, "The Basis of Moral Worth of a Human Life":

Stage 1. The value of a human life is confused with the value of physical objects and is based on the social status or physical attributes of its possessor.

Stage 2. The value of a human life is seen as instrumental to the satisfaction of the needs of its possessor or of other persons.

Stage 3. The value of a human life is based on the empathy and affection of family members and others toward its possessor.

Stage 4. Life is conceived as sacred in terms of its place in a categorical moral or religious order of rights and duties.

Stage 5. Life is valued both in terms of its relation to community welfare and in terms of life being a universal human right.

Stage 6. Belief in the sacredness of human life as representing a universal human value of respect for the individual.

Examples of statements corresponding to these stages of Aspect 3 are also presented in Table 1.

The age trends for the six stages, considered as including all aspects of morality, are indicated in the accompanying figure. It is evident that the first two types decrease with age, the next two increase until age thirteen and then stabilize, and the last two continue to increase from age thirteen to age sixteen. These age trends indicate that large groups of moral concepts and attitudes acquire meaning only in late childhood and adolescence, and require the extensive background of cognitive growth and social experience associated with the age factor.

There are two possible interpretations of these age findings. Both common sense and most psychological theory would view such age differences as the effect of increased learning of the verbal morality characteristic of the adult American culture. Some patterns of moral verbalization are presumably easier to learn than others, are perhaps explicitly taught earlier, and hence are characteristic of younger ages.

Developmental theories suggest a second interpretation. The stages of moral thinking may not directly represent learning of patterns of verbalization in the culture. Instead, they may represent spontaneous products of the child's effort to make sense out of his experience in a complex social world, each arising sequentially from its predecessors.

As an example, Tommy, the ten-year-old exemplar (in Table 1) of a Stage 1 conception of life's value, implies that one should decide whose life

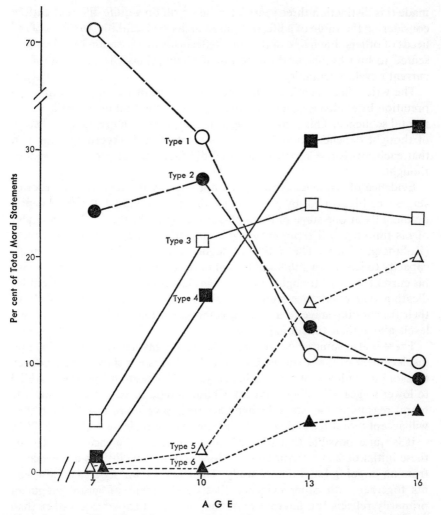

A G E

Mean Per Cent of Total Moral Statements of Each of Six Moral Judgment Types at Four Ages

to save in terms of the amount of furniture owned. While Tommy's response probably reflects his parents' high concern about acquiring or preserving furniture, his derivation of the value of life from the value of furniture is his own. The naive or primitive quality of Tommy's belief arises from a characteristic failure of younger children (usually under eight) to distinguish the value of an object to its owner and its (moral) value to others (moral "egocentrism"). As Table 1 suggests, when Tommy made this distinction three years later, he set off on a quite different path in considering the value of a life, one based on its replaceability in terms of the needs of others. Each line of thinking reflects his organization of values presented to him by his world in terms of assumptions characteristic of his current developmental level.

The writer has been led to accept this second, or developmental, interpretation by evidence suggesting that his stages form an invariant developmental sequence. This evidence suggests that use of a more advanced stage of thought depends upon earlier attainment of each preceding stage and that each involves a restructuring and displacement of previous stages of thought.

Evidence of sequence is suggested not only by the regular age order of stages (see Figure) but by patterning within the individual. If a child is predominantly at one stage of thought (for example, the third), the remainder of his thinking will represent neighboring stages, the second and fourth (Kohlberg, 1963b). The notion of sequence also implies that the child's capacity to learn new modes of thought are contingent on their match with his current stage of thought. Turiel (1964) has conducted an experiment indicating that children assimilate adult moral reasoning one level above their functioning stage to a much greater extent than moral reasoning two levels above their functional stage.

There is also some evidence that higher stages involve reorganization and displacement of lower stages. Use of higher stages is a sign of the tendency to avoid using lower stages; higher stages do not seem to be simply added to lower stages (Kohlberg, 1963a). Children tend to accept and assimilate moral reasoning one stage higher than their own more readily than they will accept moral reasoning one stage lower than their own (Turiel, 1964).

It is quite possible that the notion of invariant sequence suggested by these initial data is oversimplified. More definite conclusions are expected from an ongoing longitudinal study. The evidence for sequence, however, fits together with other evidence that development of moral judgment primarily reflects the internal patterning of social experience rather than the effects of direct teaching.

If the age development of moral ideology and judgment were a matter of verbal learning, the age factor would presumably be largely a matter of verbal intelligence or verbal mental age. If broader factors of social experience were involved, age would be expected to be highly related to moral development even with verbal intelligence controlled. The latter expectation appears to be true. Moral judgment is moderately correlated with I.Q. ($r = .31$) but quite highly related to age, with intelligence controlled ($r = .59$).

Intellectual development, then, is an important condition for development of moral thought, but level of moral thought can be clearly distinguished from general intellectual level. Level of moral judgment appears to be a quite unitary or consistent personal characteristic distinct from intelligence or specific subcultural background and beliefs. The child's stage of verbal moral judgment is quite consistent, whether a family situation or a military situation is involved, and whether the child is in favor of complying with a rule or violating it (Kohlberg, 1964a).

How may such a level of maturity of moral judgment, distinct from intellectual maturity, be interpreted or defined? One general answer is that a more mature judgment is a more *moral* judgment. This does not mean that a child who utters mature judgments is a more moral person, as judged by the standards of his community. It means that his judgments more closely correspond to genuine moral judgments as these have been defined by philosophers.

While philosophers have been unable to agree upon any ultimate principle of the good which would define "correct" moral judgments, most philosophers agree upon the characteristics which make a judgment a genuine moral judgment (Hare, 1952; Kant, 1949; Sidgwick, 1901; Mandelbaum, 1954). Moral judgments are judgments about the good and the right of action. Not all judgments of "good" or "right" are moral judgments, however; many are judgments of esthetic, technological, or prudential goodness or rightness. Unlike judgments of prudence or esthetics, moral judgments tend to be universal, inclusive, consistent, and to be grounded on objective, impersonal, or ideal grounds (Kohlberg, 1958). "I don't like him because he doesn't look nice"; "Cadillacs are good because they're expensive"; "It's not right to steal because you'll get put in jail"—these are statements about good and right which are not moral judgments, since they lack these characteristics. If we say, "Cadillacs are good because they're expensive," we are making an economic or esthetic judgment and we are not prepared to say that everyone should have them or that everyone should feel they are good; that they are good in terms of some impersonal ideal standard shared by others; and that everyone should buy a Cadillac whether he wishes to or not. If we say that an act is "morally right," we are also prepared to assert these implications of our judgment of good and right.

In this sense we can define a moral judgment as "moral" without considering its content (the action judged) and without considering whether it agrees or not with our own judgments or standards. The general direction of development in western culture seems to be toward making judgments which are genuine moral judgments. The majority of the 32 aspects of maturity defined in the Kohlberg studies, as well as the validated Piaget dimensions, correspond to these aspects of a moral judgment as defined by philosophers.

Such an interpretation of the direction of development of moral judgment implies that development is in many ways the same, regardless of the child's nation (in western culture), social class, peer group, or sex. While such a belief flies in the face of prevalent notions of unlimited cultural relativism, it is somewhat supported by empirical evidence. The Piaget studies indicated similar trends of development in various nations, in various social classes within nations, and among boys and girls. The Kohlberg studies indicated the same basic stages of moral judgment in middle- and working-class children, in Protestants and Catholics, in popular and socially isolated children, in boys and girls, and in Formosan Chinese and American children (Kohlberg, 1964a). The statement that the same stages of judgment were found means that children's answers could be categorized the same as to stage without overlooking obviously new kinds of responses, that individual children were consistent in stage regardless of group membership, and that the age order of the stages was the same in all social groups.

The most conspicuous general differences between the social groups were developmental differences which paralleled age differences, rather than differences in cultural values or beliefs[5] (Kohlberg, 1958, 1964a). In both the social class and peer group comparisons, the children involved in more extensive social participation or responsibilities (the middle-class children and the popular children) were on the whole more mature in moral judgment.[6] This was not due to the fact that the middle-class children (or the popular children) heavily favored some one type of thought, which could be seen as corresponding to the prevailing middle-class pattern (or the prevailing youth culture pattern). Instead, middle-class and working-class children seemed to move through the same sequences, but the middle-class children seemed to move faster and farther.

These findings contrast with many sociological notions as to how group memberships determine moral development. It is often thought that the child gets some of his basic moral values from his family, some from the

[5] In the case of religious groups, specific value differences were more apparent. Differences between Protestants and Catholics were not apparent in general level of development of moral judgment. Other studies have shown that exposure to parochial schools increases intentionality of moral judgment on Piaget's tests, but this is equally true for Protestant and Catholic parochial schools (Boehm and Nass, 1962: Brink, 1963).

[6] Adolescent boys were also significantly more mature than girls, a finding consistent with the notion that roles entailing more participation and responsibility should stimulate greater maturity. Other evidence suggests that this sex difference does not appear until early adolescence (Kohlberg, 1964b).

peer group, and others from the wider society, and that these basic values tend to conflict with one another. Instead of participation in various groups causing conflicting developmental trends in morality, it appears that participation in various groups converges in stimulating the development of basic moral values, which are not transmitted by one particular group as opposed to another. The child lives in a total social world in which perceptions of the law, of the peer group, and of parental teachings all influence one another. While various people and groups make conflicting *immediate demands* upon the child, they do not seem to present the child with basically conflicting or different *general moral values*. In the course of "normal" development, the conflicts between demands of groups and individuals constitute the material for the discrimination and development of such general moral values.

The institutions with moral authority (law, government, family, the work order) and the basic moral rules are the same regardless of the individual's particular position in society. The child's position in society does to a large extent, however, determine his interpretation of these institutions and rules. Law and the government are perceived quite differently by the child if he feels a sense of potential participation in the social order than if he does not. The effect of such a sense of participation upon development of moral judgments related to the law is suggested by the following responses of sixteen-year-olds to the question, "Should someone obey a law if he doesn't think it is a good law?" A lower-class boy replies, "Yes, a law is a law and you can't do nothing about it. You have to obey it, you should. That's what it's there for." (For him the law is simply a constraining thing that is there. The very fact that he has no hand in it, that "you can't do nothing about it," means that it should be obeyed.)

A lower middle-class boy replies, "Laws are made for people to obey and if everyone would start breaking them. . . . Well, if you owned a store and there were no laws, everybody would just come in and not have to pay." (Here laws are seen not as arbitrary commands but as a unitary system, as the basis of the social order. The role or perspective taken is that of a storekeeper, of someone with a stake in the order.)

An upper middle-class boy replies, "The law's the law but I think people themselves can tell what's right or wrong. I suppose the laws are made by many different groups of people with different ideas. But if you don't believe in a law, you should try to get it changed, you shouldn't disobey it." (Here the laws are seen as the product of various legitimate ideological and interest groups varying in their beliefs as to the best decision in policy matters. The role of law-obeyer is seen from the perspective of the democratic policy-maker.)

While class differences in perspective are especially pronounced with regard to law and generalized social authority, they are also evident in the areas of family and friendship relationships. Peer-group participation differences are similar to class differences but somewhat more pronounced in the family and friendship areas. Thus neither the view that the child gets some values from family and some from peers, nor theories like Piaget's which stress role-taking in one type of group rather than another, should obscure the elements of stimulation of moral development that appear common to them all.

The picture of moral development emerging from the moral judgment findings contrasts in several ways with the picture derived from the findings on moral conduct. Judgment does not appear to become "moral" until early adolescence, while "morality" of conduct appears to develop early. Individual differences in level of moral judgment are quite general and stable; morality of conduct is more specific to the situation and more unstable over time. Moral judgment appears to develop in the same direction regardless of social groups; moral conduct appears to develop in line with specific social class and peer-group norms.

Discrepancies between moral conduct and moral verbalizations are often taken as indicating that moral judgments are statements made to "put up a front" and that they develop independently of basic moral conduct or of conscience feelings. Such a view of the divorce of judgment and conduct seems to spring from the findings noted earlier that children's verbal statements of knowledge and belief that a moral act is right are almost useless predictors of performance of that act.

The fact that when the chips are down children do not do what they say does not mean that *development* of judgment and *development* of conduct go along on two independent tracks, however. Verbal judgments may not be "trustworthy" reports of conduct but they may still reflect the same basic developmental processes. There are moderately good correlations between level of moral judgment and experimental measures of resistance to cheating, and between judgment level and teacher's ratings of conscience ($r=.31$) and fairness with peers ($r=.51$). (See Kohlberg, 1964a.) These correlations of conduct with moral judgment—level of personal thought and ideology—seem to be at about the same level as the Hartshorne and May correlations of conduct with moral *knowledge*—awareness of conventional standards ($r=.34$). Furthermore, one can predict an aspect of moral conduct, for example, honesty, from moral judgment about as well as one can predict it from another aspect of moral conduct, for example, service.

The judgment-conduct correlations reinforce the general implications of the conduct-ego-strength findings. Both suggest that moral character, the general consistency in moral conduct, is to a large extent a product of maturity factors in decision making. We do not know the extent to which maturity of moral judgment represents the same factors discussed earlier as "ego strength."

We have so far discussed moral character as resistance to temptation or conformity to cultural imperatives in the face of selfish interests or impulses. In the resistance to temptation situations usually studied, external social pressures are in line with such cultural imperatives. In fact, however, the individual's direction by moral principles may often stand in opposition to social pressures by peers or adults. The child's ability to maintain direction by his own moral beliefs in the face of such pressure is usually termed "moral autonomy" or "moral courage." There is some evidence that such autonomy of judgment, unlike resistance to temptation, increases with age and other maturity variables, that it cuts across specific situations or specific pressuring groups, adult or peer, and that it correlates quite well with maturity of moral judgment ($r = .44$).

The same gross variables which favor advance in moral judgment, favor resistance to temptation and moral autonomy. These include intelligence, social class, and peer-group status (Kohlberg, 1964a). The findings on moral conduct, as well as moral judgment, then, suggest a considerable convergence of the influence of various social participation groups in moral development, though not in immediate reactions to moral situations.

THE DEVELOPMENT AND FUNCTIONING OF GUILT AND OTHER REACTIONS TO TRANSGRESSION

Many psychological writings use such terms as "conscience," "superego," and "moral character" interchangeably and center all these terms on notions of guilt or anxiety. Our review of research on moral character and judgment indicates that such simple equations are unwarranted, and that anxiety or guilt feelings may not be the most direct key to understanding the development of moral character or moral judgment. Nevertheless, guilt reactions are obviously important aspects of morality, and we must now consider the findings which clarify their complex role in moral development. In this discussion, we shall touch upon the relation of types of discipline to guilt, although a more direct and detailed review of these findings is presented in Wesley Becker's chapter in this volume. Guilt responses have formed the central focus of research on moral learning through processes of punishment and identification with parents. Several studies in this area are reported in books by Bandura and Walters (1959); Miller and Swanson (1960); Sears, Maccoby, and Levin (1957); Sears, Rau, and Alpert (1964); and Whiting and Child (1953).

Much theoretical and popular discussion has used the term "guilt" to include all painful reactions after transgression. Recently, however, extensive efforts have been made to discriminate conceptually between various types of transgression reaction, such as shame, fear, anxiety, and guilt (Erikson, 1950; Piers and Singer, 1953; Whiting, 1959). Research results clearly indicate the need to make such distinctions, since different types of transgression reactions have different relations to both child-rearing conditions and to moral behavior. When all types of reaction to transgression have been combined to get general measures of intensity of guilt, unstable and confusing findings have resulted.

Our knowledge of the varieties of transgression reactions comes mainly from free projective responses to stories in which the "hero" violates a rule when there is no chance of detection. The child is asked to complete such stories, telling what happens to the hero and how he feels. A condensed example of such a story (Allinsmith, 1960; Bandura and Walters, 1959), and of major varieties of completion responses, is presented in Table 2.

Evidence discussed in detail elsewhere (Kohlberg, 1963a) suggests that transgression story reactions fall into three main functional types. The first type includes punishment, fear, and hiding—emotions which represent

TABLE 2. EXAMPLES OF MAJOR TYPES OF ADOLESCENT COMPLETIONS
OF A TRANSGRESSION STORY

> Bill saved up $10 for a catcher's mitt. When he arrives at the store, he sees the sales clerk going down the stairs to the cellar. The clerk doesn't see Bill. Bill looks at the gloves, and just as he sees one he likes, he reaches for his money. It's gone, he realizes he has lost it. He feels awful. It occurs to Bill that the mitt would just fit under his jacket. He hides the mitt and walks out of the store. Now you finish the story.

Fear and hiding: "He walks out of the store, then he starts running. All the time he wonders if anybody saw him. He finally gets home and waits a couple days and nothing happens."

Restitution or fixing: "He walks away, but he soon realizes that it wasn't right so he goes to return the mitt. When he gets in the store he realizes it would give him a bad name if he said he took the mitt. So he goes near the other mitts, drops the mitt and picks it up and says, 'A dropped mitt'."

Punishment: "The clerk came up from the cellar, ran outside and caught Bill."

Confession: "He goes home with the mitt and tells his father he bought it. He's got it for three weeks, then it gets on his conscience and he goes in the store and tells the clerk about it."

Self-criticism and remorse: "He takes it home but he's not proud of himself. If he was really honest he wouldn't have taken it. If he took it, he wouldn't respect himself for doing that."

anxiety about punishment rather than guilt. Since the stories explicitly rule out the possibility of detection, such anxiety is unrealistic. These tendencies to express "moral anxiety" in terms of fantasies of harm to a transgressor also do not seem to serve a directly moral function, and do not correlate with nondelinquency, resistance to temptation, or morality of judgment (Bandura and Walters, 1959; Burton, 1958; Kohlberg, 1963b).

A second type of response is the direct expression of self-blame or self-judgment, true "guilt" in ordinary language. This response does seem to play a direct moral function, since it is correlated with experimental resistance to temptation (Grinder and McMichael, 1963; MacKinnon, 1938), avoidance of delinquent acts (Bandura and Walters, 1959; McCord and McCord, 1956), and development of moral judgment (Johnson, 1963).

A third intermediate type of response is best represented by confession. This response seems to represent something in between the internal moral reaction of self-criticism and the externally focused anxiety represented by a preoccupation with punishment. In some contexts, confession is correlated with resistance to temptation (Grinder, 1962; Rebelsky, Allinsmith, and Grinder, 1963). In some contexts, it is not (Burton, Maccoby, and Allinsmith, 1961; Rau, 1964). Confession may be an expression primarily of concern about the judgment of others rather than an act based on self-judgment, but it does represent a tendency to be upset by imagined disapproval of others even though one could "get away with it" (Rebelsky, 1963).[7] Hence one would expect the relationship of confession to resistance to temptation to depend upon the situational context of the act and its relationship to significant others.

The trends of age development for these three types of reaction suggest that they represent different levels of maturity. Studies of the early school years report that punishment fantasies occur early and decline with age, while confession increases with age (Maccoby and Whiting, 1960; Wright, Hill, and Alpert, 1961). Direct guilt or self-criticism is reported as very rare in these studies of younger children, but is found in a majority of children aged twelve to thirteen (Aronfreed, 1961; Hoffman, 1963).

These age findings concerning the slow development of the capacity for internal guilt or self-criticism pose something of a problem for moral theories which trace guilt to early experiences of punishment. It seems self-evident that self-induced pain after transgression (guilt) must largely originate from experiences of transgression-related pain caused by others (punishment). Some core experiences of punishment, or at least of blame,

---

[7] As is indicated later, some studies have reported high confession as associated with use of love-withdrawal discipline techniques, which suggests that confession does represent such a concern about disapproval or loss of affection after transgression.

are presumably necessary for the development of guilt reactions. Punishment, however, does not directly produce guilt, since the young punished child does not develop guilt. Furthermore, there does not appear to be a direct relationship between amount of punishment and amount of guilt. We are also not able to say that the more psychologically painful the punishment, the more likely it is to produce guilt. Physical punishment seems to show a low but significant positive correlation with children's use of punishment fantasies as consequences of transgression (Maccoby and Whiting, 1960), but does not relate positively to types of transgression reaction more representative of guilt. Even for punishment reactions, young children whose parents report they never use physical punishment may make heavy use of it in doll play transgression stories. It seems that punishment fantasies in these children may be related to a need to insist upon the power of parents and other authorities (Piaget, 1932; Rau, 1964).

Punishment by love withdrawal (ignoring, isolation, mother's statements that she doesn't like the child when he is bad, and so on) has been thought to be especially critical in producing guilt, because loss of love is believed to be more psychologically painful or anxiety arousing than physical punishment, and because it would be expected to lead to implicit role-taking or identification with the parent's disapproval (Sears, Maccoby, and Levin, 1957). Use of love-withdrawal discipline has been found to be correlated with the child's tending to confess (Burton, Maccoby, and Allinsmith, 1961; Sears, Maccoby, and Levin, 1957), although some studies do not report such a relation (Hoffman, 1963). Love withdrawal has not been found to relate to self-critical guilt, however (Aronfreed, 1961; Hoffman, 1963).

In a recent review of the literature, Hoffman (1963) suggests that the parental techniques of discipline which relate to self-critical guilt are not the infliction of psychological or physical pain extrinsic to the act, for example, the use of physical force or love withdrawal. Rather than such sanctions, the use of psychological induction of remorse by reasoning and pointing out the harm caused to others has been found to be correlated with internal guilt (Hoffman, 1963; Allinsmith and Greening, 1955). Such techniques involve the direct stimulation of the child's capacity for moral self-judgment and guilt, rather than the creation of guilt out of punishment.[8]

Presumably discipline is effective in inducing guilt only within a context in which a child is capable of, and is stimulated to make, moral self-judgments. The relation between self-critical guilt and maturity of moral judgment (Johnson, 1963, Kohlberg, 1963b) is consistent with this interpreta-

---

[8] Aronfreed (1963, 1964), however, has found experimental analogues of self-criticism related to timing of an experimental punishment of candy withdrawal, as well as finding it related to the experimenter's use of evaluative labels. We do not yet know how these experimental findings relate to natural situations of guilt-formation.

tion. These findings suggest that more mature or internal forms of transgression reactions, for example, self-criticism, are less direct reflections of punishment experiences than are immature forms, and that they are related to existential and developmental factors such as age and social class participation (Aronfreed, 1961) and to stimulation by the parent's moral communications. This conclusion needs qualification in terms of the methods used to measure guilt. The story-completion method generally used has been considered "projective," but it is clearly designed to elicit reactions of appropriate guilt rather than of unconscious or inappropriate guilt. Efforts to measure unconscious or genetically early guilt reactions with this method have been largely unsuccessful. Successful study of the role of early punishment and genetically primitive forms of guilt in later conscience development may require extensive longitudinal study.

The fact that punishment does not directly produce guilt has often been interpreted as indicating that processes of identification are required to transform punishment-anxiety into internal guilt. In this context, identification has meant the general tendency to take the role of the punishing and criticizing other. That is, in order to criticize or punish himself after transgression, the child must take the role of another toward himself. Otherwise, he would continue to view himself and the situation as he did when he performed the act. For self-criticism to be guilt, the child must "take the role of the other" in a deep or internalized sense, regardless of whether the other knows about his transgression. Such identification has been variously hypothesized to result from needs to substitute for an absent or rejecting love object (Freud, 1930; Sears, Maccoby, and Levin, 1957), from needs to defend against fear of aggression (A. Freud, 1937), or from "status envy" needs (Whiting, 1960).

Like concepts of discipline, concepts of identification must be broken down into types. The most relevant distinction seems to the writer to be between personal identification—the wish to be like the parent as an individual—and positional identification—the wish to occupy the parent's sex, authority, or family roles as figures of power or possessors of resources (Slater, 1961). Research findings suggest that personal identification is related to moral learning, while positional identification is not.

Interview measures of personal identification have been found to relate to internalized moral judgments and to guilt (Hoffman, 1963; Heinicke, 1953) as well as to nondelinquency (Glueck and Glueck, 1950; Bandura and Walters, 1959). Parental warmth would be expected to favor personal identification, as seems to be the case (Faigin, 1953; Payne and Mussen, 1956). Like personal identification, parental warmth has also been found to relate to guilt (Hoffman, 1963), to internal moral judgment (Hoffman,

1963), and to nondelinquency (Glueck and Glueck, 1950).[9] In contrast, measures of positional identification such as identification with the same sex role and with the adult authority role do not relate to moral conduct or guilt (Goethals, 1955; Maccoby, 1961; Rau, 1964; Terman and Miles, 1936).

These findings are consistent with the theory that conscience identification derives from the substitute satisfaction of dependency needs (Sears Maccoby, and Levin, 1957). However, these findings may be more easily explained without assuming covert imitative processes (Kohlberg, 1963a). That is, a child should more readily accept the values of an adult who is liked or accepted, and an adult should be better liked if he is himself accepting and nurturant. The greater acceptance of moral standards by warmly treated children does not appear to lead to greater moral control in terms of these standards, however. None of the relevant studies finds parental warmth related to resistance to temptation (Burton, Maccoby, and Allinsmith, 1961; Grinder, 1962; Rau, 1964) and, as we have noted earlier, degree of acceptance of standards need have little relationship to degree of self-restriction in terms of these standards.

The superego-identification interpretation suggests that internal conscience and guilt require the unique dependency-love tie of the young child to his parent. In contrast, the interpretation that affectional relationships (or identification) with parents is important in moral development *because positive and affectional relations to others are in general conducive to role-taking and acceptance of social standards* does not necessarily require this particular parent-child relationship. This latter interpretation is more consistent with the stage-development theories of Piaget, Baldwin, and Mead, discussed earlier. The data most relevant to this issue come from studies of the moral attitudes of children reared in institutions, foster homes, and kibbutzim.

Orphanage children (Goldfarb, 1955) and children deprived of any stable caretaking figures or family life (Redl and Wineman, 1952; Bowlby, 1947) have been found to show defects in moral attitudes. In these studies, however, as indicated in the chapter by Leon Yarrow in this volume, the environmental conditions were depriving in many additional ways. More crucial data on this issue come from studies comparing kibbutz children with control group children in Israel. While kibbutz-reared children have regular contact with their parents in the evenings and holidays, they live in a nursery with other children and their care and socialization is entrusted to a nurse-caretaker (metapeleth). The children grow up with stable affec-

---

[9] Both sets of findings are true primarily for boys, but they appear to hold equally for relations to both mother and father.

tional ties to parent-figures in a stable and socially stimulating environment, but the relations are less conflictful and intense (Rabin, 1958, 1959) and the source of socialization or "moral" demands (the metapeleth) are relatively distinct from the source of continuing affectional relations (the parents). As might be expected, in this setting moral values are more peer-group oriented than in the non-kibbutz setting (Faigin, 1958; Luria, Goldwasser, and Goldwasser, 1963).

The maturity of moral judgment of kibbutz children on Piaget's dimensions, however, is similar to that of family-reared Israeli children.[10] Reports of naturalistic observation of social behavior of kibbutz children are conflicting with regard to level of internal moral control (Spiro, 1958), but in general, kibbutz-reared adults appear to fill positions of moral responsibility equivalent to those of non-kibbutz reared persons. The kibbutz data, then, seem to suggest that an intense relationship to parents may not be necessary for the level of moral conduct and judgment expected in western societies.

With regard to guilt, the findings are more ambiguous. Kibbutz children display as much confessional guilt on story completion tests as family-reared rural controls (Luria, Goldwasser, and Goldwasser, 1963). The kibbutz children, however, do not describe as intense general negative consequences of transgression as family-reared city children (Rabin and Goldman, 1963). Since neither study used a measure with much claim to validity as an index of internal guilt, and since the control groups involved differed, urban versus rural, it is difficult to draw conclusions from these studies. They do suggest that kibbutz children are not grossly lacking in guilt reactions or a "superego," but that they react less intensely to some common transgressions. This, of course, may be a matter of group ideology, rather than of the quality of the parent-child relationship.

The writer would conclude from these studies on children reared without intense parent-child relationships that the child's identification with his parents is basically similar in nature to his role-taking and identification in other close social relationships. Because most societies make the parent-child relationship so important to the child, it is undoubtedly more crucial for the formation of moral attitudes than are the child's other social relationships. In American children there is a stage in middle and late childhood in which moral role-taking is primarily focused upon the parents (Ausubel, 1952; Kohlberg, 1958). This is probably due to the child's awareness that the parent is the legitimate and final authority for him within our society. As the adolescent moves into more complex and egalitarian role-

---

[10] S. Kugelmass, personal communication.

taking systems, moral role-taking or identification with parents is largely replaced by role-taking of those whom the social order, moral principles, and the moral situation then deem most relevant.

MORAL FACTORS IN DELINQUENCY AND NEUROSIS

A real problem is posed in integrating the findings on moral conduct and guilt in normal children with psychiatric thinking about psychopathology in childhood and adolescence. In the psychoanalytic view, neuroses and learning blocks may represent inhibitions closely linked to childhood guilt; while delinquent and other self-damaging acts may represent the need for punishment (Fenichel, 1945; Flugel, 1955). Other psychiatric and psychoanalytic thinkers have stressed the role of a pathological absence of superego or guilt feelings in the psychopathic delinquent (McCord and McCord, 1956).

Such clinical interpretations are difficult to integrate with the findings on normal children, which suggest that the formation of strong guilt tendencies may not be a necessary or universal part of childhood development and that moral conduct may be regulated more by ego strength, moral judgment, and situational expectations and reinforcement than by fixed guilt feelings. While the research studies on moral factors in delinquency and neurosis are limited, it is worthwhile to review them with regard to these basic issues.

Delinquency

Interview and story-completion data indicate that both lower- and middle-class delinquents are low in the late developing self-critical guilt reactions (Bandura and Walters, 1959; McCord and McCord, 1956). It should not be concluded from this finding that delinquents lack a superego, however, in the sense that they lack genetically early or unconscious forms of transgression reactions. No differences were found between delinquents and controls in transgression story responses of punishment, self-damage, or confession (Bandura and Walters, 1959; Woodbury, unpublished study). The observed differences in self-critical guilt seem to be largely the result of the delinquents' current moral attitude rather than of fixed personality defects. After one year of milieu or residential therapy, delinquents tested in the therapeutic institution seemed quite similar to lower-class controls in story self-blame reactions (McCord and McCord, 1956).

The attitude behind the delinquent's failure to express mature guilt appears to be his anticonventional or amoral ideology. In addition to expressing less self-critical reactions to transgression stories, delinquents express less moralizing judgments about the transgressor. A not atypical delinquent response to an incomplete story about finding a wallet on the street is:

"The kid boots the purse and makes off with the money, you know; looks for identification, takes the money, and leaves the purse. That's what I would do. Why work if you can steal it. That ain't the right attitude, but it's one way of getting it" (Bandura and Walters, 1959).

This apparently amoralistic ideology of the serious delinquent has been viewed by sociologists such as Cohen (1955) as the result of the delinquent's attachment to a group code which is deviant from conventional legal norms. The assumption has been made that the gang's code is moral, though nonlegal, and that the delinquent morally internalizes the gang code rather than (or in addition to) the conventional code. This view appears to be only partially true. The gang has a code which the delinquent obeys, but it is not perceived as being a *moral* code, by the delinquent, nor is it conformed to for internalized moral reasons. Rather, delinquents tend to perceive conformity to both the law and the gang as matters of external pressures and opportunistic advantage. Serious delinquents in the Kohlberg study (1958) tended to respond in consistently "premoral" fashion whether legal norms or gang norms were involved. Thus "not ratting" on a friend tended to be justified in the same external terms (retaliation, being ridiculed, and so on) as conformity to more conventional norms.

The 24 small city lower-class delinquents in the Kohlberg study were markedly less mature in moral judgment than matched controls, tending to be at the first two "premoral" stages of judgment. In most cases their judgments seemed to show simple developmental arrest which allowed no basis for discriminating between moral and nonmoral (gang) forms of "rightness," both being based on force and social pressure. In other cases, they had formed definite antimoral ideologies, expressed in such statements as John's, that: "Laws are made by cowards to protect themselves. Everybody is a crook at heart. You can take a child from birth and raise him to be any type of character. We raise people to kill rabbits, we could just as well raise them to kill people. As far as I am concerned what is right is to go by my own instinct." Such a relativistic antimoral ideology is not an expression of the ready-made code of a deviant subgroup, since it was not expressed by other members of John's gang. Instead, it represents an articulated individual philosophy involving considerable rationality and sophistication but continuous in basic assumptions with much of the Stage 2 thinking of normal children of eight to ten.

In addition to developmental defects and distortions in moral judgment and guilt reactions, a number of "nonmoral" deficiencies have been found to characterize delinquents, for example, ego deficits, lack of affectional reactions, and strong aggressive impulses. Such aspects of the delinquent's personality and situation which are not specifically moral are probably of far greater significance than are moral factors in the causation of delinquency. Moral ideology and self-concept factors deserve emphasis, however, because they color the whole life and personality of delinquents in stable and distinctive ways. Persons concerned with rehabilitating delinquents are perennially upset by their apparent indifference to reforming. While weak ego and other nonmoral factors are probably major factors in "getting into trouble," they do not prevent a desire for reform. In contrast, a deviant or immature moral ideology and self-concept make rehabilitative efforts extremely difficult.

Like the findings on delinquent character, the findings on the social environment of delinquents suggest an exaggeration of factors in "normal" moral misconduct. The picture is similar to, but more extreme than, that of the poor-character families in the Peck and Havighurst study. Parents of delinquents tend to be more punitive than parents of nondelinquents, although they do not differ in extent of "firmness" of socialization and home demands. They are less warm and affectionate and more inconsistent and neglectful than parents of nondelinquents. Delinquent boys tend to have overtly hostile relationships with their fathers. These differences hold regardless of social class (Glueck and Glueck, 1950; Bandura and Walters, 1959). Parent-child relationships appear to be part of a larger pattern of moral deviance and criminality (Glueck and Glueck, 1950), of subtler defects in moral judgment and attitudes "projected" onto children (A. Johnson, 1959), and of general family and social disorganization.

Such a family environment obviously seems nonconducive to any form of ego development or moral learning. In regard to moral ideology, delinquent "developmental arrest" is probably the result of living in a world which fits all too well the simplistic interpretations of early stages of moral thought. The child of eight to twelve begins to discriminate clearly between indifferent moral concerns and self-interest, both in his own conduct and that of others. Many normal children of this age (especially in the lower class) perceive themselves, their peers, and the external authorities as largely motivated by power, pleasure, and self-interest factors. If such children are also led by home conditions to perceive their parents as not only severely frustrating them, but as frustrating them out of selfish impulse and motives, they are likely to form a totally amoral view of the world. Among the small Kohlberg sample of delinquents, most of those who became adult recidivists were either amoralistic, or else fairly openly expressed the idea that their delinquent acts were "just" retaliations for grievances toward their parents.

In addition to family and social environmental factors, the actual performance of delinquent acts is an important factor in the crystallization of a premoral or antimoral ideology and associated decrements in guilt reactions. Delinquent action probably leads less to a positive identification with a deviant role than to a neutralization of its "badness." The delinquent group tends to harden, systematically, new members against sensitivity to sympathy, fear, disapproval, and guilt. In addition, the general tendency to maintain consistency between behavior and attitudes may lead to more positive evaluations of deviant acts after their performance (Festinger, 1957). In normal children, projective "guilt" reactions do not appear to increase after yielding to minor transgressions (cheating), while resisting transgression appears to increase both "guilt" reactions and moral condemnation of the act, presumably as a justification for renouncing the rewards of transgression (Burton, 1958; Mills, 1958; Rebelsky, Allinsmith, and Grinder, 1963).

Neurosis

Among the most far-reaching and fundamental issues in the study of morality are those concerning the role of guilt in the genesis of neurosis. It is obvious that neurotics suffer from strong feelings of anxiety, depression, low self-esteem, and inhibition. To a considerable extent, psychoanalysis views these feelings as expressions of guilt about repressed aggressive and incestuous wishes. It is held that since the child believes forbidden wishes are almost as evil and dangerous as forbidden acts, all children accumulate considerable guilt. When these wishes are especially strong and when strong repressive or conscience-producing forces exist, intense guilt and neurotic symptoms may result. Other theorists, such as Mowrer (1952), have held that neurotic symptoms may be the indirect expression of repressed guilt caused by real, rather than fantasied, transgressions. Both theories suggest that neurotics might be expected to show more general signs of conscious or unconscious guilt than normals (though the theories do not *necessarily* imply this conclusion).

The research findings on guilt and moral factors in neurosis are sparse, but they do suggest limitations to the notion that neurotics suffer from too much guilt or moral restraint. There is little reason to believe that neurotics are more scrupulous in their moral ideals or more morally restrained in their conduct than normal people. Neurotic children were slightly (nonsignificantly) lower than normal controls in development of moral judgment (Kohlberg, unpublished study), and paper and pencil tests of neurotic symptoms have been found to relate negatively though only slightly to honest behavior (Hartshorne and May, 1928). Thus, although neurotics may, in general, be more dissatisfied with themselves or show greater dis-

crepancies between their real and ideal selves than normals, these discrepancies may not necessarily exist with regard to moral issues.

Of more basic interest, neurotic and learning-block children referred to
a child guidance clinic did not display significantly more indicators of guilt
on either TAT pictures or story-completion items than normal or behavior-
problem children (Kohlberg, unpublished study; Woodbury, unpublished
study). These findings suggest that neurotic symptoms may not be associated with a generally guilty personality. It is still possible, of course, that
specific symptoms are associated with specific forms of guilt, for example,
incest guilt, without giving rise to a general or pervasive tendency toward
guilt. As previously mentioned, the story-completion method taps general
guilt about transgressions which the culture believes guilt-worthy, rather
than tapping neurotic or inappropriate guilt.

THE RELATION OF MORAL IDEOLOGIES TO PERSONALITY INTEGRATION

Underlying discussions of moral development, one may find various
assumptions as to the role of morality in personality integration. These
have varied from the view that morality or conscience is the highest integrative force in the personality to the view that it is basically a restrictive,
conflict-creating force and "that what the world calls its code of morals
demands more sacrifices than it is worth" (Freud, 1925). The relations
obtained empirically between moral character and ego strength in normal
children, together with the absence of signs of a generally overstrong conscience in neurotics, suggest that moral development and control are not
generally purchased at the expense of other aspects of personality development and functioning.

The concept of the punitive superego, however, has led psychoanalytically oriented thinkers to hypothesize relations between certain types of
moral systems and high personality conflict. In particular, recent researchers have focused upon the cognitive and social functioning of persons with
"authoritarian" (Adorno et al., 1950), "conventionalistic" (Hoffman,
1961), or "stereopathic" (Stern, 1962) sociomoral ideologies, as opposed to
"democratic-humanistic" ideologies. These researchers have generally held
that "authoritarianism" is a moral ideology representing defenses against
awareness of conflicts between moral repressive forces (superego) and
"natural" ego and id forces in the personality. Born out of conflict and
defense, and hence irrational, the authoritarian moral ideology is believed
to impose further restrictions upon receptivity to experience and effective
cognitive functioning.

The rationale for this view is that the authoritarian ideology represents the subordination of the ego to the superego. Because the "authoritarian" is insecure about the effectiveness of his own internal moral control, he is believed to exaggerate the value and power of external authority and to project his own uncontrolled or "immoral" impulses upon "evil" members of various outgroups. These tendencies are expressed in a variety of beliefs represented on the authoritarianism or "F" scale, including strong belief in social and religious authorities, adherence to conventional rules, punitive attitudes toward criminals and deviants, belief in the prevalence of evil in the world, and the denial of unconventional inner feelings. In contrast, the democratic-humanist ideology is thought to represent a morality based upon, and integrated with, the ego. According to Sanford (1959), "It is quite likely that the chief opponent of authoritarianism is an internalized superego which is genuinely integrated with the ego."

Research analysis (Sanford, 1959, 1962) suggests that authoritarian beliefs do cluster together to form a type of ideology (although high scores on the F-scale are largely a result of nonideological factors of test-taking set). While authoritarian beliefs are highly associated with racial and national prejudice and with politico-economic conservatism, authoritarianism may be defined independently of these social and political attitudes.

There are few studies which bear directly upon the notion that authoritarianism reflects a personality type in which there has been a "failure of the superego to be integrated with the ego," while humanism reflects a personality type in which such integration has occurred. Some relatively direct evidence on this point has been gathered by Hoffman (1961) with regard to a similar moral typology. Hoffman defined three types of preadolescent response to moral judgment situations: an external type (judging in terms of punishment), a conventional type (judging in terms of upholding the rules), and a humanistic type (judging in terms of consequences to the interests and feelings of others). The external morality is viewed as the product of a weak superego, the conventional morality as based upon superego repression, and the humanistic morality as based upon the integration of ego and superego. Groups of conventionals and humanists (who were equated for age, class, and I.Q.) showed equal guilt on story completions, and equal identification with parents on a questionnaire. Conventionals, however, showed more blocking on a sentence-completion test involving disapproved feelings, which suggested that they repressed superego-alien impulses more severely. In conjunction with the authoritarianism studies and the Peck and Havighurst study, the Hoffman findings indicate that a strongly conventionalistic or authority-maintaining moral ideology is associated with such restrictions of ego functioning as repression of free ideation and rigidities in problem-solving.

Two differing, though not contradictory, interpretations of these general findings have been advanced. The first, already outlined, explains both the "irrationality" of the conventional ideology, and the associated cognitive restrictions as the results of relatively fixed defenses against repressed impulses. A second interpretation (Loevinger, 1959) explains the authoritarian-conventional moral ideology as a normal late childhood "stage" of moral judgment, similar to Kohlberg's Authority Maintaining Stage 4. In adults, such a moral ideology would reflect the results of restriction of general intellectual and social stimulation toward development of moral thought.

In support of the superego defense interpretation, Adorno and his colleagues (1950) found that authoritarian adults described their parents' attitudes and child-rearing practices as impulse-repressing and denying. Hoffman (1963) found that parents of conventional children made high use of love-withdrawal techniques of discipline, in contrast to parents of humanistic children who more often used reasoning in backing up moral demands. These findings, taken together, suggest that conventional or authoritarian persons may have had experiences which make awareness of hostility toward parental authority a source of anxiety, hence a stimulus for the evocation of defenses.

In support of a more developmental interpretation of these moral ideologies, there is evidence of an age decline of authoritarian attitudes in middle-class youths, as well as a negative correlation of authoritarianism with social class and I.Q. (Sanford, 1959, 1962). While in part these negative correlations of authoritarianism with age, I.Q., and social class probably represent superficial test sophistication and increased collegiate "other-directedness" and tolerance, they may also reflect the positive development of principled moral judgment. A correlation of —.52 was found between the F-scale and the Kohlberg moral judgment scale. Both scales also related to a behavioral measure of moral independence of authority; the F-scale related negatively and the moral judgment scale positively.

It seems likely that both interpretations have merit, but we are not yet able to offer a view of personal moral ideology which combines personality type and developmental considerations into a single framework.

IMPLICATIONS FOR CONCEPTS OF MORAL EDUCATION

Our review of research has so far ignored issues of value and philosophy in the moral domain. The writer believes that research conceptions of morality can neither be understood nor applied without some consideration of these issues.

Studies of moral character, resistance to temptation, and conscience strength have defined and measured morality in terms of conformity to an external standard, the standard of the culture. Researchers have recognized that these cultural standards may not really be the ultimate standard of the right in this domain, and that the moral child as measured by the researcher might not be the moral child in the eyes of parents, the therapist, the teacher, or others seeking information. Differences in conceptions of moral value need not seriously limit the usefulness of research, however, if the *process* of moral learning is the same regardless of the values taught by the parent or moral educator.

Unfortunately, the number of worthwhile generalizations which can be made in these terms are few now, and will probably continue to be few, regardless of research progress in this field. We have mentioned that it is safe to tell parents that rejecting their children, being harsh and unreasoning, and using strong physical punishment are unlikely to produce effective learning of parental expectations in moral or other domains of socialization. Beyond this minimum, the conditions of effective learning of particular types of moral behavior may be quite specific to the particular desired type of behavior. A technique effective in prohibiting cheating may be ineffective in prohibiting disobedience (Rau, 1964). A technique such as physical punishment effective in preventing cheating at age five in the home may be ineffective in preventing it later (at age twelve), in the home or in the school (Burton, Maccoby, and Allinsmith, 1961; Grinder, 1963). A technique effective in preventing a child from committing a transgression (stopping and punishing the child in the act) may be quite different from the technique effective in getting the child to criticize himself for committing the act (Aronfreed, 1963; Aronfreed and Reber, 1963).

Such highly specific information about moral learning—even if the research adequately provided it—could not be translated into useful advice because the parent does not know "his values" in such detail. He does not really know whether he wants to engender inhibition of a behavior or longer-range guilt about it; whether he wants the child to conform now or whether he can wait; whether it is more important that the child should be obedient or more important that he should stand up for his own views. Most importantly, he does not know how much he should specifically train his child in his own moral values and how much he should provide a "happy home" and rely on the "natural" development of the child's morality. These problems become even more crucial to the teacher and the therapist, who have no real warrant for imposing their own moral values upon the child, but cannot escape making decisions as to what is good for the child's development.

It is evident, then, that research findings cannot be translated into direct "how to" advice prescribing definite actions. Following the detailed analysis of this issue by John Dewey (1939), however, the writer would contend that social scientists can contribute to *clarification* of moral education decisions, both of ends and of techniques, without imposing their values upon others. Such scientific clarification depends upon communicating an accurate and comprehensive general view of the nature of moral development and functioning to parents and educators in terms they can themselves relate to the specific decisions of value and practice they must make.

A basic starting point in such clarification is a consideration of what research has indicated as to the meaning of terms like morality and moral development. People disagree on what moral development is, a disagreement evident in the diversity of conceptions of morality employed in research. They also disagree as to whether morality is a damper on children's happiness necessary to keep society running and parents comfortable, or whether it is the core of higher personality development. Finally, they disagree as to whether or not moral character terms are scientifically useful in understanding children's misconduct, a question basic to any notion of moral responsibility.

These disagreements as to the nature of morality spring from the multiplicity of standards which can be used in judging the morality of an action. Sociologists have pointed out that delinquent actions may be motivated by the need to "do right" or conform to standards, to both the standards of the delinquent gang and the great American standard of fast success. A psychiatrist has suggested that "While from the standpoint of society, behavior is either 'good' or 'bad,' from the standpoint of the individual it always has some positive value. It represents the best solution for his conflicting drives that he has been able to formulate" (Josselyn, 1948). From either the sociological view or the view expressed by Josselyn, moral character terms are external value judgments useless for understanding the child. According to both views, misconduct or good conduct must be understood, like other conduct, in terms of the child's needs, his group's values, and the demands of the situation.

The research results suggest some validity to these criticisms of the use of moral character terms. Specific acts of conformity or deviance in themselves primarily reflect situational wishes and fears rather than the presence or absence of conscience or moral character. Nevertheless, there is evidence that delinquency or repeated misconduct tends to indicate deficits or retardation of general moral judgment capacities, of related guilt capacities, and the lack of internal ego control rather than simply reflecting subculturally relative values, or situational or emotional conflicts. While everyday judgments of moral character and worth are often psychologically erroneous, they do correlate with important consistencies in personality and development, which are positive from almost any viewpoint. These consistencies are indicated by the observed correlations among various character traits and between moral conduct and both maturity of moral judgment and internal guilt reactions.

On the basis of the age-development data, the writer suggested a definition of moral maturity as the capacity to make decisions and judgments which are moral (that is, based on internal principles) and to act in accordance with such judgments. While any conception of moral education must recognize that the parent cannot escape the direct imposition of behavior demands and moral judgments upon the child, it may be possible to define moral education primarily as a matter of stimulating the development of the child's own moral judgment and its control of action. Because there appears to be considerable regularity of sequence and direction in the development of moral judgments in western cultures, the stimulation of moral development may be distinguished from the simple imposition of arbitrary cultural or personal standards upon the child. This means, in the first place, the stimulation of the child's use of his current capacities for moral judgment and of his use of these judgments in guiding and criticizing his action. It means, in the second place, the stimulation of developmental change of moral judgment to the next level of maturity.

Among other things, such an aim suggests the desirability of appropriate match between the adult's moral judgments and reasoning and the child's level of judgment. While adult predispositions probably more often lie in the direction of unrealistic expectations of moral maturity, the opposite errors are also quite apparent. The writer has found teachers telling thirteen-year-old children not to cheat "because the person you copied from might have it wrong and so it won't do you any good." Most of these children were capable of advancing much more mature reasons for not cheating. As Turiel's study (1964) suggests, children are almost as likely to reject moral reasoning beneath their level as to fail to assimilate reasoning too far above their level.

A more basic question of "match" and timing in moral development involves the matching of moral expectations to the child's developing status as a moral agent. There is a great deal of consensus among parents of all social classes as to their ideals of character for their children as adults (Kohn, 1959), but a great deal of variation and confusion in translating these into expectations for young children's conduct. The issue is customarily discussed in terms of "techniques of child rearing," that is, whether it is more effective to make early strong demands or late "permissive" demands. No very definitive answer can be given to the question viewed in terms of effectiveness of techniques. As we saw, early or strong parental training demands for neatness, absence of aggression in the home, care of property, and the like have little value in promoting later resistance to temptation, nondelinquency, or guilt capacities, although they also apparently do no harm in this regard. In addition, we saw little predictiveness of early non-aggressiveness and "unselfishness" to adolescent possession of these virtues. Because of such uncertainties of outcomes in adult moral character, parents are constantly tempted to make moral demands and judgments of children in terms of conformity to their own convenience at the moment, instead of in terms of ideals of character and maturity in the future. There is, however, some slight evidence that future character is promoted by parents' ability to make this distinction.[11] The issues of moral education facing parents are not so much what socialization demands to make when, but when to treat socialization demands as moral demands involving moral judgments and moral sanctions, and when to treat them as matters of the parents' or child's convenience. The research findings on the slow age development of moral judgment, ego strength, and self-criticism suggest the wisdom of a gradualistic view of the child as morally accountable.

The general considerations discussed are potentially as applicable to the school situation as to the home. Recent research provides little reason to revise the conclusions of Hartshorne and May and others that formal or conventional character education classes or programs in the school or church have little or no effect upon children's moral conduct. In light of the long, slow, and continuously shifting development of moral ideology and judgments, and the observed relationships between moral judgment and conduct, it is, however, possible to argue that character education procedures might have a long-range impact on moral ideology and conduct not revealed in measures of immediate moral conformity or resistance to temptation. More importantly, the fact that classes or meetings for conventional "character education" appear to be ineffective should not be taken to mean that the teacher and the school do not have a very considerable impact upon the child's moral development. Whether or not "character education" exists as an explicit goal of schoolroom teaching, a great deal of the school-room process involves moralizing by teachers to pupils and teachers con-

---

[11] While strong training demands which serve the parents convenience (cleanliness, chores, neatness, aggression in the home) are, if anything, negatively related to moral response, strong demands for behavior usually viewed as more basic to adult character (obedience, achievement, aggression outside the home) are, if anything, positively related to moral responses (evidence summarized in Kohlberg, 1963a).

stitute the primary adult source of moral evaluation and of moral reasoning outside the home. In Russia, where the entire classroom process is explicitly defined as "character education," that is, as making good socialist citizens, the teacher appears to have an extremely strong influence upon children's moral standards (Bronfenbrenner, 1962).

Without suggesting the Russian moral indoctrination approach, it seems safe to suggest that a conscious interest by teachers in stimulating moral development would provide a valuable supplement to the concrete focus upon negative and immediate classroom behavior, upon maintaining discipline, and upon expressing personal values and prejudices. In part, this interest might be effected by supplementing the discussion of the immediate and trivial by a discussion of more important though more remote but related issues. Perhaps more importantly, a conscious interest in stimulating moral development would involve consideration of all the values appealed to by the teacher in terms of their impact upon the child's moral thinking and character. This would involve placing in perspective the intellectual achievement values which are of necessity the central focus of the school. If the teacher trains the child to think getting a good mark is an absolute good, she must consider what nonarbitrary basis the child might have for thinking cheating is bad. The American teacher seems to be moving increasingly toward a position as the "priest of future success." As he does, the teacher has increasing responsibility for stimulating conceptions of success which involve some moral dimensions.

REFERENCES

ADORNO, T. W., FRENKEL-BRUNSWICK, E., LEVINSON, D. J., & SANFORD, R. N. *The authoritarian personality.* New York: Harper, 1950.

ALBERT, E. M. & KLUCKHOHN, C. *Selected bibliography on values, ethics, and esthetics in the behavioral sciences and philosophy, 1920-58.* Glencoe, Ill.: Free Press, 1959.

ALLINSMITH, W. A. Moral standards: II. The learning of moral standards. In D. R. Miller and G. E. Swanson (Eds.), *Inner conflict and defense.* New York: Holt, 1960. Pp. 141-176.

ALLINSMITH, W. A. & GREENING, T. C. Guilt over anger as predicted from parental discipline: a study of superego development. *Amer. Psychologist*, 1955, **10**, 320. (Abstract)

ARONFREED, J. The nature, variety, and social patterning of moral responses to transgression. *J. abnorm. soc. Psychol.*, 1961, **63**, 223-241.

ARONFREED, J. The effect of experimental socialization paradigms upon two moral responses to transgression. *J. abnorm. soc. Psychol.*, 1963, **66**, 437-448.

ARONFREED, J. The origins of self-criticism. *Psychol. Rev.*, 1964, in press.

ARONFREED, J. & REBER, A. The internalization of social control through punishment. Paper read at meetings of the Society for Research in Child Development, Berkeley, Calif., April, 1963.

ARONSON, E. & CARLSMITH, J. M. Effect of the severity of threat on the devaluation of forbidden behavior. *J. abnorm. soc. Psychol.*, 1963, **66**, 584-588.

AUSUBEL, D. P. *Ego development and the personality disorders.* New York: Grune & Stratton, 1952.

BACH, G. Young children's play fantasies. *Psychol. Monogr.*, 1945, **59**, No. 2.

BALDWIN, J. M. *Social and ethical interpretations in mental development.* New York: Macmillan, 1906.

BANDURA, A. & WALTERS, R. H. *Adolescent aggression.* New York: Ronald Press, 1959.

BARNDT, R. J. & JOHNSON, D. M. Time orientation in delinquents. *J. abnorm. soc. Psychol.*, 1955, **51**, 343–347.

BOBROFF, A. The stages of maturation in socialized thinking and in the ego development of two groups of children. *Child Developm.*, 1960, **31**, 321–338.

BOEHM, L. & NASS, M. L. Social class differences in conscience development. *Child Developm.*, 1962, **33**, 565–575.

BOWLBY, J. *Forty-four juvenile thieves: their characters and home life.* London: Baldiere, 1947.

BRINK, J. Moral development of students in Protestant, Catholic, and public schools. Unpublished paper, 1963.

BRONFENBRENNER, U. Soviet methods of character education: some implications for research. *Amer. Psychologist*, 1962, **17**, 550–565.

BURTON, R. V. Temptation influences on fantasy. Unpublished paper, 1958.

BURTON, R. V. The generality of honesty reconsidered. *Psychol. Rev.*, 1963, **70**, 481–500.

BURTON, R. V., MACCOBY, E. E., & ALLINSMITH, W. A. Antecedents of resistance to temptation in four-year-old children. *Child Developm.*, 1961, **32**, 689–710.

CARUSO, I. H. La notion de responsabilité et du justic immanente chez l'enfant. *Arch. de Psychologie*, 1943, **29**, Entire No. 114.

CATTELL, R. B. *Personality: a systematic theoretical and factual study.* New York: McGraw-Hill, 1950.

COHEN, A. *Delinquent boys.* Glencoe, Ill.: Free Press, 1955.

DEWEY, J. *The philosophy of John Dewey.* J. Ratner (Ed.). New York: Modern Library, 1939.

DURKIN, D. Children's concepts of justice: a comparison with the Piaget data. *Child Developm.*, 1959, **30**, 59–67.

ERIKSON, E. *Childhood and society.* New York: Norton, 1950.

FAIGIN, H. Child rearing in the Rimrock community with special reference to the development of guilt. Unpublished doctoral dissertation, Harvard Univ., 1953.

FAIGIN, H. Social behavior of young children in the kibbutz. *J. abnorm. soc. Psychol.*, 1958, **56**, 111–130.

FENICHEL, O. *The psychoanalytic theory of neurosis.* New York: Norton, 1945.

FESTINGER, L. *A theory of cognitive dissonance.* Evanston: Row, Peterson, 1957.

FLUGEL, J. C. *Man, morals, and society: a psycho-analytical study.* New York: Internat. Univ. Press, 1955.

FREUD, A. *The ego and the mechanisms of defense.* London: Hogarth Press, 1937.

FREUD, S. Some sources of resistance to psychoanalysis. *Collected papers of.* . . . Vol. V. London: Hogarth Press, 1950. (Originally published, 1925.)

FREUD, S. *Civilization and its discontents.* London: Hogarth Press, 1955. (Originally published, 1930.)

FROMM, E. *Escape from freedom.* New York: Rinehart, 1947.

GLUECK, S. & GLUECK, E. *Unravelling juvenile delinquency.* New York: Commonwealth Fund, 1950.

GOETHALS, G. W. A study of the relationships between family esteem patterns and identification, the internalization of values, and aggression of a group of four-year-old children. Unpublished doctoral dissertation, Harvard Univ., 1955.

GOLDFARB, W. Emotional and intellectual consequences of psychological deprivation in infancy: a reevaluation. In P. H. Hoch and J. Zubin (Eds.), *Psychopathology of childhood.* New York: Grune & Stratton, 1955.

GRIM, P., KOHLBERG, L., & WHITE, S. Some relationships between conscience and attentional processes. Unpublished paper, 1964.

GRINDER, R. Parental childrearing practices, conscience, and resistance to temptation of sixth grade children. *Child Developm.*, 1962, **33**, 802–820.

GRINDER, R. Relations between moral judgment and resistance to temptation in conscience development. Paper read at meetings of the Society for Research in Child Development, Berkeley, Calif., April, 1963.

GRINDER, R. & MCMICHAEL, R. Cultural influences on conscience development: resistance to temptation and guilt among Samoans and American Caucasians. *J. abnorm. soc. Psychol.*, 1963, **66**, 503–507.

HARE, R. M. *The language of morals.* New York: Oxford Univ. Press, 1952.

HARRIS, D. B. & VALASEK, F. The measurement of responsibility in children. *Child Developm.*, 1954, **25**, 21–28.

HARROWER, M. E. Social status and moral development. *Brit. J. educ. Psychol.*, 1934, **4**, 75–95.

HARTMANN, H. *Psychoanalysis and moral values.* New York: Internat. Univ. Press, 1960.

HARTSHORNE, H. & MAY, M. A. *Studies in the nature of character:* Vol. I, *Studies in deceit;* Vol. II, *Studies in self-control;* Vol. III, *Studies in the organization of character.* New York: Macmillan, 1928–1930.

HAVIGHURST, R. J. & NEUGARTEN, B. L. *American Indian and white children.* Chicago: Univ. of Chicago Press, 1955.

HAVIGHURST, R. J. & TABA, H. *Adolescent character and personality.* New York: Wiley, 1949.

HEINICKE, C. M. Some antecedents and correlates of guilt and fear in young boys. Unpublished doctoral dissertation, Harvard Univ., 1953.

HENDRY, L. S. Cognitive processes in a moral conflict situation. Unpublished doctoral dissertation, Yale Univ., 1960.

HOFFMAN, M. L. Progress report: techniques and processes in moral development. Detroit: Merrill-Palmer Inst., 1961, mimeographed.

HOFFMAN, M. L. Early processes in moral development. Paper read at Social Science Research Council Conference on Character Development, New York. November 1–3, 1963.

JANIS, M. The development of moral judgment in preschool children. Yale Univ. Child Study Center, 1961, dittoed.

JOHNSON, A. M. Juvenile delinquency. In S. Arieti (Ed.), *American handbook of psychiatry: Vol. I.* New York: Basic Books, 1959. Pp. 840–856.

JOHNSON, R. A study of children's moral judgments. *Child Developm.*, 1962, **33**, 327–354.

JOHNSON, R. Guilt and development of moral judgment. Unpublished paper, 1963.

JONES, V. Character development in children: an objective approach. In L. Carmichael (Ed.), *Manual of child psychology.* New York: Wiley, 1954. Pp. 781–832.

JOSSELYN, I. M. *Psychosocial development of children.* New York: Family Service Assn., 1948.

KAGAN, J. & MOSS, H. A. *From birth to maturity.* New York: Wiley, 1962.

KANT, I. *Fundamental principles of the metaphysics of morals.* Trans. by T. K. Abbott. New York: Liberal Arts Press, 1949.

KOHLBERG, L. The development of modes of moral thinking and choice in the years ten to sixteen. Unpublished doctoral dissertation, Univ. of Chicago, 1958.

KOHLBERG, L. Moral development and identification. In H. Stevenson (Ed.), *Child psychology. 62nd Yearb. nat. soc. stud. Educ.* Chicago: Univ. of Chicago Press, 1963 (a).

KOHLBERG, L. The development of children's orientations toward a moral order: I. Sequence in the development of moral thought. *Vita Humana*, 1963, **6**, 11–33 (b).

KOHLBERG, L. The development of children's orientations toward a moral order: II. Social experience, social conduct, and the development of moral thought. *Vita Humana*, 1964, in press (a).

KOHLBERG, L. Sex differences in morality. In E. E. Maccoby (Ed.), *Sex role development*, New York: Social Science Research Council, 1964, in press (b).

KOHN, M. Social class and parental values. *Amer. J. Sociol.*, 1959, **64**, 337–351.

LERNER, E. *Constraint areas and the moral judgment of children.* Menasha, Wis.: George Banta Pub. Co., 1937 (a).

LERNER, E. Perspectives in moral reasoning. *Amer. J. Sociol.*, 1937, **43**, 249–269 (b).

LOEVINGER, J. A theory of test response. *Proc. 1958 Invitation Conf. Test Prob.*, 1959, 36–47.

LURIA, Z., GOLDWASSER, M., & GOLDWASSER, A. Response to transgression in stories by Israeli children. *Child Developm.*, 1963, **34**, 271–281.

MACCOBY, E. E. The taking of adult roles in middle childhood. *J. abnorm. soc. Psychol.*, 1961, **63**, 493–504.

MACCOBY, E. E. & WHITING, J. W. Some child-rearing correlates of young children's responses to deviation stories. Unpublished paper, Stanford Univ., 1960.

MACFARLANE, J., ALLEN, L., & HONZIK, N. *A developmental study of behavior problems of normal children between 21 months and four years.* Berkeley: Univ. of Calif. Press, 1954.

MACKINNON, D. W. Violation of prohibitions. In H. W. Murray (Ed.), *Explorations in personality.* New York: Oxford Univ. Press, 1938. Pp. 491–501.

MACRAE, R., JR. A test of Piaget's theories of moral development. *J. abnorm. soc. Psychol.*, 1954, **49**, 14–18.

MANDELBAUM, M. *The phenomenology of moral experience.* Glencoe, Ill.: Free Press, 1954.

McCORD, W. & McCORD, J. *Psychopathy and delinquency.* New York: Grune & Stratton, 1956.

McDOUGALL, W. *An introduction to social psychology.* London: Methuen, 1908.

MEAD, G. H. *Mind, self, and society.* Chicago: Univ. of Chicago Press, 1934.

MEDINNUS, G. R. Immanent justice in children: a review of the literature and additional data. *J. genet. Psychol.*, 1959, **90**, 253–262.

MILLER, D. R. & SWANSON, G. E. *Inner conflict and defense.* New York: Holt, 1960.

MILLS, J. Temptation and changes in moral attitudes. Unpublished doctoral dissertation, Stanford Univ., 1958.

MISCHEL, W. Delay of gratification and deviant behavior. Paper read at meetings of the Society for Research in Child Development, Berkeley, Calif., April, 1963.

MOWRER, O. H. Identification: a link between learning theory and psychotherapy. In *Learning theory and personality dynamics.* New York: Ronald Press, 1952. Pp. 573–616.

MOWRER, O. H. *Learning theory and the symbolic processes.* New York: Wiley, 1960.

MURPHY, L. B. *Social behavior and child personality.* New York: Columbia Univ. Press, 1937.

PAYNE, D. E. & MUSSEN, P. Parent-child relations and father identification among adolescent boys. *J. abnorm. soc. Psychol.*, 1956, **52**, 358–362.

PECK, R. F. & HAVIGHURST, R. J. *The psychology of character development.* New York: Wiley, 1960.

PIAGET, J. *The child's conception of the world.* London: Routledge, Kegan Paul, 1928.

PIAGET, J. *The moral judgment of the child.* Glencoe, Ill.: Free Press, 1948. (Originally published, 1932.)

PIERS, G. & SINGER, M. *Shame and guilt: a psychoanalytic and a cultural study.* Springfield, Ill.: Charles C Thomas, 1953.

RABIN, A. I. Some psychosexual differences between kibbutz and non-kibbutz Israeli boys. *J. proj. Tech.*, 1958, **22**, 328–332.

RABIN, A. I. Attitudes of kibbutz children to family and parents. *Amer. J. Orthopsychiat.*, 1959, **29**, 172–179.

RABIN, A. I. & GOLDMAN, H. Severity of guilt and diffuseness of identification. Paper read at meetings of American Psychological Association, Philadelphia, September 2, 1963.

RAU, L. Conscience and identification. In R. R. Sears, L. Rau, & R. Alpert, *Identification and child-rearing*. Stanford, Calif.: Stanford Univ. Press, in press.

REBELSKY, F. G. An inquiry into the meaning of confession. *Merrill-Palmer Quart.*, 1963, **9**, 287–295.

REBELSKY, F. G., ALLINSMITH, W. A., & GRINDER, R. Sex differences in children's use of fantasy confession and their relation to temptation. *Child Developm.*, 1963, in press.

REDL, F. & WINEMAN, D. *Controls from within*. Glencoe, Ill.: Free Press, 1952.

RICKS, D. & UMBARGER, C. A measure of increased temporal perspective. Paper read at meetings of the Eastern Psychological Association, April, 1963.

SANFORD, N. The approach of the authoritarian personality. In J. McCary (Ed.), *Psychology of personality*. New York: Evergreen Books (Grove Press), 1959.

SANFORD, N., ADKINS, M., COBB, E., & MILLER, B. *Physique, personality, and scholarship*. Monograph of the Society for Research in Child Development, 1943, **8**, 1–705. (Summarized in R. G. Barker, J. S. Kounin, and H. F. Wright (Eds.), *Child behavior and development*. New York: McGraw-Hill, 1943. Pp. 567–589.)

SEARS, R. R., MACCOBY, E. E., & LEVIN, H. *Patterns of child-rearing*. Evanston, Ill.: Row, Peterson, 1957.

SEARS, R. R., RAU, L., & ALPERT, R. *Identification and child-rearing*. Stanford, Calif.: Stanford Univ. Press, in press.

SEARS, R. R., WHITING, J. W. M., NOWLIS, V., & SEARS, P. S. Some child-rearing antecedents of aggression and dependency in young children. *Genet. psychol. Monogr.*, 1953, **47**, 135–203.

SIDGWICK, H. *Methods of ethics*. London: Macmillan, 1901.

SLATER, P. Toward a dualistic theory of identification. *Merrill-Palmer Quart.*, 1961, **7**, 113–126.

SPIRO, M. *Children of the kibbutz*. Cambridge, Mass.: Harvard Univ. Press, 1958.

STERN, G. Environments for learning. In N. Sanford (Ed.), *The American college*. New York: Wiley, 1962. Pp. 690–773.

TERMAN, L. M. & MILES, C. C. *Sex and personality*. New York: McGraw-Hill, 1936.

TURIEL, E. An experimental analysis of developmental stages in the child's moral judgment. Unpublished doctoral dissertation, Yale Univ., 1964.

TURNER, W. Altruism in children's behavior. In R. Kuhlen & G. Thompson (Eds.), *Psychological studies in human development*. New York: Appleton-Century, 1952.

WALTERS, R. H. & DEMKOW, L. Timing of punishment as a determinant of response inhibition. *Child Developm.*, 1963, **34**, 207–214.

WEBB, E. Character and intelligence. *Brit. J. Psychol.*, Monogr. Suppl., 1915, **1**, No. 3.

WHITING, J. W. M. Sorcery, sin, and the superego: a cross-cultural study of some mechanisms of social control. In M. R. Jones, (Ed.), *Nebraska symposium on motivation*. Lincoln: Univ. of Nebraska Press, 1959. Pp. 174–195.

WHITING, J. W. M. Resource mediation and learning by identification. In I. Iscoe & H. W. Stevenson (Eds.), *Personality development in children*. Austin: Univ. of Texas Press, 1960. Pp. 112–126.

WHITING, J. & CHILD, I. *Child training and personality: a cross-cultural study*. New Haven: Yale Univ. Press, 1953.

WRIGHT, J., HILL, J., & ALPERT, R. The development and expression of conscience in fantasy by school children. Paper read at meetings of the Society for Research in Child Development, Pennsylvania State University, 1961.

Genetics and Behavior Development

GERALD E. McCLEARN

University of California, Berkeley

ANY PARENT, and any practitioner in fields having to do with children, has intimate knowledge of individual differences. Some children are docile, others aggressive; some learn readily, others are dull; some are easily toilet trained, others are not. Individual differences are ubiquitous; indeed, the prediction that they will be found in any study appears to be one of the safest predictions that can be made.

In some research contexts these individual differences have been regarded as a nuisance—"error variance" which adds a haze of uncertainty to what otherwise would be precise functional relationships or exact predictions. In other contexts individuality becomes a matter of primary concern.

For the interpretation and explanation of individuality, the theoretical frame of reference provided by the behavioral sciences has been, on the whole, an environmentalistic one. A key factor in this development was J. B. Watson's (1924) aggressive denial of the role of hereditary determinants in behavior. His challenging offer to produce people to specification by appropriate manipulation of environment—a bluff which, in the nature of things, could never be called—was accepted as though it were a demonstrated accomplishment. Because of Watson's great influence, and for a variety of other reasons (see Dobzhansky, 1962; McClearn, 1962; Pastore, 1949), psychology in particular and behavioral sciences in general moved to a polar position with respect to the nature-nurture issue. The movement was not unanimous, of course. Postulations of "constitutional determinants" or "familial tendencies" in one or another behavior have often been made. Moreover, a continuing research effort has provided a steady accumulation of facts relating to the role of heredity in determining various behaviors in animals and man. Since about 1950 this field of behavioral genetics has undergone a rapid development. Evidence for a hereditary component is now available for a broad range of behaviors in a wide variety of organisms—from geotaxis in fruit flies to intelligence in human beings.

433

The impact of these specific behavioral genetic findings has undoubtedly been augmented by the widespread interest throughout the scientific community in recent remarkable advances at the biochemical frontiers of genetics research. The result is that many behavioral scientists have begun to question the old clichés of environmentalism, and to adopt a conceptual framework with a balanced view of the collaboration of genetic and environmental factors in determining behavioral characteristics. This chapter attempts to provide such a conceptual framework for the field of child development. To this end, the basic principles of genetics most relevant to the study of behavior will be reviewed, the general types of information available on behavioral inheritance will be indicated, and specific researches on heredity and behavioral development in animals and man will be discussed. The literature review can only be representative, not exhaustive; and in many cases references will be made to secondary sources that provide reviews, bibliographies, and contextual material rather than to original papers.

While an attempt has been made to define essential technical terms as they first appear in the text, the reader will also find a brief glossary of the more important ones preceding the "References."

BASIC PRINCIPLES OF GENETICS

When it is said that a certain trait is inherited, the empirical evidence upon which the statement is based may be of several kinds. For example: under uniform environmental conditions, inbred strains may differ with respect to the characteristic; the attempt to breed selectively for the trait may be successful; a 3:1 ratio of unaffected to affected individuals may be discovered in families; a correlation may exist between parents and offspring; the mean difference between identical twins may be less than that between fraternal twins. Yet from whatever observational basis, the conclusion that a trait is subject to genetic influence implicitly carries many notions with it. In fact, the very phrase "is inherited" must be understood as a convenient, short expression for a highly complex idea. A cumbersome but more adequate approximation of the intended meaning might be as follows. Under given environmental conditions, individuals possessing a certain gene pair or pairs will, through biochemical processes initiated and sustained by the gene products, in interaction with the environment, develop attributes measurably different from other individuals with a different gene pair or pairs. Even this statement must be regarded as incomplete, but it serves to suggest the complexity of relationships involved, and it provides a starting point for a more detailed examination of the nature of inheritance.

The Genetic Elements

In the very early period of research in Mendelian genetics, the genes were inferred entities—elements or factors hypothesized to account for observable phenomena. While this situation did not long persist—and, as we shall see later, much is now known about the chemical nature of the hereditary material—it will be convenient to begin the discussion of the transmission of genetic factors without reference to their physical attributes.

Any given gene exists in two or more alternate forms called *alleles*. We may represent one allele as *A1* and another as *A2*. Each individual possesses two alleles, one having been contributed by each parent. There will therefore be three types of individuals in a population, with respect to these particular alleles: *A1A1*, *A1A2*, and *A2A2*. We may portray the relationship between these different genetic constitutions, or *genotypes*, and the level of the observable attribute (*phenotype*) that these particular alleles affect by Figure 1.

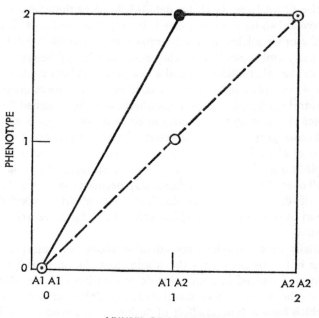

FIGURE 1.   Diagrammatic Representation Showing Two of the Many Relationships That May Exist Between Genotype and Phenotype

The solid line portrays a dominant situation, the dashed line an additive situation.

The abscissa is graduated in terms of the number of $A2$ alleles present, and the ordinate indicates an arbitrary scale of phenotypic values. For some traits it is found that the genotype-phenotype relationship is as shown in the solid line. A large difference exists between the homozygotes, that is, the $A1A1$ individuals and the $A2A2$ individuals. But the heterozygote, $A1A2$, assumes a value indistinguishable from that of one of the homozygotes ($A2A2$ in this case). This relationship is described as *dominance*, with the $A2$ allele being called *dominant* and the $A1$ allele called *recessive*.

Another possible form of relationship is shown by the dashed line of Figure 1, where the heterozygote is intermediate to the homozygotes. This situation is called an *additive* one. If the heterozygote is distinguishable from the homozygotes, but is not exactly intermediate, *incomplete dominance* is said to exist.

The use of two alleles in the illustrations above should not be taken to indicate that this is the only, or even the usual, state of affairs. A particularly instructive example of a situation in which several allelic forms exist for one locus (that is, a multiple allelic series) is the agouti series in the mouse. (See Grüneberg, 1952, for details.) Some of the alleles which have been discovered so far are symbolized A^y, A^w, A, a^t, and a. A^y is dominant over all the other alleles. In the homozygous condition (A^yA^y), it causes death in early embryological development; but in the heterozygous state with any of the other alleles, it results in a golden yellow coat. A^w is dominant over A, a^t, and a, and results in a coat which is white or cream colored on the ventral surface, but agouti elsewhere. A is the so-called "wild type" allele which, in homozygous condition or as a heterozygote with a, gives the well-known gray-bellied agouti coat color characteristic of many house mice. The a^t allele is dominant over a and results in an animal with a smooth black dorsal surface and a tan ventral surface. The homozygote aa is black all over. An interesting relationship between the A and a^t alleles has been described. A appears to be dominant over a^t with respect to the determination of dorsal coat color, but recessive as far as ventral coat color is concerned.

This allelic series provides considerable scope for variability in coat coloration but is by no means the whole story. Some 15 different allelic series may be involved in coat color determination in mice (Grüneberg, 1952). One other series may be mentioned. The albino series has at least five alleles, which have a general effect of "diluting" the coat color. The allele that is dominant over all of the other members of the series is symbolized C, and the allele recessive to all others is c. C permits the full expression of color as determined by other genes. But c^i (intense chinchilla), c^{ch} (chinchilla), c^e (extreme dilution) mute the effects of other genes to varying degrees. The homozygous *cc* condition completely inhibits color formation, and results in an albino animal, regardless of the allelic combinations present for any of the other coat-color genes.

Many other multiple-allelic series are known in the mouse and other experimental animals. Several have also been described in man, relating to various blood-group factors, hemoglobin characteristics, color-blindness, and hemophilia. (See Stern, 1960, Ch. 11.) It is important to note, with respect to multiple allelic series, that in spite of the abundance of allelic forms of the gene any given individual can normally possess no more than two.

Transmission of Genes

In the process of reproduction each parent contributes to the offspring only one allele of each of the many genes he possesses. This mechanism permits—indeed, it guarantees—recombination of genetic factors in successive generations. It is the basis for the heterogeneity upon which natural selection, the fundamental process of evolution, depends.

There are two principal genetic laws pertaining to the process of genetic transmission. The first, the law of *segregation*, may be illustrated in the following manner.

Consider a single gene with two allelic forms, *A1* and *A2*. Assume that *A2* is dominant over *A1*, and that the phenotypic character influenced by these alleles can be represented by showing *A2A2* and *A1A2* as stippled squares, and *A1A1* as an unstippled square, as in Figure 2. Two homozygous parents are shown, *A1A1* and *A2A2*. In the process of reproduction each parent can generate and transmit only one allele of this particular gene in the sex-cells or "gametes." When the gametes of both parents unite, the hybrid offspring (designated F1, or first filial generation) will all be genotypically *A1A2*. Also, by virtue of the dominance relationship, they will all resemble the *A2A2* parent phenotypically. Each of the F1 individuals can produce two kinds of gamete, *A1* and *A2*; and, if mating occurs between two members of the F1, the gametes will unite at random to produce one *A2A2* genotype, two *A1A2* genotypes, and one *A1A1* genotype. Because of dominance, the well-known ratio of 3:1 is obtained in phenotypic expression.

The fundamental point is that the genetic determinants are particulate entities which do not alter each other's essential genetic nature, although at the level of phenotypic measurement the influence of one allele may be overridden by another through dominance. In Figure 2, for example, the F2 individual who is genotypically *A1A1* has the same phenotype as his

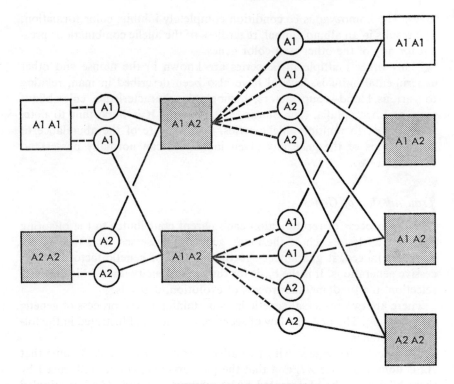

FIGURE 2. Segregation

Individuals are represented as squares; gametes as circles. See text for explanation.

A1A1 grandparent, in spite of the fact that his *A1* alleles had spent one entire reproductive cycle in intimate association with *A2* alleles.

While the law of segregation pertains to the separability of alleles of the same gene in transmission from one generation to the next, the *law of independent assortment* concerns the pattern of transmission of two or more genes considered simultaneously. In essence, independent assortment means that segregation occurs for each gene independently of other genes. This may be illustrated by elaborating the previous example. Suppose that, in addition to the gene pair *A1-A2*, we are concerned with a *B* gene, existing in two allelic forms, *B1* and *B2*. Figure 3 represents the phenotypic expression of the *B* genes by shape. *B2* is dominant and determines "squareness." Homozygous *B1B1* individuals are "triangular." With the phenotype determined by the *A* genes represented by presence or absence of stippling, as in the previous example, we may therefore represent an *A1A1B1B1* indi-

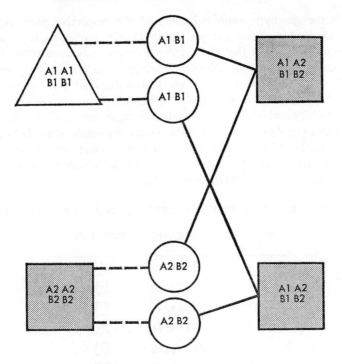

FIGURE 3. Independent Assortment

Characteristics of the individuals are represented by square or triangle. Gametes are shown as circles. See text for explanation.

vidual as an unstippled triangle, and a *A2A2B2B2* individual as a stippled square. Figure 3 shows the consequences of a mating between individuals of these genotypes.

The *A1A1B1B1* parent can produce gametes of only one kind, namely, *A1B1*; the *A2A2B2B2* parent, likewise, can produce only *A2B2* gametes. The offspring are uniform in genotype, all being *A1A2B1B2*, but because of dominance relationships postulated they will resemble the *A2A2B2B2* parent phenotypically. Each of the F1 offspring can produce four kinds of gamete with respect to these genes: *A1B1*, *A1B2*, *A2B1*, and *A2B2*. When these gametes unite at random, the outcome will be as shown in Table 1. There are, of course, 16 possible combinations of the different gamete types. But because the order in which the alleles is written is immaterial (that is, *A1A2=A2A1*), we are concerned here with combinations rather than permutations—and therefore only nine distinct genotypes are listed. The relative frequency with which each of these genotypes will occur is given in the genotype ratio column and the respective phenotypes are shown adjacent to each genotypic listing. One important basic principle to be pointed out here is that the same phenotype may arise from different genotypes. If we combine all like phenotypes we obtain the phenotypic ratio shown in the last row of Table 1. The essential point of the law of independent assortment is that, during gamete formation, equal numbers of all possible combinations of the alleles are produced. That is, in spite of the fact that the *A1A2B1B2* individuals were the result of an *A1B1* gamete uniting with an *A2B2* gamete, these particular gamete forms are no more frequent in the gametes produced by the *A1A2B1B2* individual than are the "recombinant" gametes *A1B2* and *A2B1*.

TABLE 1.   INDEPENDENT ASSORTMENT IN AN F2 GENERATION

GENOTYPE RATIO	GENOTYPE	PHENOTYPE
1	A1 A1 B1 B1	△
2	A1 A1 B1 B2	□
1	A1 A1 B2 B2	□
2	A1 A2 B1 B1	△ (shaded)
4	A1 A2 B1 B2	■ (shaded)
2	A1 A2 B2 B2	■ (shaded)
1	A2 A2 B1 B1	△ (shaded)
2	A2 A2 B1 B2	■ (shaded)
1	A2 A2 B2 B2	■ (shaded)

PHENOTYPE RATIO — 9 ■ : 3 △ : 3 □ : 1 △

These constitute the basic features of Mendelian inheritance. Their generality is somewhat circumscribed by special situations which are described in most genetic textbooks. One of the limiting features of independent assortment, the *linkage* of genes, is of sufficient importance to warrant further consideration in the next section.

The Physical Basis of Genetic Transmission

Genetic material is not scattered haphazardly in the organism. Cytological research has revealed that the genes are linearly arranged on small string-like bodies called *chromosomes*, which are in the nuclei of the cells. A given gene occupies a particular site or *locus*, on a specific chromosome.

In the somatic cells, the chromosomes are arranged in homologous pairs, one of each pair coming from each parent.

The number of pairs varies from species to species, and does not appear to be particularly related to phyletic status. To illustrate, the kangaroo has 6 pairs, the mouse 20, the rat 21, the fruit fly 4, the dog 39, and man 23. Figure 4 shows a photomicrograph of the chromosomes of a normal human male. In the bottom half of the figure, the chromosomes are arranged into appropriate pairs. Each chromosome appears double because the preparation was made at a stage in which each chromosome had duplicated itself. This duplication is an essential part of two fundamental processes, *mitosis* and *meiosis*. In *mitosis*, the chromosomes duplicate themselves so that four sets are contained within a single cell: two paternal sets and two maternal sets. When the cytoplasm of the cell divides, two sets, one maternal and one paternal, go into each daughter cell. This mechanism is, of course, basic to growth and must recur many times in generating a multicellular animal from a single fertilized ovum. (See one of the general genetic references for details of the *mitotic* process.)

Meiosis occurs in gametogenesis. As in mitosis, chromosomal duplication provides four sets of chromosomes within a single cell. Subsequent cytological processes, however, eventuate in four daughter cells instead of two. The daughter cells then develop into gametes, each with one complete chromosome set. (In oogenesis, some become polar bodies.) It is important to note, however, that it is not usual for a complete paternal set or complete maternal set to find its way into a gamete. A random process apparently operates wherein the probability of each individual chromosome in a particular gamete having come from the paternal (or maternal) set is 0.5, independently of whether any other chromosome came from the paternal (or maternal) set. Thus there will be a binomial distribution of gametes with varying proportions of maternal and paternal chromosomes. (This generalization is modified by the phenomenon of "crossing-over" described below.)

The fact that genes are linearly arranged on chromosomes imposes a restriction on independent assortment. If the locus for the *A* gene happens to be on the same chromosome as the locus for the *B* gene, the genes are said to be *linked*. Then, if an *A1A2B1B2* individual had received these alleles by one chromosome which contained *A1B1* and another which contained *A2B2*, the segregation of the *A1* allele into a gamete would imply that the *B1* allele would also go into that same gamete. Linkage is not complete, however. In the meiotic process, a phenomenon called "crossing-over" can occur. This is illustrated diagrammatically for a single chromosome pair in Figure 5. In I, the two chromosomes are represented as having eight loci.

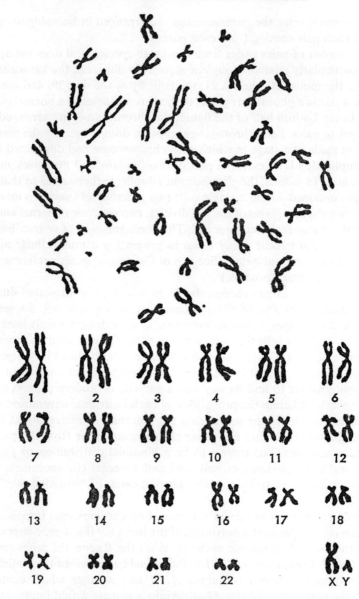

FIGURE 4. Chromosomes of Normal Human Male

The upper portion of the figure shows the original preparation. In the lower portion, the chromosomes have been arranged in pairs and the identifying numbers are shown. (Reproduced from Hamden, D. G. The chromosomes. In Penrose, L. S. (Ed.), *Recent advances in human genetics*. Boston: Little, Brown, 1961. Used with permission of author and publisher.)

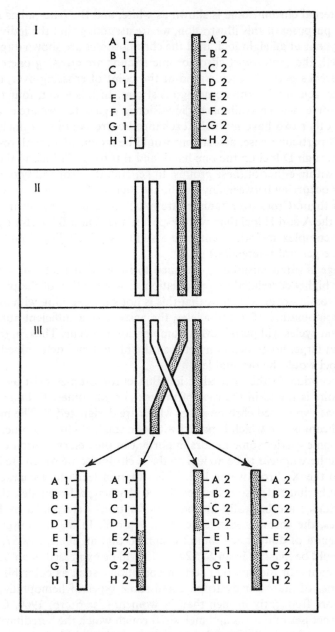

FIGURE 5. Linkage and Crossing-Over

See text for explanation.

The maternal chromosome is shown as white, and the paternal as shaded. For the purposes of this illustration, we are assuming that the individual is heterozygous at all eight loci. In II the chromosomes are shown duplicated, and in III, the centermost chromosome strands are crossing one over the other. Breaks occur in each strand at the point of crossing-over, and the ends may rejoin with the homologous strand. In this event, four types of chromosomes will be available for inclusion in a gamete: two are unaltered, and the other two have mutually exchanged corresponding segments.

In this particular case, assortment would be independent with respect to the A through D loci on the one hand, and E through H loci on the other, but not within either of these groups. In general, the probability of a crossing-over occurring between any two linked loci is a function of the distance between them. Cross-over gametes are much more likely to occur with respect to the A and H loci than with respect to the A and B loci, for example.

More complex meiotic events are also known, including double crossover. (See general references.)

Linkage is often mistakenly assumed to imply that traits must be perfectly or highly correlated in a population. Consideration of the phenomenon of crossing-over will show that this is not so. Beginning with any particular combination of linked alleles, the passage of a sufficient number of generation cycles will permit every combination to occur. Thus, in the population at large, no association between the phenotypes determined by the linked loci would be detectable.

An exception to the generalization that chromosomes exist as homologous pairs is found in the case of the sex chromosomes. In humans, the female has two paired chromosomes which are designated X. The male has one X chromosome which is paired with one small Y chromosome. The Y chromosome carries some factors important in the determination of maleness, but there appear to be no loci on the Y chromosome which are homologous to the X chromosome loci. This situation leads to a characteristic type of inheritance for so-called sex-linked characters. In females, the rules of inheritance are basically the same as for traits determined by loci on *autosomes*, the chromosomes other than X or Y. In males, however, the phenomenon of dominance cannot occur, so that an allele, say *S1*, whose effect would be masked in an *S1S2* female, will be expressed in an *S1* male. This accounts for the fact that certain conditions, such as color-blindness, some types of muscular dystrophy, and some types of hemophilia, occur much more frequently in men than in women. (See Stern, 1960, Ch. 13.)

The processes of mitosis and meiosis, through which the hereditary material is passed from cell generation to cell generation within individuals and from one generation of individuals to the next, are of necessity exquisitely precise and accurate. Mistakes can and do occur, however. One type of error is of particular interest for the present topic. Nondisjunction, a failure of the duplicated strands of one chromosome to separate and enter different daughter cells, sometimes occurs in meiosis. The result is that one gamete will contain the usual complete set plus one extra chromosome, while another gamete will contain one chromosome less than the full set. When these gametes unite with normal ones, the resulting individuals are termed *trisomic* or *monosomic*, respectively. We shall have occasion later to refer to abnormalities caused by this type of failure in transmission of genetic material.

Quantitative Inheritance

For many years there was a dispute over the applicability of the Mendelian laws, which were worked out with respect to qualitatively differing phenotypes, to the inheritance of quantitatively varying characteristics. For example, the condition of dwarfism is recognizable as a qualitative deviation in stature. In "normal" individuals, however, there is an enormous range of body height, continuously distributed. There was adequate evidence that normal variation in height was influenced by hereditary factors, but none of the Mendelian ratios could be calculated from these normally distributed data.

The resolution of the problem was provided by the multiple factor hypothesis, which postulated that a continuously varying trait could be influenced by many loci, each of which made but a relatively small contribution to the phenotypic end product.

To illustrate this point, we may return to a simplified model. In Table 1 we considered a situation involving two loci in which each locus determined a separate character. Now we will suppose that both loci influence the same quantitative character. Assume that each allele labeled "1" contributes nothing to the trait, and that each allele labeled "2" contributes one unit. If there are no interactions between the two loci (and ignoring any environmental effects for the moment), the phenotypic array shown in Table 2 would be obtained. Statistically, this situation may be represented by a binomial expansion, and, if the number of postulated loci were increased, the distribution would come to resemble a normal distribution very closely.

The kinds of intra- and interlocus interaction that have been described for qualitative characters presumably can occur also in these multiple factor or *polygenic* situations, and these interactions can have an effect on the phenotypic distributions. Furthermore, environmental effects must be considered. While environmental variation may cause little difficulty in classifying individuals with respect to a qualitative, single-locus condition, it may

TABLE 2. TWO-LOCUS ADDITIVE MODEL FOR POLYGENIC INHERITANCE

RATIO	GENOTYPE	PHENOTYPIC VALUE	FREQUENCY DISTRIBUTION	
			PHENOTYPE	FREQUENCY
1	A1 A1 B1 B1	0	0	1
2	A1 A1 B1 B2	1		
1	A1 A1 B2 B2	2	1	4
2	A1 A2 B1 B1	1		
4	A1 A2 B1 B2	2	2	6
2	A1 A2 B2 B2	3		
1	A2 A2 B1 B1	2	3	4
2	A2 A2 B1 B2	3		
1	A2 A2 B2 B2	4	4	1

form a substantial portion of the variability found in a population with respect to a quantitative characteristic. An exceptionally favorable environment may raise the phenotypic value of a genotypically average individual,
or a poor environment may lower it. Thus an individual's relative phenotypic position in a distribution is partly attributable to his environment,
and partly to his genotype. The relative contribution of each of these
sources to the total variability of a trait in a population will vary from trait
to trait, and from population to population.

It is apparent that the classical analytical methods, appropriate to qualitative characters, are not applicable to polygenically determined characters.
A statistical approach is required, and the methodologies developed deal
with means, variances, and covariances.

A fundamental concept of quantitative genetics is *heritability*, which is
symbolized h^2. If we denote the total phenotypic variance as V_P, the genetic
variance as V_G, and the environmental variance as V_E, we may write
(ignoring some complexities of interactions):

$$V_P = V_G + V_E$$

Both of the right-hand terms may be further partitioned. For example, we
might distinguish long-term environmental effects from short-term effects.
Likewise the V_G term may be regarded as the sum of V_A, an additive component, V_D, a dominance component, and V_I, an epistatic (interlocus interaction) component. Of these, the V_A component is of the most practical and
theoretical value, for it provides the principal basis of response to selective

breeding, of parent-offspring resemblance, and other quantitative genetic phenomena.

Heritability may be defined as the ratio, V_A/V_P; that is, it is the proportion of the total phenotypic variance which is of the additive genetic kind.

Heritability may be estimated in many ways. For example, if mating in a population is random, and environmental effects are randomly distributed among all members of the population, the regression of the mean of the offspring on the mean of the parents will provide an estimation of h^2. The regression of offspring on a single parent will estimate one-half h^2, and the intraclass correlation of full siblings will overestimate h^2 by an amount dependent upon dominance effects.

The restrictive assumptions concerning mating pattern and environmental effects can be met with relative ease in experimental studies on animals, but studies on human beings, where mating is not random and where genotype-environment correlations often exist, are much more difficult to interpret.

The foregoing discussion of quantitative genetics has provided little more than a glimpse of the field. For detailed presentations, see Falconer (1960), Kempthorne (1957), Lerner (1958), and Mather (1949).

Gene Action

It is a long way from particulate entities on the chromosomes in the nucleus to a phenotype such as body weight, coat color, learning ability, or activity level. Investigations of the intermediate processes between genotype and phenotype comprise the fields of physiological and biochemical genetics. Developments in these fields have been extremely rapid in the past few years; indeed, the pace of research is such that any review will inevitably be incomplete. Whole new areas of exploration have recently been opened up, and the natural result is that many unanswered questions are exposed along with the answers or tentative answers to older questions. In this section, I shall therefore attempt to provide only a general picture of the field.

Biochemical Genetics

The field of biochemical genetics began in 1902, when Garrod described alcaptonuria, a rare human condition (2nd ed., 1923). A distinguishing feature of this condition is that the urine turns black upon exposure to air. This reaction is due to the fact that alcaptonurics excrete an abnormally large amount of homogentisic acid (alcapton) in the urine. Biochemical considerations led to the conclusion that this characteristic was due to a defect in the metabolic sequence whereby tyrosine is converted to carbon dioxide and water. The fact that more than one affected individual was frequently found in the same family led to the suggestion that the condition was inherited.

Several other examples of "inborn errors of metabolism" were soon discovered, and studies on other organisms and other characters followed. (See Beadle, 1951.) Speculation arose that genes might, in some cases, be related to enzymes. Strong support was given to this hypothesis by a series of experiments on the bread-mold fungus, *Neurospora crassa* (Beadle, 1945). This organism was peculiarly suited for this type of research because normally it can synthesize all of the amino acids, purines, pyrimidines, polysaccharides, lipids, and so on, necessary for growth on a medium containing only inorganic salts, sugar, biotin, and a nitrogen source. Various mutated strains are unable to grow on the minimal diet; and it is possible, by selectively adding substances to the medium, to discover which compound these organisms are unable to synthesize. In this manner, with these "nutritional mutants" it has proved possible to trace the metabolic sequences, and by genetic analyses, demonstrate that single genes control single steps in metabolism.

From the results of these and other studies, the unifying "one gene—one enzyme" hypothesis was provisionally accepted. Essentially, this hypothesis stated that each gene had its primary effect in determining the specificity of one enzyme, and each enzyme was determined by a single gene. Different alleles, then, could result in quantitatively different enzyme productions, or a qualitative change in the enzyme produced. The concept has more recently been extended to include all proteins and may be expressed as follows: each gene specifies the sequence of amino acids found in a single protein. (See Yanofsky and St. Lawrence, 1960.)

In the past few years, great progress has been made with respect to the understanding of the molecular constitution of the gene and the mechanism of gene action. It has long been known that an important component of chromosomes is *deoxyribonucleic acid (DNA)*. DNA constitutes about 40 per cent of the chromosomes, and it is evidently not present in other parts of the cell. Since the genetic material had been localized in the chromosomes, and not elsewhere, this finding strongly suggested that DNA was, in fact, the molecular manifestation of the genes. Studies with microorganisms have provided conclusive evidence that DNA is the material basis of heredity (Avery, MacLeod, and McCarty, 1944).

The Watson-Crick hypothesis (Watson and Crick, 1953a,b) postulates a structural model of DNA which provides possible explanations of how genes accomplish their two basic types of activity: self-reproduction and protein determination. According to this model, DNA has a double-helix structure as shown in Figure 6. The helices are long chains of organic bases linked to each other by phosphate groups and the sugar deoxyribose. Spacing between the helices is maintained by hydrogen-bonded base pairs formed from the purines, adenine and guanine, and the pyrimidines, cytosine and thymine. The configurations of these bases are such that only pairings between thymine and adenine on the one hand, and cytosine and guanine on the other, will satisfy the spatial requirements. Each unit of phosphate, sugar, and base is called a nucleotide. The base pairs may occur in any sequence, and the diversity of possible linear arrangements provides the scope for the differentiation that characterizes the hereditary material.

The basic ingredients from which DNA is constituted are available in the cellular milieu. Thus, if the helices separate, as shown on the right of Figure 6, complementary bases will become attached to the now separated

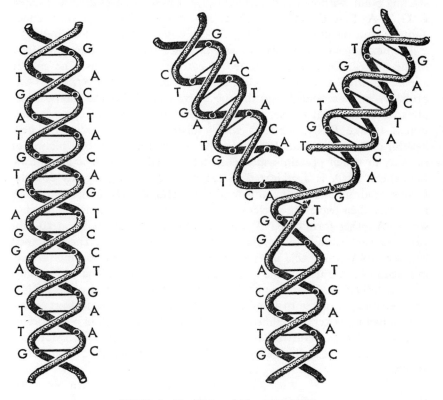

FIGURE 6. The Watson-Crick model of DNA

See text for explanation. (Reproduced from Dobzhansky, T. *Mankind evolving.* New Haven: Yale University Press, 1962. Used with permission of author and publisher.)

original bases. Eventually, two entirely new strands will be formed, each identical to the other and to the (now nonexistent) parental molecule. In this manner, the genetic material can make the duplications necessary for growth and for reproduction.

There is great current interest in how the genetic information is "coded" by the base pair sequence. Since the information must ultimately be expressed in terms of amino acid sequences in proteins, and since there are 20 different amino acids, the code must be such that by using only four "letters" all 20 amino acid "words" can be written. Several possibilities have been suggested for such a code. One of these proposed codes, for which considerable experimental support has been provided, is that of Crick (1962). Briefly, the conclusions are that groups of three consecutive bases specify an amino acid, and that the message is read from a fixed starting point, without overlap. That is, if the first six bases are represented C G T A T A, then C G T codes one amino acid while A T A codes another, and the combinations G T A and T A T are not utilized.

The next question concerns the way in which the information contained in the nuclear DNA is transmitted to cytoplasmic proteins. The answer appears to involve another nucleic acid, *ribonucleic acid* or *RNA*. RNA is probably single-stranded, and the successive nucleotides are composed of phosphate, the sugar ribose, and the bases adenine, guanine, cytosine, and uracil. Unlike DNA, RNA is widely distributed throughout the cell. Several different kinds of RNA have been described. A broad picture of the way in which protein synthesis is determined by DNA is as follows. Messenger RNA is synthesized in the nucleus, presumably by complementary pairing against the unwound DNA strands. The messenger RNA molecules then leave the nucleus, and in some way are attached to ribosomes. Another form of RNA, transfer RNA, evidently exists in 20 subvarieties, each capable of combining with one amino acid. The combined transfer RNA-amino acid units assemble in order on the ribosome surface, in a sequence dictated by the messenger RNA molecule. The amino acids become linked into a protein chain, which is then released from the RNA and becomes available to fulfill its role in cellular biochemical processes.

This picture is very simplified, and details may be found in a number of general references (Hurwitz and Furth, 1962; Kornberg, 1962; McElroy, 1961; Pardee, 1962; Sinsheimer, 1962; Sutton, 1961, 1962; Zamecnik, 1962).

Mutation

The above description has portrayed the process of duplication as one which results in exact copying, and this is usually the case. Occasionally, however, mutation results in a change in base sequence. These mutations will then be copied in subsequent mitosis and meiosis. This mechanism is the explanation for the existence of different allelic forms of a gene. Mutation occurs at low "spontaneous" rates, but may be greatly accelerated by high energy radiation and certain chemical compounds. (See Auerbach, 1962.) The result of a mutation will be the substitution of a different amino acid in the synthesized protein, which, in turn, may result in a quantitative or qualitative alteration in the biochemical activity of the protein.

A particularly instructive example may be cited from the recent work on hemoglobinopathies in man. Individuals with the serious and often fatal condition of "sickle-cell anemia" were found to have a type of hemoglobin different from that of normal individuals. Genetic studies have shown that the difference is due to one locus. Studies of the molecular nature of hemoglobin have shown that it is a large molecule composed of some 560 amino acids, and it has been found that the sickle-cell hemoglobin differs from normal hemoglobin only in the substitution of valine for glutamic acid in one particular location. Thus the genetic difference at one locus results in the change of only one amino acid in a complex molecule, yet the difference can be a matter of life or death.

Other hemoglobin abnormalities have been identified, and the reader is referred to Rucknagel and Neel (1961) for a review of this rapidly developing area of research.

Environment

To this point, for convenience of exposition, relatively little has been said of the role of environment in the production of a phenotype. But environment and genotype play interacting and supportive roles, and the understanding of genetic mechanisms without consideration of the contribution of environment is no more possible than the converse. A good illustration of this fundamental point can be made from the data of Krafka (1919), shown in Figure 7. Krafka studied the effects of rearing Drosophila in different temperatures on the expression of two genotypes which result in reduction of number of eye facets. The data for two temperatures, 15° and 27° Centigrade, are replotted in Figure 7. On the left, comparison is made between the two genotypes for each temperature. The magnitude of the effect of the genetic difference is expressed by the difference in heights of the bars, and it is immediately apparent that the size of the genetic effect is very much dependent upon the environmental conditions under which it is assessed. At 15° C, the difference is great; at 27° C, the difference is considerably reduced. On the right of the figure, the same data are shown with the emphasis on the effect of environment. The difference in rearing temperature has a large influence on phenotype for one genotype, and a small effect for the other genotype.

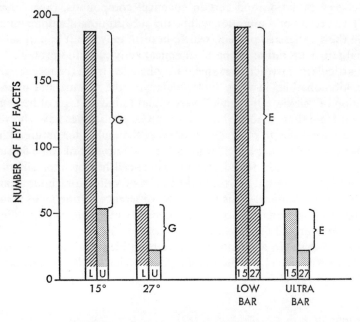

FIGURE 7.   Genotype and Environment Interaction

L and *U* represent *low-bar* and *ultra-bar* genotypes, respectively. *15* and *27* refer to rearing temperature. *G* and *E* brackets illustrate the difference attributable to genetic and to environmental differences, respectively. Replotted from Krafka, J. The effect of temperature upon facet number in the bar-eyed mutant of Drosophila. (Part I. *J. gen. Physiol.,* 1919, **2,** 409–432.)

Several other examples may be cited to emphasize the point. There is a dominant gene in Drosophila which produces an abnormal abdomen when the flies emerge from the pupa case in a moist medium. When the medium is dry, however, all of the emerging flies are phenotypically normal. (See Srb and Owen, 1952, p. 78.)

In the Himalayan rabbit, which has a white body and black extremities, it has been shown that deposition of pigment is due to the lowered temperature of the extremities. If these animals are kept in a warm cage, they develop no black pigment. If an area on the dorsal skin is artificially cooled, this normally white area develops black pigment. (See Sinnott, Dunn, and Dobzhansky, 1958, p. 25.)

There are skeletal variants among strains of mice. Ninety per cent of the animals of one strain have 25 presacral vertebrae, and 90 per cent of another have 26. The hybrids between these strains differ, depending on the strain of the mother. When fertilized ova of these reciprocal hybrids are transplanted to the uteri of animals of a third strain the differences between them disappear. The uterine environment obviously is influential in determining this characteristic (Green and Green, 1953).

As a general principle, the description of the phenotypic effect of different genes is incomplete without specification of the environmental circumstances. Equally, no description of the effect of an environmental manipulation can be regarded as complete without specification of the genotypes of the organisms to which such manipulation was applied.

Environment must be broadly conceived. It includes much more than the obvious intrauterine and postnatal factors. One part of a developing embryo may exert environmental influences over another part; a given cell is part of the environment of another cell; and, indeed, some cytoplasmic contents of the cell exert environmental influences over other cytoplasmic contents of the same cell (Weiss, 1962).

An instructive illustration of genotype-environment interaction is provided by a series of studies on the teratogenic effect of cortisone in mice. Fraser and associates (1954) reported the incidence of cleft palate in the offspring of mice of two strains, which were injected with cortisone during pregnancy. The greatest sensitivity was found to be when the series of four daily injections was begun on the eleventh day of gestation. Under this condition 100 per cent of the A-strain offspring, but only 17 per cent of the offspring of the C57BL strain, had cleft palates. This finding clearly demonstrates a genetic difference in susceptibility to an environmental agent, but further study revealed that part of the effect is attributable to maternal genotype and part to foetal genotype. The offspring of A mothers and C57BL fathers are genetically identical to the offspring of C57BL mothers and A fathers (except for the sex chromosomes of the male offspring). The former group showed an intermediate incidence (43 per cent) of cleft palate under the standard conditions, but the latter group showed only a 4 per cent incidence. Thus animals of essentially identical genotypes were differentially affected, depending on the genotype of their mother.

That this "maternal effect" is not a complete explanation of the difference in incidence between the original parent strains is shown by comparing the incidence of the A animals (100 per cent) with that of the offspring of A mothers and C57BL fathers (43 per cent). Both of these groups had A uterine environments, but the former was homozygous for the sensitive genotype, and the latter heterozygous.

GENES AND DEVELOPMENT

One of the most interesting problems in biology concerns the way in which ontogenesis can result in a highly differentiated organism, all of whose cells have been derived from a single cell, and all of which contain the same genetic information. In part, the answer is probably to be found in the fact that the cytoplasmic contents of the fertilized egg are not uniformly distributed. Definite systematic gradients exist in the concentration of various of these intracellular particles (Shumway and Adamstone, 1954; Waddington, 1956; Wagner and Mitchell, 1955). The initial cleavages of the developing egg result in unequal distribution of cytoplasmic contents. With this early differential in composition, subsequent development will give rise to differences in chemical processes in various cell-lines. In some cases, a gene-produced enzyme may encounter none of its appropriate substrate, with the result that the gene has no effect upon that cell. Lacking the product of the absent chemical reaction, the chemical milieu of the cell is further altered. Cells become progressively more differentiated, with some substrates available in profusion, and others absent or present in only small concentrations.

The effects of extracellular environmental factors are also differential. Some cells will be close to the surface of the embryo, and can participate more readily in direct gaseous exchange with the environment. Other cells are subjected to different physical forces by virtue of being enclosed by surrounding cells.

Concepts arising from recent research on microorganisms may ultimately contribute greatly to the understanding of developmental processes of multicellular organisms. Jacob and Monod (1961) have reviewed the evidence for the existence of *regulator* genes, which have functions different from the *structural* genes thus far described. A regulator gene evidently produces a repressor substance which becomes associated with part of the DNA chain, thus preventing the formation of the messenger RNA. The net effect, of course, is failure to produce the protein coded by that particular RNA. The repressor substance itself may be inactivated by other substances, however, with the result that the protein synthesis can proceed. By postulating various types of interrelationships among regulator genes, structural genes, and their products, Monod and Jacob (1961) have shown how metabolic processes of a cell can be switched on and off; how one of two interrelated potential metabolic pathways can permanently block the other; how an oscillation from one pathway to another can occur; and so on.

Although detailed confirmation is required in multicellular organisms, the mechanisms proposed provide attractive working hypotheses concerning the processes of development.

As a consequence of factors and processes of this nature, differentiation of embryonic tissues proceeds. As it does, the embryonic phenomena of induction occur, in which further development of one tissue depends upon the presence of other tissues. Many studies have shown that the ultimate expression of a genetic condition can be traced to failures of induction. As an example, consider the defective condition in mice known as *Kreisler*, which is determined by a recessive gene. In early development there is a shifting of the auditory pits, so that the ear vesicles do not come into contact with the myelencephalon, as is normally the case. The consequences are defective differentiation of the labyrinth of the ear, shortening of the semicircular canals, absence of the ductus endolymphaticus with a resulting increase in endolymphatic pressure, and formation of cysts in the subarachnoid space. Development of the pons, rhombencephalon, and cerebral hemispheres is grossly affected by the cysts. Many of the affected mice die early, but some reach maturity. Their behavior is abnormal, with head tremors and turning in small circles being characteristic (Grüneberg, 1952).

Often it is possible to show that a number of diverse symptoms can be related, through a "pedigree of causes," to a single primary defect. The classical example of this has been provided by Grüneberg (1947) with respect to a genetic condition in mice. The various developmental relationships for the condition are shown in Figure 8. The syndrome is traceable, ultimately, to a defect in cartilage formation; yet it is expressed in skeletal, respiratory, and circulatory anomalies. In a similar manner, also in mice, Falconer, Fraser, and King (1951) related abnormal pinnae, kinked tails, corneal ulceration, respiratory disorders, and abnormal coat texture, together with other abnormalities, to the effect of the recessive gene "*crinkled*" on hair follicle development.

The phenomenon of multiple effects of a gene has been termed *pleiotropy*. While in many cases the effects can be related through sequential developmental processes, it is also possible that the same genes can have different, more or less primary effects in widely separated organs or tissues by virtue of the differentiated cytoplasms of the different tissues. (See Hadorn, 1961.) Thus, function of a gene might be highly specific at the level of protein synthesis; but through the complex interrelationships of ontogenesis, it may have manifold effects at higher levels of phenotypic measurement.

Much of the evidence on the genetic control of the developmental process has been derived from studies of abnormalities, such as those described above. The literature is extensive and has recently been reviewed by Hadorn (1961), to whom the interested reader is referred for more details.

Of course, the discovery of an allele which results in an abnormality of development does not imply that the normal allele is alone responsible for

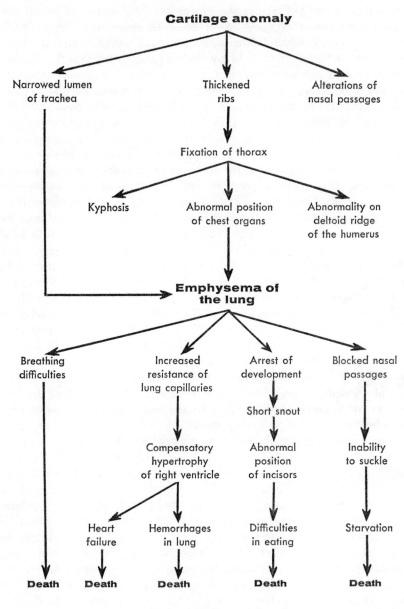

FIGURE 8.   A "Pedigree of Causes"

After Grüneberg in Sinnott, Dunn, and Dobzhansky's *Principles of genetics*. 5/e. New York: McGraw-Hill, 1958. P. 352.

the direction of the normal developmental process. It requires less to wreck a piece of machinery than to construct it. Just as we have seen that a single gene can have many phenotypic effects, a given phenotype can be the end result of the functioning of many genes.

Waddington (1957) has considered in detail the problem of polygenic influence on development. Two points may be singled out as of primary interest for the present topic. The first refers to canalization of development. If a particular tissue is developing along its usual path, and is shifted from it by some experimental procedure, there is a strong tendency for development to return to the original path. While this "canalization" is usually discussed in regard to histogenesis and morphogenesis, there is no reason to believe that the phenomena do not occur with respect to behavior which is mediated by the organs resulting from the morphogenesis. An important aspect of canalization is that its effectiveness is under genetic influence. Individuals with some genotypes are better able to return to normal development after displacement than are others with different genotypes. The situation may be analogized to a ball rolling down a trough. Some troughs are V-shaped, and the course of the ball can be deflected only with difficulty. Other troughs are U-shaped, with more latitude for the ball to be diverted from side to side. In this analogy the shape of the trough, the width of its bottom, and the steepness of its sides are genetically determined, and the environment may be regarded as forces at right angles to the direction in which the ball is rolling. The ball itself is the tissue, or organ, or organism undergoing development.

The second important point is related to the notion of critical periods in development. At various levels, the trough forks, offering alternate routes. Very often, one of the alternatives will be favored by being deeper or more directly aligned, so that there is a higher probability of that route being taken. Yet forces applied to the ball at the critical juncture can increase the probability of the alternate pathway being followed. Thus there exist critical periods in development during which environmental factors, which have only modest effects at other times, can substantially alter the course of subsequent development.

This physical analogy is offered in the spirit of a simplified model, and its limitations are acknowledged. Nevertheless, it serves as a convenient frame of reference for thinking about developmental processes. The reader should consult Waddington (1957) for other conceptualizations and the experimental data upon which they are based.

This section has described some current theories, and a few examples, of the way in which genetic factors influence development. The principal point is that an adult characteristic is not "inherited" as a full-blown static entity, but is the result of a developmental "trajectory" which is determined by the complex interaction of both genetic and environmental factors.

BEHAVIORAL GENETICS

Having reviewed briefly some basic principles of genetics, we may now turn to research dealing directly with behavioral genetics. The literature is too extensive for a thorough review to be undertaken here. Instead, researches will be cited which are fairly representative of content and methodology.

Animal Research

Much of the research in behavioral genetics of animals has employed highly inbred strains. The logic of these studies is quite straightforward. By strict inbreeding the genetic variability within an inbred strain is reduced, theoretically approaching zero as the number of consecutive inbred generations increases. Thus, with certain reservations (see Falconer, 1960), all of the animals within a highly inbred strain will be genetically like each other, and will be homozygous at all loci. The probability that any inbred strain could develop the same homozygous genotype as another separately maintained strain, is so small that it may be taken to be zero. Thus, although the number and nature of the loci involved is unknown, we can be sure that different inbred strains differ in genotype. If different strains are reared and tested under environmental circumstances as uniform as possible, behavioral differences which appear may therefore be attributed to this genotypic difference.

Strain differences have been described in a wide variety of behavioral characteristics. In mice, for example, differences among various inbred strains have been established in aggressiveness (Ginsburg and Allee, 1942); locomotor activity (Thompson, 1953; McClearn, 1959; Bruell, 1962); learning ability (King and Mavromatis, 1956; Lindzey and Winston, 1962); audiogenic seizure susceptibility (Hall, 1947; Fuller and Smith, 1953); and alcohol preference (McClearn and Rodgers, 1959). Similarly, studies on rat strains have revealed differences in food-hoarding behavior (Stamm, 1954); locomotor activity (Carr and Williams, 1957); learning (Myers, 1959); and alcohol preference (Myers, 1962). Other studies have successfully sought strain differences in sex drive of guinea pigs (Valenstein, Riss, and Young, 1954); in maternal behavior of rabbits (Sawin and Crary, 1953); and habitat selection of *Peromyscus* (Harritt, 1952). Studies of dogs have also revealed breed differences in learning ability (Fuller, 1955), and social behavior (Mahut, 1958; Pawlowski and Scott, 1956).

Strain differences provide the rather limited information that genotypic differences can produce phenotypic differences in the trait under consideration. Further information has frequently been sought by cross-breeding. Comparison of parent strains with derived F1, F2, and backcross generations, for example, can provide estimates of the degree of genetic determination of the trait. Estimates of environmental variance may be obtained from the variances of the parent strains and F1, since within these groups there is no genetic variance, according to the model. In the F2 generation, there is genetic segregation, and thus genetic variance in addition to environmental variance. Appropriate subtraction can provide an estimate of the amount of genetically produced variance in the F2 generation, and this can be expressed as a proportion of the total phenotypic variance to provide an index of the degree of genetic determination. (See Falconer, 1963. This quantity differs from heritability as defined earlier on page 446, in that the numerator in this case includes all genetic variance and not just additive genetic variance.) Fuller and Thompson (1960), for example, found that approximately 60 per cent of the variation in activity scores of an F2 generation derived from C57BR/a and A/Jax strains was genetic in origin.

Another major procedure in research with animals has been selective breeding. If the individual differences within a heterogeneous population are based in part on additive genetic variance, then the mating of like extremes over a number of generations should result in a shift in the mean of the characteristic. In practice, selection is usually carried out in both upward and downward directions, so that both a "high" line and a "low" line are derived. The rate of change in means over the generations of selection, the symmetry or lack of symmetry of the changes in mean in the "high" and "low" lines, and other features of the response to selective breeding are of theoretical interest in quantitative genetics. In addition, a selection program generates animals that can be used in research upon correlated characters, biochemical intermediates, and so on.

There have been several selection studies in behavioral genetics. Tryon (1940) and Heron (1935, 1941) were both successful in breeding for "maze-bright" and "maze-dull" rats. The animals from these studies were used in later experiments on the generality of the "brightness" and "dullness" (for example, Searle, 1949); motivational differences and differential error tendencies (R. E. Harris, 1940); brain biochemistry (Rosenzweig, Krech, and Bennett, 1960), and so on. In other studies, selection has been carried out for high and low degrees of "emotionality" (Hall, 1938; Broadhurst, 1958) and activity of rats (Rundquist, 1933); audiogenic seizure susceptibility of mice (Frings and Frings, 1953); and phototaxis (Hirsch and Boudreau, 1958) and geotaxis (Hirsch, 1962) in fruit flies.

In view of the number of organ systems known or presumed to be involved in most behavior patterns, polygenic systems have probably been involved in most of the studies mentioned. As pointed out on page 455, however, a single locus is sometimes found to have a large effect (usually resulting in an "abnormality") on phenotypes for which normal variation is polygenically determined. Examples with behavioral connotations include the neurological mutants of the mouse, which result in various types of incoordination and deficiencies of motor control and which involve various kinds of neural or sensory maldevelopment (see Grüneberg, 1952); and the effects of single genes on mating behavior in Drosophila (Bastock, 1956).

The studies mentioned in this brief review illustrate the broad range of behaviors in which a genetic role has been demonstrated. Indeed, the demonstration of genetic influence is now rather commonplace, and represents only the first (though necessary) step in a research project.

Human Research

A substantial portion of the literature on human behavioral genetics has been derived from one or another type of study involving twins. The basic logic of twin studies is clear. MZ (monozygotic or identical) twins have identical genotypes, whereas DZ (dizygotic or fraternal) twins have genotypes no more similar than those of ordinary siblings. Because there is no genetic difference between MZ twins, any phenotypic difference must be environmental in origin. Differences between members of DZ twin pairs are both environmental and genetic in origin. If one can assume that the effects of environment are no greater and no less in DZ than in MZ twins, the mean intrapair difference of a group of MZ twins can be subtracted from that of a group of DZ twins, and the residual will be a measure of the effects of genetic differences. (To avoid obvious difficulties arising from differences in rearing male and female children, DZ pairs of like sex only are usually used in such comparisons.) The relative sizes of the estimates of environmental and genetic contributions may be used to obtain a type of heritability estimate. In twin studies involving more or less qualitative and dichotomous categories, comparisons are made in terms of *concordance* (both members of a twin pair alike), and *discordance* (members of a twin pair unlike).

A number of behavioral studies involving comparison of MZ and DZ twins have been reported. Many studies have measured both intellectual and personality variables (for example, Newman, Freeman, and Holzinger, 1937; Vandenberg, 1962). The typical finding has been that the mean intrapair difference for DZ twins exceeds that for MZ twins more in the case of intelligence measures than in personality trait measures. This indicates that there is, in general, a larger genetic component in intellectual than in personality traits. Within each of these general domains, however, some measures or factors have higher genetic components than others. Among other results, for example, Vandenberg (1962) found that scores on the Primary Mental Abilities Tests on Number were more heritable than those on Memory; and Gottesman (1962) found evidence of an appreciable genetic component on the Social Introversion but not on the Hysteria scale of the Minnesota Multiphasic Personality Inventory.

Abnormalities of behavior have also been explored by the twin-study technique. Several studies, for example, have been concerned with schizophrenia. (See Rosenthal, 1962, for review.) Although the concordance values and the interpretation differ somewhat from study to study, all of these studies show a much higher concordance in MZ twins than in DZ twins.

Other twin methods make use of MZ twins only. By comparing the intra-pair differences of MZ twins reared apart with those of MZ twins reared together, the effectiveness of long-term environmental differences can be investigated. (See, for example, Newman, Freeman, and Holzinger, 1937.) In the co-twin control method, one member of a MZ twin pair is subjected to a training program or some other specific environmental treatment, and the co-twin is retained, untreated, as a control subject. This approach has been used principally in studies on acquisition of skills (for example, Gesell and Thompson, 1929).

Rosenthal (1959) has made yet another use of MZ twins in using concordance or discordance to classify subgroups of schizophrenia with presumed differences in etiology. The assumption was made that schizophrenia in discordant MZ cases was largely environmental in origin, and that in concordant MZ cases it had a significant genetic etiology. The families of MZ twin pairs discordant with respect to schizophrenia were then compared to the families of concordant MZ pairs. Differences were found between the two classes of family, with incidence lower, onset later, and prognosis more favorable in the families of the discordant MZ twins.

Another approach to the study of inheritance in humans is the examination of correlations among relatives. By virtue of the fact that relatives will share some alleles but differ in others, correlations greater than zero but less than unity are expected on genetic grounds alone. In studies on physical characteristics such as body weight or height, parent-offspring and sibling correlations are typically found to be about 0.50. In behavioral characteristics, values of this same order of magnitude have been found on intelligence test scores (for example, Jones, 1928; Roberts, 1941) but lower values are typically found in the case of personality indices (for example, Crook, 1937). This finding is in accord with the results from twin studies cited above.

Another human research method involves the study of adopted children. The basic reasoning is that "own" children living with their parents may resemble their parents or siblings both because of commonly shared genes and the common environmental milieu (which includes parents and siblings). Adopted children, on the other hand, will resemble their adoptive parents and siblings only because of the environmental effects; and they will resemble their own, biological parents and siblings only because of genetic similarities. Appropriate comparisons should therefore permit the estimation of the relative effects of genes and environment.

The effect of environment was revealed, for example, by the finding that the correlation of siblings adopted into different homes was lower than the correlation of siblings living together (Freeman, Holzinger, and Mitchell, 1928). The role of genotype was shown in another study (Burks, 1928) in which the correlations of mental ages of parents with I.Q. scores of children were greater for parents and "own" children than for parents and adopted children.

Developmental processes are implicated in a longitudinal study by Skodak and Skeels (1949). These investigators obtained I.Q. scores of 63 adopted children at four age levels, and compared these scores to the I.Q.'s of true mothers. The correlation increased from zero at about two years of age to 0.35 at about seven years of age. The mean I.Q. of the adopted children was substantially higher than that of true mothers, however.

Because I.Q. measures were unfortunately not available for all of the true mothers or adoptive mothers, education level of the adults was employed as an indirect index of intelligence in other comparisons. The correlation of child's I.Q. with true mother's educational level rose from essentially zero at two years to 0.31 at four years, and remained fairly stable thereafter. The corresponding correlations with adoptive mother's education level, or with adoptive father's education level, did not significantly differ from zero at any age level.[1]

Honzik (1957) obtained data showing increasing correlations of chilren's I.Q. with parent's education level in a sample of children reared by their true parents. Comparison with the data of Skodak and Skeels revealed a striking similarity in the pattern of increasing relationship to true

---

[1] Correlations reported by Kagan and Moss (1959) do not show a uniform increase in the resemblance between child's I.Q. and parent's education or I.Q. These findings are of limited relevance to the issue under discussion, however, since the earliest measurements taken were at three years of age. (Measures were also taken at six and ten years.) By three, the correlations of the studies cited above were already appreciable and the rate of increase had begun to taper off.

parents for both groups. Thus the rate of increasing resemblance to true parents and the resemblance in the final level attained appears to be the same whether children are reared by their true parents or not.

Logical and Methodological Considerations

In the interests of brevity and continuity, the preceding discussion of the general methodologies in behavioral genetics has disregarded a number of difficulties of interpretation. Appreciation of these difficulties is of the highest importance, however, not only for the behavioral geneticist but also for others who must evaluate the relevance of genetic research for their own specialties. Although a detailed analysis cannot be undertaken here, some examples of the types of logical and methodological problems encountered will be provided.

It is particularly important that the impossibility of absolute answers to the "nature-nurture question" be appreciated. Not only is a question that asks if a trait is due to heredity *or* environment logically indefensible; a question that inquires as to the proportional contribution of genetic and environmental sources of variance can receive only a relative answer. Estimates of heritability refer to a specifically defined trait in a particular population at a certain time and under certain environmental conditions. Such an estimate *may* have broader application; but whether it does is an empirical matter. This relativity is made apparent by considering some extreme hypothetical situations. Suppose that a highly inbred population, in which all individuals were genetically identical, were placed in a highly diversified environment. In this population, all variance would arise from environmental sources, and the heritability would be zero. A genetically heterogeneous population in an absolutely uniform environment would vary only for genotypic reasons, and the heritability would be unity. If this genetically heterogeneous population were placed in the diversified environment, the total variability would be due to both sources of variance, and the heritability would be some value between zero and one.

Thus no eternal reality is revealed by the finding that x per cent of the variance of an F2 is due to genetic differences. In laboratory settings environments are controlled in as stable a state as possible unless some specific feature of the environment is under study. In less controlled circumstances—or in a more heterogeneous population, or even in another F2 derived from different parent strains—the proportional contributions of heredity and environment could differ.

Similarly, in the comparison of MZ and DZ twins, the genotypic diversity is limited to that which can occur among siblings and the range of environmental factors to that occurring within families. A heritability estimate from such a situation should not be applied uncritically to the general population.

In addition to such basic limitations in the type of scientifically meaningful statements that can be made, many assumptions of the logical models are incompletely met in practice. For example, it is basic to twin-study logic that DZ twins are not exposed to greater environmental differences than are MZ twins. In reality, they are. In addition, the unambiguous interpretation of parent-offspring correlations requires, among other things, that mating be at random with respect to the trait. It is well established, however, that husband-wife correlations are of considerable magnitude in many behavioral traits. A fundamental assumption in most procedures is also that genotype and environment are uncorrelated. Yet the likelihood that correlations do exist is great. Parents transmitting genes for schizophrenia susceptibility, for example, may also rear their children in a schizogenic manner; parents transmitting genes for intelligence probably also provide environmental support for intellectual attainment. This same problem of correlation of genotype and environment confounds interpretation of many adopted-child studies in which selective placement resulted in the assignment of children of presumed "better" genetic endowment to superior adoptive homes.

Though animal research is less troubled than human research with these specific problems, it has some of its own. For example, practically all research with inbred strains, or with generations derived from inbred strains, is based upon the assumption that all of the strains involved are homozygous at all loci (or at least at all loci influencing the trait under investigation). Even in theory the complete fulfillment of this assumption is only approached with increasing number of consecutive generations of inbreeding. The occurrence of mutations will provide a further barrier to complete homozygosity. Furthermore, there is evidence (Lerner, 1954) that the superior vigor and fitness of heterozygotes, as compared to homozygotes, can lead to differential survival and reproduction within a strain—with the result that the level of homozygosity actually attained is less than that computed on theoretical grounds.

Insofar as these and other failures to meet assumptions completely are necessary consequences of biological or social facts, and are not alterable by the researcher, the only solution appears to be to assess with precision the degree to which the assumptions are not fulfilled and to make adequate compensation in analysis. A complementary aim might be to develop models that do not make the same assumptions.

Another type of problem relates to procedural matters, such as determination of zygosity of twins, sampling requirements, and the like. In these problems, identification of shortcomings often permits corrections and the result is a steady increase in the adequacy of research design. For example, in early twin studies it was not possible to distinguish like-sexed DZ twins from MZ twins on criteria other than general physical resemblance. Investigators were reduced to circular reasoning in identifying the MZ twins on the basis of close similarity, and in then examining their similarity. Improvements in independent criteria of resemblance permitted more adequate diagnosis in later work. As a result, the more recent studies (for example, Sutton, Vandenberg, and Clark, 1962; Gottesman, 1962) have been able to utilize the extensive current knowledge concerning inheritance of a number of blood types to diagnose zygosity with great precision.

Some of the difficulties of obtaining representative samples in genetics research are illustrated with respect to twin studies on schizophrenia in a recent, thorough review by Rosenthal (1962). For example, obtaining cases on the basis of consecutive admissions to mental hospitals results in different concordance rates than does sampling from resident patient populations (pp. 118–119).

Obviously, these few examples can only be suggestive of the methodological considerations pertinent to behavioral genetics research. Detailed discussions will be found in most general texts in genetics. Two recent books by Burdette (1962, 1963) deal specifically with methodology. Fuller and Thompson (1960) also discuss methodological problems from the point of view of behavior study.

HEREDITY AND BEHAVIOR DEVELOPMENT

The studies in the preceding section were selected to provide a representative (though necessarily a sketchy) picture of the breadth of behavior patterns which have been investigated from the genetic point of view. As we have seen, the interpretation of many of the studies is not without some ambiguity, but the overall conclusion must be that heredity plays a basic and fundamental role in behavioral processes.

In this section the intent is to provide a somewhat more detailed examination of several phenotypes that relate to behavioral development. In some of these studies, the developmental process was explicitly investigated. In others, the trait investigated represents an arrest or abnormality of the developmental processes. These studies of abnormalities are not only of interest in their own right, but also instructive in elucidating the types of mechanisms through which genes can influence both abnormal and normal development.

Animal Research

One type of study involves a description of the developmental aspects of a particular behavior in two or more genetically distinct strains, breeds, or subspecies reared in standard environments. King and Shea (1959), for example, studied responses of two subspecies of deermice on an elevated maze. Significant differences were discovered at early ages, but these differences disappeared by thirty days of age. Detailed analyses suggested that the results could be explained in terms of differential rates of maturation in activity and the clinging response.

Another approach has been to investigate the effects of environmental variables, applied during development, on later behavior of genetically different groups. The importance of hereditary factors is revealed in these studies by group differences in response to the variable. In one such study, King and Eleftheriou (1959) subjected animals from the *gracilis* and *bairdii* subspecies of deermice to systematic handling (by automatic machine) for ten minutes daily from the age of three days until the age of twenty-five days. At about seventy-nine days, all animals were tested for activity level, and a week later were placed in a shock-avoidance conditioning situation. In comparison with control animals, the treated subjects from both *gracilis* and *bairdii* displayed more exploratory activity, but the treatment effect was significantly greater in *bairdii*. In the conditioning apparatus, *gracilis* treated animals made more responses than their controls, but *bairdii* treated animals made fewer.

A further example is provided by a study on learning in different mouse strains (Lindzey and Winston, 1962). Animals of the C57BL and C3H strains that had been "gentled" by systematic handling were compared to control animals as to their performance in a maze. The gentled C57BL animals were much superior to the control C57BL's, but the treatment had practically no effect on the C3H animals.

The effects of infantile trauma were also explored by Lindzey, Lykken, and Winston (1960). Four strains of mice were exposed, at the age of four to eight days, to a loud auditory stimulus. The animals were then compared in adulthood on responses to several tests of temperament. For the measure of emotionality, the effect of the noxious stimulation was fairly uniform in the different strains, but in a test for timidity the effects varied from strain to strain.

In yet another organism, the guinea pig, two inbred strains and one genetically heterogeneous group were studied in an experiment on the effects of social versus isolated rearing upon adult sexual behavior (Valenstein, Riss, and Young, 1955). A striking effect of isolated rearing was found in one of the inbred strains in an overall sexual behavior index, with no significant effect being demonstrated in the other groups.

As a final example from animal research, we may consider the experiment by Freedman (1958) in which the effects of "indulgent" and "disciplinary" rearing regimes were compared in four breeds of dogs: Shetland sheepdogs, basenjis, wirehaired fox terriers, and beagles. The indulged pups were never punished and were encouraged to undertake various kinds of activity. The disciplined pups were restrained and taught to sit, stay, and come on command. These rearing conditions were applied daily from the third to the eighth week, at which time all animals were given the test situation. Food was placed in a bowl and, for three minutes, the dog was prevented from eating by a slap on the hindquarters and a shouted "No" from the experimenter. The experimenter then left the room, and the time until the animal began to eat was recorded.

This test situation was repeated for eight days. The effect of mode of rearing was large for the beagles and terriers, with the indulged animals requiring much longer to begin to eat than the disciplined animals. For the basenjis and Shetland sheepdogs, the mode of rearing was ineffective. All basenjis ate quickly, and all Shetland sheepdogs avoided the food, regardless of condition of rearing.

The general conclusion to be drawn from these studies is that the same environmental treatment may have quite diverse outcomes, depending upon the genotype of the individual receiving the treatment.

Human Research

For a long time there was animated discussion over the mode of inheritance of amentia. Gradually, it was recognized that a number of discrete conditions could be differentiated within this general category. Subsequent research has made clear that different varieties of "feeblemindedness" may have widely differing etiologies. Those in which hereditary factors play a predominant role vary from single-gene conditions through conditions involving chromosomal abnormalities. Other conditions, particularly the less severe ones not involving stigmata, appear to be the lower end of the normal distribution of intelligence. Here, environmental factors undoubtedly have an important effect, and so also do genetic factors. Segregation of the multiple genetic factors underlying intelligence will inevitably result in individuals with many "unfavorable" alleles, just as it generates individuals with exceptionally good genic endowments. Finally, of course, there are conditions in which obvious environmental factors have played a decisive role.

Phenylketonuria. One of the best understood conditions of mental defect is phenylketonuria. An example of "inborn errors of metabolism," it was shown by Fölling in 1934 to involve the excretion of large quantities of phenylpyruvic acid in the urine. Almost immediately thereafter, Penrose (1935) and Jervis (1937) showed it to be inherited in a recessive manner. The existence of the biochemical anomaly inspired research into the metabolic pathway involved. The crucial defect was found to be a reduced ability to convert phenylalanine, an essential amino acid, into tyrosine (Jervis, 1947, 1953) because of a lack of the appropriate enzyme, phenylalanine hydroxylase. This results in an accumulation of phenylalanine in the body fluids, and abnormal amounts of a variety of other substances related to phenylalanine metabolism. (See Knox and Hsia, 1957.) For some time, it was unclear whether the mental symptoms were the result of an excess of some metabolites resulting from the block, or a deficiency of some product which could not be formed in normal quantities because of the block (Jervis, 1954). Evidence now strongly supports the view that there is a toxic effect of phenylalanine or some of its derivatives, but the exact identity of the responsible compound has yet to be established.

The possibility of rational therapy was suggested by these findings, and several studies have been performed in which those suffering from phenylketonuria have been fed diets free of phenylalanine (Armstrong and Tyler, 1955; Bickel, Garrard, and Hickmans, 1954; LaDu, 1959; Woolf, Griffiths, and Moncrieff, 1955). The results have been quite encouraging, with normal chemical findings subsequent to the administration of the artificial diet. Mental development has also been observed to improve, although insufficient time has elapsed to determine if it is completely normal.

It appears that the best therapeutic results may be expected if the special diet is begun at an early age. To this end, it becomes important to identify the condition in neonates. Since the phenylpyruvic acid in the urine reacts with a ferric chloride solution to form a green color, a simple screening test is available. But, since the biochemical abnormalities do not appear until after protein feeding has been begun, this test is not effective in the maternity hospital, and there are some further practical problems in routine screening procedures (Farquhar, Kaneas, and Tait, 1962). Nevertheless, with the special diet commercially available and early detection feasible, at least amelioration of the disease is possible.

Since phenylketonurics are homozygous for a recessive allele, their parents, although normal mentally, must each be heterozygous. For purposes of genetic counseling, it is important to be able to identify such heterozygous "carriers." A normal relative of a phenylketonuric, for example, might wish to know if he is homozygous or heterozygous for the normal allele. By means of procedures developed by Hsia and his coworkers (1956), such identification is now possible. The relative of a phenylketonuric and his or her spouse can be tested and the probability of affected children being born can be assessed.

Other mental deficiency syndromes. Other types of mental deficiency have also been intensively studied. Of these, only a few can be mentioned. Infantile amaurotic idiocy (Tay-Sachs disease) is another recessive condition. It involves progressive neural degeneration and optic nerve atrophy beginning at a few months of age. Death ensues by about two years of age. The biochemical derangement in this case involves lipid metabolism.

A similar condition is juvenile amaurotic idiocy. This is also determined by a recessive gene and presents a symptom pattern very much like that of infantile amaurotic idiocy—except that the age of onset is between about two and ten years of age, and the deterioration may last for several years before death occurs. (See Penrose, 1954.)

Another syndrome involving neural degeneration is Huntington's Chorea. This condition, however, is inherited as a dominant. The age of onset may vary from ten to seventy years of age; but in the typical case, it begins between the thirtieth and fiftieth years. Progressive neural degeneration is accompanied by involuntary movements, and usually by mental impairment. The late onset of Huntington's Chorea poses special problems in genetic counseling, since in many cases the affected individual will already have had children. Since the condition is dominant, one-half of the children, on the average, will be expected to have received the allele causing the abnormality. Some promise that a palliative therapy might be ultimately attainable is given by the work of Kempinsky and associates (1958), who found some reduction in choreic movements following administration of reserpine.

These three abnormal conditions illustrate a fundamental point concerning the genetics of development: in general, presence at birth is not a criterion of inheritance. The effects of genes may not be manifest until advanced developmental stages. Indeed, we must regard the genetic role in development as persisting from conception to death.

Böök (1953), Jervis (1952), and Penrose (1954) provide reviews of these and other types of mental defect.

Chromosome anomalies. In very recent years methodological developments have made possible some striking advances in human cytology. In particular, it has been possible to relate certain chromosomal abnormalities to specific syndromes. A discussion of Mongolism will serve as a brief introduction to this topic and we shall also consider sex chromosome abnormalities. Details should be sought in the references cited.

Mongolism is characterized by such a distinctive syndrome that it has been recognized as a clinical entity for decades. Studies on its causation had been rewarded with most confusing results until recent advances in cytology made detailed study of human chromosomal complements possible. The first descriptions of chromosomal anomaly associated with Mongolism were made practically simultaneously by Lejeune, Gauthier, and Turpin (1959) and Jacobs and associates (1959). Instead of the normal 46 chromosomes (22 pairs of autosomes plus one pair of sex chromosomes), patients with Mongolism were found to have 47 chromosomes. The extra chromosome was found to be an autosome, identified as number 21. (See Figure 4; also consult Harnden, 1961; Ford, 1962; and Appendix II of Burdette, 1962, for discussions of the problems of chromosome identification and nomenclature.) This finding has since been confirmed in a large number of cases. (See Hamerton, 1962, for a review.) There appear to be at least two ways in which the extra chromosomal material can be transmitted. Nondisjunction has already been described (see page 445). Another mechanism appears to be translocation, in which part of chromosome 21 becomes attached to another chromosome. The net effect is similar in both mechanisms in that extra genetic material from chromosome 21 is present.

Mongolism thus represents an unusual genetic situation. The terminology of Mendelian genetics—which permits description of phenylketonuria as recessive, Huntington's Chorea as dominant, and so on—is not directly applicable. A large amount of extra genetic material involving many loci is the causal factor. How this extra material exerts its detrimental effects is not yet known, but the ultimate explanation undoubtedly will be in terms of enzyme mechanisms. In view of the fact that Mongolism presents a picture of generalized developmental arrest (Penrose, 1954, p. 184), elucidation of the causal mechanisms should provide new insights into the control of normal developmental processes.

Abnormalities of autosomes besides number 21 have been discovered in other clinical conditions. Two other syndromes involving multiple congenital abnormalities are evidently associated, respectively, with trisomy of chromosome 17 or 18, and one of the 13–15 chromosomes. Similarities among these chromosomes do not permit unequivocal identification at the present time.

In addition to the autosomal trisomy syndromes just discussed, anomalies of sex chromosomal complement have been described in conditions of abnormal sexual development. In patients showing the Klinefelter syndrome, involving breast development and absence of spermatogenesis in males, it is often found that the sex chromosome constitution is XXY. In Turner's syndrome, involving sexual infantilism in presumptive females, the chromosome complement has been found in many cases to include only one X chromosome and no Y chromosome. Individuals possessing XXX, XXXY,

XXXXY, XXYY, and XXXX sex chromosomes have been described (Miller, 1961; Polani, 1962; see also Sohval, 1963).

Genetics and "Normal" Development

The more dramatic examples of genetic influence on human development are provided by the abnormalities discussed above. It is probable that the medical and psychological problems involved have spurred research on these conditions. In addition, the relative ease of identification and classification of affected individuals, and the fact that some of the conditions have a straightforward single-locus genetic basis, have made for better understanding of these abnormalities than of normal variation in development. We may reasonably expect the same principles to apply in the development of normal characteristics, however. Although there is currently less direct evidence than one might wish, some data are available to illustrate pertinent points.

Sontag and Garn (1956/57) studied developmental patterns of a variety of physical traits and of I.Q. in sibling groups. Certain patterns of development were found to be characteristic of families. An example is given of four siblings, all of whom showed rapid growth, large size, slow motor development, and incoordination. The authors emphasize that the familial similarities may be found in the pattern or sequence of developmental events rather than in the chronological timing.

We have already noted that genes do not always show their effects in the earliest stages of life. An example in normal development may be that of intelligence. The studies of Skodak and Skeels (1949) and of Honzik (1957), discussed earlier, found the correlation between the child's I.Q. and the educational level of his biological parent increased between infancy and early childhood. Bayley (1954) also reports a similar trend, as does Hindley (1961). Hindley found the correlation between child's I.Q. and mother's education rose from 0.26 at age six months to 0.43 at age five years; and with father's education, the correlation rose from 0.18 to 0.40. It would be premature, however, to conclude from these studies that the genetic component does increase with age, since the validity of I.Q. tests with very young children is highly questionable. Thus it is possible that the increasing correlations between child I.Q. and parent education result from the increasing validity of the tests rather than the emergence of the genetic contribution. The resolution of this problem awaits the development of more adequate procedures for testing the intelligence of infants. (See Escalona and Moriarity, 1961.)

Jarvik and his colleagues (1957) compared senescent identical and fraternal twin pairs on various psychological test scores obtained approximately eight years apart. In the original test series, the mean intrapair difference was greater for fraternal twins than for identical twins on all tests: vocabulary, digit symbol, block design, similarities, tapping, and digit span. In the retest series, the same general picture emerged for all tests except digit span. These results demonstrate the influence of hereditary factors even during the process of senescent decline, and serve to reemphasize that genetic factors operate throughout the entire life span. Although the number of cases is too small for definitive statements to be made, the greater intrapair difference of identical twins in the retest of digit span suggests, in accord with the theoretical considerations given earlier, that the relative contributions of genetic and environmental factors may differ for different mental processes.

CONCLUSION

Limitations of space have permitted the presentation of only a fragment of the available evidence concerning the influence of genotype on behavior. A thorough review is provided by Fuller and Thompson (1960). In this chapter I have attempted to present not so much a review as a documented frame of reference.

There are two essential points which could profitably be incorporated into the *Weltanschaung* of all theorists, researchers, and practitioners in the behavioral sciences. The first pertains to individuality. With the number of loci in man estimated to be between ten thousand and one hundred thousand, the possible number of genotypes far exceeds the number of persons now living, plus those who have ever lived, in all of human history. Excepting identical twins, and other identical multiple births, each human being is a unique and unrepeatable event. Add the effects of environment to this genotypic heterogeneity, and individuality is further enhanced. This uniqueness of the individual has implications of the highest importance for both theory and practice. A theoretical formulation which assumes the genetic equivalence of all men (or rats) is excluding a whole realm of potentially important determinants. Children of some genotypes may thrive under authoritarian upbringing; others may be stifled under any regime but a permissive one; the word method of teaching reading may be optimal for pupils of some genotypes, and the phonic system may be superior for others. In short, what is sauce for a goose may not only not be sauce for a gander, it may be poison to a different goose.

This situation complicates things considerably. Theories which ignore individuality cannot be expected to provide answers to the problems of a specific individual—unless research has clearly demonstrated that *for the specific trait in question*, genetic differences may be ignored without too great a distortion. It is dangerous in the extreme to assume in advance that this is so.

The second point may be stated briefly, since it has already been elaborated in considerable detail. We have seen that genotype and environment interact in development. It is inappropriate to view the behavioral repertoire as composed of those traits that are inherited and those that are not. All traits have environmental and genetic components. Thus it is appropriate only to inquire as to the relative proportion of the population variability which is due to differences in genetic and environmental factors. The hoary "nature-nurture controversy" must be replaced by a concept of "nature-nurture collaboration." Understanding of the dynamics of behavior cannot be achieved by ignoring either source of variation.

GLOSSARY

Allele—One of two or more alternative forms of a gene occupying a particular locus.

Autosome—Any chromosome other than the sex chromosomes.

Crossing-over—Exchange of corresponding material between homologous chromosomes.

Diploid—Having two chromosome sets.

Epistasis—Interaction between genes at different loci.

Gamete—A mature sex cell (egg or sperm).

Gametogenesis—The process of gamete formation.

Genotype—The entire genetic complement of an individual.

Haploid—Having one chromosome set.

Heterozygous—Condition in which members of a pair of genes are in different allelic forms.

Homozygous—Condition in which both members of a pair of genes are in the same allelic form.

Independent assortment—Segregation of alleles at one locus uninfluenced by segregation of alleles at another locus.

Linkage—Restriction on independent assortment due to different loci being on the same chromosome.

Locus—Position on a chromosome occupied by allelic forms of a given gene.

Meiosis—A process involving two successive cell divisions in which the chromosome number is reduced from diploid to haploid.

Mitosis—Process by which daughter nuclei resulting from cell division are provided with full chromosomal complements.

Multiple alleles—A series of three or more alternative states of a gene.

Multiple factors—Two or more loci acting upon a single trait.

Mutagenic—Resulting in or capable of causing mutation.

Mutation—Alteration in hereditary material.

Phenotype—Observable or measurable characteristic.

Pleiotropy—Situation in which a single gene has measurable effects on different phenotypes.

Polar body—Small cells produced during oogenesis (gametogenesis of eggs) that do not develop into functional gametes.

Polygene—Multiple factor.

Segregation—Separation of members of a pair of genes during meiosis and random combination with other genes at fertilization.

Sex chromosomes—Chromosomes particularly involved in sex determination; in man, females have two homologous X chromosomes, males have one X and one nonhomologous Y chromosome.

Trisomy—Having one extra chromosome.

Zygote—The cell produced by union of gametes.

REFERENCES

The references are divided into two sections. The first lists those which the author regards as particularly suitable, either because of completeness of coverage or particular clarity of exposition, for the student of behavior who is interested in further study of genetics. The second section lists all references cited in this chapter.

SELECTED REFERENCES

General Genetics and Methodology

BURDETTE, W. J. (Ed.) *Methodology in human genetics.* San Francisco: Holden-Day, 1962.

BURDETTE, W. J. (Ed.) *Methodology in mammalian genetics.* San Francisco: Holden-Day, 1963.

SINNOTT, E. W., DUNN, L. C., & DOBZHANSKY, T. *Principles of genetics.* (5th ed.) New York: McGraw-Hill, 1958.

SRB, A. M. & OWEN, R. D. *General genetics.* San Francisco: W. H. Freeman, 1952.

Quantitative Genetics

FALCONER, D. S. *Introduction to quantitative genetics.* Edinburgh: Oliver & Boyd, 1960.

LERNER, I. M. *The genetic basis of selection.* New York: Wiley, 1958.

Developmental Genetics

HADORN, E. *Developmental genetics and lethal factors.* London & New York: Wiley, 1961.

WADDINGTON, C. H. *The strategy of the genes.* New York: Macmillan, 1957.

Human Genetics

NEEL, J. V. & SCHULL, W. J. *Human heredity.* Chicago: Univ. Chicago Press, 1959.

PENROSE, L. S. (Ed.) *Recent advances in human genetics.* Boston: Little, Brown, 1961.

STERN, C. *Principles of human genetics.* San Francisco: W. H. Freeman, 1960.

Biochemical Genetics

HARRIS, H. *Human biochemical genetics.* Cambridge, England: Cambridge Univ. Press, 1959.

SUTTON, H. E. *Genes, enzymes, and inherited diseases.* New York: Holt, Rinehart & Winston, 1961.

Behavioral Genetics

BROADHURST, P. L. Experiments in psychogenetics. In H. J. Eysenck (Ed.), *Experiments in personality.* Vol. I. New York: Humanities Press, 1960. Pp. 3–102.

CASPARI, E. Genetic basis of behavior. In A. Roe & G. G. Simpson (Eds.), *Behavior and evolution.* New Haven: Yale Univ. Press, 1958. Pp. 103–127.

FULLER, J. L. & THOMPSON, W. R. *Behavior genetics.* New York: Wiley, 1960.

McCLEARN, G. E. The inheritance of behavior. In L. J. Postman (Ed.), *Psychology in the making.* New York: Knopf, 1962. Pp. 144–252.

REFERENCES CITED

ARMSTRONG, M. D. & TYLER, F. H. Studies on phenylketonuria: I. Restricted phenylalanine intake in phenylketonuria. *J. clin. Invest.,* 1955, **34,** 565–580.

AUERBACH, C. *Mutation: an introduction to research on mutagenesis.* Vol. 1. Edinburgh: Oliver & Boyd, 1962.

AVERY, O. T., MACLEOD, C. M., & MCCARTY, M. Studies on the chemical nature of the substance inducing transformation of pneumococcal types. *J. exp. Med.*, 1944, **79**, 137–158.

BASTOCK, M. A gene mutation which changes a behaviour pattern. *Evolution*, 1956, **10**, 421–439.

BAYLEY, N. Some increasing parent-child similarities during the growth of children. *J. educ. Psychol.*, 1954, **45**, 1–21.

BEADLE, G. W. Biochemical genetics. *Chem. Rev.*, 1945, **37**, 15–96.

BEADLE, G. W. Chemical genetics. In L. C. Dunn (Ed.), *Genetics in the twentieth century.* New York: Macmillan, 1951. Pp. 221–239.

BICKEL, H., GARRARD, J., & HICKMANS, E. M. The influence of phenylalanine intake on the chemistry and behavior of a phenylketonuric child. *Acta Paediat. Upps.*, 1954, **43**, 64–77.

BÖÖK, J. A. Oligophrenia. In A. Sorsby (Ed.), *Clinical genetics.* London: Butterworth, 1953.

BROADHURST, P. L. Studies in psychogenetics: the quantitative inheritance of behaviour in rats investigated by selective and crossbreeding. *Bull. Brit. psychol. Soc.*, 1958, **34**, 2A. (Abstract)

BROADHURST, P. L. Experiments in psychogenetics. In H. J. Eysenek (Ed.), *Experiments in personality.* Vol. I. New York: Humanities Press, 1960. Pp. 3–102.

BRUELL, J. H. Dominance and segregation in the inheritance of quantitative behavior in mice. In E. L. Bliss (Ed.), *Roots of behavior.* New York: Harper, 1962. Pp. 48–67.

BURDETTE, W. J. (Ed.) *Methodology in human genetics.* San Francisco: Holden-Day, 1962.

BURDETTE, W. J. (Ed.) *Methodology in mammalian genetics.* San Francisco: Holden-Day, 1963.

BURKS, B. S. The relative influence of nature and nurture upon mental development: a comparative study of foster parent-foster child resemblance and true parent-true child resemblance. *Yearb. nat. Soc. Stud. Educ.*, 1928, **27**, Part I, 219–316.

CARR, R. M. & WILIAMS, C. D. Exploratory behavior of three strains of rats. *J. comp. physiol. Psychol.*, 1957, **50**, 621–623.

CASPARI, E. Genetic basis of behavior. In A. Roe & G. G. Simpson (Eds.), *Behavior and evolution.* New Haven: Yale Univ. Press, 1958. Pp. 103–127.

CRICK, F. H. C. The genetic code. *Sci. Amer.*, 1962, **207**, 66–74.

CROOK, M. N. Intra-family relationships in personality test performance. *Psychol. Rec.*, 1937, **1**, 479–502.

DOBZHANSKY, T. *Mankind evolving.* New Haven: Yale Univ. Press, 1962.

ESCALONA, S. K. & MORIARITY, A. Predictions of school-age intelligence from infant tests. *Child Developm.*, 1961, **32**, 597–605.

FALCONER, D. S. *Introduction to quantitative genetics.* Edinburgh: Oliver & Boyd, 1960.

FALCONER, D. S. Quantitative inheritance. In W. J. Burdette (Ed.), *Methodology in mammalian genetics.* San Francisco: Holden-Day, 1963. Pp. 193–216.

FALCONER, D. S., FRASER, A. S., & KING, J. W. B. The genetics and development of "crinkled," a new mutant in the house mouse. *J. Genet.*, 1951, **50**, 322–344.

FARQUHAR, J. W., KANEAS, E. T., & TAIT, H. W. Problems of routine screening for phenylketonuria. *Lancet*, 1962, **2**, 498–500.

FÖLLING, A. Uber Ausscheidung von Phenylbrenztraubensaure in den Harn als Stoff-weekselanomalie in Verbindung mit Imbezillitat. *Ztschr. f. physiol. Chem.*, 1934, **227**, 169–176.

FORD, C. E. Methods in human cytogenetics. In W. J. Burdette (Ed.), *Methodology in human genetics.* San Francisco: Holden-Day, 1962.

FRASER, F. C., KALTER, H., WALKER, B. E., & FAINSTAT, T. D. The experimental production of cleft palate with cortisone and other hormones. *J. cell. comp. Physiol.,* 1954, **43,** 237–259.

FREEDMAN, D. G. Constitutional and environmental interactions in rearing of four breeds of dogs. *Science,* 1958, **127,** 585–586.

FREEMAN, F. N., HOLZINGER, K. J., & MITCHELL, B. C. The influence of environment on the intelligence, school achievement, and conduct of foster children. *Yearb. nat. Soc. Stud. Educ.,* 1928, **27,** Part I, 103–217.

FRINGS, H. & FRINGS, M. The production of stocks of albino mice with predictable susceptibilities to audiogenic seizures. *Behaviour,* 1953, **5,** 305–319.

FULLER, J. L. Hereditary differences in trainability of purebred dogs. *J. genet. Psychol.,* 1955, **87,** 229–238.

FULLER, J. L. & SMITH, M. E. Kinetics of sound-induced convulsions in some inbred mouse strains. *Amer. J. Physiol.,* 1953, **172,** 661–670.

FULLER, J. L. & THOMPSON, W. R. *Behavior genetics.* New York: Wiley, 1960.

GARROD, A. E. *Inborn errors of metabolsim.* (2nd ed.) London: H. Frowde, Hodder & Stoughton, 1923.

GESELL, A. & THOMPSON, H. Learning and growth in identical infant twins: an experimental study by the method of co-twin control. *Genet. Psychol. Monogr.,* 1929, **6,** 1–124.

GINSBURG, B. E. & ALLEE, W. C. Some effects of conditioning on social dominance and subordination in inbred strains of mice. *Physiol. Zool.,* 1942, **15,** 485–506.

GOTTESMAN, I. I. Differential inheritance of the psychoneuroses. *Eugenics Quart.,* 1962, **9,** 223–227.

GREEN, E. L. & GREEN, M. C. Modification of difference in skeletal types between reciprocal hybrids by transplantation of ova in mice. *Records Genet. Soc. America,* 1953, **22,** 76. (Abstract)

GRÜNEBERG, H. *Animal genetics and medicine.* New York: Paul B. Hoeber, 1947.

GRÜNEBERG, H. *The genetics of the mouse.* The Hague: Martinus Nijhoff, 1952.

HADORN, E. *Developmental genetics and lethal factors.* London & New York: Wiley, 1961.

HALL, C. S. The inheritance of emotionality. *Sigma Xi Quart.,* 1938, **26,** 17–27.

HALL, C. S. Genetic differences in fatal audiogenic seizures between two inbred strains of house mice. *J. Hered.,* 1947, **38,** 3–6.

HAMERTON, J. L. Cytogenetics of Mongolism. In J. L. Hamerton (Ed.), *Chromosomes in medicine.* London: Little Club Clinic Dev. Med. 5. National Spastics Society and Heinemann Medical Books, 1962. Pp. 140–183.

HARNDEN, D. G. The chromosomes. In L. S. Penrose (Ed.), *Recent advances in human genetics.* Boston: Little, Brown, 1961.

HARRIS, H. *Human biochemical genetics.* Cambridge, England: Cambridge Univ. Press, 1959.

HARRIS, R. E. An analysis of the maze-learning scores of bright and dull rats with reference to motivation factors. *Psychol. Rec.,* 1940, **4,** 130–136.

HARRITT, T. V. An experimental study of habitat selection by prairie and forest races of deer mouse *Peromyscus maniculatus. Contr. Lab. Vert. Biol.,* Univ. of Michigan, 1952, **56,** 53.

HERON, W. T. The inheritance of maze learning ability in rats. *J. comp. Psychol.,* 1935, **19,** 77–89.

HERON, W. T. The inheritance of brightness and dullness in maze learning ability in the rat. *J. genet. Psychol.,* 1941, **59,** 41–49.

HINDLEY, C. B. Social class influences on the development of ability in the first five years. *Proc. XIV Internat. Congr. Applied Psychol.,* Copenhagen, 1961. Pp. 29–41.

HIRSCH, J. Individual differences in behavior and their genetic basis. In E. Bliss (Ed.), *Roots of behavior.* New York: Harper, 1962. Pp. 3–23.

HIRSCH, J. & BOUDREAU, J. C. Studies in experimental behavior genetics: I. The heritability of phototaxis in a population of *Drosophila melanogaster*. *J. comp. physiol. Psychol.*, 1958, **51**, 647–651.

HONZIK, M. P. Developmental studies of parent-child resemblance in intelligence. *Child Developm.*, 1957, **28**, 215–228.

HSIA, D. Y-Y., DRISCOLL, K. W., TROLL, W., & KNOX, W. E. Detection by phenylalanine tolerance tests of heterozygous carriers of phenylketonuria. *Nature*, 1956, **178**, 1239–1240.

HURWITZ, J. & FURTH, J. J. Messenger RNA. *Sci. Amer.*, 1962, **206**, 41–49.

JACOB, F. & MONOD, J. On the regulation of gene activity. *Cold Spring Harb. Symp. on Quant. Biol.*, 1961, **26**, 193–209.

JACOBS, P. A., COURT BROWN, W. M., BAIKIE, A. G., & STRONG, J. A. The somatic chromosomes in Mongolism. *Lancet*, 1959, **1**, 710.

JARVIK, L. F., KALLMANN, F. J., FALEK, A., & KLABER, M. M. Changing intellectual functions in senescent twins. *Acta Genetica et Statistica Medica*, 1957, **7**, 421–430.

JERVIS, G. A. Introductory study of fifty cases of mental deficiency associated with excretion of phenylpyruvic acid. *Arch. Neurol. Psychiat.*, 1937, **38**, 944–963.

JERVIS, G. A. Studies of phenylpyruvic oligophrenia. The position of the metabolic error. *J. Biol. Chem.*, 1947, **169**, 651–656.

JERVIS, G. A. Genetic factors in mental deficiency. *Amer. J. hum. Genet.*, 1952, **4**, 260–271.

JERVIS, G. A. Phenylpyruvic oligophrenia: deficiency of phenylalanine oxidizing system. *Proc. Soc. exp. Biol., N. Y.*, 1953, **82**, 514–515.

JERVIS, G. A. Phenylpyruvic oligophrenia (phenylketonuria). *Proc. Assn. Res. nerv. ment. Dis.*, 1954, **33**, 259–282.

JONES, H. E. A first study of parent-child resemblance in intelligence. *Yearb. nat. Soc. Stud. Educ.*, 1928, **27**, Part I, 61–72.

KAGAN, J. & MOSS, H. A. Parental correlates of child's I.Q. and height: cross-validation of the Berkeley Growth Study results. *Child Developm.*, 1959, **30**, 325–332.

KEMPINSKY, W. H., BONIFACE, W. R., MORGAN, P. P., & BUSCH, A. K. Reserpine in chronic progressive (Huntington's) Chorea. *Proc. Amer. Acad. Neurol.*, Tenth Annual Meeting, Philadelphia, 1958.

KEMPTHORNE, O. *An introduction to genetic statistics*. New York: Wiley, 1957.

KING, J. A. & ELEFTHERIOU, B. E. Effects of early handling upon adult behavior in two subspecies of deermice, *Peromyscus maniculatus*. *J. comp. physiol. Psychol.*, 1959, **52**, 82–88.

KING, J. A. & MAVROMATIS, A. The effect of a conflict situation on learning ability in two strains of mice. *J. comp. physiol. Psychol.*, 1956, **49**, 465–468.

KING, J. A. & SHEA, N. J. Subspecific differences in the responses of young deermice on an elevated maze. *J. Hered.*, 1959, **50**, 14–18.

KNOX, W. E. & HSIA, D. Y-Y. Pathogenetic problems in phenylketonuria. *Amer. J. Med.*, 1957, **22**, 687–702.

KORNBERG, A. Biologic synthesis of deoxyribonucleic acid. In J. M. Allen (Ed.), *The molecular control of cellular activity*. New York: McGraw-Hill, 1962. Pp. 245–257.

KRAFKA, J. The effect of temperature upon facet number in the bar-eyed mutant of drosophila. Part I. *J. Gen. Physiol.*, 1919, **2**, 409–432.

LADU, B. N. The importance of early diagnosis and treatment of phenylketonuria. *Ann. intern. Med.*, 1959, **51**, 1427–1433.

LEJEUNE, J., GAUTHIER, M., & TURPIN, R. Etude des chromosomes somatiques de neuf enfants mongolions. *C. R. Acad. Sci., Paris*, 1959, **248**, 1721–1722.

LERNER, I. M. *Genetic homeostasis*. New York: Wiley, 1954.

LERNER, I. M. *The genetic basis of selection*. New York: Wiley, 1958.

LINDZEY, G., LYKKEN, D. T., & WINSTON, H. D. Infantile trauma, genetic factors, and adult temperament. *J. abnorm. soc. Psychol.*, 1960, **61**, 7–14.

LINDZEY, G. & WINSTON, H. Maze learning and effects of pretraining in inbred strains of mice. *J. comp. physiol. Psychol.*, 1962, **55**, 748–752.

MAHUT, H. Breed differences in the dog's emotional behaviour. *Canad. J. Psychol.*, 1958, **12**, 35–44.

MATHER, K. *Biometrical genetics*. New York: Dover, 1949.

McCLEARN, G. E. The genetics of mouse behavior in novel situations. *J. comp. physiol. Psychol.*, 1959, **52**, 62–67.

McCLEARN, G. E. The inheritance of behavior. In L. J. Postman (Ed.), *Psychology in the making*. New York: Knopf, 1962. Pp. 144–252.

McCLEARN, G. E. & RODGERS, D. A. Differences in alcohol preference among inbred strains of mice. *Quart. J. Stud. Alcohol.*, 1959, **20**, 691–695.

McELROY, W. D. *Cellular physiology and biochemistry*. Englewood Cliffs, N. J.: Prentice-Hall, 1961.

MILLER, O. J. Developmental sex abnormalities. In L. S. Penrose (Ed.), *Recent advances in human genetics*. Boston: Little, Brown, 1961.

MONOD, J. & JACOB, F. General conclusions: teleonomic mechanisms in cellular metabolism, growth, and differentiation. *Cold Spring Harb. Symp. on Quant. Biol.*, 1961, **26**, 389–401.

MYERS, A. K. Avoidance learning as a function of several training conditions and strain differences in rats. *J. comp. physiol. Psychol.*, 1959, **52**, 381–386.

MYERS, A. K. Alcohol choice in Wistar and G-4 rats as a function of environmental temperature and alcohol concentration. *J. comp. physiol. Psychol.*, 1962, **55**, 606–609.

NEEL, J. V. & SCHULL, W. J. *Human heredity*. Chicago: Univ. Chicago Press, 1959.

NEWMAN, H. H., FREEMAN, F. N., & HOLZINGER, K. J. *Twins: a study of heredity and environment*. Chicago: Univ. Chicago Press, 1937.

PARDEE, A. B. Aspects of genetic and metabolic control of protein synthesis. In J. M. Allen (Ed.), *The molecular control of cellular activity*. New York: McGraw-Hill, 1962. Pp. 265–278.

PASTORE, N. *The nature-nurture controversy*. New York: King's Crown Press, 1949.

PAWLOWSKI, A. A. & SCOTT, J. P. Hereditary differences in the development of dominance in litters of puppies. *J. comp. physiol. Psychol.*, 1956, **49**, 353–358.

PENROSE, L. S. Inheritance of phenylpyruvic amentia (phenylketonuria). *Lancet*, 1935, **2**, 192–194.

PENROSE, L. S. *The biology of mental defect*. (Rev. ed.) London: Sidgwick & Jackson, 1954.

PENROSE, L. S. (Ed.) *Recent advances in human genetics*. Boston: Little, Brown, 1961.

POLANI, P. E. Sex chromosome anomalies in man. In J. L. Hamerton (Ed.), *Chromosomes in medicine*. London: Little Club Clinic Dev. Med. 5. National Spastics Society and Heinemann Medical Books, 1962. Pp. 140–183.

ROBERTS, J. A. F. Resemblances in intelligence between sibs selected from a complete sample of an urban population. *Proc. 7th Internat. Congr. Genetics*, Edinburgh, Scotland, 1941. P. 252.

ROSENTHAL, D. Some factors associated with concordance and discordance with respect to schizophrenia in monozygotic twins. *J. nerv. ment. Dis.*, 1959, **129**, 1–10.

ROSENTHAL, D. Problems of sampling and diagnosis in the major twin studies of schizophrenia. *Psychiat. Res.*, 1962, **1**, 116–134.

ROSENZWEIG, M. R., KRECH, D., & BENNETT, E. L. A search for relations between brain chemistry and behavior. *Psychol. Bull.*, 1960, **57**, 476–492.

RUCKNAGEL, D. L. & NEEL, J. V. The hemoglobinopathies. In A. G. Steinberg (Ed.), *Progress in medical genetics*. Vol. 1. New York: Grune & Stratton, 1961.

RUNDQUIST, E. A. Inheritance of spontaneous activity in rats. *J. comp. Psychol.*, 1933, **16**, 415–438.

SAWIN, P. B. & CRARY, D. D. Genetic and physiological background of reproduction in the rabbit: II. Some racial differences in the pattern of maternal behavior. *Behaviour*, 1953, **6**, 128–146.

SEARLE, L. V. The organization of hereditary maze-brightness and maze-dullness. *Genet. Psychol. Monogr.*, 1949, **39**, 279–325.

SHUMWAY, W. & ADAMSTONE, F. B. *Introduction to vertebrate embryology.* (5th ed.) New York: Wiley, 1954.

SINNOTT, E. W., DUNN, L. C., & DOBZHANSKY, T. *Principles of genetics.* (5th ed.) New York: McGraw-Hill, 1958.

SINSHEIMER, R. L. The structure of DNA and RNA. In J. M. Allen (Ed.), *The molecular control of cellular activity.* New York: McGraw-Hill, 1962. Pp. 221–244.

SKODAK, M. & SKEELS, H. M. A final follow-up study of one hundred adopted children. *J. genet. Psychol.*, 1949, **75**, 85–125.

SOHVAL, A. R. Chromosomes and sex chromatin in normal and anomalous sexual development. *Physiol. Rev.*, 1963, **43**, 306–356.

SONTAG, L. W. & GARN, S. M. Human heredity studies of the Fels Research Institute. *Acta Genetica et Statistica Medica*, 1956/57, **6**, 494–502.

SRB, A. M. & OWEN, R. D. *General genetics.* San Francisco: W. H. Freeman, 1952.

STAMM, J. S. Genetics of hoarding: I. Hoarding differences between homozygous strains of rats. *J. comp. physiol. Psychol.*, 1954, **47**, 157–161.

STERN, C. *Principles of human genetics.* San Francisco: W. H. Freeman, 1960.

SUTTON, H. E. *Genes, enzymes, and inherited diseases.* New York: Holt, Rinehart & Winston, 1961.

SUTTON, H. E. Metabolic defects in relation to the gene. In W. J. Burdette (Ed.), *Methodology in human genetics.* San Francisco: Holden-Day, 1962. Pp. 287–303.

SUTTON, H. E., VANDENBERG, S. G., & CLARK, P. J. The hereditary abilities study: selection of twins, diagnosis of zygosity and program of measurements. *Amer. J. hum. Genet.*, 1962, **14**, 52–63.

THOMPSON, W. R. The inheritance of behaviour: behavioural differences in fifteen mouse strains. *Canad. J. Psychol.*, 1953, **7**, 145–155.

TRYON, R. C. Genetic differences in maze-learning ability in rats. *Yearb. nat. Soc. Stud. Educ.*, 1940, **39**, Part I, 111–119.

VALENSTEIN, E. S., RISS, W., & YOUNG, W. C. Sex drive in genetically heterogeneous and highly inbred strains of male guinea pigs. *J. comp. physiol. Psychol.*, 1954, **47**, 162–165.

VALENSTEIN, E. S., RISS, W., & YOUNG, W. C. Experimental and genetic factors in the organization of sexual behavior in male guinea pigs. *J. comp. physiol. Psychol.*, 1955, **48**, 397–403.

VANDENBERG, S. G. The hereditary abilities study: hereditary components in a psychological test battery. *Amer. J. hum. Genet.*, 1962, **14**, 220–237.

WADDINGTON, C. H. *Principles of embryology.* London: Allen & Unwin, 1956.

WADDINGTON, C. H. *The strategy of the genes.* New York: Macmillan, 1957.

WAGNER, R. P. & MITCHELL, H. K. *Genetics and metabolism.* New York: Wiley, 1955.

WATSON, J. B. *Behaviorism.* New York: Norton, 1924. (Rev. ed., 1930.)

WATSON, J. D. & CRICK, F. H. C. A structure for deoxyribose nucleic acids. *Nature*, 1953, **171**, 737–738 (a).

WATSON, J. D. & CRICK, F. H. C. Genetical implications of the structure of deoxyribonucleic acid. *Nature*, 1953, **171**, 964–967 (b).

WEISS, P. From cell to molecule. In J. M. Allen (Ed.), *The molecular control of cellular activity.* New York: McGraw-Hill, 1962. Pp. 1–72.

WOOLF, L. I., GRIFFITHS, R., & MONCRIEFF, A. Treatment of phenylketonuria with a diet low in phenylalanine. *Brit. J. Med.*, 1955, **1**, 57–64.

YANOFSKY, C. & ST. LAWRENCE, P. Gene action. *Ann. Rev. Microbiol.*, 1960, **14**, 311–340.

ZAMECNIK, P. C. Soluble ribonucleic acid and protein synthesis. In J. M. Allen (Ed.), *The molecular control of cellular activity.* New York: McGraw-Hill, 1962. Pp. 259–264.

Some Neural Substrates of Postnatal Development

MADGE E. SCHEIBEL AND ARNOLD B. SCHEIBEL

U.C.L.A. Center for Health Sciences and Brain Research Institute

THE INCREASINGLY HECTIC PACE of scientific endeavor is reflected in virtually all the skilled disciplines drawing on reservoirs of empirically derived data. Medicine and its allied branches are, perhaps, affected by this continuing revolution more than any of the applied biological sciences. As a result, the therapist, whatever his training or persuasion, is under continuous (at times unbearable) pressure to "keep up with the latest," lest his attitudes and therapeutic skills not reflect the most useful, and most publicized, facets of medical science. Even more compelling are the inner needs of the individual, freighted with clinical or therapeutic responsibility, to see a little more clearly into some of the substrate phenomena which influence and determine his own effectiveness, or lack of it.

In rising measure, this quest takes him to the findings of basic laboratory science where concepts may be discussed in unfamiliar idiom and the results at issue seem far from his daily concern. Yet the experience of the past supplies sufficient proof that such data, however exotic, must eventually become his concern—and it is in that context that this article is offered.

Considerations of space and the nature of the clinician's own needs preclude an exhaustive review. Rather, it is our intention to select such highlights as may suggest direction and feeling tone in a rapidly growing field of enquiry. The nature of neurophysiological investigation virtually presupposes some familiarity with basic concepts on the reader's part, if only at a nostalgic level, and some unfamiliarity with terms and ideas of very recent currency. It is hoped the reader's interest will help him surmount difficulties in the material or the reviewers' inadequacies in making it comprehensible.

Four general areas of neurophysiologic investigation relevant to problems of development will be considered. These include reflex activity, spontaneous electrocortical activity (the EEG), evoked cortical responses, and

481

autonomic function. Behavioral studies and conditioning, pathoneuro-physiology, and developmental and pathological anatomy are, at best, referred to in passing as being essentially beyond the scope of the review. And no mention at all is made of the burgeoning field of developmental biochemistry, which is outside the reviewers' area of competence.

A historical preview will not be offered, for the entire field of enquiry is still young. Most of the significant material will appear in its contextual, if not temporal, frame in the discussions that follow. It should also be borne in mind that the research being reviewed deals, essentially, with the import of measurable electrical impulses in the human or animal nervous system during early stages of development.[1]

NEURONAL MATURATION AND REFLEX ACTIVITY

Axonal Conduction

The ontogenetic development of reflex activity is significantly related to three sets of factors. They are: (a) the physiological and structural characteristics of the sensory and motor fibers that make up the limbs of the arc; (b) the nature and profusion of connections established within the neuraxis; and (c) the degree of control established by descending elements from hierarchically higher (suprasegmental) mechanisms. The earlier observations by Hursh (1939) have been amplified by the more extensive studies of Skoglund (1960a, b, c, d, e), demonstrating that conduction velocity and refractory period of peripheral nerve fibers show progressive changes with growth in the immediate postnatal period. In general, muscle nerves develop more quickly than the large fibers of skin nerves, and the latter more quickly, in turn, than the gamma efferents,[2] though all fibers seem to have approximately the same conduction velocity at birth. As one example quoted by Skoglund (1960b), the conduction velocity of fibers in kitten gastrocnemius nerve varies from 9 to 12 meters per second at birth, and reaches adult values of 70 to 115 meters per second at the end of the fourth month. The absolute refractory period of individual fibers decreases by a factor of 4 or 5 during the same period to an adult value of the order of 0.2 to 0.4 milliseconds. Increasing firing rates of such fibers clearly reflect these changes and contribute to more polished sensori-motor patterns. Until essentially adult values are achieved, however, reflex latency is demonstrably

---

[1] This review includes material through January, 1963.

[2] Gamma efferents: small diameter motor fibers which innervate fusiform cells of the muscle spindle sensory apparatus. By varying the length of these contractile elements, gamma efferents control the sensitivity (adjust the gain) of the entire muscle and tendon proprioceptive system. Thus sensory messages from muscle tissue retain a high degree of sensitivity whether the muscle-tendon mass is relaxed or in contraction.

longer (Wilson, 1962), as can be shown by the delayed appearance of the excitatory post-synaptic potential in ventral horn motoneurons following stimulation of dorsal roots.

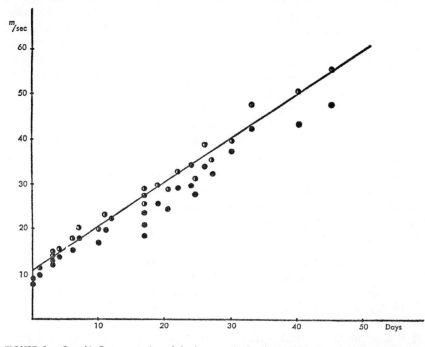

FIGURE 1. Graphic Representation of the Increase in Conduction Velocity of the Fast Afferents in Gastrocnemius Muscle Nerve as a Simple Linear Function of Postnatal Age in Days (Half-filled Circles)

The filled circles represent conduction velocity of the peak of the first potential wave. Reflex time decreases as conduction velocity increases and adult values for both are achieved by the second to fourth month of extra-uterine life in the cat. (Reproduced from Skoglund, S. The spinal transmission of proprioceptive reflexes and the postnatal development of conduction velocity in different hindlimb nerves in the kitten. *Acta Physiol. Scand.*, 1960, **49**, 318–329 (b).)

Structural Changes

A number of structuro-functional changes are involved in maturation of the impulse-carrying capacity of nerve fibers. These clearly include progressive increase in fiber diameter, changes in the membrane, and development of the fiber investments including the myelin sheath where it exists. However, Ulett, Dow, and Larsell (1944, p. 9) have shown that:

. . . myelinization of the fibers of the corpus callosum and cortico-ponto-cerebellar tracts is not essential for the conduction of the nerve impulses produced by electrical stimulation and that conduction of such impulses precedes myelinization by several days in the rabbit.

It must be assumed, rather, that myelinization and the development of mature nodal structures of Ranvier contribute to increased conduction velocity (and thereby to overall conduction efficiency), setting the stage for the internodal type of saltatory conduction demonstrated conclusively by Tasaki (1953). That the rate and degree of myelinization itself may be affected by neuronal function is shown by Langworthy (1933), whose data demonstrated that the optic nerve of kittens unilaterally blindfolded at birth showed appreciably less myelin investment than that of the contra-lateral normally stimulated eye. Similarly, Clark (1942) reported failure of development of certain retinal elements in animals restricted to an environ-ment of blue light from birth, stressing once more that utilization of all neural elements significantly affects their structural and functional status.

Specific data supplied by Noback and coworkers (1962) provide a de-tailed study of the ontogenetic development of large axons in the medullary pyramid of the kitten, expressed in conduction velocity and fiber diameter. The sequence of values reported by these investigators runs as follows:

1st postnatal week (pnw), 1 M/sec., 2 u; 2nd pnw, 2–3 M/sec., 2 u; 4th pnw, 15–20 M/sec., 4–6 u; 7th pnw, 35–50 M/sec., 4–6 u; 14th pnw, 70–90 M/sec., 7–10 u; adult, 70–90 M/sec., 10–16 u. . . (Noback, Housepian, and Purpura, 1962, p. 263).

It is interesting to observe that conduction velocity has increased by a factor of almost 100, while fiber diameter is increasing only five to eight times.

Proprioceptive End-Organs

Muscle and tendon receptors in the newborn kitten characteristically respond to stretch in short bursts. A more mature tonic pattern of response becomes apparent only after seven to ten days, with gamma-efferent con-trol demonstrable even later (seventeen days) in the postnatal sequence. Skoglund (1960c) believes this progression from phasic to tonic response mirrors changes both in the physical characteristics of immature muscle and in the electrical characteristics of the nerve fiber. The picture is some-what complicated by the cranio-caudal and proximo-distal maturation sequence in neuromuscular phenomena which has been noted by a number of workers (Coghill, 1929, 1930, 1943; Barron, 1941; Skoglund and Vallbo, 1960). In this regard sustained discharges seem to appear earlier in proximal muscles about the hip and spine than in distal muscle groups, and stretch reflexes in the limbs begin to threaten the prenatal supremacy of flexor responses earlier in the forelimbs than in the hind (Skoglund, 1960a). It is interesting to recall that the residua of strokes usually follow this sequence in reverse, leaving proximal musculature relatively more intact than distal, and flexor tone often more obvious (especially in the arms) than extensor tone.

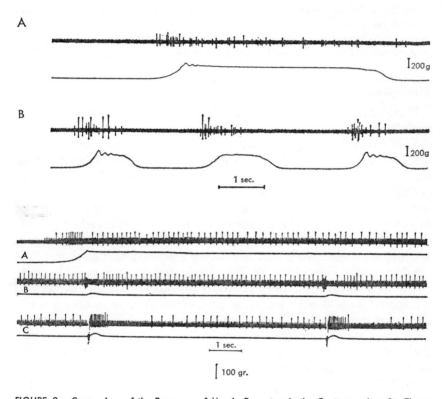

FIGURE 2.   Comparison of the Response of Muscle Receptors in the Gastrocnemius of a Three-Day Cat (A and B, Upper Group) with Twenty-three Day Cat (A, B, and C, Lower Group), as Recorded in Thin Filaments of the First Sacral Dorsal Root

UPPER GROUP: (A) Response to an 8 mm. stretch of the muscle kept at constant length until released. Discharge is irregular and decays with time. (B) Three short pulls of the muscle set up a brief discharge each time. LOWER GROUP: (A) Muscle stretched 8 mm. and kept at constant length. Notice sustained discharge during the increased tension in contrast with the earlier records. Ventral root shocks of twice and ten times threshold for alpha motoneuron fibers are administered in B and C respectively, and show patterns of tonic and phasic response in combination including a brief phase of post-excitatory depression (over one second in C). These response patterns are similar to those of the adult. (Reproduced from Skoglund, S. The activity of muscle receptors in the kitten. *Acta Physiol. Scand.*, 1960, **50**, 203–221 (c).)

Skoglund (1960a,c) relates the erratic motor activity, ataxic gait, and lack of sustained supporting reactions of the postnatal organism to a number of these already-mentioned stigmata of neuromuscular immaturity. Among these, the lack of sustained gamma-efferent driving of muscle spindles figures prominently.

> The first walking trials are accompanied by an intention tremor of slow frequency. This could mean that when the muscle contracts and the spindles are unloaded in the presence of weak or lacking gamma support they would soon be silenced. As a consequence the stretch reflex diminishes and the spindles firing anew when pulled upon as the contraction weakens. In this way the observed tremor would be self-generating. . . (Skoglund, 1960c, p. 219).

Maturation of Neuropil

If evidence is available for progressive postnatal development of extra-medullary receptors, conductors, and effectors, there are equally impressive, if incomplete, data suggesting a plastic intraneural matrix at birth which shows continuous change for a considerable period. In an investigation of synaptic boutons on the ventral horn cells of spinal cord, Tiegs (1926) found very few endings in the spinal cord of newborn kittens, though there were indications that the number increased rapidly with age. In general accord with this are the data of Kuypers (1962) which indicate that in infant rhesus macaques, the bulk of direct cortico-motoneural connections are established postnatally during a period encompassing at least the first eight months of life. Windle (1930), studying fiber density in newborn kitten spinal cord, found relatively small concentrations of fibers in the ventral horn at birth but noted progressive increase in density thereafter, a change mirrored in the development of longitudinal fiber masses throughout the grey matter of the cord. Fiber density was correlated with the degree of behavioral maturity of the kitten. As an apparent expression of the cranio-caudal progression of maturation mentioned before (Coghill, 1929, 1930, 1943), nerve fiber density appeared greater in cervical than in lumbar cord areas. These differences had disappeared in the two-month-old kitten. Roughly similar findings were reported by Rexed and Sourander (1960). Using the Nauta method to study degenerating fibers from sectioned dorsal roots, they noted that the number of degenerating collaterals streaming into the ventral horn increased with age. However, all such data are subject to the same criticism: the presence of a fiber does not necessarily attest to its functional state.

Malcolm (1955) and Skoglund (1960b) showed through physiological means that the muscle-spindle afferents from hind limbs in the kitten had already established monosynaptic connections with the spinal ventral horn cells at birth. However, early facilitation following a maximum homo-synaptic conditioning volley is missing in the newborn (Skoglund, 1960d), probably because of the prolonged refractory phase (up to 10 milliseconds) of immature fibers (Hursh, 1939). Eccles (1957) states that the initial op-portunity for temporal facilitation is lost within 10 milliseconds, so it must be assumed that a considerable number of dorsal root collaterals, though histologically identifiable, are functionally immature or nonfunctioning during this period.

Maturation of Reflex Activity

Skoglund's work (1960d) indicates that at birth the efferent side of the reflex arc appears better developed functionally than the afferent side and that there is progressive elaboration of the intramedullary connections of the dorsal root collaterals. However, the relatively minor depressant effect on ventral horn motoneurons produced by antidromic stimulation of ven-tral roots argues for incomplete development of the recurrent collaterals here, so that both limbs of the arc must be considered incomplete in the newborn.

In the kitten and in most newborn mammals, flexor activity shows a marked preponderance over extensor responses (Skoglund, 1960a). Al-though no completely satisfactory explanation exists for this phenomenon, experiments of Eccles and Lundberg (1959) and of Skoglund (1960a) sug-gest that at least two possibilities may be considered. Supraspinal control of spinal reflexes seems to be defective or lacking at birth. Postnatal develop-ment of supraspinal inhibition playing upon interneurons, which ordinarily are inhibitory to the extensors, must be awaited. This dawning disinhibition of the extensor system probably advances *pari passu*, with postnatal devel-opment of discharges from muscle receptors which also helps to redress the flexor-extensor balance.

One other factor of relevance is the absence of post-tetanic potentiation in the two-neuron arc of the newborn. Skoglund (1960c) has shown that this probably depends on a combination of factors, including fiber imma-turity (slow conduction and long refractory period) and immature intra-medullary termini. At about the time fiber conduction achieves a rate of 30 meters per second, potentiation can be demonstrated along with the development of tonic firing patterns from muscle spindles.

Arutyunyan (1962) reports similar results, describing post-tetanic po-tentiation in the monosynaptic arc in kittens by the ninth or tenth day after birth. With age the duration and intensity of the response increases, indicating progressive maturation of the mechanisms upon which post-tetanic phenomena depend. Furthermore, he finds that intravenous eserine enables post-tetanic potentiation to be demonstrated as early as the third day. The fact that this cholinesterase-inhibiting substance precociously unmasks the phenomenon underlines the relationship of this type of reflex potentiation to acetylcholine mediators in synaptic structures.

Maintenance of muscular tone is coordinately achieved by the gamma efferents working on the spindles and these in turn on the tonic ventral horn cells, thereby providing the physiologic ingredients for the tonic stretch reflex. All of these mechanisms must be operative for the animal to achieve an upright position and walk.

Although the scope of this review will not allow us to examine the formidable literature on behavior and conditioning, a recent article by Caldwell and Werhoff (1962) on classical conditioning in newborn rats deserves mention within a physiological frame. These workers observed that when newborn albino rats were conditioned to a vibrotactile stimulus paired with an electric shock, the UCS-CS interval resulting in optimal performance in the newborn varied markedly from that in the adult. In newborn animals a 1200-millisecond interval proved optimal, compared to 300 to 600 milliseconds for the adult. The investigators attributed the longer interval in the former to neural immaturity, referring in particular to low speed of neural conduction and incomplete myelinization.

Theoretical Formulations Concerning Reflex Activity

Global reflex patterns of the pre- and postnatal organism follow a fairly consistent and increasingly well-understood progression. Much of our knowledge in this area is due to G. E. Coghill (1930, 1943), some of whose findings, in epitome, will be synthesized with similar investigations of the Russian school as exemplified by the work of A. A. Volokhov (1959). Coghill (1930, p. 640) summarizes his position in these words:

> . . . From the lowest to the highest vertebrates there is a common law according to which the individual attains its progressive adjustment to its environment. This law or pattern of development consists in the expansion of a primarily integrated total pattern of action within which partial patterns arise by individuation through restriction of both the field of motor action and the field of adequate stimulation.

The initial total pattern follows general laws of development already sketched out for the prenatal organism, moving in a rostro-caudal direction along the axis of the body, and only later migrating laterally to include progressively more distal parts of the extremities. "The progressive individuation of the partial pattern within the total pattern of action obviously hangs on inhibition" (Coghill, 1943, p. 465). A sequence of responses to tactile stimulation of a fetal limb have been described, which begins with excitation of the entire animal with the exception of the limbs which are still relatively nonmotile, to "reflex" movement localized to the stimulated limb in conjunction with nonresponse of the remainder of the body. The latter is interpreted by Coghill (1943) and apparently by Volokhov (1959) as inhibition of the total action pattern. The source of such reflex-individuating selective inhibition is suggested as coursing from higher centers and more specifically, by Volokhov, from cortex.

The same principle of individuation or place-specificity seems to supply a frame within which maturation of the sensory side of the action pattern may be understood. As an example, Minkowski (1923) reports that in an earlier phase of development of the plantar reflex, flexion of the foot and toes follows a touch to both dorsal and plantar surfaces of the foot. "There is a progressive reduction of the reflexogenous zone to the definitive focal area . . . [which] . . . is to be regarded as a process of growth in the interface, so as to speak, between the receptor and effector functions." As will be seen elsewhere, the progressive narrowing or focusing down upon a neural zone of the function(s) attributed to it is a general characteristic of neural maturation.

In all cases, however, there seems to be a consensus that endogenous movements antedate reflex activity. Thus Windle and Griffin (1931, p. 175) conclude that "spontaneous motor activity always involved a part of the body before reflex response could be elicited locally or at a distance from the point stimulated." And when reflex responses become available to the organism they are, as already noted, flexor in nature. Coghill (1943, p. 485) concludes:

> . . . Not only is flexion the primary form of response in development, but in its earliest expression it is essentially nociceptive—an avoiding reaction. Extension, which has to do preeminently with posture and locomotion appears later, relatively much later, than flexion in ontogenetic development.

The conclusions of Volokhov (1959) seem in general agreement with this developmental schema. However, as more patterned reflex responses appear in the immediate prenatal period, they are identified as (a) protective-defensive, (b) food-motor, and (c) postural-tonic and righting reflexes. Food-motor reflexes characterized by sucking and swallowing movements are seen in the rabbit fetus at the twenty-second to twenty-sixth day of development, while postural-tonic and righting reflexes appear in the last ten days of prenatal life. Defensive movements of a washing, scratching, shaking, and licking nature, presumed due to mechanical or thermal stimulation of skin zones, are detected from five to eight days before birth and even earlier in guinea pigs.

In early postnatal life all such reflexes are initially intensified and then, after thirty to forty days of extra-uterine life, become markedly weakened and fractionated by descending inhibitory influences, primarily from the cortex. Opinions seem to differ on the intra-uterine function of such reflex patterns; but whatever their import at that time, they serve as indices of the increasing complexity of the underlying neural substrate.

SPONTANEOUS ELECTROCORTICAL ACTIVITY (THE EEG)

From the time that Hans Berger first placed electrodes on his son's head (Brazier, 1961) and recorded the immature electroencephalograph, the spontaneous EEG has proved to be a powerful and effective tool in the study of maturation in the central nervous system. A sizable literature has developed on this theme, including a large group of well-documented studies on the human newborn and a more scattered group of communications devoted to electrocortical development in a number of laboratory animals. Differences in recording techniques and laboratory procedures have contributed to some of the difficulties in this area. However, increased recognition of the significance of ontogenetic studies has stimulated neurophysiological investigation of the postnatal organism. As a result, the past five years have produced a relatively large mass of correlatable structural and functional data in a number of mammals. Developmental time scales and (in some cases) pattern detail vary, but a comprehensive picture has begun to emerge, based on the sequence of development of structural entities and physiological phenomena.

Since the pioneering report of Lindsley (1936), all investigators are in essential agreement that the most significant developmental change in the EEG is a progressive increase in frequency from birth to maturity. The pace of this progression in frequency depends largely on the species involved. The degree of EEG development at birth is dependent partly on species and significantly on the level of development at birth of the individual organism. A number of investigators including Ellingson (1958), Ellingson and Wilcott (1960), and the Scheibels (1962) have stressed the wide variability at term among individuals of the same species, and even of litter mates, reflecting a host of genetic and intra-uterine factors operative upon each individual.

Maturation of EEG Activity in Animals

In the guinea pig, rhythmic potentials can first be recorded from fetal cortex at the forty-sixth day of gestation (term sixty-six days) according to Flexner, Tyler, and Gallant (1950), and between the forty-eighth and fifty-sixth days according to Jasper, Bridgman, and Carmichael (1937). It is at this time that neuroblasts differentiate into neurons and the neuronal membrane becomes permeable to sodium. Flexner's group suggests that certain aspects of the EEG resemble the adult tracing as early as twenty days before birth, notably in development of strychnine spikes, although it is by no means clear that the adult spontaneous pattern is achieved until the postnatal period.

Crain (1952) followed the development of the EEG in rats, reporting spontaneous electrical activity and experimentally elicited strychnine spikes at three to four days and an essentially normal adult record at seven to ten days, in good agreement with Schadé's (1957) figure of eight to eleven days. Bures's study (1957) of the maturational aspects of long-term potentials and spreading depression in rat cortex suggests that clear-cut and reproducible spreading depression, as described by Leão (1944), can be demonstrated between the fifteenth and twentieth postnatal day and may represent an even more definitive index of maturation than the development of 8- to 13-per-second (alpha) activity.

In the rabbit, according to Schadé (1959, 1960), the first six to eight postnatal days are marked by high-frequency oscillations of low amplitude, interrupted by irregular 1.0- to 2.5-per-second waves and many silent periods—although some electrical activity can apparently be recorded as early as the thirty-first day of gestation (Bradley et al., 1960). No regional differences in the EEG can be identified at this time (Kornmuller, 1935; Schadé, 1959).

> Between 8 and 15 days after birth the high-frequency pattern is replaced by waves of larger amplitude and low frequency. The slow waves become predominant, and in animals of 10 and 12 days the spindles develop. The appearance of the 12.5–15.0 spindles is a sign of maturity of the EEG. The electrical activity becomes practically mature and indistinguishable from the pattern of the adult animal 10–15 days after birth (Schadé, 1959, p. 27).

Schadé (1959, 1960) apparently shares Bures's (1957) opinion on the significance of spreading depression as an index of cortical maturity. He finds that even with the strongest stimuli (topical application of crystals of HCl and 12 volts D.C. stimulation) it is impossible to elicit the Leão effect before twenty-four to thirty days of age, or roughly twice the time necessary to achieve an adult alpha pattern in the EEG. On the basis of several

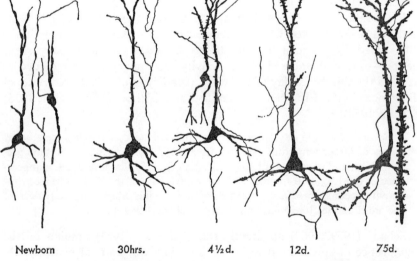

Cx.

2

5

11

15

30

50uV

1 sec.

93

Newborn   30hrs.   4½d.   12d.   75d.

FIGURE 3.   Structural and Functional Aspects of Maturation of Cerebral Cortex in the Cat

Successive EEG tracings from second through ninety-third day of postnatal life show progression from slow irregular rhythms (two to four per second) to a mature alpha-rich record in the third month. Spindle bursts are seen in the eleven-day tracing and thereafter. The series of groups of data, Schadé (1959) concludes that full maturation of the spontaneous EEG correlates with the development of the apical dendrites in deeper cortical layers, and that spreading depression occurs only when the apical dendrites reach their full development at the pial surface.

In young dogs, Charles and Fuller (1956) were unable to differentiate between sleeping and waking patterns before the eighteenth to twentieth day; although Petersen and Himwich (1959) have found what appear to be sleep spindles separated by low-amplitude irregular waves as early as the first postnatal day in curarized pups. However, more recent data from this laboratory (DiPerri, Himwich, and Petersen, in press) suggest a different situation in chronic nonparalyzed preparations. (See below.) In general, EEG development in the dog parallels that in other species, though maturing at a slower rate than that of rat, rabbit, and cat.

Detailed study of EEG development in chronically implanted, freely moving newborn kittens by the Scheibels (1959, 1961, 1962) reveals irregular 4- to 6-per-second rhythms alternating with slower patterns, presumably as the level of consciousness varies. Some differentiation between the sleeping and waking EEG is noted in these studies; the sleeping state, furthermore, seems characterized behaviorally by the presence of phasic muscle twitches or generalized jerks that are reflected in the EEG. Faster rhythms approaching alpha frequencies gradually develop over the first ten days to two weeks, and adult rhythms are achieved between the third and fifth weeks of life. The appearance of isolated spindle bursts between the fifth and seventh days are interpreted as ". . . early physiological evidence of developing synaptic relations between nonspecific corticipetal fibers and still immature apical dendrites" (A. B. Scheibel, 1962). More specifically, temporal relations are demonstrated between the appearance of spines on the apical shafts, the histological evidence of axo-dendritic contacts increasingly effected through them by the nonspecific afferents, and physiological support for developing nonspecific thalamic control over cortical potentials (The Scheibels, 1959, 1961, 1962). As is evident above, these investigators also use spindle bursts as a measure of the maturational level but differ

---

Caption for Figure 3 Continued

drawings below summarize the development of cortical pyramidal cells during the postnatal period. Apical and basilar dendrite systems which are present to varying degrees at birth reach full development in the third month, while cell bodies achieve final size and shape somewhat earlier. Of particular interest are the spiny projections of the dendrites which can first be seen in the latter part of the first week. Their development on all portions of the dendrites (except near the cell body) are apparently related to the presynaptic fibers effecting contact with them. In the case of the apical dendrites, nonspecific (reticulo-cortical) fibers form an important part of the presynaptic contingent and can be seen effecting increasingly more intimate contact with the apical shafts in these drawings. (Reproduced from Scheibel, A. B. Neural correlates of psychophysiological development in the young organism. In J. Wortis (Ed.), *Recent advances in biological psychiatry.* Vol. IV. New York: Plenum Press, 1962. Pp. 313–327.)

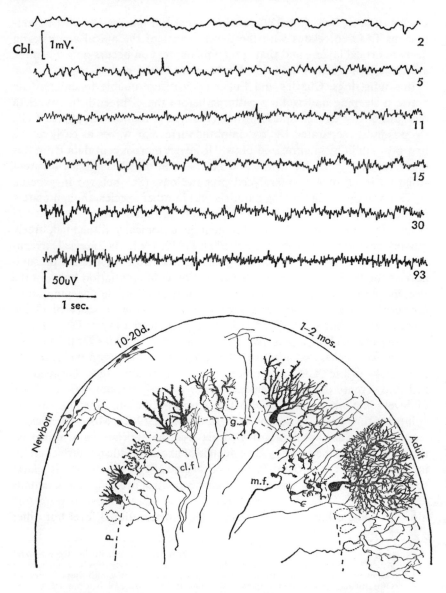

FIGURE 4.   Structural and Functional Aspects of Maturation of the Cerebellar
Cortex in the Cat

Successive tracings summarize development of electrical activity from an amorphous, at times almost isopotential record through increasingly rapid frequencies, culminating in the rapid, approximately 300-per-second activity of mature cerebellar cortex by the end of the third month. On a single cerebellar folium, progressive developmental stages of cortical cells from Schadé (1959) in identifying them as characteristic of an earlier stage of postnatal development. However, in addition to the different mammalian species being studied, Schadé's preparations were under light urethane anaesthesia. Both factors probably figured in the difference in conclusion regarding the epoch signaled by spindling.

Further data on the significance of spindling and the development of sleep-wakefulness cycles come from the work of Jouvet (1962), who has called attention to the phenomenon of paradoxical sleep. During this stage the organism apparently enters a state of unconsciousness more profound than that of typical spindle, slow-wave sleep, characterized by a low-voltage, fast (that is, paradoxical) EEG; complete loss of tone in neck muscles (cat), as revealed by the electromyogram; heightened threshold to arousal stimuli; and characteristic random eye movements, associated by some investigators with dreaming (Dement and Kleitman, 1957). Jouvet finds that if the entire neocortex of the adult preparation is removed, spindle and slow-wave phenomena disappear and the animal seems to pass in and out of paradoxical sleep patterns without the usual intervening slow-wave phase. In the first few postnatal days of life, he finds the young kitten acting like a neodecorticate preparation, incapable of generating spindle-rich, high-voltage, slow-wave patterns. Within the first week or two, spindles begin to appear as cortical (and cortico-thalamic) mechanisms mature. It is only at this time that meaningful differentiation between sleep and waking states can be made in the young kitten; however, as the eyes open and motor patterns mature, ancillary clues become available. In any case, these important observations of Jouvet probably help to explain the many differences of opinion among investigators working with various species, especially the kitten, as to when adequate EEG differentiations can be made between wakeful and sleeping states. They also accord well with very recent observations of DiPerri and associates (in press), who do not find sleep spindles in the EEG of the implanted unrestrained, sleeping pup until the seventh week of life.

The significance of paradoxical (phase I, activated, rhombencephalic) sleep remains unclear and there is still no consensus on whether this state

---

Caption for Figure 4 Continued

and fibers are shown. Development of the dendritic tree of the Purkinje cell (P) and the climbing fiber (Cl. F.) system follow each other closely. These elements bear intimate synaptic relationship to each other. Similar maturation patterns are seen in the granule cell (g)—mossy fiber (m. f.) pair. Full development of cerebellar cortical electrical activity probably depends to some extent on maturation of all of these elements and of the cerebellar neuroglia (not shown), but it is probable that physiological activity of the cerebellum is under way before histological maturity is achieved. (Reproduced from Scheibel, M. E. and Scheibel, A. B. Some structuro-functional substrates of development in young cats. (To be published in Galesburg Symposium on *Brain development and biogenic amines*. Elsevier Press.)

represents the most profound sleep level, or a superficial one verging on wakefulness. Recent unpublished observations by Roffwarg and Dement (1963) and by Parmalee and associates (1963) identify paradoxical sleep states as early as the thirty-sixth week after conception. It appears that at term, the infant may spend up to 50 per cent of his sleeping time in this rhombencephalic phase whereas at maturity (eighteen years) the figure has dropped to 18 per cent. This evolution suggests that the sleep pattern associated with low-voltage fast EEG rhythms is archaic both ontogenetically and phylogenetically and that dream activity which has come to be associated with it, represents an add-on function, developing only as the individual begins to experience and interact with his environment. Additionally, the fact that rotary eye movements can be recorded as easily in the thirty-sixth to fortieth week infant as in the adult throws into question the interpretations of some investigators (Dement and Kleitman, 1957) that these represent ocular following of the visual imagery in dreams.

The Scheibels (1961) have also reported on the development of spontaneous electrical activity in cerebellar cortex and brain-stem reticular formation. At one day of age, kitten cerebellar cortex shows amorphous 2- to 5-per-second rhythms without recognizable form, alternating with virtually isopotential runs. By the fifteenth day, 10- to 30-per-second rhythms ride the slower one-half to one-per-second baseline fluctuations. At one month, up to 50-per-second frequencies are seen; by the end of the third month, a histologically mature cerebellar cortex generates the adult 300-per-second pattern. Unlike the cerebellar cortex, the reticular formation shows a high degree of histological maturity at birth although there is some increase in axon-dendrite complexity and further axon myelinization. Nonetheless, the neonatal electroreticulogram appears as primitive as the cerebellar record and matches its development over the first two weeks. Thereafter the frequency spectrum tops off at 30 to 50 per second which, with some variation, represents the adult pattern. They conclude:

> . . . In the first 2 to 3 weeks of life an immature cerebellar cortex and a relatively mature r.f. share the same electrical patterns. Congruence of patterning breaks down after the first month as increasing maturation of specialized elements in cerebellar cortex enable faster intrinsic rhythms (Scheibel and Scheibel, 1961, p. 320).

The EEG in the Human Infant

By now there are probably several hundred titles which bear reference to some aspect of development of the EEG in the human infant. Particular note might be made of papers by Lindsley (1938, 1939); J. P. Smith (1937); Henry

(1944); Hughes, Davis, and Brennan (1951); Hughes, Ehemann, and Brown (1948); Kellaway (1952a,b); Melin (1953); Cornil and Corriol (1949); Fischgold and Berthault (1953); Dreyfus-Brisac *et al.* (1956, 1958); and Ellingson (1958). Within limits, most descriptions resemble the early ones of Lindsley (1936) who watched the slow, poorly organized cortical rhythm of the newborn child progressively develop pattern and increase in frequency to adult alpha rhythms between the tenth and twelfth years of life. He described brief runs of what appeared to be alpha waves[3] over the visual cortex, appearing as early as the third to sixth postnatal month, and attributed these to beginnings of visual activity. J. P. Smith (1937) also noted presumptive alpha rhythms by the sixth postnatal month and suggested that they were hidden by higher voltage, low-frequency cortical potentials. These observations have more recently been confirmed (according to Brazier, 1961) by Dovey, using an electronic analyzer to demonstrate the presence of alpha-band frequencies masked by the large, slow waves of the six-month-old cortex. Activity is obvious first over the sensory-motor Rolandic areas (J. P. Smith, 1937; Ellingson, 1958), attesting to the relatively more advanced development of cortical mechanisms here compared with occipital and prefrontal stations. Asynchrony between hemispheres is quite common in the newborn, being most obvious in the temporal regions, and least noticeable over the convexity.

Sureau, Fischgold, and Capdevielle (1949) have raised questions as to whether the EEG in the newborn infant reflects differences between sleeping and waking states. J. P. Smith (1937), Hughes and associates (1948), and Ellingson (1958), among others, have clearly shown that such differences can be recognized. The latter describes a low-voltage record in the wakeful infant, resembling the alert state in adults. As the baby becomes progressively more quiet while still awake:

> . . . fragmentary rhythmic elements and some irregular slow waves appear. As the eyes close, the slow waves become more prominent, increasing in voltage. When the baby is lying quietly, breathing regularly, and moving only occasionally or not at all (presumably asleep), slow waves of mixed frequency and usually irregular contour predominate and may become very prominent, although there are considerable individual differences. . . (Ellingson, 1958, p. 32).

Fast spindle bursts (15 to 25 per second) may be seen occasionally in both sleeping and waking infants, often more prominently in the recordings of prematures and usually of rather low amplitude (Ellingson, 1958).

[3] As originally used by Lindsley, the term *alpha* was applied to occipitally derived waves of any frequency. Today, investigators and clinicians limit the term to rhythmic 9- to 11-per-second wave activity, no matter what the topographical derivation. However, the majority of workers agree that alpha activity is most obvious over the occipital area and tends to lead in phase from this area.

The presence of sleep-like patterns in the quiet but open-eyed infant has led Ellingson (1958) to suggest that at this stage of development, the presence of open eyes may prove less reliable as a criterion of wakefulness than in older children. This could explain why some investigators have reported little or no difference between sleeping and waking EEGs in infants, and may also bear relation to that state called *hypnagogic* by Kellaway (1952b). This investigator described striking 4- to 5-per-second drowsy rhythms in older children who appeared still awake behaviorally, though such findings await confirmation by others. In any case, the distinct series of transition stages between wakefulness and profound sleep seen in older children and adults appears much less evident in the newborn. This entire field of enquiry is under more detailed examination by Parmalee and associates (1963).

The EEG in the Fetus and Premature Infant

Serial studies of the premature EEG have added considerably to an understanding of the early developmental period, especially in the hands of Dreyfus-Brisac and associates (1956, 1957, 1958, 1959). Dreyfus-Brisac has commenced systematic recording at the presumed lower limit of fetal viability (four and one-half to five months), but quotes Okamoto and Kirikae (1951) as having detected transamniotic fast activity as early as the fiftieth day of human fetal life. Between the fifth and seventh months of fetal life, the EEG of the extra-uterine fetus is described as "paroxcystic" (Dreyfus-Brisac, 1959), without periodicity or differentiation between sleeping and waking states. There is complete hemispheric independence and total lack of reactivity (to applied stimuli). During this period, however, rapid modification of the pattern can be described, including a progression from "spatio-temporal anarchy" characterized by bursts of high-voltage, slow 0.5-per-second waves alternating with low-voltage bursts of 5- and 8-per-second waves and erratic frontal spikes. By the seventh month:

> . . . discontinuity is less marked and for the first time a spatial organization of activity appears on each hemisphere. Slow waves (1 c/s) with 10- to 14-per-second and 10- to 20-microvolt rapid frequencies superimposed, appear in rolando-occipital and in all interhemispheric derivations except the bifrontals. They are accentuated in bursts without regular periodicity (Dreyfus-Brisac, 1959, pp. 31–32).

Maturational Epochs in EEG Activity

At the eighth month of fetal life, the first important maturative stage is achieved. This epoch is characterized by the appearance of developing interdependence between hemispheres; clear-cut differentiation between sleeping and waking states (Hughes *et al.*, 1948; Dreyfus-Brisac, 1959); reactivity of the wakeful record on photic stimulation (Ellingson, 1958); and a gradual increase in voltage and rhythmicity through the third postnatal month. During this period, there is stepwise development (Dreyfus-Brisac, 1957, 1959) of the sleeping EEG but without parallel evolution in the waking record, suggesting progressive differentiation at different structural levels (Dreyfus-Brisac and Blanc, 1956).

A second important stage in EEG development is noted at the third postnatal month of life and is characterized by (a) the development of "topographical organization of activity with occipital predominance" (Dreyfus-Brisac, 1959); (b) the appearance of regular sinusoidal rhythms, which increase from a 2- to 4-per-second frequency at three months to seven to nine cycles at three years with concomitant voltage decrease, thereby resembling mature alpha activity in all respects except frequency; (c) increasing occipital reactivity to photic stimulation (Dreyfus-Brisac, 1959; Ellingson, 1958);

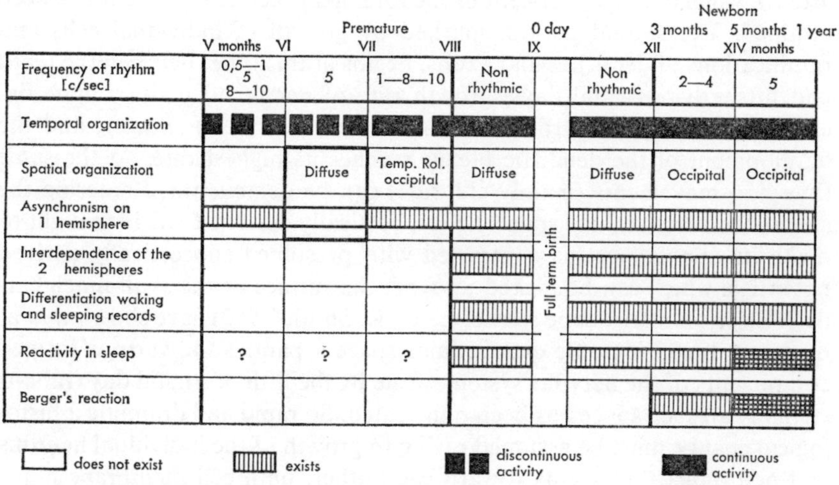

	V months	VI	Premature VII	VIII	0 day IX	Newborn 3 months XII	5 months	1 year XIV months
Frequency of rhythm [c/sec]	0,5—1 / 8—10	5	1—8—10	Non rhythmic		Non rhythmic	2—4	5
Temporal organization	discontinuous activity					continuous activity		
Spatial organization			Diffuse	Temp. Rol. occipital	Diffuse	Diffuse	Occipital	Occipital
Asynchronism on 1 hemisphere	exists		exists			exists		
Interdependence of the 2 hemispheres				exists		exists		
Differentiation waking and sleeping records				exists		exists		
Reactivity in sleep	?	?	?	exists		exists		continuous activity
Berger's reaction						exists		continuous activity

(Between column IX and XII, vertically: **Full term birth**)

Legend: ☐ does not exist   ▥ exists   ■■ discontinuous activity   ▰▰ continuous activity

FIGURE 5. Summarizing Diagram Showing the Evolution of EEG Patterns of Sleep and Reactivity from the Fifth Month after Conception to Two Years of Age

Note that the EEG prior to the eighth month following conception is considered completely unorganized, lacking in characteristic wave forms (except for "paroxcystic" subcortical bursts) and without sleep-wakefulness differentiation. The latter response is first seen as a flattening in the record about the eighth month at which time occipital activity is most marked. Most of the wave phenomena seen in mature, wakeful, drowsy, and sleeping records become recognizable in the first six to nine months of postnatal life. (Reproduced from Dreyfus-Brisac, C. Electroencephalography in infancy. In F. Linneweh (Ed.), *Die physiologische Entwicklung des Kindes*. Berlin, Gottingen, Heidelberg: Springer, 1959. Pp. 29–40.)

(d) greater differentiation of sleep-waking EEG patterns, including the appearance of well-defined sleep spindles (Fischgold, 1959); and (e) development of diffuse arousal reactions upon opening of the eyes or presentation of attention-provoking stimuli.

A third maturational epoch in EEG development is reached at the age of three years (Dreyfus-Brisac, 1957, 1959) at which time the child's sleep record comes to resemble those of sleeping adults. Beyond this point characteristics of wave amplitude and frequency, interhemispheric phase relations, and reactivity to sensory stimuli progressively approximate the mature record.

Concept of the Critical Period

The presence of critical periods in the development of the EEG reflects an increasing awareness of such ridgepoints in a number of developmental sequences. Schadé (1960) has drawn attention to several critical points in the histological development of rabbit cortex. The first phase, characterized by neuron proliferation, comes to a close a day or two before birth or just after it, when about 95 per cent of the total nerve cell complement has been attained. The second period, marked by growth of individual cells and ramifications of dendrites and axons, begins at this time. Between the tenth and fifteenth postnatal days, growth rate of nerve cell body volume decreases markedly, the growth of nuclear volume ceases entirely, and the development of the dendritic plexus reaches its highest rate. At the same time, ion movements (mainly chloride) can be demonstrated entering the apical dendrites and the spontaneous, cortically derived EEG is thought to make its appearance (as contrasted with presumed subcortically derived potentials which can be picked up from the surface of the skull much earlier). Electron microscope studies by K. R. Smith (1963) have shown that at birth a still considerable extracellular space separates the various formed components of the nervous system, while by the fifth postnatal day (rabbit) virtually all such space has been obliterated. So rapid and dramatic a histological change must be assumed owing to growth of the individual neurons and neurological elements toward each other, until cell membrane abuts on cell membrane and the extracellular compartment is completely occupied by the increasing bulk of neural components. Chemical and physiological implications of such a change must be formidable and it may well be that Schadé's observation regarding chloride entry into dendrites (see above) is but one sequela of increasingly intimate neuronal-glial appositions.

Reflecting the development of critical periods in histological, neurophysiological, and biochemical maturation are the increasingly recognized critical epochs in development of behavior. The relationship of these latter phenomena to the substrate mechanisms still largely eludes us, although intuition and successful correlation in a few areas argue that such interrelations will eventually be found. An extended survey of critical period phenomena in behavior is beyond the scope of this review, but it is worth recalling that three major groups have been identified. These include optimal periods for (a) learning, (b) infantile stimulation, and (c) formation of basic social relationships (Scott, 1962). Although the principle of "criticality" is sometimes regarded as an artifact of classification, it should be recognized that:

> Both growth and behavioral differentiation are based on organizing processes. This suggests a general principle of organization: that once a system becomes organized, whether it is the cells of the embryo that are multiplying and differentiating, or the behavior patterns of a young animal that are becoming organized through learning, it becomes progressively more difficult to reorganize the system. That is, organization inhibits reorganization. Further, organization can be strongly modified only when active processes of organization are going on and this accounts for critical periods of development (Scott, 1962, p. 957).

EVOKED CORTICAL RESPONSES

The use of the cortical evoked potential as an index of maturation in the central nervous system has proved to be of increasing importance to workers in this field since the study of Ulett, Dow, and Larsell (1944). These workers demonstrated that transcallosal and cortico-ponto-cerebellar conduction was not directly dependent on myelinization, but that evoked wave form and latency did depend on the degree of maturation of the fiber system. Building on these observations, E. J. Bishop (1950) discovered that in young rabbits, strychnine-induced cortical spikes have already acquired their mature triphasic form at birth, though difficult to elicit in the first twenty-four hours after birth. Durations are longer and amplitudes less than in the adult, however, and longer (recovery?) intervals occur between each spike complex. The most rapid shortening in spike duration occurs during the preliminary postnatal phase of histological maturation in cortical axonal and dendritic neuropil, and appreciably precedes the first appearance of myelin in internal capsule and subcortical white matter. Bishop concludes that although the capacity for generating cortical spikes is present at birth, their relatively long duration (low degree of cortical synchrony) and very low repetition rate probably account for the apparent difficulty in recording typical paroxysmal spikes from infants with convulsive disorders.

That strychnine spikes can be generated by very immature prenatal cortex is suggested by the observations of Flexner's group (1950), indicating that as early as the forty-sixth day of gestation (term sixty-six days) guinea pig cortex can respond with recognizable spikes to fragments of strychnine-soaked filter paper placed on the surface. Although these authors do not supply detailed evidence, and their published records are limited to one figure made up of EEG strips, the appearance of their immature spikes seems to agree with Bishop's (1950) in being triphasic in nature and of fairly long duration. Unlike the latter's, however, their records seem to suggest that bursts of five to ten spikes per second are obtainable from fetal cortex. Whether this discrepancy represents species variation, differences in recording technique, or true relative hyperirritability of fetal cortex remains to be determined.

Cortical response to specific sensory stimuli and to electrical shocks gives the investigator a higher measure of control over the evoked phenomena and has been used with increasing frequency in the past decade. Hunt and Goldring (1951) elicited essentially surface negative responses from visual cortex to electrical stimulation of the optic nerve in newborn rabbits. The corresponding response to light flashes did not occur until the seventh postnatal day. This coincides with time of onset of myelinization in the optic tract.

Similar findings have been reported by Marty (1962) in a long and detailed study of sensory responses of cortex. He concludes that cortex will respond earlier to electrical shock to the optic tract than to flashes of light, because central transmission and integrative mechanisms mature earlier than the peripheral receptors themselves. Similar conclusions are drawn regarding rates of maturation of the components of the auditory system. However, the somesthetic system seems capable of adequate levels of responsiveness from periphery to most central stations even in the prenatal period (Marty, 1962), which may represent a meaningful adaptation of the organism to the increasing problems of later intra-uterine life.

By the tenth postnatal day, Hunt and Goldring (1951) found that electrical and light-flash-induced responses were similar in form and followed a parallel course to maturity. These workers concluded, as did Marty (1962), that a certain minimal degree of retinal maturity was necessary to allow for initiation of sufficiently synchronized afferent volleys. They also described progression of the evoked cortical response from a surface negative to the mature surface positive form, observations made repeatedly by subsequent investigators (see below) with varying interpretations.

The relatively late-appearing, light-evoked response in rabbit cortex can be found earlier in the newborn kitten and human infant. Ellingson and

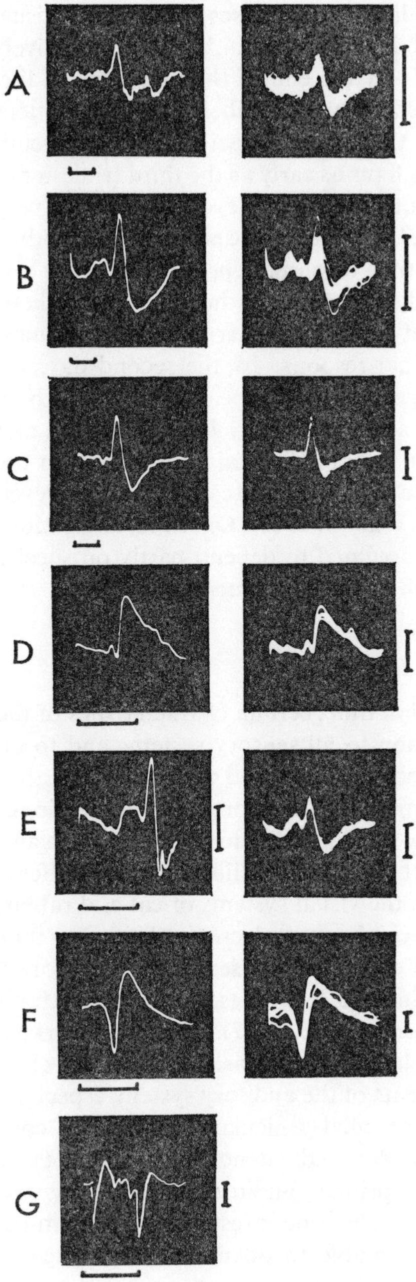

FIGURE 6. Progressive Maturation of the Visual Evoked Cortical Response from Surface Negative to Surface Positive Configuration

Single responses are shown on the left; superimpositions of eight to twenty responses on the right. (A) Eight-day-old negative response. (B) Eight-day-old (different series) negative response preceded by initial small positive wave. (C) Fifteen-day-old negative response. (D) Large negative wave preceded by small negative-position complex. (E) Twenty-two-day-old small positive response now precedes the negative wave. (F) Thirty-five-day-old semimature, surface-positive response with long latency. (G) Thirteen-week-old typical adult surface positive initial response, followed by a second response to stimulus 100 milliseconds later. Calibration: negative deflections are up; horizontal calibration lines indicate one hundred milliseconds; vertical calibration lines indicate 100 microvolts. (Reproduced from Ellingson, R. J. and Wilcott, R. C. Development of evoked responses in visual and auditory cortices of kittens. *J. Neurophysiol.*, 1960, **23**, 363–375.)

Wilcott (1960) reported "very long latency responses . . . in the visual cortex of the cat on about the second day of life . . . ," with progressively shorter latency discharges identifiable by the end of the first week of life. Similar responses have been reported by the Scheibels (1962) in kittens at one and one and a half days, while the former investigators noted identifiable cortical responses in the human fetus as early as the third trimester of pregnancy. Not only does the time of onset of the evoked response vary markedly among mammalian species, but in the same species and individual the evoked phenomena may vary in time of onset depending on what system is stimulated. Thus while the evoked response of the kitten somesthetic cortex may be demonstrated in the first day of life (Scherrer and Oeconomos, 1954; Grossman, 1955), and the visual response by the second day, the analogous auditory cortical discharge may not appear until the fifth to tenth day after birth (Rose, Adrian, and Santibanez, 1957; Ellingson and Wilcott, 1960). Furthermore, auditory responses attain adult form in the cat by the fourth to fifth week, while visual responses have not achieved this stage at six weeks (Ellingson and Wilcott, 1960). Once more variations in the results here reported must be assumed to depend partly on species variation, and partly on the technique of the experimenter.

Specific Parameters of the Evoked Response

Despite such variations in maturation time, certain characteristics of the evoked cortical response seem common to all sensory systems and to all species. As the neuraxis matures, latency of the evoked discharge decreases. Scherrer and Oeconomos (1954) estimate that the cortical somesthetic response latency in the cat may decrease by a factor of ten between birth and the adult state. Ellingson and Wilcott (1960) and Ellingson (1958) offer a similar figure for latency reduction in the visual systems of cat and rabbit, while response latency in the human visual system decreases by two to four times over a similar span. Latency of evoked responses in auditory cortex of the cat decreases by a factor of three to five times, according to both Ellingson and Wilcott (1960) and Rose's group (1957). The latter workers attribute the progressive shortening of latency to increased conduction velocity in the various subcortical components of the auditory system, especially those peripheral (downstream) to the medial geniculate body. Their conclusion is buttressed on carefully determined latency measurements at round window, medial geniculate, and primary auditory cortex. They suspect coincidentally decreasing nuclear delay due, presumably, to maturation of synaptic mechanisms but are unable to document these suggestions.

Ellingson (1960, p. 675) has shown, furthermore, that response latency in the human infant is inversely correlated to age up to a body weight of about twelve pounds ($r = -.80$):

> Curves of response latency vs. age and of response latency vs. body weight are 2-legged rather than monotonic, the breaks in the curve occurring at 4 weeks post-term and 9 pounds respectively. This phenomenon may reflect either a growth spurt in the visual system or different developmental rates in the two parts (scotopic and photopic?) of the visual system.

A second common characteristic has to do with the wave form and polarity of the evoked cortical response. With the exception of the human visual cortex (Ellingson, 1958), the primitive evoked discharge is initially surface negative, occasionally double, with the first component often higher than the second. A small positive wave appears somewhat later— although in kitten auditory cortex, according to Ellingson and Wilcott (1960), it may be present at earliest demonstration of the auditory evoked response. Recognizable early positive components are visible by the middle or end of the second week in the kitten (Marty, Contamin, and Scherrer, 1958; Ellingson, 1958, 1960; the Scheibels, 1961, 1962; Purpura, 1961a,b) and the normal surface positive pattern is achieved by the twentieth to fortieth day when neocortex in this species closely resembles the mature structure, as shown by usual staining techniques. However, Purpura's work (1961b) suggests that these statements regarding polarity and form of the evoked response in primary receptive areas of cortex may not apply to associative or elaborative areas of neocortex.

Neural Substrates of Evoked Cortical Activity

A number of investigators have speculated on the structural basis of this progression from immature surface negative to mature surface positive evoked phenomena in receptive cortex. Hunt and Goldring (1951) and Ellingson (1960) suggest that this progression may be due to changes occurring with growth, in the nature of impulse patterns barraging the cortex and/or to changes in the responses of cortical cells to the corticipetal stimuli. Purpura (1961a,b) hypothesizes that initial surface negativity generated in superficial axodendritic pathways represents depolarization following directly upon the afferent barrage, which at this stage of development is applied largely to the apical pyramidal shafts. Later, as the basal dendrite system is elaborated and synaptic mechanisms are activated here, depolarization (p.s.p.) in these deeper dendrite masses results in initial surface positivity as potential theory would demand. This replaces the earlier negative wave as the initial component of the response. That minor surface positive components are present even at birth though usually swamped by the larger negative component is demonstrated, according to Purpura, by the application of gamma amino butyric acid (GABA). He concludes:

> The absence of a significant surface-positivity in the specific response of somesthetic cortex appears to be due to the weak p.s.p.'s evoked in the cortical depths in the immediate neonatal period. Later in development when axosomatic synapses and synaptic contacts on basilar dendrites are more numerous, the early surface-positivity becomes prominent. . . . The surface positivity probably reflects predominantly the activity of subsurface depolarizing axosomatic synapses (Purpura, 1961c, p. 128).

The position of Anokhin seems to differ only in emphasis.

> The negative phase of the evoked potential depended on quite different neural structures from those responsible for the positive phase. . . . We think this first event (the negative component) is phylogenetically very old and that it travels through the spino-thalamic pathway. . . . This branch is found to reach maturation first before the neurons from the specific thalamic nuclei which have synaptic connections of the axosomatic kind (Anokhin, 1961, pp. 151–152).

A somewhat different interpretation has been advanced by the Scheibels (1961, 1962). Like Purpura and Anokhin, they remain within the general framework of potential theory but emphasize the intercalation of a "new" neuropil field generated by developing short-axoned (Golgi II) cells in the receptive sectors of sensory cortex.

> . . . We suggest that initial surface negative responses are . . . due to superficial dendrite activity. . . . The developing complexity of the terminal arbors and then of the local granule cell axon plexus produces neuropil fields of growing complexity whose activity is increasingly manifest by initial surface positivity. This probably represents not only a masking of the previously seen initial negativity but an actual displacement of it caused by the interposition of a short-axoned neuropil buffer between the specific afferent system and the pyramidal components of the cortex (A. B. Scheibel, 1962, pp. 321–322).

What apparently constitutes a third characteristic of the developing evoked potential has been reported by Marty and associates (1958) who describe an increasing focalization of the evoked potential with maturation. Thus visual evoked responses, which could be recorded over the posterior half of the lateral hemisphere at birth, become increasingly localized to the classical (adult) visual receptive areas during the initial weeks of postnatal life. Detailed studies of Purpura (1961b,c) on the ontogenetic development of the superficial cortical response (SCR) do not appear to throw light on this problem. However, data reported by Mountcastle (1957) and by the Scheibels (1958) may be of relevance. The former investigator has found that in somatic sensory cortex, cell columns of the order of one millimeter in diameter appear related to single peripheral points of stimulation. This apparently represents the degree of fineness of grain of the representational mosaic in sensory cortex. The Scheibels (1958) noted that individual nonspecific (reticulo-cortical) projection fibers divide deep to cortical grey matter, then rise vertically to the pial surface, apparently dividing the cortex into cylindrical shaped fields, each of which is about one millimeter in diameter. They have suggested that these nonspecific corticipetal projections may play a role in delimiting and sharpening sensory field localization at the cortical level. Since this system is imperfectly developed at birth, and only beginning to effect synaptic articulations with the apical dendrite shafts during the first week of life, the progressive focalization described by Marty and associates (1958) may be a function of maturation of this system and/or of cortical association fibers whose terminal patterns are similar.

Early Effects of Repetitive Stimulation

A number of investigators have commented on the inability of newborn cortex to follow rapid repetitive stimuli of any kind (Hunt and Goldring, 1951; Scherrer and Oeconomos, 1954; Grossman, 1955; Ellingson, 1958; the Scheibels, 1959, 1962; Purpura, 1961a, b, c). Hunt and Goldring (1951) observed that in the visual system "fatigability as determined by the amplitudes of responses to repetitive stimuli (maximal strength) at 1-second intervals was very marked in the youngest animals but had largely disappeared by 16 days." Similar observations were made by Scherrer and Oeconomos (1954) for the somesthetic system of kittens and by Ellingson (1958) in newborn infants.

DoCarmo (1960) examined the effects of repetitive stimuli applied directly to the cortex of rabbits and found evidence of following at frequencies as high as 20 per second, although the cortical wave forms were immature and did not attain adult configuration until eighteen days after birth. Recruitment elicited from the ventral anterior nucleus at 6 per second regularly showed marked diminution in amplitude of all responses following the first one, until the eleventh postnatal day when classical recruitment phenomena began to appear, manifested by greater amplitude of the second spike than the first. At eighteen days, an essentially adult picture finally supervenes.

A more ambitious study of recruitment in immature kitten cortex by Purpura (1961a, b, c) has revealed interesting cyclic phenomena in the cortical response which are difficult to explain. Following DoCarmo (1960), he describes an initial wave followed by three to five minimal responses. Continued stimulation at 5 per second "results in the development of an extraordinarily complex series of stages consisting in initial stabilization of responses, then abrupt transition to a stage in which responses alternate in amplitude." This sequence is sufficiently regular as to allow for oscilloscope trace superposition. (See Figure 7.) Furthermore, "doubling the stimulus frequency did not alter the orderly evolution of these various stages. It would appear from this that at certain stimulus frequencies the transition from one stage to another is dependent on the total number of stimuli applied to the responding synaptic organization and not on stimulus frequency per se" (Purpura, 1961b). This sequence of alterations is apparently not seen after the first postnatal week, when typical recruitment phenomena begin to be observed.

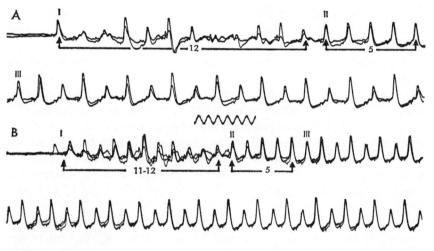

FIGURE 7.   Complex Cortical Response in One-Day Kitten (Acute Preparation) to Repetitive Thalamic Stimulation

Five-per-second stimulation (A) and ten-per-second stimulation (B) in intralaminar thalamic nucleus evokes a series of negative waves on anterior supra-sylvian gyrus. Following a period of varying response heights (phases I and II), a series of responses appear showing regular alternation in amplitude. These three phases appear with regularity (note superimposition of traces) and disappear after the 10th week to be replaced by mature recruitment phenomena. (Reproduced from Purpura, D. P. Structure and function of cortical synaptic organizations activated by corticipetal afferents in newborn cat. In M. A. B. Brazier (Ed.), *Brain and behavior, First Conference.* Madison, N. J.: Madison Printing Co., 1961. Pp. 95–138.)

The classical mode of cortical activation (arousal) by high-frequency stimulation in the brain-stem reticular core (Moruzzi and Magoun, 1949) has been investigated by the Scheibels (1959, 1962) in chronically implanted newborn kittens. For the first seven to fourteen days after birth, slow frequencies (10 to 20 per second) were found generally more effective than fast (100 to 300 per second) in producing short runs of cortical low-voltage, fast activity. Following this period, fast frequencies became increasingly effective while the slow frequencies were more likely to produce recruitment-like phenomena or a simple type of cortical "following reaction," depending on the precise location of the stimulating electrode tip in the brain-stem reticular formation. (See Figure 8.)

Additionally, in the immediate postnatal period they reported "inability to produce more than one or two sequences of activation at any one time without doubling or tripling the stimulating voltage. Some hours of 'recovery' are necessary between attempts at cortical activation" (A. B. Scheibel, 1962). This rapid fatigue or habituation effect was considered due to immaturity of the synaptic mechanism, and apparently represents one more facet of "faulty" response of the immature nervous system to repetitive stimulation. Development of adult cortical activation patterns and recruitment phenomena can justly be considered reliable criteria of cortical maturation. (See Figure 8.)

AUTONOMIC FUNCTION

Studies on the development of the autonomic nervous system and autonomic function have, until recently, received scant attention in the clinical frame, despite their evident relevance to the clinician and therapist. We shall refer to only two of these studies, selected as prototypic of their kind.

It has been known for some time that a regular waxing and waning of a number of physiologic functions over the 24-hour (circadian) cycle does not exist until after birth (body temperature, motility, sleep-wakefulness). Development of postnatal rhythmicity of function might represent either postnatal maturation of a group of endogenous functions—thereby representing only one more inevitable step in maturation—or alternatively could reflect the impact of the postnatal environment. Hellbrugge (1960) examined this problem in a group of normal newborn children, keeping careful records of day-night patterns of a number of physiologic functions for the first several months to several years of life, commencing in the last trimester of pregnancy where possible. These measurements included pulse rate, body temperature, sleep-wakefulness patterns, electrical skin resistance, urine excretion, potassium and sodium excretion, and feeding inter-

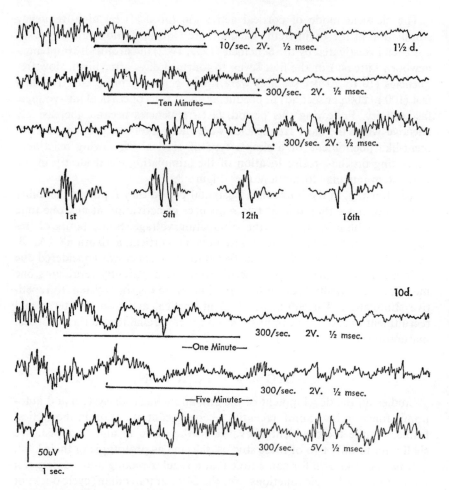

FIGURE 8.   Effects of Slow and Fast Repetitive Mesencephalic Reticular Stimulation on Cerebral
Cortex in the One- and One-half and Ten-day-old Kitten

In the first group of three tracings, 10-per-second tegmental stimulation effectively desyn-
chronizes the cortex, while a following 300-per-second stimulation is effective only after a much
longer latency. Ten minutes later, another 300-per-second stimulus appears almost totally ineffective. The second group of three traces taken at the age of ten days suggests that the cortex
is still capable of only one or two activations without a lengthy intervening period of rest. The
first stimulus at 300-per-second is effective in flattening the record, while the second is totally
ineffective (one minute later). A third attempt is equally ineffective five minutes later, even
though stimulating voltage is more than doubled. The group of four evoked potentials in the
middle of the figure demonstrate that cortex will continue to respond to a group of individual
stimuli when a suitable interval separates each stimulus from the last. In this case, the interval
was 10 seconds. (Reproduced from Scheibel, A. B. Neural correlates of psychophysiological
development in the young organism. In J. Wortis (Ed.), *Recent advances in biological psychiatry.* Vol. IV. New York: Plenum Press, 1962. Pp. 313–327.)

vals. The author's general conclusion, apparently more intuitive than rigorous, seems to be that the final emergence of autonomic rhythms depends on a combination of factors, stemming largely from an inherent periodicity implicit in the organization of the individual, but importantly modifiable by the postnatal environment. Hellbrugge's specific conclusions bear quotation.

1. Different physiologic functions develop a certain day and night rhythm independently from each other.
2. The day and night rhythm of the different functions becomes apparent at different times after birth.
3. During the development of day and night periodicity an increase in the range of oscillation occurs in all physiologic functions.
4. This increase of range in some cases is caused more by the increase of the upper width of oscillation during the light hours, in others by the increase of the lower width of oscillation during the dark hours.
5. The decrease of the night values in nearly all functions occurs between five and seven p.m.
6. With the broadening of the nightly lowering, the morning rise in the different physiologic functions during development necessarily sets in at a continuously later time.
7. In man, also, the monophasic day-night rhythm seems to originate out of polyphasic cycles. As the origin of these cycles in sleep and wakefulness, the spontaneous period of twenty-five hours seems to be the most likely one (Kleitman and Engelmann, 1953).
8. For the development of day and night rhythm the maturity of the child at birth is of essential importance. Day and night periodicity develops later in premature than in children born at term (Hellbrugge, 1960, pp. 321–322).

In a series of investigations first reported in 1955, Richmond and his associates (1955, 1959, 1962a,b) have been evaluating certain types of responses in infants, selected to reveal aspects of autonomic function. The responses selected were those which might be most descriptive of the infant as a total organism at the time and which might enable predictions about its patterns of reactivity in later years.

Using infant cardiac rate as one index of reactivity, they found that swaddling of the neonate decreased motor activity, heart rate, and respiratory activity, and tended to increase the stability of the heart rate. The workers speculate that these effects may be related to a general decrease of proprioceptive inputs with concomitant decrease in levels of activity of reticular formation, hypothalamus, and cortex (Lipton, Steinschneider, and Richmond, 1960). Using a group of cardiotachometric techniques worked out for the program, these workers (Lipton *et al.*, 1961a) measured changes in heart rate to a standardized test stimulus (5-second air-stream delivered to the umbilicus). Prestimulus rates, rate of increase following stimulus, and rate of return to baseline following stimulus were considered significant parameters and provided clues to subsequent behavior and total autonomic reactivity of the individual (Lipton *et al.*, 1961b). Homeostatic effectiveness, expressed in part by the differences between pre- and post-stimulus heart rates and by the post-stimulus return, were found to vary widely between individuals (Richmond *et al.*, 1962a). Using somewhat similarly structured tests with adults, Freeman (1939) had earlier concluded that physiological recovery from experimental loads could be of use in predicting individual capacity to withstand conflict and related types of nervous tension in living situations. Thus the investigation of individual variation in autonomic function has been used in the adult as well as in the infant in developing insights into the individual's probable response to environmental stress.

Richmond and Lipton (1959) report that heart-rate change with stimulus showed an inverse relationship to prestimulus rate, that is, greatest increases occurring after lowest prestimulus rates, thereby stressing the importance of knowledge of the prior physiologic state of an organism. The nature and amount of the cardiac reaction was shown to vary with the stimulus used. Thus "cold immersion produced greater responses than air on the abdomen, and air on the anal region gave less reaction" (Richmond and Lipton, 1959).

In other experiments it could be shown that hungry infants showed more marked cardiac reactions than recently fed subjects, which suggests the effect of the internal milieu upon reactivity, and that degree of motor activity and/or interaction with the environment also significantly affected the response. These workers express their confidence that:

> Autonomic endowment . . . can be described in the newborn period if one preserves an approach which accounts for the prestimulus state of the organism. Such observations will provide further measures of interindividual differences and in longitudinal studies of child development, permit more appropriate interpretation of data (Richmond and Lipton, 1959, p. 101).

CONCLUSIONS

These groups of apparently disparate data emphasize the subservience of the immature individual, at both prenatal and postnatal epochs, to his intrinsic physiologic limitations. The low velocity of nerve fiber conduction and the immaturity and paucity of neonatal intramedullary connections limit repetitive activity and conduction in synaptic systems, severely restricting temporal and spatial summation, and virtually preventing post-tetanic potentiation. Since these three phenomena are considered by many to be essential for learning activity, from a neurophysiologic point of view, it can be seen that the capabilities of the infant are initially restricted largely to innate behavioral devices. Inability of the very young child to institute any type of progressional or anti-gravity activity is clearly not solely the result of lack of practice. Such inability is due more importantly to incomplete intramedullary articulation between receptor and effector fibers, relative absence of modulating forces from supra-spinal centers, and inadequate and primitive activity patterns in proprioceptive mechanisms and their own gain-adjusting (gamma-efferent) apparatus.

Even the involuted, hyperflexed appearance of the newborn infant reflects not simply the residua of intra-uterine packing but a very real imbalance of neurally determined flexor-extensor tone. It is difficult to escape the concept of the infant as a qualitatively different organism, operating through large blocks of relatively undifferentiated, mass muscular effort, triggered by a relatively small number of stereotyped stimuli. The progressive increase of upper-echelon neural control over these cruder, downstream mechanisms, effects (largely by inhibition) increasingly precise motor patterns, progressively more appropriate to the stimuli. In some respects the progressive revelation of a mature sensory-motor repertoire resembles psychoanalytically postulated personality development, where progressively elaborating ego and superego forces exert expanding control and modulation over the id-instinctual forces to enable more realistic interaction with the environment.

The progressive development of the spontaneous EEG and evoked cortical potential phenomena bear witness, at another level, to the anatomic-physiologic inadequacies of the newborn child. In the last two and one-half to three months before term, when a still thin and highly immature cerebral pallium, not yet beyond its first critical point and still proliferating actively, produces anarchic bursts of many frequencies, it is almost certainly the already massive subcortical tissue of the thalamus and basal ganglia which are erratically firing through. As the pallium begins to approach final neonatal thickness, the first critical point is attained and passed, and axo-dendrite sprouting replaces somal reproduction. The new electrical activity of the cortex begins to take precedence, muffling then drowning out subcortical activity and, except during neurosurgical intervention, the observer is not likely again to see undiluted samples of deep activity.

The time necessary to achieve an adult EEG alpha frequency appears, in most cases, to be the measure of the maturational process and underlines the tremendous difference in time scales between rabbit (ten to fifteen days) and man (about twelve years). Yet at birth the human brain is relatively farther along in development than the rat or rabbit. One can only wonder at the impressive certainty and speed with which a cortical organ can be shaped, following the birth of a relatively helpless, closed-eyed, rabbit fetus. Starting at a somewhat higher developmental plateau at parturition, the same process in the human infant takes over 250 times as long. This enormously longer period of development in the young human organism is but one expression (and in itself one cause) of a remarkably lengthy and effective period of acquired learning.

The relatively great length of this part of human life and the emergence of the concept of successive critical periods—each apparently optimal for acquisition of certain affectual, intellectual, or social techniques—suggest possibilities for more effective exploitation of these epochs in the training of the child. Carried back farther in the ontogenetic sequence, increasingly fine-grained analyses of the type sketched out by Schadé (1960) might eventually localize periods critical in development of various biochemical and enzyme systems. Conceivably, manipulations of maternal physiology and/or affect, just prior to such periods, might be used to enhance certain characteristics or faculties of the unborn fetus. Such critical time-linked processes are recognized even today in some instances, in the known-to-be deleterious effects of certain viruses (German measles), physical agents (X-ray irradiation), or chemicals (Thalidomide) during the first trimester of pregnancy.

Progressively more discriminative correlation between EEG frequency and evoked wave form could achieve greater clinical significance with the perfection and widening availability of electronic frequency analyzers and response averaging devices. In late realization of Hans Berger's dream, fragments of evidence are becoming available, suggesting that some forms of mental retardation (Gibbs and Gibbs, 1962; Chapman, 1963) and severe characterological defect (Kennard et al., 1955, 1957) may reflect in form and pattern of cortical waves. If future work bears out these observations, they may eventually be related to the period of developmental distortion or arrest which they represent, thereby holding out hope for discovery of preventive measures. In each case, more precise knowledge of the sequence of development spells out its own clinical relevance. It is the clinician's responsibility to recognize the areas of suggested correlation and convert them into rational therapeutic means.

REFERENCES

ANOKHIN, P. K. The multiple ascending influences of the subcortical centers on the cerebral cortex. In M. A. B. Brazier (Ed.), *Brain and behavior. First conference.* Madison, N. J.: Madison Print. Co., 1961. Pp. 139–170.

ARUTYUNYAN, R. S. Development of post-tetanic potentiation facilitation in a monosynaptic spinal arc during early postnatal ontogeny. *Fiziologicheskii Zhurnal SSSR imenti I. M. Sechenova,* 1962, **48**, 922 ff. (Quoted from English translation in *Transl. Suppl. Fed. Proc. Amer. Soc. exp. Biol.,* 1963, **22**, 290–293.)

BARRON, D. H. The functional development of some mammalian neuromuscular mechanisms. *Biol. Rev.,* 1941, **16**, 1–33.

BISHOP, E. J. The strychnine spike as a physiological indicator of cortical maturity in the post-natal rabbit. *EEG Clin. Neurophysiol.,* 1950, **2**, 309–315.

BRADLEY, W., KAISER, I., MORRELL, F., & NELSON, E. Maturation of electrical activity in the central nervous system. In P. Bowman & H. Mautner (Eds.), *Mental retardation. Proceedings of first international conference.* New York: Grune & Stratton, 1960. Pp. 98–111.

BRAZIER, M. A. B. *A history of the electrical activity of the brain: the first half-century.* New York: Macmillan, 1961.

BURES, J. The ontogenetic development of steady potential differences in the cerebral cortex in animals. *EEG Clin. Neurophysiol.,* 1957, **9**, 121–130.

CALDWELL, D. F. & WERHOFF, J. Classical conditioning in newborn rats. *Science,* 1962, **136**, 1118–1119.

CHAPMAN, L. Unpublished data, 1963.

CHARLES, M. S. & FULLER, J. L. Developmental study of the electroencephalogram of the dog. *EEG Clin. Neurophysiol.,* 1956, **8**, 645–652.

CLARK, W. E. L. The anatomy of cortical vision. *Transac. Ophthal. Soc.,* 1942, **62**, 229–245.

COGHILL, G. E. *Anatomy and the problem of behavior.* Cambridge, England: Cambridge Univ. Press, 1929.

COGHILL, G. E. The structural basis of the integration of behavior. *Proc. nat. Acad. Sci.,* 1930, **16**, 637–643.

COGHILL, G. E. Flexion spasms and mass reflexes in relation to the ontogenetic development of behavior. *J. comp. Neurol.,* 1943, **79**, 463–486.

CORNIL, L. & CORRIOL, J. L'electroencephalogramme des enfants de moins de trois ans. *Sem. Hop., Paris,* 1949, **25**, 2745–2747.

CRAIN, S. M. Development of electrical activity in the cerebral cortex of the albino rat. *Proc. Soc. exp. Biol., N. Y.,* 1952, **81**, 49–51.

DEMENT, W. & KLEITMAN, N. Cyclic variations of EEG during sleep and their relation to eye movements, body motility and dreaming. *EEG Clin. Neurophysiol.,* 1957, **9**, 673–690.

DIPERRI, R., HIMWICH, W. A., & PETERSEN, J. The evolution of the EEG in the developing brain of the dog. In *Galesburg symposium on brain development and biogenic amines.* Amsterdam: Elsevier Press, in press.

DOCARMO, R. J. Direct cortical and recruiting responses in postnatal rabbit. *J. Neurophysiol.,* 1960, **23**, 496–504.

DREYFUS-BRISAC, C. Activité électrique cérébrale du foetus et du très jeune premature. *Proc. 4th Internat. Meeting, EEG & Clin. Neurophysiol., Bruxelles.* In *Acta Med. Belg.,* 1957, 165–171.

DREYFUS-BRISAC, C. Electroencephalography in infancy. In F. Linneweh (Ed.), *Die physiologische Entwicklung des Kindes.* Berlin, Gottingen, Heidelberg: Springer, 1959. Pp. 29–40.

DREYFUS-BRISAC, C. & BLANC, C. Electroencephalogramme et maturation cérébrale. *L'encephale,* 1956, **45**, 205–245.

DREYFUS-BRISAC, C., SANSON, D., BLANC, C., & MONOD, N. L'electroencephalogramme de l'enfant normal de moins 3 ans: aspect fonctionnel bioelectrique de la maturation nerveuse. *Etudes Neo-Natales*, 1958, **7**, 143–175.

ECCLES, J. C. *The physiology of nerve cells*. Baltimore: Johns Hopkins Press, 1957.

ECCLES, J. C. & LUNDBERG, A. Supraspinal control of interneurones mediating spinal reflexes. *J. Physiol., London*, 1959, **147**, 565–584.

ELLINGSON, R. J. Electroencephalograms of normal full-term newborns immediately after birth, with observations of arousal and visual evoked responses. *EEG Clin. Neurophysiol.*, 1958, **10**, 31–50.

ELLINGSON, R. J. Cortical electrical responses to visual stimulation in the human infant. *EEG Clin. Neurophysiol.*, 1960, **12**, 663–677.

ELLINGSON, R. J. & WILCOTT, R. C. Development of evoked responses in visual and auditory cortices of kittens. *J. Neurophysiol.*, 1960, **23**, 363–375.

FISCHGOLD, H. Personal communication, 1959.

FISCHGOLD, H. & BERTHAULT, F. Electro-encephalogramme de l'epilepsie du nouveau-né et du nourrison. *Etudes Neo-Natales*, 1953, **2**, 59–79.

FLEXNER, L. B., TYLER, D. B., & GALLANT, L. J. Biochemical and physiological differentiation during morphogenesis: X. Onset of electrical activity in developing cerebral cortex of fetal guinea pig. *J. Neurophysiol.*, 1950, **13**, 427–430.

FREEMAN, G. L. Toward a psychiatric Plimsoll mark: physiological recovery quotients in experimentally induced frustration. *J. Psychol.*, 1939, **8**, 247–269.

GIBBS, E. L. & GIBBS, F. A. Extreme spindles: correlation of electroencephalographic sleep pattern with mental retardation. *Science*, 1962, **138**, 1106–1107.

GROSSMAN, C. Electro-ontogenesis of cerebral activity. Forms of neo-natal responses and their recurrence in epileptic discharges. *Arch. Neurol. Psychiat., Chicago*, 1955, **74**, 186–202.

HELLBRUGGE, T. The development of circadian rhythms in infants. In *Symposium on quantitative biology*. Vol. XXV. Cold Spring Harbor, L. I., N. Y.: Long Island Biological Assn., 1960. Pp. 311–323.

HENRY, C. E. Electroencephalograms of normal children. *Monogr. Soc. Res. Child Developm.*, 1944, **9**, No. 39.

HUGHES, J. G., DAVIS, B. C., & BRENNAN, M. L. Electroencephalography of the newborn infant: VI. Studies on premature infants. *Pediatrics*, 1951, **7**, 707–712.

HUGHES, J. G., EHEMANN, B., & BROWN, U. A. Electroencephalography of the newborn: I. Studies on normal, full-term, sleeping infants. *Amer. J. Dis. Child.*, 1948, **76**, 503–512.

HUNT, W. G. & GOLDRING, S. Maturation of evoked responses of the visual cortex in the postnatal rabbit. *EEG Clin. Neurophysiol.*, 1951, **3**, 465–471.

HURSH, J. B. The properties of growing nerve fibers. *Amer. J. Physiol.*, 1939, **127**, 140–153.

JASPER, H. H., BRIDGMAN, C. S., & CARMICHAEL, L. An ontogenetic study of cerebral electrical potentials in the guinea pig. *J. exp. Psychol.*, 1937, **21**, 63–71.

JOUVET, M. Récherches sur les structures nerveuses et les mécanismes réponsables des differents phases du sommeil physiologique. *Arch. Ital. Biol.*, 1962, **100**, 125–206.

KELLAWAY, P. The development of sleep spindles and of arousal patterns in infants and their characteristics in normal and certain abnormal states. *EEG Clin. Neurophysiol.*, 1952, **4**, 262–287 (a).

KELLAWAY, P. Electroencephalographic diagnosis of cerebral pathology in infants during sleep: I. Rationale, technique, and the characteristics of normal sleep in infants. *J. Pediat.*, 1952, **41**, 262–287 (b).

KENNARD, M. A., RABINOVITCH, M. S., & FISTER, W. The use of frequency analysis in the interpretation of the EEG's of patients with psychological disorders. *EEG Clin. Neurophysiol.*, 1955, **7**, 29–38.

KENNARD, M. A. & SCHWARTZMAN, A. E. A longitudinal study of electroencephalographic frequency patterns in mental hospital patients and normal controls. *EEG Clin. Neurophysiol.*, 1957, **9**, 263–274.

KLEITMAN, H. & ENGELMANN, T. G. Sleep characteristics of infants. *J. appl. Psychol.*, 1953, **6**, 269–282.

KORNMULLER, A. E. Die biolelektrischen Erscheinungen architektonischer Felder der Grosshirnrinde. *Biol. Rev.*, 1935, **10**, 383–426.

KUYPERS, H. G. J. M. Corticospinal connections: postnatal development in the rhesus monkey. *Science*, 1962, **138**, 687–688.

LANGWORTHY, O. R. Development of behavior patterns and myelinization of the nervous system in the human fetus and infant. Publ. Nos. 139–143, *Carnegie Inst., Washington*, 1933.

LEÃO, A. A. P. Spreading depression of activity in the cerebral cortex. *J. Neurophysiol.*, 1944, **7**, 359–390.

LINDSLEY, D. B. Brain potentials in children and adults. *Science*, 1936, **84**, 354.

LINDSLEY, D. B. Electrical potentials in the brains of children and adults. *J. genet. Psychol.*, 1938, **19**, 285–306.

LINDSLEY, D. B. A longitudinal study of the occipital alpha rhythm in normal children: frequency and amplitude standards. *J. genet. Psychol.*, 1939, **55**, 197–213.

LIPTON, E. L., STEINSCHNEIDER, A., & RICHMOND, J. B. Autonomic function in the neonate: II. Physiologic effects of motor restraint. *Psychosom. Med.*, 1960, **22**, 57–65.

LIPTON, E. L., STEINSCHNEIDER, A., & RICHMOND, J. B. Autonomic function in the neonate: III. Methodological considerations. *Psychosom. Med.*, 1961, **23**, 461–471 (a).

LIPTON, E. L., STEINSCHNEIDER, A., & RICHMOND, J. B. Autonomic function in the neonate: IV. Individual differences in cardiac reactivity. *Psychosom. Med.*, 1961, **23**, 472–484 (b).

MALCOLM, J. L. The appearance of inhibition in the developing spinal cord of kittens. In H. Waelsch (Ed.), *Biochemistry of the developing nervous system: proceedings first international neurochemical symposium.* New York: Academic Press, 1955. Pp. 104–109.

MARTY, R. Developpement post-natal des réponses sensorielles du cortex cérèbral chez le chat et le lapin. Thesis presented to the Faculty of Sciences, Univ. of Paris, 1962. Masson et cie., ed. Pp. 1–264.

MARTY, R., CONTAMIN, F., & SCHERRER, J. Cortical response to photic stimulation in the new-born cat. *EEG Clin. Neurophysiol.*, 1958, **10**, 761.

MELIN, K. A. The EEG in infancy and childhood. *EEG Clin. Neurophysiol.*, 1953, Suppl. No. 4, 205–211.

MINKOWSKI, M. Zur entwicklungsgeschichte, Lokalisation, und Klinik des Fussohlenreflexes. *Schweiz. Arch. f. Neur. u. Psychiat.*, 1923, Bd. 13, S 475–514.

MORUZZI, G. & MAGOUN, H. W. Brain-stem reticular formation and activation of the EEG. *EEG Clin. Neurophysiol.*, 1949, **1**, 455–473.

MOUNTCASTLE, V. B. Modality and topographic properties of single neurons of cat's somatic sensory cortex. *J. Neurophysiol.*, 1957, **20**, 408–434.

NOBACK, C. R., HOUSEPIAN, E. M., & PURPURA, D. P. Ontogeny of large pyramidal neurons with axons in the medullary pyramidal tract (cat). *Anatom. Rec.*, 1962, **142**, 263.

OKAMOTO, Y. & KIRIKAE, T. EEG studies in brain of foetus, of children of premature birth, and newborn. Together with a note on reactions of foetus brain upon drugs. *Folia Psychiat. Neurol. Jap.*, 1951, **5**, 461. Cited by C. Dreyfus-Brisac, Electroencephalography in infancy. In F. Linneweh (Ed.), *Die physiologische Entwicklung des Kindes.* Berlin, Gottingen, Heidelberg: Springer, 1960. Pp. 29–40.

PARMALEE, A. H. Unpublished data, 1963.

PETERSEN, J. C. & HIMWICH, W. A. Biochemical and neurophysiological development of the brain in the neo-natal period. *The Physiologist*, 1959, **21**, 93. Cited by W. A. Himwich. *Internat. Rev. Neurobiol.*, 1964, in press.

PURPURA, D. P. Ontogenetic analysis of some evoked synaptic activities in superficial neocortical neuropil. In E. Florey (Ed.), *Nervous inhibition. Proceedings of an international symposium*. New York: Pergamon Press, 1961 (a).

PURPURA, D. P. Analysis of axodendritic synaptic organizations in immature cerebral cortex. *Ann. N. Y. Acad. Sci.*, 1961, **94**, 604–654 (b).

PURPURA, D. P. Structure and function of cortical synaptic organizations activated by corticipetal afferents in newborn cat. In M. A. B. Brazier (Ed.), *Brain and behavior. First conference*. Madison, N. J.: Madison Print. Co., 1961. Pp. 95–138 (c).

REXED, B. & SOURANDER, P. Cited by S. Skoglund, Central connections and functions of muscle nerves in the kitten. *Acta Physiol. Scand.*, 1960, **50**, 222–237.

RICHMOND, J. B. & LIPTON, E. L. Some aspects of the neurophysiology of the newborn and their implications for child development. In L. Jessner & E. Pavenstedt (Eds.), *Dynamic psychopathology in childhood*. New York: Grune & Stratton, 1959. Pp. 78–105.

RICHMOND, J. B., LIPTON, E. L., & STEINSCHNEIDER, A. Autonomic function in the neonate: V. Individual homeostatic capacity in cardiac response. *Psychosom. Med.*, 1962, **24**, 66–74 (a).

RICHMOND, J. B., LIPTON, E. L., & STEINSCHNEIDER, A. Observations on differences in autonomic nervous system function between and within individuals during early infancy. *J. Amer. Acad. Child. Psychiat.*, 1962, **1**, 83–91 (b).

RICHMOND, J. B. & LUSTMAN, S. L. Autonomic function in the neonate: I. Implications for psychosomatic theory. *Psychosom. Med.*, 1955, **17**, 269–275.

ROFFWARG, A. & DEMENT, W. Unpublished data, 1963.

ROSE, J. E., ADRIAN, H., & SANTIBANEZ, G. Electrical signs of maturation in the auditory system of the kitten. *Acta Neurol. Latinoamer.*, 1957, **3**, 133–143.

SCHADÉ, J. P. *Electro-area-grafic van de cortex cerebri*. Amsterdam, 1957. Cited by J. P. Schadé, Maturational aspects of EEG and of spreading depression in the rabbit. *J. Neurophysiol.*, 1959, **22**, 245–257.

SCHADÉ, J. P. Maturational aspects of EEG and of spreading depression in the rabbit. *J. Neurophysiol.*, 1959, **22**, 245–257.

SCHADÉ, J. P. Origin of the spontaneous electrical activity of the cerebral cortex. In J. Wortis (Ed.), *Recent advances in biological psychiatry*. Vol. I. New York: Grune & Stratton, 1960. Pp. 23–42.

SCHEIBEL, A. B. Neural correlates of psychophysiological development in the young organism. In J. Wortis (Ed.), *Recent advances in biological psychiatry*. Vol. IV. New York: Plenum Press, 1962. Pp. 313–327.

SCHEIBEL, M. E. & SCHEIBEL, A. B. Structural substrates for integrative patterns in the brain-stem reticular core. In H. H. Jasper *et al.* (Eds.), *Reticular formation of the brain*. Boston: Little, Brown, 1958. Pp. 31–55.

SCHEIBEL, M. E. & SCHEIBEL, A. B. Development of reticulo-cortical control in the newborn. *Amer. Acad. Neurol., Abstracts of 11th annual meeting*, 1959. P. 29.

SCHEIBEL, M. E. & SCHEIBEL, A. B. Neural correlates of psychophysiological development in the young organism. *Anatom. Rec.*, 1961, **139**, 319–320.

SCHEIBEL, M. E. & SCHEIBEL, A. B. Some structuro-functional correlates of maturation in young cats. *EEG Clin. Neurophysiol.*, 1962, **14**, 429.

SCHEIBEL, M. E. & SCHEIBEL, A. B. Some structuro-functional substrates of development in young cats. In *Galesburg symposium on brain development and biogenic amines*. Amsterdam: Elsevier Press, in press.

SCHERRER, J. & OECONOMOS, D. Réponses corticales somesthetiques du mammifère nouveau-né comparées à celles de l'animale adulte. *Etudes Neo-Natales*, 1954, **3**, 199–216.

SCOTT, J. P. Critical periods in behavioral development. *Science*, 1962, **138**, 949–958.

SKOGLUND, S. On the postnatal development of postural mechanisms as revealed by electro-myography and myography in decerebrate kittens. *Acta Physiol. Scand.*, 1960, **49**, 299–317 (a).

SKOGLUND, S. The spinal transmission of proprioceptive reflexes and the postnatal development of conduction velocity in different hindlimb nerves in the kitten. *Acta Physiol. Scand.*, 1960, **49**, 318–329 (b).

SKOGLUND, S. The activity of muscle receptors in the kitten. *Acta Physiol. Scand.*, 1960, **50**, 203–221 (c).

SKOGLUND, S. Central connections and functions of muscle nerves in the kitten. *Acta Physiol. Scand.*, 1960, **50**, 222–237 (d).

SKOGLUND, S. The reactions to tetanic stimulation of the two-neuron arc in the kitten. *Acta Physiol. Scand.*, 1960, **50**, 238–253 (e).

SKOGLUND, S. & VALLBO, A. Cited by S. Skoglund, The activity of muscle receptors in the kitten. *Acta Physiol. Scand.*, 1960, **50**, 203–221.

SMITH, J. P. The EEG during infancy and childhood. *Proc. Soc. exp. Biol. Med.*, 1937, **36**, 384–386.

SMITH, K. R. Fine structure of the central nervous system of the fetal and postnatal rabbit, with special reference to the extra cellular space. *Anatom. Rec.*, 1963, **145**, 288.

SUREAU, M., FISCHGOLD, H., & CAPDEVIELLE, G. L'EEG du nouveau-né de 0 à 36 heures. *Rev. Neurol. Paris*, 1949, **81**, 543–545.

TASAKI, I. *Nervous transmission.* Springfield, Ill.: Charles C Thomas, 1953.

TIEGS, O. W. The structure of the neuron junctions of the spinal cord. *Austrian J. exp. biol. med. Sci.*, 1926, **3**, 69–79.

ULETT, G., DOW, R. S., & LARSELL, O. The inception of conductivity in the corpus callosum and the cortico-ponto-cerebellar pathway of young rabbits, with reference to myelinization. *J. comp. Neurol.*, 1944, **80**, 1–10.

VOLOKHOV, A. A. Development of unconditioned and conditioned reflexes in ontogenesis. *21st Internat. Congr. Physiol. Sci.*, 1959. Pp. 248–254.

WILSON, V. E. Reflex transmission in the kitten. *J. Neurophysiol.*, 1962, **25**, 263–276.

WINDLE, W. F. Normal behavioral reactions of kittens correlated with the postnatal development of nerve-fiber density in the spinal gray matter. *J. comp. Neurol.*, 1930, **50**, 479–504.

WINDLE, W. F. & GRIFFIN, A. M. Observations on embryonic and fetal movements of the cat. *J. comp. Neurol.*, 1931, **52**, 149–188.

Contributors

Authors

WESLEY C. BECKER, PH.D. Professor, Department of Psychology, University of Illinois.

BETTYE M. CALDWELL, PH.D. Research Associate, Department of Pediatrics, Upstate Medical Center, State University of New York; Lecturer in Psychology, Syracuse University.

JOHN D. CAMPBELL, PH.D. Social Psychologist, Laboratory of Socio-Environmental Studies, National Institute of Mental Health.

JAMES J. GALLAGHER, PH.D. Professor, Institute for Research on Exceptional Children, University of Illinois.

JEROME KAGAN, PH.D. Chairman, Department of Psychology, The Fels Research Institute; Associate Professor, Antioch College.

LAWRENCE KOHLBERG, PH.D. Assistant Professor, Department of Psychology, and member of the Committee on Human Development, University of Chicago.

ELEANOR E. MACCOBY, PH.D. Associate Professor, Department of Psychology, Stanford University.

GERALD E. McCLEARN, PH.D. Associate Professor, Department of Psychology, University of California, Berkeley.

ARNOLD B. SCHEIBEL. University of California Center for Health Sciences and Brain Research Institute, Los Angeles.

MADGE E. SCHEIBEL. University of California Center for Health Sciences and Brain Research Institute, Los Angeles.

IRVING E. SIGEL, PH.D. Chairman of Research, The Merrill-Palmer Institute; Associate Professor of Psychology, Wayne State University.

JOAN W. SWIFT, PH.D. Research Director, The Thresholds, Chicago.

LEON J. YARROW, PH.D. Director, Infant Research Project, Family and Child Services of Washington, D. C.

521

JERRY HIRSCH, PH.D. Professor, Department of Psychology, University of Illinois.

ALFRED J. KAHN, D.S.W. Professor, Columbia University School of Social Work.

WILLIAM KESSEN, PH.D. Associate Professor, Department of Psychology and Child Study Center, Yale University.

J. CLAYTON LAFFERTY, PH.D. Clinical Psychologist, Wayne County Board of Education, Detroit.

RICHARD W. OLMSTED, M.D. Chairman, Department of Pediatrics, University of Oregon.

SALLY PROVENCE, M.D. Associate Professor of Pediatrics, Child Study Center, Yale University; Instructor, Western New England Institute of Psychoanalysis, New Haven.

JULIUS B. RICHMOND, M.D. Professor and Chairman, Department of Pediatrics, Upstate Medical Center, State University of New York.

L. JOSEPH STONE, PH.D. Professor, Department of Child Study, Vassar College.

RUTH UPDEGRAFF, PH.D. Professor, Institute of Child Behavior and Development, State University of Iowa.

STEPHEN B. WITHEY, PH.D. Program Director, Institute for Social Research; Professor, Department of Psychology, The University of Michigan.

Author Index

525

Heinze, S., 360, 364, 381
Hellbrugge, T., 509, 511, 516
Hellman, I., 106, 107, 133
Hellmer, L. A., 174, 176, 178, 181, 190, 205
Hendrix, G., 372, 379
Hendry, S., 388, 429
Henry, C. E., 496, 516
Herbst, E. K., 261, 288
Heron, W. T., 459, 477
Hertzig, M. E., 77, 87
Herzberg, F., 156, 164
Hetherington, E. M., 47, 52, 53, 84
Hickmans, E. M., 468, 476
Hicks, J. A., 263, 285
Highberger, R., 278, 279, 285
Hildreth, G., 140, 164
Hilgard, J. R., 94, 104, 109, 133, 262, 263, 285
Hill, A. B., 285
Hill, J., 411
Hill, R. J., 311, 320
Hill, W. F., 185, 186, 206
Himeno, Y., 269, 285
Himmelweit, H. T., 328, 330, 332, 339, 343, 345, 347
Himwich, W. A., 493, 515, 518
Hindley, C. B., 471, 477
Hindman, E., 380
Hirsch, J., 459, 477, 478, 523
Hissem, I., 262, 285
Hitchcock, E. A., 95, 135, 140, 166
Hoefer, C. A., 14, 24, 26, 84, 253, 255, 285
Hoffman, H. N., 237, 245
Hoffman, L. W., 9, 95, 116, 133, 144, 166, 303, 319
Hoffman, M. L., 169, 178, 181, 183, 187, 188, 206, 411, 412, 413, 420, 421, 422, 429
Holland, J., 352, 379
Hollenberg, E., 178, 198, 206
Hollingshead, A. B., 297, 298, 299, 319
Holt, R. R., 229, 246
Holway, A. R., 26, 31, 45, 51, 84
Holzinger, K. J., 460, 461, 462, 477, 479
Honkavaara, S., 231, 232, 234, 235, 245
Honzik, M. P., 35, 84, 140, 141, 164, 280, 286, 392, 393, 430, 462, 471, 478
Hood, W. R., 304, 321
Hopper, H. E., 59, 84
Horowitz, E. L., 254, 271, 282, 285, 302, 319
Horowitz, F. D., 276, 285, 306, 319
Horrocks, J. E., 305, 319, 322
Hosken, B., 139, 140, 165, 172, 206
Housepian, E. M., 484, 517
Hovland, C. I., 140, 152, 164
Howard, A., 181, 194, 200, 207
Howells, J. G., 94, 95, 104, 133
Hoyt, J. M., 276, 286, 297, 302, 320
Hsia, D. Y-Y., 468, 478
Hsu, F. L. K., 295, 319

Huang, I., 233, 234, 245
Hughes, B. O., 253, 286
Hughes, J. G., 497, 499, 516
Hunt, D. E., 209, 210, 239, 245
Hunt, J. McV., 211, 212, 218, 220, 223, 245, 305, 319, 355, 379
Hunt, R., 254, 255, 283
Hunt, W. G., 502, 505, 507, 516
Hurlock, E. B., 230, 245, 292, 319
Hursh, J. B., 482, 487, 516
Hurwitz, J., 450, 478
Huschka, M., 44, 45, 48, 49, 50, 52, 84
Huston, A. C., 268, 283, 337, 347
Hytten, F. E., 24, 28, 64, 84

Ilg, F. L., 20, 84, 219, 245
Inhelder, B., 211, 212, 220, 222, 223, 236, 239, 245, 247, 248, 350, 379
Irvine, E., 275, 285
Irwin, O. C., 100, 101, 131

Jack, L. M., 273, 275, 285
Jackson, E. B., 27, 29, 30, 56, 84, 85, 112, 133
Jackson, K., 95, 124, 132
Jackson, P. W., 267, 284, 352, 365, 367, 368, 369, 379
Jackson, T. A., 227, 245
Jacob, F., 454, 478, 479
Jacobs, P. A., 470, 478
Jahoda, G., 234, 245
Jakubczak, L. F., 312, 319
Janis, I. J., 140, 152, 164
Janis, M., 397, 429
Janke, L. L., 156, 164
Jarvik, L. F., 471, 478
Jasper, H. H., 491, 516
Jay, P., 146, 164
Jelliffe, D. B., 23, 84
Jenkins, J. J., 140, 141, 143, 165
Jennings, E., 380
Jennings, H. H., 313, 319
Jersild, A. T., 139, 165, 254, 260, 261, 262, 270, 285
Jervis, G. A., 468, 469, 478
Jessner, L., 116, 133
Joel, W., 254, 285
Johnson, A. M., 418, 429
Johnson, D. M., 390, 428
Johnson, H. M., 255, 285
Johnson, M. W., 260, 261, 267, 285
Johnson, R. C., 223, 245, 398, 399, 411, 412, 429
Jones, H. E., 253, 285, 461, 478
Jones, M. C., 152, 161, 165, 166, 298, 319
Jones, V., 383, 429
Jorgensen, A. P., 253, 285
Josselyn, I. M., 424, 429
Jouvet, M., 495, 516

Subject Index